Teaching:
Vantage Points for Study

Dr. Charles E. Alberti

Dedicated to
P.C., J.F.B., R.C., and R.R.C

Second Edition

Teaching: Vantage Points for Study

Edited by
RONALD T. HYMAN
Rutgers University

J. B. LIPPINCOTT COMPANY
Philadelphia • New York • Toronto

371.1
H996t

ISBN: 0-397-47300-1

Library of Congress Catalog Number 73-21695

Printed in the United States of America

1 3 5 7 9 10 8 6 4 2

Library of Congress Cataloging in Publication Data

Hyman, Ronald T   comp.
    Teaching: vantage points for study.

    Includes bibliographical references.
    1. Teaching—Addresses, essays, lectures.
I. Title.
LB1025.H985   1974   371.1'008   73-21695
ISBN 0-397-47300-1

Contents

Preface

Since the publication of the first edition of this collection, teachers and students alike have kindly offered helpful comments and suggestions for revision. I have incorporated many of these in this new, expanded and updated edition. Yet, the general idea behind the book remains the same: teaching deserves and needs serious study; teaching demands a plurality of approaches; and an anthology on teaching needs a focus which will invite readers to explore in some depth the several themes presented.

Nine vantage points now constitute the framework for this second edition: communications, social climate, cognitive processes, learning and cognitive development, psychological climate, games, aesthetics, nonverbal communication, and strategies.

Approximately half of the articles are new, and three of these were written especially for this second edition. The rationale for the inclusion of two new vantage points—nonverbal communication and learning and cognitive development—will, I am sure, be apparent to all who are familiar with the educational literature of the past decade. Furthermore, in revising the original seven vantage points, I have included recent articles which broaden the scope of the book. New selections represent the main thrusts of psychology—behaviorism, psychoanalysis, and humanistic psychology; and new material aids in the discussion of "open education."

Thus, I have maintained the overall format of the first edition and have chosen articles that maintain a balance between the empirical and nonempirical study of teaching. Also, as in the original edition, an overview to each section introduces the articles, shows connections between them, and suggests directions for further study.

I hope that this book will encourage the readers to broaden and continue their study of teaching.

I wish to thank Bea Mayes for her help, Richard Heffron of J. B. Lippincott Company for his assistance, and my many students for their encouragement.

RONALD T. HYMAN

New Brunswick, New Jersey
February 1974

Introduction

Changes in the field of education within the last two decades have opened up a new area of study that focuses on the process of teaching. This area is to be distinguished from other efforts focusing on teacher personality traits, on teacher effectiveness, and on how people learn. It has been primarily descriptive rather than evaluative. This expression of interest in understanding the nature of teaching has taken many forms because of the diversity of the people who constitute the corps of investigators. The result has been the publication of articles, research reports, and conference papers in scattered places. The purpose of this book is to make available significant and representative material from this growing body of literature on the analysis of teaching.

Reasons for Studying Teaching

It is reasonable to ask about the need and motivation behind this interest in teaching. Obviously, there is no single set of answers; several factors are salient and deserve attention. First, men engage in some activities for their own sake, activities that offer their own intrinsic satisfaction. The study of teaching is one of these, and if there were no further justification, this motive would suffice.

Second, educators and psychologists have openly acknowledged that

1

the focus on teacher effectiveness for the past fifty years has yielded very little helpful knowledge. Philip Jackson, an educational psychologist, has put it this way:

> First is the lamentable, but undeniable, fact that our search for the good just doesn't seem to have paid off. Almost all of the noble crusades that have set out in search of the best teacher and the best method—or even the better teacher and the better method—have returned empty-handed. The few discoveries to date (it would be unfair—and, . . . imprudent as well—to deny that there have been any) are pitifully small in proportion to their cost in time and energy. For example, the few drops of knowledge that can be squeezed out of a half century of research on the personality characteristics of good teachers are so low in intellectual food value that it is almost embarrassing to discuss them (13:8–9).

The shift, as noted, has been from studying teaching effectiveness and teacher personality to analyzing the teaching process itself, with the hope that this approach will yield clues to what constitutes effectiveness. The ultimate aim is still the improvement of teaching.

Third, educators have finally taken to heart the exhortations of the psychologists not to rely on learning psychology as the sole means of understanding teaching. The psychologist Jerome S. Bruner stated in his 1963 speech to the national Association for Supervision and Curriculum Development that its members should investigate teaching in their search for clues for improving the curriculum of our schools. He said, "I find that the dependence upon learning theory among educators is as touching as it is shocking" (5:524). Bruner went on to explore four possible aspects of a theory of instruction.

A similar statement was made seventy-one years earlier, in 1892, by William James, the father of modern psychology. In his *Talks With Teachers,* James pointed out that psychology by itself will not enable teachers to teach well.

> I say moreover that you make a great, a very great mistake, if you think that psychology, being the science of the mind's laws, is something from which you can deduce definite programmes and schemes and methods of instruction for immediate schoolroom use. . . . To know psychology, therefore, is absolutely no guarantee that we shall be good teachers. To advance to that result, we must have an additional endowment altogether, a happy tact and ingenuity to tell us what definite things to say and do when the pupil is before us. That ingenuity in meeting and pursing the pupil, that tact for the concrete situation, though they are the alpha and omega of the teacher's art, are things to which psychology cannot help us in the least (14:23–24).

It has taken many years for James's insight to have its effect on teachers.

Fourth, it is hoped that a study of teaching will eventually lead us to a theory of teaching that will serve as a guide for teachers; it will direct them in their teaching of skills, knowledge, and values. B. O. Smith and his associates did not formulate a theory of teaching from their investigations, but they did come up with some concepts which "might become elements of a teaching theory" (22:1).

Fifth, educators recognize that teaching is a common phenomenon in our society and an integral part of our efforts to sustain our cultural heritage and democracy. As an activity in which close to two million citizens in this country engage, and which serves or influences in turn about a quarter of our population, it deserves study. It follows that we should now as much about teaching as we can.

Studying teaching because it is vital to us provides a particular motivation. It asks us to look for the significant in the interaction between teacher and pupil. What we learn about teaching has definite implications for our future. Vital self-interest is what Bettelheim says was his reason for studying the activity around him in a German concentration camp. What he learned helped him to keep his freedom for making decisions, which, he says, is the essence of humanity. In a sense, he was able to become the master of his condition. Bettelheim's experience can be applied to teaching, though admittedly his situation was extreme.

Inside the camps I did not study my behavior, nor did I study my fellow prisoners or question them because I intended to make a disinterested survey of a problem that had roused my scientific interest. Quite the contrary; not detached curiosity, but vital self interest induced me to study my own behavior and the behavior I noticed around me. To observe and try to make sense out of what I saw was a device that spontaneously suggested itself to me as a way of convincing myself that my own life was still of some value, that I had not yet lost all the interests that had once given me self respect (3:111).

Observational Frameworks: Need and Types

The question thus becomes "How do we observe the activity around us in order to make sense out of it?" We know that observation is selective. People simply cannot observe everything, for "what goes on in the world at large at any time or the human phase of it is too vast in extent and too complicated in intension to be fully described or understood in any finite time. . . . Each observer or recorder is restricted to some fragment of what is going on. The best we can attain is some indication of what is outwardly visible from a single point of view for a limited time" (6:24). Since we cannot observe everything, we select what we will observe and do so from a particular orientation. Newspaper accounts and legal eye-witnesses are constant reminders of this basic fact in communications—that different people select different things to see. Historians, for example, are aware of this relativism, and it has become a part of their professional preparation to examine the various frameworks employed by different historians writing on a common topic or period.

In this light, it is clear that if we are to understand a person's description, explanation, or evalution of teaching, we need first to understand the nature of his vantage point. As Belth has stated, frameworks are "windows through which we see the world and our own transaction with the world, and they make that world meaningful to us in their own terms. No man ever sees the world other than through some conceptual system, whether he is aware of this or not" (2:61).

When we observe a teacher at work, we need to know the framework he is employing if we are to understand his actions. "Consider now an observer, O, of N's behavior. If O wants to predict how N is going to act, he must familiarize himself in terms of which N is viewing the situation. . . ." (24:91). By way of illustration, let us examine two types of frameworks commonly utilized when people observe others.

Max Black in his book *Models and Metaphors* (4) identifies four kinds of models: scale, analogue, mathematical, and theoretical. Of these four, the most frequently used in the field of education today is the analogue. Let us turn to this type of framework first. Here, we look at teaching *as if* it were, for example, psychotherapy, gardening, or an athletic game. Then what we can say about psychotherapy, athletics, or gardening we will also be able to say about teaching, once we have shown that they have common features. This type of *as if* thinking can be very fruitful.

Analogies are a means of transferring to a new situation the "structure or web of relationships" of the original one (4:222). They are a means of explaining how the various parts of something fit together. We form relationships between events, objects, people, and abstractions by considering them as similar to others we already know. Analogies provide a means of organizing the incoming raw data in some meaningful way, particularly when we encounter novel and/or complex situations. In order to make sense of what he sees on his trip, the tourist will often say, "That looks like _____ back home."

But in spite of the help they offer, analogies also yield problems. The very path that leads to easy and quick understanding can also lead to error and confusion if we are not careful. To avoid trouble, we must be judicious in the use of analogies. "An adequate analogue model will manifest a point-by-point correspondence between the relations *it* embodies and those embodied in the original: every incidence of a relation in the original must be echoed by a corresponding incidence of a correlated relation in the analogue model" (4:222). By this criterion, surely few analogies, if any, are adequate. Most analogies have only partial correspondence with the original situation. Trouble arises when we accept and act upon complete correspondence when, in fact, it cannot be demonstrated. The analogy that does not hold completely is potentially misleading. We must drop it before we stretch it beyond its helpful limits. If not, we come to believe that certain relationships exist when they do not.

A good analogy can also narrow our scope. When we find an adequate analogy that seems fruitful to us, it is easy to forget that it is only one way of looking at teaching. The use of a single analogy to view teaching is obviously inadequate, since teaching is very complex. By their nature, complex situations require us to consider them along several avenues of approach.

Many people, recognizing the pitfalls present in the use of analogies, choosen not to employ them when discussing teaching. Instead, they frequently use implicit analogies or what Stephen Pepper calls "root metaphors" (16:91) and Max Black calls "archtypes" (4:241). In this second type of framework, a person takes the key words, expressions, concepts, and categories from an area he knows, and "in terms of these categories he proceeds to study all other areas of fact whether uncriticized or previously criticized" (16:91). In this way, someone may even unwittingly speak of "planting" the "seed" of knowledge to watch it "grow" in the "sunshine" of the "green" classroom. Indeed, the word *kindergarten* is a result of this root metaphor.

Why we must identify and understand the model, whether analogy or root metaphor, from which a person views teaching is clear. The framework leads us to focus on certain aspects of teaching. It suggests that we ask certain questions about teaching. It is the guide to enquiry, the guide for collecting data about teaching (20:25). And, most importantly, it "can even, in particular situations, imply action to be taken" (2:91). Surely, we wish to understand why teachers and observers ask certain questions. Surely, we wish to understand the actions they take. As Susanne K. Langer says:

> The formulation of experience which is contained within the intellectual horizon of an age and a society is determined, I believe, not so much by events and desires, as by the *basic concepts* at people's disposal for analyzing and describing their adventures to their own understanding. Of course, such concepts arise as they are needed to deal with political or domestic experience; but the same experiences could be seen in many different lights, so the light in which they do appear depends on the genius of a people as well as on the demands of the external occasion. Different minds will take the same events in very different ways (15:3).

It is appropriate to mention that the recognition of the need of a framework is not restricted to the philosophers. Several educational psychologists and curriculum specialists, as well as numerous social and natural scientists, have written on this matter. Reference to one who writes about his observations of the classroom will suffice. Ralph Tyler, a curriculum researcher of considerable experience, stated in his paper to the First Annual Phi Delta Kappa Symposium on Educational Research:

If when one entered a classroom he had no prior conceptualization of teaching and learning, he would see children and an adult, he would hear several children and the adult speaking, he would note physical items in the room, movements of people and the like. What gives it meaning for the investigator of classroom instruction is a "model" which he conceives, a simplified picture of the structure and process of classroom instruction. This model usually includes such elements as a teacher, pupil, objectives of instruction, methods of teaching, materials of instruction, learning outcomes. If he holds such a model in mind, he has a basis for focusing his observations and for arranging and analyzing his data. This development of a formal model provides a way of viewing the complex phenomenon in a fashion which permits scientific study (23:57).

The Concept of Teaching

To this point, we have discussed teaching without defining the term. To proceed beyond this point, we will have to consider definitions. The literature on teaching contains various uses of the word; and if we are to understand that literature, we need to be aware of the issues involved in defining it (11; 12). An effort has been made by some analytic educational philosophers to clarify the concept of teaching since such a clarification is obviously necessary for effective communication among educators. It is also needed by the empirical researcher, since the notion of teaching that he accepts guides his endeavor. Marie Hughes, in a paper on the assessment of teaching, writes, "There are many ways to analyze the records of actions in the classroom situation. The manner of analysis is controlled to a large degree by the definition accepted for teaching" (10:26). Questions, then, about the definition of teaching are not trivial but central to our concern.

Three typical definitions will suffice to illustrate the scope of teaching.

1. Smith: Teaching is a system of actions intended to induce learning (21:88).

2. Gage: By teaching, we mean, for the present purpose of defining research on teaching, any interpersonal influence aimed at changing the ways in which other persons can or will behave (8:96).

3. Scheffler: Teaching may be characterized as an activity aimed at the achievement of learning and practiced in such manner as to respect the student's intellectual integrity and capacity for independent judgment (19:131).

The definitions by Smith and Gage are clearly broader than Scheffler's. They allow for such actions as indoctrinating, lying, propagandizing, advising, and mothering to be counted as teaching. Even "brainwashing," with all its negative connotations, can fit these two definitions, for it does induce learning and change the ways people behave.

Scheffler's definition is obviously narrower. It does attempt to separate "teaching" from "indoctrinating" and other synonyms; it rightly puts an emphasis on manner; yet this very narrowness raises many questions by answering one. What constitutes intellectual integrity? How shall we measure and know the student's capacity for independent judgment? By what criteria shall we know when the teacher's actions respect the student's intellectual integrity and capacity for independent judgment? If we so restrict teaching to such narrow behavior, what shall we call the multitude of other actions which a teacher performs? Is there an implication that indoctrinating and training are not desirable in the classroom? For example, in light of Scheffler's definition shall we say that the following four statements by a teacher constitute teaching?

1. Robbing and murdering are bad.
2. The United States was justified in revolting against England in 1776.
3. The way to read and write English is to go from left to right.
4. The United Nations is an effective agency for maintaining world peace. It is a step towards world government.

The second issue involves the relation of teaching to learning. The question here is whether learning must result if we are to call the teacher's actions "teaching." The three definitions cited earlier all keep teaching and learning apart. That is, teaching is seen as aiming at or intending to bring about learning. Other definitions make "teaching" dependent on the successful outcome called "learning." That is, if there is no learning, there is no teaching. This notion stems from the comparison of teaching with selling, i.e., selling is to teaching as buying is to learning. If no one buys, no one sells. Similarly, if no one learns, no one teaches.

Currently, most educators accept the intentional rather than the successful use of teaching. Nevertheless, the research and writing of some reflect the opposite view. Indeed, the relation between teaching and learning remains unsettled. We do not know exactly how and to what extent teaching contributes to or causes learning. Part of the problem is that we are not certain *which* learning we are talking about (can there be no learning at all when a teacher acts?) and just what constitutes learning.

From this brief discussion of only two issues involved in defining "teaching," it is clear that the wider issue is tangled and complex. Several writers, especially Green (9), have attempted to resolve the problems by using different terms for discussing teaching. Yet in spite of the further analysis we still have no precise way of deciding what we will and will not call teaching.

In the selections that follow, the reader will find various explicit and implicit meanings of "teaching." The author's concept of teaching becomes a part of his frame of reference, and along with the analogies and root metaphors he uses we must seek it out. His concept of teaching serves as a criterion for what he deems appropriate in the classroom. If a teacher holds one concept, he will behave one way; if he hold another concept, he will behave differently. The concept guides his behavior. Winch's statement regarding war in his chapter on concepts and actions is also appropriate to the concept of teaching.

The idea of war, for instance . . . was not simply invented by people who wanted to *explain* what happens when societies come into armed conflict. It is an idea which provides the criteria of what is appropriate in the behavior of members of the conflicting societies. Because my country is at war there are certain things which I must and certain things which I must not do. My behavior is governed, one could say, by my concept of myself as a member of a belligerent country. The concept of war belongs *essentially* to my behavior (24:127–128).

To understand, then, what is written about teaching, we must know the writer's vantage point and his concept of teaching.

Overview of the Selections

The selections that follow have been chosen and grouped according to selected vantage points on teaching: communications, social climate, cognitive processes, learning and cognitive development, psychological climate, games, aesthetics, nonverbal communication, and strategies. These vantage points reflect the editor's way of viewing and comprehending the growing literature on teaching. These seem to him the major vantage points on teaching. They do overlap in some ways; they do have elements in common. The intention has not been to create a definitive instrument for classifying all studies on teaching, but to provide a means of organization that will reveal the points of view and concepts underlying each selection. Other vantage points are not included here because of limited space and because of their relative lack of development. These nine major vantage points illustrate the work already done on teaching and suggest the potential of future work.

Within each section, the articles may differ from one another in several respects, and this possibility should be kept in mind when reading. Some authors employ an empirical approach to studying teaching. They have developed instruments to measure selected aspects of teaching and present the data that was collected with them. Others have concentrated on an analytic and/or speculative study of teaching. Some of these have a fully developed framework but lack the field work for collecting data.

Some selections focus on the teacher, and others on the pupils. Still others record and analyze the behavior of both the teacher and the pupils. Most focus on verbal behavior in the classroom as the prime means of communication, considering it to be a representative sample of the total classroom behavior. Others include or focus on the nonverbal behavior considering it too significant to omit in spite of the many limitations inherent in dealing with it.

Some have chosen to go to the classroom to study teaching. Few, if any, of the recent empirical studies have been conducted under laboratory conditions. Some who work directly in the classroom rely on audio tape recordings to catch the ephemeral talk of the teacher and pupils. They then categorize the discourse when listening and/or reading a typescript of the recording. Others categorize the discourse as it occurs "live" without using any means of preserving it. Some study elementary school students, while others work with students in secondary school. Some study teachers in one subject area, while others focus on teachers from several academic fields. Some study gifted students, while others use heterogeneously grouped pupils.

In this way, these selections represent a wide range of approaches to the study of teaching. The decision about which path to take reflects the judgment of the author. Obviously, the study of teaching welcomes a multitude of approaches. Certain studies seem more fruitful than others, but each offers some insight into the nature of teaching not otherwise available.

Section Overviews

The introductions to the nine sections are intended to place each vantage point in context, introduce the separate articles, show connections between them, and suggest some possible directions for further study. The purpose of these "overviews" is not to point out the main ideas of the various selections or to summarize them. To do so would be to usurp the main task of each reader. The reader is urged to read the articles carefully, for each was chosen for the insights it contributes toward the understanding of teaching.

Examining Observation Instruments

Virtually all of the recent empirical work on teaching conducted in the classroom comes from trained observers using an observation instrument to gather data. This is one salient characteristic of the recent surge of interest in teaching. Therefore, the reader should be aware of some central issues regarding observation instruments used for gathering data about teaching.

Obviously, the prime question concerns the vantage point of the instrument. This is the concern of the earlier part of the introduction and does not need much more explication here. Suffice it to repeat that the observer using an instrument or the reader of data obtained from someone else's use of an instrument must ask himself what is the vantage point of that instrument. For example, does the instrument focus on psychological climate? Cognitive processes? Nonverbal communication?

The next issue concerns the type of instrument. Currently, researchers and practitioners are using three different kinds of observation instrument, the category system, sign system, and rating scale. In characterizing these types Rosenshine and Furst state, "When an event is recorded each time it occurs, the instrument is labeled a *category system;* when an event is recorded only once if it occurs within a specified time period, regardless of how often it occurs during that period, the recording instrument is called a *sign system.* Observers using *rating* instruments are expected to estimate the frequency of specified events or constellations of events only once, usually at the end of an observation session. The estimations are usually made on a five-or-seven-point scale, one end of which represents high frequency (usually containing phrases such as 'most of the time' or 'strongly agree'), and the other end represents low frequency ('seldom' or 'strongly disagree')" (18:132).

In a category system the observer classifies each observed unit of teaching behavior into the categories provided. Each unit of observed behavior, therefore, must fit into one of the categories. The instruments developed by Bellack (Section 3), Flanders (Section 2), and Tyler (Section 5), are examples of category systems. In a sign system and rating scale the observer looks out only for the specified teaching items. In a sign system a specified behavior may or may not even occur during the observation period. The instruments developed by Brown and his associates (see Webb in Section 3) and Solomon (Section 4) are examples of sign systems. Similarly, in a rating scale the specified item may or may not pertain to the particular observation period. The instrument developed by Tuckman (Section 5) may be considered a rating scale rather than a category or sign system.

Among the early observation instruments it was possible to distinguish among these three types according to the level of inference required by the user. Inference "refers to the process intervening between the objective data seen or heard and the coding of those data on an observation instrument" (17:281). For example, if a sign system has a large number of specific, concrete behaviors, it requires a low level of inference "to interpret a teacher's action as instance of 'answering pupil's question' or 'illustrating on the board.' In contrast it demands a higher degree of inference to interpret a teacher's statement as serving a controlling function or facilitating function" (1:8).

As researchers have combined elements of these three types in their newly developed instruments, it is no longer possible to make clear-cut distinctions according to inference. Whereas it was once possible to generalize that rating scales required higher levels of inference by the observers than category systems, it is now possible to make this claim accurately. Some items in category systems now require high inference levels while others require low levels; and this applies also to sign systems and rating scales (18).

Until further research clearly distinguishes among these three types according to inference level and the value of one type over another, we will have to examine each instrument on its own characteristics. The observer should be aware that (1) rating scales require him not only to make judgments because of such words as warm, cold, fair, and unfair but also to estimate the frequency or degree of particular quality; (2) that rating scales and sign systems generally are associated with units of teaching behavior specified according to an arbitrary period of time rather than a communication event or activity (see below); and (3) many, but not all, category systems utilize a communication event or activity rather than time as the unit of teaching behavior to be classified.

Another key issue in observation instruments concerns the unit of behavior. Unit of behavior refers to the segment of teaching behavior about which the observer will make a record. How will the observer know when to record data? In general, observation instruments have two types of units of behavior, an arbitrary time unit and a communication event or activity.

An arbitrary time unit requires the observer to record during or at the end of a pre-specified period of time. For example, Flanders' (Section 2) instrument requires the observer to categorize teaching behavior at least once every three seconds; Lewis, Newell, and Withall's (Section 1) instrument utilizes a ten-second period of time; Solomon's (Section 4) instrument uses a two-minute observation period; and Tuckman's (Section 5) instrument uses a time span of approximately forty-five minutes. Time units provide an easy-to-learn unit of behavior and a regularity in recording verbal and/or nonverbal data. On the other hand, time units may fragment the teaching situation and hence not reflect the general flow of teaching. Time units seem inappropriate for observing teaching strategies, for example, since it is unlikely that a strategy will be discernible in a three-second, ten-second, or any given arbitrary time unit.

A communication event or activity unit requires the observer to make a record whenever an event or activity occurs. For example, Taba's (Section 9) instrument requires the observer to categorize with every "thought unit"; Bellack's (Section 3) instrument requires the observer to categorize whenever a new pedagogical move and/or change of speaker occurs; and French and Galloway's (Section 1) instrument requires the observer to make a record with every communication event. Such units are often difficult to learn and require much training. However, they generally grow out of the purpose of the instrument and the categories in it. Hence, they become an integral part of the instrument rather than an attachment to it.

These three key issues and others, which do not require much explication here, appear as questions in the list below which an observer might well ask.

1. What is the vantage point of the instrument? That is, what concepts underpin the instrument and thus guide the observer in collecting data. For example, is it psychological climate? Strategies?

2. What type of instrument is it? That is, is it a category system or a sign system or a rating scale?

3. What is the unit of behavior? That is, when does the observer make a record? What type is it? If it is a time unit, which one specifically is it? If it is a communication event or activity, which one specifically is it?

4. Are measurements with this instrument reliable? That is, do trained observers agree about the records they make? Reliability is necessary if objectivity is to be attained. And objectivity is desirable. What degree of agreement is to be considered acceptable is a matter of judgment, however. What is acceptable depends, too, on the method for statistically arriving at a percentage of agreement.

5. Is the instrument fruitful? That is, do the items fit teaching in such a way as to give new insights and valuable data about this complex act called teaching?

6. Is the instrument applicable to other situations? That is, if the instrument was developed in a particular research project, can other researchers and practitioners apply the instument? Can the instrument be used with ease by people not intensively trained by the developers of the instrument?

In regard to category systems in particular:

7. Are the categories all-inclusive? That is, do all instances of the observed behavior fit into one of the categories? If it is not possible to categorize a specific instance of behavior, then the set of categories is incomplete and requires further expansion.

8. Are the categories mutually exclusive? That is, are the categories

so precisely defined that each is distinct from the other? If so, then each instance of behavior fits into one and only one category. This is necessary in order to achieve reliability among observers.

9. Are the categories useful? Reliability obviously must not be achieved at the expense of having so few categories or such obvious ones ("teacher talks," "pupil talks") that the usefulness of the data would be limited (7:197). On the other hand, if there are too many categories, reliability is likely to decrease along with a decrease in the utility of the instrument. A large set of categories would require so much skill on the part of the observers that its usefulness in the future would be severely limited. As Flanders says, "somewhere between too many and too few categories is an optimum number" (7:197). This optimum number depends on many factors, including the vantage point, the purpose of the observation, and the skill of the observers.

Outcome of Studying Teaching

From this collection, the reader should gain new insights into teaching. These should help him to clarify and define his ideas about teaching and to review these ideas from a new and broader perspective. This gain in precision and breadth should lead to new questions, and these, in turn, to new answers; thus the reader may be encouraged to modify his own views about teaching.

In any case, he should be better able to understand, assess, and compare the teaching that he reads about and sees, and he should be in a better position to explore the possibilities of devising and using instruments of research based on the various selections.

Summary

This book has many purposes. It provides an anthology of articles on teaching grouped according to the authors' frames of reference. It breaks new ground by presenting in readily available form material to be used by pre-service and in-service teachers as they study the multiple vantage points from which educators view teaching. It offers the reader the prospect of new insights into teaching. It suggests the acknowledgment of a new field in education for which no name presently exists. (Perhaps the term *pedagography* would be appropriate.) This book is the result of a new effort to shed light on teaching and is presented in the hope that it will help some improve their own teaching, enlist some as "pedagographers," and encourage others to join the growing corps of investigators of teaching. It is offered as a seed rather than as a harvest.

1. Bellack, Arno A. "Methods for Observing Classroom Behavior of Teachers and Students." Paper written for discussion at the conference on Methods of Determining Criteria for the Evaluation of Comprehensive Schools sponsored by Padagogisches Zentrum, Berlin, November 12-15, 1968. Mimeographed.

2. Belth, Marc. *Education as a Discipline: A Study of the Role of Models in Thinking.* Boston: Allyn and Bacon, 1965.

3. Bettelheim, Bruno. *The Informed Heart.* New York: The Free Press of Glencoe, 1960.

4. Black, Max. *Models and Metaphors.* Ithaca, N.Y.: Cornell University Press, 1962. Chapter 13.

5. Bruner, Jerome S. "Needed: A Theory of Instruction." *Educational Leadership,* 20:523-532, May, 1963.

6. Cohen, Morris R. *The Meaning of Human History.* LaSalle, Ill.: Open Court Publishing Company, 1947.

7. Flanders, Ned. "Some Relationships among Teacher Influence, Pupil Attitudes, and Achievement." *Contemporary Research on Teacher Effectiveness.* Edited by Bruce J. Biddle and William J. Ellana. New York: Holt, Rinehart and Winston, 1964. Pages 196-231.

8. Gage, N. L. "Paradigms for Research on Teaching." *Handbook of Research on Teaching.* Edited by N. L. Gage. Chicago: Rand McNally and Company, 1963. Pages 94-141.

9. Green, Thomas F. "A Topology of the Teaching Concept." *Studies in Philosophy and Education,* 3:284-319, Winter, 1964-65.

10. Hughes, Marie M. "Utah Study of the Assessment of Teaching." *Theory and Research in Teaching.* Edited by Arno A. Bellack. New York: Bureau of Publications, Teachers College, Columbia University, 1963. Pages 25-36.

11. Hyman, Ronald T., ed. *Contemporary Thought on Teaching.* Englewood Cliffs, N.J.: Prentice-Hall, 1971.

12. Hyman, Ronald T. *Ways of Teaching,* 2d ed. Philadelphia: J. B. Lippincott Company, 1974.

13. Jackson, Philip W. "The Way Teaching Is." *The Way Teaching Is.* Washington, D.C.: National Education Association, 1966. Pages 7-27.

14. James, William. *Talks to Teachers on Psychology and To Students on Some of Life's Ideals.* New York: W. W. Norton, 1958.

15. Langer, Susanne K. *Philosophy in a New Key.* New York: Mentor Book, 1942.

16. Pepper, Stephen C. *World Hypotheses.* Berkeley: University of California Press, 1942.

17. Rosenshine, Barak. "Evaluation of Classroom Instruction." *Review of Educational Research,* 40:279-300, April, 1970.

18. Rosenshine, Barak, and Norma Furst. "The Use of Direct Observation to Study Teaching." *Second Handbook of Research on Teaching.* Edited by Robert M. W. Travers. Chicago: Rand McNally and Company, 1973. Pages 122-183.

19. Scheffler, Israel. "Philosophical Models of Teaching." *Harvard Educational Review,* 35:131-143, Spring, 1955.

20. Schwab, Joseph J. "Structure of the Disciplines: Meanings and Significances." *The Structure of Knowledge and the Curriculum.* Edited by G. W. Ford and Lawrence Pugno. Chicago: Rand McNally, 1964. Pages 6-30.

21. Smith, B. Othanel. "A Concept of Teaching." *Language and Concepts in Education.* Edited by B. Othanel Smith and Robert H. Ennis. Chicago: Rand

McNally and Company, 1961. Pages 86-101.

22. Smith B. Othanel. "Toward A Theory of Teaching." *Theory and Research in Teaching.* Edited by Arno A. Bellack. New York: Bureau of Publications, Teachers College, Columbia University, 1963. Pages 1-10.

23. Tyler, Ralph W. "The Contribution of the Behavioral Sciences to Educational Research." *First Annual Phi Delta Kappa Symposium on Education Research.* Edited by Frank W. Banghart, Bloomington, Ind.: Phi Delta Kappa, 1960. Pages 55-70.

24. Winch, Peter. *The Idea of a Social Science.* New York: Humanities Press, 1958.

1 *Communications*

Overview

That teaching involves communication is a truism which nobody challenges, whatever his concept of teaching. Yet only recently have educators begun to analyze teaching with the help of concepts from communications theory. This lag is partly due to the relative newness of communications, cybernetics, and information theory as fields of study in themselves. These areas have developed only within the last quarter of a century.

The six selections in this first vantage point of Communications represent a wide range of approaches and purposes. Gerbner sees communications as the process which humanizes man; he presents a model of this process and considers its implications for teaching. The Packers view communication in the teaching-learning process with the aid of concepts drawn from cybernetics, making particular use of information bits, uncertainty, entropy, and feedback. Lewis, Newell, and Withall employ communications concepts identified in an earlier article by Lewis dealing with mental health in the classroom. Zahorik studies just the perception by the pupils of their teachers' verbal feedback. French and Galloway examine the function of different communication events in teaching. Greenberg looks at the flow of a teacher's communication and the resulting interaction patterns. As in other sections, these articles supplement one another so as to yield a broad application to the study of teaching from this perspective.

It is important to note that these selections do not present teaching *as if it* were communication. They describe teaching as one instance of human behavior that involves communications. That is, teaching is a specific case of a more general abstraction called communication. This procedure is in contrast to other selections in this book, which, for example, say that teaching may be likened to short-story writing or psychotherapy or a game or a computer. Hence, the selections in this chapter cannot be critized as using inadequate analogies for teaching. Teaching involves communications in a special way, and it is the task of educators to identify it. Indeed, this is precisely the task of the current surge of investigations on teaching.

All the complex models of communication have as their base a quite simple model that may be diagrammed as follows:

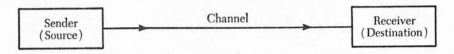

This diagram may be slightly embellished by the addition of three more concepts:

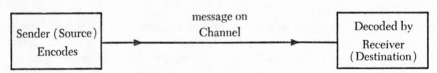

This simple model applies to verbal communication that, we are reminded by our authors, concerns cognitive, affective, and skill behavior as well as nonverbal behavior such as physical actions, facial expressions, written symbols, and a speaker's tone qualities. This simple scheme serves as the foundation of the models by Gerbner and the Packers.

It is necessary to remember that, though all the articles emphasize verbal communication, their ideas apply to nonverbal behavior as well. Their emphasis in no way implies that verbal communication is more important than nonverbal communication. Rather, verbal behavior is the prime means of human communication. This notion is advanced by Flanders in the section on classroom social climate as justification for coding only verbal behavior in teaching.

The concept of a communications system described by the Packers calls to mind the four pedagogical moves by Bellack and his associates, for these moves also constitute a system; two of Bellack's pedagogical moves (structuring and soliciting) are initiatory, while two (responding and reacting) are reflexive. Indeed, Bellack has combined these moves into various teaching cycles (see Section 3) which resemble Green-berg's interaction patterns. Zahorik's concept of feedback is similar to Bloom's (Section 4) concept of reinforcement. French and Galloway refer to that unique combination of Flanders' and Galloway's formula-tions which is included in this book in Section 8. Thus, the ideas from this vantage point tie in with other systems.

Lewis, Newell, and Withall present a study based on an instrument for classifying the dominant intention of classroom communication (primarily verbal communication). They utilize four concepts of com-munication presented by Lewis in an earlier article which they cite. These concepts are receptiveness, accuracy, mobility, and responsive-ness. The authors give examples for each category to assure observer agreement. The reader is alerted to the fact that the unit of behavior in this study is a ten-second time interval, as opposed to the "communica-tive event" employed by French and Galloway. Furthermore, the results of this study conducted with graduate students are consistent with a parallel study with undergraduates also conducted at the Uni-versity of Wisconsin.[1]

This section, more than any other, illustrates a major point of this book. Perception of events is selective, and meaning varies according to the receiver's point of view. This is particularly evident in the articles by Zahorik and Gerbner. It is also stressed by the Packers when they ask the teachers to consider which messages that they are transmitting to the pupils are in reality being received. For the Packers, this act of determin-ing which message is received distinguishes the teacher from the scholar. This idea of selectivity applies as well to what the teacher receives in feedback from the pupils.

Gerbner makes the point that if we do not provide for free selection, a representative context, and equitable availability in communication, we manipulate rather than educate. He asks us to challenge cherished assumptions so as to lead the pupil to self-direction. In his study with undergraduates cited earlier, Withall reports "many of the hard core educational values and procedures by which student teachers are guided seem to have been derived in part from their elementary and high school teachers and from the cooperating or master teacher in whose classroom they teach during their student teaching experience."[2] This, too, is a call for research on ways to change teachers' communicating skills and values in order to improve their teaching.

This need for change is particularly significant in light of Zahorik's statements about feedback. (1) "The results concerning general feed-

[1]John Withall, "Mental Health-Teacher Education Research Project," *Journal of Teacher Education*, 14:318–325, September, 1963.
[2]Ibid., p. 323.

back usage suggest that teacher verbal feedback during the interactive classroom situation is a rather rigid behavior. Only a few types of feedback are used with regularity and these types may be less informational than others which are used infrequently."[3] (2) "The types of feedback that are regularly used are not necessarily the types that are the most valuable for provoking feeling and providing information on correctness, explanation, and direction." (See Zahorik's selection.)

Further research on teaching from this communications perspective is clearly needed. Many questions for research are raised. For example, what are the effects of various kinds of "noise" on classroom communication? (*Noise* is used here in its technical sense to mean any additional information transmitted to the receiver not sent by the sender. That is, more information is in the output than in the input.) Are there different effects for the various subject-matter fields, age levels of pupils, and ability levels of pupils? How much redundancy does the teacher need to provide in order to eliminate the lack of communication due to "equivocation," which refers to the situation where there is more information transmitted than received? Does the amount of redundancy needed change according to subject-matter area, age level of pupils, and ability level of pupils? Is it different for communication of cognitive matters, affective concerns, and motor skills? Will learning increase if formal feedback procedures are instituted that go beyond the usual written examination? Will learning increase if students are taught to assess communication, as suggested by Gerbner? These are but several of the questions that need answers. Obviously, it is fruitful to talk about teaching in these communications terms.

[3]John A. Zahorik, "Classroom Feedback Behavior of Teachers," *Journal of Educational Research*, 62:149, December, 1968. See also his article on feedback in the May-June, 1970, issue (Volume 63, Number 9) of this same journal.

1 A Theory of Communication and Its Implications for Teaching

George Gerbner

Is there a "communication approach" to human problems? If the answer is yes, what is it? What are reasons for taking such an approach? What are reasons for the development of it? What can such an approach contribute to understanding and judgment? And what implications can be derived for teaching and for the curriculum?

These are the questions I would like to reflect upon with you.

Let me define communication as social interaction performed through messages. Messages may be defined as formally coded or symbolic or representational events which are of some shared significance in a culture, and which are produced for the purpose of evoking significance.

My distinction between the "communication approach" and other approaches to human behavior rests, therefore, on the extent to which (1) messages are germane to the process studied, and (2) concern with the production, nature, and uses of messages is central to the approach employed. If there is a "communication approach" or theory or discipline, it can be distinguished from others in that *it makes the nature and role of messages in life and society its central organizing concern.*

Reprinted with permission from *The Nature of Teaching*, edited by Louise M. Berman. Copyright © 1963 by the University of Wisconsin-Milwaukee. (Numbering has been retained as in original article.)

There are many reasons for studying the nature and role of messages in life and society. Some are traditional. Certain familiar reasons include the acquisition or improvement of communication skills, appreciations, tactics, and the knowledge itself which messages and message systems signify and convey. The same reasons underlie our studies of language, composition, rhetoric, literature, art, and various other modes of verbal and non-verbal expression.

Another and less familiar reason exists for studying the nature and role of messages in life and society. Although applicable to all ages, this new reason is the outgrowth of the historical and cultural circumstances of the twentieth century. As the industrial revolution has transformed man's relation to society, the communication revolution—an extension of the industrial revolution to the mass-production of messages—has transformed man's relation to culture. This transformation has brought about the need to re-examine basic assumptions about the nature and role of messages in life and society, to inquire into the humanizing potentials of communications and of communication systems. That need is, in my view, the basic reason and historical rationale for the emergence of a "communication approach" to human problems.

This approach is primarily analytical and critical. It does not necessarily take the objectives of communicators or existing institutional goals as its point of departure or standard of value. Rather, it attempts to raise questions about all these components as parts of total communication situations to be assessed in order to arrive at a fuller understanding of the humanizing potentials of messages in communication, and of communications in culture. A by-product of this effort might be the improvement of skills, appreciations, and tactics. But the end result should be an improvement of standards.

It is in this way that I would like to approach a theory of communication and its implications for teaching. First, we shall consider, in a very brief outline, a view of communication as a humanizing process. Then I will sketch the development of a theory and model of communication not inconsistent with the demands placed upon theory in our view of the humanizing functions of communication. Our model will help illustrate some operational elements and relationships in communication on the process level; it will help answer the question: What happens when we interact through messages?

Next we shall ask: What *should* happen when we interact through messages? What are the desirable qualities of our operational elements and relationships in the light of our view of communication as a humanizing process? What communication and teaching functions serve these values?

After discussing communication and its implications for teaching on the value level, we shall conclude with some suggestions on the institutional level. The question there is: What happens when industrial institutions mass-produce message systems making up much of the popular culture in which all educational enterprises operate? What are some roles and responsibilities of formal education in the new cultural situation?

Communication, a Humanizing Process

How did *Homo sapiens* become human?

A hundred million years of evolution is compressed in the word "comprehend." It stems from the expression "to grasp with the forehand." The ability to grasp with the hand and with the mind literally developed hand-in-hand.

Life in damp tropical forests freed the forearms of a certain group of primates from the burden of carrying the body, and made them into hands—strong, sure, and delicate instruments. Exceptionally deft manipulation required an exceptionally large and complex control system—the human brain. The needs of hand-brain coordination made it possible to develop the brain capacity necessary for holding an image long enough to reflect on it, store it, and retrieve it. This capacity is the prerequisite for the production and use of messages, and thus for human communication.

The invasion of glaciers robbed hominoids of their arboreal paradise and forced them to taste the fruits of a new type of knowledge. Huddled in cold valleys, flooded even during the warm spells, hardpressed to develop resources of collaboration, community, and communication, *Homo sapiens* transformed himself into what we would recognize as human. He emerged from the Ice Ages a pretty accomplished artist, scientist, and organizer.

Communication played, and plays, a unique part in the human transformation. The original "wisdom of *Homo* the "*sapiens*" stems from his symboling ability which arose, along with his tool-making talents, from marvelous hand-brain coordination and development put to communal uses. This symboling ability is the capacity to produce messages; to record, represent, and re-create aspects of the human condition; to encode, share, and decode significance; and thus, to extend the scope of consciousness beyond the reach of the senses, and to create a vision of human potentialities and requirements beyond that of any living species.

Communication infuses the other humanizing processes of collaboration and community with our most uniquely human characteristics. It does that by performing certain specialized functions in society and culture. I call these the humanizing functions of communication.

Humanizing Functions of Communications

The shaping of sounds, forms, images, and stories into language, magic, legend and ritual arose from the needs of survival through living and working together. One function of these communication activities was to make work easier, life meaningful, ways of looking at life and the world convincing to those born into a culture. Let me call this the *art* function of communication as a social enterprise. Man the communicator as artist informed and inspired, frightened and entertained as he helped all to bear the hardships, share the joys, avoid the dangers, and celebrate the accomplishments of communal life. He made the truths of the tribe—or of the culture—believable and compelling.

From the taming of fire to the sowing of seeds man learned not only the arts of making truths believable, but also the importance of making beliefs truer. Man reached out, got burned, and fled in panic. But not always. For he could also reflect and so he could contemplate an abstract proposition: Which end of a burning stick could be seized with impunity? Let me call this the *science* function of communication as a social enterprise. Man the communicator, as scientist, undertakes to assess the validity of propositions. His function is, therefore, to make beliefs truer.

The art of moving men and the science of moving mountains confer the power to move men to move mountains. The distribution and use of this power is the third social function in communication. It is the *organizing* or administrative, or governmental function. Man the communicator as organizer is responsible for the structure of conscious reflective choices. He deals with the production, availability, and selection of messages. He decides the balance of representations available; he stacks the decks of any message system; he controls the purpose, nature and extent of freedoms built into those systems. As the humanizing role of the communicator as scientist is to make beliefs truer, and as artist to make truths more believable, his responsibility as administrator is to organize the energy and power of message systems to promote liberating ends and to make knowledge freer.

This is my view of communication as a humanizing process. I submit that theories and models of communication become useful in a general way if they have some relevance to problems of conceptual organization, judgment, and action in the humanizing process.

A Communication Model: The Process Level

If communication is interaction through messages, we must be able to *produce* messages, and we must be able to *perceive* messages. In other words, we must be able to perceive events in a special way, and produce events in equally unique ways reflecting that special type of perception.

If we draw circles for elements and bars for interactions between the elements, a diagram can be made of a communication act.

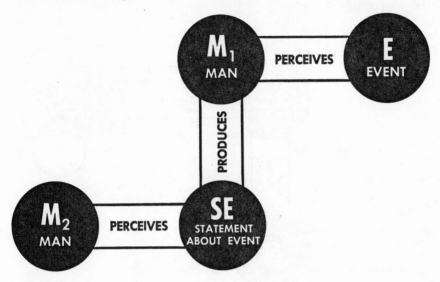

FIGURE 1

Figure 1 is the skeleton of a basic communication act. A man perceives an event (horizontal dimension) and produces a statement about it (vertical dimension); another man perceives the statement (horizontal dimension).

Let us now look more deeply into this process, first along the perceptual (horizontal) dimension. Events (including statements) must be *available* to be perceived; you can't play the game without cards. (But the kind of cards available will, of course, determine the kind of game played.)

Secondly, the event (or statement) must be *selected* for perception. We cannot attend to all things; attention is selective. Choices depend upon availability of items. But choices also depend upon a third element of the perceptual field: context.

Context describes the method in which parts of a whole are woven together in time and space. It is the way the deck is shuffled. It affects chances of selecting any one event in a series or field of events. In addition, the context of presentation (structure of the outside field) and the context of interpretation (structure of the inside field) affect the meaning we attribute to perceptions.

Availability, context, and selection lead us from the world outside to the world inside. Let us draw a smaller circle inside "man" (M) standing for the event (or statement) "as perceived" (E' or SE'). If we also write in some of the terms of perception, the horizontal dimension of our model takes on certain changes.

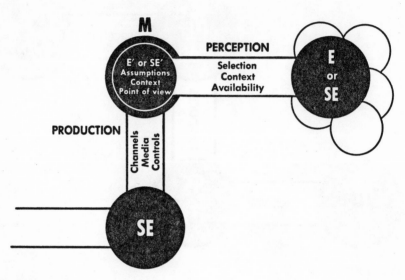

FIGURE 2

As Figure 2 shows, I am suggesting that we perceive in terms of prior *assumption,* that we fit our perceptions into a *context* of our own, and that we can only perceive (or conceive of) something from where we are—from a *point of view.* Let me illustrate.

If I ask you the shape of Figure 3, chances are you will say it is a trapezoid. If I ask you the shape of a window, chances are you will say it is rectangular, even if you see it from a side view. Yet, if you see the window from a side view, its shape might look something like Figure 4. And the shape of Figure 4 is the same as the shape of Figure 3.

Why does that happen? We live in a world of rectangular shapes (some would say squares); but trapezoids are rare. So when we see a trapezoid in a familiar *context,* we *assume* that "really" it is a rectangular object seen from a *point of view* which makes rectangles appear trapezoidal.

We learn to perceive things in this way. We learn this unconsciously; but we learn this way of perceiving so well that sometimes we see a rectangle in perspective, even when looking at a shape we *know* is really trapezoidal. The assumptions, contexts, and points of view which have formed the terms of our perceptions make it difficult to see some things as they "really" are. Figure 5 shows that our "window" is not, in fact, rectangular. But it is easier to assume that the yardsticks are cheating, or even that the hands holding the "window" in Figure 6 are of different

FIGURE 3

size, than to see a trapezoidal window. Every perception, therefore, is a judgment based on past experience and present expectation.

The significance of these statements for communication is two-fold. First, the messages we produce reflect the terms upon which we perceive. (The history of perspective drawing, for example, shows a growing awareness of these terms.) Secondly, the way we perceive messages will be determined both by the terms of perception *built into* messages, and the assumptions, contexts, and points of view *brought to* the perception of messages.

FIGURE 4

FIGURE 5

We can now complete our basic diagram of a communication act.

Figure 7 shows that an event (or statement) available in a certain context is selected for perception in terms of the perceiver's assumptions, context, and point of view. The perceiver is also a communicator; he uses some means and controls (channels, media, *etc.*, as I am using language and print on this paper) to produce a statement about the event. In this way the process continues.

FIGURE 6

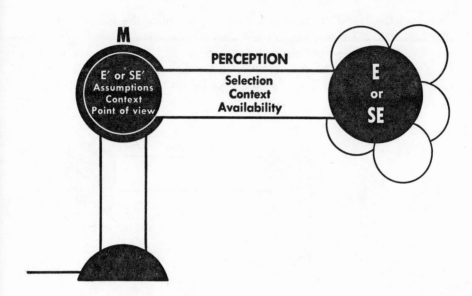

FIGURE 7

Failure to understand terms implicit in our messages may leave us in the dark about what happens, and why, as the exchange goes on. . . .

The Job of the Teacher

What is the job of the teacher? Is it to cultivate existing assumptions, whatever they might be, in order to put across the desired "message"? This is, in effect, what some lists of "helpful hints" on "effective communication" tell us. This is what much narrowly conceived and superficially interpreted research on communication "effects" tells us. But cultivating existing assumptions in order to put across the desired "message" is manipulation, not education.

Often the teacher cannot honestly convey his message without challenging cherished assumptions. And, at times, unexamined assumptions implicitly reflected in messages counter and negate the explicit "lessons." Therefore, the analysis of messages in teaching first leads to self-analysis: What am I communicating besides what I think I am teaching? Am I talking about "a government of laws and not of men"—but from a Lone Ranger point of view? Do I need monsters to make a unit on space travel or on life on other planets more believable? If so, I may be an "effective" communicator, but I should not be in the classroom. I should not be in the classroom for the simple reason that successfully manipulating people, even into the "right" conclusions, only impoverishes the bases of self-direction and, therefore, negates the aims of education.

People learn best not what their teachers think they teach or what their preachers think they preach, but what their cultures in fact cultivate. We "teach" many things, most of them short-lived. But we cultivate

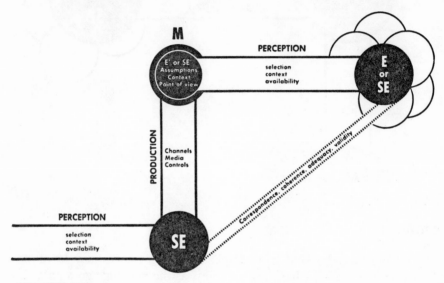

FIGURE 11

the assumptions, contexts, and points of view in terms of which we communicate all things. These terms are likely to be the most lasting and least examined parts of our lessons. So the questions I ask as I reflect on teaching as a communication process are these: What approach to the subject and to learning itself did I cultivate when I only meant to transmit a few "facts"? What perspectives on man, life, and the world did I present when I only meant to teach English or geography or math or physics?

The Value Level

These questions bring us to the level of values. That teaching has elements of art, science, and organization is no news to anyone. It should not be surprising, then, that teaching has the values of these activities as humanizing functions in communication.

Let us develop a value-oriented version of our communication model. First, we shall supply a dimension missing from the operational version of the model, but present in every real communication situation: the relationship between the statement (now conceived as a single specific proposition) and what the statement is "about." This is the hypotenuse of our model, shown in Figure 11. This relationship may be characterized by the presence or absence of qualities of correspondence, coherence, adequacy, or validity attributed to the message.

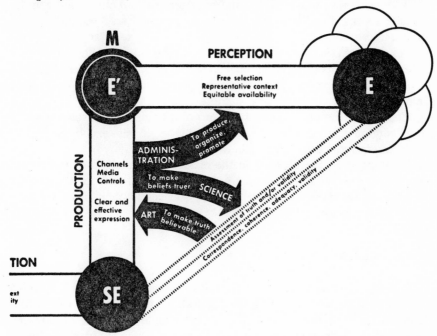

FIGURE 12

Now let us ask the question: What *should* happen as we interact through messages? What are the desirable, the humanizing qualities of each of the three dimensions of our communication model? And how do the functions of organization, science, and art serve these qualities?

Along the perceptual dimension we have selection, context, and availability as operational elements. What do we ask of these? We ask that selection be as *free* as possible, that context be as *representative* as possible, and that availability be as *equitable* as possible. So the ideal (even if troublesome) criterion of value along this dimension is *free selection in a representative context of pertinent evidence.*

The hypotenuse of our model is the relationship between statements and what statements are "about." Here we consider it desirable to *assess* qualities of *truth and validity* built into our messages.

The production dimension relates the terms of our perception and cognition—our "beliefs"—to the statements we make. Here we want skillful use of channels, media, controls, etc. to reflect these "beliefs" in effective forms. We want to produce *clear and believable messages.*

Figure 12 shows these qualities of the three dimensions. It also indicates how the functions of administration, science, and art serve these qualities.

The teacher as administrator and organizer of communication activities uses means, facilities, and controls to promote free selection in a representative context of pertinent evidence. The teacher as scientist assesses the truth qualities of information and the validity of assumptions, contexts, and points of view implicit in statements. The teacher as artist uses his skills and materials to express true and valid beliefs in clear and convincing forms.

Combining the humanizing functions of administration, science, and art in communication, the teacher thus strives to make choices freer, beliefs truer, and truths more believable.

Scrutiny of communication in the classroom is analysis of messages and processes. It leads, on one hand, to self-analysis, and, on the other, to a concern with the full range of consequences implicit in communication as a humanizing process.

The Institutional Level

Finally, we come to the institutional level. Concrete historical developments give our concern with communication processes and values its urgency and relevance. If it is true that most people learn best what their cultures cultivate, a revolution in culture has brought about a transformation in learning and altered the position of the teacher and the school in society.

The industrial revolution has shifted into the communications phase. Message-systems which provide many of the raw materials of our consciousness (and of the terms of our perceptions) have become mass-produced, institutionalized commodities. Bigness, fewness, and costliness in cultural, as in any other, mass production brought centralization of control, standardization of product, streamlined efficiency of technique. These changes meant increasing penetration of influence into many spheres of life and across many previous boundaries of place, time, and social status. We can safely say that never before could so many people in so many places know and talk so much about the same things at the same time.

The shape of human affairs has changed. Instead of the slow filtering down process, we have the almost simultaneous introduction of information, ideas, and products at all levels of society. Mass production and distribution of communications to scattered, heterogeneous audiences means potential enrichment of cultural horizons incredible by all previous standards. But it also means that the assumptions, contexts, and points of view which cultivate our perceptions of what is real, what is important, and what is right, now roll off the assembly line bearing a brand name, a corporate image, a marketing approach.

The words of Andrew Fletcher, uttered in 1704, reverberate in the halls of the Academy and, at times, of Congress. "I believe," he said, "that if a man were permitted to write all the ballads, he need not care who should make the laws of the nation." For ours is a revolution in the writing of all the ballads.

The mass media have increasingly taken over democratic national responsibilities for transmitting the cultural heritage, for illuminating the realities of today, and for setting the agenda of tomorrow.

How did the mass media fulfill that responsibility? As well as could be expected, perhaps even better. Being free from public control but lacking guarantees of public support in using that freedom, the mass media must, on the whole, merchandise such gratifications as can be profitably cultivated under the circumstances.

How does formal education find its place and its responsibilities in the new cultural situation? I think we have only begun to diagnose the situation. There is little doubt that we can and should find ways of using the riches available to all for the first time in the history of cultures. It has often been pointed out that we should also help make some order out of the distortions, confusions, and general cultural chaos characterizing the new situation. But all these worthy activities do not go to the heart of the problem.

The new situation is a radical transformation of the ways members of our species became human. Seen in that light, the problem is not only that of tastes, appreciations, discriminating consumership. The problem is also the organization of culture, with all its humanizing functions, both as a public and a private matter. The task is one of citizens' building and molding social institutions for democratic human purposes. We have opportunities to exercise policy choices in the field of popular culture, or to let these choices go by default. The difference is likely to affect our survival as a nation; and, if we survive, it is certain to determine the outcome of our experiment with self-government.

A role education can play in communication on the institutional level is to prepare itself, and the new peneration of citizens, to exercise such choices. It makes little difference whether we think about such studies under the heading of Social Science or Citizenship or English or Mass Media. It is more important that they be conceived as part of general education on all levels rather than only as training in the specific applied skills of communication or of consumership.

Such studies should develop ways of observing modern cultural institutions mass-producing images of man, life, and the world, and of the uses we make of them. They should examine circumstances of cultural production and consumption, and consider what kinds of humanizing aims can be fulfilled under what kinds of conditions. These considerations should result in the development of standards for the citizen as well as for the consumer.

I might now summarize my attempt to present a theory of communication and its implications for teaching as follows: The reasons for the emergence of a "communication approach" rest, I believe, in the trends and developments of the last century. Such an approach or theory or discipline makes the nature and role of messages in life and society its central organizing concern. It attempts to analyze what happens in communication as a teaching process, and to assess the values of what happens. Then the approach turns to the institutional developments from which it sprang. It uses the insights of process and of value to find the place of the school, the role of education, and the responsibilities of the teacher in the new culture in which both we and our students live and grow and learn.

References

Certain aspects and topics in this paper have been developed in greater detail (although in earlier formulations) in the following articles:

GERBNER, GEORGE. "The Individual in a Mass Culture," *Saturday Review,* XLIII (June 18, 1960), 11–13, 36–37. Also (abridged) in *The Executive,* IV (1960), 14–16, and *The National Elementary Principal,* XL (February, 1961), 49–54.

————. "Education and the Challenge of Mass Culture," *Audio-Visual Communication Review,* VII (Fall, 1959), 264–278.

————. "Content Analysis and Critical Research in Mass Communication," *Audio-Visual Communication Review,* VI (Spring, 1958), 85–108.

————. "Toward a General Model of Communication," *Audio-Visual Communication Review,* IV (Summer, 1956), 171–199.

The following sources may be useful to those interested in further exploration of the perceptual aspects, especially the "window" and other similar demonstrations.

CANTRIL, HADLEY. *The "Why" of Man's Experience.* New York: Macmillan, 1950.

KILPATRICK, FRANKLIN P. (ed.). *Explorations in Transactional Psychology.* New York: New York University Press, 1961.

2 Cybernetics, Information Theory and the Educative Process

C. Kyle Packer and Toni Packer

Norbert Wiener coined the word *cybernetics* to designate ". . . the entire field of control and communication theory, whether in the machine or in the animal. . . ."[1] This science and the closely related field of information theory have brought about a sharpening of concepts and rapid development of new ideas as well as a mushrooming of applications, usually in the direction of automation.

But do the concepts that are basic to cybernetics and to information theory have any relevance to education?

One might first think of automatic computing machines and of the fact that some theorists have attempted to draw parallels between these machines and the human brain. This sort of thing will not be attempted here. Rather, it will be suggested that certain concepts taken from cybernetics and from information theory do appear to have a relevance to the teaching-learning process. This is in the nature of a preliminary study which appears to show that further work in this field might bear fruit.

[1]Wiener, Norbert. *Cybernetics* (Cambridge: Technology Press, M.I.T., and New York: John Wiley & Sons, Inc., 1948), p. 19.

Reprinted with permission from *Teachers College Record*, 61:134–142, December, 1959.

These concepts may bear on the teaching-learning process in several ways (*a*) on our *theory* of the process; (*b*) on our *study* of the process— our experimentation; (*c*) on our *knowledge* of the process; and (*d*) on our *attitude* as participants in the process.

We shall take certain concepts singly, in so far as possible, and, though not attempting a survey of cybernetics and of information theory, try to explain the concepts and their potential significance.

Feedback

Feedback is a term that antedates the term cybernetics. Classical examples of feedback are the governor of a steam engine (Watt, 1788) and the household thermostat. Essentially, including feedback in a system means that we use part of our output (the power of our steam engine or the heat of our furnace) to cause a change (in the flyballs of the governor or in the contacts of the thermostat) which, in turn, causes our system to stay within certain bounds.

To make this form of control clearer, contrast it with, say, an automatic washing machine. There is no control which judges the performance (in terms of cleanliness) and determines whether to continue or to stop the washing process. We set the controls according to our intentions. *We* must then judge the results and reset the controls if necessary. *We*, that is, are the means by which feedback does in some measure occur. Thus with a push-button radio, we can set the push button to bring in rather accurately a certain station. When we want that station we push that button. Since there is no feedback by which the actual performance of the radio changes in any manner the setting, no further change in setting will occur. If we wish to tune the station better, *we* have to do it, perhaps at the same time recalibrating our push button.

The very usefulness of the push-button radio, however, shows that this method of control is quite satisfactory in certain systems.

Wiener has cited a dramatic example of feedback in the control system of an elevator. The obvious conclusion of what is essential in such a system very well illustrates the principle of feedback:

It is important that the release for opening the door be dependent on the fact that the elevator is actually at the door; otherwise something might have detained it, and the passenger might step into the empty shaft. This control of a machine on the basis of its *actual* performance rather than its *expected* performance is known as *feedback*. . . .[2]

[2]Norbert Wiener, *The Human Use of Human Beings*, Rev. Ed. (Boston: Houghton Mifflin, 1954), p. 24.

Immediately preceding this example, Wiener states this generalization:

For any machine subject to a varied external environment to act effectively it is necessary that the information concerning the results of its own action be furnished to it as a part of the information on which it must continue to act.[3]

Tustin, using the familiar thermostat as an illustration, contrasts a feedback loop with an open control sequence, by considering the placement of the thermostat in one case indoors, and the other outdoors.[4] In the open control sequence, with the thermostat outside, the room temperature may not stay within the desired range. The two systems may be diagrammed as in Figures 1 and 2.

FIGURE 1 Open Control Sequence

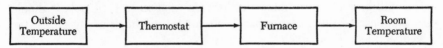

Feedback, diagrammed in Figure 2, shows a circularity which may be described as its characteristic feature.

FIGURE 2 Feedback Loop

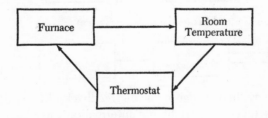

It would appear that feedback, especially in the light of Wiener's generalization quoted above, may be a concept useful to a theory of the teaching-learning process. Clearly the learner needs information concerning the results of his behavior furnished to him as part of the information on which he continues to act. It is not enough that he *intended* to act thus; he needs to know how he *actually* performed.

This difference between the intended pattern of performance and the actual pattern of performance becomes a new input which changes

[3] Wiener, *op. cit.*, p. 24.
[4] Arnold Tustin, "Feedback," in *Automatic Control*, by the editors of *Scientific American* (New York: Simon & Schuster, 1955), pp. 11–13.

both the amount and the direction characteristics of the pattern of performance so that it approximates more closely the pattern desired.[5]

The feedback principle reveals the kind of information needed for improved performance even more explicitly than does the principle of "immediate knowledge of results." Not only the correctness or incorrectness but the deviation, the amount and direction of error, is essential to the system involving feedback.

There are, indeed, cases in which the knowledge of results implies the amount and direction of corrective action, but it is only this implied information which makes feedback successful, not merely the correct model itself. It is thus clear that marking, grading, testing, and so on are rather poor feedback designs in the teaching-learning system.

We have spoken only of the learner, but the concept of the teaching-learning process which has been accepted as the framework for these ideas from cybernetics implies a close link between teacher and learner. This will be referred to later, but here, in relation to feedback, it should be emphasized that the teacher is often the "mechanism" by which the feedback loop is completed.

We are thus contrasting a system which might be diagrammed as in Figure 3 or Figure 4 with the system shown in Figure 5.

FIGURE 3 Open Control Sequence in Main and Subsystems

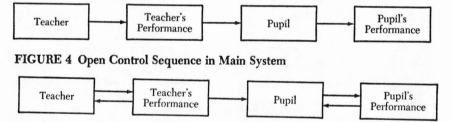

FIGURE 4 Open Control Sequence in Main System

That is to say, in a system involving feedback (Figure 5) the pupil's performance is taken as part of the information on which the teacher

FIGURE 5 Feedback Loop in Main and Subsystems

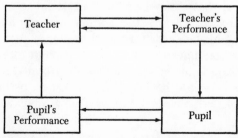

[5]Wiener, *Cybernetics*, p. 13.

continues to act, and some of this information, coming back to the pupil, is the difference between the pupil's actual performance and the given pattern.

The role of information and messages is the very heart of cybernetics, for as Wiener states,

Control . . . is nothing but the sending of messages which effectively change the behavior of the recipient.

It is this study of messages, and in particular of the effective messages of control, which constitutes the science of *Cybernetics*. . . .[6]

And in referring to the link between communication and control, Wiener emphasizes that feedback is essential, for effective control necessitates our receiving messages that our orders have been received, understood, and obeyed.[7]

Without here discussing control or degree of control in the teacher-learner relationship, the need for these return messages in this relationship is patently clear. Certain examples of bad teaching—from emotional outbursts such as "That's the third time he's done these problems and he still hasn't solved them right!" to the almost emotionless ramblings of the absent-minded professor in the lecture hall—show that basically we realize that complete lack of feedback results in a poor teaching-learning situation.

Feedback, in its very simplest form, may be a sort of right or wrong criticism which leaves the figuring out of the pattern to the learner. Parental do's and don'ts may function at this rather simple level. The child may, of course, be getting incidentally other clues which do facilitate his learning. This predisposition to learn is not an in-built characteristic of machines, however, and Wiener has contrasted systems utilizing the simple feedback of the control engineers with systems constructed on the basis of his more generalized conception of feed-back:

If . . . the information which proceeds backward from the performance is able to change the general method and pattern of performance, we have a process which may well be called learning.[8]

Perhaps we could contrast the controlling methods and teaching methods by contrasting feedback of the right-wrong, do-don't type with feedback which gives information as to how the performance could be modified so as to achieve the correct performance.

[6]Wiener, *The Human Use of Human Beings* (Boston: Houghton Mifflin, 1950), pp. 8–9.
[7]See Wiener, *The Human Use of Human Beings*, 1954, p. 16.
[8]Wiener, *The Human Use of Human Beings*, 1954, p. 61.

Conditions may be such that feedback causes oscillation or "hunting," and a breakdown of the system.[9] This may well have a parallel in certain teacher-pupil situations which result in poorer pupil performance, but these considerations will not be elaborated in this discussion.

Some guideposts to the further study of feedback are provided by both Nagel[10] and Tustin,[11] and we may apply their suggestions to the teacher-pupil situation in somewhat the following way: We need to know how to measure performance or to compare it to some standard and, in a sufficiently short time to be effective, alter our methods so as to effect a change in the conditions under which the pupil or student is performing. We must know how to transmit information effectively, know the conditions under which breakdown may occur, and develop ways to predict outcomes in order to prevent such oscillatory behavior from developing.

"Bits" of Information, or Halving Uncertainty

Modern digital computers operate on the binary number system, a number system based on two rather than on the customary ten. In information theory too the binary digit has become the essential unit; the term binary digit being contracted to the word *bit*, which is defined precisely so as to provide an exact standard with which to measure the amount—not the quality—of information. Essentially, if there exists uncertainty and we receive information which *halves* that uncertainty, we have received one *bit* of information.

The nurse's first remark to the nervous father waiting outside the delivery room reduces his uncertainty by one-half. Of the two possibilities, a boy or a girl, her remark that "It's a boy" halves the uncertainty, thus providing one *bit* of information.* Of course this is a simplified view of the situation for the purpose of an example. Other uncertainties exist for the nervous father, and other information is contained in the nurse's remark. Her statement tells that the birth process is complete, her manner may show that all is well, and so on.

In this example, halving the uncertainty made for complete certainty. This is the unusual case. If one hundred possibilities exist, information reducing the uncertainty to fifty would convey one *bit* of information, but would not provide complete certainty. Thus if we know that something

[9]Wiener, *Cybernetics*, p. 14.
[10]Ernest Nagel, "Self-Regulation," in *Automatic Control*, by the editors of *Scientific American* (New York: Simon & Schuster, 1955), pp. 3–4.
[11]Tustin, *op. cit.*, p. 14.
*The logarithmic relation of uncertainty to possibility is seen in the fact that *one* possibility means *no* uncertainty: the logarithm of one is zero.

appears in a 100-page book, the statement that it is on a right-hand page provides one *bit* of information.

Although we may not be in position to measure precisely the amount of information contained in each statement we make, the concept of reducing uncertainty is a useful one in a theory of the teaching-learning process. For the process of teaching and of learning is a process of reducing uncertainty. Furthermore, it will be clear that in order to reduce uncertainty surely and efficiently, the teacher must know some of the uncertainties in the minds of students, know the subject well enough to differentiate among the set of possible messages which includes the misconceptions, and have the skill to communicate in such a manner as to reduce these uncertainties.

These three factors already have been given attention by skilled teachers. Certain features can be brought out in the light of the concepts taken from information theory. First of all, no matter how well organized a certain body of knowledge is, the uncertainties to be considered are primarily those of the student. Ashby states that ". . . the act of 'communication' necessarily implies the existence of a *set* of possibilities, i.e., more than one. . . ."[12] Further:

> . . . we must give up thinking . . . about "this message." We must become scientists, detach ourselves, and think about "people receiving messages." And this means that we must turn our attention from any individual message to the set of all the possibilities.[13]

The fact that two and two are four seems clear and definite, and may be communicated and explained by a few well-chosen examples. However, if one is aware of the need to know the uncertainties in the pupils' minds, one should observe carefully the various thrusts, guesses, and inaccuracies made by the pupils. The pupil must be given ample chance to express his own thinking, not for grading or marking, but so that the teacher gets information on the pupil's uncertainties in order to reduce them.

We do not, in fact, convey any information unless we reduce the uncertainty in the pupil's mind. Statements, no matter how well chosen, convey information only when they reduce uncertainties. That is to say, the information is not contained in the statement *per se.*

It is clear that a statement made to a class of thirty students conveys, in all likelihood, a different amount of information to each. A statement about a deciduous conifer would convey a different amount of informa-

12W. Ross Ashby, *An Introduction to Cybernetics* (London: Chapman & Hall, Ltd.; New York: John Wiley & Sons, 1956), p. 123.
13*Ibid.*, p. 124.

tion to those who knew something about conifers, but not about the larch, from that conveyed to those who knew about the larch.

The set of possible messages has variety to the extent that the elements of the set are distinguishable. However, the variety in a set is in part determined by the powers of discrimination of the observer.[14] The discriminations made by one pupil will not be the same as those made by another. Their two sets of discriminations being different means that different amounts of information are contained in what appears to be the same message. Some people seem to get more out of puns, poetic allusions, or coded messages than others do, owing to differences in their powers of discrimination. In certain cases, satisfactory communication may necessitate altering either the sender's message or the receiver's powers of discrimination.

This presents a different-from-the-usual picture of the communication problem in the teacher-learner situation. *The set of possible messages* is a different base of operation from *the message*. Clearly, then, the teacher's function includes knowing not merely the subject, or message, but the other possibilities—the set—from which this message is selected. The various responses and questions of pupils assume a new significance as clues to this set from which we are selecting our message.

This concept of the teacher's function may, in part, account for the fact that a scholar well versed in his field may be a poor teacher. If he is so oriented toward his subject matter and all of its ramifications that he fails to observe the uncertainties of his students, he may make statements which, though they would be highly informative to certain persons, only slightly reduce the uncertainties of his students and hence convey little information to them. On the other hand, knowing his field well, he may be in a better position to detect crucial uncertainties in his students' thinking and to reduce these with particularly apt and informative remarks.

Moreover, good teachers know that parroted statements do not prove learning. They contain little information because they do not reduce the teacher's uncertainty about the uncertainty of the pupil. In "Mending Wall," Robert Frost speaks of the proverbial masking understanding and preventing investigation:

> He moves in darkness as it seems to me,
> Not of woods only and the shade of trees.
> He will not go behind his father's saying,
> And he likes having thought of it so well
> He says again, "Good fences make good neighbours."[15]

[14]*Ibid.*, pp. 124–26.
[15]From *Complete Poems of Robert Frost*, Copyright, 1930, 1949, by Henry Holt and Company, Inc. By permission of publishers.

Coupling

In the foregoing remarks on feedback and on *bits* of information, it is clearly evident that the teacher and the student are linked in a system in which reciprocal communication is of utmost importance.

This process has been described as "coupling." According to Ashby,

The coupling is of profound importance in science, for when the experimenter runs an experiment he is coupling himself temporarily to the system that he is studying.[16]

If this is true, then the teacher-student or teacher-class coupling is certainly a vital concept in studying the teaching-learning process.

When individual components are coupled, each affects the conditions or the input of the other. The resultant combination is a *new system*. The teacher-class system must be regarded as a system of coupled components, not as two unrelated systems operating by chance along the same time-scale.

This concept is useful in studying the teaching-learning process or in studying a particular teacher-class system. It should be helpful in reforming the teacher's attitudes toward his role in the classroom.

Coupling which results in a system in which each component affects the other is coupling with feedback. This is in contrast to the system in which one component dominates the other; that is, a system in which one component affects the other without the other affecting it.

Systems with interacting components were considered in the section on feedback. Again, in the discussion on bits of information, coupling was indicated to be essential to the communication process. There it was pointed out that reducing uncertainty of pupils involved getting information as to their uncertainties; that is, information must be communicated back and forth between teacher and student. Thus conceived, mistakes of the students are not unfortunate circumstances, but part of the information on which the teacher bases his teaching.

Further, the instructor who examines the total system in which he and the students are coupled will observe different relationships from those observed by the instructor who examines the students as an independent, non-coupled system. Observations on the teacher or parent as part of a coupled system have been made by Davis and Dollard,[17] based upon Hull's concept of "circular reinforcement,"[18] and by Porter.[19]

[16]Ashby, *op. cit.*, p. 48.

[17]Allison Davis and John Dollard, *Children of Bondage* (Washington, D. C.: American Council on Education, 1940), pp. 281–85.

[18]Clark Hull, Abstract of S-R Sessions of Monday-Night Group, 1938–39 (Institute of Human Relations, Yale University, 1939), p. 4. Mimeographed.

[19]E. H. Porter, Jr., *Therapeutic Counseling* (Boston: Houghton Mifflin Co., 1950), pp. 45–48.

Entropy and Disorganization

Here we shall be concerned with an apparent law with which human beings are battling in their whole efforts to achieve organization: the law that disintegration is constantly occurring. This is certainly true in any system of communication and should be taken for granted in the class-room. It may well bear on our attitudes as participants in the teaching-learning process, for, if nothing else, the expected can be approached with forethought and planning.

As long ago as 1824 Carnot showed that while the energy changes in a steam engine resulted in no loss of energy, they did result in a state in which that part of the energy of the steam going to the condenser was no longer available for work. The thermodynamic processes of even the most efficient heat engine result in this "unavailable energy." Clausius, in formulating mathematically the unavailable energy (1854) as the product of two factors, introduced the term "entropy" for the one factor, "temperature" being the other. It has been shown that entropy must either remain constant (and then only under theoretically ideal conditions) or increase, but it could never decrease. That is to say, the entropy of the universe increases, hence the universe is "dying" because more and more energy becomes unavailable. These ideas have been promulgated by and been the concern of many workers since the second law of thermodynamics was stated, following the work of Carnot.

At the risk of oversimplification, the essential ideas are that in practice all energy changes are accompanied by some energy being converted into heat. Further, heat cannot be transformed completely into other forms of energy, with the result that it becomes unavailable: it is and will remain heat. Heat does not flow from a colder to a hotter body, but only in the reverse direction. As a result of all this, the temperature will tend to reach an average, a uniform level, a state of equilibrium. In terms of probability: the improbable, the ordered, states will disappear and only the more probable, random, or disordered states will persist in the universe. Entropy thus has been viewed as a measure of randomness, of disorganization, of the "most probable states."

Shannon and Wiener pointed out the similarity of the form of probability calculations of the information in a message with the formula for entropy as a measure of thermodynamical probability. Our approach in making analogies and comparisons should be cautious, but the relevancy to our undertaking crops out in many statements of authorities. For example, Wiener stated:

That information may be dissipated but not gained, is, as we have seen, the cybernetic form of the second law of thermodynamics.[20]

[20]Wiener, *The Human Use of Human Beings,* 1954, p. 78.

And again:

. . . we can show by general observations that phonetic language reaches the receiving apparatus with less over-all information than was originally sent, or at any rate with not more than the transmission system leading to the ear can convey; and that both semantic and behavior language contain less information still.[21]

This tendency toward deterioration is part and parcel of the act of communication; hence our concern in education. Wiener points out that

The commands through which we exercise our control over our environment are a kind of information which we impart to it. Like any form of information, these commands are subject to disorganization in transit. They generally come through in less coherent fashion and certainly not more coherently than they were sent. In control and communication we are always fighting nature's tendency to degrade the organized and to destroy the meaningful; the tendency, as Gibbs has shown us, for entropy to increase.[22]

Educators should not be surprised at this natural tendency being in action in the classroom. It falls largely to us to fight this; enlisting the aid of the pupil if we can, but in no case blaming him for this natural phenomenon.

The implication to education may be even broader:

As entropy increases, the universe, and all closed systems in the universe, tend naturally to deteriorate and lose their distinctiveness, to move from the least to the most probable state, from a state of organization and differentiation . . . to a state of chaos and sameness. . . . But . . . there are local enclaves whose direction seems opposed to that of the universe at large and in which there is a limited and temporary tendency for organization to increase.[23]

Education, in perpetuating the culture of the group, may tend to aid the increase of entropy—to increase, that is, the sameness of cultural patterns. However, to the extent that it provides centers for the birth and growth of these local enclaves in which organization and differentiation increase, itends to cause entropy to decrease. The dual aspects of culture and of education—stability and change—have been pointed out by others.[24]

[21]*Ibid.*, p. 81.
[22]*Ibid.*, p. 17.
[23]*Ibid.*, p. 12.
[24]Melville J. Herskovits, *Man and His Works* (New York: Alfred A. Knopf, 1952), pp. 40, 491.

The Field of Cybernetics

In his work *On Human Communication*, Colin Cherry writes:

... it was apparent during the years immediately preceding the Second World War that the ideas, basic concepts, and methods of communication engineering were of wide applicability to other specialized branches of science. The lead was taken by Norbert Wiener who, with Rosenblueth, called attention to the great generality of the concept of *feedback*, which had been studied intensively by communication engineers for twenty years, and emphasized that this concept provided a useful relationship between biological and physical sciences. They referred to this general study as *cybernetics*. . . .[25]

Ashby states that

Cybernetics . . . treats, not things but *ways of behaving*. It does not ask "What *is* this thing?" but "*What does it do?*" . . . Cybernetics deals with all forms of behaviour in so far as they are regular, or determinate, or reproducible.[26]

One must consider whether the teacher-pupil or teacher-class system could be studied from the standpoint of cybernetics as has been suggested in this article. Surely, if such a study is to be fruitful, it must go beyond mere analogies. Further, a good theoretical groundwork should not be compromised by liberties taken to make "applications."

Ashby has described "two peculiar scientific virtues of cybernetics" which may strengthen claims here presented:

One is that it offers a single vocabulary and a single set of concepts suitable for representing the most diverse types of system. . . .
The second . . . is that it offers a method for the scientific treatment of the system in which complexity is outstanding and too important to be ignored.[27]

There is no doubt that the systems with which we are concerned in the teaching-learning process are extremely complex. Clear concepts expressed in adequate terminology in a framework that is broad enough to encompass the complexity of the systems we study may be the result of the application of the methods and concepts of cybernetics to the teaching-learning process.

[25]Colin Cherry, *On Human Communication* (Cambridge: Technology Press, M.I.T., and New York: John Wiley & Sons, 1957), p. 56.
[26]Ashby, *op. cit.*, p. 1.
[27]*Ibid.*, pp. 4–5.

3 An Analysis of Classroom Patterns of Communication

W. W. Lewis, John M. Newell, and John Withall

The purpose of this paper is to (a) describe the origins and use of a set of observational categories for studies of interaction in the classroom and (b) report the sensitivity of these categories to the classroom communication behaviors of two instructors teaching according to two predetermined instructional methods or foci. Although a number of systems for this purpose are already available (1, 3, 6), they are structured around concepts like dominative-integrative or teacher-centered versus learner-centered behavior. The studies being described here are rather specifically oriented toward the description of classroom interaction as a process of communication acts (4).

Communication acts are defined broadly to include the exchange of information, directions, concepts, or evaluations between two or more persons. It seemed desirable to develop a set of categories that would be primarily descriptive rather than evaluative. The descriptive categories were intended to minimize the degree of inference by an observer in recording the interaction in a classroom. At the same time it seemed

Reprinted with permission of authors and publisher: Lewis, W. W., Newell, J. M. and Withall, J. "An Analysis of Classroom Patterns of Communication." *Psychological Report*, 1961, 9:211–219.

necessary to use a set of categories comprehensive enough to cover any communication act likely to occur in a classroom. The Bales Interaction Process Analysis categories (2) seemed to hold some promise in meeting those needs. However, the use of the Bales categories in recording behavior in elementary and secondary school classrooms suggested some serious limitations, primarily the large proportion of responses being categorized as "asking for orientation" and "giving orientation." In order to make finer discriminations in this behavioral setting, new categories were added and some of the old ones were dropped or redefined. Following several revisions, 13 categories were selected. There is no relationship implied among any of the 13 categories except that they are mutually exclusive. That is, there is no continuum, such as "asking–giving" or "thinking–feeling," underlying the numbering of the categories.

In order to test the usefulness of the observational categories in discriminating activity characteristics in classrooms, two small experimental classes, each with a different instructor, were formed. The general objective of both classes was to help classroom teachers understand children's behavior. However, each instructor intentionally used a different instructional method to achieve his objective. The observational categories were used systematically with both classes to see what differences could be demonstrated.

Method

The Instructional Approaches

The two instructional methods will be referred to as (a) the case-study method and (b) the student-centered method. The stated intent of the instructor using the case-study method was to employ case studies, done by the students in his class, to develop and elaborate concepts relevant to an understanding of children's behavior in the school classroom. The initiation of activities, pacing, and evaluation of learning experiences in the case-study approach were controlled largely by the instructor. He assigned readings, case histories, and a final examination to the students in his group.

The stated intent of the instructor using the student-centered method was to provide an opportunity for his students to discuss their pupils, themselves, or issues of importance to them personally. He attempted to respond at a level of personal significance to whatever material was raised spontaneously by members of the class. Topics for discussion, readings, and tasks related to the discussions were not assigned by the instructor using the student-centered method, but were left to the initiative of the individual students.

The students in the two groups were all enrolled for credit in a graduate course at the University of Wisconsin dealing with guidance practices in the public school. All were employed full time as teachers or administrators in a suburban community of Madison, Wisconsin. In one group there were 6 elementary teachers, 2 elementary principals, and 1 high school teacher; 3 men and 6 women. In the other group were 4 elementary teachers, 1 music teacher, 1 elementary principal, and 1 high school teacher; 2 men and 5 women. The students had been assigned to one of the two instructional groups by shuffling their course cards and dealing the cards into two piles. The two groups met in separate rooms at the same building, at the same hour, and for the same length of time. There were 14 meetings, each lasting approximately 150 minutes, for each of the groups.

The Observational Categories

The 13 categories are designed to be applied during the process of communication in the classroom, either in a live observation of an actual classroom, or to tape recordings of classroom behavior. An observer is asked to make a series of judgments about the dominant intent of the initiator of each act of communications. He is asked to project himself into the role of the recipient of the communication act and decide what was the dominant intent of the person speaking. Both verbal and non-verbal aspects (where detectable) of the behavior are used in making the judgment. An arbitrary time interval, 10 sec., is used as the unit of behavior which is judged by the observer.

A brief description and illustrations of each of the categories follow.

1. *Asks for Information.* An act having as its major intent the eliciting of a response which presumably may be evaluated for accuracy, either by objective operation, general acceptance, or reference to an authority (such as the teacher or a text book).

Examples.—Asks question about content of lesson; asks for report; asks for confirmation of response previously given; asks for repetition of what has been said; offers incomplete statement with the expectation that another will finish it; asks any question in such a way as to imply that there is a "right" answer; asks name of an object; asks for definition; asks for enumeration.

2. *Seeks or Accepts Direction.* An act implying willingness to consider suggestion or direction from another, or if suggestion or direction has already been offered, an act or statement indicating compliance.

Examples.—Asks how to begin an assigned task; asks what to do next; asks which procedure to follow; asks for volunteers; follows directions of another; agrees with suggestion or direction, indicates that direction will be followed at some future time; asks for permission for a specific act.

3. *Asks for Opinion or Analysis.* An act intended to elicit problem-structuring statements from others, either affective-evaluation or cognitive-interpretive.

Examples.—Asks for opinion, wish, feeling, belief, or preference; asks for evaluation of behavior; requests for interpretation or explanation of some phenomena without implying that there is one "correct" answer; requests for elaboration or examples of a concept; requests for statement of relationships between concepts; non-directive leads or questions to facilitate self-exploration by others; reflection of feeling or alternate meaning of what another has said for purposes of clarifying meaning; asks for interpretation of another's personal experience (as distinguished from asking for a report of experience).

4. *Listens.* Five seconds or more out of any 10-sec. interval where an individual is listening or attending to another individual is given a listening score (less than 5 sec. is not scored).

5. *Gives Information.* An act intended to convey, confirm, or inform "facts" which may be evaluated by objective operation, general acceptance, or reference to an authority.

Examples.—Giving data such as names, dates, speed, capacity, etc. relevant to a topic under discussion; attempting to provide information requested by another; confirming the accuracy of others' responses; denying the accuracy of others' responses; gives report on what one has seen, heard, read, etc.; gives repetition of what has been said; names object; gives definition; gives enumeration.

6. *Gives Suggestion.* An act intended to structure action or indicate alternatives for others which, at the same time, implies autonomy for others by providing more than one alternative or allowing for refusal.

Examples.—Offering a procedure in a tentative way; offering two or more procedures, leaving choice to others; stating a preferred behavior without indicating that the preference holds for others; volunteers own services.

7. *Gives Direction.* An act intended to structure some action of another in which compliance seems to be taken for granted, or in which non-compliance would probably elicit some form of disapproval.

Examples.—Calling class to attention; calling attention to some detail; getting attention of another by calling his name; routine administrative directions or orders; stating expectation of behavior to be followed; setting limits on behavior; stating consequences of behavior; granting a request; denying a request.

8. *Gives Opinion.* An act intended to structure or give direction to a topic under discussion by use of speaker's internal, private, or unstated criteria.

Examples.—States opinions, wish, feeling, belief, or preference; makes a statement or asks a question reflecting a personal point of view; verbalizes introspective processes; gives criticism or evaluation of a behavior or concept; agrees or disagrees with opinion voiced by another.

9. *Gives Analysis.* An act intended to structure or give direction to a topic under discussion by reference to a frame of reference or a criterion that is explicitly stated and external to speaker's personal point of view.

Examples.—Gives interpretation or explanation of some phenomena without implying that it is the only "correct" way of looking at it; elaborates or gives examples of a concept; points out relationships between examples and concepts or between two or more concepts; points out discrepancies between concept and examples; proposes hypothetical example or case to illustrate a point or raise a question.

10. *Shows Positive Feeling.* An act which implies positive evaluation of some behavior or interaction in the observational field, regardless of whether the referent is the self or some other person.

Examples.—Any friendly act or overture, such as greeting or responding to a greeting; praising, approving, encouraging, rewarding, or showing active attention to others; sharing or sympathizing with others, expressions of satisfaction, enjoyment, or relief; joking or laughing "with" others.

11. *Inhibits Communication.* An act which implies unwillingness or inability to engage in the ongoing process of communication, regardless of whether the act stems from negative evaluation, internal tension, or disinterest.

Examples.—Does not respond when response would ordinarily be expected; is cool, aloof, or disinterested in what is going on; is inattentive to or ignores a question or request; does not comply with a request; shows tension by blocking, "fright," etc.; accepts criticism or rebuff without reply.

12. *Shows Negative Feeling.* An act which implies active negative evaluation of some behavior or interaction in the observational field, regardless of whether the referent is the self or some other person.

Examples.—Disapproving, disparaging, threatening, discouraging another's behaviors; lowering another's status; defending or asserting self; poking fun, belittling, or laughing "at" others; expressing fear, rage, hostility, disappointment, discouragement, displeasure, unhappiness, etc.

13. *No Communication.*[1] The behavior occurring in the classroom is not relevant to teacher-pupil communication during a 10-sec. interval.

Procedure in Applying Categories

The observer makes his judgments sequentially, as they occur in the classroom interaction, assigning at least one category score to each 10-sec. interval within a predetermined length of time. When there is a shift in the inferred intent of the communicator within any given 10-sec. interval, the interval is assigned an additional category score, or more if necessary. After the observer completes his recording for a time sample, he tabulates the number of occurrences of each category and makes a summary of the communication pattern during the time of observation in the form of frequencies for each category.

The observational categories were used on selected samples from both instructional approaches. Sessions 3, 7, and 12 were arbitrarily designated as early, middle, and late segments of the course. Within each of these sessions, for each instructional approach, a 24-min. sample was taken at a point beginning 10 min. after the session started, and another 24-min. sample was taken at a point beginning 10 min. after a coffee break midway through the session. Following this procedure, each 48-min. sample is used to represent the communication pattern in the early, middle, and the late stages of each group's development. The observers worked from tape recordings which were collected routinely in all of the group meetings.

Two independent category records were made on each time sample, one on the communication acts of the instructor in the class, the other on the communication acts of the students in the class. In this way, three records of category frequencies, representing early, middle, and late sessions, were collected for each instructor, and three records of category frequencies were collected for the students as a group in each class.

An estimate of inter-judge reliability was obtained by having two observers independently categorize 24-min, samples from tape recordings of three different instructors, the two reported on here and one other. The frequency of use of the 13 categories was tabulated for each instructor. The agreement between the two observers, quantified as rank-order correlation coefficients for each of the three instructors, was .99, .97, and .98.

Analysis of the Data

An attempt to assess the overall similarity of the communication patterns of the two instructors, between sessions for the same instructor and between instructors for the same session, was carried out by comparing

[1]Since the completion of this study, an additional category, 14, Perfunctory Agreement or Disagreement, has been added.

the ranking of category use by each instructor. Each session was treated separately to establish ranking of categories. The rankings were compared by means of Spearman's *rho* (5, pp. 202-213). Since the frequency of occurrence of some of the 13 categories was not large, the rank-order correlation coefficients for the instructors are based on categories 1 + 5, 3, 4, 6 + 7, 8, and 9, and for the students on categories 1, 2 + 3, 4, 5, 6 + 7, 8, 9, and 10.

T A B L E 1   Rho$_S$ Showing Similarity of Category Frequencies in Early, Middle and Late Sessions for Case-Study Group

Sessions	Instructor	Students
Early-middle	.94*	.96**
Early-late	.89*	.82*
Middle-late	.94*	.90**

*p < .05   **p < .01

Table 1 shows high inter-session consistency for the case-study instructor, indicating little change in his overall pattern of communication from session to session. Table 2 shows low inter-session consistency for the student-centered instructor, suggesting that his pattern of communication, at least in its broad outlines, was somehow different in the early

T A B L E 2   Rho$_S$ Showing Similarity of Category Frequencies in Early, Middle and Late Sessions for Student-Centered Group

Sessions	Instructor	Students
Early-middle	.26	.73*
Early-late	.56	.96**
Middle-late	.81	.73*

*p < .05   **p < .01

T A B L E 3   Rho$_S$ Showing Similarity of Category Frequencies Between Groups During the Same Session

Sessions	Instructor	Students
Early	.89*	.89**
Middle	.49	.85*
Late	.24	.78*

*p < .05   **p < .01

session from what it was in the middle session, and that the late session was still different from either the early or middle one. The data reported in Table 3 confirm the impression of change in the pattern of communication by the student-centered instructor. In the early session, both instructors were alike in their communication patterns but they became progressively dissimilar in the middle and late phases of the group meetings.

A comparison of communication patterns of students in the two groups was also based on ranking of category use. For students, the *rhos*, also reported in Tables 1, 2, and 3, do not reflect any change. Each group was alike in use of communication categories in early, middle, and late sessions, and the groups were similar to each other in each of the three sessions.

Differences of content in the communication patterns of the two groups were analyzed by comparing the proportion of the total responses for each category during a single session. The third and twelfth sessions were arbitrarily designated as the early and late samples in the series of meetings. Categories for which significant differences in proportions were

T A B L E 4 Significant Differences in Use of Categories by Instructors in Early and Late Sessions (Proportion of Total Responses)

	Case-Study	Student-Centered	Z	p
Early Session				
Listening	.60	.73	4.41	<.01
Asking For and Giving Information	.16	.08	3.09	<.01
Giving Analysis	.15	.09	2.33	<.05
Late Session				
Listening	.58	.71	3.37	<.01
Giving Directions and Suggestions	.09	.01	4.64	<.01
Giving Opinion	.03	.10	3.86	<.01
Giving Analysis	.10	.02	3.48	<.01

T A B L E 5 Significant Differences in Use of Categories by Students in Early and Late Sessions (Proportion of Total Responses)

	Case-Study	Student-Centered	Z	p
Early Session				
Listening	.33	.16	5.28	<.01
Giving Opinion	.16	.28	3.80	<.01
Late Session				
Listening	.28	.14	5.12	<.01
Giving Information	.24	.52	8.20	<.01

obtained between the case-study and the student-centered classes are reported in Table 4 for the instructors and in Table 5 for the students. The categories that are not included in the two tables are those in which the proportion of responses did not differ significantly or in which the category's proportion of the total number of responses for the session was so small that differences appeared to be spurious.

Table 4 shows that, although both instructors spent over half of their time listening, in both sessions sampled, the student-centered instructor spent a significantly greater proportion of his time listening than did the other instructor, both in the early and late sessions. He also gave more opinions in the late session. The case-study instructor asked for and gave more information in the early session, gave more directions and suggestions in the late session, and gave more analysis in both sessions.

The responses of the students in both groups, in Table 5, seem to suggest again that differences between instructors are more marked than differences among their students. For example, the proportion of students' listening responses in both sessions simply mirrors the greater verbal activity of the case-study instructor on both occasions.

Discussion

The two procedures used in analyzing observational data on the two instructional groups, namely, (a) ranking category usage in each group and (b) proportional usage of each category by both groups, reflect expectations based on the stated intent of the instructors. The case-study instructor intended to structure the interaction of his group around the analysis of material collected by his students on children in their classrooms. The student-centered instructor's intent was to pursue the personal meaning of whatever questions were raised spontaneously by members of his class.

The analysis of broad communication patterns showed that both instructors started out in about the same way, and that the case-study instructor continued the same pattern into middle and late sessions of the group meetings. The student-centered instructor progressively modified his pattern of communication through the middle and late sessions. No such change was noticeable in the broad communication patterns of the students in either group. Another method of analysis of the communication categories indicated more specifically some of the differences between the two groups. While both groups were in fact "discussion" groups, as indicated by the consistent categorization of over half of both instructors' behaviors as listening, the student-centered instructor did more listening, in both early and late sessions, than the case-study instructor. The higher level of verbal activity by the case-study instructor and perhaps his concern with the cognitive structuring of the discussions, are shown in his more frequent use of the categories of asking for and giving information, giving directions and suggestions, and giving analysis. A clue to the nature of the changing behavior of the student-centered instructor is given in the difference between the two instructors in the late session that was not present in the early session. The student-centered instructor gave more opinions than the case-study instructor, and more opinions than he himself had given in the early session, which suggests that he was moving out of the role of discussion "leader" as the sessions progressed and into the role of "participant," while the case-study instructor was maintaining his role of moderator or director of the discussion throughout the sessions. There is very little evidence of differences between the two groups of students, or of change by students within either group, that cannot be interpreted as a reflection of differing levels of verbal activity of the instructor in the group.

The 13 observational categories seem to be useful in making discriminations between instructional groups in which it may be presumed that different patterns of communication are occurring. The two methods of analyzing data based on the observations, (a) looking at relative use of all categories and (b) comparisons of use of each category, suggest interpretations that are consistent with each other and that are consistent with the intent of each of the instructors. The next step in the use of the categories is to apply them to undergraduate courses in teacher education where the method of instruction is intentionally varied from one class to another.

Summary

This is a report on the development of a set of observational categories for the study of classroom interaction and on the reliability of these categories in describing the classroom communication behaviors of two instructors teaching according to two predetermined and describable instructional foci. The study was conceived within the framework of viewing classroom interaction as a series of communication acts, verbal and non-verbal, between teacher and learners.

References

1. H. H. Anderson & H. M. Brewer. Studies of teachers' classroom personalities; I. Dominative and socially integrative behavior of kindergarten teachers. *Appl. Psychol. Monogr.*, 1945, No. 6.

2. R. F. Bales. *Interaction process analysis.* Cambridge, Mass.: Addison-Wesley, 1950.

3. N. A. Flanders. *Interaction analysis in the classroom: a manual for observers.* Univer. of Minnesota, College of Education, August, 1960.

4. W. W. Lewis. Selected concepts of communication as a basis for studying mental health in the classroom. *J. Communication*, 1961, 11, 157-162.

5. S. Siegel. *Nonparametric statistics for the behavioral sciences.* New York: McGraw-Hill, 1956.

6. J. Withall. The development of a technique for the measurement of social-emotional climate in classrooms. *J. Exp. Educ.*, 1947, 17, 347-361.

4 Communication Events: A New Look at Classroom Interactions

Russell L. French and Charles M. Galloway

In recent years, a number of educators and researchers have profitably focused their attention on the behavior of the classroom teacher in an attempt to gain insight into the teaching-learning process. Vast amounts of behavioral data, greatly enriching our knowledge of "the way teaching is," have been contributed through these efforts. In short, the study of teacher behavior has yielded significant data concerning teacher-pupil relationships and classroom interaction.

However, it has probably occurred to every serious student of classroom behavior that most observational systems of behavioral analysis reduce teacher and pupil verbal and nonverbal expressions to their lowest level of meaning. Undoubtedly, many observers using the available systems feel the need for some larger rubric from which specific behaviors will gain a proper perspective in relationship to the totality of the teaching-learning act.

Growing out of this need for a broader perspective have been a number of attempts to place both teaching and teacher behavior in a communication framework. Indeed, Hyman (1968) has concluded: "Teaching is a specific case of a more general abstraction called communication."

Many of those who have attempted to place teacher behavior in a communication framework have displayed a logical tendency toward grouping behaviors into communication entities. For example, Smith and Meux (1962) and Galloway (1962) have suggested that teacher-pupil interactions can be viewed as "episodes." Lewis, Newell, and Withall (1961) described "communication acts." Bellack (1963) used the concept of "teaching cycles." And Openshaw and Cyphert (1966) have referred to "classroom encounters."

Most conceptualizations of communication entities have been defined in terms of (a) the characteristics of behaviors or activities in progress or (b) arbitrary allotments of time. However, a classroom observer soon becomes aware that teacher-pupil interactions have varying functions. To look at classroom interactions in light of their functions suggests the concept of communication events.

Communication Events

A communication event can be defined as a sequence of teacher-pupil communicative behaviors separated from preceding and succeeding sequences of behaviors (events) by naturally occurring boundaries. As defined by Galloway (1962), these boundaries are: (a) a variation or change in the direction of a teacher's communicative behavior; (b) a change in the teacher's behavior toward a new interaction; (c) the occurrence of a significant or potent act which appears influential; and (d) social intervention in which an interruption is instigated by either a pupil or the teacher. As implied, communication events are composed of both verbal and non-verbal behaviors by both teachers and pupils. It is not uncommon to find an entire event composed entirely of non-verbal behaviors.

Observation of elementary and secondary classrooms suggests that what goes on there may be described as communication events which are institutional, task-oriented, personal, or mixed in nature.

Institutional Events

Institutional events are those which relate to managing the classroom and meeting the expectations of the institution. Perhaps Jackson (1968) has best delineated this kind of event by posing a series of questions relevant to their recognition in most classrooms. These questions are: (a) "Who may enter and leave the room?" (b) "How much noise is tolerable?" (c) "How to preserve privacy in a crowded setting?"

(d) "What to do when work assignments are prematurely finished?"
(e) "How far to go in establishing classroom-social etiquette?"
The following are illustrative institutional events:

1. A verbal and/or nonverbal reprimand to a student for chewing gum because this action is against school rules.

2. Teacher handing back quiz papers and explaining grading procedures.

3. Teacher calling roll and pupils responding verbally and nonverbally.

4. Pupils and teacher preparing for the use of a motion picture.

5. Teacher announcement and/or explanation of school events or activities.

6. Teacher calling for, signing, and discussing with pupils absence excuses.

7. Teacher cueing pupils verbally and/or nonverbally in an attempt to maintain silence or order and pupils responding.

8. Teacher directing pupils to begin their homework; pupils feigning industrious activity.

9. Teacher verbal and/or nonverbal direction to pupils in how to leave the classroom for some particular purpose.

Task Events

Task events focus on the teaching and learning of subject matter content whether cognitive, affective, or skill-oriented. Task events are characterized by stating, asking, showing, acknowledging, and clarifying communicative behaviors on the part of both teachers and pupils, and some key words related to these behaviors are suggestive of the work of Bloom (1956) and Sanders (1966): remembering, understanding, applying, analyzing, synthesizing, and evaluating.
Illustrative task events include:

1. A teacher-pupil discussion of the functions of Congress.

2. A teacher demonstration of how to read a weather map.

3. Teacher explanation of the factors influencing the Battle of Gettysburg while pupils take notes.

4. Teacher aiding individual pupils during an independent study period.

5. A student report on inflation.

6. A laboratory exercise in which pupils are using microscopes with the teacher assisting them.

Personal Events

Personal events are those in which personal needs, goals, and emotions of a pupil, a group of pupils, and/or the teacher provide the central focus. Davitz (1964) has provided a rather extensive list of emotional expressions relevant to these events. The list includes admiration, affection, amusement, anger, boredom, cheerfulness, despair, disgust, dislike, fear, impatience, joy, satisfaction and surprise.

Typical personal events are:

1. Pupil expressions of frustration and teacher response to these.

2. Teacher expression of personal interest in or concern for a pupil or his problems.

3. Pupil expression of affection toward the teacher and teacher response, either verbal or nonverbal.

4. Angry dialogue between two pupils concerning actions on the playground.

Mixed Events

Mixed events also occur in classrooms. These contain elements of more than one of the event types previously described. While one might classify mixed events according to the elements which they contain (task-personal events, institutional-personal events, etc.), this would appear to be a somewhat difficult and useless procedure. Interaction and communication become distorted when the focus of an event becomes complex and when participants are no longer aware of the specific nature of the event. Therefore, the descriptive category "mixed events" better describes the function of these behavioral sequences than does any further breakdown of the category.

Coding Communication Events

Personal, institutional, task, or mixed events can involve the teacher with a single pupil or with a group of pupils. Since any attempt to identify the focus and intent of interaction in the classroom at any given time must include clarification of the number of participants involved, communication events must be classified as *individual* (interaction between the teacher and one pupil) or *group* (interaction between the teacher and several pupils).

A simple identification of classroom communication events involves a coding scheme utilizing the symbol I to signify institutional events, P for personal events, T for task events, and M for events which cannot be clearly defined (events mixed in nature). Further, institutional, task, or personal events involving the teacher with a single student (individual events) are indicated by the symbol i placed after the symbol characterizing the basic nature of the event (for example, Ti, Pi, Ii).

An important aspect of a communication event is its duration. This facet is captured by tallying the appropriate reference symbol at the initiation of the event and marking continuance of the event with dots tallied at three-second intervals. If this system is used, an observer's coding of a group-task event occupying 20 seconds of classroom time would resemble this: T

.

.

.

.

.

.

Recent Findings Relevant To Classroom Communication

Although research employing the PIT model (title derived from the first letter of each major communication event type previously described) has, as yet, been limited, application of the model to video tapes representing 1360 minutes of interaction in junior high school classrooms has determined the significance of the model and yielded some interesting data.

The 1360 minutes (23 hours) of interaction analyzed contained a total of 1705 separate communication events. Each 40-minute class period (34 periods in all) contained an average 50.4 events.

Of the total 1705 communication events, 1173 were task-oriented, with 794 of these being group-centered task events, and 379 involving the teacher with only one pupil. Single group task events averaged 73.9 seconds in duration, while individual task events occupied approximately 37.6 seconds each. Of the 50.4 events per class period, 34.5 were task-oriented. Task events, either group or individual, accounted for 69.2 percent of all events recorded.

In the junior high school classrooms observed, institutional events numbered 420. Of this total, 249 institutional events involved the teacher with the whole class or a significantly large group of pupils. Individual institutional events constituted 171 of the institutional event total. Twenty-five percent of all events recorded were institutional events, and an average of 12.6 institutional events occurred per 40-minute class period. Single group-centered institutional events averaged 30.3 seconds in length, and each individual institutional event was approximately 11.8 seconds long.

The video tapes made of junior high school English, mathematics, science, and social studies classes yielded a total of 65 personal events, of which 21 could be classified as group personal events, and 44 were individual personal events. Group personal events took up 30.5 seconds each, while individual personal events were alloted 16.1 seconds. Personal events represented only 3.8 percent of all interaction, and an average of only 1.9 such events occurred per 40-minute class period.

The junior high school teachers observed engaged in 47 mixed events, only two of which could be designated individual mixed events. Approximately 2.6 pecent of all events recorded were mixed in nature, with a 40-minute class period yielding an average of 1.4 such events. Interestingly, most of these occurred during independent study activties scheduled near the end of the class period.

While none of the above statistics are particularly meaningful without knowledge of the communication goals of the participating teachers and the interaction strategies which they were attempting to implement, the data are indeed interesting. However, further research is needed before it can be known how truly representative these statistics are in describing communication patterns in junior high school classrooms and what variations exist in elementary and secondary classrooms.

Suggested Applications of the PIT Model

It is quite clear that the PIT model provides another perspective for descriptive research in classroom interaction, but it also appears that the model has practical utility for classroom teachers, supervisors, and administrators.

Due to its simplicity of nature and application and the fact that it can be easily learned, the PIT model offers the classroom teacher a means of analyzing his communication, particularly when video tape is available as a means of recording classroom activity.

Given specific teacher goals and intents, supervisors and administrators can employ the model as one means of aiding teachers in improving their instruction and classroom communication. Further, the model may be used to gain insight into communication patterns appropriate and promising to teaching and learning at various grade levels, in various subject areas, and among various types of learners.

Finally, the PIT model may be used in combination with Flanders' Interaction Analysis, French and Galloway's IDER System, or several other behavioral analysis systems to provide the observer with a clear picture of both individual teacher and pupil behaviors and broader communications patterns. Much can be gained from knowledge of the behaviors teachers commonly use to open and close particular types of communication events, behavioral patterns typically found in particular event types, etc. Indeed, some research of this kind has already been undertaken.

References

Arno A. Bellack and J. R. Davitz, in collaboration with H. M. Kliebard and R. T. Hyman, *The Language of the Classroom: Meanings Communicated in High School Teaching.* New York: Teachers College, Columbia University, 1963. (USOE Cooperative Project 1947.)

Benjamin Bloom *et al. A Taxonomy of Education Objectives: Cognitive Domain.* New York: David McKay Company, Inc., 1956.

Joel R. Davitz. *The Communication of Emotional Meaning.* New York: McGraw-Hill Book Company, 1964.

Charles M. Galloway. "An Exploratory Study of Observational Procedures for Determining Teacher Nonverbal Communication." Unpublished dissertation. Gainesville: University of Florida, 1962.

Ronald T. Hyman, editor. *Teaching: Vantage Points for Study.* Philadelphia: J. B. Lippincott Company, 1968.

Philip W. Jackson. *Life in Classrooms.* New York: Holt, Rinehart and Winston, Inc., 1968.

W. W. Lewis, John M. Newell, and John Withall. "An Analysis of Classroom Patterns of Communication." *Psychological Reports* 9: 211-19; October 1961.

M. Karl Openshaw and Frederick R. Cyphert, in collaboration with Norman V. Overly and Edgar Ray Smith. *Development of a Taxonomy for the Classification of Teacher Classroom Behavior.* Columbus: The Ohio State University Research Foundation, 1966. (USOE Cooperative Research Project 2288.)

Norris M. Sanders. *Classroom Questions: What Kinds?* New York: Harper & Row, Publishers, 1966.

B. O. Smith and Milton O. Meux. *A Study of the Logic of Teaching.* Urbana, Illinois: University of Illinois, 1962. (USOE Cooperative Research Project 258.)

5 The Teacher As Communicator

Selma Greenberg

Overview

To describe, to analyze, to evaluate, and finally to modify one's teaching behavior is the task Hofstra University's School of Education has set for pre-service teachers during their student teaching experience. To provide the knowledge, skills, abilities, and materials necessary for the successful accomplishment of this goal is the specific task we set for ourselves. To help our students with the difficult task of achieving ability to modify their classroom verbal behavior we have found the use of an objective system for analyzing classroom interaction to be an essential part of our program. The classroom interaction system that we have been using for the past ten years is one developed by Robert Spaulding. It is particularly suited to our needs because it is fast, effective, and easy to use, like many modern remedies. Spaulding's system focuses exclusively on the teacher's activities, posits verbal interaction as the central and representative classroom activity, and concentrates on the form classroom verbal communication takes over time.

This article by Selma Greenberg of Hofstra University was prepared expressly for this second edition. It is based on *Discovering New Dimensions in the Teaching Process* by Greta Morine, Robert S. Spaulding, and Selma Greenberg (Scranton: International Textbook Company, 1971).

Assumptions

Most classroom interaction systems like Spaulding's assume that it is the teacher who sets the classroom verbal pattern. The teacher is seen as the initiator and director of the class's verbal flow. The students are viewed as the reactors and/or responders to patterns originally established by the teacher. While all systems of classroom interaction tend to focus on the teacher to a greater or lesser degree, Spaulding's system focuses exclusively upon the teacher's communication. Thus, when *a child speaks,* the coder records this communication as *the teacher listens.* Since our aim is to have each student develop self-analytic abilities within the teaching role, this exclusive focus on the teacher's activities found in the Spaulding code is positive for our purposes. Additionally, our pre-service students, spend a semester prior to student teaching studying classroom activity from the viewpoint of the child, and thus, we believe, a balance is achieved. The students, at that time, use a coding system also developed by Spaulding for studying the children.

Recently Spaulding has modified and merged his two systems of coding for research purposes. We, however, continue to teach their use separately, for we feel that within our particular instructional design the dual form facilitates learning. Nevertheless, the exclusive concentration on the teacher's activity reduces the objectivity of the coding system, for to code a child speaking as *teacher listens* is to make a judgment about the teacher's behavior in the absence of sufficient behavioral cues.

Like Marshall McLuhan, Spaulding holds that "the medium is the message." His system is solely concerned with the form classroom communication takes. Thus, when using the Spaulding system, one gains no information as to what verbal material constitutes the content of the verbal interaction. The information gained from the use of the system is descriptive of the *process* of communication alone. We use the Spaulding system in a larger program which contains, in addition, a system for analyzing goals and objectives and another system for analyzing questions. Thus, we believe that we provide the necessary content balance for the content-free Spaulding system.

Since the Spaulding system differentiates those statements intended to effect cognitive processing from those statements intended to effect affective responses, it is subject to some criticism. Critics argue that the separation of affect and cognition is not only artificial but positively harmful in that it suggests the incorrect notion that affect and cognition can be separate. Although we believe that the separation of statements whose intent is to influence cognition from those whose intent is to influence affect is artificial, we do not see evidence that it is harmful. Rather, we tend to believe that this dichotomy, for purposes of analysis and instruction, has been helpful to the student.

Key Concepts and Coding System

The notion of constructing a graphic picture of the classroom communication process as it unfolds over time is the unique aspect of the Spaulding system, especially since this is made possible without the aid of machinery or complex materials. The coding system is recorded on an easily reproduced *flow chart,* and therefore, when we code a sample of the lesson, we speak of *flowing* it. In a parallel fashion we speak of the *flow* of classroom communication. Time becomes a central focus for the users of this code. In the way we have used the code, samples of hourly or three-quarter hourly classroom interaction are recorded every second in three three-minute segments with each segment of nine minutes receiving a distinct notation. Thus, 540 distinct bits of information will be produced from nine minutes of coding. This is how we have chosen to use the flow chart, but it is possible to code as much or as little of a lesson as is required or desired. It is also possible to code less frequently than every second. Some students, unable to develop the speed required to code each second, code either every other second or every third second. We have found, though, that if one codes at less frequent intervals than every third second, too much information is lost, and the resulting description of the classroom *flow* is quite distorted. A similar distortion takes place when coding becomes erratic, because typically it is easier to code long monologues rather than rapid interaction. If coding is nonrhythmic, the picture of the flow of classroom interaction that emerges suggests that more monologues have taken place than has actually been the case.

Since the code itself is quite simple, the time needed to learn its content is brief. However, considerably more time is needed to learn to record at the requisite speed and with the necessary rhythm. Therefore, our students' time is spent on learning the process of coding rather than the content.

Our code is divided into three parts, each represented by a letter. The first part or letter indicates the major teaching activity that is being engaged in. There are five categories of major teaching activities in the first part:

A—Approval
D—Disapproval   } AFFECTIVE DOMAIN

I—Instruction
L—Listening   } COGNITIVE DOMAIN
O—Observing

The second part or letter indicates at whom or to whom the activity is directed. The code choice for the second letter is:

> C—Class
> Gr—Group
> B—Boy
> G—Girl

The third part or letter of the code indicates the subcategory of activity within the major activity which is being engaged in. If the major category is A (Approval) or D (Disapproval), the third letter would indicate what is being approved or disapproved. The code choices are:

> R—Response
> B—Behavior
> P—Person

If the major activity is either Instruction or Listening, the cognitive domain, the third letter would be:

> P—Presenting
> E—Eliciting
> R—Recording
> M—Management

The major teaching activity category, Observing, is a broad one which includes all nonverbal activity. That is, when a teacher is neither speaking nor listening to a student speak, this nonverbal event is coded Observing. Furthermore, since there are no subcategories for this category, the coder uses only two letters. The first letter is O for Observing, and the second letter is C, Gr, B, or G, to indicate who is being observed. In short, if the major category is Observing, there is no third part.

Let me now illustrate the use of this coding system. If a teacher were to say to the class, "What language might we be speaking if the whole world went to a single language system?" this would be coded ICE (Instruction to the Class—Eliciting).

The complete coding system appears in Figure 1.

FIGURE 1. The Spaulding Interaction System

	Major Categories		*Subcategories*
AFFECTIVE DOMAIN	APPROVAL OR DISAPPROVAL	R—	approval or disapproval of a child's *response* to a question or comment by the teacher or another child—generally related to the content of the lesson

		B—	approval or disapproval of a child's *behavior* or activity—generally related to classroom management
		P—	approval or disapproval of a child as a *person* or of the child's personal characteristics
COGNITIVE DOMAIN	INSTRUCTION	P—	*presenting* information related to the content of the lesson
		E—	*eliciting* a response related to the content of the lesson (questioning)
		R—	*recording* information related to the content of the lesson
		M—	*management* of routine aspects of the lesson, such as directing students to turn to a certain page, assigning homework, giving directions for directing movement of students or supplies around the room, such as passing out books, collecting papers, changing location
COGNITIVE DOMAIN	LISTENING	P—	listening to a student *presenting* information related to the content of the lesson
		E—	listening to a student *eliciting* information related to the content of the lesson
		M—	listening to a student presenting or eliciting information related to routine aspects (*management*) of the lesson
	OBSERVING		observing the activity of students

Procedures

When a flow chart is prepared, the first two letters of the code are already indicated, and the coder need only locate the correct spot in order to place the third letter of the code appropriately. The *flow chart* is constructed in a series of dots. An unused flow chart looks like this:

A(pproval)   Class   ....
              Group ....
              Boy   ....
              Girl   ....

D(isapproval) Class   ....
              Group ....
              Boy   ....
              Girl   ....

I(nstruction) Class   ....
              Group ....
              Boy   ....
              Girl   ....

L(istening)   Class   ....
              Group ....
              Boy   ....
              Girl   ....,

O(bserving)   Class   ....
              Group ....
              Boy   ....
              Girl   ....

When the coder has located the correct spot to record the third letter of the code, it is placed above the dot, like this E. If an action continues over time, an x is placed above the dots which follow to indicate that the same action is being carried out through time. If a teacher is asking the class a question for five seconds, the coder locates the major category "Instruction, the Class line, and marks an E on the first vacant vertical column of dots and follows it with four x's, like this: Exxxx.
. . . . .

Earlier it was indicated that the teacher's question, "What language might we be speaking if the whole world went to a single language system?" is coded **ICE**. On a flow chart this question would look like this:

A Class   ....
   Group   ....
   Boy   ....
   Girl   ....

D Class   ....
   Group   ....
   Boy   ....
   Girl   ....

I Class   Exxxx xxx
   Group   ....
   Boy   ....
   Girl   ....

L Class   ....
   Group   ....
   Boy   ....
   Girl   ....

O Class   ....
   Group   ....
   Boy   ....
   Girl   ....

Suppose a girl responds to this question in the following way. "Since there are more people in China than in any other country, I think Chinese might be the language we would speak if the whole world were on one language system." The coder locates the next available vertical line of dots (in this case the ninth dot), the Listening line appropriate to the sex of the child responding, and codes the response. Thus, the coding of the question and the response would appear on the flow chart like this:

A Class   ....
   Group   ....
   Boy   ....
   Girl   ....

D Class   ....
   Group   ....
   Boy   ....
   Girl   ....

I Class   Exxxx xxx., ...

   Group   ....

   Boy   ....

   Girl   ....

L Class   ....

   Group   ....

   Boy   ....

   Girl   ....Px xxxxx xxx ..

O Class   ....

   Group   ....

   Boy   ....

   Girl   ....

The *interaction pattern* is another major concept in the Spaulding code. Spaulding's interaction pattern has three parts and a single structure. It always begins with a teacher's question or elicitation, includes the teacher's listening to the child's response, and terminates with whatever reaction the teacher makes to the response that has been given. When the coding of the segment is completed, the coder inspects the flow chart to determine the existence of interaction patterns. The identified patterns are then encircled. To demonstrate, let us return to our sample teacher's question, "What language might we be speaking if the whole world went to a single language system?" and to the student's response, "Since there are more people in China than in any other country, I think Chinese might be the language we would speak if the whole world were on one language system." Let us imagine the teacher's reaction to that response to be, "Susan, considering today's political realities, it would be interesting to speculate whether this is a possibility." When coding this reaction, the coder finds the Instruction category, finds the fourth line, places a P (Presenting) on the next available vertical dot (in this case the nineteenth), and follows it with seven x's to indicate that the reaction took approximately eight seconds to complete.

When the coding of the segment is complete, the flow chart is inspected for instances of interaction patterns. Then each is identified by being encircled. Thus the complete interaction pattern is coded and identified like this:

```
A  Class   .....  .....  .....  .....  .....  .....
   Group   .....  .....  .....  .....  .....  .....
   Boy     .....  .....  .....  .....  .....  .....
   Girl    .....  .....  .....  .....  .....

D  Class   .....  .....  .....  .....  .....  .....
   Group   .....  .....  .....  .....  .....  .....
   Boy     .....  .....  .....  .....  .....  .....
   Girl           .....  .....  .....  .....

I  Class   Exxxx xxx..  .....  .....  .....
   Group   .....  .....  .....  .....  .....
   Boy     .....  .....  .....  .....  .....
   Girl    .....  .....  ..... ...Px xxxxx x....

L  Class   .....  .....  .....  .....  .....
   Group   .....  .....  .....  .....  .....
   Boy     .....  .....  .....  .....  .....
   Girl    .....  Px xxxxx xxx  .....

O  Class   .....  .....  .....  .....  .....
   Group   .....  .....  .....  .....  .....
   Boy     .....  .....  .....  .....  .....
   Girl    .....  .....  .....  .....  .....
```

Findings and Conclusions

Since our desire is to have the student teacher develop skills of self-analysis, the coding is typically done by the student teacher from an audio tape of the student's own teaching. Because we believe that the Spaulding system is minimally value-laden, we believe it can be used to study one's teaching communication from many different theoretical viewpoints and value positions. We feel that the students will have a versatile analytic tool when they learn this system.

Our interpretation of current research into classroom teaching has led us to urge students to use this system to reduce teacher talk; reduce judgmental statements, whether positive or negative; increase cognitive instruction while decreasing management remarks; frame questions which require extensive responses; and react to questions by probing, presenting additional materials by asking other children to respond rather than simply giving an affirmative or negative judgment. We ask the students to ask themselves these kinds of questions when they have completed the coding of their lesson:

1. How is class time divided between teacher-talking and teacher-listening?
2. How much time is spent in the affective domain? What proportion is negative?
3. How much of the instructional time is spent in management comments?
4. How frequently are questions asked?
5. What is the relation of time spent asking questions to time spent listening to responses?
6. What happens to students' responses? Are they evaluated by teacher? Are they the stimulus for other questions from teacher or students? Are they the stimulus for other statements by teacher and/or students?

In 1968 Greta Morine reported on a study which examined the effects of our program on first-year teachers.[1] Our graduates in their first year of teaching were compared with the graduates of similar institutions who were teaching in the same schools and with experienced teachers who had been judged excellent by their peers. According to Morine, "Hofstra graduates showed less teacher talk and more listening to student talk than expected . . . the experienced teachers also showed less teacher talk and more student talk than expected but did not go as far in this direction as the Hofstra graduates . . . . The non-Hofstra graduates showed more teacher talk and less listening to student talk than expected." The differences were significant at the .001 level. Hofstra graduates also repeated student responses less than the other groups and reacted to student responses by asking follow-up questions to a significantly greater extent than the other two groups. In the use of disapproval, Hofstra graduates were slightly below the expected levels, non-Hofstra graduates well below the expected level, and the "judged good" experienced teachers well above the expected level. Hofstra graduates were high in the use of approval, although we had not stressed this, and non-Hofstra graduates were below the expected level.

In summary, the results of this study led us to believe that the Spaulding system used in conjunction with our other instruments of analysis and evaluation had helped us to affect teaching behavior in a direction we believe to be positive.

[1] Greta Morine, "Evaluating the Curriculum: Problems and Prognosis" (paper presented at the annual meeting of the American Educational Research Association in Chicago, 1969), mimeographed.

Future Use

While stating that the Spaulding system is useful from differing value and theoretical positions, it must here be asserted that its structure reflects the current structure of classroom life. That is, it is focused on verbal behavior; it posits the teacher as a central authority figure; it assumes whole-class or large-group instruction; and it suggests that classroom communication has a question-answer format. One might speculate as to whether or not its use might create a limiting mind set which militates against a consideration of radically different alternative classroom structures. A class in which communication is highly individualized, in which communication is totally conversational, and in which children share authority with the teacher is not a suitable setting for the use of a coding system such as this. However, it is probably the case that no present classroom coding system would be useful if classroom structure shifted dramatically.

Additionally, I have come to believe that the practice of conducting classroom communication as an eternal oral short-answer quiz is particularly harmful to youngsters. I now believe that questions which have "right" or "wrong" answers would be better asked in written form or in a much more private encounter than the typical whole-class setting. Finally, as a feminist whose consciousness has been raised, I've been more and more offended by the unnecessary boy/girl discrimination in the code. This discrimination has been helpful in using the code to demonstrate differential treatment teachers exhibit toward boys and girls. (Research shows that teachers ask boys more questions as well as giving them more negative feedback.) However, for general use it will just have to go!

6 Pupils' Perception of Teachers' Verbal Feedback

John A. Zahorik

The pupils have arrived. The bell has rung. The classroom door has been closed. Teaching and learning are going on. As teachers go about the task of teaching, they display a great variety of verbal behavior. They provide information, ask questions, give directions, issue reprimands, offer praise, put on demonstrations, and state opinions.

These verbal behaviors can take many forms. Teachers can ask various types of questions, give many kinds of directions, issue many sorts of reprimands, or offer many classes of praise. It seems reasonable to believe that some verbal behaviors may be more appropriate, more valuable, or more effective than others in promoting pupils' learning.

The question of the comparative value of various educational procedures is usually resolved by resorting to experimental research. The standard model for conducting research is the test-teach-test model. One practice or method is pronounced more valuable than another on the basis of the pupils' performance on a test. The practice of basing judgments on performance is not unlike the practice in laboratory research of making judgments by studying a rat running a maze or depressing a

Reprinted with permission from *The Elementary School Journal*, 71:105–114, November, 1970. Copyright © 1970 by the University of Chicago.

bar. But pupils are not rats. One can observe the behavior of pupils as one can observe the behavior of rats. One can also talk to pupils and have them express their feelings, their thoughts, and their perceptions. Rats rarely speak to mortals.

The practice of evaluating classroom precedures by using the test-teach-test model is valid and useful, but children are sensing, responsive human beings who can communicate. Why not ask them what they think about a procedure? Why not solicit their perceptions about a particular behavior? Why not make judgments by direct means as well as by indirect means such as a test performance?

This paper reports a study in which pupils' perceptions were solicited. Pupils were asked about teacher verbal feedback—about responses that teachers made to pupils.

In this study *teacher verbal feedback* means teachers' oral remarks about the adequacy or the correctness of a pupil's statements solicited or initiated in the development of subject matter. Theoretically teacher verbal feedback can have a considerable effect on the pupils' learning and system control. From a teacher's verbal feedback a pupil can acquire information about the effectiveness of his behavioral output, adjust and change his future output, and gain a measure of control over his behavior.

In a previous study the writer investigated the frequency with which teachers used various types of verbal feedback and the relationship of feedback to several teaching-learning variables (1). In the investigation reported here the verbal feedback of fifteen teachers was examined with an instrument that had twenty-five categories. Of these twenty-five categories, which are identified in Table 1, thirteen (1.0 through 8.0) describe direct feedback, eleven (9.0 through 13.0) describe indirect feedback, and one (14.0) describes miscellaneous feedback. The instrument identifies more than twenty-five types of feedback, however, for the categories represent feedback elements rather than feedback types. A feedback type may be composed of only one element or category. Type 13.0 (lesson progression) answers this description: in this type of response, the teacher simply moves on to a new topic. Or a feedback type may be composed of several elements. One possible combination is 1.1-4.0-13.0 (simple praise-confirmation, positive answer, and lesson progression). In this type of response, the teacher mildly praises the pupil, repeats his answer approvingly, and moves on to a new topic.

In this study *direct feedback* was defined as oral remarks that have a major purpose of conveying information to the pupil about the value of his behavior. *Indirect feedback* was defined as oral questions and statements that have a primary purpose other than providing feedback, but questions and statements from which the child can infer the value of his behavior.

According to the results of this study, teachers' verbal feedback is a rigid behavior. Although the teachers used 175 different types of feedback, they used only 16 types regularly. As Table 2 shows, these sixteen types provided mainly simple positive feedback (1.1 and 4.0), response development feedback (9.1 and 9.3), and lesson development feedback (11.1 and 13.0). The fifteen teachers gave little direct negative, elaborate, clue, and explanation feedback.

The results further showed that teachers' verbal feedback is complex behavior. Besides being related to the value of the pupil's response, feedback is related to the type of teacher solicitation made, the purpose of the part of the lesson in which the feedback occurred, and the grade level of the pupils and the teachers.

From these results, the problem of the present study emerged: What do the regularly used types of feedback and several rarely used types of feedback means to pupils?

T A B L E 1.   Categories of Teacher Verbal Feedback

Categories	*Examples*
1.0 Praise-confirmation	
1.1 Simple praise-confirmation	"Good," "Yes," "All right"
1.2 Elaborate praise	"That's very good thinking, Tom."
1.3 Elaborate confirmation	"O. K., that's what the truck is used for."
2.0 Reproof-denial	
2.1 Simple reproof-denial	"No," "Uh uh"
2.2 Elaborate reproof	"You aren't using your head."
2.3 Elaborate denial	"That couldn't possibly be the correct answer."
3.0 Praise-confirmation and reproof-denial	"Yes and no," "Maybe"
4.0 Positive answer	"South America" (after pupil responds with "South America" to question concerning the location of Peru)
5.0 Negative answer	
5.1 Negative answer repetition	"Central America?" (after pupil responds with "central America" to question concerning the location of Peru)
5.2 Statement of correct answer	"Peru is in South America" (after pupil responds with "Central America" to question concerning the location of Peru)
6.0 Positive answer and negative answer	"So, you think that they're developing a civilization."

TABLE 1. *Continued*

Categories	*Examples*
7.0 Positive explanation	"Thailand is correct because the 'h' is silent." (after pupil responds with "Tiland" to question concerning pronunciation of Thailand)
8.0 Negative explanation	". . . the 'h' is silent and so is the 'a'." (after pupil responds with "Thailand" to question concerning pronunciation of Thailand)
9.0 Response extension: development	
9.1 Response development solicitation without clues	"Why is he named that?" (after pupil responds with "Lord Snowdon" to question concerning the name of Princess Margaret's husband)
9.2 Response development solicitation with clues	". . . and what happens to that beak after he catches lots of fish?" (after pupil responds with "long and big" to question concerning the unusualness of a pelican's beak)
9.3 Response development statement	". . . and in Washington they'll stop at President Kennedy's grave." (after pupil responds with "Washington, D.C." to question concerning where some visitors plan to spend time in our country)
10.0 Response extension: improvement	
10.1 Response improvement solicitation without clues	"Great what?" (after pupil responds with "Great" to question concerning what country Princess Margaret is from)
10.2 Response improvement solicitation with clues	"Great what? It's another name for England." (after pupil responds with "Great" to question concerning what country Princess Margaret is from)
10.3 Response improvement statement	". . . probably 80 to 90 per cent of all the people of Southeast Asia are farming in some way." (after pupil responds with "a few are farmers" to question concerning occupations in Vietnam)
11.0 Solicitation repetition: several answers	
11.1 Several-answers solicitation without clues	". . . another one, Alice?" (after pupil responds with "zinc" to question concerning resources of Vietnam)

TABLE 1. *Continued*

Categories	*Examples*
11.2 Several-answers solicitation with clues	". . . another one, Bob? One that aluminum is made from." (after pupil responds with "zinc, coal, and iron" to question concerning resources of Vietnam)
12.0 Solicitation repetition: one answer	
12.1 One-answer solicitation without clues	". . . Betty?" (after pupil responds with "Russia" to question concerning which country is aiding South Vietnam)
12.2 One-answer solicitation with clues	". . . think of who has soldiers over there, Jim?" (after pupil responds with "France" to question concerning which country is aiding South Vietnam)
13.0 Lesson progression: different topic	"What is the chief source of food in Vietnam, Susan?" (after pupil responds with "Mekong" to question concerning the name of the Vietnamese river on which dams are being built)
14.0 Miscellaneous feedback	

Collecting Data

To get information about pupils' perceptions of teachers' verbal feedback, an instrument containing twenty-eight segments of classroom dialogue was developed. Each segment consisted of three parts: teacher solicitation, pupil response, and teacher verbal feedback. The segments were taken verbatim from the fifteen lessons used to examine feedback usage and relationships in the previous study. Of the types of feedback in the twenty-eight segments, sixteen were the frequently used types reported in Table 2, and twelve were rarely used types, which appeared to be highly informational. Three of the rarely used types were negative types, two were mixed or neutral, three were elaborate, two gave clues, and two gave explanations.

These twenty-eight segments containing twenty-eight types of feedback were presented in written form to a randomly selected group of forty-two third- and sixth-grade pupils. The pupils were from the fifteen classes of the earlier investigation. Since the lesson originally taught to the fifteen classes was the same lesson at each grade level, all the pupils were familiar with the content of the segments.

The instrument was administered to small groups of pupils. Each segment was read aloud while the pupils read silently. The pupils were asked to pretend that the teacher speaking in the transcript was their teacher and that they were the boy or girl who was speaking.

After the reading of each segment, the pupils were asked to think about the teacher's feedback and make four judgments: Did they feel good, not good, or did they have no feeling as a result of the feedback? Did the feedback tell them whether the answer was right, wrong, or did it not tell? Did the feedback tell them why the answer was right, wrong, or did it not tell? Did the feedback tell them how to improve their right answer, correct their wrong answer, or did it not tell?

Pupils' perceptions were sought to determine something of the reinforcement, motivation, and cognitive information value of the various types of feedback. According to Ausubel (2), feedback, or knowledge of results, facilitates learning because of the reinforcement, motivation, and cognitive information it can provide. The first judgment or perception was designed to measure the value of the response in reinforcing and motivating. The other three judgments were designed to measure cognitive information value.

T A B L E 2.   Frequencies and Per Cents of Use of the Sixteen Most Frequently Occurring Types of Teacher Verbal Feedback

Feedback Type*	Frequency	Per Cent
4.0-13.0	183	8.46
9.1	179	8.28
1.1-13.0	168	7.77
1.1-4.0-13.0	125	5.78
13.0	110	5.09
1.1-11.1	101	4.67
4.0-9.1	100	4.63
4.0-9.3-13.0	95	4.39
4.0-11.1	73	3.38
9.3-13.0	64	2.96
1.1-4.0-11.1	63	2.91
1.1-9.3-13.0	61	2.82
1.1-4.0-9.3-13.0	52	2.41
11.1	51	2.36
1.1-9.1	49	2.27
10.1	47	2.17
Total 16 types	1,521	70.35
TOTAL 175 types	2,162	100.00

*The titles of the categories which comprise the feedback types are: 1.1, simple praise-confirmation; 4.0, positive answer; 9.1, response development solicitation without clues; 9.3, response development statement; 10.1, response improvement solicitation without clues; 11.1 several-answers solicitation without clues; and 13.0, different topic lesson progression (1:149).

Pupils' Perceptions

Tables 3 and 4 summarize pupils' perceptions of the twenty-eight types of teacher verbal feedback as determined by responses to four questions on the value of the feedback.

As Table 3 shows, the pupils felt that the sixteen types of frequently used feedback provoked some feeling and provided some information on correctness, but provided almost no explanation or direction. The types of feedback that nearly all the pupils perceived as provoking feeling were 1.1-11.1 (simple praise-confirmation and several-answers solicitation without clues), 1.1-4.0-11.1 (simple praise-confirmation, positive answer, and several-answers solicitation without clues), 1.1-9.3-13.0 (simple praise-confirmation, response development statement, and different topic lesson progression), 1.1-4.0-9.3-13.0 (simple praise-confirmation, positive answer, response development statement, and different

T A B L E   3.   Frequencies of Pupil Judgments of Feeling, Correctness, Explanation, and Direction for the Most Frequently Occurring Types of Teacher Verbal Feedback

Feedback Type*	Feeling			Correctness			Explanation			Direction†		
	+	−	0	+	−	0	+	−	0	+	−	0
4.0-13.0	24	2	16	30		12	9		33	2		40
9.1	13	9	20	7	6	28	1	2	39	1		41
1.1-13.0	25	2	15	32	1	9	3		39	4	1	37
1.1-4.0-13.0	29	1	12	36		6	8	1	33	9		33
13.0	8	20	14	6	12	24	1	3	37	1	1	40
1.1-11.1	38	2	2	38		4	4		38	1		41
4.0-9.1	15	11	16	16	4	22	1	1	40	3	1	38
4.0-9.3-13.0	31	1	10	27	1	14	21	1	20	11	1	30
4.0-11.1	11	9	22	20	1	21	8		34	1	3	38
9.3-13.0	14	10	18	12		30	2		40	5	3	34
1.1-4.0-11.1	34	3	4	38		3	13		28	2		39
1.1-9.3-13.0	33	2	7	41		1	16		26	9	1	32
1.1-4.0-9.3-13.0	38	1	3	36		6	25		17	14	2	26
11.1	5	20	17	4	9	29	1	3	38	1	2	39
1.1-9.1	35		7	36		6	8	1	33	5		37
10.1		28	14	2	16	23	1	6	34	3	4	35

*The titles of the categories which comprise the feedback types are: 1.1, simple praise-confirmation; 4.0, positive answer; 9.1, response development solicitation without clues; 9.3, response development statement; 10.1, response improvement solicitation without clues; 11.1, several-answers solicitation without clues; and 13.0, different topic lesson progression.

†The meanings of the symbols of the four kinds of judgments are: + = positive feeling or positive correctness, explanation, or direction information; − = negative feeling or negative correctness, explanation, or direction information; and 0 = no feeling or no correctness, explanation, or direction information.

TABLE 4.   Frequencies of Pupil Judgments of Feeling, Correctness, Explanation, and Direction for a Variety of Infrequently Occurring Types of Teacher Verbal Feedback

Feedback Type*	Feeling			Correctness			Explanation			Direction†		
	+	−	0	+	−	0	+	−	0	+	−	0
12.1	3	25	14	3	19	20	2	7	33	6	5	30
5.2-13.0	4	24	14	4	23	15		11	31	5	14	23
2.1-5.1-11.1		34	7		40	1		22	19	1	7	33
3.0-11.1	7	21	14	7	19	15	1	8	33	1	7	34
4.0-10.1	9	13	20	13	9	20	5	7	30	3	7	32
1.3-11.1	16	4	22	28	3	11	6	3	33	1		41
1.2-13.0	42			42			8		34	3		39
2.3-12.1	2	28	12	1	36	5		16	26		8	33
10.2	3	31	8		30	12		16	26	4	17	21
9.2	10	11	21	12	6	24	3	1	38	11	6	25
8.0-12.1	2	33	7		37	5		33	9		16	26
4.0-7.0-13.0	32	4	6	29	4	9	25	1	16	8	1	33

topic lesson progression), and 1.1-9.1 (simple praise-confirmation and response development solicitation without clues). Those types that nearly all the pupils saw as providing information on correctness were these same types with the addition of type 1.1-4.0-13.0 (simple praise-confirmation, positive answer, and different topic lesson progression). For the remaining types of feedback the pupils either had mixed reactions on feeling and correctness, or they believed that the types did not convey feeling and information on correctness.

The types of feedback that nearly all the pupils saw as stimulating feeling and as giving information on correctness contained simple praise-confirmation (1.1). None of the types that were seen as not stimulating feeling or giving information contained simple praise-confirmation with the exception of Type 1.1-13.0 (simple praise-confirmation and different topic lesson progression). Apparently, if pupils are to feel good about an answer or to believe that their answer is correct or appropriate, the teacher's verbal feedback must contain such phrases as "All right," "Fine," or "Good." Repeating the correct answer approvingly, develop-

*The categories representing the feedback types are: 1.2, elaborate praise; 1.3, elaborate confirmation; 2.1, simple reproof-denial; 2.3, elaborate denial; 3.0, praise-confirmation and reproof-denial; 4.0, positive answer; 5.1, negative answer repetition; 5.2 statement of correct answer; 7.0, positive explanation; 8.0, negative explanation; 9.2, response development with clues; 10.1, response improvement solicitation without clues; 10.2, response improvement solicitation with clues; 11.1, several-answers solicitation without clues; 12.1, one-answer solicitation without clues; 13.0, different topic lesson progression.

†The meanings of the symbols of the four kinds of judgments are: + = positive feeling or positive correctiness, explanation, or direction information; − = negative feeling or negative correctness, explanation, or direction information; and 0 = no feeling or no correctness, explanation, or direction information.

ing the response, and other feedback elements without accompanying simple praise-confirmation do not seem to have this effect.

In relation to explanation and direction information, of the sixteen types of frequently used feedback, only two were seen as valuable by at least a majority of the pupils: 1.1-4.0-9.3-13.0 (simple praise-confirmation, positive answer, response development statement, and different topic lesson progression) and 4.0-9.3-13.0 (positive answer, response development statement, and different topic lesson progression). A slim majority of the pupils perceived these two types as conveying explanation information. Perhaps response development statement (9.3) was interpreted as an explanation.

As Table 4 indicates, the pupils viewed many of the rarely used types of feedback as provoking feeling and providing information on correctness, and also as providing explanation and direction information. More pupils perceived many of these twelve types as conveying feeling and information on correctness, explanation, and direction than perceived the sixteen frequently used types as accomplishing these purposes.

Of the twelve rarely used types of feedback, the following are negative types: 12.1 (one-answer solicitation without clues), 5.2-13.0 (statement of correct answer and different topic lesson progression), and 2.1-5.1-11.1 (simple reproof-denial, negative answer repetition, and several-answers solicitation without clues). As Table 4 shows, of these types, Type 2.1-5.1-11.1 was viewed by nearly all the pupils as stimulating feeling and providing information on correctness. A majority also saw this type as imparting explanation information. Simple reproof-denial (2.1) is present in this type of feedback and not in the other two negative types. Perhaps if pupils are to know that an answer is wrong and to experience negative feeling, the teacher must use feedback that contains expressions such as "no," "Uh uh," or "That's wrong," just as if pupils are to know that an answer is correct and to feel good, the teacher may have to use simple praise-confirmation. Although there appears to be little difference between pupils' perceptions of the two negative types without simple reproof-denial and their perceptions of Type 10.1 (response improvement solicitation without clues), the only negative type of the frequently used sixteen types, the difference between the children's perceptions of 2.1-5.1-11.1 and 10.1 is great. Type 2.1-5.1-11.1 conveys much more feeling and information than Type 10.1.

Feedback types 3.0-11.1 (praise-confirmation and reproof-denial and several-answers solicitation without clues) and 4.0-10.1 (positive answer and response improvement solicitation without clues) are neutral or mixed types of feedback. The pupils had ambivalent reactions about the feeling and the correctness conveyed by these types. Most of the pupils also indicated that these types did not provide explanation or direction.

Feedback types 1.3-11.1 (elaborate confirmation and several-answers solicitation without clues), 1.2-13.0 (elaborate praise and different topic lesson progression), and 2.3-12.1 (elaborate denial and one-answer solicitation without clues) are elaborate types. Of these types, the perceptions of Type 1.2-13.0 are the most striking. Every one of the forty-two pupils judged this type as arousing feeling and providing information on correctness. None of the sixteen types of frequently used feedback stimulated a unanimous response to any of the four questions. Apparently, elaborate praise (1.2) conveys more feeling and information on correctness than simple praise-confirmation (1.1). With the exception of the information on correctness provided by Type 2.3-12.1, the other perceptions of these three types of elaborate feedback were either mixed or indicated that feeling and information were not provided.

Two other types of infrequently used feedback are 9.2 (response development solicitation with clues) and 10.2 (response improvement solicitation with clues). These are clue types. As Table 4 shows, pupil reactions to all four questions are mixed for these two types with the exception of explanation information for Type 9.2. However, the number of pupils who felt that Type 10.2 provided direction was greater than for any other type of feedback, including the sixteen types frequently used.

The remaining types of feedback, types 8.0-12.1 (negative explanation and one-answer solicitation without clues) and 4.0-7.0-13.0 (positive answer, positive explanation, and different topic lesson progression), are explanation types. The majority of the pupils indicated that they felt either good or not good as a result of these types of feedback and that these types provided information on correctness. More important, however, is the fact that the pupils judged Type 8.0-12.1, and to a lesser extent Type 4.0-7.0-13.0, as providing explanation. Type 8.0-12.1 imparted more explanation information than any other type of feedback including the sixteen frequently used types. In addition, this type conveyed information on direction to a relatively large group of pupils.

From these pupils' perceptions of a variety of twenty-eight types of teacher verbal feedback, it can be seen that the types of feedback that are regularly used are not necessarily the types that are the most valuable for provoking feeling and providing information on correctness, explanation and direction. Several types of infrequently used feedback such as the direct negative of simple reproof-denial, elaborate praise, a particular kind of clue, and explanations are more valuable. When the perceptions of elementary-school pupils are used as evidence, it appears that the sixteen types of frequently used feedback provide some reinforcement-motivation and limited cognitive information. Other types of feedback, however, provide more reinforcement-motivation and extensive as well as limited cognitive information.

Suggestions for Teaching

Although no hard and fast prescriptions for teaching can be drawn from these pupils' perceptions, they do generate some speculative suggestions for teacher verbal feedback during the teaching-learning act.

One general suggestion is that teachers use a wide variety of types of feedback rather than only a limited range of types. The types of feedback frequently used are not the types that provide the most reinforcement-motivation and cognitive information.

In addition to this general suggestion, the following specific suggestions are proposed:

1. If it is important that pupils experience positive feeling and know that an answer is correct, teachers might consider responding directly and specifically with elaborate praise or simple praise-confirmation. Elaborate praise appears to be more effective than simple praise-confirmation, but simple praise-confirmation does convey feeling and information on correctness. Neutral or mixed types of feedback or types of feedback that contain only indirect feedback or positive answer repetition may not be helpful for this purpose.

2. If it is important that pupils experience negative feeling and know that an answer is incorrect, thought should be given to using simple reproof-denial. Elaborate reproof may be more valuable for this purpose, but pupils' perceptions of elaborate reproof were not obtained. Indirect negatives such as 10.1 (response improvement solicitation without clues) may not be helpful. A request that the responding pupil or another pupil improve, change, or correct an answer does not convey feeling and information on correctness as simple reproof-denial does. Actually, there seems to be greater agreement on feeling than on correctness. This finding has interesting implications for those who feel that direct negatives cause pupils to overreact, while soliciting improvement does not.

3. If it is important that pupils have direction and guidance for future responses, consideration might be given to using types of feedback that contain clues (10.2 and, to a lesser extent, 9.2). Few types of feedback that do not contain clues seem to provide this information.

4. If it is important that pupils know why an answer is correct or incorrect, thought should be given to using types of feedback that contain explanations (7.0 and 8.0). Again, few types of feedback that do not contain explanation seem to provide this information.

Pupils' perceptions appear to shed some light on the meaning of particular teacher verbal behaviors. Research on pupils' perceptions, and perhaps teachers' perceptions, of many teacher verbal behaviors in addition to feedback might uncover knowledge that would be useful in promoting pupils' learning.

References

1. John A. Zahorik, "Classroom Feedback Behavior of Teachers," *Journal of Educational Research*, 62 (December, 1968), 147-50.

2. David P. Ausubel. *The Psychology of Meaningful Verbal Learning*, pp. 203-6. New York: Grune and Stratton, 1963.

2 *The Social Climate*

Overview

Educators who view teaching from the vantage point of classroom social climate employ such concepts as leadership, power, interaction, influence, authority, and role. They ask such questions as: How does the teacher manifest his leadership position in the classroom? In what ways does the teacher use his power? What patterns of teaching influence can we identify in the classroom? Who is recognized as having the authority for making classroom decisions? In what ways do teachers respond to the social needs of the students? What roles does the teacher perform as he teaches? In what activities do people interact in the classroom?

Of all the vantage points for studying teaching, this one of classroom climate is by far the most common one taken by educators. More empirical studies have been made on teaching from this perspective than from any other. This background of research gained strength in the 1930s from the work on the dynamics of youth groups done by Kurt Lewin and his associates, Lippitt and White. The early leading researcher on teaching was H. H. Anderson, who, with his associates, studied "dominative" and "integrative" contacts in nursery school. Most of the subsequent research on classroom climate (and youth groups as well) utilizes these two categories of behavior established years ago. This debt is evident in the material included in this section.

Flanders, in summarizing research projects on social classroom climate, has presented a short and insightful synthesis of these two teacher behavior patterns labeled Integrative Pattern and Dominative Pattern.

Integrative Pattern	*Dominative Pattern*
a. Accepts, clarifies, and supports the ideas and feelings of pupils	a. Expresses or lectures about own ideas as knowledge
b. Praises and encourages	b. Gives directions or orders
c. Asks questions to stimulate pupil participation in decision-making	c. Criticizes or deprecates pupil behavior with intent to change it
d. Asks questions to orient pupils to schoolwork	d. Justifies own position or authority[1]

The selections that follow demonstrate the significance of understanding social climate. In our democratic society citizens learn how to use and deal with authority, power, and leadership, in large measure, from their school experiences. Outside the home, the classroom is the one group, and adult-led at that, which each person must join at one time or another. The student learns social values by being personally involved with the teacher and his classmates and by observing the interactions of others about him. He learns how power is used, for example, and what the consequences of power are. In short, the interaction with the teacher and with his classmates teaches the pupil social skills, knowledge, and values.

This perspective has yet another significance. For years many people have been claiming that the climate of the classroom, which is set by the teacher, affects the cognitive achievement of the students. Many claim that when a teacher follows a more "democratic" pattern of behavior the students achieve more. Although the empirical research on this point is inconclusive,[2] we can say that different teachers have different patterns of behavior and that these patterns result in varying student behaviors. That is, certain types of teacher action facilitate certain pupil action. Besides, the democratic pattern, even if it does not yield more cognitive achievement, may yield more emotional and aesthetic growth. A need therefore exists to study the relationship between teacher behavior that involves authority, power, influence, and leadership and the cognitive, emotional, and aesthetic behavior of pupils.

[1] Ned A. Flanders, *Teacher Influence, Pupil Attitudes, and Achievement,* Cooperative Research Monograph no. 12. U.S. Department of Health, Education, and Welfare, Office of Education (Washington, D.C., 1965).

[2] Richard C. Anderson, "Learning in Discussion: A Resume of Authoritarian Democratic Studies," *Harvard Educational Review,* 29:201–215, Summer, 1959. Note that Flanders' study here does claim more achievement for pupils with teachers who are indirect (democratic).

R. S. Peters,[3] the British philosopher of education, has clearly demonstrated the various uses of the word *authority* in educational matters. He distinguishes between a teacher who is *in authority* for purposes of social control within the social structure of the schools and a teacher who is *an authority* because of his special competence in a subject or skill area. He further distinguishes being *in authority* from *being authoritarian*, which he claims is a repressive form of the use of social authority. In the selections included here, the reader should note which of these three forms of the word *authority* is being used by the authors.

Two of these selections—Flanders and Hughes—are empirical studies dealing with this matter of authority and influence. They present their instruments and their results, all based on the concepts of teacher power, the superior-subordinate relationship in the classroom, and teacher-pupil interaction.[4] Flanders studied junior high school classes, while Hughes studied classes in elementary school. Flanders categorized behaviors at the end of each three-second period, and Hughes employed the concept of functions performed by the teacher for the pupil as her unit of analysis. The studies were conducted in different sections of the country (Utah and a west coast state by Hughes; Minnesota by Flanders) and in different years. Flanders categorized teacher and pupil behavior, and Hughes categorized only teacher behavior. Flanders categorized only verbal behavior, while Hughes used both verbal and non-verbal behavior. Hughes drew up narrative records and categorized them afterwards, while Flanders categorized behavior "live" in the classroom.

The study by Flanders is no doubt the best-known research on classroom observation today. His Interaction Analysis instrument is widely used by other researchers because of its simplicity and the ease in obtaining acceptable observer reliability. It is unique in that, as the identified categories are paired off, the observer can readily plot the patterning of a class verbal behavior in a matrix, or a ten-by-ten table, showing the hundred possible sequences of category pairs. Flanders' category system is presented along with the selection by Chapline, which is an illustrative analysis of a matrix plotted from an actual junior high school social studies class. The Chapline article is important, for it shows the reader how to plot and analyze a matrix. This technique is an essential ingredient of all the studies done by Flanders and his many followers.

The reader should be alerted to one category in Marie Hughes' study in particular. Development of content is defined as the response the teacher makes to the data put into the situation by the pupil. The teacher may elaborate on, clarify, add to, accept, stimulate further, and even evaluate material offered by the pupil. In this way, Hughes's "con-

[3] R. S. Peters, "The Authority of the Teacher," *Comparative Education*, 3:1–12, November, 1966.

[4] See the overview to the Communications section for additional comment on the concepts utilized here.

tent" category is unique. It is quite different from other content as categorized in studies in this chapter and other chapters. Her other categories, such as positive affectivity and negative affectivity, are similar to those used in other research studies.

The selection by Adams and Biddle presents the framework of their study of teaching from a social science vantage point. In taking a position similar to that of an anthropologist studying the behavior setting of a group, these authors focus on the interaction of members of the group. Their branching framework, depicted in the selection, presents the transactional process of the classroom. The framework attends to the verbal dimension of the classroom but, significantly, also examines the nonverbal aspect of behavior labeled as location. (For this reason the reader should keep this selection in mind when he reads Section 8 on Nonverbal Communication.)

In this selection from their book Adams and Biddle do not present the lengthy and complex set of results from their empirical study. Suffice it to report here that in terms of behavior a classroom is a "remarkably busy place." In terms of role, the behavior changes rapidly, about once every eighteen seconds during an average lesson. (For details the reader may wish to see Chapters 4–7 in the authors' book *Realities of Teaching.*)

This change of role fits well with the article by Morine and Morine. The Morines intensively develop the "sociological concept of role" and show how a teacher plays multiple roles in teaching. They examine six major teaching roles and briefly mention five other roles the teacher plays in the classroom. The teacher shifts his role in teaching, according to the Morines, as he perceives changes in expectations of him.

Although the Morines do not develop their own observational instrument for measuring role functions, role expectations, and role behaviors, they draw upon the empirical findings of other researchers. They refer to such researchers as Flanders (this section), Taba (Section 9), Rogers (Section 5), and Ausubel (see Gagné in Section 4).

The reader would do well to compare the various roles identified by the Morines with the various vantage points constituting this book. For example, note the similarity between the Teacher as Counselor and the Psychological Climate vantage point. Also, note the similarity between the Teacher as Diagnostician and the Learning and Cognitive Development vantage point. The reader may wish to use the same set of questions the Morines have developed at the beginning of their selection as he himself studies the other articles constituting the vantage points of this book.

In all of these selections the point is made that the teacher shifts his behavior as he perceives changes in the teaching situation. The need to constantly perceive and analyze changes in the classroom is similar to Dewey's point in *Democracy and Education,* the teacher must know his subject matter so well that he can focus on diagnosing the ongoing discussion:

> When engaged in the direct act of teaching, the instructor needs to have subject matter at his fingers' ends; his attention should be upon the attitude and response of the pupil. To understand the latter in its interplay with subject matter is his task, while the pupil's mind, naturally, should be not on itself but on the topic at hand. Or to state the same point in a somewhat different manner: The teacher should be occupied not with the subject matter in itself but in its interaction with the pupils' present needs and capacities.[5]

Suggestions for further work leap forth from these selections. One will suffice here to demonstrate that a vast amount of research is still needed. Flanders states that no teacher has a pure pattern of influence in the classroom. That is, no teacher manifests only direct influence or indirect influence over the pupils. Rather, each teacher's is a mixture of different types of verbal influence, the proportions of which determine the teacher's style. Hughes, on the basis of her notion of what kind of people she would like pupils to become[6] and of what the impact of the teacher on the pupils is, has outlined in her full report the following model of good teaching:

Controlling Functions	20–40%
Imposition	1–3%
Facilitating	5–15%
Content Development	20–40%
Personal Response	8–20%
Positive Affectivity	10–20%
Negative Affectivity	3–10%

The question then becomes what pattern or mixture of teacher-influence behavior is most likely to bring out the desired learning in the classroom? This question, no matter which of the six following frameworks we use, is but one of the many significant problems that will require much investigative energy and ingenuity.

[5] John Dewey, *Democracy and Education* (New York: Macmillan Company, 1961), p. 183.

[6] See the selections by Rogers (Section 5), Hallman (Section 7), Gallagher and Aschner (Section 3), and Maccia (Section 3) for views expressing approaches virtually the same as Hughes's.

7 Teaching

Greta Morine and Harold Morine

Teaching and the Concept of Role

The purpose of this analysis of teaching is to describe teaching as one very important component of the modern elementary school. The elementary school is a social institution that is strongly affected by changes and conflicts in the society as a whole. In turn, the school effects changes in the groups who work within it—teachers, administrators, and pupils.

The terms used here to describe the school are mainly sociological terms. If the school is viewed from a sociological perspective, then it is fitting to describe teaching from the same perspective. Therefore, the sociological concept of role is used to analyze the process of teaching as it occurs in the modern elementary school.

"Role" refers to a set of expectations and a set of behaviors that are associated with an acquired or assigned status. A given role performs particular functions for the social group in which it is carried out. Any one individual may function in a variety of roles throughout his lifetime

Reprinted with permission from Chapter 11 of *The Elementary School in the United States,* The Seventy-second Yearbook of the National Society for the Study of Education, Part II. Chicago: University of Chicago Press, 1973.

or at any given point in his lifetime. Thus, a woman (assigned status) may display one set of behaviors when functioning in her role as daughter (assigned status), another set when functioning in her role as wife (acquired status), and a third when functioning in her role as an author (acquired status).

The three principal aspects of the concept of role as defined here are: a role involves a function; a role is associated with a set of expectations and a set of behaviors; an individual may play a variety of roles. All of these aspects of role can be applied to teaching.

"Teacher" can be and has been perceived as a unitary role consisting of several basic functions and a set of related behaviors and expectations. A more productive application of the concept of role is to draw an analogy between the teacher and the individual. Just as we can perceive the individual as functioning in a variety of social roles, so we can perceive the teacher as functioning in a variety of instructional roles. Each possible instructional role performs a particular function for the pupils with whom it is carried out. Each instructional role has an associated set of expectations and an associated set of behaviors, though there are usually discrepancies between the expected behaviors associated with the role and the actual behaviors exhibited by the individual performing the role. Any given teacher can be perceived as having a repertoire of instructional roles. Some teachers may have extensive repertoires, while others have very limited ones.

If teaching is perceived as a set of instructional roles, then an analysis of teaching as it exists in the elementary school today must consider the following questions:

1. What are the instructional roles teachers are asked to perform?
2. What are the expectations associated with each role?
3. How valid are these expectations, and what are the actual behaviors associated with each role?
4. What functions can each role serve? . . .

Instructional Roles

The Teacher As Reporter

The instructional role of *reporter* of information and events is a time-honored one. In preliterate societies much of the transmission of knowledge from generation to generation was conducted by the process of storytelling. Abelard, in the twelfth century, used a method that involved reporting both sides of a philosophical issue. St. Thomas Aquinas advocated the use of logical demonstration wherein the speaker or reporter stated a question, presented the views of authorities, and suggested his own solution. The modern counterpart of this ancient instructional role is the well-known lecture method.

ROLE EXPECTATIONS. Much of the research and analysis dealing with the lecture method is related to college teaching, but some of the same expectations hold for use of this role in the elementary school. The teacher as reporter is expected to be well organized, to speak clearly, to use varied emphasis and intonation, to give many illustrations and examples of the major points, to maintain eye contact with the pupils, and to summarize carefully.[1] It is generally agreed that the teacher as reporter should communicate enthusiasm and interest for his topic as well as knowledge about it.

Ausubel has advocated use of this instructional role in the elementary school. He has three very important role expectations: that this role be used to transmit the basic concepts of each discipline separately; that the teacher should present the most general and inclusive ideas of the discipline first; that the teacher should relate each new concept to previously learned content.[2]

It is generally expected that the teacher as reporter communicates orally and that the communication is mainly one-way. The concomitant role for the pupil is to listen. In the elementary school it is usually recommended that the oral presentation be accompanied by some visual illustrations, such as pictures, slides, transparencies, or key words written on the chalkboard.

VALIDITY OF ROLE EXPECTATIONS. Not all of the expectations associated with the role of teacher as reporter have been demonstrated to have real consequence for pupils' learning. Teacher enthusiasm and clarity do appear to make a difference in children's achievement.[3] However, the importance of organization has not been clearly demonstrated. Studies have shown that randomly organized presentations are comprehended as well as logically organized ones.[4]

The expectation that the elementary teacher when lecturing or reporting uses mainly one-way communication has not been fully substantiated in studies of classroom interaction. Gage notes that "classroom discourse is the most prevalent and the most loosely defined teaching method. It consists of a mixture of brief and informal lectures with dis-

[1]James W. Brown and James W. Thornton, Jr., *College Teaching: Perspectives and Guidelines* (New York: McGraw-Hill Book Co., 1963), pp. 138–52.

[2]David P. Ausubel, *The Psychology of Meaningful Verbal Learning* (New York: Grune and Stratton, 1963), p. 79.

[3]Rosenshine and Furst, op. cit., pp. 44–46.

[4]Wayne N. Thompson, *Quantitative Research in Public Address and Communication* (New York: Random House, 1967), pp. 65–68.

cussions and recitations."[5] Flanders and many others have reported that teachers talk some 65 to 75 percent of the time in this type of classroom discourse.[6] It would seem to follow that pupils are talking 25 to 35 percent of the time. Apparently, what actually occurs in the elementary school classroom when the teacher tries to function in the role of reporter is a somewhat modified form of the lecture method, with presentation of information being punctuated by feedback from pupils.

FUNCTIONS OF ROLE.   The role of reporter can be an effective instructional role when it is performed well and when it is performed *intermittently*. Variation in teaching behavior seems to be associated with more positive attitudes and higher achievement of pupils. But teachers who use the modified lecture pattern almost exclusively tend to have classes that achieve less well.[7]

A presentation of information can transmit knowledge efficiently to large groups, especially when the presentation is followed by discussion in small groups. One pattern of use for this role would be to have a skilled reporter present a concept to a large group of pupils, using Ausubel's *advance organizer* strategy.[8] Following the presentation, discussion groups aimed at helping pupils integrate the new concept with previously learned material would be led by teachers skilled in use of this strategy. This pattern of use would seem to be a practical one in elementary schools that are organized for team teaching and differentiated staffing (see chapter 9).

The Teacher As Model

The instructional role of *model* also has antecedents that go far back in time. Anthropologists note that a basic form of the socialization process in most societies is children's imitation of adult activities. Both physical and social skills are learned in this manner. In ancient Athens, the rhetoricians used systematic imitation as a method of teaching young men to speak effectively. There is also some evidence that moral values are learned through imitation of and identification with adult models,[9] and teachers historically have been expected to display exemplary moral behavior. In modern use of this role the elementary teacher models a variety of physical skills for children to learn through imitation.

[5]Gage, "Teaching Methods," op. cit., p. 1450.

[6]Ned Flanders and Anita Simon, "Teacher Effectiveness," in *Encyclopedia of Educational Research*, 4th ed., ed. Robert L. Ebel (Toronto: Collier-Macmillan, Ltd., 1969), p. 1429.

[7]Rosenshine and Furst, op. cit., p. 45.

[8]Joyce and Weil, op. cit., pp. 174–77.

[9]Albert Bandura and Frederick J. McDonald, "The Influence of Social Reinforcements and the Behavior of Models in Shaping Children's Moral Judgments," *Journal of Abnormal Social Psychology* 67 (1963): 274–82.

ROLE EXPECTATIONS. The teacher as model of particular physical or psychomotor skills is expected to be adept at the skill he is modeling. Some of the skills that teachers are expected to model include: "perfect" handwriting in manuscript and/or cursive on chalkboards and on paper; ball-handling skills appropriate for seasonal team sports such as dodge ball, kickball, baseball, football, basketball; artistic skills such as cutting, pasting, painting, charcoal sketching; handicraft skills such as sewing, knitting, macrame, tie-dyeing, weaving; woodworking skills such as sawing, hammering, planing, sandpapering; musical skills such as tone-matching, song-singing, instrument-playing.

The teacher as model is also expected to exemplify social roles that children need to learn, and portray the values and attitudes that the society wants its youth to develop.

VALIDITY OF ROLE EXPECTATIONS. There is a serious question whether it is possible for a teacher to fulfill the expectations of others when performing the role of model. An individual teacher may possess many of the psychomotor skills that children need to learn, but he rarely possesses them all. The probability is high that he possesses only a few.

Modeling of social roles is an area of some controversy. With the changing sex roles in the society today, it is difficult for any teacher to know what social roles to model. Elementary school teachers (largely women) have been accused of overplaying the female role and contributing to the "feminization" of the American male.[10] According to this view, the elementary teacher models and rewards behavior typical of the American female, such as showing preference for verbal communication, sedentary activities, and cooperation (conformity to group norms). More masculine behavior, such as high-level physical activity, frequent physical confrontations, competition, and showing independence of authority, is rarely displayed by the teacher and tends to be punished when it is displayed by pupils.

Recently, the followers of women's liberation movements have joined the attack by noting the stereotyped sex roles that are portrayed in children's textbooks.[11] Surely it will not be long before they begin to protest the model of the female portrayed by the elementary teacher herself. For, while the classroom teacher (usually female) has some independence, even a kindergarten child knows that it is the principal (usually male) who holds the real power in the school. And, while the number of male teachers in elementary schools has increased somewhat in recent years, the number of females in administrative positions has not.

[10]Patricia C. Sexton, "Education and Effeminacy," *School and Society* 116 (1968): 273–74.

[11]Phylis Alroy et al., *Dick and Jane As Victims: Sex Stereotyping in Children's Readers* (Princeton, N.J.: Women on Words and Images, 1972).

Modeling of values and attitudes is an equally controversial area. The modern multicultural society no longer agrees that inculcation of middle-class values and attitudes is an appropriate function of the elementary school. Subcultures are demanding teachers for their children who can understand and model the values of their culture. Thus, black children need black teachers, Chicano children need Chicano teachers, and Asian children need Asian teachers. Less militant groups of the various subcultures continue to argue for integrated classrooms, where children can learn to understand and appreciate the differences that exist in a multicultural nation. In such classrooms it would not seem to be appropriate for the teacher to model a "preferred" value system.

FUNCTIONS OF ROLE. How can the elementary school teacher deal with the dilemmas surrounding the role of teacher as model? One way would be to limit the roles he attempts to model. He can model effectively psychomotor skills that he does possess, for example, and solicit the help of other teachers or of volunteers and paraprofessionals to model the skills he does not possess.

He can model social roles that are desirable for the classroom and which have no sexist connotations. For example, research suggests that teachers expect their pupils to be good listeners but that teachers rarely portray this role themselves.[12] A useful social role to model would be the role of listener, with the teacher portraying skills in paraphrasing and checking comprehension of the messages being sent by pupils.

Teachers legitimately can model intellectual roles.[13] They can show through their behavior that they value scholarship, the indeterminate situation, the excitement of moving from the known to the unknown, or the unique solution. They can be caught once in a while reading a book. They can show children that a teacher's hypothesis may fail to bear fruit, that a teacher can come up against an intellectual stone wall but refuse to quit in the face of frustration. The one value which teachers can model safely is the value of thinking and learning.

The Teacher As Problem-setter

The instructional role of *problem-setter* has its historical roots in the Socratic method. The first step in a Socratic dialogue was to get the learner to question his own knowledge. In the early 1800s, Herbart formulated his version of the inductive method, which required pupils to develop generalizations from information that the teacher organized and presented. John Dewey's project method aimed at engaging learners in problem-solving activities that were related to concerns about the

[12]Flanders and Simon, op. cit., p. 1429.

[13]Harold Morine and Greta Morine, *Discovery: A Challenge to Teachers* (Englewood Cliffs, N.J.: Prentice-Hall, 1972).

real world of the child. These varied approaches to problem-setting all have their counterparts in modern instructional practice. Some educators group all the modern manifestations of this role under the term *inquiry methods*. Space does not permit a discussion of all the variations of this particular role, and this analysis focuses upon the role performed by the teacher when using inductive discovery as a form of problem-setting.

ROLE EXPECTATIONS. While teaching strategies used in various discovery methods can differ markedly, most versions of this aspect of the problem-setter role expect that the teacher will provide pupils with data or examples from which a basic principle or generalization can be drawn. In some instances, the teacher is expected to ask open questions that will lead pupils to generate such data.[14] When the data have been examined by pupils, it is expected that the teacher will guide discussion so that pupils suggest relationships among the data and evaluate each other's ideas. The teacher is expected to refrain from such evaluation but may compare the ideas of different pupils in an objective manner. When pupil agreement is reached, the teacher is expected to encourage pupils to revise faulty generalizations by providing new data or new insights about old data. Throughout the discovery process the teacher is expected to accept and make use of pupils' ideas and to refrain from presenting his own conclusions.

VALIDITY OF ROLE EXPECTATIONS. The research on the effectiveness of this version of the problem-setter role is not conclusive since studies of discovery methods have tended to be irrelevant, poorly designed, or negative in their findings. A much more structured method called "guided discovery" does seem to facilitate learning and retention.[15] Studies of teaching behavior do appear to support the effectiveness of this type of instructional role. Flanders cites several studies that indicate a relationship between teacher statements that make use of pupils' ideas and pupils' achievement and attitudes toward school.[16]

There is some question as to how well teachers (and researchers) understand and execute the expectations of the advocates of discovery methods. Many seem to construe the inductive discovery version of the problem-setter role in an extreme form, depriving learners of all cues and leaving them completely unguided in their search for concepts or principles.[17] While the indirect patterns of classroom interaction identified by Flanders are related to higher achievement, most teachers studied

[14]Hilda Taba, *Teacher's Handbook for Elementary Social Studies* (Reading, Mass.: Addison-Wesley Publishing Co., 1967), p. 92.

[15]David P. Ausubel, *Educational Psychology: A Cognitive View* (New York: Holt, Rinehart & Winston, 1968), pp. 497–504.

[16]Flanders and Simon, op. cit., p. 1426.

[17]Gage, "Teaching Methods," op. cit., p. 1456.

tended not to use these indirect patterns.[18] Experienced supervisors note that many teachers attempting to use discovery methods resort to telling pupils the answer if the desired generalization is not quickly reached. The lack of evidence to support the effectiveness of discovery methods may be related to the fact that researchers have not yet differentiated the most important factors affecting discovery learning, and that teachers have not yet learned to play this version of the problem-setting role as effectively as they might.

FUNCTIONS OF ROLE. The instructional role of problem-setter can be used in interaction with individuals and with small or medium-sized groups. It is used appropriately in any subject area where the learning of thinking skills is as important an objective as learning content. Gage notes that there is considerable evidence to support the notion that structured or guided discovery can be used in teaching "some aspects of some subjects with advantages for learning, retention, and transfer."[19] He suggests that strategic use of this version of the problem-setter role will increase interest, involvement, and problem-solving ability without an unreasonable expenditure of time.

One way to apply this suggestion would be to use a form of the problem-setter role and the reporter role in an alternating cycle. Pupils could be encouraged to develop generalizations related to a given set of data. When they have evaluated their own generalizations, the teacher could present those of scholars in the field and compare the generalizations and the data organizations of the scholars with those developed by pupils. If this plan were followed, the teacher as reporter would need to point out the disagreements existing among scholars, so that children would learn to question the validity of knowledge generated by authorities in the same way that they question the validity of the knowledge they generate themselves.

The Teacher As Counselor

The instructional role of *counselor* was advocated by Pestalozzi in the late 1700s. He hoped to release pupils' spirits and increase their efficiency by showing them that they were loved. The child study movement in the 1940s was another forerunner of this role. At this time, teachers became very aware of the personal and social development of their pupils and sought to engage them in activities that would facilitate this development. Jersild's studies of children's self-perceptions led him to advocate classroom discussions of common personal and social problems.[20] The modern advocates of similar instructional roles include Carl Rogers

[18]Flanders and Simon, op. cit., p. 1429.
[19]Gage, "Teaching Methods," op. cit., p. 1456.
[20]Arthur T. Jersild, *In Search of Self* (New York: Teachers College Press, 1952).

(student-centered teaching), William Glasser (reality therapy), and William Schutz (awareness or sensitivity training).[21]

ROLE EXPECTATIONS.   While advocates of the counselor role differ somewhat in the strategies they recommend, they agree that a fundamental aspect of education is the task of finding personal identity and self-worth. They expect the teacher to facilitate this task by providing pupils with the opportunity to explore their feelings in open discussions. The teacher may begin such discussions by asking an open-ended question or by leading pupils in a brief exercise designed to stimulate sensory awareness. As pupils discuss the question or their reactions to the awareness exercise, the teacher is expected to be accepting, supportive, and nonjudgmental.

In Glasser's "Classroom Meeting," the role of counselor takes on some additional complexities. The teacher must be warmly involved with the group rather than objective and detached. He must get the child and the group to make judgments about their behavior, although he himself remains nonjudgmental. He must assist children in planning a better course of action for their future behaviors and may suggest some alternatives to be considered. He endeavors to get the children to make a commitment to follow the course of action they select, and once the commitment is made, he supports it by exercising discipline, rather than by excusing children for nonperformance.[22]

VALIDITY OF ROLE EXPECTATIONS.   There seems to be general agreement among elementary school counselors that the classroom teacher does have an important guidance function.[23] Relatively few classroom teachers have had any training to fulfill this function, however. When Jersild recommended classroom discussion on personal problems, he also recommended that teachers get training in counseling themselves.[24] Present-day advocates of the counselor role do not always stress the need for such training. But it is not an easy matter for the teacher to subordinate his own feelings and problems to those of his pupils unless he has had a prior opportunity to develop some insights into his own feelings.

Many teachers have interpreted the counselor role as being completely separate from instruction. They hope to develop positive self-concepts in children by focusing on affect alone, forgetting that self-concept is always related to achievement of some standard of behavior.

[21]Joyce and Weil, op. cit., pp. 208–9.

[22]Ibid., pp. 225–26.

[23]Harold F. Cottingham, "Counseling—Elementary Schools," in *Encyclopedia of Educational Research*, 4th ed., ed. Robert L. Ebel (Toronto: Collier-Macmillan Ltd., 1969), p. 235.

[24]Arthur T. Jersild, *When Teachers Face Themselves* (New York: Teachers College, Columbia University, 1955).

Some teachers interpret the idea of helping pupils find their own direction to mean that pupils will select the goals and activities that the teacher had in mind to begin with. These teachers are usually disappointed in their expectations.

There is little evidence of the effectiveness of these techniques with children, for several reasons. Proponents of the counselor role are prone to rely on self-reports rather than more objective forms of evaluation. The goals are long-term rather than immediate, so that changes that are achieved tend to be gradual and difficult to observe. The recent educational "movements" associated with this role have not been on the scene long enough to produce much evaluative research. Some adherents of the movement argue that results should *not* be evaluated. "Don't analyze it" is their rallying cry.

FUNCTIONS OF ROLE. The instructional role of counselor can be used with small or medium-sized groups. It can be used to deal with pupil problems that are related to the school setting.

Glasser recommends use of this role in dealing with academic problems as well as social problems. A "Classroom Meeting" can be used to find out what students do and do not know about a topic they have been studying. It can be used to learn what topics are interesting and thought-provoking to children. Rogers suggests that each class might open with a variant of the question, "What do we want to do today?" Problem-solving activities then develop around individual questions posed by pupils.

One way to apply these suggestions would be to use the counselor role to involve pupils in planning and evaluation of their own instruction. Group planning can be very time-consuming, but it is possible to alternate between teacher-directed and student-directed activities. One organization that has been tried in many schools is to have teacher-directed study of "survival" or basic skill subjects during the morning hours and student-directed activities such as interest centers or "uncommon learning centers" in the afternoon hours.[25]

The Teacher As Diagnostician

In the seventeenth century Comenius used an instructional method that involved developing materials sequentially and providing pupils with immediate correction. Thorndike in the early 1900s viewed immediate feedback and reinforcement as a necessary condition of learning. But Skinner is the man most widely associated with modern interpretations of the instructional role of *diagnostician*. Both programmed instruction and behavior modification have their basis in the assumption that teachers

[25]Harold Morine and Greta Morine, *A Primer for the Inner City School* (New York: McGraw-Hill Book Co., 1970).

can diagnose pupil needs and prescribe stimulus and reinforcement conditions in order to foster attainment of those needs.

ROLE EXPECTATIONS. The teacher as diagnostician is expected to determine pupils' cognitive levels in various subject areas, state specific behavioral objectives to be achieved, select or produce the appropriate instructional material to achieve these objectives, and evaluate individual performance at the end of the instruction. With many programmed instructional materials, these teacher tasks are simplified by the provision of diagnostic tests and specific instructions as to sequencing of materials.

The role of diagnostician is used also in dealing with children's social learning. In this case, the teacher is expected to identify both the undesirable behavior that is to be decreased and the desirable behavior that is to be increased. The prescription or treatment that the teacher then applies involves ignoring the undesirable behavior, rewarding the desirable behavior, and isolating the child without comment for behavior that is dangerous or unacceptable.

With the move toward accountability in education, the instructional role of diagnostician has become increasingly important. For example, the Stull Bill in California mandates that teacher effectiveness be judged on pupil achievement of the behavioral objectives agreed upon by the teacher and administrator. This criterion of effectiveness is to be used for decisions about tenure and salary increases.

VALIDITY OF ROLE EXPECTATIONS. There is a good deal of research available on programmed instruction. It leaves no doubt that students who use programmed materials learn. They learn from different kinds of programming and from different kinds of materials. Some of them even like the programs. But the most common finding of the studies is that there is no significant difference between the instructional conditions being compared.[26]

Supposedly this instructional role calls for attention to individual differences. Since pupils work independently on programs, the programs can be suited to their own individual attainment levels. But the studies of effectiveness of programmed instruction generally fail to include individual difference variables such as aptitude, personality, and interests, and thus little is known about these as correlates of learning scores.[27] Therefore, a teacher attempting to prescribe the most effective instruction for a particular pupil has little assurance that programmed lessons will be the most effective type of material. One study has shown that with high-aptitude students, instruction from an innovative teacher

[26]Lawrence M. Stolurow, "Programmed Instruction," in *Encyclopedia of Educational Research*, 4th ed., ed. Robert T. Ebel (Toronto: Collier-Macmillan Ltd., 1969), p. 1020.

[27]Ibid.

plus a program is most effective, while with low-aptitude students a conventional teacher alone produces better results.[28]

The expectation that teachers are able and willing to state specific behavioral objectives is open to some question. In recent years many of the teacher education materials produced by the national research and development laboratories have been aimed at retraining teachers to use this skill.[29] But it is evident from talking to teachers in the classroom that most of them feel woefully inadequate to the task and that many of them object to it strongly on the grounds that it is "behavioristic" or "mechanistic" rather than "humanistic."

The validity of expectations with regard to the instructional role of diagnostician applied to the affective realm is slightly more positive. Spaulding has identified six behavioral "styles" of children and set up treatment schedules for each style, with the general objective of moving children toward a style of independent, self-directed behavior.[30] He has demonstrated that teachers can be trained to use the treatment schedules, that the treatment schedules are effective in changing children's behavior, and that the resultant behavior change acts to reinforce the teacher's newly acquired behavior patterns.[31]

However, there is evidence that untrained teachers tend to be more aware of negative than positive behavior in the children they observe and teach.[32] Coding of interactive behavior indicates that teachers tend to disapprove social behavior of children and approve cognitive behavior. They rarely approve social behavior or disapprove cognitive behavior in their verbal interchanges.[33] Thus, it is apparent that most teachers need some special training to use the instructional role of diagnostician in relation to children's social behavior in the classroom.

As in the case of programmed instruction, many teachers object to the use of behavior modification techniques on the grounds that they represent an antihumanistic approach to education. While these views may be naïve, they must nevertheless be taken into account as a set of circumstances conditioning what teachers will and will not incorporate readily into their pedagogical skills.

[28]Ibid.

[29]Bruce Joyce et al., *Materials for Modules: A Classification of Competency-Oriented Tools for Teacher Education* (New York: Teachers College, Columbia University, 1971), pp. 29–31.

[30]Robert L. Spaulding, *Educational Intervention in Early Childhood*, Durham Education Improvement Program Final Report, vol. 1 (Durham, N.C.: Duke University, 1971), pp. 30–46.

[31]Ibid., pp. 50–57.

[32]Ibid., p. 171.

[33]Greta Morine, Robert Spaulding, and Selma Greenberg, *Discovering New Dimensions in the Teaching Process* (Scranton, Pa.: Intext Educational Publishers, 1971), p. 84.

FUNCTIONS OF ROLE. The instructional role of diagnostician in the cognitive realm can be used in settings where individualized instruction and independent learning are the pattern. It can be used in teaching basic skill areas, where general agreement exists as to the necessity of pupil attainment of specific knowledge. It can be used in subject areas where programmed materials and diagnostic tests are well developed. At present there is a variety of such materials available to teach mathematics and reading at the elementary level.

The instructional role of diagnostician in the affective realm can be used in interaction with individuals and small groups. It can be used in settings where agreement exists as to what is desirable social behavior. It is most effectively used when there are support personnel available to observe and code the behavior of teacher and child and provide the teacher with feedback during the initial stages of treatment. This fact would seem to recommend its use in team-teaching situations or in schools that have paraprofessionals or volunteer teaching assistants available.

The diagnostician role can be used in conjunction with some of the other roles discussed previously. For example, the instructional role of diagnostician (cognitive realm) can be used in teacher-directed settings to teach basic skill subjects while the role of counselor is being used to facilitate student-directed learning in other subject areas. The role of diagnostician (affective realm) can be used to change children's social behavior at the same time that the role of problem-setter is being used to facilitate their learning of intellectual skills.

The Teacher As Systems Manager

The instructional role of *systems manager* may have its historical roots in Froebel's concern for human development and his belief that teaching should always be two-sided—giving and taking, prescribing and following, active and passive, firm and yielding. These would seem to be the characteristics exemplified in the best British infant schools and the most successful open classrooms in American elementary schools today.[34] It is in the open classroom that the role of systems manager is most frequently played.

ROLE EXPECTATIONS. The teacher as systems manager is expected to select, produce, or procure a wide variety of instructional materials for independent use by children. He is to organize time and space in the classroom so that these materials are readily available to children. He is to encourage freedom of movement, freedom of conversation, and freedom of choice of learning activities. He is to assist children when

[34]Joseph Featherstone, "Open Schools: Tempering a Fad," *New Republic* 165 (September 25, 1971): 17–21.

they need assistance, guide them when they need guidance, instruct them when they need instruction, and leave them alone when they need to be left alone. At times he is to make decisions about what it is that children need, and at times he is to help children make these decisions. As the children make choices and use the instructional materials, the teacher is to keep records of the experiences that they have and to evaluate the learning that is taking place.

Since efficient operation of this kind of instructional setting usually requires a smaller adult-child ratio than the traditional classroom, the teacher as systems manager is also expected to manage the activities of other adults in the classroom. These other adults may be paraprofessionals, teacher aides, parent volunteers, or student teachers. In dealing with them the teacher is expected to select a limited function for each that will support the total system and which is in keeping with the particular talents that each possesses. He is then expected to define their roles clearly for them, train them to function in these roles, and evaluate their performance periodically.

VALIDITY OF ROLE EXPECTATIONS. The research on effectiveness of the instructional role of systems manager is no more conclusive than the research on other roles. Children in formal schools do slightly better on conventional achievement tests than do children in informal schools, possibly because formal schools teach children to take tests. It does not appear that informal settings are harmful to the development of conventional academic skills. Pupils in informal settings do display more "initiative, critical thinking, ability to express [themselves] in writing, and capacity to pursue [tasks] on [their] own."[35]

The observable behavior of teachers in many "open" schools does not match well with expectations of the systems manager role. It is a common phenomenon to see open-space schools and classrooms where bookcases and filing cabinets have replaced the absent walls and protect one teacher from the view of another. The desks in these "rooms" are in rows or clusters. Teachers stand in the middle of the class and talk to everyone at once, only now they operate under the handicap of acoustical planning that makes it impossible for students on the fringes of the group to hear them clearly. In older buildings where walls have been removed to make two typical classrooms into one large open room, the amount of movement that occurs from one half of the room to the other is usually minimal. Teachers find it difficult to adapt to new uses of space and new patterns of trust and cooperation, and they have not received much help in retraining themselves in these uses.

[35]Joseph Featherstone, "Open Schools: The British and Us," *New Republic* 165 (September 11, 1971): 20–25.

The expectation that teachers will manage other adults in the classroom effectively has not been completely fulfilled, either. The fact is that most elementary school teachers are in the profession because they enjoy working with children. They resist demands that they reduce the time they spend with children in order to direct and evaluate the efforts of other adults. They feel that the advantages of more adults in the classroom will be lost if all of the adults are not spending their time interacting with children. As a result, many teachers do not have a very clear idea of what the other adults are actually *doing* with the children.

FUNCTIONS OF ROLE.   The instructional role of systems manager can be used most effectively in educational settings where active support and cooperation are furnished by parents, administrators, and other teachers. It is not a role that a teacher can learn or perform easily on his own. The teacher as systems manager may work with a medium-sized group, but the more typical pattern is to have several teachers playing this role with large groups of children.

The roles of problem-setter, model, and diagnostician can be played within the context of the systems manager role. For example, an optional activity in an open-classroom setting can be a group lesson where discovery teaching strategies are used. Another optional activity might be a group lesson where the teacher is modeling a particular set of skills, such as a construction activity where woodworking skills are being taught. The teacher as diagnostician (cognitive realm) may prescribe one or two activities for each child during the course of a day, leaving them free to schedule other activities according to their own interests. The teacher as diagnostician (affective realm) would spend part of his time giving approval to children who were involved in productive, independent work in the open-classroom setting.

Other Instructional Roles

There are many other instructional roles that a teacher can be called upon to perform. The teacher as *policeman* may be expected to maintain law and order in the classroom, playground, cafeteria, or hall. The teacher as *critic* may be expected to evaluate the creative productions of children on the basis of a variety of external criteria and to report these evaluations to the "audience" of classmates, parents, and administrators. The teacher as *consumer* may be expected to shop wisely in the commercial world of the educational supermarket and to follow carefully the directions on the packages of prepared "foods." The teacher as *artist* may be expected to use his technical skills in innovative ways, creating a "canvas" that displays his unique perception of the world for the children to view and explore. The teacher as *experimenter* may be expected to hypothesize about the effects of various strategies, collect data about classroom behavior, search for relationships between data, and develop his own instructional theory.

Sometimes it seems that there are no limits to the roles an elementary teacher may be expected to perform. It is clear, however, that there are definite limits to the roles that teachers *do* perform. The discrepancy between expectations and behavior exists in the performance of instructional roles just as surely as it exists in the performance of other social roles.

It also is clear that there rarely is any conclusive evidence that the roles teachers are expected to perform are related to improvement of educational outcomes. Each of the eleven roles mentioned in this chapter has a group of advocates who can point to a number of logical and psychological reasons why the particular role they prefer will lead to a better environment for children. What they cannot point to is a number of instances where that particular role has been demonstrated to be more effective than any other particular role.

8 Teacher Influence, Pupil Attitudes, and Achievement

Ned A. Flanders

Early Research on Classroom Climate

The term "classroom climate" refers to generalized attitudes toward the teacher and the class that the pupils share in common despite individual differences. The development of these attitudes is an outgrowth of classroom social interaction. As a result of participating in classroom activities, pupils soon develop common attitudes about how they like their class, the kind of person the teacher is, and how he will act in certain typical situations. These common attitudes color all aspects of classroom behavior, creating a social atmosphere, or climate, that appears to be fairly stable, once established. Thus, the word "climate"[1] is merely a

[1]Climate is assessed either by analyzing teacher-pupil interaction and inferring underlying attitudes from the interaction, or by the use of a pupil-attitude inventory and predicting the quality of classroom interaction from the results. Its precise meaning, as commonly used, is seldom clear—just as its synonyms, "morale," "rapport," and "emotional tone," are also ambiguous. To have any meaning at all, the word is always qualified by an adjective, and it is in the choice of adjectives that researchers become reformers and too often lose their objectivity.

Reprinted with permission from *Teacher Influence, Pupil Attitudes, and Achievement* by Ned A. Flanders, Cooperative Research Monograph No. 12. U.S. Department of Health, Education, and Welfare, Office of Education, Washington, D.C., 1965.

shorthand reference to those qualities that consistently predominate in most teacher-pupil contacts and in contact among the pupils in the presence or absence of the teacher. . . .

One contribution of research on classroom climate has been the identification of different kinds of verbal statements that the teacher uses. This information has been used in the development of our system of interaction analysis.

A less consistent contribution of this early research concerns the words used to designate patterns of teacher behavior. In fact, there is quite a choice: H. H. Anderson—"dominative" and "integrative;" R. Lippitt and R. K. White—"authoritarian," "democratic," and "laissez-faire;" J. Withall, N. A. Flanders, H. V. Perkins—"teacher-centered" and "student-centered;" and M. L. Cogan—"preclusive" and "inclusive."[2] All these come from a short stroll in the conceptual garden of psychology; an overnight hike could extend the list indefinitely. Faced with such a choice, we might first pause to discuss the concepts used in this type of research.

Concepts used to describe teacher influence refer to a series of acts occurring during some time period. When a particular series occurs again and again, it becomes familiar to an observer and he can identify it. We call such a series a "pattern" of influence.

It is interesting to distinguish between an influence pattern and the concept of "role," as it is commonly used in the literature of social psychology. The difference is in the degree of behavioral specificity that is implied. For example, it may be said that a teacher plays in the classroom a "democratic" or "authoritarian" role. These concepts not only connote value judgments, but they are so abstract that they fail to denote very much about the behavior of the teacher. If someone tries to create either role, his choice of influence patterns depends primarily on his personal and often unique understanding of the concept. Such a choice involves too many alternatives; specificity is lacking.

The only path through these difficulties is to increase understanding by insisting that the concepts used have explicit behavioral meaning. . . . Certain concepts that refer to the teacher's behavior . . . will be pre-

[2]The Measurement of Domination and of Socially Integrative Behavior in Teacher's Contact with Children," *Child Development*, 10,2, 73–89; "The Social Climate of Children's Groups," in Barker, R. G., Kounin, J. S., and Wright, H. F., eds. *Child Behavior and Development*. New York: McGraw-Hill, 1943, pp. 458–508; "The Development of a Technique for the Measurement of Social-Emotional Climate in Classroom," *Journal of Experimental Education*, 17, March 1949, 347–61; "Personal-Social Anxiety as a Factor in Experimental Learning Situations," *Journal of Educational Research*, 45, Oct., 1951, 100–110; "Climate Influences Group Learning," *Journal of Educational Research*, 45, October, 1951, 115–119; "Theory and Design of a Study of Teacher-Pupil Interaction," *The Harvard Educational Review*, 26,4, 315–342.

sented. In each instance, a description of behavior in a social setting will be given first. Next, concepts will be used to abstract the behavior events, and in the process, a theoretical definition of the concept will become clear. Finally, the procedures used in this study to measure or quantify the concept will be briefly stated.

The reader may wish to evaluate the development of these concepts by applying the following criteria. First, what are the concepts that are given theoretical meaning by analysis of the behavior that commonly occurs in a classroom? Second, are the procedures used for quantifying behavior that is associated with a concept (a) practical: that is, can they be used in a classroom; (b) representative: that is, do they adequately sample all behavior that could logically be associated with the concept; and (c) reliable: that is, can the error factor be determined and is it low, compared with the differences studied? Third, can the concepts be organized into hypotheses or principles (cause and effect statements) to predict behavior or the consequences of behavior?

Concepts For Describing Teacher Influence

Teacher influence exists as a series of acts along a time line. It is most often expressed as verbal communication. In this study we assume that verbal communication constitutes an adequate sample of the teacher's total influence pattern. A single act of a teacher occupies a segment of time. Before this act a particular state of affairs exists; after the act is completed, a different state of affairs exists. Some acts are more potent than others and have greater consequences. Furthermore, a long series of similar acts may have more extensive effects than just an isolated few.

A researcher is free to choose concepts that will be used to describe the state of affairs before and after an act, and concepts that will be used to describe the act itself.

Suppose a teacher says, "Please close the door," to a student. The chances are that the student will close the door. Before this act of influence, the student was engaged in some activity, such as thinking or reading. But since he was expected to comply with the teacher's command, he interrupted his train of thought to get up and close the door.

Actually, this sequence of behavior is as complex as we wish to make it. We could theorize about the social expectations that exist when a teacher makes what adults call a reasonable demand of a student. Much could be said, if we had the facts, about how past contacts with other authority figures have helped to form this particular student's reactions to a command. It might be that the student resented this intrusion and chose to push the door so that it slammed, rather than gently closing it. A lesser degree of resentment could be expressed by an audible sigh followed by slow movements.

Because of all the concepts that could be used to describe behavior, there is a choice here along a continuum. The genotypic concepts that describe inner motives or feelings are at one end, and the phenotypic concepts that describe more superficial aspects of behavior are at the other end. The choice should fit the purpose. A psychiatrist would prefer certain concepts for his purposes that would probably be too genotypic for the majority of interpretations that a teacher needs to make.

Our choice in this instance leads to the following explanation. The teacher exerted *direct influence,* which restricted the *freedom of action* of the student, making him momentarily more *dependent* on the teacher. From this illustration we hope the reader will understand that an act of direct influence restricts freedom of action, usually by focusing on a problem and, in this case, it made the student more dependent on teacher influence for a short period of time.

By the way, you the reader may have felt uneasy when you thought of a teacher's restricting the freedom of action of a student. These are terms that often elicit value judgments. However, it seems sensible to assert that a student's freedom of action is restricted when he is told to shut the door. Nevertheless, it is difficult to make an objective description of such events.

Now, suppose the same door is open, but with a completely different script. The teacher asks, "Does anyone feel a draft in here?" Johnny says, "Yes, it's cold. I think it's coming from this open door." The teacher says, "Well, since it seems cold, please close the door." So Johnny gets up and closes the door.

The second example includes the same command and ultimately leads to the same compliance, yet most of us would agree that the state of affairs would be different at the termination of the episode. Consider, too, differences after a series of such episodes, extending over hours, days, weeks, or the school year.

Again we face a choice in conceptualizing the behavior. Our choice is as follows: The command, "Close the door," was modified first by a question, "Does anyone feel a draft in here?" second, by a student response, "Yes, it's cold. I think it's coming from this open door," the latter phrase being a student-initiated idea; and third, by the teacher's acknowledging the student's idea, "Well, since it seems cold . . ." Taken all together, the teacher's acts of influence are more indirect than direct. While the student's freedom of action was restricted, his perception of this restriction was probably modified in the second example because he was solving a problem that he had helped to identify, rather than merely complying with the command of an authority figure. In fact, the teacher's behavior encouraged the student's initiative and, in this sense, his freedom of action was expanded. Later on, after more examples are given, we hope it will become clear that an act of indirect influence expands freedom of action and usually makes a student less dependent on the teacher. He often has greater orientation to a problem, because he helped to identify it.

Most teachers who hear these ideas expressed immediately conclude that indirect influence is superior to direct influence. We believe that the basis of this value judgment lies less in the ideas just expressed than in the social pressures that affect teachers' self-concepts. Most teachers apparently want to believe that they are "indirect teachers," even before they hear how these concepts are defined or are told about any research findings. If being an indirect teacher means consistently using indirect influence, we can state categorically that no such teacher exists, because no teacher employs a pure pattern of influence. All teachers establish some kind of balance based on a combination of direct and indirect influence.

At this point, further objection often arises. It seems obvious that any "intelligent teacher" would prefer to have his students "problem-oriented," as illustrated in the second episode, rather than "authority-oriented," as illustrated in the first episode. (The quotation marks are used here to emphasize how quickly abstract value judgments enter the discussion.) Our experience would suggest that, in the long run, most teachers want the students in their classes to react to the demands of problem-solving rather than to their own authority. Yet does it necessarily follow that indirect influence is superior to direct influence? Is the student in the first illustration any less "problem-oriented" than the student in the second?

Our system of interaction analysis provides an explicit procedure for quantifying direct and indirect influence that is closely related to the teacher behaviors identified by research on classroom climate. Direct influence consists of those verbal statements of the teacher that restrict freedom of action, by focusing attention on a problem, interjecting teacher authority, or both. These statements include lecturing, giving directions, criticizing, and justifying his own use of authority. Indirect influence consists of those verbal statements of the teacher that expand a student's freedom of action by encouraging his verbal participation and initiative. These include asking questions, accepting and clarifying the ideas or feelings of students, and praising or encouraging students' responses. . . .

*Concepts For Describing Teacher Flexibility And
Homogeneous Classroom Activities*

Anyone who has observed many hours in a classroom soon notices that classroom interaction occurs in a sequence of activity periods. First, there may be a routine 3 to 5 minutes for settling down to work. Next, perhaps, homework is corrected and handed in. Next, a student or group may give a report. This may be followed by a 15-minute discussion, and so on. We have found it advantageous to tabulate interaction analysis data separately for these periods.

The main reason for separating data from different activities is that we can then discover whether a teacher shifts his balance of direct and indirect influence in various activity periods. Is a teacher more indirect when new material is being introduced? Is he more indirect when helping diagnose difficulties? Is he more direct when supervising seatwork? What about evaluating homework or test results?

Identifying activity periods is almost a second system of categorization that is superimposed on the system for classifying verbal statements. In junior-high academic classrooms, we use 5 activity categories: introducing new material; evaluating homework, tests, or learning products; other class discussion; supervising seatwork or group activities; and routine clean-up, passing of materials, or settling down to work. In general, a change from one activity to another is indicated by the statements made, a change of class formation, or a change in the communication pattern.

Tabulating data separately for homogeneous activities permits us to define teacher flexibility and measure it. Teacher flexibility is a measure of the change a teacher makes in his verbal influence from one activity period to another. We measure this by noting the ratio of indirect influence (I) to direct influence (D) in one activity period and comparing it with the corresponding ratio in other activity periods. If we wish to avoid a measure which is a ratio of a ratio, that is, an I/D ratio as a percent divided by a percent, we can compare changes in the percent of indirect influence across different activities, and then make the same comparison for direct influence. Unfortunately, this does not eliminate the statistical problems. Distributions of I/D ratios, comparative percents of indirect statements, and raw tallies all form a "J"-shaped curve. . . .

Hypotheses of Teacher Influence for This Study

In the long run, the purpose of testing hypotheses about teacher influence is to establish principles of teacher behavior that can guide a teacher who wishes to control his own behavior as part of his plan for classroom management. Each principle, if it is to be useful, must be a cause-and-effect statement. Accordingly, this report will express principles in statements that adhere to the following general pattern: if such and such is true, then action "X" will produce result "Y."

This study is concerned with the following hypotheses, which will be stated in terms of the concepts described in the preceding section:

Hypothesis One: Indirect teacher influence increases learning when a student's perception of the goal is confused and ambiguous.

Hypothesis Two: Direct teacher influence increases learning when a student's perception of the goal is clear and acceptable.

Hypothesis Three: Direct teacher influence decreases learning when a student's perception of the goal is ambiguous.

In these three hypotheses, the concept *learning* refers to the development of skills and understandings that can be measured by pre- and post-tests of achievement. In this project, tests were administered before and after a 2-week unit of study, so that an operational definition of learning consists of final achievement, adjusted for initial ability.

By way of brief review, the dynamic explanation of these hypotheses rests on the following reasoning: First, indirect influence increases learning when goals are ambiguous because less disabling dependence develops. During the initial stages of learning, goals are ambiguous. Indirect influence increases student freedom of action, allowing the student the opportunity to question goals and the procedures for reaching them. The net effect of this participation in clarifying goals is less compliance to authority *per se* and more attention to problem-solving requirements, or at least a more balanced orientation for those students who have high dependence-proneness.

Second, direct influence increases learning when goals are clear because the criteria for accepting or rejecting teacher influence as well as various alternative actions can be recognized in terms of the problem-solving requirements. The student is presumably oriented toward the problem; direct teacher influence is likely to be oriented toward the problem and be helpful; and the net effect is more efficient action toward problem solution. Dependence on the teacher remains steady or is decreased as a result of successful progress toward the goal.

Third, direct influence decreases learning when goals are ambiguous because it increases dependence sharply. The primary response of the student is compliance with teacher authority when goals are unclear. This, in turn, develops dependence. Unless the student understands the goal that the teacher has in mind, he has no other acceptable alternative, given our present cultural expectations. The high dependence that quickly develops means that the student is oriented more toward pleasing the teacher than toward meeting the problem-solving requirements.

These hypotheses are generalized predictions across a range of individual differences. The interaction between a teacher and a particular student in a specific situation is modified by unique personality characteristics and situational factors. . . .

Classroom Interaction Analysis

The spontaneous behavior of a teacher is so complex and variable that an accurate description of it is most difficult to obtain. Even trained observers struggle with the same biases that distort the testimony of witnesses at the scene of an accident. Too often an observer's preconceptions of what he thinks should happen allow him to perceive certain behaviors but prevent him from perceiving others. Interaction analysis is an observation procedure designed to minimize these difficulties, to permit a systematic record of spontaneous acts, and to scrutinize the process of instruction by taking into account each small bit of interaction.

Classroom interaction analysis is particularly concerned with the influence pattern of the teacher. This might be considered a bias, but it is a bias of purpose and interest. Our purpose is to record a series of acts in terms of predetermined concepts. The concepts in this case refer to the teacher's control of the students' freedom of action. Our interest is to distinguish those acts of the teacher that increase students' freedom of action from those acts that decrease students' freedom of action, and to keep a record of both. The system of categories is used by the observer to separate those acts which result in compliance from those acts which invite more creative and voluntary participation; at the same time, it prevents him from being diverted by the subject matter which is irrelevant to this study.

Interaction analysis is concerned primarily with verbal behavior because it can be observed with higher reliability than most nonverbal behavior. The assumption is made that the verbal behavior of the teacher is an adequate sample of his total behavior; that is, his verbal statements are consistent with his nonverbal gestures, in fact, his total behavior. This assumption seems reasonable in terms of our experience.

The Procedure

The observer sits in the classroom in the best position to hear and see the participants. At the end of each 3-second period, he decides which of a prescribed set of numbered categories best represents the communication events just completed. He writes this category number down while simultaneously assessing communication in the next period. He continues at a rate of about 20 to 25 observations per minute, keeping his tempo as steady as possible. His notes are merely a sequence of numbers written in a column, top to bottom, so that the original sequence of events is preserved. Occasionally, marginal notes are used to explain the class formation or any unusual circumstances. When there is a major change in class formation, the communication pattern, or the subject under discussion, the observer draws a double line and indicates the time. As soon as he has completed the total observation, he retires to a nearby room and writes up a general description of each separate activity period. This includes the nature of the activities, the class formation, and the position of the teacher. The observer also notes any additional facts that seem pertinent to an adequate interpretation and recall of the total observation period.

The Categories

There are 10 categories in the system. Seven are assigned to teacher talk and two to student talk. The 10th category covers pauses, short periods of silence, and talk that is confusing or noisy. The category system is outlined below.

Of the seven categories assigned to teacher talk, categories 1 through 4 represent indirect influence, and categories 5, 6 and 7, indirect influence.

Indirect influence encourages participation by the student and increases his freedom of action. To ask a question (category 4) is an invitation to participate and express ideas, opinions, or facts. It is true that a question can be so phrased as to leave very little freedom of action, but at least the student can refuse to answer, a reaction which reflects more freedom than does passive listening. The more general a teacher's question, the greater the opportunity for the student to assert his own ideas.

When the teacher accepts, clarifies, or uses constructively the ideas and opinions of students (category 3), they are encouraged to participate

CATEGORIES for interaction analysis, 1959†

TEACHER TALK

INDIRECT INFLUENCE

   1.° ACCEPTS FEELING: accepts and clarifies the tone of feeling of the students in an unthreatening manner. Feelings may be positive or negative. Predicting or recalling feelings are included.

   2.° PRAISES OR ENCOURAGES: praises or encourages student action or behavior. Jokes that release tension, but not at the expense of another individual, nodding head or saying "um hm?" or "go on" are included.

   3.° ACCEPTS OR USES IDEAS OF STUDENT: clarifying, building, or developing ideas suggested by a student. As teacher brings more of his own ideas into play, shift to category 5.

†For some illustrative modifications of this 1959 set of categories see: Gertrude Moskowitz in *Foreign Language Annals*, 1:218–235, 1968; Richard L. Ober in *Systematic Observation of Teaching* (Prentice-Hall, 1971), p. 39; Elizabeth Hunter in *Classroom Interaction Newsletter*, 6:23, November, 1970; and Ned A. Flanders in *Analyzing Teaching Behavior* (Addison-Wesley, 1970), p. 34.

TEACHER TALK   Continued

INDIRECT INFLUENCE   *Continued*

4.* ASKS QUESTIONS: asking a question about content or procedure with the intent that a student answer.

DIRECT INFLUENCE

5.* LECTURING: giving facts or opinions about content or procedure; expressing his own ideas, asking rhetorical questions.

6.* GIVING DIRECTIONS: directions, commands, or orders which students are expected to comply with.

7.* CRITICIZING OR JUSTIFYING AUTHORITY: statements intended to change student behavior from unacceptable to acceptable pattern; bawling someone out; stating why the teacher is doing what he is doing; extreme self-reference.

STUDENT TALK

8.* STUDENT TALK—RESPONSE: talk by students in response to teacher. Teacher initiates the contact or solicits student statement.

9.* STUDENT TALK—INITIATION: talk initiated by students. If "calling on" student is only to indicate who may talk next, observer must decide whether student wanted to talk.

SILENCE

10.* SILENCE OR CONFUSION: pauses, short periods of silence and periods of confusion in which communication cannot be understood by the observer.

further. Often teachers act as if they do not hear what a student says; to acknowledge and make use of an idea is a powerful form of recognition. To praise or encourage student participation directly (category 2) is to solicit even more participation by giving a reward. The ability to use the feeling tone of a student constructively, to react to feeling and clarify it (category 1), is a rare skill. Teachers with this ability can often mobilize positive feelings in motivation and successfully control negative feelings that might otherwise get out of hand.

All the actions falling into categories 1 through 4 tend to increase and reward student participation, and to give students the opportunity to become more influential. The net effect is greater freedom of action for the students.

Direct influence increases the active control of the teacher and often stimulates compliance. The lecture (category 5) focuses the attention of

*There is NO scale implied by these numbers. Each number is classificatory, designating a particular kind of communication event. To write these numbers down during observation is merely to identify and enumerate communication events, not to judge them.

the students on ideas chosen by the teacher. To give directions or commands (category 6) is to direct the activities of the class with the intent of obtaining compliance. Category 7 refers to criticizing student behavior or justifying the teacher's use of authority. These actions concentrate authority in the hands of the teacher. Direct influence tends to increase teacher participation and to estabish restraints on student behavior. The ensuing restriction of freedom may occur in the form of compliance to the teacher or of adjustment to the requirements of problem-solving activities. The net effect is less freedom of action for the students.

The division of student talk into categories 8 and 9 provides an automatic check on freedom of student action within the system of categories. Ordinarily, but not always, a pattern of direct teacher influence is associated with less student talk, which generally consists of responses to the teacher (category 8). A pattern of indirect influence is ordinarily associated with more student talk, which is often initiated by the students (category 9). The use of only two categories to record all kinds of student talk neglects a great deal of information, but the major purpose of these categories is the analysis of teacher influence. The greatest information will accrue from observation if category 9 is used sparingly and only on those occasions when the communication is truly student-initiated.

For example, the act of a student in answering a specific question asked by a teacher obviously falls into category 8. Even the act of giving an oral report may be placed in this category when the student is restricted to a specific outline and is probably responding to the teacher's directions.

Category 9 should be used by the observer only to indicate the student's spontaneous expression of his own ideas. General questions are often a clue that a student may be initiating his own ideas. When a teacher calls on a student who voluntarily raised his hand to speak and asks, "Have you anything to add, Robert?" the chances are that the use of category 9 is correct.

The purpose of category 10 is to record short pauses, silences, and periods of confusion as they occur during classroom interaction. It is not intended to record periods of silence or confusion lasting for more than 2 minutes. The continuous use of this category to designate long periods of silence serves no useful purpose.

The system of categories is designed for situations in which the teachers and the students are actively discussing schoolwork. It is an inappropriate tool when the verbal communication is discontinuous, separated by fairly long periods of silence, or when one person is engaged in prolonged lecturing or in reading aloud to the class. In situations in which two-way communication does not exist and is not likely to exist, the observer should stop and make a note of the exact time at which spontaneous interaction lapsed and the reasons for the interruption. The observer must remain alert to the resumption of spontaneous interaction.

Marking Activity Periods

Teacher influence is a pattern that is constantly changing over time. The most effective teachers, in fact, have a large repertoire of behaviors, and systematic observation shows that they can present many different influence patterns.

The identification of activity periods is one way that flexibility can be studied. In effect, a second system of categories is super-imposed on the 10 interaction categories; this second system is likely to be different in each research study. For example, it may be sufficient in a study of high school mathematics classes to indicate periods of (a) settling down to work, (b) introducing new material, (c) teacher-directed discussion or work on material that is not new, (d) supervision and direction of individual seatwork, and (e) periods of evaluation, in which homework and test results are discussed.

In an elementary classroom, it would be reasonable to keep interaction data collected during show-and-tell separate from reading instruction, and these in turn from arithmetic, music, games, penmanship, etc.

If interaction analysis is to be used to discover whether a teacher's pattern of influence in planning work with students is different, for example, from his influence pattern while supervising work already planned, then even finer discriminations would be necessary to identify the boundaries of the required time periods. . . .

The Tabulation of Interaction Matrices

A trained observer records his data as a series of numbers instead of the hash marks used in early training. For example, the school bell rings and the following interaction occurs. The numbers written down by the observer are indicated in parentheses.

Teacher: "Class! The bell has rung. May I have your attention please! (category 6)

During the next 3 seconds talking and noise diminish. (category 10)

Teacher: "Jimmy, we are all waiting for you." (category 7) Pause.

Teacher: "Now, today we are going to have a very pleasant surprise, (category 5) and I think you will find it very exciting and interesting. (category 1)

Have any of you heard anything about what we are going to do? (category 4)

Pupil: "I think we are going on a trip in the bus that's out in front." (category 8)

Teacher: "Oh! You've found out! How did you learn about our trip?" (category 4) Etc.

By now the observer has written down 6, 10, 7, 5, 1, 4, 8, and 4. As the interaction proceeds, the observer will continue to write down numbers. To tabulate these observations in a 10×10 matrix, the first step is to make sure that the entire series begins and ends with the same number. The convention we use is to add a 10 to the beginning and end of the series, unless the 10 is already present. Our series now becomes 10, 6, 10, 7, 5, 1, 4, 8, 4, and 10. This procedure is followed in order to produce a finished matrix in which the sum of column 1 equals the sum of row 1, the sum of column 2 equals the sum of row 2, in short, so that the sums of the columns and rows are equal, respectively.

The number 10 is used because it will affect the interpretation of teacher influence the least. One of our less sympathetic critics has suggested, however, that this convention is necessary in order to begin and end an observation in confusion!

The numbers are tallied in the matrix one pair at a time. The row is designated by the first number, and the column is designated by the second number. The first pair is 10–6; the tally is placed in the row 10, column 6 cell. The second pair is 6–10; this is tallied in the row 6, column 10 cell. The third pair is 10–7, the fourth pair is 7–5, and so on. Each pair overlaps with the next and the total number of observations, N, always will be tabulated by $N - 1$ tallies in the matrix. In this case we started a series of 10 numbers and the series produced 9 tallies in the matrix. The tabulation is shown in Figure 2-3.

Each matrix should include all of the observations for the elapsed time of a single activity period, or all the numbers between a double line.

For example, 1 hour's observation in a secondary class may yield a separate matrix for each of the following time periods: first, 5 minutes of routine announcements, getting settled down, taking the roll, etc.; second, 15 minutes of going over homework and reviewing the previous day's assignment; third, 15 minutes for the introduction of some new material and discussion of this material; fourth, 10 minutes to discuss one student's progress on a special assignment; and fifth, 8 minutes of starting on the next day's homework, with the teacher giving help to individual students.

A total matrix for the 53-minute class may also be desirable. In an elementary school, natural units of activity would also be tabulated in separate matrices. A particular research design may require combining matrices of the same activity for subsequent analyses. . . .[3]

[3]For an illustration of the uses of a matrix in interpreting a teacher's interaction pattern, the reader should see the article by Chapline on page 127. R.T.H., editor.

Second

	1	2	3	4	5	6	7	8	9	10	Total
1				/							1
2											0
3											0
4								/		/	2
5	/										1
6										/	1
7					/						1
8				/							1
9											0
10						/	/				2
Total	1	0	0	2	1	1	1	1	0	2	9

First

FIGURE 2-3

Summary of Results

Before summarizing the results of this project, let us review its three main hypotheses, which were first listed on page 117:

(1) Indirect teacher influence increases learning when a student's perception of the goal is confused and ambiguous.

(2) Direct teacher influence increases learning when a student's perception of the goal is clear and acceptable.

(3) Direct teacher influence restricts learning when a student's perception of the goal is ambiguous.

The significant differences in achievement[4] support the generalization that the teaching methods we have called indirect produce more achievement. Our classification of teachers as indirect is based on an above-average proportion of indirect to direct acts of influence over an extended period of time. This evidence alone does not prove or disprove the three main hypotheses, even though it does have important implications for teaching.

The support of hypotheses 1 and 2 comes from the following reasoning. First, students of teachers who used an above-average proportion of indirect to direct acts of verbal influence learn more. Second, teachers

[4]Flanders' project studied 15 seventh-grade social studies teachers (381 pupils) and 16 eighth-grade mathematics teachers (363 pupils) teaching 2-week units of study. R.T.H., editor.

with an above-average proportion of indirect influence also show more variability in adapting their influence to different types of classroom activities and to the different stages of learning that exist in a 2-week unit of study. Finally, the adaptations made by these more flexible teachers follow the shifts of teacher influence described in hypotheses 1 and 2.

Hypothesis 1 states that indirect teacher influence increases learning when a student's perception of the goal is ambiguous. We assume that learning goals are ambiguous during the initial stages of a 2-week unit of study. The indirect teachers provided more activities that permitted students to express their own opinions and develop initiative during the beginning stages of the unit. Their verbal influence during these stages was much more indirect than their overall 2-week average, and also much more indirect than the initial and overall averages of direct teachers. This evidence clearly supports hypothesis 3.

Hypothesis 2 states that direct teacher influence increases learning when a student's perception of the goal is clear and acceptable. As learning progressed, the more flexible, indirect teachers decreased their use of activities that expanded student initiative and increased their use of activities that restricted student initiative. At the same time they made adjustments in their own patterns of teacher influence so that they became more direct, compared only to their own average, as learning progressed. This evidence clearly supports hypothesis 2.

Hypothesis 2 has, in one sense, too much evidence to support it. The students whose teachers employed an above-average proportion of direct influence consistently showed less achievement. These teachers showed less flexibility in adapting their influence to difference types of classroom activity and to the different stages of learning in a 2-week unit of study. The evidence concerning direct influence is so consistent that the following modification of hypothesis 3 is justified: direct influence decreases learning, except when goals have initially been clarified and made acceptable by the use of indirect influence.

In planning this project, we anticipated that different types of students would react differently to direct and indirect influence. However, no differences were found in achievement between dependent-prone and independent-prone students. We also found that students classified by IQ scores into the top quartile, middle 50 percent, and bottom quartile did not respond differently to teachers whom we classified as direct or indirect. The one exception to this, which occurred in social studies and which indicated that high-IQ students were more sensitive to differences in direct and indirect influence, was not supported in larger samples. The possibility still exists that different types of students develop different attitudes toward teachers who use different patterns of influence. For example, a preliminary analysis of M.S.A.I.[5] scores, not reported here, indicated a significant sex difference.

Perhaps the conclusion that needs to be emphasized most in this summary is that the students who achieved the most and who had significantly higher scores on our revised classroom attitude instrument were in classes which were exposed to *flexible* patterns of teacher influence. This flexible pattern included periods of predominantly direct influence as well as periods of predominantly indirect influence. This characteristic flexibility was associated with a higher overall i/d average. Our data show that a sustained above-average pattern of direct influence restricts learning and produces less desirable attitudes. It is obvious that as teacher influence deviates from this narrow pattern, the overall i/d must increase. These deviations are what we have called flexibility.

[5]Minnesota Student Attitude Inventory. R.T.H., editor.

9 A Case Study in Interaction Analysis Matrix Interpretation

Elaine B. Chapline

Interaction Analysis, developed and expanded by Flanders for the analysis of teacher-pupil verbal interactions within the classroom, has a unique form in which data can be described and interpreted. Summarization of class sessions can be made succinctly through the production of ten-by-ten matrices. Each cell on the matrix depicts the frequency with which a particular verbal sequence occurred during a session. These matrices may be constructed for a part or for all of a class session. In order to interpret matrix data appropriately, additional information which spells out the purposes of the lesson and the nature of the learning activity are important. These extra-matrix cues serve as a frame of reference within which inferences about teacher influence may be drawn.

A matrix (Figure 2) which can serve as a case study in matrix interpretation was developed from an audio-tape recording of a ninth-grade social studies class. This lesson took place during a regular forty-five-minute class period and was recorded by the classroom teacher. It was the first lesson on a new area of content, and was a discussion lasting

This article by Elaine B. Chapline of Queens College was written expressly for this book and is published here for the first time. This article relates specifically to the article by Ned A. Flanders.

through the class period. The verbal behavior was categorized by a trained observer using Flanders' ten categories.

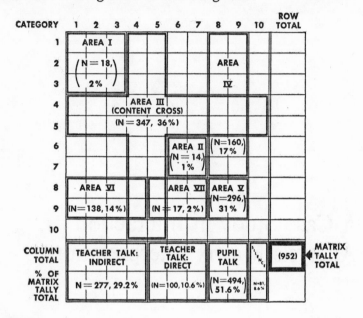

FIGURE 1

Description

Matrix interpretation initially involves developing an overview of the ways in which matrices can be descriptively summarized and of the nature of specified areas within the matrix (see Figures 1 and 2).

Category totals, matrix tally total (i.e., total of sequential pairs entered on the matrix, N = 952), and the percentage of each of the ten categories are figured initially. Since the totals in columns and rows for each category should coincide, the accuracy with which the matrix has been produced can be checked. Next, percentage of teacher talk (i.e., categories $1 + 2 + 3 + 4 + 5 + 6 + 7$) and pupil talk (i.e., categories $8 + 9$) and of category 10 are calculated. The percentages of teacher talk which reflect indirect influence $(1 + 2 + 3 + 4)$ and direct influence $(5 + 6 + 7)$ are then spelled out separately. The I/D ratio (categories $1 + 2 + 3 + 4$ divided by categories $5 + 6 + 7$) provides a gross indication of the nature of a teacher's influence. The i/d ratio, as developed by Flanders, is calculated by dividing categories $1 + 2 + 3$ by $6 + 7$. It serves to focus on teacher influence without the presence of the categories which are most content-laden (i.e., categories 4 and 5). Steady-state cells occur on the diagonal across a matrix. These reflect the degree to which a specific verbal act was maintained for longer than three seconds. They are cells 1-1 (i.e., row one, column one), 2-2, 3-3, etc. In the illustrative case, they account for 38 percent of the tally total.

CATEGORY	1	2	3	4	5	6	7	8	9	10	ROW TOTAL
1				1							1
2		4	8	27	3	3		27	21	4	97
3		1	5	16	14				7	1	44
4		1	2	26	8	1		65	21	11	135
5			5	18	27	2		3	14	9	78
6			1	3	1	14		1		1	21
7								1			1
8		48	10	14	5		1	109	15	4	214
9		40	11	15	10	1		2	170	31	280
10	1	3	2	16	9			6	32	12	81
COLUMN TOTAL	1	97	44	135	78	21	1	214	280	81	952 ← MATRIX TALLY TOTAL
% OF MATRIX TALLY TOTAL	.1	10.2	4.6	14.3	8.3	2.2	.1	22.7	28.9	8.6	100.0

29.2 Indirect				10.6 Direct			51.6		8.6	
Teacher Talk							Student Talk		Sil-ence	

I/D = 2.76
i/d = 6.43
I/D8,9 = 8.1

FIGURE 2

The matrix areas which portray specific classroom behaviors are identified in Figure 1. Area 1 encompasses the tallies of categories 1–3 used in an extended, sustained fashion, that is, those which continue beyond three seconds. In the illustrative case, Area I accounts for 2 percent of the total tallies. Area II consists of the tallies of cells 6-6, 6-7, 7-6, and 7-7. These involve extended use of direct influence and account for one percent of the total. Area III has been labeled "content cross" by Flanders. In this case, 36 percent of the interaction is included in this area, which incorporates all the tallies in categories 4 and 5.

Area IV consists of those cells in which student responses followed directly from teacher behaviors. For example, cell 4-8 indicates that a student response followed a teacher question, and cell 6-9 indicates that a student initiation followed a teacher direction. This area aids in understanding how the students entered into the lesson following teacher activity. Area V, 31 percent in the illustration, describes extended student talk.

The teacher's response to or use of student statements through indirect means is portrayed in Area VI, 14 percent, while teacher response through direct means is portrayed in Area VII, 2 percent.

Interpretation

Inferences about the nature of a lesson may be drawn from matrix data through the formulation of hypotheses about what happened during the lesson. These hypotheses should be held tentatively or until they can be confirmed or refuted through the use of additional data.

In the illustrative lesson, information provided by the matrix in Figure 2 lists the tally total (952), percentage of teacher talk (39.8), pupil talk (51.6) and category 10 (8.6), I/D ratio (2.76), and i/d ratio (6.43). These items are helpful in establishing a general description of this lesson. Verbal participation was active, and the pace of the lesson was fairly rapid, as indicated by the tally total. That is, a large number of category transitions took place, obviously, within three-second intervals during forty-five minutes.

Thus far on the basis of the information notes, this lesson may be described as one in which students spoke quite a bit and in which the teacher used a great deal of indirect influence. The nature of this indirect influence comes into focus in the i/d ratio, in which the frequent use of facilitating statements (categories 1–4) and minimal use of controlling statements (categories 5–7) is revealed. The $I/D_{8,9}$ ratio (i.e., categories 1–4 divided by categories 5–7 for rows 8 and 9 only) provides further evidence for this by pointing out the preponderance of the teacher's acceptance of and use of student ideas directly following student talk. Yet the steady-state cells suggest that there were opportunities provided for the development and elaboration of ideas during the lesson.

In any matrix analysis, when dealing with the data in the multiple cells, a series of questions about how the lesson was carried out may be raised. For example, how may this lesson have started? What emerges as a frequent pattern of verbal interaction? From where did the ideas (or content) seem to come? How did the teacher seem to respond to student ideas? How did the students seem to respond to the teacher's ideas? What seemed to be the teacher's general role in this lesson?

The "classroom game" typically involves the teacher's taking initiative in starting a lesson. (See selections by Bellack and his associates.) A matrix cue about the beginning of interaction patterns may frequently be found in the teacher's use of categories 4, 5, or 6. The frequency of tallies in any cell in the matrix serves to call attention to the vitality of this particular verbal sequence in a lesson. In this matrix, the frequent use of brief, specific questions is suggested by the heavy loading in cell 4-8. Some questions which were probably broad and which sought responses involving the pupil's own ideas were also used (see cell 4-9). Pupils also got into the interaction via their direct initiative while the teacher was talking (cell 5-9). These may have been questions raised by the pupils or reactions to what the teacher was saying. The frequent use of encouragement and/or praise (cells 2-8 and 8-2) suggests that the teacher may have been supporting continuation or expansion of pupil talk. This may have taken the form of a brief statement that served to encourage an individual pupil to continue or to elaborate on what he was saying.

The sequence of classroom events in this lesson is suggested by the nature of category 8 (Areas V, VI, VII). In a considerable number of instances, pupil talk continued longer than three seconds. That is, there were answers which involved some extension of ideas and which took longer than three seconds to speak (cell 8-8). There were some instances in which a pupil's answer led to elaborations which were not sought in the original question (cell 8-9).

The teacher's responses to the pupils' statements suggest that she was equally encouraging and accepting of ideas which were directly elicited by her questions and those which pupils initiated themselves. This may be seen by comparing the frequencies in cells 8-2 and 8-3 with 9-2 and 9-3. Also, she responded similarly to pupil responses and pupil initiations with questions and explanations, as seen by comparing cells 8-4 and 8-5 with cells 9-4 and 9-5. The almost complete absence of criticism or directions in response to pupil talk (cells 8-6, 8-7, 9-6, 9-7) suggests that the teacher found ways to use most of the ideas pupils expressed. If a student gave an incorrect response, for example, the teacher appears to have provided correction or clarification through statements other than criticisms. It seems plausible that some corrections could have been made through questioning (cells 8-4 and 9-4), clarification (cells 8-3 and 9-3), or explanation (cells 8-5 and 9-5).

The teacher's explanations and use of lecturing provide an interesting area for examination in this matrix (see column 5). During this lesson, the teacher frequently brought information into the discussion after a pupil's idea was expressed (cells 8-5, 9-5, 3-5). There appears to have been little straight lecturing by the teacher (cell 5-5), but rather a pattern in which the input of information and ideas was carried out by pupils and teacher.

The pupils' reaction seems to have been characterized by responsiveness, which the teacher judged as appropriate. The sheer quantity of pupil talk suggests considerable participation in the lesson. The presence of pupil-to-pupil talk (cells 9-10 and 10-9) (These cells are used to denote pupil-to-pupil talk. This is to be distinguished from extended pupil talk, which appears in cell 9-9.) suggests that pupils were involved in the learning activity and interacting. This inference is based on the high quantity of acceptance and the lack of criticism (Areas VI and VII). Since the precise nature of the students' responsiveness is not identified on Interaction Analysis matrices, there is an alternative hypothesis regarding this teacher's reactions to the students. It may have been that the teacher did not respond with correction or criticism to the students' behavior even though these actions were not focused on the learning activity.

The quantity of category 10 (8.6 percent) and its meaning in this lesson is of specific interest. Some of the tallies indicate change of pupil speaker (cells 9-10 and 10-9), as noted above. There were instances, however, in which 10's follow questions and explanations. These may have been brief pauses in the sequence. They may also have reflected simultaneous speech in which one category could not be assigned by the observer. If this "bubbling over" of more than one speaker did occur, it was not viewed by the teacher as cause for exercise of control via directions or criticism as shown by the lack of any tallies in cells 10-6 and 10-7. The teacher's most frequent reactions to behavior classified as category 10 were questioning and explaining (10-4 and 10-5). One pattern which may have emerged is: question asked, brief pause, and question restated or explained.

With the quantity of pupil talk as high as it was, it does not seem plausible that this was a lesson characterized by many silences or pauses. The likelihood seems greater that the 10's reflect some pauses, some transitions of speaker, and some simultaneous verbal activity which the teacher seems to have dealt with as a matter of course. She seems to have accepted the expressions (cells 10-1, 10-2, and 10-3) which were classified as 10's. She may have picked up one speaker's comments and have responded to those on several occasions.

The use of directions and/or the giving of assignments (category 6) was limited, as shown by the low percentage of 2.2. About one-third of the directions appear to have grown out of some other verbal behavior, namely, teacher encouraging, questioning, and explaining, and pupil ideas.

Summary

This illustrative lesson is characterized by considerable pupil talk and facilitation of pupil talk by the teacher. The teacher generally appears to have been serving as a question-raiser, encourager and clarifier, and information-giver. The matrix suggests that pupils were exercising considerable influence on the nature of the lesson. While there seems to have been a fairly rapid pace, there was time taken for expansion of ideas by both teacher and pupils.

The format used for interpreting this illustrative matrix may be applied generally. When skill in matrix interpretation has been developed, a marked feeling for probable specific ingredients of a lesson will result. Additional extra cues from the direct observer and information from the teacher on his objectives and purposes is necessary in order to select among plausible alternative hypotheses. In this way, it is possible to interpret a lesson quite accurately from a matrix.

10 What is Teaching? One Viewpoint

Marie M. Hughes

Psychologists, other researchers, and curriculum workers are in agreement that a most important variable in the classroom is that of the teacher.

The teacher behavior in the classroom that is most pervasive and continuous is, of course, the verbal action. The verbal and the nonverbal behavior of teachers is, according to Mary Aschner, "the language of responsible actions designed to influence the behavior of those under instruction" (1).

Indispensable data then for a description and analysis of teaching are verbatim records of what the teacher said and did and the response made by a child or group, including children's initiatory actions directed toward the teacher.

Data of This Study

The data of this study (2) were secured from 41 elementary teachers— 7 men and 34 women. These teachers had classrooms in 19 buildings in 8 school districts.

Reprinted with permission of the Association for Supervision and Curriculum Development and Marie M. Hughes, from *Educational Leadership*, 19:251–259, January, 1962. Copyright © 1962 by the Association for Supervision and Curriculum Development.

The representativeness of the group may be judged from the fact they received their training degrees in 22 different states. Their age range was 25 to 50 years; their teaching experience, 5 years to 30 years; with a bimodal distribution at the ninth and fifteenth years. They were career teachers and judged good by supervisory and consultant staff members.

Three 30-minute records were secured from each of the teachers by two observers working at one time in the classroom with the teacher's cooperation and knowledge of the exact time the observers would arrive to take the record. In general, the records were taken several days apart.

A brief episode from one 30-minute record may provide a more adequate picture of the data with which we worked:

Record #2620, page 2:

T.: Carl, do you remember the day you came to school and said you could play a tune on the piano? It was a tune we all knew and so we sang it with you. You found out you could play the same tune on the tone bells. I wonder if you'd play the same tune for us today.

T.: My! We like to sing with you. Can we start our music time by your playing again and our singing with you? Why don't you play it on the tone bells?

Carl: I'd like to play it on the piano.

T.: Well, all right, you may play it on the piano if you'd rather. Do you want to play it all through once or shall we start right off together?

Carl: I'll play it through. (Played on piano "Mary Had a Little Lamb" with one hand.)

T.: That was very nice!

Carl: I think you could sing with me.

T.: All right, we'd be glad to. (Carl played and children sang.) Thank you, Carl.

Carl: You could even do all of it.

T.: You mean we could sing all of the verses?

Carl: I can even do "followed her to school one day . . . etc."

T.: I'm sure you can, Carl. Thank you very much.

What does the teacher do? It is obvious that there is a wide repertoire of behavior open to the teacher.

The teacher *tells* people what to do.

The teacher *sets* goals, the specifics of attention. "Today, we shall do the 25 problems on page 90."

The teacher *gives* directions. "Take your books out and open them to page 90." "Do not write your name."

The teacher *reprimands.* "Take your seat, Johnny."

The teacher *accuses.* "You didn't work very hard."

The teacher *admonishes.* This is, of course, before anything happens.

"Don't forget to close the door." "Make sure you look up your words."

The teacher *supports* and *encourages.* "That's nice." "Good." "Fine." "O.K." "I knew you could do it."

The teacher *grants* or *denies* requests.

The teacher *clarifies* and *eleborates* on the problem or content under discussion.

The teacher *asks* questions.

The teacher *gives* cues.

There are many ways to categorize or organize the verbal behavior and nonverbal behavior of a teacher. It is the point of view of this investigator that the superior-subordinate relationship in the teacher-learner situation, with its culturally bestowed power position over the child, makes it impossible for the teacher to act in the classroom without performing a *function*[1] for some child group, or the entire class as recipients. It is the teacher who holds the power to give aid or withhold aid; to judge and to punish; to gratify or to deny; to accept or to ignore the response of a child.

Actually, children who are not participants in a given episode of interaction with the teacher do respond to his behavior (3, 4).

The presumptuousness of looking at teacher behavior from the standpoint of functions performed for the child is recognized. The 30-minute consecutive record often made it possible to follow actions and reactions through an episode and many times several episodes. In addition, for a four year period there had been consistent effort through interviews and paper and pencil tests to discover children's views of typical classroom situations. To date, responses have been secured from some 1400 fifth and sixth graders in three states (5, 6). Interviews have been held with younger children, and with junior high youths.

As expected, children react in an individual manner; however, there is a great range of intensity of reaction. In general, there is a high degree of emotionality, with children responding to elements in the situations that were not intended or foreseen by adults. Another tentative finding was that for any given teacher behavior, from 7 to 20 percent of those to whom it was directed appeared to make no response. They were not involved or they failed to identify with the situation when given the opportunity in interviews or paper and pencil test. The mode for this noninvolvement was 14 percent. Most of the teachers are, of course, aware of the phenomenon of one or more children seeming not to be "with it."

[1]See the addendum to this article for a detailed outline of the seven functions as identified in Figure 1. R.T.H., editor.

Description of Teaching

Figure 1 presents the mean distribution of teaching acts performed by the teachers during three 30-minute periods of teaching. It is immediately clear that the largest number of teaching acts falls within the category of controlling functions. Figures 2 and 3 present the mean distributions of teaching acts for teachers who are among the highest and those who are among the lowest in the exercise of control in the classroom. Since the present report is devoted largely to an exposition of Controlling Functions, and the Development of Content, a brief definition of the other categories may be useful.

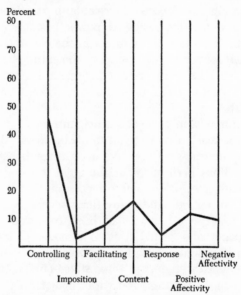

FIGURE 1 Mean Distribution of Teaching Acts for 90 Minutes Observation for 35 Teachers

Teacher Imposition: These are acts where the teacher projects himself into the situation. For example: In a few classrooms without routine procedures for supplies, the teacher might say over and over again, "Keep your seat, I'll bring it to you." Another is the expression of evaluation; e.g., on reading a story in a foreign locale, "Their names are certainly queer." Moralizing is another act that falls in this category. As may be noted in the figures, very few teaching acts fall in this category.

Facilitating: These acts may be thought of as management functions that are relatively neutral. All statements that designate time, change of schedule and so forth. Those information seeking acts that are nonevaluative; that is, the child is free to have or not have it, e.g.: "Who brought lunch money?" Rhetorical questions of "Wasn't that fun?" "Did you enjoy it?" "We're finished, aren't we? " Such questions, if they evoke a response, secure a chorus of "yes" or "no" as expected. More often than not the teacher does not wait for an answer.

These management functions differentiate least among teachers and are the most stable with a teacher's series of records.

Personal Response includes meeting the individual requests of children, listening to their personal interests and experiences unrelated to the content under consideration.

These are all positive responses and most often are interactions between a teacher and a single child.

Positive and Negative Functions need little comment since they are the praise and reproof categories. It is realized that the use of positive and negative reinforcement controls behavior; however, by their very nature these teaching acts are, as a group, more affectively-laden. Therefore, it was deemed desirable to trace them out separately.

Although space does not permit an elaboration of these last three categories, it is hypothesized that they have much to do with the personal liking or not liking of the teacher. There is something in a personal response that conveys the idea, "You count—you are important enough for me to listen to you, and to do something just for you."

Approval and acceptance were expressed most often in a stereotyped manner: "Fine," "Yes," "O.K.," "Good," "All right." Such expressions without a definite referent served the purpose of allaying tension. It was one way of saying "All is well."

It is hypothesized that the acceptance of reprimands of any degree of intensity depends to a large extent on the teacher's use of *public criteria*. If he makes clear the elements in the situation that call for certain required behavior, children may protest, but they can accept the reprimand as just. Consistency of teacher behavior is another element in fairness.

In general, more acts of positive affectivity were recorded for teachers than of negative affectivity; however, Figure 2 depicting teachers high in control, shows two teachers who were more negative than positive in their teaching. The gross differences in distribution of teaching acts shown in Figures 2 and 3 suggest that the classroom is quite different for the children in attendance.

Controlling Functions

Our study showed that the teaching acts most frequently performed were those of control. By control, reference is not limited to discipline.

Since these teachers were considered good teachers, their classes were well organized and generally attentive. By control is meant goal setting, directing the children to the precise thing to which they give attention. Not only is the content named for children, but they are held to a specific answer and processes of working. Such control is firm and pervasive. In many classrooms the control might be considered implacable. Sixty-eight percent of the teachers had one or more of their records with 50 percent or more of their teaching acts categorized as controlling. The teacher most often wanted only one answer and refused all others. For example, a third grade was reporting on books read, then classifying them according to theme. One little girl made a few remarks about her book and then said, "It's a fantasy." The teacher immediately replied, "You mean imaginative, don't you?" No reward for the use of a divergent word or a suggestion of any relationship or differentiation between the two.

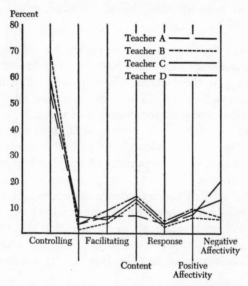

FIGURE 2 Distribution Patterns of Teaching Acts for 4 Teachers High in Controlling

The control of content is exercised by the teacher in the structure of the *what* to give attention to. In a third grade arithmetic class each child had a foot rule. The teacher structured the group by saying, "Today, we are going to study the middle line. What is it called?" Several children answered, "One-third," "a fourth," "a half." One boy was busy measuring some paper on his desk and said, "This is 6¼ inches." (Correct) The teacher replied, "Just the middle line today. We just talk about the half."

As long as the question or statement that structures the class or the individual requires but *one* answer, the teacher is in absolute control.

Nothing more may properly occur until the next question is asked. Such structure of content appears to evoke memory but little more in mental activity.

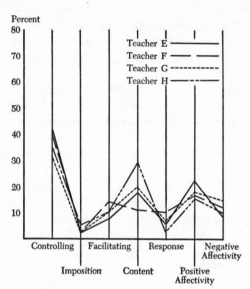

FIGURE 3 Distribution Patterns of Teaching Acts for 4 Teachers Low in Controlling

When structure is open, more than one answer is possible. Indeed, there may not be an absolutely right answer. For example, "What might happen if the new highway went across the state by one route instead of another?" Closed structure of content resulted in question and answer between teacher and class—it was strictly recitation. Open structure, with more than one answer possible, resulted in participation of several pupils before re-entry of the teacher in the situation. In other words, more ideas were generated and more pupils became involved in the work.

Control as Regulation of Who

Another phase of controlling behavior is that of regulating who will do what; answer questions, give the report, take lunch money to the office, etc. Such regulation can serve indirectly as punishment or as reward.

"Your work is finished, so you take the books to Mrs. Jones." At least a criterion of choice, "your work is done," is made public. In one episode the children were sharing their stories with one another and the teacher regulated after each story with, "Whom shall I choose, whom shall I ask to go next?" A child would then be named. As teacher choices followed one another, the excitement mounted over who was to be next and not over the content of the stories.

Other teachers set up some *neutral* manner of regulating. "Write your names on the board when you are ready and we shall take them in order." Another teacher had children put a slip on a spindle. Their stories were then read in order of completion. Some teachers made charts of committees who worked at the various housekeeping and management chores a week at a time.

We found in one sixth grade that the students considered the teacher unfair. He was perplexed, so we tried to find out why this perception. It turned out that Lou and Hazel always got to answer the telephone. They sat next to the office and could answer without moving about unduly. This fact had not been shared with the children; consequently, all they saw was unfairness.

The use of *Public Criteria* for the controlling actions of the teacher is suggestive. It ameliorates the power of the teacher. It gives the authority an impersonal embodiment.

Control Over Many Activities

The controls exercised are expressed in all kinds of activities. It was difficult to get hold of the criteria used by teachers in their expression of control.

A child was making cut-out paper pears to be placed in a cornucopia poster filled with fruits and vegetables. The teacher said, "Why don't you make them bigger?"

> *Child:* I made them like they are on my grandfather's farm.
> *T.:* Get the picture from my desk and make them big like that.

The teacher judged in cases of altercation or conflict of interest. Incidentally, the conflict of interest was frequently between teacher and child or group. To illustrate, a teacher said:

> *T.:* Who do you wish to have help you with your reading?
> *Child:* Madeline.
> *T.:* How about Susan?
> *Child:* Jane.
> *T.:* Let's see. Mary would be a good one. Yes, go sit with Mary.

A junior high school teacher working with the English class putting out a paper said:

> *T.:* Here are some interesting things about the Navy that we could put in the paper. Who wants to write it?

Agnes: I will. I read it and thought the boys might like it.
T.: No, you already have three things in. I'll write it myself.

We hypothesize that consistent use of *Public Criteria* might aid in reducing the conflicts with authority. *Public Criteria* are situationally placed:

T.: There is time for *one* story before noon.
T.: We had trouble with a certain kind of problem yesterday; therefore, we will work on similar problems today.
T.: The children using the saws are on the barn committee and must have them until they finish; therefore, you have to wait.

Public Criteria can also express the conventions and accepted ways of doing. "You have too many erasures on your paper to read it easily," instead of "I won't take a paper that looks like that."

Place of Controlling Functions

This investigator believes that it is the business of the teacher to manage (control, if you prefer) the classroom so that learning for all the children present may proceed. Controlling functions will undoubtedly constitute between 30 and 40 percent of a teacher's behavior; however, the power component may be ameliorated through the use of:

Open-structure that permits some choice or requires more than one answer.
Increased Regulation (*who* is to respond) that is neutral or done with public criteria that expresses the reason for the choice.
Directions that are clear with limits so to reduce repetition of directions and lessen the number of reprimands.
Rules that are group developed, situationally oriented, and enforceable. They should make sense to children.

Development of Content

There is a relationship between the development of content and the nature of the control exercised by structure. When the structure permits no exploration on the part of children it serves to delimit and restrict.

A primary class was reading about a baby elephant. They discussed its age and other things pertaining to the picture of the baby elephant. Finally Ben spoke up and said:

Ben: Look, here is an elephant with a tusk.
T.: Yes, that elephant is on the other page. Read this page and find out what Baby Elephant did when she got to the monkey cage.

It might have been profitable to raise the question why one elephant had tusks and the other did not. It can be hypothesized that the mental processes evoked by the different situations are likewise different.

In another class the teacher and class were looking at a large map of the two hemispheres, when one child asked where the local town was. The teacher replied, "It is about here, but can't be seen on this map. I'll get you one and you can find it and other towns you know."

The teaching acts that develop content elaborate and add to the content or problem under consideration. Response is made to the data placed in the situation by the children. It is believed that children involved in content have something to say. They are encouraged in this by the teacher who respects their efforts. The teacher *stimulates* by offering several suggestions of ideas or of activities that might be done. The choice of doing, however, remains with the child. (It is, of course, proper to give a direction or an assignment, which then would be an act of control.)

Evaluation that keeps content as a referent is in this category. To illustrate, "You have used several kinds of sentence structure in your composition. Very good." The phrase, "That's good," spoken after a child has read the composition does not tell him whether he was good to have written it at all, or good to have read it, or just good to have gotten through the episode. In terms of compositions, he has received nothing definite that helps him move ahead with his writing. He has received teacher approval. With most of the evaluation made in the form of generalized approval or disapproval, such expressions foster dependence on teacher instead of judgment and interest in the content.

If children and youth are to become interested in subject matter for its own sake, do they not need to link their own experience and make their own personal inquiry in relationship to it? If children are not listened to, how can one know what concepts are developed or what interpretations are made?

An upper grade discussion had been going on concerning early California Indians.

> *T.:* Incidentally, did the California Indians have a pretty easy life?
> *Arthur:* No.
> *T.:* Yes they did, Arthur. Don't you remember? Who can tell me about it?

What logic was Arthur using in his reply? Was it strictly subjective, "I wouldn't have liked it," or had he assessed the situation with some judgment?

When do children use a variety of mental processes such as making comparisons, explaining with some logic, noting relationships, generalizing from a series of data? What kind of questions and teacher responses evoke what mental activity (7)?

Perhaps teachers need to develop what might be called *creative use of interruptions.*

Not long ago a mother reported the disgust of her kindergarten son whose teacher allegedly told him that he couldn't talk about dinosaurs until third grade. The child had been to the Dinosaur Monument and Museum with his family. While there, the father had bought each boy a book which had been read at home.

One can conjecture all kinds of reasons why the teacher did not wish to get off on dinosaurs. However, the question remains, "In what situations do teachers act in ways that children can see them as people who *aid* in their personal quest for knowing? Since this child's dinosaurs were tied to Vernal, Utah, it might have been very stimulating to listen to his story and also mention the Berea Tar Pits within the city of Los Angeles, as another locale where bones had been found.

It is, of course, possible that the child wanted attention only. Even so, the school can meet such personal needs of children through the use of their explorations and inquiries in the development of content. It is suggested that children's questions and remarks be integrated with the lesson plan of the teacher.

The present study of teaching found that the most prevalent series of teaching acts were in question-answer test or recitation situations. Far too many such situations were spent in working for the specific answer wanted by the teacher.

Of the total group of 41, only 3 teachers had all of their records with 20 or more of their teaching acts in this category of development of content. Seventy-four percent of all records had 20 percent or less of teaching acts falling in this category of exploration, amplification, utilization of children's questions and remarks, evaluation and stimulation. This category has been described as working with the content or problem and called *development of content.*

Some relationships of one category to another may be of interest. Development of Content and Negative Affectivity correlate −.42 significant at the .001 level in social studies. This relationship is not unexpected, since teachers who use many acts of Negative Affectivity are not responsive to children's ideas and explorations even in subject matter.

Personal Response is correlated −.35 with Controlling and a −.38 with Negative Affectivity. Again, this is not unexpected and it holds for all records regardless of kind of work the classes were doing.

The point of view expressed in this report is that teaching may be described in terms of functions the teacher behavior, verbal and nonverbal, performs for the child, group or class to whom it is directed. It was found possible to categorize such teaching acts in seven categories:

Controlling, Imposition, Facilitating, Development of Content, Personal Response, Positive Affectivity, and Negative Affectivity.

Control of the class was exercised in varied activities, but particularly in terms of *what* to give attention to and *who* was to do what; also, the how of doing was prescribed and enforced.

Management of the classroom for learning is the teacher's job; therefore control functions are necessary. It was suggested, however, that the power component the teacher holds may be reduced with changes in verbal behavior.

In dealing with subject matter, little attention was given to children's exploratory remarks or their questions. The questions teachers used for structure were usually closed; that is, asked for one *right* answer. It was suggested that one right answer evoked the use of recall as a mental process instead of stimulating a larger range of mental activity.

It was suggested that *responsiveness* on the part of the teacher to children's remarks, questions, personal experience (data they place in the situation), would lead them to greater involvement in content (subject matter) and stimulate use of higher mental processes.

Teachers demonstrated different patterns in teaching. Different patterns do affect the learning of children (8, 9).

References

1. Mary Jane Aschner. "The Language of Teaching." In: *Language and Concepts in Education,* Edited by O. Smith and R. Ennis. Chicago: Rand McNally Co., 1961. 124 p.
2. Marie M. Hughes and Associates. *The Assessment of the Quality of Teaching: A Research Report.* U. S. Office of Education Cooperative Research Project No. 353. Salt Lake City: The University of Utah, 1959.
3. J. Kounin and P. Gump. "The Ripple Effect in Discipline." *The Elementary School Journal,* Fall 1958, p. 158-62.
4. J. Kounin, et al. "Explorations in Classroom Management." *Journal of Teacher Education,* June 1961, p. 235-46.
5. Arthur Carin. "Children's Perceptions of Selected Classroom Situations." Doctorial Dissertation, University of Utah. June 1959.
6. Elena De Vaney. "Perceptions Among Teachers and Students of Varying Cultural Backgrounds." Doctoral Dissertation, University of Utah. October 1960.
7. M. J. McCue Aschner. "Aasking Questions to Trigger Thinking." *NEA Journal,* September 1961, p. 44-46.
8. Ned Flanders. *Teacher Influence: An Interaction Analysis.* U. S. Office of Education Cooperative Research Project No. 397. Minneapolis: University of Minnesota, 1960.
9. Pauline Sears. "What Happens to Pupils Within the Classroom of Elementary Schools." Paper read at American Educational Research Association meeting, Los Angeles, June 30, 1960.

Addendum: The University of Utah Revision of the
Provo Code for the Analysis of Teaching*

All of the teaching functions that form the *Code for the Analysis of Teaching* have been identified from actual records of teaching. The *University Revision* added several functions to the original Provo Code and reorganized the larger categories to include the two categories of Imposition of Teacher and Functions of Personal Responsiveness.

The University Revision of the Provo Code for the Analysis of Teaching contains thirty-three functions that teachers perform in the classroom in interaction with children. These thirty-three functions have subscripts that describe the manner in which the functions are performed. We have retained this rather cumbersome but very useful Code so that the description of teaching might be as complete as possible. The Outline of the Code on the following pages includes the subscripts used.

These thirty-three functions are subsumed under seven large categories. . . .

OUTLINE OF THE
UNIVERSITY OF UTAH REVISION OF THE PROVO CODE
FOR THE ANALYSIS OF TEACHING

CONTROLLING FUNCTIONS

Structure	Regulate
open	open
closed	closed
intervention	global
sequential	routine
orientation	neutral
ongoing	sequential
public criteria	direction
	public criteria

Standard Set	Judge
recall	direction
teacher edict	punish
group developed	turn back
universal	just

*Reprinted with permission from *The Assessment of the Quality of Teaching in Elementary School: A Research Report* by Marie M. Hughes and Associates. U.S. Department of Health, Education, and Welfare, Office of Education, Cooperative Research Project No. 353. Salt Lake City, University of Utah, 1959.

IMPOSITION OF TEACHER

Regulate Self
Moralize
Teacher Estimate of Need

Inform Appraisal
Inform

FACILITATING FUNCTIONS

Checking
   information
   routine
   involvement

Demonstrate
Clarify Procedure

FUNCTIONS THAT DEVELOP CONTENT

Resource
   routine
   child initiative

Stimulate
   one
   three
Structure, turn back

Content-Agree

Clarify
   just
   content
   generalize
   summarize
Evaluate
   just
   negative
   positive
   with discrimination

FUNCTIONS THAT SERVE AS RESPONSE

Meets request
   routine
   makes arrangements
Clarify Personal
   problem
   experience

Interprets
   situation
   feelings
Acknowledges Teacher
   Mistake

FUNCTIONS OF POSITIVE AFFECTIVITY

Support
   just
   stereotype
   specific

Solicitous

Encourage

Does For Personal

FUNCTIONS OF NEGATIVE AFFECTIVITY

Admonish

Reprimand
    public criteria
Accusative

Threat

Negative Response Personal
    public criteria

Verbal Futuristics
    public criteria

Ignore

11 The Classroom Scene

Raymond S. Adams and Bruce J. Biddle

The kind of interpretation used in the current study had few of the characteristics of conventional interpretations of classroom behavior. We did not even start from the assumption that the classroom *had* to be either a place where teaching *or* learning goals were being fulfilled. Instead, we took a position similar to that taken by anthropologists when they look at group behavior and seek to determine how people interact. Taking such a position forced us to develop new terms to describe aspects of the situation. These terms are best understood once a broad general description has been given.

Our General View

At the outset we accepted the idea that the classroom is a *behavior setting*. As such, the classroom has many unique qualities that distinguish it clearly from other social groups. The members of its "society" live only part of their lives there, and within it they neither seek nor get full and complete satisfaction of all their spiritual and temporal needs. Teachers are members of this society because they achieve a limited fulfillment, mostly vocational or economic; pupils are constrained to be members because forces more powerful than they decree it.

Once within the boundaries of the classroom, the "unnaturalness" of the social situation is apparent. For here, in unbalanced distribution, are a number of children often neatly confined within a limited age range, and one adult, probably female, who asserts power far beyond the limits that reason might (democratically) lead one to expect. We have here a system—characterized by some confusion—which tries bravely to be "all things to all pupils" but which often only succeeds in stressing examinable results that are subsequently, and sometimes naively, equated with "education."

The classroom has a number of artifacts. These may vary from chalk to cheese. However, most of them are thought to be relevant to a task or process that is peculiar to educational settings in general. This process involves interaction among the individuals who comprise the personnel. The stated purpose of the process is to change the behavior of the individuals who constitute the majority group (students), especially in the areas of meanings (knowledge), norms (socially sanctioned behavior), and values (general concepts of good and bad, right and wrong).

In its personnel, then, the manner in which they are constrained, the idealistic nature of its task objectives, and the procedures by which attempts are made to achieve the objectives, the classroom is manifestly different from other social groups.

A Closer Look

What is it then that makes classrooms similar from a behavioral point of view? As we see it, similarity resides in the nature of the interaction process that occurs between the members. However, interactions can occur in a variety of ways. Some are short, others are drawn out. Some are concerned with weighty issues, some with trivia. More importantly, sometimes a series of interactions may be seen as fulfilling a discernible and perhaps unique function. For example, the full exposition of a Pythagorean theorem may entail quite a number of interactions, one after another. Such sequences are, educationally, more significant than the single interaction. To recognize their distinctive character, we called these educationally significant combinations of interactions, *transactions*, and the process (reasonably enough) the *transactional process*.

In order that transactions may occur, communication among the personnel or between the personnel and the artifacts, must exist. Without communication (defined in its broadest terms), transactions would be impossible. This assumption leads automatically to a number of questions. For example: If there is communication, what is it about? In what manner is it undertaken? Who is involved in the communication process? To what extent? Are there distinctive communication networks? What patterns do they exhibit? What effect does the distribution of members have on the pattern of communication? At a more practical level there are other questions. For example: How much subject matter is being presented? How much time is being spent on organization and control? Are the children being challenged to think? How much does the teacher dominate the situation? Do children participate equally in the interaction?

Up to this point the transactional process has been defined somewhat loosely as *what conventionally goes on in classrooms* or, more precisely *what kind of behavior is common to most classrooms*. The term then is strictly behavioral. It is still imprecise, however, because we have yet to specify what does happen in classrooms. So far we have provided a blanket term so that we have a name by which to call it. But this blanket term covers a number of more specific behaviors. These specific behaviors now need to be described in detail and some definition of other terms also is necessary.

Words and Our Meanings

Transactions have both *functional* and *structural* characteristics. At the risk of grossly oversimplifying a complex process, function is taken here to mean how communications are given and what they are about. Structure means who gives the communication, to what extent, and under what conditions.

Function

The functions of transactions can be examined from two points of view: their *content* and their *mode* or manner. Each will be dealt with in turn.

There are three basic kinds of content: subject-matter content, sociation content, and organization content.

SUBJECT-MATTER CONTENT.   Two kinds of subject matter are taken into account in this section of the conceptual map: scheduled subject matter and nonscheduled matter. *Scheduled subject matter* refers to contents of communications that directly relate to the kind of lesson specified at the time. For example, in an "arithmetic lesson" scheduled subject matter means communications about arithmetic. However, many communications in classrooms do not bear on the subject ostensibly being taught. Thus, even an arithmetic lesson can be punctuated by excursions into social studies, biology, literature, and the like. Such subject-matter digressions are classified as *nonscheduled subject matter*.

SOCIATION CENTER. In this study "sociation" applies to the trans-action where content either focuses on the process of being sociable or clearly represents recognized social conventions. "Good morning class," "how do you do," are communications of the latter kind. In the case of the former, exhortations to "be good citizens," "be tidy workers," "stop fighting," "be well mannered," "be nice," are all appropriate examples. Such communications are concerned with aspects of behavior that psychologists recognize as affective.

ORGANIZATION CONTENT. Whenever the content of any communication is devoted to matters that directly involve the administration of the classroom, the appropriate content category is "organization." Under this heading fall communications that are concerned with controlling and directing personnel or property in the setting. It covers the numerous teacher directives that help (or hinder) the functioning of the classroom.

Given information on the extent to which attention is devoted to the three different contents, it would be possible to make statements like this one: "In this classroom fifteen percent of the total time is devoted to organizational procedures, two percent to matters concerned with interpersonal behavior, seventy percent to scheduled subject matter, and thirteen percent to nonscheduled subject matter." This kind of information has two principal uses. First, once enough classrooms are sampled we will know how classroom time conventionally is spent. Second, the discovery of marked differences between classrooms may lead to an explanation of the reasons for many educational outcomes. For instance, presumably children who are engaged in a greater amount of scheduled matter should be better informed. Those whose attention is directed toward sociation should be more socially sensitive and better adjusted, and so on.

However, content is only one of a number of aspects that have been conceptualized. Mode is the next. The mode concept is less easy than content to illustrate in that it represents a relatively novel interpretation. Again there are three kinds: information dissemination, intellectualization, and operation.

INFORMATION DISSEMINATION MODE. Information dissemination refers to all communications devoted to the conveying of information. Statements concerned with providing facts, clarifying facts, demonstrating facts, exhibiting evidence, and the like, all fall under this heading.

Some of our reasons for isolating information dissemination may be gleaned by reflecting briefly on the nature of examination scripts and upon the average textbook. They demonstrate the fact (if it needed demonstration) that acquiring information is of prime importance in education. Factual knowledge is regarded highly. Necessarily then, factual information features prominently in the teaching-learning intercourse. Facts are presented, interpreted, explained, elaborated, illustrated, and repeated with monotonous inevitability. This is what information dissemination is about.

INTELLECTUALIZATION MODE. Intellectualization refers to all communications devoted expressly to the procedures involved in considering, in reasoning, and in indulging in deductive and inductive thought. It also includes those nonlogical procedures such as expressing attitude, opinion giving, judgment making, interpretation making, assessing, and evaluating. It should be noted that *the focus is on the procedure itself* and not on what the individuals concerned might be presumed to be thinking. As such, intellectualization is quite distinct from the "intellectualizing" that is usually (sometimes optimistically) inferred as lying behind communications made by individuals.

We fixed on the idea of intellectualization because it seems apparent that one of the conceits that many teachers at all levels permit themselves is that they teach their students "to think." Furthermore, whether it is due to their efforts or not, children *do* learn how to think, at least in some fashion. We assume therefore that a proportion of the communications occurring in classrooms must focus on the actual procedure by which the members become familiar with the processes of thinking, reasoning, forming opinions, and so on. Intellectualization *statements* are characterized by the use of phrases such as "the reason for," "it follows from this," "because of," and so on. Intellectualization *questions* tend to be of the "why" and "by what means" kind. Intellectualization also includes those untidy, illogical, and frequently unsystematic but nonetheless intellectual communications which give evidence of opinions, prejudices, judgments, and interpretations. This is *irrespective of the quality* of the opinion, judgment, or evaluation itself.

Again, this component of intellectualization is distinguished from information dissemination by its emphasis on the nature of the procedure rather than the "facts" that might confirm or deny the judgment.

OPERATION MODE. The third subcategory refers to those classroom processes which cannot be classified under the other two headings and which appear to exist merely for the sake of the experience itself. Group singing is classified under this heading. Any practice activities (reciting arithmetic tables, practicing a motor skill, doing writing drills) also are included. So too are creative activities such as painting (without instruction) and dancing. Group quizzes, tests, and examinations also are located under this heading. Such activities often are ritualized in classrooms. They persist over time often with little variation. They carry their own momentum in that they circumscribe and prescribe behavior. At such times, group behavior becomes more overtly homogeneous. These are the occasions when uniformity reigns and conformity is the norm.

In a somewhat limited sense, the three mode concepts represent "knowing," "understanding," and "doing." To have on record the extent to which "knowing," "understanding," and "doing" feature in classrooms seems potentially useful. The prospect of differentiating classrooms on this basis also looks promising because it offers the opportunity for comparing the educational outcomes of classes which stress practice, those which stress understanding, and those which stress organization.

Structure

The structure of transactions is viewed a little differently from its function. Structure refers to an order that persists among the parts of a system, hence to ordered features of the transactions. There are four different kinds of structure. They will be dealt with in turn.

COMMUNICATION STRUCTURE. Theoretically the number of classroom members involved in any one communication exchange could range from two to everybody in the group. During certain kinds of exchanges, however, some members may not be involved in the communication network at all; these are the *disengaged*. At other times no communication of any kind may be in evidence. These different states of affairs have been accommodated by identifying different communication groups. These groups are differentiated on the basis of the extent to which they command the attention of class members. When more than fifty percent of the class are attending to a single communication, this is called a *central group*. A group with fewer than fifty percent has been called a *peripheral group*. Any member who is *not involved* actively in any of these groups is recognized as belonging to a *residue*. Taken together, the various groups within a classroom form a communication structure, a pattern that may give evidence of considerable change and variation over time.

The selection of communication structure can be justified on a priori grounds. For example, since Dewey and Kilpatrick, the idea of the classroom as a stage upon which the virtuoso teacher gives a continuing performance has undergone reform. Numerous teaching methods have relegated lecturing to a subservient position. Yet controlling some thirty children poses its own problems and, it must be admitted, children are not always the best agents to convey an educational message. Consequently, lecturing to the "whole class" is still a recognizable teaching activity. Nevertheless, the degree to which "whole class" activities occur, and the extent to which they dominate the situation is unknown. To

contrast classrooms where lecturing is infrequent with others where it is
not holds potential interest. Here again it would be intriguing to compare
educational outcomes in classrooms where, say, a great deal of (un-
official) peripheral group activity occurs, with others where it does not.

Communication structure patterns occur over time. They also occur
through the individuals who are in the classroom setting. In our research,
personnel involved in communication groups have been identified in two
ways: according to the *positions* they hold, and according to the *roles*
they play.

POSITIONS. Only two *"positions"* have been specified. They are,
obviously enough, (1) *teacher* and (2) *students*. This rather gross categorization was sufficient for the purposes of this study. In future studies
it should be possible to identify a number of other positions that differentiate one student from another so that we become concerned with
discussion-leaders, monitors, errand boys, and so on.

ROLES. Three different *communicating roles* were also specified
for communication groups. They are respectively *emitter, target,* and
audience. An *emitter* is the person who speaks first when a communication group is set up. The *target* is a person or group to whom the emitter
addresses himself. The *audience* consists of those members who are attending to the communication.

Role and position are complementary. Any role can be identified according to whether a teacher or student is performing it, and teachers
and students may be identified according to the roles that they play.

The use of these positions and role concepts claims legitimacy from
sociological convention. A number of researchers[1] have noted that the
teacher dominates the classroom. Consequently, to discover the extent to
which he undertakes an emitter role as distinct from an audience or
target role has many implications for modern educational development.
For instance, if the teacher is characteristically the *deus ex machina,*
when the machines themselves—teaching machines—begin to take over,
what effect will this have on the whole configuration of classroom interaction? If the teacher as principal emitter organizes his ideas on the
basis of adult logical systems which, as Piaget suggests, children are
incapable of comprehending, what are the consequences in terms of
developing patterns of thinking?

In contrast with the teacher-dominated classroom, schools like Sum-
merhill have long advocated a truly child-centered classroom education.
But what does this mean in patterns of interaction? Are pupils continuously independent? Is there no group-structured activity? Are there no

[1]The authors cite here Bellack, Flanders, and Jackson. For Bellack see Section 3;
for Flanders see Section 2; and for P. W. Jackson see his *Life in Classrooms* (New
York: Holt, Rinehart and Winston, 1968). R.T.H., editor.

lectures? Once again, to determine the operating characteristics of different kinds of classrooms—the different ways they run the show—opens up the possibility of relating educational outcomes with what actually occurs.

LOCATION. Finally, at any point in time each person in the classroom occupies a particular location. Structure, therefore, can also be regarded as a geographical distribution of the members. By plotting where the actors are, it is possible to arrive at a clear picture of where the action occurs in each classroom. Is it, for instance, distributed (democratically) throughout the room? Is it confined to a few select locations? To what extent do the "props" in the situation (blackboard, bookcase, teacher's desk) determine where the action is? Plotting locations makes answers to such questions possible. Oddly enough, social science has not been particularly concerned with the demography of small groups. Hall (1959) has made some provocative comments about the significance of nonverbal (demographic) aspects of interaction but, by and large, demography has been left to those who are interested in large societies.

Panorama

In brief review of the discussion so far, the structural aspects of the classroom may perhaps be regarded as the web on which the tapestry of the transactional picture is to be woven. It limits the extent of the picture, dictates the degree of fineness of work, and provides the foundation framework that will determine the durability of the finished product. Nonetheless, the appeal and beauty of the work will owe little to it. Elegance will derive mainly from the functional character of the classroom. Function will constitute the woven pattern, the blending of forms, the balance of color, the over-all design.

There is one final definitional act that has to be undertaken. The foregoing discussion lists a number of different kinds of individual and collective behaviors. Because we will refer to such behavior-states repeatedly from here on, they need a generic designation. It is at this point that we run up against one of social science's problems. The kind of term needed has to cover both individual behaviors and behaviors engaged in by a number of people at once. Unfortunately, there are few terms in the English language that refer unequivocally to collective behavior. (Cohesiveness is an excellent one in that it has no equivalent for individuals —it is impossible for one person to cohere.) The solution offered for the particular problem here is to call all these kinds of behaviors whether collective (for instance, communication structure, role allocation) or individual (teacher location, teacher role assignment, and so on), by the

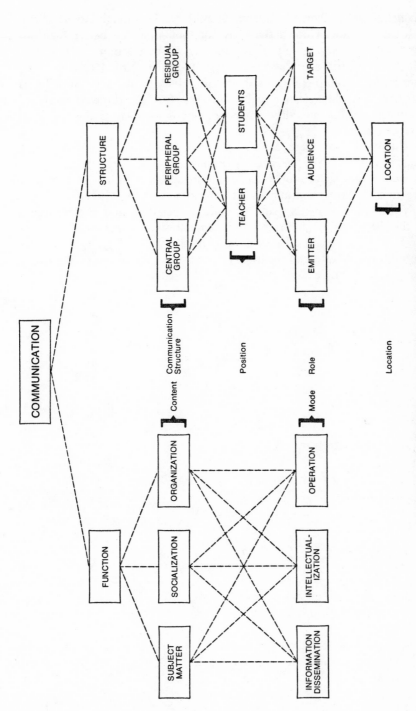

FIGURE 2-1 The Transactional Process of the Classroom

term *activities.* However, this term should not be thought to have any overtones of value. One "activity" is not thought to be better than another. One "activity structure" is similarly no better than its brethren. In fact the existence of "activities" is not even regarded as essentially better than the complete nonexistence of activity of any sort. Activity, as it is used here then, is not to be mistaken for "self-directed activity," "activity-period," or "activity-corner" or any other pedagogically approved activity term.

The ideas that were contained in the conceptual framework just discussed have been represented in Figure 2.1 as a model or paradigm. The model starts at the top with "communication" which is then broken down into its functional and structural parts. The functional part comprises the three contents (subject matter, sociation, and organization) and the three modes (information dissemination, intellectualization, and operation). The structural part consists of the kinds of group structures (central, peripheral, and residual); positions (teacher and student); roles (emitter, target, and audience); and location.

3 *The Cognitive Processes*

Overview

The cognitive processes perspective directs us to seek answers to such questions as: What content is it that teachers and pupils talk about? To what aspect of the topic at hand do teachers and pupils devote their discourse? What are the various types of logical thinking processes manifested in classrooms? How can we empirically specify examples of the operations of the intellect? What types and examples of creative, productive thinking can we locate in classroom discourse? When we say, "This teacher really teaches the pupils how to think," what is it that he teaches the pupils to do? What are the cognitive skills that teachers and pupils perform in their verbal behavior?

In spite of the fact that the development of "good thinking" has always been an aim of teaching (consider the popular phrase "teach the children *how* to think, not *what* to think"), the examination of teaching from this vantage point represents a comparatively new approach. There were several attempts in the first quarter of the century to investigate the use and types of questions that teachers ask, but these were done via questionnaires to teachers rather than by actual observation. For some unknown reason these studies were not refined during the next thirty years. In the late 1950s educators again began to look at teaching by focusing on the thought processes, logical operations, and content of classroom teaching. The reason for this particular resurgence at that time is difficult to pinpoint. Yet it is probably not merely coincidental that it came at the time when many Americans began concentrating

161

their demands on the content of teaching as the arms and space races went into high gear.

The selections that follow show teaching as a complex activity. Indeed, the central aim of each of the following selections is to shed light on this complexity. These studies define the basic concepts of the cognitive perspective. Gallagher and Aschner write about productive thinking. Maccia considers actual and hypothetical thinking. Bellack and his associates discuss pedagogical, substantive, substantive-logical, and instructional meanings. Webb, representing the group at the University of Florida, presents the cognitive skills identified by Bloom and his associates in their work on the cognitive domain. Denny presents a system to describe creative thinking, using, in part, categories based on the work of Guilford.

The further significance of these selections comes from the categories each has constructed to define the basic concepts operationally. With these well-defined categories it is possible to talk meaningfully and specifically about the thinking manifested in classroom discourse. Without such categories, productive thinking, for example, is so general a concept that it is virtually impossible to identify examples of it. Therefore, the reader needs to pay careful attention to these attempts to describe in behavioral terms classroom content, logic, and thinking.

The taxonomy by Bloom and his associates, utilized as the theoretical foundation for the selection by the Florida group, requires special attention. Although it is perhaps the most widely known set of cognitive categories, it is also perhaps the most widely misunderstood. By definition a taxonomy is a set of categories arranged into a sequential and cumulative order. When Bloom first published his work, he entitled it "Taxonomy" because he believed that the categories did constitute a hierarchical order. Later, however, in another book,[1] Bloom and his associates reported uncertainty about their taxonomy. "It is to be hoped that new research will emerge which will determine more clearly whether the group has developed a *classification* scheme or a *taxonomic order.*"

In short, Bloom and his associates are not sure that their categories constitute a set of cumulative levels. Perhaps the categories are not a taxonomy but only a simple classification system. If the categories are but a classification system, then it is indeed inappropriate to speak about cognitive *levels.* That is, for example, we cannot say that synthesis is a higher level of thinking than analysis and application. This is so despite the reference to cognitive levels by Webb in her article. Nevertheless, whether we have a taxonomy or only a classification system, the Florida research presented by Webb deserves our serious attention because even as a classification system the concepts are useful.

[1]David R. Krathwohl, Benjamin S. Bloom, and Bertram B. Masia, *Taxonomy of Educational Objectives: Handbook II: Affective Domain* (New York: David McKay Company, 1964), p. 12.

As a result of the complexity of this cognitive aspect of teaching, the systems devised to quantify it are themselves intricate. One crucial element of the intricacy is the type of basic unit of behavior employed by Bellack and Gallagher and Aschner. These researchers do not employ the dimension of time as a methodological means for breaking up the classroom discourse into small units in which to locate and categorize cognitive processes. Bellack and his associates use the pedagogical move, while Gallagher and Aschner use the thought unit. The use of such units of behavior, as opposed to a simple time unit, requires much more skill and training in order to achieve competence and reliability. The investigators have not chosen units based on time since they feel it is inappropriate when focusing on cognitive behavior. They believe that time units divide the discourse into fragments inconsistent with the flow of classroom thinking. The reader, then, must give careful attention to the definitions of these units of behavior.

In Bellack's research the unit of behavior takes on considerable importance. It becomes more than just a unit of discourse. It becomes a concept with which to view teaching. Bellack, therefore, devotes much of his article to describing and analyzing his four pedagogical moves. Furthermore, he uses these moves to create a new concept, the teaching cycle, with which it is possible to discuss patterns in classroom teaching. Thus, Bellack's unit of behavior has assumed over the years an importance which matches that of his cognitive categories.

Both Denny and Webb employ time units for breaking up the classroom discourse. Denny breaks the discourse into two-minute intervals, while Webb uses six-minute intervals. Denny uses a combination of a category system and a sign system, while Webb uses a straight sign system for both teacher and pupil.

In regard to the systems devised, the reader needs to keep two factors in mind. First, the sets of categories in these selections overlap. For example, the evaluative category of Gallagher and Aschner's productive thinking is quite similar to Bellack's opining and justifying and to Bloom's evaluation. Yet the concept of productive thinking is not the same as the concept of logical operations. Maccia's hypothetical thinking is similar to Gallagher and Aschner's divergent thinking. Other examples of overlapping will be apparent.

Second, these studies use similar terminology but not always with the same definitions. The overlaps in categories and terminology stem in part from the common area of endeavor and in part from the fact that these investigators are in fairly close contact with each other through their reports, correspondence, and conferences.

All of the selections concentrate on the verbal behavior of teaching. They do so because verbal behavior is the prime medium through which teachers and pupils express their thoughts. Moreover, due to the intricacy of the instruments, the systems by Bellack and Gallagher and Aschner rely on tape recordings to preserve the classroom discourse. This method allows for slowing down the pace of the discourse in order to get at its meaning. Live discourse simply occurs too fast to permit the analysis in terms of these multifaceted concepts.

In light of all these points there is no denying that these instruments for analyzing cognitive behavior are impractical for the day-to-day needs of the untrained classroom teacher. But this does not invalidate the worth of these studies. If the systems do not serve his daily needs, the teacher can use these concepts and categories for informal analysis and as a guide to his planning for classroom activities, or he can try to simplify the instruments and the procedures to fit his own peculiar situation. Or he can rely on a corps of trained observers that can serve a group of teachers. These studies may serve as the foundation for less cumbersome instruments in the future. As in other fields, first attempts are often complicated but lead to simpler systems as more people apply their talents to the task.

The multidimensional study by Bellack and his associates is included in this section because it is primarily a system for content analysis of classroom language. It analyzes the substantive topic under study and the logical operations performed with that topic. Elsewhere in this book the results of this research are presented as *The Classroom Game*. This is consistent with the notion of the language game that these investigators borrowed from Wittgenstein for their framework, as they explain in the selection here.

These selections raise questions for research. For example, is it possible to devise an instrument and to train observers to gather data pertinent to Maccia's concepts of actual thinking and hypothetical thinking in the classroom? Surely, if hypothetical thinking is as important to our democracy as Maccia claims, we need to know under what conditions it occurs and can occur most effectively. Similarly, we need to conduct studies parallel to those of Bellack, and Gallagher and Aschner, but with different age groups, to see if the age factor correlates with varying results. Are children of eight or ten mature enough to engage in hypothetical thinking or divergent thinking?

We also need to create experimental conditions to see if certain teaching techniques affect the results. For example, what occurs if the teacher deliberately restrains from speaking reacting moves as categorized by Bellack? What occurs if the teacher deliberately asks fewer questions? What happens if the teacher does not define new terms? These are but a few suggestions of the many follow-up studies that we need to conduct. The alert reader will certainly come up with many more.

12 The Language of the Classroom

Arno A. Bellack and Joel R. Davitz in collaboration with
Herbert M. Kliebard, Ronald T. Hyman, and Frank L. Smith, Jr.

Purpose and Procedures

The purpose of this research was to study the teaching process through analysis of the linguistic behavior of teachers and students in the classroom. Observation of what goes on in elementary and secondary schools reveals that classroom activities are carried on in large part in verbal interaction between students and teachers; few classroom activities can be carried on without the use of language. This study, therefore, focused on language as the main instrument of communication in teaching. The major task was to describe the patterned processes of verbal interaction that characterize classrooms in action. A subsidiary aim, viewed primarily as an exploratory phase of our general line of research, was to study

Reprinted with permission. Selected from *The Language of the Classroom: Meanings Communicated in High School Teaching,* Parts 1 and 2. Part 1, Arno A. Bellack and Joel R. Davitz in collaboration with Herbert M. Kliebard and Ronald T. Hyman; Part 2, Arno A. Bellack in collaboration with Ronald T. Hyman, Frank L. Smith, Jr., and Herbert M. Kliebard. U.S. Department of Health, Education, and Welfare, Office of Education, Cooperative Research Projects No. 1497 and No. 2023. New York, Institute of Psychological Research, Teachers College, Columbia University, 1963 and 1965.

linguistic variables of classroom discourse in relation to subsequent pupil learning and attitude change.

The subjects were 15 teachers and 345 pupils in Problems of Democracy classes studying a unit on international trade. The 15 classes, located in seven high schools in the metropolitan New York area, ranged in size from 15 to 35 pupils, with a mean of 23 pupils. To establish reasonable limits within which the classes could carry on their work and to provide a relatively stable basis both for testing changes in knowledge and for analyzing the substantive meanings of the classroom discourse, a unit of instruction was selected for the participating classes. This unit was based on the first four chapters of the pamphlet *International Economic Problems*, written by Dr. James Calderwood.[1] Teachers were asked to teach in any manner they believed appropriate; no effort was made to control their methods of instruction. The experimental class sessions consisted of four periods on four successive days during the regular school schedule. Transcriptions of tape recordings of four sessions for each of the 15 classes served as the basic data for the analysis of the verbal interaction of teachers and pupils.

Theoretical View of Classroom Behavior

We began with the assumptions that the primary function of language is the communication of meaning and that describing linguistic events in the classroom in terms of the meanings expressed by teachers and students is a potentially fruitful direction for research. Our conception of the nature of meaning was derived in large measure from Wittgenstein's view that "the meaning of a word is its use in the language."[2] Equation of meaning and use suggested that the basic problem was to identify the distinctive functions language actually serves in the verbal interplay between pupils and teachers.

In searching for the meaning of what teachers and students communicate in the classroom, we found it helpful to identify (1) what the speaker was doing *pedagogically* with the words he spoke at a given time; (2) *what* he was saying (i.e., the content of his statement); and (3) the *feeling tone* or emotional meaning conveyed by the communication. That is, in analyzing the utterance of a teacher or of a student at a given point in class discussion, we were first of all concerned with the pedagogical significance of what the speaker was saying—whether, for example, he was structuring the class discussion by launching or focusing

[1] James D. Calderwood, *International Economic Problems*, Minneapolis, Curriculum Resources Inc., 1961.

[2] Ludwig Wittgenstein. *Philosophical Investigations*. Oxford, Basil Blackwell, 1958. p. 20.

attention on a topic or problem, eliciting a response from a member of the class, responding to a question posed by a previous speaker, or reacting to a comment previously made. Second, we were interested in identifying the content of the communication—what topic was under discussion, what information the question called for, what explanation was being offered, or what assignment was being made. Furthermore, in addition to the pedagogical function of the language and the content of the message, we were concerned with both the explicit and the implicit emotional aspects of the speaker's vocal expression.

The basic methodological problem was to devise the means whereby these three dimensions of meaning could be defined operationally. In dealing with this problem, we were again influenced by Wittgenstein's approach to language. In his view, "the *speaking* of language is part of an activity, or a form of life."[3] Language is adaptable to many uses and functions in carrying on activities that are essentially linguistic in nature. Wittgenstein refers to these activities as "language games," a metaphor used to point up the fact that linguistic activities assume different forms and structures according to the functions they come to serve in various contexts. A game has a definite structure, and there are certain moves that a player is bound to make insofar as he is playing the game at all. These are some of the verbal activities that he identifies as language games:[4]

> Giving orders and obeying them
> Reporting an event
> Forming and testing a hypothesis
> Play acting
> Making a joke and telling it
> Making up a story and reading it

Carrying the game metaphor a step further, Wittgenstein observes that verbal activities in various contexts follow language rules that govern the use of words in these activities. Learning to participate in various types of language activities is therefore very much like learning to play a game. Participants have to learn the rules, the purpose of the rules, and how the various parts of the game are related; only if one learns these rules can he play the game successfully.

Viewing classroom discourse as a kind of language game was a useful approach for purposes of this research, in that it suggested a framework for analysis within which the various dimensions of meaning could be defined in operational terms. Teaching is similar to most games in at least two respects. First, it is a form of social activity in which the players

[3]*Ibid.*, p. 11.
[4]*Ibid.*, p. 11–12.

—teachers and pupils—fill different but complementary roles. Furthermore, teaching is governed by ground rules of play which guide the actions or moves made by participants. We reasoned that if we could identify the various types of verbal moves teachers and students make in playing the game of teaching and the rules they implicitly follow in making these moves, we would be in a position to investigate the functions these verbal actions serve in classroom discourse and hence the meanings which are communicated.

Examination of the transcripts of classroom discussions suggested that the actions that characterize the verbal interplay of pupils and teachers could be classified in four major categories. We labeled these basic verbal actions *pedagogical moves* and classified them in terms of the functions they serve in classroom discourse:

> *Structuring.* Structuring moves serve the pedagogical function of setting the context for subsequent behavior by launching or halting —excluding interaction between pupils and teachers and by indicating the nature of the interaction. For example, teachers frequently begin a class period with a structuring move in which they focus attention on the topic or problem to be discussed during that session.
> *Soliciting.* Moves in this category are designed to elicit a verbal response, encourage persons addressed to attend to something, or elicit a physical response. All questions are solicitations, as are commands, imperatives and requests.
> *Responding.* These moves bear a reciprocal relationship to soliciting moves and occur only in relation to them. Their pedagogical function is to fulfill the expectation of soliciting moves. Thus, students' answers to teachers' questions are classified as responding moves.
> *Reacting.* These moves are occasioned by a structuring, soliciting, responding, or another reacting move, but are not directly elicited by them. Pedagogically, these moves serve to modify (by clarifying, synthesizing or expanding) and/or to rate (positively or negatively) what has been said previously. Reacting moves differ from responding moves, in that while a responding move is always directly elicited by a solicitation, preceding moves serve only as the occasion for reactions. Rating by a teacher of a student's response, for example, is designated a reacting move.

As we proceeded with the anlysis of the data in terms of pedagogical moves, it became evident that these moves occur in certain cyclical patterns or combinations which we designated *teaching cycles*. A teaching cycle begins either with a structuring move or with a soliciting move, both of which are *initiating* maneuvers; that is, they serve the function of getting a cycle underway. In contrast, responding and reacting moves are *reflexive* in nature; a responding move is elicited by a soliciting move and a reacting move is occasioned by a preceding move and therefore they cannot begin a cycle. A cycle frequently begins, for example, with a soliciting move by the teacher in the form of a question, continues with a responding move by the student addressed, and ends with a rating reaction by the teacher. A cycle might also get underway with a structuring move by the teacher in which he focuses attention on the topic to be discussed, continue with a question related to this topic, and end with responding moves by one or more pupils. The concept of teaching cycles makes it possible to identify patterns in the verbal exchange between teachers and students and thus to describe the ebb and flow of the teaching process as it develops over time.

In addition to meaning from the viewpoint of the pedagogical significance of what teachers and students communicate, we were also interested in the dimension of meaning represented by the content of the messages communicated. Analysis of the classroom protocols from this point of view revealed that teachers and students communicate four functionally different types of meanings: (1) *substantive meanings* with associated (2) *substantive-logical* meanings; and (3) *instructional meanings* with associated (4) *instructional-logical* meanings.

Substantive meanings refer to the subject matter discussed in the class; that is, specific concepts such as multilateral trade and generalizations involving, for example, the relation between specialization and the factors of production. Substantive-logical meanings refer to the cognitive processes involved in dealing with the subject matter, such as defining, explaining, fact stating, interpreting, opining and justifying. Instructional meanings refer to the social-managerial aspects of the classroom, such as assignments, materials and routine procedures which are part of the instructional process. Instructional-logical meanings refer to distinctively didactic verbal processes such as those involved in rating negatively and positively, explaining procedures, and giving directions.

As we developed techniques for analyzing classroom discourse in terms of pedagogical units, we attempted to develop parallel methods for determining the emotional meanings of each of these units. This approach, however, did not prove feasible; instead, a procedure utilizing larger time samples of the discourse was developed. This provided a reliable basis for characterizing the emotional style of the discourse in terms of dimensions of meaning suggested by Osgood, Suci and Tannenbaum[5]: (1) valence; (2) strength; and (3) activity.

[5]Charles Osgood, George J. Suci, and Percy H. Tannenbaum. *The Measurement of Meaning.* Urbana, University of Illinois Press, 1957.

Analysis of the Data

Coding System

The four types of pedagogical moves described above were the basic units of analysis. Within each pedagogical move the four types of meanings described in the preceding section were identified when they appeared in the discourse and were coded according to categories 3 through 8 summarized below.[6]

(1) SPEAKER: indicates source of utterance
  Teacher (T); *Pupil* (P); *Audio-Visual Device* (A)

(2) TYPE OF PEDAGOGICAL MOVE: reference to function of move
  Initiatory Moves
   Structuring (STR): sets context for subsequent behavior, launches, halts/excludes
   Soliciting (SOL): directly elicits verbal, physical, or mental response; coded in terms of response expected
  Reflexive Moves
   Responding (RES): fulfills expectation of solicitation; bears reciprocal relation only to solicitation
   Reacting (REA): modifies (by clarifying, synthesizing, expanding) and/or rates (positively or negatively); occasioned by previous move but not directly elicited; reactions to more than one previous move coded REA
   Not Codable (NOC): function uncertain because tape inaudible

(3) SUBSTANTIVE MEANING: reference to subject matter topic (Based on a content analysis of the pamphlet by Calderwood)
  Trade (TRA)
   Trade—Domestic and International (TDI)
   Trade—Money and Banking (TMB)
   Trade—Who Trades with Whom (TWH)
  Factors of Production and/or Specialization (FSP)
   Factors of Production—Natural Resources (FNR)
   Factors of Production—Human Skills (FHS)
   Factors of Production—Capital Equipment (FCS)
   Factors Other Than Natural Resources, Human Skills, and Capital Equipment Occurring in Discussion of Reasons for Trade (FRE)

[6]Italics indicate actual coding terminology.

Imports and/or Exports (IMX)
  Foreign Investment—General (FOR)
    Foreign Investment—Direct (FOD)
    Foreign Investment—Portfolio (FOP)
Barriers to Trade (BAR)
  Barrier—Tariffs (BAT)
  Barrier—Quotas (BAQ)
  Barrier—Exchange Control (BAE)
  Barrier—Export Control (BAX)
  Barrier—Administrative Protectionism (BAA)
Promoting Free Trade (PFT)
Relevant to Trade (REL)
Not Trade (NTR)

(4) SUBSTANTIVE—LOGICAL MEANING: reference to cognitive process involved in dealing with the subject matter under study

Analytic Process: use of language or established rules of logic
  Defining-General (DEF): defining characteristics of class or term with example of items within class explicitly given
    Defining-Denotative (DED): object referent of term
    Defining-Connotative (DEC): defining characteristics of class or term
    Interpreting (INT): verbal equivalent of a statement, slogan, aphorism, or proverb

Empirical Process: sense experience as criterion of truth
  Fact Stating (FAC): what is, was, or will be without explanation or evaluation; account, report, description, statement of event or state of affairs
  Explaining (XPL): relation between objects, events, principles; conditional inference; cause-effect, explicit comparison-contrast; statement of principles, theories or laws

Evaluative Process: set of criteria or value system as basis for verification
  Opining (OPN): personal values for statement of policy, judgment or evaluation of event, idea, state of affairs; direct and indirect evaluation included
  Justifying (JUS): reasons or argument for or against opinion or judgment
  Logical Process Not Clear (NCL): cognitive process involved not clear

(5) NUMBER OF LINES IN 3 AND 4 ABOVE

(6) INSTRUCTIONAL MEANINGS: reference to factors related to classroom management

Assignment (ASG): suggested or required student activity;
reports, tests, readings, debates, homework, etc.

Material (MAT): teaching aids and instructional devices

Person (PER): person as physical object or personal experiences

Procedure (PRC): a plan of activities or a course of action

Statement (STA): verbal utterance, particularly the meaning,
validity, truth or propriety of an utterance

Logical Process (LOG): function of language or rule of logic;
reference to definitions or arguments, but not presentation
of such

Action-General (ACT): performance (vocal, non-vocal, cognitive, or emotional) the specific nature of which is uncertain or complex

Action-Vocal (ACV): physical qualities of vocal action

Action-Physical (ACP): physical movement or process

Action-Cognitive (ACC): cognitive process, but not the language or logic of a specific utterance; thinking, knowing,
understanding, listening

Action-Emotional (ACE): emotion or feeling, but not expression of attitude or value

Language Mechanics (LAM): the rules of grammar and/or
usage

(7) INSTRUCTIONAL-LOGICAL MEANING: reference to cognitive processes related to the distinctly didactic verbal moves in the instructional situation

Analytic Process: see (4) above

Defining-General (DEF)

Defining-Denotative (DED)

Defining-Connotative (DEC)

Interpreting (INT)

Empirical Process: see (4) above

Fact Stating (FAC)

Explaining (XPL)

Evaluative Process

Opining (OPN): see (4) above

Justifying (JUS): see (4) above

Rating: reference to metacommunication; usually an evaluative reaction (REA)

Positive (POS): distinctly affirmative rating

Admitting (ADM): mild or equivocally positive rating

Repeating (RPT): implicit positive rating when statement (STA) is repeated by another speaker; also for SOL to repeat vocal action (ACV)

Qualifying (QAL): explicit reservation stated in rating exception

Not Admitting (NAD): rating that rejects by stating the contrary; direct refutation or correction excluded

Negative (NEG): distinctly negative rating

Positive/Negative (PON): SOL requesting positive or negative rating

Admitting/Not Admitting (AON): SOL asking to permit or not permit procedure or action

Extralogical Process: SOL expecting physical action or when logical nature of verbal response cannot be determined

Performing (PRF): asking, demanding, explicit directive or imperative

Directing (DIR): SOL with or without stated alternatives; asking for directive, not permission for specific action

Extralogical Process Not Clear (NCL): extralogical process involved not clear

(8) NUMBER OF LINES IN 6 AND 7 ABOVE

Each pedagogical move is coded as follows:

(1)/(2)/(3)/(4)/(5)/(6)/(7)/(8)

(1) Speaker
(2) Type of Pedagogical Move
(3) Substantive Meaning
(4) Substantive-Logical Meaning
(5) Number of Typescript Lines in (3) and (4)
(6) Instructional Meaning
(7) Instructional-Logical Meaning
(8) Number of Typescript Lines in (6) and (7)

Coding the Protocols

The following excerpt from one of the coded protocols illustrates the coding procedures and interpretation of the coded information.[7]

Excerpt From Protocol

Teacher (Move #1): Now, in order to pacify, or help satisfy, certain groups in American industry and American politics who want high protective tariffs, or who are clamoring for protection, we have inserted into our reciprocal

[7]For a full one-page excerpt see the addendum to this article. R.T.H., editor.

agreements two—what you might call—safeguards which are coming up now as President Kennedy looks for greater authority in the tariff business. (Move #2): What have we inserted in here to give an element of protection or to stifle the outcries of American businessmen who want protection? Two clauses which we call . . . ? Yes?

Pupil (Move # 3). The peril point and the escape clause.

Teacher (Move #4): Right. The peril point and the escape clause.

Code

Move #1 T/STR/BAT/XPL/5/-/-/-
Move #2 T/SOL/BAT/FAC/2/-/-/-
Move #3 P/RES/BAT/FAC/1/-/-/-
Move #4 T/REA/BAT/-/-/STA/POS/1

Interpretation

The teacher focuses on a substantive area by explaining something having to do with tariffs to the extent of five lines (Move #1). He then solicits for two lines with the expectation that a factual response on tariffs will be given (Move #2). A pupil gives a one-line response by stating a fact about tariffs (Move #3). The teacher positively evaluates the statement by the pupil (Move #4).

The entire segment of discourse is an example of a teacher-initiated cycle (STR SOL RES REA).

Reliability

The results . . . indicate a consistently high degree of reliability for all major categories of analysis; agreement ranged from 84 to 96 per cent [between pairs of coders]. Thus, the data strongly support the conclusion that the system devised in this research for a content analysis of classroom discourse is highly reliable.

Emotional Meanings

The semantic differential technique was used to describe each teacher's emotional style in terms of the meanings he conveyed along three dimensions: valence, activity, and strength.[8] Since it seemed reasonable to assume that our interpretations of the emotional meanings expressed by teachers would be quite different from those of the typical high school students who participated in the research, it was decided that emotional meanings should be analyzed from the point of view of student observers. Judges in this part of the study were 11th grade students in a communications class in a senior high school similar to those who participated in the experimental classes. Because of the confidential nature of the tape recordings, ratings were obtained only for thirteen teachers who con-

---

[8]Osgood, Suci, and Tannenbaum. *op. cit.*

sented to have recordings of their classes played for persons other than regular members of the research staff. These ratings served as the basis for analyzing the emotional meanings communicated by the teachers. The correlations [of reliability between sets of judges] obtained are valence, r. 81; activity, r. 75, and strength, r. 84. The results thus indicate adequate internal consistency.

Results

Perhaps the most striking aspects of the results are the remarkable similarities among many of the teachers and classrooms and the stability of individual classes over the four sessions. The data reveal a consistent and generally stable pattern of pedagogical discourse.

1. Teachers dominate the verbal activities of the classrooms studied. The teacher-pupil ratio in terms of lines spoken is approximately 3 to 1; in terms of moves, the ratio is about 3 to 2. The volume of total verbal output is thus considerably greater for the teacher than for the pupil.

2. The pedagogical roles of the teacher and the pupil are clearly defined in terms of the frequency of behavior in each category of pedagogical moves. The teacher is responsible for structuring the lesson, for soliciting responses from pupils and for reacting to pupils' responses. The pupil's primary task is to respond to the teacher's solicitation. Occasionally the pupil reacts to preceding moves, but he rarely uses the reacting move to rate previous action. Only infrequently does the pupil solicit a response from the teacher or from another pupil. Seldom does the pupil spontaneously structure the discourse; when he uses a structuring move he frequently presents it as the fulfillment of a specific assignment made by the teacher, which usually involves a debate or a report.

Pedagogical Move		Total	Percentage of moves by teachers	Percentage of moves by pupils	Percentage of moves by audio-visual devices
Soliciting	SOL	100.	86.0	14.0	0
Responding	RES	100.	12.0	88.0	0
Structuring	STR	100.	86.0	12.0	2.0
Reacting	REA	100.	81.0	19.0	0
	N (SOL)	= 5,135			
	N (RES)	= 4,385			
	N (STR)	= 854			
	N (REA)	= 4,649			

3. Structuring moves account for about six per cent of the discourse in terms of moves spoken. Soliciting, responding and reacting each

account for approximately 30 per cent of the moves. The classes vary somewhat from this pattern, but for the four moves the distribution of variations is fairly restricted, with most classes clustering within a few percentage points of each other. Furthermore, in each of the classes the proportion of moves devoted to each of the pedagogical moves tends to be generally stable over the four sessions. This reflects a consistent style of play within each class.

4. Analysis of teaching cycles centers on the dimensions of initiator (teacher or pupil) of the cycle, pattern of pedagogical moves within the cycle, and the rate at which cycles occur. Classes vary in the extent to which teachers initiate teaching cycles; generally, teachers initiate about 85 per cent of the cycles. Analysis of cycle pattern indicates that the basic verbal interchange in the classroom is the soliciting-responding pattern. Teachers often shape and frame this basic pattern with reacting moves and occasionally with structuring moves, although teachers differ in the extent to which they use the structuring and reacting moves. Classes also differ in the rate at which verbal interchanges take place; the average rate is slightly less than two cycles per minute.

5. In approximately two-thirds of the moves and about three-fourths of the lines speakers refer to or talk about substantive material, that is, the subject matter of international trade. Of all the categories of analysis, classes vary most widely in the substantive meanings expressed. This finding was not anticipated, since the major restriction imposed on the teachers by the research procedure was specification of the substantive material to be covered.

6. With respect to the substantive-logical meanings, approximately one-half of all moves involve empirical meanings (fact stating and explaining). Speakers use the analytic mode (defining and interpreting) and the evaluative mode (opining and justifying) much less frequently; each of these two modes accounts for about one-tenth of the moves in any class. Thus, a major portion of the discourse in the classes studied is devoted to stating facts about and explaining principles and problems of international trade, while considerably less of the discourse is concerned either with defining terms and interpreting statements or with expressing and justifying personal opinions about economic issues.

7. In almost one-half of the moves and approximately one-fourth of the lines of the discourse, speakers convey instructional meanings. It is chiefly the teacher who expresses the instructional meanings. A large proportion of these meanings might be viewed as metacommunications, in that they involve teacher comments about preceding comments by pupils. Other instructional categories that occur with relative frequency are procedures, materials, and assignments. All other instructional categories account for very little of the discourse.

8. The instructional-logical meanings that occur most frequently involve fact stating, usually about procedures, assignments, and other instructional matters. A substantial proportion of statements in this area also deal with teachers directing pupils to perform various actions. Almost all of the remaining instructional-logical entries involve some form of rating reaction by the teacher.

9. With respect to the analysis of emotional meanings, teachers maintain a relatively stable emotional style, insofar as the dimensions of potency and activity are concerned, and, to a lesser degree, in terms of valence. Teachers thus tend to be consistent over time in the kinds of emotional meanings they convey to students.

The Language Game of Teaching[1]

These results provide a description of the language game of teaching. Despite the fact that the rules of this game are not explicitly stated for any of the players, teachers and students in the classrooms under study obviously follow a set of implicit rules with few deviations. These rules define the teaching game. Although classes differ somewhat in details, for the purposes of an initial description of the classroom game, the results indicate that common elements underlie much of the teaching game, in that pupils and teachers follow a consistent set of language rules.

The classroom game involves one player called the teacher and one or more players called pupils. The object of the game is to carry on a linguistic discourse about subject matter, and the final "payoff" of the game is measured by the amount of learning displayed by the pupils after a given period of play. In playing the game, each player must follow a set of rules. If one plays the role of teacher, he will follow one set of rules; if one plays the role of pupil, he will follow a somewhat different, though complementary, set of rules. In fact, the first rule, which might be called "the rule of rules," is that if one is to play the game at all, he will consistently follow the rules specified for his role.

Within the general set of rules defining the game, there are individual differences among teachers and classes in style of play. In one classroom, the teacher or pupils may specialize in one kind of move or sequence of moves, while in another class the players may specialize in a slightly different pattern of discourse. Notwithstanding these variations in style and differences in specialization of moves, the game is played by a consistent set of general rules. These rules are rarely made explicit during the course of play; more often, they are defined implicitly by the ways

[1]A fuller description of The Language Game of Teaching is presented in Section 6, p. 347 of this book. R.T.H., editor.

in which teachers and pupils use these moves. It follows then that if one is to understand the rules of classroom behavior, he must study the functions that the pedagogical moves actually serve in the discourse of teachers and pupils.

Another way to interpret these data is to consider the sequence of pedagogical moves that occurs most commonly in the typical game. This sequence is, essentially, the solicitation-response teaching cycle which is shaped and framed by structuring and reacting moves. The most common type of verbal interchange in the classroom involves a teacher's solicitation and a pupil's response, which is usually followed by an evaluative reaction by the teacher. If this sequence does indeed define a general pattern of classroom discourse, it would seem to be important to investigate this sequence of moves in greater detail, to evaluate its pedagogical effectiveness, and to devise methods of increasing the effectiveness and efficiency of both teachers' solicitations and teachers' reactions.

A ONE-PAGE EXCERPT FROM A PROTOCOL

T: However, to get back to our main point once more, in talking about the U.S. role in, in all this international trade. Our export trade is vital to us. Our import trade is vital to us, and it would upset and shake American economy to a tremendous extent if we were to stop importing or stop exporting. T|REA|IMX|XPL|9|PRC|FAC|2
Let's turn to American investments abroad. You suppose we do invest much money outside of the U.S.? T|STR°|FOR|-|-|PRC|FAC|2
T|SOL|FOR|FAC|2|-|-|-|
P: Yes. P|RES|FOR|FAC|1|-|-|-|
T: In what ways, in what fields? How would it be done? T|SOL□|FOR|XPL|2|-|-|-|
P: Well, a lot of the big companies here in the U.S. will set up companies over in other countries, and that way they can give the workers over there a chance to work

and to sell their products and
the foreign countries can get
the tax off that.⌐———————— P|RES|FOD|XPL|9|-|-|-|

T: I think you put the most important thing last, but that's
true.⌐The branch office in a T|REA|FOD|-|-|STA|QAL|2
foreign country, which in-
volves the exportation of
American capital, is so often
done to avoid paying what? ⌐——— T|SOL■|FOD|XPL|5|-|-|-|

P: Taxes.⌐———————————— P|RES|FOD|XPL|1|-|-|-|

T: What kind of taxes?⌐———————— T|SOL•|FOD|FAC|1|-|-|-|

[*This move begins a STR-SOL-RES teaching cycle.
�口This move begins a SOL-RES-REA teaching cycle.
■This move begins a SOL-RES teaching cycle.
•This move begins a new teaching cycle which is not completed in this short
excerpt. In the full report it turned out to be an SOL-RES teaching cycle. R.T.H.,
editor]

13 A Preliminary Report on Analyses of Classroom Interaction

James J. Gallagher and Mary Jane Aschner

The introduction of many innovations in curriculum and methods has changed the face of American education and has increased interest in methods of evaluation of educational programming. The purpose of the present article is to present a new approach—one involving analysis of classroom interaction—which may be useful in arriving at such an evaluation.

The educational literature teems with examples of past evaluations of educational programs, most of them focused primarily upon the *product*. The measure of the success of a given program was the standing of the child at the end of a period of a kind of educational treatment, or the amount of change the child achieved over a given period of time. Such methods of evaluation have been especially common in research evaluating the usefulness of ability grouping or acceleration. Methods of teaching reading have also been frequent objects of evaluation. In a comparison of reading-method X with reading-method Y, one common procedure has been to obtain two groups of children, presumably com-

Reprinted with permission from the *Merrill-Palmer Quarterly of Behavior and Development*, 9: 183–194, July 1963.

This research has been supported by the Elizabeth McCormick Fund and the Cooperative Research Branch of the U.S. Office of Education.

parable on important variables, with one group being placed in a class-room where they would receive reading-method X, and the other group where they would receive reading-method Y. The children would be tested on reading skills both at the beginning and at the end of the experiment. Such a procedure has been curiously sterile in producing improvements in reading programs and other areas of educational curriculum and planning as well. Why?

Let us suppose that the group mentioned above, who received reading-method Y, obtained scores on reading ability that were superior to those of the group who underwent reading-method X. We may then conclude that there were certain variables at work in the total environment provided by reading-method Y which were superior to those operative in the environment in which reading-method X was applied. The problem confounding the educator lies in the multitude of possible factors that could have been responsible for the resulting differences in the experimental and control group test scores. Was it the organization of content that brought about the improvement? Was it a superior teacher, or his enthusiasm for the new method? Or was the change due to one small part of the total instructional method rather than to the whole? Could not the same benefits be obtained perhaps, merely by adopting only one part of program Y?

Yet faced with such results, the educational administrator must often limit his decision to either accepting or rejecting method Y. This, in short, is the basic defect in attempts that have been made to use the product of the program—or the children's achievement gain—as the criterion for the effectiveness of programming.

An alternative method of evaluation consists in analyses of the teaching process as it goes on in the classroom. Such analyses can be accomplished in the examination of teacher-pupil interaction and of the developmental processes of learning. In analyzing these interaction sequences, it is possible to identify—and to describe—fruitful or fruitless teaching procedures in a way that has not been possible under the conventional "prepost test" type of study.

Prior Interest in Sequence Analysis

Interest in the process of verbal interaction is not new; the present study has profited from the experiences of two different lines of investigation. Rogers (1951) and Snyder (1947) pioneered a series of investigations into the process of psychotherapy through the classification of the verbal interactions of client and counselor relationships. Rogers has commented, "Let it be said at the very outset that in the present stage of our knowledge we do not really know what is the essential process of therapy." Practically all counselors and therapists believe that there is a flow and sequence in the process of counseling itself, but it has not been thoroughly investigated.

In a more specifically educational setting, Aschner (1961) using in-class analysis techniques, has discovered certain conventions and ground rules that tend to shape the course and contexts of classroom operation. Smith (1961) has investigated classroom interaction in an attempt to identify the logical dimensions of the teaching process. Smith points out the importance of studying both teacher and pupil behavior, as well as their mutual interaction. His view of the present state of knowledge of the teaching process is quite similar to that expressed by Rogers.

> Our knowledge of the act of teaching as well as that of taking instruction is meager. Neither of these acts has been investigated sufficiently to justfy from a scientific standpoint fundamental changes in teaching. . . . The act of teaching has received far less attention than its central role in pedagogy would seem to require (pp. 93-94).

There are two major prerequisites to an efficient analysis of the teaching process: (a) some type of classification system which enables the investigator to label teacher-pupil and pupil-pupil interactions, and (b) a theoretical structure which provides a basis for evaluating teacher behaviors in terms of their effectiveness. By using a particular frame of reference or theoretical structure, the investigator can evaluate a given instance of teacher-pupil interaction or a sequence of such interactions to see how closely the observed sample of behavior approximates the theoretical ideal or goal. Other investigators have adopted similar approaches in the study of the classroom or of a particular type of educational program (Flanders, 1960; Spaulding, 1962; and Suchman, 1961).

A Research Project on Productive Thinking

The present research is investigating productive thought processes in gifted children, as these are evidenced within the context of classroom verbal interaction. The definition of productive thinking used in this study is similar to that formulated in the theoretical structure developed by Guilford (1956). We define "productive thinking" as consisting in those divergent, convergent and evaluative operations whereby the individual draws upon available past and present acts, ideas, associations and observations in order to bring forth *new* facts, ideas and conclusions. Productive thinking, so defined, includes both the creative and critical-analytic dimensions of reasoning. The basic data for the present study of verbal interaction were obtained through tape recording five consecutive classroom sessions in 12 classes of intellectually superior children of junior high school age, in a variety of subject matters: Social Studies, Mathematics, Science and English.

The Guilford Classification System

Guilford's *Structure of Intellect* (1956), was developed through a series of studies using factor analytic methodology. The parameters of this theoretical structure consist in the *operations* of thinking, the *content* within which these operations are performed and the *products* which result from the performance of these operations upon the content. Guilford has identified four types of content in his theoretical structure: *figural, symbolic, semantic* and *behavioral*. Figural content is represented by geometric patterns and designs which convey no intrinsic meaning. Symbolic content is made up of signs and signals which convey meaning by representing other things, such as numbers or formulae. Semantic content represents meaning as conveyed in spoken and written language. Behavioral content is identified as the physical actions and social behaviors of the individual. The present research concentrates primarily upon the areas of symbolic and semantic content, since these are emphasized in a school setting.

As products of thinking, Guilford lists *units, classes, relations, systems, transformations* and *implications*. For example: The apple (*unit*) is a tree-grown fruit (*class*). If the wind blows much harder, the roof will be torn off our house (*implication*). A brick has little in common with an ordinary book (*association*), but I could use it for a book-end (*transformation*). The more people there are who want something, the higher the price will be (*system*). The last three of these product categories represent, in reality, more complex combinations of the first three, placed in various relationships with one another.

The present category system was constructed primarily on the operations of intellect as Guilford has described them. Five primary categories have been developed. These are: cognitive memory (*C-M*), convergent thinking (*CT*), divergent thinking (*DT*), evaluative thinking (*ET*), and routine (*R*). The routine category consists in the familiar and conventional interpersonal maneuverings of speakers in the management activities of the classroom setting, and in a number of categories defining behaviors—verbal and otherwise—expressing affect and feeling tone.

In addition to the tape recordings of the classroom proceedings, two observers were present in the classroom during each recorded session, and took extensive notes on the classroom activities. They noted, for example, such things as blackboard diagrams and written material, textbook references, charts, and demonstration apparatus materials. In addition, they tried to identify the more obvious attitudinal dimensions of interaction between teacher and class, such as censure, praise, frustration, humor, etc. Each transcribed classroom session has been classified, unit by unit, by trained judges working with the scoring manual developed for this purpose (Aschner, Gallagher, *et al.*, 1962). These codings are then transferred to a flow chart for more extensive analysis. In order that the reader have some idea of the dimensions of each of these areas of cognitive behavior in the classroom, a brief description is given below.*

Cognitive-memory operations represents the simple reproduction of facts, formulae, or other items of remembered content through use of such processes as recognition, rote memory and selective recall. Some examples of cognitive-memory performance would be seen in the following:

T.: Will you tell us what is the first question on the guidesheet?
Bill: What is the "spoils system"?

T.: What were some of the main points covered in our discussion about mercantilism?
Mary: One of the things we learned was that there was an attempt to keep a favorable balance of trade.

T.: Does anybody remember who was the sixteenth President of the United States?
Bob: Abraham Lincoln.

All of the above are examples of teacher-student interchanges that do not require the student to integrate or associate facts; the questions dealt with are all of the kind that can be handled by direct reference to the memory bank. The sole duty of the student is to select the appropriate response from his store of remembered items. While factual information is clearly indispensable to the development of higher thought processes, it is also obvious that it would be a sterile and uninteresting class that dealt exclusively with this type of question, never moving into the challenge and excitement of more complex operations.

Convergent thinking represents the analysis and integration of given or remembered data. It leads to one expected end-result or answer because of the tightly structured framework through which the individual must respond. Some examples of convergent thinking follow:

T.: If I had six apples and gave John two, how many apples would I have left?
Bob: Four.

*See the addendum to this article for a more complete description of the categories. R.T.H., editor.

T.: Can you sum up in one sentence what you think was the main idea in Paton's novel, *Cry The Beloved Country?*

Pete: That the problem of the blacks and the whites in Africa can only be solved by brotherly love; there is no other way.

Thus, convergent thinking may be involved in the solving of a problem, in the summarizing of a body of material, or in the establishment of a logical sequence of ideas or premises—as, for example, in reporting the way in which a machine works, or in describing the sequence of steps by which the passage of a bill through Congress is accomplished.

Divergent thinking represents intellectual operations wherein the individual is free to generate independently his own data within a data-poor situation, or to take a new direction or perspective on a given topic. Some examples of divergent thinking would be:

T.: Suppose Spain had not been defeated when the Armada was destroyed in 1588 but that, instead, Spain had conquered England. What would the world be like today if that happened?

Sam: Well, we would all be speaking Spanish.

Peg: We might have fought a revolutionary war against Spain instead of England.

Tom: We might have a state religion in this country.

These examples represent teacher-stimulated divergent thinking, but it need not always be teacher-generated. In a regular discussion of the "spoils system," a student may come up with the following:

Well, sure, the spoils systems might be a good thing when a political party is getting started, but what about when there's no party system—like in the United Nations?

Here the student reveals his ability to take off from an established fact or facts and see further implications or unique associations that have not been requested or perhaps even thought of by the teacher. Instances of this type of self-initiated student behavior would also fall under the general category of divergent thinking.

Evaluative thinking deals with matters of judgment, value and choice, and is characterized by its judgmental quality. For example:

T.: What do you think of Captain Ahab as a heroic figure in Moby Dick?

Bob: Well, he was sure brave, but I think he was kind of mean the way he drove the men just because he had this crazy notion of getting back at Moby Dick.

T.: Is it likely that we will have a hard winter?

Mary: Well, I think that the pattern of high pressure areas suggests that we will.

T.: Who was the stronger President, Jackson or Adams?
Mike: Adams.

In the first of the above examples, the student is asked to construct a value dimension of his own in terms of what he considers "heroic," and then to make a judgment as to where on this value dimension he would place Captain Ahab. In the second response, the student is asked to make an estimate or to give a speculative opinion or assessment of probability. A third possibility involves entering a qualification or disagreement, wherein the respondent would offer a modification of a prior judgment of another student; or he may state a counter-judgment, in which he declares direct opposition to the statement of the previous speaker.

The final category, routine, contains a large number of miscellaneous classroom activities. Included here are the attitudinal dimensions of praise and censure of others and of self. Also present are dimensions of *structuring*, a kind of prefatory remark, telling in advance what the speaker intends to say or do, or what he expects someone else to say or do. Other characteristic occurrences, such as humor, as well as the ordinary, "routine" classroom management behaviors—even to requests to close the door or asking what time it is—are included in this primary category.

The excerpt given below represents about one and a half minutes of recorded classroom activity in a science class. The discussion concerned the relationship between gravitational attraction and the weight of a body in space.

[1] *Doug:* All right, then, so that if you weighed one-fourth as much as 10 lbs. you'd weigh 2.5 lbs., and since you go 4,000 miles from—and every time to weigh one-fourth as much, you would go 4,000 miles further than 12,000 miles, and that is 16,000.

T.: At this point, I weigh 10 lbs., 16,000 miles out from the center of the earth.

[2] *Doug:* You said from the surface.

T.: No, it is measured from the center of the earth. 12,000 miles from the surface would be 16,000 miles from the earth.

Doug: Oh.

[3] *T.:* Are you with me now?

Doug: I thought you said to double the distance. . . . (remainder of Doug's comment unclear.)

T.: No, you've got to double that distance every time. So, for example, in order to find out where I would weigh one-quarter as much as I do on the earth, I've got to double that distance. In order to find out where I weigh one-quarter as much as I weigh here, I've got to double that entire distance. So it's . . . 20 . . . 32,000 miles from the center of the earth or it's 28,000 miles from the earth's surface. Now, can you see that if I keep on doing this, and you can see that as I keep on doing this, I'll never, never, ever—Don—as you see that I keep on doing this, I'll never get to a point where I'll weigh nothing. [4] It would always be one-quarter of something. It would always be a small number. I can go out there forever and there will still be a small, a small fraction of an ounce that I would weigh. In other words, the gravitational attraction of any object never stops. It just keeps on going out. It gets less very rapidly but it never gets to nothing. Peter?

[5] *Peter:* Well, it's just like the rabbit who was being chased by the hound and the hound caught up by half as much each time and he never got there but he kept gaining more and more, half as much each time—closer.

[6] *T.:* (Addressing the class) You all understand that problem? /[7] If I'm chasing one of you and every five minutes I get half the distance to you, I'll never reach you. I'll keep getting half the distance to you, but I'll never get there, because there will always be something—some distance between us.

The numbered remarks above represent typical features of teacher-student interaction behavior. These merit a closer consideration:

1. In this instance, Doug is giving a typical example of convergent thinking; he is spelling out the steps that he is following to obtain a solution to the problem.

2. Here, Doug is making a request for clarification, and is also actually questioning the correctness of the teacher's approach. This is a type of response that is usually observed only in the more self-assured students—youngsters who do not hesitate to express their doubts about the correctness of the teacher's position.

3. This type of teacher behavior is classified in the routine category and is called "monitoring-feedback." It is one type of teacher behavior in which the teacher attempts to ascertain whether or not the student or the class as a whole understands the point that he is trying to make.

4. In this instance, the teacher—after a long clarifying explanation—sets forth the general rule or principle underlying the phenomenon that they are discussing. Depending upon one's philosophy, one might suggest, in this instance, that it might have been better for the teacher to elicit the general rule from the students rather than to state it himself.

These are the sorts of points that can be brought under discussion through the use of tapescripts. In this way an experienced teacher, or a teacher-in-training, has the opportunity to examine his own performance and that of the students in the cool and quiet aftermath of the class session. Using tapescripts in this way is not unlike using motion pictures of football games to view on the day after the game, in order to find out why certain plays were successful while others were not. The teacher can profit greatly from a close study of the responses of his students to the ways in which he carries on instruction.

5. Despite the fact that this class sequence centers upon convergent thinking processes, some students, Peter for instance, are irrepressible; such students can be counted upon to come up with unique or unusual associations, as Peter does here by bringing in a highly appropriate analogy. This type of divergent thinking performance is far from com-

monplace, even among groups of highly talented students.

6. This is an example of teacher clarifying behavior in which he restates the analogy that Peter presented, thus to make sure that the students all grasped the point that Peter was trying to make.

7. The diagonal line between the first and second sentences of the teacher's remarks represent the division between thought units on the tapescript. In addition to being a promising tool for research in classroom interaction, the tapescript also provides, as we have said, an opportunity for the teacher to look over both his own performances and those of his students, in order to detect weak points in his own presentation, and to discover particular student problems that escaped him in the swift moment-by-moment pace of the classroom session itself.

Table 1 shows the total thought units classified in one social studies classroom over five consecutive 56-minute sessions. In this class, the boys seemed to be consistently more fluent verbally, and in the flow of ideas in all expressive areas. Using the Mann-Whitney U test, this difference between boys and girls was significant at the .10 level in the area of divergent thinking and total production, and approximated that level in

T A B L E 1   Sex Differences in Expressed Thoughts in Social Studies Class for Gifted Children

		Expressed Thought Processes (Five Consecutive Class Sessions)				
		Cogni- tive Memory	Conver- gent Thinking	Diver- gent Thinking	Evalua- tive Thinking	Total
Boys (N = 10)	Mean Percent of Total	12.8 36	7.7 22	8.9 25	5.6 16	35.0
Girls (N = 9)	Mean Percent of Total	8.0 39	5.1 25	4.1 20	3.1 15	20.3
Teacher	Total Percent of Total	262 52	100 20	31 6	107 22	500
Boys vs. Girls* Mann Whitney U		25.5	28.0	24.0	28.5	24.0

*A U of 24 significant at .10 level.

the three other areas. Despite these differences in production, the proportion of the different thought processes used was quite similar in boys and girls. The interpretation to be applied to these proportions must await further analyses and comparisons with other classroom groups and other teachers.

The teacher's proportion of total thought productions (questions and statements) was rather similar to the students. She produced a higher percentage of cognitive-memory and evaluative responses, but a lower proportion in convergent and divergent thinking. Many of the teacher's cognitive-memory responses represented attempts to clarify and add to student statements, rather than a mere doling out of facts.

The low percentage of teacher divergent questions in comparison with student responses is described in more detail in Figure 1. Figure 1 indicates the relationship of the thought processes expressed by the students to the types of teacher questions posed during the five class sessions.

Although divergent production is presented in this figure, similar graphs can be made for each area of cognitive operation. It can be noted that 17 per cent of the teacher's total question-asking activities was done in divergent thinking in class session I, as opposed to 4 per cent in class session II, and 11 per cent in class session III, etc. It it interesting to note that the profile of the divergent production of both girls and boys follows the same general pattern as that of the teacher. In those sessions during which the teacher asks for more divergent production, the percentages of responses in this area are correspondingly high. When the amount of divergent production requested stays below 5 per cent, the decrease in divergent production by the students is marked.

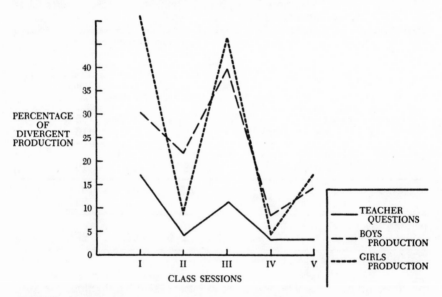

FIGURE 1 Relation of Teacher Questions to Student Divergent Thinking Production.

It may be noted however, that only a slight increase in the teacher's percentage of divergent questions brings forth a large increase in divergent production in the students. This results from the fact that a single question, such as "What would happen if the United States were colonized from the West coast to the East instead of vice versa?", can bring forth as many as fifteen or twenty responses, each related to divergent production on the part of these gifted students.

While the boys produced more divergent responses than the girls, the ratio of their total responses to the divergent area was about the same, as seen in Figure I. In addition to capturing much of the general flavor of the varieties of intellectual operations that occur in the classroom context, it is also possible to trace profiles of individual children, and to determine whether certain students may have problems in expressing themselves in a given area of intellectual operation. Further analyses will also deal more directly with the sequential patterns of teacher-student interaction, as distinguished from that quantification of total, over-all results, as indicated in Table 1 and Figure 1.

The long range goals of the present research include:

1. The construction of a reliable classification system by means of which the verbal interaction of teachers and pupils can be analyzed in any classroom, regardless of subject matter content or student ability level. It may be possible eventually to investigate the question of whether there are fundamental differences in expected   intellectual operations from one subject matter to another—for example, from science to social studies, or from mathematics to English. Such differences might explain, in part, the reason why some students are able to perform quite well in one subject area and yet perform poorly, or in a mediocre way, in other areas.

2. It is hoped that through an analysis of classroom interaction it will be possible to identify examples of certain kinds of highly desirable intellectual performance. It should then be feasible, working backward from these criterion cases, to see what types of teacher behavior or pupil behavior preceded and hence may have stimulated these desirable outcomes. In this manner it may be possible to gain insight into effective methods of teaching for higher conceptual performance, and thus to lay the groundwork for experimental studies in which teachers could—through the strategic use of certain kinds of behavior—seek to raise the level of intellectual productivity of gifted children and, indeed, of children at all levels of ability.

3. Attempts will be made to relate the in-class performance of the children in this study to a wide variety of measures of intellectual aptitude and personality characteristics, measures which were administered to them prior to tape recording their classroom sessions.

4. Measures of family attitudes and behavior will also be related to

individual in-class performances through family interviews and question-naires designed by the sociologist on the project staff.

The eventual goal of the project is to arrive at a description of the intellectual processes that occur in the classroom and, through this, to acquire not only a greater understanding of the teaching process itself, but also to work out more effective ways of training teachers for the stimulation of productive thought processes.

References

Mary Jane Aschner. The language of teaching. In B. O. Smith and R. H. Ennis (Eds.), *Language and concepts in education.* Chicago: Rand McNally, 1961.

Mary Jane Aschner, J. J. Gallagher, W. C. Jenne, Joyce Perry, Helen Farr, & Sibel Afsar. A system for classifying thought processes in the context of class-room verbal interaction. (Mimeographed, Institute for Research on Exceptional Children, University of Illinois, 1962).

N. A. Flanders. *Teacher influence, pupil attitudes and achievement.* Min-neapolis: U. of Minnesota Press, 1960. (Final report, Cooperative Research Project No. 397).

J. P. Guilford. The structure of intellect. *Psychol. Bull.,* 1956, 53, 267-293.

C. R. Rogers. *Client-centered therapy.* Boston: Houghton Mifflin, 1951.

B. O. Smith. A concept of teaching. In B. O. Smith and R. H. Ennis (Eds.), *Language and concepts in education.* Chicago: Rand McNally, 1961.

R. L. Spaulding. Some correlates of classroom teacher behavior in ele-mentary schools. Address given at A.E.R.A. meeting, Atlantic City, New Jersey, February 20, 1962.

W. U. Snyder. *A casebook of non-directive counseling.* Boston: Houghton Mifflin, 1947.

J. R. Suchman. Inquiry training: building skills for autonomous discovery. In W. C. Morse and G. M. Wingo, *Psychology and Teaching.* Chicago: Scott Foresman, 1961.

Addendum: Secondary Classification Categories*

I. ROUTINE (R)

This category includes routine classroom procedural matters such as management of the classroom, the structuring of class discussion and approval or disapproval of the idea or the person.

*Reprinted with permission from *Productive Thinking of Gifted Children* by James J. Gallagher, U.S. Department of Health, Education, and Welfare, Office of Education; Cooperative Research Project No. 965. Urbana, Institute for Research on Exceptional Children, College of Education, University of Illinois, 1965.

The full classification system and instructions are presented in a supplementary publication, Aschner-Gallagher System for Classifying Thought Processes in the Con-text of Classroom Verbal Interaction (Urbana, Ill.: University of Illinois, 1965). R.T.H., editor.

MANAGEMENT

Mq— *Question:* Requests or invitations to speak; calling for questions, as in "Anybody have a question?"

Mp— *Procedure:* Announcements or procedural instructions, given or requested for individuals or the group as a whole.

Ma— *Aside:* Incidental or parenthetical comment; gratuitous content.

Mnc— *Nose-Counting:* Calling for or responding with a show of hands for a tally or canvas.

Mfb— *Feedback:* Request for or response with signs from group as to whether or not the speaker's actions or remarks are clearly understood.

Mw— *Work:* Non-verbal actions or seatwork going on in connection with current discussion or class proceedings.

X— Unclassifiable response primarily due to technical recording difficulties.

STRUCTURING

Sts— *Self-Structuring:* Conventional prefatory move to signal content and purpose of one's own next remarks or behavior.

Sto— *Structuring Other(s):* Engineering next speech or actions of others(s). Monitoring other's performance. Pump-priming to keep discussion going on a point already before the class.

Stf— *Future Structuring:* Forecast of future activity, study, learning, etc. beyond this particular class session.

Stc— *Class Structuring:* Focusing class attention on point to be emphasized or taken up; laying groundwork for question or problem; probing, pushing, adding data for bogged-down class (teacher only).

VERDICT

Ver— *Verdict:* (+ or −) Impersonal praise or reproach on quality of *academic* performance of individual or group.

Verp— *Personal Verdict:* (+or −) Personal praise or reproach of individual. (Occasionally by T on whole class) Negative Verp generally on deportment.

Agr— AGREEMENT: (+ or −) Acceptance or rejection of content; conceding a point; *not* permission-giving nor procedural.

S— SELF REFERENCE: Speaker's personal report or comment upon or about self. Often conventional device; cautionary tactic.

Du— DUNNO: Explicit indication that one does not know.

Mu— MUDDLED: Speaker confused, mixed up, flustered.

Hu— HUMOR: Remark of evident witty, humorous, or comic intent; response (usually laughter) to same.

II. COGNITIVE-MEMORY (C-M)

C-M operations represent the simple reproduction of facts, formulas and other items of remembered content through use of such processes as recognition, rote memory and selective recall.

Scr— SCRIBE: Giving a spoken or written spelling or exemplification of a work or expression.

RECAPITULATION

Req— *Quoting:* Rote recitation or literal reading from text, paper or notes in hand.

Rep— *Repetition:* Literal or nearly verbatim restatement of something just said.

Rec— *Recounting:* Narration of past extra-class occurrence.

Rev— *Review:* Recitation of material which occurred or was discussed in current or past class session.

CLARIFICATION

Clm— *Clarifying Meaning:* Rendering a previous statement more intelligible either by (a) restating or rephrasing or (b) adding informative details.

Clq— *Clarifying Qualification:* Rendering a previous statement more accurate either by (a) "Entering a rider" upon the remark or (b) entering an explicit correction.

FACTUAL

Fs— *Fact Stating:* Requests for and recitations of items taken to be matters of fact.

Fd— *Fact Detailing:* Spinning out further a prior assertion of fact or other statements (As, Exr) in which factual items were mentioned.

Fm— *Factual Monologue:* Reporting of factual material in the form of a monologue during which verbal exchange is conventionally excluded.

III. CONVERGENT THINKING (CT)

Convergent thinking is thought operation involving the analysis and integration of given or remembered data. It leads to one expected result because of the tightly structured framework which limits it.

TRANSLATION

> Tr— *Translation:* Shift of conceptual material from symbolic or figural content to semantic, or vice versa.

ASSOCIATION

> As—*Association:* Involving likenesses and differences; degrees of comparison; and relationships of direction, spatial position and/or classification, etc.

EXPLANATION

> Exr— *Rational Explanation:* Asking or telling why X is the case; why Y caused X, etc. Substantiating a claim or conclusion by citing evidence.
> Exv— *Value Explanation:* Asking or telling why X is good, bad, useful, important, etc. Justifying a rating, viewpoint, or value-based judgment by giving reasons why.
> Exn— *Narrative Explanation:* Step-by-step account of how something is done, how a mechanism works, or of what led up to an event or given outcome.

CONCLUSION

> Gen— *Generalization:* Integration of prior remarks by slightly more general reformulation.
> Cons— *Summary Conclusion:* Summary reformulation, often serial or enumerative, of material treated in discussion or reading.
> Conl— *Logical Conclusion:* Calling for a deductively drawn implication from material presented.

IV. EVALUATIVE THINKING (ET)

Evaluative thinking deals with matters of value rather than matters of fact and is characterized in verbal performance by its judgmental character.

Ura— *Unstructured Rating:* A value judgment produced or requested on some idea or item in terms of a scale of values provided by the respondent.

Uju— *Unstructured Judgment:* A value judgment produced or requested on some idea or item wherein the value dimension has already been provided.

STRUCTURED

Svp— *Structured Probability:* An estimate or speculative opinion is given or requested as to the likelihood of some occurrence or situation.

Svc— *Structured Choice:* Speaker calls for or declares his position as a choice between alternatives (not between *Yes or No* answers).

QUALIFICATION

Qj— *Qualified Judgment:* An offer or request for a rider or modification to a prior value judgment. Also, attempts to make more precise the value dimension discussed.

Q-c— *Counter Judgment:* Speaker declares a directly opposed position with respect to value statement of a previous classroom speaker.

V. DIVERGENT THINKING (DT)

In a Divergent Thinking sequence, individuals are free to independently generate their own ideas within a data-poor situation, often taking a new direction or perspective.

El— ELABORATION: Structured or free (s or f). Building upon a point already made; filling out or developing a point, but not shifting to a new point, often by concocting instances or examples.

Ad— DIVERGENT ASSOCIATION: (s or f) Constructing a relationship between ideas, casting the central idea into sharper and often unexpected perspective, by comparisons, analogies, etc.

Imp— IMPLICATION: (s or f) Extrapolation beyond the given, projection from given data—typically by antecedent—consequent or hypothetical construction—to new point(s) of possibility.

Syn— SYNTHESIS: Spontaneous performance, tying in, integrating the current central idea with an entirely new point or frame of reference. May be a variation or reversal of a previous conclusion.

Double Paired Ratings: The complex nature of verbal classroom interaction often requires the combination of more than one of the above described categories.

14 Hypothetical Thinking in Education

George S. Maccia

The rude awakening brought about by recent advances in Russian technology has brought on a flood of charges and counter-charges about the condition of education in the American schools. It has been said often that schools are developing a "group-mindedness" among our youth which depreciates individual excellence and effort. As a remedy some are calling for a return to hard "facts" and the so-called mind-sharpening disciplines of mathematics and science. Against the sound and fury of current controversies, I suggest that the solution to the problem for education in democracy does not lie in the reemphasis of certain specific subject contents severely taught. Furthermore, it lies only partially in social adjustment. It lies, rather, in the development of the quality of thinking on the part of individual students.

Whether shaping satellites or democracy, individuals who think creatively and build co-operatively are necessary. Creative thinking employs both analysis and synthesis. Analysis and synthesis form part of the activities in which students are engaged in our nation's schools. In our classrooms experience is examined, distinctions are noted, categories are proposed, concepts are formed, concepts are related, and re-formed.

"Hypothetical Thinking in Education" by George S. Maccia is reprinted with permission from *Educational Theory*, 10: 182–186, July, 1960.

Yet, creative thinking, unfortunately, is not emphasized in any great measure either in current educational practices or in current proposals for improvement. Certainly, individual differences in physiological equipment, cultural backgrounds, and in motivation do account in part for the small measure of creative thinking achieved in our schools. One might argue, indeed, as many do, that only a few are gifted. Nevertheless, I aver that there is a mind-set in much of our current methodology which shackles thought.

In our current methodology we have come to prize two notions about formal education both of which have been shaped to operate within a machinery of mass production. On the one hand we assert the primacy of subjects rooted in traditions of classical literature which we call the Humanities. On the other hand we assert the primacy of subjects rooted in traditions of naive empiricism which we call the Sciences. In the Humanities we dish out the gems of the past in order to preserve our heritage and to provide models for 'liberal' thinking. In the Sciences the most abstract conceptions are forced into ill-fitting models of actual experience in order to support the contention that experience teaches. Such methods, unfortunately, assure that meanings are confined to what is said to be actual, e.g., the descriptions of the writings of yesterday's creative thinkers and the quantitative relating of particular events. In both cases we cripple our youth by building around them a wall of actual experience too high for them to see what lies beyond. The creative man must re-make his experience. He must leap the wall and explore the region of the possible.

The thesis of this paper is that thinking analytically at any level of human discourse involves not only thinking in terms of what is actual, but also thinking in terms of experience which is not actual. In other words, thinking in terms of possibles is equally involved and is of utmost importance. The earth satellites remind us every ninety minutes or so of the necessity to think the possible.

If credence is to be given the claim that our current methodology in education cripples our youth, further explanation of what I mean by *thinking in terms of what is actual* and *thinking in terms of what is possible* is in order.

Thinking What Is Actual

Thinking in terms of the actual is the thinking we do when we describe particular objects or events. Our thoughts about the actual take the form, "Here is a . . ." That is to say, they are expressed in categorical statements. For instance, "Here is a black crow" is such a statement. Furthermore, thinking in terms of the actual leads us to summarize our descriptions about experience. We set forth descriptive generalizations such as, "All crows are black." When descriptive generalizations are a part of science, they are known as empirical laws. Boyle's law—"At constant temperature, the volume of a gas varies inversely with the external pressure" is an example from the physical sciences.

Thinking what is actual is, of course, a necessary skill for the isolation of objects and events from experience and for the grouping together of isolates of like kind. Descriptive generalizations are important tools in analytical thinking. They are used widely in everyday affairs, as well as in science. Descriptive generalizations, unfortunately, are often regarded as the essence of thinking and of science. Consider the following statements: "Science," one student reported on an examination paper, "is a factual study built on definite concrete knowledge"; "The study of science is a purely physical task," reported another. How often have you read or heard similar statements about science? If more evidence is required that descriptive generalizations are often regarded as the essence of science, I refer the reader to any of the several textbooks in the teaching of elementary science methods. And for evidence that it is not uncommon in education to place a premium upon thinking in terms of what is actual, I suggest that the reader examine the current crop of textbooks on audio-visual methods in education.

Thinking What Is Possible

Thinking what is possible is hypothetical thinking. Such thinking is characterized in part by the employment of conditional propositions which are of the form, "if p then q." A proposition of this form is suppositional.

In the sciences conditional statements are often about inferred entities—e.g., statements about molecules or atoms or electrons. Consider the following statement: "If the kinetic energy of a gas is increased then molecules travel at a higher rate of velocity." The inferred entity, molecule, which is talked about in the preceding statement differs from an actual entity. It is derived, not observed. Thus, the statement is suppositional rather than actual.

Hypothetical thinking also employs the contrary-to-fact statement which differs from the conditional statement in being expressed in the subjunctive mood. For example, the chemist states: "If the temperature were to fall to − 273°C there would be zero volume." This statement does not relate directly to what is actual. All known substances solidify at a temperature above − 273°C, thereby fixing observable volume at some definite value greater than zero. Every schoolboy and every physical scientist uses the concept of Absolute Zero, a concept which is derived from the proposition just stated. Although the schoolboy may be, the scientist is not disturbed by the obvious discrepancy between his thinking and his experience of the actual. The scientist knows that he can describe the actual with greater certainty by considering what is possible, rather than by solely considering what is actual.

Hypothetical Thinking and Problem Solving

We have seen that analytical thinking has, at least, two characteristics: description of the actual and consideration of the possible. It is now my intention to point out that problem solving relies more on hypothetical thinking than it does on description of particulars and descriptive generalizations.

Much is made of the importance of contact between the thinker and something actual. Emphasis is placed upon experience of the actual. It must be noted that the experience of the possible is justifiable in science, only so far as it is rooted in what is actual. Such a prescription is necessary if wild speculation is to be avoided. Some educators place too high a premium, however, on description and descriptive generalizations. Problem solving is looked upon merely as a guess concerning the conclusions of the study which are to be expressed in the form of descriptive generalizations. Such a procedure would never conclude with a derived entity such as Absolute Zero, for the particulars which could be observed say nothing directly about it—indeed, they are all against such a formulation. Absolute Zero is a hypothetical entity, remains a hypothetical entity, but it provides, nevertheless, part of the means for solving certain kinds of problems.

The function of hypothetical thinking in problem solving has been minimized. The emphasis upon particulars tends to restrict thinking to that which is descriptive of what is actual and places a premium upon the weighting of hypothetical thinking on the side of the greatest number of particulars. I am not suggesting that particulars be ignored. I am suggesting that we can value particulars too highly, and may fall into the error of Comté. As Peirce put it: "Comté's own notion of a verifiable hypothesis was that it must not suppose anything that you are not able directly to observe. From such a rule it would be fair to infer that he would permit Mr. Schlieman to suppose he was going to find arms and utensils at Hissarlik but would forbid him to suppose that they were either made or used by any human being, since no such beings could ever be detected by direct percept. He ought on the same principle to forbid us to suppose that a fossil skeleton had ever belonged to a living ichthyosaurus." (V.579)[1]

[1]*Collected Papers of Charles Sanders Peirce*, ed. by Hartshorne and Weiss.

The history of science reveals that frequently in theory construction fruitful hypothetical thinking runs counter to what is suggested by the greater body of particulars. We are all now aware of the tremendous impact of Einstein's hypothetical thinking in our everyday world. His thinking grew out of the findings of the Michelson-Morley experiments and these, in turn, ran counter to the greater body of particulars then known about physical phenomena. Consider also De Broglie, who turned his back on the particulars and hypothesized phase waves which are mathematical devices not directly related to particulars, but which make possible mathematical reconciliation of waves and particles existing together in mechanical motion. Schroedinger, in developing his generalized wave mechanics, likewise hypothesized special conditions that are totally absurd in so far as our actual spatial experience is concerned. He postulated nine dimensions for the helium atom and 279 dimensions for an atom of uranium, thereby resolving some of the contradictions in the wave-particle theory of matter.

Dirac's solution was even further removed from the particular than either De Broglie's or Schroedinger's. His mathematical symbols were completely general and did not define or represent any actual conditions or events. Algebraic axioms, some restrictive assumptions, the deductions from these assumptions, and the relations between the equations evolved from the entire set of building blocks for his solution to the wave-particle problem. Dirac's solution for the integration of scattered and contradictory data provides a case for problem solving which is greatly removed from the naive conception of problem solving often propounded in what is called the "Method of Science."

Doing things and being done by things is not the be all and end all of problem solving. Seeing possible relations within a system of thought seems to provide significant contributions to the solutions of problems.

Hypothetical Thinking and Education

In requesting that a closer look be given to hypothetical thinking and its role in the solving of problems, I do not suggest that counting angels on pinheads is a fruitful educational exercise. Thinking about the actual is one aspect of analytical thinking. It is a necessary aspect, for it anchors hypothetical thinking ultimately to experience to which all men can attest. What I would warn against is the tendency to think what is actual so rigidly that only one possible set of relations is seen. In order to solve problems, analytical thinking must include what is possible. The thinker must not only allow for different relationships, but must break the bonds of conventional relationships and alter patterns of thinking which have become habitual or which follow exclusively the suggestions which appear to be called for by particulars.

In order to illustrate my meaning, consider the following example:

Problem

. . .

. . .

. . .

You are asked to connect the dots in the figure by means of four straight lines drawn continuously. In order to accomplish this integration, the individual must surmount certain conventions or patterns of integration which are suggested by the apparent relation of the dots:

(1) the dots mark off the area within which the lines are to be drawn,

(2) each line must pass through the same number of dots, and

(3) the figure is completely closed within the configuration of the dots. The solution to this particular problem requires thinking which considers relationships which are not suggested by the dots themselves. A reorientation is required. The solver of this problem must think what is possible. In other words, hypothetical thinking is required, as the solution reveals.

If the foregoing analysis of the nature of hypothetical thinking has merit certain conclusions follow for education. More emphasis should be placed upon hypothetical thinking. Students should be confronted by situations which call for the reorientation of his experience. He must be asked to see possible relations. He should be encouraged to think suppositionally.

Solution

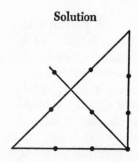

Some steps in this direction have been taken in the physical sciences. Students are asked to solve problems of the following sort:

(1) You have a closed box which contains an infinite supply of oxygen. In the box is a lighted candle which is fastened to the bottom of the box. The box is dropped off a cliff and falls freely for several thousand feet. What would happen inside the box?

(2) You are falling freely in space. In each hand you hold a bar of the same kind of metal. One of the bars is a magnet. How can you tell which bar is the magnet?

In order to solve these problems, the student must think what is actual. He must know the particulars of science in their ordinary relationships. But it is not the knowledge of particulars alone which brings the solution. The student must think in terms of a world of experience in which there is no gravity and deduce what is possible in such a world. In other words, the student must think hypothetically.

Reorientation of thinking seems to be the first step to thinking creatively. Once reorientation occurs, habitual patterns of thinking are no longer relied upon exclusively. Insights about possible relationships, hitherto undreamed, are allowed. The thinker, whether he be a scientist or a poet, becomes free to create new theories or new language forms. In this way a new world of experience is synthesized.

Thus, it appears that education has a twofold task. First, activities should be provided which enable the student to acquire mastery of the tools, methods, and relationships which have been developed for ordering experience. Second, the student should be involved in activities which will enable him to obtain a sensitivity to possible relationships which are outside the experience in which he normally operates. The student must deal with the possible.

15 Taxonomy of Cognitive Behavior: A System for the Analysis of Intellectual Processes

Jeaninne Nelson Webb

How do students and teachers spend their time in the classroom? What goes on there? These are the kinds of questions that systematic observation of classroom behavior attempts to answer. Systematic observation provides a framework through which teaching-learning behavior can be viewed and assessed. The social-intellectual environment of the classroom is exceedingly complex; diverse observational systems have been developed to enable researchers to quantify and analyze the factors which combine to create this complexity.

The systematic observation movement has been directed largely towards observation of verbal interaction which provides measurement of the social-emotional climate of the teaching-learning acts. This focus has produced invaluable data. Yet no matter how precise and valid the information, interaction analysis has permitted only a one dimensional view of classroom behavior. It has long been assumed that the school's main task has been to promote intellectual activity; hence the analysis of

Reprinted with permission from *Journal of Research and Development in Education*, 4: 23–33, Fall, 1970.

cognitive behavior is of major importance in investigating the educational process.

The problems in developing an instrument to identify and quantify cognitive behaviors systematically have been difficult to solve. The search for a system which would enable an observer to efficiently and effectively view and record cognitive behavior in relevant terms has been an arduous one. The *Taxonomy of Cognitive Behavior (TCB)*,* an observational system designed to measure the cognitive behavior of both students and teachers in a classroom, is the outgrowth of this search. Based upon a widely used and accepted theory of cognition, the *Taxonomy of Educational Objectives: Cognitive Domain,* Bloom (1956), it is a sign system of items organized in a somewhat hierarchical order from the more simple to the more complex of cognitive activities.

The *Taxonomy of Cognitive Behavior* reflects, as does the Bloom *Taxonomy,* an instructional theory which postulates the teacher's basic task in the classroom as the guidance of students in the acquisition of knowledge and the development of intellectual abilities and skills. This theory demands the student go beyond the mere ingestion of facts and information, to acquire methods and techniques for using them. The learner's task has been defined as a search for appropriate information and methods from previous experiences which are brought to bear on new problems. (Bloom, 1956) This requires 1, a background of knowledge or procedures which can be utilized; 2, some analysis or understanding of the new situation; 3, facility in discerning the appropriate relations between previous experiences and new situations; 4, skills in the design and application of techniques to meet the new situation; and finally, 5, critical abilities in judging the worth or value of the outcome of the endeavor. In other words, the student must acquire both knowledge and the intellectual abilities and skills to deal with them.

Few educators would disagree that this is, indeed, the basic task of the schools. Yet it has been suggested that the acquisition of knowledge has dominated education, that the majority of our institutions and their teachers emphasize the acquiring of information and neglect the development of cognitive processes which are needed in dealing with knowledge. With the *Taxonomy of Cognitive Behavior,* it is possible to more precisely define and measure this allegation. The *TCB,* used by trained observers in classroom situations, provides data which indicate the kinds of intellectual behavior both students and teachers are evidencing and to some extent the frequency with which they occur. Through the use of the *TCB,* it can be discovered if the acquisition of information is the central focus of teachers and students or if they are engaged in cognitive

*Developed by Bob Burton Brown, Richard Ober, Robert Soar, and Jeaninne Webb, University of Florida, 1967.

behaviors which go beyond the memorization and recall of facts and information.

In addition to describing the intellectual range of the classroom activities, data from the *TCB* can also make an important contribution to instructional theory. When the same classroom behavior is observed and analyzed with both cognitive and climate dimensions, the relationships between social-emotional and intellectual behavior can be identified and examined. This kind of information enables the theorist to develop researchable hypotheses in which teaching behaviors can be systematically varied to identify more specific relationships among teacher/ student affective and cognitive behaviors.

Theoretical Foundation

If an observation system is to yield useful information, it must be based upon an explicated theory or rationale. Bloom's *Taxonomy* was chosen as a widely used and accepted theory of cognition on which to base the *Taxonomy of Cognitive Behavior*.

The items which comprise the *TCB* reflect seven levels of thinking or cognitive behavior. They are labeled knowledge, translation, interpretation, application, analysis, synthesis and evaluation. These levels follow the system developed by Bloom and others, with the exception of the translation and interpretation levels which Bloom included under the heading of comprehension. However, translation and interpretation represent distinct kinds of thinking and are treated as separate levels in this instrument.*

These levels of cognitive behavior are assumed to represent increasingly complex intellectual skills and are hierarchical in nature.† The knowledge level is represented by almost one-third of the instrument's items, the basis on which successive cognitive behaviors are built. Within this level, the items have been subdivided into three separate categories, (1) knowledge of specifics, (2) knowledge of processes to deal with specifics and (3) knowledge of universals and abstractions. They include those behaviors which emphasize remembering, recognition and recall. Each of the three categories requires the knowledge of progressively more abstract material but all are at the memory level; they do not require the learner to deal with the information. No hierarchy is assumed among the items within this level or any of the others, but rather between the seven levels.

*A precedent for this distinction was set by Norris Sanders in his book *Classroom Questions: What Kinds?* in which he has used the Bloom system to categorize the types of questions teachers ask. Harper & Row Book Co., 1966.

†See the Overview to this section for comment and clarification. R.T.H., editor.

The second level, translation, is dependent upon the learner's possession of relevant knowledge. The task is to convert communication into known terms; it requires the understanding of the literal message in the communication. Communication is used here in its broadest sense; it could be a demonstration, a field trip, a musical work, a verbal message or in pictorial or symbolic form. Closely related to comprehension is the third level, interpretation. At the interpretation level the individual not only identifies and comprehends ideas as in translation but also understands their relationships. It goes beyond repetition and rephrasing of the parts of a communication to determine the larger and more general ideas contained in them. Hence the person who can restate ideas in his own words but cannot summarize them has reached the translation but not the interpretation level.

The upper levels of the *Taxonomy of Cognitive Behavior* represent behavior in which the individual must deal with knowledge in some manner. At the fourth level, application, he must know the information he is working with well enough to be able to demonstrate its use in a new situation. The task is to bring to bear upon given material or situations the appropriate information to solve a problem. Application, as distinguished from comprehension, involves transfer of training. It is based upon the person's being able to apply previous learning in a new or novel situation without having to be shown how to use it. The fifth and sixth levels, analysis and synthesis, represent contrasting intellectual tasks. At the analysis level, there is an emphasis on the breakdown of material into parts in order to detect the relationships of the parts and the way they are organized. Whereas at the synthesis level, the individual puts together elements and parts in order to form a whole in such a way as to constitute a pattern or structure that was not evidenced before. This entails recombining parts of earlier experiences into a new organization, one that is unique to the synthesizer. In analysis, the person takes apart a given whole; in synthesis he creates a whole.

Evaluation is the last level of the *TCB*. It is the level which describes activities of conscious judgment-making. It involves the use of criteria or standards to determine the worth or value of methods, materials or ideas. Evaluations must be distinguished from opinions which are usually made from an emotional or affective base. Only judgments supported by clear criteria or specific evidence are to be recorded in the evaluation level.

Thus the theory represented by the *Taxonomy of Cognitive Behavior* postulates that the learner must acquire knowledge (the lowest level) and be able to comprehend it (the second and third levels) before he can deal with it in some manner (represented by upper levels).

A clarification needs to be made at this point; simplicity and complexity are not synonymous with concreteness and abstractness. It is perfectly possible to deal with concrete objects at a complex intellectual level or to have knowledge of a highly abstract idea, which would represent the lowest cognitive level. The assumption that intellectual abilities grow increasingly complex in nature does not suggest that the upper levels are only present in the cognitive behavior of the mature individual. Rather they can occur in some form at each developmental stage, although the younger child will deal with more concrete information as he performs these activities. The *TCB* observation system subscribes to the theory that intellectual development involves both the acquisition of knowledge and its utilization. There are distinct and discrete intellectual abilities which must be employed in this utilization; these abilities can be discriminated and may occur in some form at each developmental stage of the child.

Development of the Taxonomy of Cognitive Behavior

To be adequately based on theory, an observational system must meet the criterion of comprehensiveness. The items or categories which comprise the system must be so designed that its theoretical foundation is thoroughly represented and the kinds of cognitive activities which occur in classroom situations be included. It must also be comprehensive in the sense that it can be used at all levels of the educational system, from nursery school through higher education and in all subject matter areas.

In an effort to meet this criterion, the *TCB* in its present form has undergone several revisions. Initially over ninety items were written in an attempt to include all of the cognitive behaviors which could possibly occur in the classroom at each of the levels of the hierarchy. This original compilation of items was then examined to discover those which tended to overlap or describe the same behavior. Duplications were removed, the language was clarified and overlapping items were combined. The instrument was then given a dry run by a group of potential observers using videotaped episodes of classroom behaviors. Through experiences derived from these sessions in which items were discussed, clarified and revised, a form similar to the present instrument was developed to be tested in the field. A group of twelve observers was then trained to use the instrument; training was accomplished in sessions in which videotapes of classroom teaching were observed and recorded by observer-trainees. As these observers were a highly select group which had participated in the original developmental sessions, their familiarity with and knowledge of the theoretical foundation of the instrument expedited the training. Reliability of observers was established by computing between-observer agreement a far from rigorous measure of reliability but one which was believed to be adequate for a field test.

The first field test of the instrument was made in a single school system in which there were one hundred and thirty-two classrooms at all grade levels, first through twelfth, and in all subject matter areas. Each teacher was visited for a single, thirty minute period. The observations produced 132 scores which represented the cognitive behavior of both teachers and students. The unique feature of this field trial was that the *Taxonomy* was used in conjunction and simultaneously with two other observation instruments, the *Reciprocal Category System* and the *Teacher Practices Observation Record*. Thus there were three records made of the same classroom situations during each observation period. Factor analysis of the resulting data revealed that the *Taxonomy of Cognitive Behavior* did measure aspects of classroom behavior which were not tapped by the other systems. As would be expected, correlations were found between certain pupil and teacher cognitive behaviors and factors of the other two systems; however there was a clear indication that the *TCB* reflected aspects of behavior not mirrored by the other systems.

Results of the field test were encouraging. It had been possible to train observers to use the instrument with a respectable degree of precision, thus establishing the communicability of the system, at least with selected observers. To be of practical use in the field an observation system must not be so esoteric in language or design that it can only be used by those who develop it.

It was also possible to begin to put some faith in the validity of the instrument. The results of gathering and analyzing data collected from the same classroom behavior with three observation systems made it possible to conclude that each system was, indeed, assessing properties of behavior which were unrelated enough to warrant the use of each to study the teaching-learning situation. This conclusion made a tentative step towards establishing construct validity for the *TCB*. Much additional research must be done before firm statements can be made. At the present, it can only be assumed that the instrument is measuring aspects of classroom behavior different from those sampled by other systems.

This field test also proved the comprehensiveness of the instrument in measuring behavior at varying developmental stages of children. High level cognitive activities were found at all grade levels, indicating not only that the instrument could be used successfully throughout the school system but also that even very young children are capable of and do perform at the higher levels of thinking. The *TCB* proved to be comprehensive in terms of curriculum content also. It was found to be usable in subject areas dealing with the major disciplines and the non-academic areas as well.

From the experiences in using the instrument in live classroom situations, it was found that the *Taxonomy* seemed to be fairly comprehensive also in terms of representing the complexities of intellectual behavior. It seemed that categorizing specific behaviors, one of the major problems in designing instruments to assess cognition, had been solved. Within a five second interval an individual may in a single verbal response trigger several items at multiple levels. By use of a sign system this problem of categorizing such behavior has been greatly reduced. The observer does not need to make a judgment as in which single classification a behavior must be categorized. He simply responds to all of the items involved. This does not completely free him of judgments; this system, like all others, is not "observer proof." It does however free him from having to fit complex behaviors into single pigeon holes. The solution of this problem of categorizing specific cognitive behaviors is a major research contribution. The theory reflected by Bloom's *Taxonomy* had up to this time defied effective utilization in an observational system. The use of a sign system in which items that describe behaviors can be checked as they occur within a specified interval of time has proved to be a useful method of dealing with the problem.

After undergoing this rather extensive field trial, the instrument was altered slightly by both the addition, deletion and further clarification of specific items. This is as it stands now. Scoring procedures were developed which can be calculated quickly, by hand, and require no more than fourth grade mathematical skills. Each observation produces two scores, one for the teacher and one for the students. It is also possible to plot a profile which indicates the range and frequency of the various levels recorded and which provides for ease of interpretation.

Utilization of the Taxonomy of Cognitive Behavior

Training of Observers

To utilize an observation system, observers must be trained to record accurate and pertinent data. Two approaches to training can be made, depending upon how the data is to be used. In each of the instances in which the *TCB* has been used for research purposes, observers have been graduate students who began training sessions with a thorough understanding of the rationale of the system and were highly motivated to "succeed" as reliable observers. Using video-tapes of actual classroom behavior it has been possible to achieve high between-observer agreement and fairly consistent within-observer agreement after ten to twelve hours of training. Garrison (1970) reports between-observer reliability coefficients of .93-.98 using these techniques. Webb (1970) has found consistency or within-observer coefficients ranging from .80-.85 for a selected group of observer validity, in terms of agreement with criterion scores developed by the trainer, have been acceptable.

One of the problems in using video-tape to train observers has been the difficulty in finding tapes which reflect all the items on the instrument. A project is now under way to produce manuals, tapes and films which will standardize training procedures and provide criterion films from which reliability and validity estimates can easily be established.

A second approach to training has been used in the education of pre-service and in-service teachers for purposes of teacher evaluation. In this case the observers have been teachers usually selected by some outside agency who seldom have had experience with or knowledge of the cognitive theory on which the instrument is based. As the purpose of training these observers has been to sensitize them to their own classroom performance, precision of measurement has not been as important a goal as their conceptualizing the rationale of the instrument. One of the training techniques which has proved highly successful with teachers has been the production rather than recognition of behavior represented by items of the instrument. With the use of portable video recorders in training sessions, teachers can be asked to simulate lessons which will produce behavior reflected by specified items, the micro-lessons are then recorded and played back enabling the group to then make judgments as to whether the behavior was produced. Not only has this been a particularly effective training procedure, it has also produced transfer to the trainee's own classroom behavior.

These two techniques of training, recognition of behavior and reproduction of behavior, are not mutually exclusive. However, the emphasis on the type of training should reflect the goals of training: to produce highly competent observers who will gather precise and valid research data or to help classroom teachers and their supervisory personnel gain some insight into their own teaching behavior for the purposes of evaluation and professional growth.

Research

Several research studies have utilized the *Taxonomy of Cognitive Behavior* as a method for collecting classroom behavior data. Two types of information have been gained from the studies. One is descriptive in nature and indicates the levels of cognition in school classrooms observed; the second has tentatively identified some of the relationships between cognitive behavior and other factors in the teaching-learning situation.

Results from the original field study of the *TCB*, in which 132 classroom teachers were observed, reported by Wood (1969) and Bane (1969) indicate that cognitively most classroom time is spent by both students and teachers at the knowledge level. Wood reports more total behavior for both teachers and students was recorded at the lowest cognitive level (memory of specific bits of information) than all other levels combined. In a study of 71 student teachers at West Virginia University, Cunningham (1970) found similar results. The most frequent cognitive behavior for both student teachers and their pupils was at the knowledge level. The translation and interpretation levels were second and third most common for both. Teachers were found to use analysis more than application, pupils more application than analysis. Synthesis and evaluation were seldom evident. The median scores of both groups was at the knowledge level. These results are perhaps discouraging but not surprising. They reflect the common cultural expectation of schooling—the teacher as the giver of information, the student as the receiver.

Data from the *Taxonomy of Cognitive Behavior* has been analyzed to identify the relationships between intellectual behavior, classroom climate and instructional procedures. Two studies reported by Wood and others (1969, 1970) have indicated that such relationships do exist. These are highly complex and are related to many variables. One of the most interesting findings has been the relationship of teacher and student cognitive levels to student verbal behavior and instructional methods. It was found that when the teacher based his instruction on student ideas, using information and hypotheses which were student initiated, there was a close relationship between high level cognition of teacher and student. When the reverse was true—the teacher was highly directive and did not solicit or use student initiated ideas—the students remained at the lowest cognitive levels even when the teacher moved up the cognitive hierarchy.

These findings leave much for speculation and further research. Is student behavior at the higher cognitive levels related to achievement? If high level student behavior is desirable what kinds of teaching strategies are related to this variable? Would these strategies differ at grade levels or in content areas? How does non-verbal behavior fit into these relationships? The search for answers to these and a host of other questions promises to be an exciting one.

Teacher Education

The Taxonomy of Cognitive Behavior has been used in pre-service and in-service education in Florida, Alabama, Georgia and West Virginia. Pre-service teachers at the University of Alabama, University of Florida and West Virginia University have all undergone training in the use of the system as part of their professional education program. In-service teachers in many of the county school systems of Florida, the metropoli-

216 TEACHING: VANTAGE POINTS FOR STUDY

tan Atlanta region and in Alabama have also received training. Although specific purposes for the use of the system have varied from place to place, the general goal has been to provide feedback to teachers concerning their classroom behavior.

At the present a study is underway at the University of Alabama to produce hard data as to the efficacy of this use of the instrument (Webb, 1970). Preliminary results indicate training in the use of the instrument does indeed help teachers to become more analytical in viewing their own teaching practices. However, experiences in using the *TCB* for those purposes would lead those of us who have developed and used the system to insert a word of caution. For most teachers this is a totally new and foreign way to view the teaching-learning situation. Ten to twelve hours training in the use of the instrument is not enough to create any real change in performance for the majority of teachers. Knowing about the instrument is not enough. Very often the ideas inherent in the system are almost overwhelming to the teacher.

Although learning to use the *Taxonomy of Cognitive Behavior* is the first step, it is not sufficient in itself to influence a teacher's behavior. Teachers must be taught to translate the concepts of the theoretical rationale of the system and apply them in classroom situations. Feedback through the use of video-tape, audio-tape or live data collection can then help them analyze and make judgments about their teaching behavior in terms of the goals they have identified. This is a time-consuming process but one which can make a genuine impact on instruction.

Mechanics of the Instrument

The *Taxonomy of Cognitive Behavior* is illustrated in Figure 1 on pages 218 and 219. The mechanics of the system are simple. There are five separate six-minute recording periods in each thirty-minute observation. The observer records behavior as it occurs, checking each item of teacher behavior and student behavior in the appropriate column as it happens. Items which describe behaviors which did not occur or for which a discrimination cannot be made are left unmarked. A particular item is marked only once in a given six-minute period, no matter how often that specific behavior occurs. If a behavior is represented by more than one item, all items that are involved are checked. If a behavior does not fit into the framework of the instrument it is ignored. At the end of the thirty-minute period, the recorded teacher behaviors and pupil behaviors are tallied to produce a record of the cognitive activities which have taken place during the observation.

Scoring is not a complicated procedure. As the various items of cognitive activity described by the instrument do not form a continuous, evenly spaced series of increasing complexity, the best indicator of the general level of cognitive activity of teacher or students is the observed item which represents the median of the items recorded.

This median for the teacher is found by adding all the subtotals in the T total columns to find a grand total. This number is divided by two and rounded off to the nearest whole number. This figure represents the midpoint number. Starting at the top of the first page, add by counting down the T total column, and if necessary continue adding by counting down the second page, until the midpoint number is reached. Circle the item whose subtotal contains this midpoint number total. This item represents the cognitive level that has 50% of the observations lying below it and 50% of the observations lying above it as one reads from 1:00 to 7:00 on the *TCB* and represents the general cognitive activity shown by the teacher. The process is repeated to score pupil behavior.

References

Robert King Bane. An Investigation of the Relationships Between Experimental, Cognitive, and Affective Teaching Behavior and Selected Teacher Characteristics. *Unpublished dissertation,* University of Florida, Gainesville, Florida, 1969.

Benjamin S. Bloom. *Taxonomy of Educational Objectives: Handbook of Cognitive Domain,* New York: David McKay Company, Inc., 1956.

B. B. Brown and J. N. Webb. "Valid and Reliable Observations of Classroom Behavior." *Classroom Interaction Newsletter* 4:35-38, 1968.

Glennis, Cunningham. "Multidimensionality: Implications for Preparation of Teacher" paper read at A.E.R.A. meeting, Minneapolis, Minnesota, 1970.

R. J. Garrison. Identification of Verbal Creative Classroom Behaviors Utilizing a Strategy Designed to Achieve Creative Response. *Unpublished dissertation,* University of Alabama, 1970.

S. E. Wood. "A Factor Analysis of Three Sets of Simultaneously Collected Observational Data," paper read at A.E.R.A. meeting, Los Angeles, California, 1969.

S. E. Wood and Richard L. Ober. "Simultaneous Use of Four Different Observational Systems to Assess Student Teacher Classroom Behavior," paper read at A.E.R.A. meeting, Minneapolis, Minnesota, 1970.

Jeaninne N. Webb. "The Effects of Training in the Analysis of Classroom Behavior on the Self-Evaluation of Teaching Performance." U.S.O.E. project 9-D-061. University of Alabama, University, Alabama, 1970.

FIGURE 1 Florida Taxonomy of Cognitive Behavior

TOT							
T	P	T/P	T/P	T/P	T/P	T/P	**1.10** KNOWLEDGE OF SPECIFICS
							1. Reads
							2. Spells
							3. Identifies something by name
							4. Defines meaning of term
							5. Gives a specific fact
							6. Tells about an event
							1.20 KNOWLEDGE OF WAYS AND MEANS OF DEALING WITH SPECIFICS
							7. Recognizes symbol
							8. Cites rule
							9. Gives chronological sequence
							10. Gives steps of process, describes method
							11. Cites trend
							12. Names classification system or standard
							13. Names what fits given system or standard
							1.30 KNOWLEDGE OF UNIVERSALS AND ABSTRACTIONS
							14. States generalized concept or idea
							15. States a principle, law, theory
							16. Tells about orgnztn or structure
							17. Recalls name of prin, law, theory
							2.00 TRANSLATION
							18. Restates in own words or briefer terms
							19. Gives cncrt exmpl of an abstract idea
							20. Verbalizes from a graphic rprsntatn
							21. Trans vrblztn into graphic form
							22. Trans fig stmnts to lit stmnts, or vice v
							23. Trans for lang to Eng, or vice versa
							3.00 INTERPRETATION
							24. Gives reason (tells why)
							25. Shows similarities, diffrncs
							26. Summarizes or concludes frm obs of evdnce
							27. Shows cause and effect rtnshp
							28. Gives analogy, simile, metaphor
							29. Performs a directed task or process

Florida Taxonomy of Cognitive Behavior

TOT							4.00 APPLICATION
T	P	T/P	T/P	T/P	T/P	T/P	
							30. Applies previous learning to new sitn
							31. Applies principle to new situation
							32. Apply abstrct knldg in a prctcl sitn
							33. Idntifs, selects, and carries out process
							5.00 ANALYSIS
							34. Distngshs fact from opinion
							35. Distngshs fact from hypothesis
							36. Distngshs cnclsn frm stmnts wch suppt it
							37. Points out unstated assumption
							38. Shows interaction or relation of elements
							39. Points out prtclrs to jstfy cnclsn
							40. Checks hypthss with given info
							41. Dstngshs rel frm irrelvnt stmnts
							42. Detects error in thinking
							43. Infers prpse, pt of view, thghts, feelings
							44. Recog bias or propaganda
							6.00 SYNTHESIS (Creativity)
							45. Reorganizes ideas, materials, process
							46. Produces unique cmmnctn divergent idea
							47. Produces a plan, prpsd set of oprtns
							48. Designs an apparatus
							49. Designs a structure
							50. Devises scheme for classifying info
							51. Formulates hypothesis, intelligent guess
							52. Mks dedctns frm abstrct smbls, propostns
							53. Draws inductive generalizatn frm specifics
							7.00 EVALUATION
							54. Evaluates something from evdnce
							55. Evaluates something from criteria

16 The Classroom Creativity Observation Schedule (CCOS): Development and Potential

David A. Denny

Introduction

The CCOS may be considered as a way-station on the difficult road toward the development of an empirical basis for instruction designed to foster pupil creative thinking abilities. Studies of teacher personality and attention to specific training procedures for the purpose of fostering creativity have not been fruitful over an extended period. The study of specific teacher-pupil behaviors which relate to pupil creative growth is seen as a step in a series leading to the goal of developing pupil creativity. Over the years, the author and his colleagues have been engaged in a series of studies of which the development of CCOS was a part. They are not comprehensive studies and might be criticized for moving too rapidly in a forward direction without the necessary replication to validate hypotheses at the horizontal level. They form, however, the theoretical base for the development of the observation system presented here

Reprinted with permission from *Classroom Interaction Newsletter,* 8: 37–46, December, 1972.

and the interested reader should consult these sources for detailed information and rationale (Rusch, Denny and Ives, 1965; Rusch, Denny and Ives, 1967; Denny, 1968; Turner and Denny, 1969; Denny, 1966).

Although a number of studies of classroom behavior have been conducted in which one of the dependent "product" variables has been pupil creativity gain, the relationships have been often conflicting and indirect (Wodtke, 1963; Soar, 1966, 1968; Gallagher, 1965; Taba, 1964; Sears, 1963; Spaulding, 1963; Birkin, 1970).

If the model relating presage, process and product is valid, one wonders why these relationships cannot be more clearly defined. There appears to be just enough evidence to encourage researchers to continue exploration. It would appear, for example, that warm, pupil-centered teacher behavior tends to foster pupil creative thinking as opposed to task-oriented, aloof behavior (Turner and Denny, 1969; Birkin, 1970). Specific definition of behaviors with their presage and product relationships must await further development of the instruments and theoretical rationale involved. For example, the creativity measures are at best exploratory in nature and need further research and refinement (Denny, 1969, 1970). Soar has suggested that the basic paradigm of a linear relationship between certain behaviors and creativity is questionable (Soar, 1968).

Of particular interest, as far as the development of CCOS is concerned, are conclusions about measuring classroom behavior variables resulting from reviews of a decade of work with observation schedules. Two conclusions appear to support the necessity for the development of an observation system designed specifically to isolate teacher and pupil behaviors which relate to pupil creativity gain. First, it has been concluded that the teaching process is so complex and the number of variables so great that a precise list defining effective teaching is wishful thinking (Rosenshine, 1969; Simon, 1969). It will be necessary to relate specific teaching behaviors to specific goals and to explore outcomes other than "academic achievement" (Simon, 1969).

The second conclusion is that the use of simple categories which explore *either* teacher or pupil behavior is at best severely limited in process-product productiveness and in theoretical fruitfulness (Birkin, 1970; Rosenshine, 1970). Birkin specifically raises the need for a study of the effect of student behavior on teacher behavior for which there has been little or no concern in the literature. He cites overlapping process variables, but with categories limited in range of behavioral acts exclusive to *either* student or teacher. "Such limitations of coverage and built-in rigidities seriously inhibit the generation of concepts expressing classroom processes" (Birkin, 1970, p. 40). He has attempted to correct this conceptual error by utilizing the "crucial assumption" which considers significant events to be not categories per se, but the co-occurrence of categories (Birkin, 1969, p. 30).

Although the CCOS is recognized as primarily a research instrument in initial stages of development, it does direct itself to these two areas of need. It gets at specific aspects of classroom behavior hypothesized to be related to creative development. Indeed, the schedule was developed for this specific purpose since the schedules available seem to be limited in analysis of these variables. Secondly, it considers the co-occurrence of variables as it examines pupil and teacher behavior in context with one another. For example, teacher behavior is coded as a function of pupil reaction to teacher statement in some items.

Although further development of the items and format of CCOS is needed to move from the research stage, and experimental design is necessary to establish cause and effect relationships between process and product variables, CCOS appears to be a step in a needed direction in the development of observation schedules.

Description of CCOS

Type of System

CCOS combines sign and category type observation items. The observer must categorize behavior occurring during a two-minute interval. Categories indicate frequency or extent of observed behaviors during the interval. Multi-dimensionality is achieved by using rating-type procedures in which context and content are considered simultaneously with verbal and nonverbal behavior of both teachers and pupils. A low-level of observer inference is achieved, however, through a detailed manual of instructions and through a training program for observers. Experience has shown that ten to fifteen hours of observer training will result in acceptable levels of reliability.

Scoring procedures are designed to yield a total score which is positively correlated with pupil gain in creativity. Behaviors hypothesized as negatively related to pupil creativity development contribute to a low total score while behaviors hypothesized as positively related contribute to a high score. Averaging, subtracting negative behaviors and tallying of occurrences are various procedures used for the three types of items to result in a total score.

The Items—Theoretical Relationship

The revised schedule consists of eight items designed to assess classroom behavior in an equal number of hypothesized dimensions. The dimensions combine to form two major regions. A diagram of the regions and dimensions is presented in Figure 1. It will be noted that Classroom Climate and Teaching-Learning Structure is subdivided into two categories: General Provisions for Structuring the Learning Situation, and Specific Structuring for Creative Development. It will be observed that the climate region encloses the structure region indicating Classroom Climate is a prerequisite for structuring to be effective in pupil creative development. In like manner, General Provisions for Teaching-Learning Structure are considered necessary for Specific Structuring to be effective. Code letters in Figure 1 refer to items of the observation schedule which purport to measure the dimensional aspects.

A summary description of each of the eight items is located on p. 225.

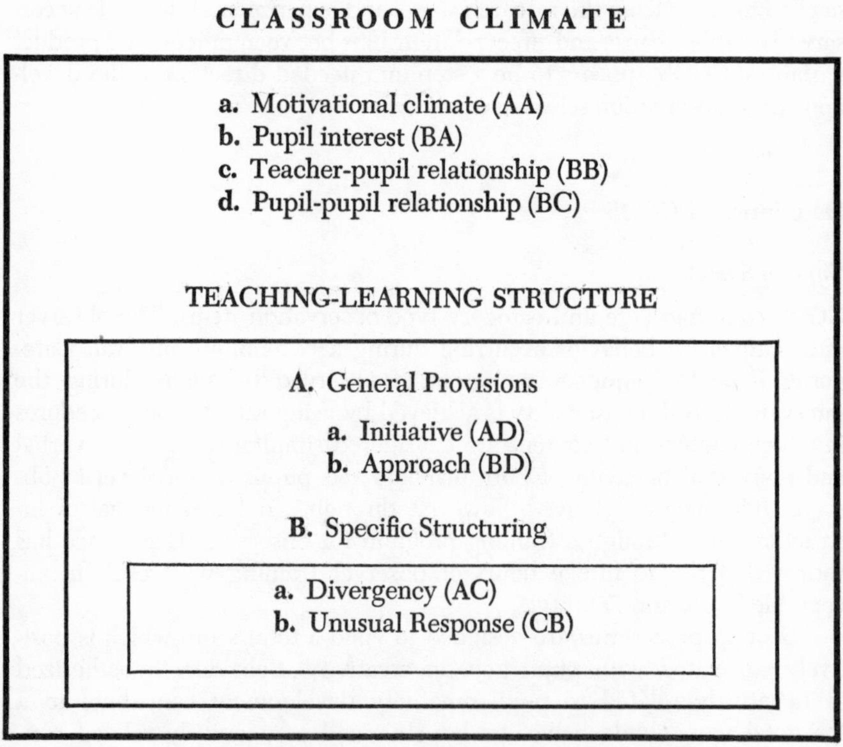

CLASSROOM CLIMATE

a. Motivational climate (AA)
b. Pupil interest (BA)
c. Teacher-pupil relationship (BB)
d. Pupil-pupil relationship (BC)

TEACHING-LEARNING STRUCTURE

A. General Provisions

a. Initiative (AD)
b. Approach (BD)

B. Specific Structuring

a. Divergency (AC)
b. Unusual Response (CB)

FIGURE 1. Hypothesized Dimensions of Classroom Interaction

Using the Schedule Score Sheet

The eight items are organized on the schedule score sheet by type of item, rather than the hypothesized relationship shown in Figure 1.

Figure 2 is a reproduction of the CCOS score sheet. It will be noted that the score sheet is divided into three schedules. Schedule A consists of three items: Motivational Climate, Divergency, and Initiative in Control. Each of these three items is a category type item in which the observer categorizes behavior according to detailed descriptions provided in the directions manual. Each of the three items has a five numeral code which specifies behaviors differing from one another in frequency and type. At the end of a two minute interval the observer records a code number for each of the three items in Schedule A which typifies the behavior occurring during that two minute interval. Schedule B consists of four items of the sign type: Pupil Interest, Pupil-Pupil, Teacher-Pupil, and Teacher Group Approach. It will be noted that Pupil Interest, and Pupil-Pupil refer to pupil behaviors; the other two items refer to teacher behaviors. During the two-minute interval, the observer circles a code number when one of the symptomatic behaviors is observed to occur. The score sheet lists an abbreviation of the symptomatic behaviors. A more detailed description of the behaviors is provided in the directions manual.

CLASSROOM CREATIVITY OBSERVATION SCHEDULE (1969 Revision)
Classroom Climate

(AA) *Motivational Climate*—Assessed on a five point scale each two minute period; from continuous threatening or punitive motivational stimuli (negative = 1) to continuous supportive, positively reinforcing stimuli (positive = 5).

(BA) *Pupil Interest*—Assessed positive or negative signs every four minutes during a two minute interval; positive signs = pupil eagerness, attention, intent work, etc.; negative signs = pupil reluctance, restlessness, irritability, etc.

(BB) *Teacher-Pupil Relationship*—Assessed positive or negative signs every four minutes during a two minute interval; positive signs = teacher responds positively, uses "we" approach, is attentive to pupil remarks, asks opinion, etc.; negative signs = teacher abrupt with pupils, uses "I" approach, cuts off pupil talk, interfered, involved few children.

(BC) *Pupil-Pupil Relationship*—Assessed positive or negative signs every four minutes during a two minute interval; positive signs = children refer positively to the success of others, share responsibility, accept overt differences in capability, etc.; negative signs = children refer negatively to the success of others, reluctant to share responsibility, make fun of others, etc.

General Structuring

(AD) *Pupil Initiative*—Assessed on a five point scale each two minute period from complete teacher domination in control of instruction (low pupil initiative = 1) to high pupil control of instruction (high pupil initiative = 5).

(BD) *Teacher Approach*—Assessed positive or negative signs every four minutes during a two minute interval; positive signs = teacher builds interest, alters pace, has materials ready, concludes lesson or phase while interest high; negative signs = fails to build interest, pace unvaried, materials not ready, children restless when concludes.

Specific Structuring

(AC) *Encouragement of Pupil Divergency*—Assessed on a five point scale each two minute period, from teacher allows only convergent thinking, giving correct responses, etc. (score of 1) to teacher's main purpose is to obtain divergent thinking (score of 5).

(CB) *Unusual Response*—One tally for each positive reinforcement of unusual pupil response whenever it occurs during the observation.

Schedule C is a simple tally of the times the teacher encourages Unusual Response. At any time during the observation when the observer perceives an occurrence of this behavior he places a tally mark on the line provided. He then returns to his scoring of schedule A or B.

A typical observation would proceed then, with the observer timing himself and at the end of two minutes recording a code number for each of the three items in Schedule A typifying the behavior during the preceding two minute interval for those items. He would observe for another two minute interval and repeat that process. Then, for the third two minute interval he would concentrate on the symptomatic behaviors described in Schedule B, circling the corresponding code number when one of the symptomatic behaviors was to occur during that interval. At any time during the observation he would interrupt to place a tally mark in Schedule C when he saw the teacher encouraging unusual response. This process is repeated until the conclusion of the observation period. The score sheet provides for thirty minutes of observation time.

At the end of the observation period the observer sums and averages to obtain a total score for the observation period. A high score is positively related to pupil gain in creativity. A maximum total score would be 32 plus whatever tallies were obtained in Schedule C, an unlimited item.

Validity and Reliability of the Classroom Creativity Observation Schedule

The present Classroom Creativity Observation Schedule is a revision of a schedule originally developed and tested in a USOE supported study in 1966 in Central Indiana (Denny, 1966; 1968). The original schedule (Denny, Rusch, Ives Classroom Creativity Observation Schedule) contained eleven items. Revisions, based on the 1966 study, have resulted in the present CCOS. The total number of items was reduced to eight by elimination of three unreliable items. Revisions were also made to improve scoring procedures and to eliminate ambiguities in wording.

Although studies using CCOS are presently in process, both in the United States and abroad, publication of reliability and validity data for the revised CCOS is not yet possible. The reader desiring more detailed statistical information should consult the original study and a concurrent construct validity study (Denny, 1966, 1968; Turner and Denny, 1969). These studies revealed satisfactory levels of reliability and validity for the original eleven item schedule. Since the present eight item instrument was revised to eliminate unreliable items and to improve objectivity, it should show substantial increases in both reliability and validity.

Preliminary communications with researchers using the revised schedule appear to support the hypothesis of increased reliability. Draheim, in a dissertation to be completed in 1972, obtained a reliability coefficient of .99 for an adaptation of the CCOS (Draheim, 1972). Spelman, doing research in Ulster, Northern Ireland, also finds favorable reliability (Spelman, 1972). As the CCOS is used in a greater variety of classrooms and examined in relation to many measures of creativity, the data regarding reliability and validity will continue to accumulate.

Conclusion

The Classroom Creativity Observation Schedule (CCOS) has been presented as an instrument in the research stage which holds promise as a means of assessing classroom variables related to pupil gain on measured creativity.

The revised CCOS should be administered to other populations and grade levels and compared with other measures of creativity. Reanalysis of the reliability and validity of each item should then be undertaken.

Causal relationships should also be explored by using an experimental design in which teachers are taught to practice behaviors designed to develop pupil creativity.

Researchers desiring to further develop and analyze the CCOS are urged to communicate with the author.

Bibliography

Birkin, T. A., "Some Educational Influences on Creativity Changes." A paper delivered at a symposium on creativity at the 41st Congress of the Australian and New Zealand Association for the Advancement of Science, Adelaide, August, 1969 (mimeo).

Birkin, T. A., "Towards a Model of Instructional Processes," in I. Westbury and A. Bellack, *Research Into Classroom Process*, Teachers College Press, 1970.

Denny, David A., *Preliminary Analysis of an Observation Schedule Designed to Identify the Teacher-Classroom Variables Which Facilitate Pupil Creative Growth*, USOE, CRP No. 6-8235-2-12-1, Indiana University, Bloomington, 1966.

CLASSROOM CREATIVITY OBSERVATION SCHEDULE (CCOS)

Classroom Creativity Observation Schedule (CCOS)

Teacher _____ Grade _____ Total Score _____

Observer _____ Date _____ From _____ to _____

TOTAL MINUTES _____

SCHEDULE A.

2-MINUTE INTERVALS

	1st	2nd	4th	5th	7th	8th	10th	11th	13th	14th	Tot.	Aver.
A. Motivational Climate (AA)												
C. Divergency (AC)												
D. Initiative in Control (AD)												

SCHEDULE B.

(PUPIL BEHAVIORS)

	3rd	6th	9th	12th	15th	Tot.	Dif./Aver.
A. Pupil Interest (Discussion) (BA)							
1. Respond eagerly — Reluctant to respond	1 2	1 2	1 2	1 2	1 2		
2. Courteous response — Rude response	3 4	3 4	3 4	3 4	3 4	+	
3. Received criticism positively — Recd. criticism neg.	5	5	5	5	5		
(work period)							
4. Work intently — Restless, etc.	1 2	1 2	1 2	1 2	1 2		
	3 4	3 4	3 4	3 4	3 4	−	
5. Promptly participates — Slowly participates	5	5	5	5	5		

C. Pupil–Pupil (BC)

		Scale						
1. Refer positively to others' success	+	1 2 / 3 4	1 2 / 3 4	1 2 / 3 4	1 2 / 3 4	1 2 / 3 4	1 2 / 3 4	1 2 / 3 4	+	— Refer neg. others' suc.
2. Help each other	—	1 2 / 3 4	1 2 / 3 4	1 2 / 3 4	1 2 / 3 4	1 2 / 3 4	1 2 / 3 4	1 2 / 3 4	—	— Reluctant help each other
3. Accept individual differences										— Make fun ind. diff.
4. Expresses appreciation of unusual response										— Derides unusual resp.

(TEACHER BEHAVIORS)

B. Teacher–Pupil (BB)

1. Responds positively	+	1 2 / 3 4	1 2 / 3 4	1 2 / 3 4	1 2 / 3 4	1 2 / 3 4	1 2 / 3 4	1 2 / 3 4	+	— Resp. neg. & abruptly
2. Teacher uses "we" approach	—	1 2 / 3 4	1 2 / 3 4	1 2 / 3 4	1 2 / 3 4	1 2 / 3 4	1 2 / 3 4	1 2 / 3 4	—	— T. uses "I" approach
3. Attentive to pupil remarks										— Inattentive to pupil
4. Attends to non-volunteers										— Not att. to non-vol.

D. Teacher Group Approach (BD)

1. Builds & sustains p. interest	+	1 2 / 3 4	1 2 / 3 4	1 2 / 3 4	1 2 / 3 4	1 2 / 3 4	1 2 / 3 4	1 2 / 3 4	+	— Not b. & s. pupil int.
2. Materials ready for use	—	1 2 / 3 4	1 2 / 3 4	1 2 / 3 4	1 2 / 3 4	1 2 / 3 4	1 2 / 3 4	1 2 / 3 4	—	— Mat. not ready
3. P's. involved at high interest										— P's. inv. after hi int.
4. Concludes while interest high										— Conc. after interest

SCHEDULE C. (tally as occur)

B. Teacher Encouragement of Unusual Responses (CB)

Tally _____   Total _____

(Revision 4/18/69—Copyright 1969, David A. Denny)

Denny, David A., "Identification of Teacher-Classroom Variables Facilitating Pupil Creative Growth," *American Educational Research Journal*, 5:365-383, May 1968.

Denny, David A., *A Detailed Analysis of Sixth Grade Creativity Test Data*, Oneonta, N.Y., State University College, 1969a.

Denny, David A., *Classroom Creativity Observation Schedule, Directions Manual*. 1969 Edition, Oneonta, New York; State University College, 1969b.

Denny, David A., "A Comparison of Two Operational Definitions of Originality and Their Relationship to Measured Intelligence," A paper presented to AERA, Minneapolis, Minnesota, March 1970 (mimeo).

Draheim, Diana, doctoral candidate, Boston University School of Education. Personal correspondence with the writer, September 1972.

Gallagher, James J., "Productive Thinking in Gifted Children," USOE, CRP No. 965, University of Illinois, Urbana, 1965.

McNemar, Quinn, *Psychological Statistics*, New York, John Wiley and Sons, Inc., 1962, pp. 285-286.

Medley, Donald M., and Mitzel, Harold E., "Application of Analysis of Variance to the Reliability of Observations of Teachers' Classroom Behavior" *Journal of Experimental Education*, 27:23-35, September, 1958.

Medley, Donald M., and Mitzel, Harold E. "Measuring Classroom Behavior by Systematic Observation," in N. L. Gage (Ed.), *Handbook of Research on Teaching*, Chicago, Rand-McNally Co., 1963, pp. 247-328.

Rosenshine, Barak, "Teaching Behaviors Related to Pupil Achievement," *Classroom Interaction Newsletter*, 5:4-17, December, 1969.

Rosenshine, Barak, "Evaluation of Classroom Instruction," *Review of Educational Research*, 40:279-300, 1970.

Rusch, Reuben R., Denny, David A., and Ives, Sammie, "Fostering Creativity in the Sixth Grade," *Elementary School Journal*, 65:262-268, February 1965.

Rusch, Reuben R., Denny, David A., and Ives, Sammie, "Fostering Creativity in the Sixth Grade and its Effect on Achievement," *The Journal of Experimental Education*, 36:80-86, Fall, 1967.

Sears, Pauline S., *The Effect of Classroom Conditions on the Strength of Achievement Motive and Work Output on Elementary School Children*, USOE, CRP No. 873, Stanford University, Stanford, California, 1963.

Simon, Anita, "Research on Teaching: Usability and Meaningfulness," *Classroom Interaction Newsletter*, 5:1-3, December 1969.

Soar, Robert S., "Teacher-Pupil Interaction and Pupil Growth," A paper presented to the American Educational Research Association, Chicago, Illinois, February, 1966 (mimeo).

Soar, Robert S., "Optimum Teacher-Pupil Interaction for Pupil Growth," A paper presented at AERA, Chicago, Illinois, February, 1968 (mimeo).

Soar, Robert S., "The Study of Presage—Process—Product Relationships: Implications for Classroom Process Measurement," A paper presented at AERA, Chicago, Illinois, February, 1968 (mimeo).

Spaulding, R. L., "Achievement, Creativity and Self-Concept Correlates of Teacher-Pupil Transactions in Elementary Schools," USOE, CRP No. 1362, University of Illinois, Urbana, 1963.

Spelman, Brendan J., post graduate researcher in education, The New University of Ulster, Coleraine County Londonderry, Northern Ireland. Personal correspondence with the writer, September, 1972.

Taba, Hilda, Levine, S., and Elzey, F., *Thinking in Elementary School Children*, USOE, CRP No. 1574, San Francisco State College, San Francisco, California, 1964, p. 207.

Turner, Richard L., and Denny, David A., "Teacher Characteristics, Teacher Behavior, and Changes in Pupil Creativity," *The Elementary School Journal*, 69:265-270, February, 1969.

Wodtke, Kenneth A., *A Study of the Reliability and Validity of Creative Tests at the Elementary School Level*, Unpublished doctor's thesis, University of Utah, Salt Lake City, December, 1963 (micro).

4 *Learning and Cognitive Development*

Overview

In the past few years we have seen rapid growth in the number of research groups attempting to implement new curriculum programs and teaching methods. The researchers, when considering the student component of their curriculum and teaching plans, have turned to learning psychologists for guidance. That is to say, they have based their curriculum and teaching plans not only on their ideas about what to teach and how to teach but also on how students learn. People planning curriculum and teaching strategies have turned to learning and cognitive development experts for help.

The three articles in this section present the key ideas on learning of some of our leading learning psychologists today, Piaget, Bruner, Skinner, Gagné, and Ausubel. These articles then go on to present ideas on teaching based on these learning perspectives. The Solomon article, based essentially on the developmental stages of Piaget and the imagery-related stages of Bruner, offers an observation system to view teaching, as does the Bloom article, based essentially on the reinforcement concept of Skinner.

Solomon takes the theories of Piaget and Bruner and develops a Taxonomy of Image Provoking Behavior (TIP). His model for this is obviously Benjamin Bloom's Taxonomy presented in Webb's selection in Section 3. Solomon goes on to use concepts from his set of categories and concepts from Benjamin Bloom's categories to present the data he has gathered from observing teachers. Richard Bloom takes two key concepts from Skinner, reinforcement and cueing, and bases his observation system on them. His data show that teachers of nursery school children do differ in their behavior.

Gagné treats learning theory without presenting an observation system. Before presenting modern conceptions of learning, Gagné offers a survey of the "older conception of learning" associated with Thorndike and Underwood and commonly based on the concepts of stimulus and response. Then Gagné outlines the modern conception of learning, "the information-processing conception."

While Solomon uses a sign system involving twelve two-minute periods to observe his teachers, Bloom uses a category system based on a teacher behavior unit. Therefore, it is interesting to compare Solomon with Webb (Section 3) and Bloom with Taba (Section 9). Also, since Bloom studies teachers of very young students, it is interesting to compare his system and results with those of Resnick (Section 9), who studies teachers of five- to seven-year-old students in an informal, open classroom. In addition, the reader would do well to compare Skinner's concept of learning with Gagné's "older conception" and "modern conception" of learning.

The reader will note that the inclusion here of the theories of Skinner and Thorndike (that is, the older conception of learning) offers the reader a view which is often called First Force, or behavioristic, psychology. Second Force and Third Force psychology viewpoints appear in Section 5, the Psychological Climate. What is more, each of these views obviously offers a different picture of teaching because the concepts constituting that perspective differ. The reader should then compare the view of teaching offered by First Force psychology, as appearing in these selections by Bloom and Gagné, with the views of teaching offered in the selections by Freud (Second Force), Tyler (utilizing Menninger, Second Force), Rogers (Third Force), and Macdonald and Zaret (utilizing Rogers, Allport, and other Third Force psychologists).

Questions for research readily leap to mind. Do teachers who personally accept Skinnerian learning theory differ from teachers who personally accept Gagné's information processing conception when observed from the vantage point of Bellack's categories (Section 3)? When observed with Galloway's nonverbal categories (Section 8)? When observed with Gallagher and Aschner's categories (Section 3)? Do teachers of nursery school children differ in their utilization of visual imagery, according to Solomon's categories, from teachers of middle school students? How can we help teachers exhibit more concrete-imagery-level behavior, more reinforcing behavior, and behavior which teaches students strategies of coding?

17 Some New Views of Learning and Instruction

Robert M. Gagné

During recent years there has been an increased recognition of, and even emphasis on, the importance of principles of learning in the design of instruction for the schools. This recognition of the central role of learning in school-centered education seems to be accorded whether one thinks of the instruction as being designed by a teacher, by a textbook writer, or by a group of scholars developing a curriculum.

When the findings of research studies of learning are taken into account, one usually finds questions about instruction to be concerned with such matters as these:

1. For student learning to be most effective, how should the learning task be presented? That is, how should it be communicated to the student?

2. When the student undertakes a learning task, what kinds of activity on his part should be required or encouraged?

3. What provisions must be made to insure that what is learned is remembered and is usable in further learning and problem solving?

Questions such as these are persistent in education. The answers given today are not exactly the same as those given yesterday, and they

Reprinted with permission from *Phi Delta Kappan*, 51: 468–472, May, 1972.

are likely to be altered again tomorrow. The major reason for these changes is our continually deepening knowledge of human behavior and of the factors which determine it. One should not, I believe, shun such changes nor adopt a point of view which makes difficult the application of new knowledge to the design of novel procedures for instruction. The opportunities for improvement seem great and the risks small.

Status of Learning Research

As a field of endeavor, research on how human beings learn and remember is in a state of great ferment today. Many changes have taken place, and are still taking place, in the conception of what human learning is and how it occurs. Perhaps the most general description, that can be made of these changes is that investigators are shifting from what may be called a *connectionist* view of learning to an *information processing* view. From an older view which held that learning is a matter of establishing *connections* between stimuli and responses, we are moving rapidly to acceptance of a view that stimuli are *processed* in quite a number of different ways by the human central nervous system, and that understanding learning is a matter of figuring out how these various processes operate. Connecting one neural event with another may still be the most basic component of these processes, but their varied nature makes connection itself too simple a model for learning and remembering.

My purpose here is to outline some of these changes in the conception of human learning and memory, and to show what implications they may have for the design and practice of instruction. I emphasize that I am not proposing a new theory; I am simply speculating on what seems to me to be the direction in which learning theory is heading.

The Older Conception

The older conception of learning was that it was always basically the same process, whether the learner was learning to say a new word, to tie a shoelace, to multiply fractions, to recount the facts of history, or to solve a problem concerning rotary motion. Edward L. Thorndike held essentially this view. He stated that he had observed people performing learning tasks of varied degrees of complexity and had concluded that learning was invariably subject to the same influences and the same laws.[1] What was this model of learning that was considered to have such broad generalizability?

One prototype is the conditioned response, in which there is a pairing of stimuli, repeated over a series of trials. The two stimuli must be presented together, or nearly together in time. They are typically associated with an "emotional" response of the human being, such as an eyeblink or a change in the amount of electrical resistance of the skin (the galvanic skin reflex). The size of the conditioned response begins at a low base-line level, and progressively increases as more and more repetitions of the two stimuli are given. Such results have been taken to indicate that repetition brings about an increasingly "strong" learned connection—with an increase in strength that is rapid at first and then more slow.

Learning curves with similar characteristics have been obtained from various other kinds of learned activities, such as simple motor skills like dart-throwing and memorization of lists of words or sets of word-pairs.

Remembering

What about the remembering of such learned activities? Is learning retained better as a result of repetition? Is something that is repeated over and over at the time of learning better recalled after the passage of several weeks or months? The curve which describes forgetting is perhaps equally familiar. Forgetting of such things as lists of nonsense syllables is quite rapid in the beginning, and after several weeks descends to a point at which only about 20 percent is remembered. A motor task is usually retained a great deal better, and after the same amount of time its retention may be as much as 80 percent.

These are the basic facts about remembering. But how is it affected by repetition? Is retention better if the original learning situation has been repeated many times? Evidence is often cited that this is so. Increasing the number of trials of repetition during original learning has the effect of slowing down the "curve of forgetting," i.e., of improving the amount of retention measured at any particular time. Underwood,[2] for example, has stated that "degree of learning" of the task to be recalled is one of the two major factors which influence forgetting in a substantial manner. The second factor is interfering associations, whose strength is also determined by their degree of learning. It should be pointed out that when Underwood uses the phrase "degree of learning" he refers to amount of practice—in other words, to amount of repetition.

At this point, let me summarize what I believe are the important implications for instruction of what I call the "older" conceptions of learning and memory. The designer of instruction, or the teacher, had to do two major things: First, he had to arrange external conditions of presentation so that the stimulus and response had the proper timing—in other words, so that there was *contiguity* between the presentation of the stimulus and the occurrence of the response. Second, he had to insure that sufficient *repetition* occurred. Such repetition was necessary for two reasons: It would increase the strength of the learned connections; the more the repetition, within limits, the better the learning. Also, repetition was needed to insure remembering—the greater the number of repetitions, the better the retention. Presumably, whole generations of instructional materials and teacher procedures have been influenced in a variety of ways by application of these conceptions of learning to the process of instruction.

Questioning Older Conceptions

During recent years, a number of significant experimental studies of learning and memory have been carried out which call into question some of these older conceptions. (Of course there have always been a certain number of individuals—voices in the wilderness—who doubted that these principles had the general applicability claimed for them.) I shall describe only a few of the crucial new studies here, to illustrate the perennial questions and their possible answers.

Does learning require repetition?

A most provocative study on this question was carried out by Rock[3] as long ago as 1957. It has stimulated many other studies since that time, some pointing out its methodological defects, others supporting its conclusions.[4] The finding of interest is that in learning sets of verbal paired associates, practice does not increase the strength of each learned item; each one is either learned or not learned. To be sure, some are learned on the first practice trial, some on the second, some on the third, and so on; but an item once learned is fully learned.

So far as school subjects are concerned, a number of studies have failed to find evidence of the effectiveness of repetition for learning and remembering. This was true in an investigation by Gagné, Mayor, Garstens, and Paradise,[5] in which seventh-graders were learning about the addition of integers. One group of children was given four or five times as many practice problems on each of 10 subordinate skills as were given to another group, and no difference appeared in their final performance. A further test of this question was made in a study by Jeanne Gibson,[6] who set out to teach third- and fourth-graders to read decimals from a number line. First, she made sure that subordinate skills (reading a number in decimal form, writing a number in decimal form, locating a decimal number on a number line) were learned thoroughly by each child. One group of students was then given a total of 10 practice examples for each subordinate skill, a second group 25 for each, and a third none at all. The study thus contrasted the effects of no repetition of learned skills, an intermediate amount of repetition, and a large amount of repetition. This variable was not found to have an effect on performance, both when tested immediately after learning and five weeks later. Those students who practiced repeated examples were not shown to do better, or to remember better, than those who practiced not at all.

Still another study of fairly recent origin is by Reynolds and Glaser,[7] who used an instructional program to teach 10 topics in biology. They inserted frames containing half as many repetitions, in one case, and one-and-a-half times as many repetitions, in another, as those in a standard program. The repetitions involved definitions of technical terms. When retention of these terms was measured after an interval of three weeks, the investigators were unable to find any difference in recall related to the amount of repetition.

I must insert a caveat here. All of the studies I have mentioned are concerned with the effects of repetition immediately after learning. They do not, however, test the effect of repetition in the form of *spaced reviews*. Other evidence suggests the importance of such reviews; in fact, this kind of treatment was found to exert a significant effect in the Reynolds and Glaser study. Note, though, that this result may have quite a different explanation than that of "strengthening learned connections."

Modern Conceptions of Learning

Many modern learning theorists seem to have come to the conclusion that conceiving learning as a matter of strengthening connections is entirely too simple. Modern conceptions of learning tend to be highly analytical about the events that take place in learning, both *outside* the learner and also *inside*. The modern point of view about learning tends to view it as a complex of processes taking place in the learner's nervous system. This view is often called an "information-processing" conception.

One example of information processing theory is that of Atkinson and Shiffrin.[8] According to this theory, information is first registered by the senses and remains in an essentially unaltered form for a short period of time. It then enters what is called the short-term store, where it can be retained for 30 seconds or so. This short-term store has a limited capacity, so that new information coming into it simply pushes aside what may already be stored there. But an important process takes place in this short-term memory, according to Atkinson and Shiffrin. There is a kind of internal reviewing mechanism (a "rehearsal buffer") which organizes and rehearses the material even within this short period of time. Then it is ready to be transferred to long-term store. But when this happens it is first subjected to a process called *coding*. In other words, it is not transferred in raw form, but is transformed in some way which will make it easier to remember at a later time. Still another process is *retrieval,* which comes into play at the time the individual attempts to remember what he has learned.

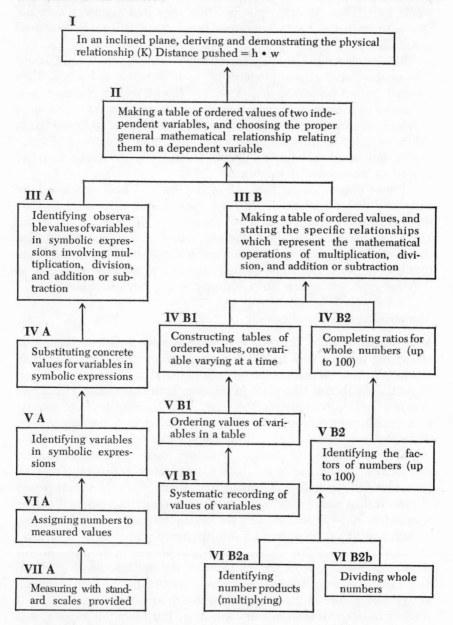

FIGURE 1 A hierarchy of subordinate intellectual skills applicable to the problem of deriving a general expression relating variables in an inclined plane (Wiegand, 1969).

It is easy to see that a much more sophisticated theory of learning and memory is implied here. It goes far beyond the notion of gradually increasing the strength of a single connection.

Prerequisites for learning

If repetition or practice is not the major factor in learning, what is? The answer I am inclined to give is that the most dependable condition for the insurance of learning is the prior learning of prerequisite capabilities. Some people would call these "specific readinesses" for learning; others would call them "enabling conditions." If one wants to insure that a student can learn some specific new activity, the very best guarantee is to be sure he has previously learned the prerequisite capabilities. When this in fact has been accomplished, it seems to me quite likely that he will learn the new skill without repetition.

Let me illustrate this point by reference to a study carried out by Virginia Wiegand.[9] She attempted to identify all the prerequisite capabilities needed for sixth-grade students to learn to formulate a general expression relating the variables in an inclined plane. Without using the exact terminology of physics, let us note that the task was to formulate an expression relating the *height* of the plane, the *weight* of the body traversing downwards, and the *amount of push* imparted to an object at the end of the plane. (Wiegand was not trying to teach physics, but to see if the children could learn to formulate a physical relationship which was quite novel to them.) The expression aimed for was, "Distance pushed times a constant block weight equals height of plane times weight of cart."

Initially, what was wanted was explained carefully to the students; the plane and the cart were demonstrated. Thirty students (out of 31) were found who could not accomplish the task; that is, they did not know how to solve the problem. What was it they didn't know? According to the hypothesis being investigated, they didn't know some *prerequisite things*. Figure 1 shows what these missing intellectual skills were thought to be.

What Wiegand did was to find out which of these prerequisite skills were present in each student and which were not present. She did this by starting at the top of the hierarchy and working downwards, testing at each point whether the student could do the designated task or not. In some students, only two or three skills were missing; in others, seven or eight. When she had worked down to the point where these subordinate capabilities *were* present, Wiegand turned around and went the other way. She now made sure that all the prerequisite skills were present, right up to, but not including, the final inclined plane problem.

The question being asked in this study was, If all the prerequisite skills are present, can the students now solve this physical problem which they were unable to solve previously? Wiegand's results are quite clear-cut. Having learned the prerequisites, nine out of 10 students were able to solve the problem which they were initially unable to solve. They now solved the problem without hesitation and with no practice on the problem itself. On the other hand, for students who did not have a chance to learn the prerequisites, only three of 10 solved the problem (and these were students who had no "missing" skills). This is the kind of evidence that makes me emphasize the critical importance of prerequisite intellectual skills. Any particular learning is not at all difficult if one is truly prepared for it.

Coding and remembering

Quite a number of studies appear in the experimental literature pertaining to the effects of coding of information on its retention. I choose as an illustration a study of Bower and Clark.[10] These investigators studied the recall by college students of 12 lists of 10 nouns apiece. In learning each list, each student was encouraged to make up a story connecting the nouns. For each student there was a yoked control who was not encouraged to make up a story but who was permitted the same amount of time to learn each list of nouns.

Here is an example of a story which one of the subjects constructed for the words *vegetable, instrument, college, nail, fence, basin, merchant, queen, scale,* and *goat:* "A vegetable can be a useful instrument for a college student. A carrot can be a nail for your fence or basin. But a merchant of the queen would scale that fence and feed the carrot to a goat."

The subjects were asked to recall each list immediately after their study of it. They recalled 99 percent under both conditions. The subjects were later asked to recall all of the lists, after they had learned all 12. In this case there was an enormous difference: The recall of the narrative group averaged 93 percent, that of the non-narrative group only 13 percent. In other words, deliberate coding had increased recall by seven times.

Retrieval and remembering

Suppose that learning has indeed occurred; what will insure that whatever has been learned will be remembered? There seems to be at least some absence of evidence that simply practicing or repeating things after they have been learned has the effect of improving retention. What the individual does when he is asked to remember something is to *retrieve* it; that is, he brings to bear a process of searching and finding, in his memory, something he is looking for. This process is probably very little understood at present, but there is increasing evidence that it does occur and that it plays a crucial role in remembering.

Some interesting work has been done on the subject of retrieval. In one experiment, Tulving and Pearlstone[11] had groups of high school students learn lists of words of various lengths: 12 words, 24 words, or 48 words. The words themselves were instances of categories, such as four-footed animals (cow, rat); weapons (bomb, cannon); forms of entertainment (radio, music); professions (lawyer, engineer), and so on. The words were presented one at a time in mixed-up order. Different lists also used one, two, or four words in each category.

Once the lists of words had been learned, recall was measured under two different conditions. In the first, the learners were simply told to write down all the words they could remember. In the second, the category names were used as cues to recall; that is, the learners were asked to write down all the words they remembered which were "forms of entertainment," all which were "four-footed animals," and so on. These extra cues worked wonders on recall. The effect was more marked the greater the number of words that had to be recalled. The differences among those learning 48 words was striking, amounting to a twofold increase.

These results show in a rather clear way how powerful is the effect of such extra cues on retrieval of information that has been learned. In this study, the words themselves can be said to have been "equally well learned" in all the groups. What was different between the groups was the aid they were given in retrieving what they had learned. This is only one of the accumulating pieces of evidence that remembering is markedly affected by retrieval at the time of recall, more than it is, perhaps, by events taking place at the time of learning.

Implications for Instruction

The contrasts between older and newer conceptions of learning and memory seem to me quite remarkable. What implications do they have for instruction? If there are indeed newly discovered ways to affect learning and remembering, how might they be put to use in the classroom and in materials of the curriculum?

First, there is the very fundamental point that each learner approaches each new learning task with a different collection of previously learned prerequisite skills. To be effective, therefore, a learning program for each child must take fully into account what he knows how to do already, and what he doesn't know how to do already. One must find out what prerequisites he had already mastered—not in a general sense, but in a very precise sense for each learner. Does this mean one must do "diagnostic testing"? Yes, that's exactly what it means. To do so, of course, one must first develop the requisite diagnostic tests. By and large, we don't have them.

Second, the most important guide to the learning that needs to be accomplished is the set of prerequisites that the student has not yet mastered. Remember here Wiegand's experiment. When she systematically saw to it that students climbed the hierarchy, skill by skill, this was what was specifically needed to get them to engage in the problem solving they were originally unable to do.

Third, do students need additional practice to insure retention? If by this is meant, "Should they be given many additional examples so that what they have learned will be 'strengthened'?," I think the evidence says it probably won't work this way. Periodic and spaced reviews, however, are another matter, and it seems likely that these have an important role to play in retention. Notice that when a review is given, the student has to exercise his strategies of retrieval.

This brings me to the final point, which concerns the processes of coding and retrieval. Probably what should be aimed for here is the learning by students of strategies of coding. These are by no means the same as what are called "mnemonic systems," although it is possible that such systems have a contribution to make in teaching us how coding might be done. For meaningful learning, it appears even more likely that notions like "advance organizers" and "anchoring ideas," as studied by Ausubel,[12] may be particularly powerful.

Similarly, retrieval strategies are also a class of objective that might be valued for instruction. From the evidence we have, I should say that retrieval strategies might very well consist in networks of superordinate categories into which newly learned specific information, or specific intellectual skills, can be placed. Having students learn to retrieve information by a process of search which first locates such superordinate networks may be a major way of providing them with the capability of good retention.

Even these two or three aspects of modern learning conceptions, it seems to me, lead to a very different view of what instruction is all about. In the most general sense, instruction becomes not primarily a matter of communicating something that is to be stored. Instead, it is a matter of stimulating the use of capabilities the learner already has at his disposal, and of making sure he has the requisite capabilities for the present learning task, as well as for many more to come.

[1] E. L. Thorndike, *Human Learning*, New York: Appleton-Century, 1931, p. 160.

[2] B. J. Underwood, "Laboratory Studies of Verbal Learning," in E. R. Hilgard (ed.), *Theories of Learning and Instruction. Sixty-third Yearbook, Part I.* Chicago: National Society for the Study of Education, 1964, p. 148.

[3] I. Rock, "The Role of Repetition in Associative Learning," *American Journal of Psychology*, June, 1957, pp. 186–93.

[4]W. K. Estes, B. L. Hopkins, and E. J. Crothers, "All-or-None and Conservation Effects in the Learning and Retention of Paired Associates," *Journal of Experimental Psychology*, December, 1960, pp. 329–39.

[5]R. M. Gagné, J. R. Mayor, H. L. Garstens, and N. E. Paradise, "Factors in Acquiring Knowledge of a Mathematical Task," *Psychological Monographs*, No. 7, 1962 (Whole No. 526).

[6]J. R. Gibson, "Transfer Effects of Practice Variety in Principle Learning." Berkeley: University of California, Ph.D. Dissertation, 1964.

[7]J. H. Reynolds and R. Glaser, "Effects of Repetition and Spaced Review upon Retention of a Complex Learning Task," *Journal of Educational Psychology*, October, 1964, pp. 297–308.

[8]R. C. Atkinson and R. M. Shiffrin, "Human Memory: A Proposed System and its Control Processes," in K. W. Spence and J. T. Spence (eds.), *The Psychology of Learning and Motivation: Advances in Research and Theory*, Vol. 2. New York: Academic Press, 1968, pp. 89–195.

[9]V. K. Wiegand, "A Study of Subordinate Skills in Science Problem Solving." Berkeley: University of California. Ph.D. Dissertation, 1969.

[10]G. H. Bower and M. C. Clark, "Narrative Stories as Mediators for Serial Learning," *Psychonomic Science*, April, 1969, pp. 181–82.

[11]E. Tulving and Z. Pearlstone, "Availability Versus Accessibility of Information in Memory for Words," *Journal of Verbal Learning and Verbal Behavior*, August, 1966, pp. 381–91.

[12]D. P. Ausubel, *Educational Psychology: A Cognitive View*. New York: Holt, Rinehart and Winston, 1968.

18 Teacher Behavior As Viewed From A Skinnerian Perspective

Richard D. Bloom

This article presents the rationale, description, and some results of a classroom observation system based on a Skinnerian learning perspective. The work of B. F. Skinner (e.g., 1938, 1953) has exerted considerable influence in American psychology. For one thing, he has made important methodological and theoretical contributions to the study of the learning process. Skinner has also been very much concerned with developing ways by which his learning theory may be usefully applied to the classroom situation as a way of maximizing student learning outcomes. Perhaps the prime example of Skinner's applied interest has been his developmental work in programmed instruction.

Skinner's views on the nature of the learning process, though parsimonious, have wide-ranging implications. These views are summarized as follows. First, the basic data of the learning process are observable responses. In turn, such behavior is subject to environmental influences which may be categorized into two major dimensions. One such influence involves the operation of reinforcing events. Conceptually

This article is an expansion and revision of one previously published in *Research Bulletin* (New Jersey School Development Council, Rutgers University). Printed with permission of the publisher and the author.

a reinforcer refers to any environmental event following a response which may strengthen that behavior. A classic example of a reinforcer is the pellet of food which is released whenever a laboratory rat presses the lever in the famous "Skinner Box." If lever-pressing increases in frequency of occurrences following food, it is assumed that food exercises a reinforcing (strengthening) effect upon that response.

In the context of the classroom, it may be postulated that a variety of teacher reactions to pupil learning efforts may exercise a strengthening effect on that behavior. Thus, a teacher's comment of "That's right, a nice job" after a pupil has responded to some learning activity might be characterized as a reinforcer for that behavior. Indeed, Skinner (1954) places considerable emphasis on knowledge of results about being correct as an important source of reinforcement by which learning-related behaviors of a student are strengthened and maintained in the classroom. He writes, "If the natural reinforcement inherent in the subject matter is not enough, other reinforcers must be employed" (Skinner, 1954).

A second environmental influence on behavior postulated by Skinner is that the environment provides cues or signals to the individual as to when it is appropriate or inappropriate to respond. Thus, again using an animal illustration, a laboratory rat can learn that lever-pressing will produce a food pellet only when a red light is on in the experimental apparatus. Extending this idea to the classroom, pupils learn to pay attention to a variety of teacher signals or cues as prompts to respond to learning activities in the classroom. A teacher raising a question to a pupil is one example of the cueing function of the classroom environment.

It is reasonable to assume that the teacher exercises considerable influence in establishing conditions which can contribute to or interfere with pupil learning. The observation scale described in this paper delineates four dimensions of teacher behavior which are hypothesized as important in mediating classroom learning outcomes. Two of these dimensions of teacher behavior—reinforcement and cueing—are derived from the Skinnerian framework described above. The following, then, are dimensions of teacher behavior used in the observation scale.

1. INFORMATION GIVING (IG). This dimension refers to any teacher behavior by which a fact or portion of a concept is verbally transmitted by the teacher to her pupils.

2. CUEING (C). This dimension refers to any teacher effort to involve pupils actively in the learning activities by asking them specific questions relevant to the curriculum lesson or by giving pupils instructions to respond motorically. This category is somewhat analogous to a programmed learning situation in which the child responds to a series of questions presented in a sequential order.

3. Reinforcement (R). This refers to any indication by the teacher of the correctness or incorrectness of a pupil's (or the class's) response to a learning activity. Included in this category are any teacher statements which guide the pupil toward the desired response. This dimension parallels a basic feature of a programmed learning situation— i.e., an immediate indication of whether a response is correct.

4. Teacher Control (TC). This refers to any effort by the teacher to maintain or redirect pupil attention in relation to a learning activity.

Method

The above dimensions were used in observing a cognitive enrichment program for underprivileged preschool children. The observations were conducted in four nurseries, each having an average enrollment of thirteen children, supervised by a teacher and her assistant. The nursery observations were limited to planned group activities involving, for example, concept teaching, object-word relationships, etc. Each observation was made for a five-minute period. When the lessons were terminated before the observation period ended, the scores were prorated for a five-minute interval. From 34 to 42 observations were obtained for each of the four teachers.

In using the observation procedure, a tally was recorded to represent a unit of a teacher's behavior corresponding to one of the dimensions described above. A unit was defined as the smallest discernible segment of a teacher's verbal or nonverbal behavior which could be classified into a particular category.

TABLE 1   Mean Percentage of Behavioral Units Distributed Among the Four Observational Categories for Each Teacher.

Teacher	Information Giving	Cueing	Reinforcement	Teacher Control
	%	%	%	%
A	64 (1924)	24 (728)	9 (260)	3 (88)
B	34 (1017)	46 (1384)	12 (360)	8 (238)
C	42 (1271)	30 (911)	16 (485)	12 (331)
D	43 (1304)	32 (967)	18 (534)	7 (195)
Mean Percentage	46	33	14	7

NOTE: The numbers in the parentheses indicate the total number of behavioral units occurring within the thirty observation periods upon which the percentages were computed.

To illustrate the categories and the manner in which the tallies were made, a brief sample from a nursery lesson is given below with the categories indicated in parentheses:

TEACHER: Yesterday, I showed you a vegetable (IG). Does anybody remember what it was (C)?
CHILD: A tomato.

TEACHER: No, it was not a tomato (R). (Teacher seats a child moving away from the group (TC). Tony, sit quietly (TC). Robert, the vegetable I brought yesterday was what (C)?
CHILD: A cucumber.

TEACHER: Yes, it was a cucumber (R). You said that word very well (R). Now let's all say cucumber (C).

A preliminary condition to be met in the construction of the scale dealt with the ability of independent observers to agree on their interpretation of the behavorial categories. Based on twenty-six five-minute observation periods (obtained in an earlier study), the inter-rater reliability correlation coefficients exceeded .90 for each of the four observation categories. To insure representativeness of the reliability data, the twenty-six observations were distributed approximately equally among the four nurseries.

Results and Discussion

The data in Table 1 indicate that the total scorable units of teacher behavior are not uniformly distributed among the four categories (x^2 = 44.44, 3 df, p<.01) with teachers spending a major portion of their time in giving information. In addition, there is a significant variation among the teachers in how their behavior is distributed among the four observational categories (x^2 = 38.62, 9 df, p<.01). Thus, for example, of the total observable behavior of teacher A, 64 percent was categorized as information giving, in contrast to 34 percent for teacher B.

Table 2 presents the intercorrelations among the observational categories. In general, the pattern of relationship suggests in part that the observed categories of teacher behavior were mutually restricting of each other. Thus, tendencies of teachers to give information reduces the likelihood of their encouraging pupil responses (cueing) or reinforcing.

T A B L E 2 Intercorrelations Between Observation Categories Based on N = 30 Observations

Variables	IG	C	R	TC
Information Giving (IG)	—	−.85	−.73	−.31
Cueing (C)		—	.49	.00
Reinforcement (R)			—	.12
Teacher Control (TC)				—

While the effectiveness of any particular style of teacher cannot be determined from the available data, some inferences may be made from an examination of interrelationships among categories. As suggested from the Skinnerian framework, it may be assumed that the ratio of reinforcing to cueing should be high for effective teaching. That is, children should be regularly and consistently informed regarding the accuracy of their responses in order to reinforce desirable behavior and extinguish incorrect response tendencies. A one way analysis of variance does show that this ratio differs significantly ($F = 3.06$, df $= 3/116$, $p<.05$) between teachers from a mean value of .56 for Teacher D to .26 for Teacher B.

In evaluating the usefulness of the observation scale, attention must be first directed to whether or not the scale differentiates among teacher styles. The very limited evidence collected so far suggests that the observation procedure does indeed detect differences between teachers, especially in regard to cueing and reinforcement dimensions. The scale must of course be validated against external criteria. As suggested above, one prediction might be that learning (as measured by standard achievement tests) would be higher in classrooms where teachers provide frequent reinforcement to the learning efforts of pupils—i.e., in classrooms where the ratio of reinforcement to cueing is high. Studies which confirm such a prediction would help establish the construct validation of the described observation scale.

References

B. F. Skinner. *The Behavior of Organisms: An Experimental Analysis.* New York: Appleton-Century-Crofts, 1938.

B. F. Skinner. *Science and Human Behavior.* New York: Macmillan, 1953.

B. F. Skinner, The Science of Learning and the Art of Teaching. *Harvard Educ. Rev.*, 24, 1954, 86-97.

19 The Analysis of Concrete to Abstract Classroom Instructional Patterns Utilizing the TIP Profile

Gerard O. Solomon

Introduction

The well prepared teacher spends countless hours reviewing materials, gathering resources, and writing objectives. Indeed, the importance placed on lesson plans both in teacher training institutions and by administrative supervisors alike places a high priority on pre-classroom planning.

While developmental levels have been considered important in respect to student readiness especially in terms of placement or grouping there has been a significant lag in the utilization of this concept in planning for and implementing instructional strategies. Lesson plans typically do not include teaching strategies but place their emphasis on subject matter. Even if the teacher has become aware of differences in student developmental level, skills for guiding learning consistent with this perception are often absent. This problem requires an attempt to reformu-

Reprinted with permission from *Journal of Research and Development in Education*, 4:52–61, Fall, 1970.

late the developmental level concept both as a research tool for isolating the variables involved and particularly to provide the practicing teacher with an "organizer" by which more appropriate instructional strategies may be designed and implemented.

Research with developmental levels has led to the observation that when a topic is presented on a concrete level by subjecting the physical senses of the students to the actual object, the degree of understanding as measured by subsequent student behavior appears to be high. Among other factors, the many ambiguities present in abstract language appear to be absent or diminished in concrete experiences. For those students having had prior concrete subject matter experiences, a presentation utilizing representational devices such as transparencies and models in lieu of an unobtainable or nonexistent concrete object tends to result in greater understanding than instruction consisting purely of abstract language behavior.

All too frequently the classroom teacher introducing new material by means of lecture finds this abstract mode of instruction does not result in the expected high degree of comprehension achieved by another group of students. Attempts at clarification may utilize vivid examples or stimulate the students to "see" what the lesson is all about. Students remaining confused may prod the teacher into drawing a picture. After doing so the remaining non-comprehending students are characterized as slow by the teacher "requiring it to be put in their hand to understand it." Thus the teacher starts abstractly and ends concretely. This example emphasizes the disharmonious relationships between the levels of some particular students and the levels and sequence of classroom instruction utilized. Clearly in this example the teacher is initially going over the heads of many of the students before dropping down to less abstract levels. For this particular student population beginning on the concrete level and ending up at the abstract might have made more sense. The nature of imagery and the role it plays in the concrete to abstract developmental levels will be outlined in the theoretical foundations to be considered next.

Theoretical Bases for the TIP Profile

Investigation of the role of imagery in teaching and learning was undertaken in 1967 and 1968. (Solomon 1968) By imagery is meant a conscious mental representation of a perceivable, absent, or non-existent object, process or concept. A person experiencing visual imagery for example can be said to be mentally looking at pictures. Likewise, an individual hearing a popular song continuously running through his mind is experiencing auditory imagery. Other types of imagery exist. The literature over a 65 year span, from (Galton 1883) to the present, is uniform in recognizing that the majority of students have mental imagery, particularly visual imagery (Brower 1947). In the light of current thought in the area of human development it is apparent that the appearance and utilization of imaging ability dovetails exactly with the development and attainment of certain cognitive levels. The developmental levels espoused by Piaget and Bruner are especially applicable.

The developmental levels of Piaget proceeding from sensorimotor to the stage of formal operations, and those of Bruner proceeding from enactive to symbolic, have this in common: they both suggest a concrete to abstract continuum. The emphasis by Bruner (1966) on the utilization of imagery in what he terms the ikonic level provides a key to a closer merging of imagery and the developmental level concept. The point made is that imagery is necessary in order to relate an ikonic "representation" to that which it represents. A student must be able to mentally picture a cat in order to comprehend a vague line drawing of the animal.

On the basis of the literature and classroom experiences, a line of research reasoning was developed as follows: according to Piaget a continuum of cognitive growth exists with students varying as to their cognitive maturity, that is, their level on the developmental continuum; according to Bruner, imagery is necessary at certain levels of cognitive growth and helpful at others; therefore, a continuum of cognitive growth can be advanced which both incorporates and adds to the developmental stages of Piaget and the imagery related stages of Bruner. The continuum may be diagrammed:

> Concrete level
> Concrete-imagery level
> Representational level
> Abstract level

The terms *concrete, representational,* and *abstrct* are used to encompass the entirety of the cognitive development continuum. These terms do not suggest a different course of development than that postulated by Piaget but are thought to be more conducive to the relating of the continuum to imagery as these terms reflect the predominant mode of behavior at each general level. A brief description of some important aspects of each of the foregoing levels of the cognitive growth continuum would be useful at this point.

The Concrete Level

Initially, children are not able to deal with that which is not present. During this stage actions and reactions are based on available perceptions. During early childhood, concrete experiences are predominately most meaningful because the child cannot deal effectively with that which is not present at the time. For that matter, imagery is not necessary to function on this level. A person does not need an image of a fish when a fish is being viewed. As was pointed out by Ausubel (1963), if an older child on a higher level of development, or even an adult on the abstract level, has not had certain actual concrete experiences, he cannot deal initially with these areas on a higher level.

The Concrete-Imagery Level

As the child matures further he can begin to mentally speculate about that which he perceives. The child will imitate the sound of an animal, the whistling of a tea kettle or the staccato beat of a drum while observing the mute object. Thus, with imagery, immediate perceptions can be enriched. The starting point, however, in this stage is always the concrete experience. Enriching his perceptions with imagery, the child begins to achieve reversibility. Reversibility could be accomplished completely, for example, when the child could break a piece of clay in two pieces and visualize its original state. The development of imaging ability is necessary then for this level. As this imaging ability becomes highly sophisticated, the child reaches the representational level.

The Representational Level

As Bruner (1966) points out, in order for a child to deal with that which is completely absent in its concrete form by substituting a representation it is necessary for him to utilize imagery to make the translation from the representation to the actual object. For what Bruner calls ikonic representation, the term *representational* is used. A child on the representational level can utilize charts and graphs and will understand a road map. Pictures of objects will completely suffice and what happens to a picture book character can be vicariously experienced by the child through imagery. A child will stretch his arms out to represent an airplane and will go zooming around the room. A representation of a soft drink such as a Coca-Cola sign will often provoke an intense enough gustatory image in the child to present a problem to an accompanying adult.

The Abstract Levels

The term abstract level is used much as Bruner uses symbolic and Piaget uses the Stage of Formal Operations. In the two abstract stages, verbal or written language can be wholly substituted for the concrete by the student. It must be pointed out that two types of language behavior are possible, one utilizing a purely abstract verbalization. Written language, being less abstract since it is closer to the concrete, can be grouped separately as the abstract imagery level. As Ausubel (1963) points out, transitions between developmental levels tend to be gradual and stages overlap. Thus the less predominant but growing abstract language development of a child in the preoperational stage is necessarily accompanied by a high degree of imagery. Verbal description given by elementary students are notably rich in image-provoking content as are verbal descriptions and essays on the secondary level. The radio jingle, "taste that beats the others cold," to sell a cola is aimed at the abstract-imagery level.

The use by teenagers of sayings gleaned from television, as "Here comes de judge" and "Sock it to me," is consistent with the use of imagery-rich abstractions typical of this level. Thus, an individual who has reached the initial stage in which abstractions predominate couples abstractions with images. Students at the high school age are in transition into the fifth stage where abstractions may be predominately used without recourse to imagery. This transition is rarely complete until mature adulthood is reached and even then, while the individual can perform on this level for extended periods of time, this rarely occurs unless some factor such as an extremely abstract occupation is present.

Cognitive Development and the Teacher-Student Relationship

Two points may be emphasized with respect to the relationship between developmental levels as previously described and the student-teacher relationship. First, although students may be on different levels of development in different subject areas, the teacher is conceded to confront more individual differences between students as they enter still higher grades. At almost any grade level, however, the teacher will be faced with students who represent various levels of cognitive maturity and thereby necessitate differing levels of teacher behavior in order to allow for these individual differences. Second, an individual may perform on any level of cognitive maturity below the highest level achieved. Difficulties occur not when a student who has achieved an abstract level in some area is presented concrete experiences but when the reverse occurs.

A teacher faced with, but not aware of or prepared to deal with the individual differences in cognitive maturity in the classroom, may present material on a level appropriate for only part of the class, going over the heads of the rest. Nearly all high school chemistry students, for example, perform well with material requiring the representational level hence one solution for a chemistry teacher would be to plan classroom activities on this level common to the entire class since those students on level above the representational can "drop down" with ease.

The teacher is not doing students any favors when he consistently institutes activities on the lowest level common to all students. Although this procedure may result in immediate understanding by all, students subjected to this procedure may not reach higher levels of cognitive maturity as soon as they otherwise might. The teacher should tempt the student into higher stages of development by exposing him to more advanced forms of cognition.

Classification of Image Provoking Behavior

With respect to imagery, the teacher presenting purely abstract or purely concrete experiences is not provoking imagery in most students. This points to the feasibility of grouping teacher behavior into image provoking and non-image provoking classifications. It can be seen that the teacher presenting concrete-imagery, representational, and abstract-imagery experiences does not provoke imagery in those students who have achieved these respective levels of cognitive growth and this grouping would constitute the imagery grouping. Combining the possible modes of imagery with the image provoking levels yields the following *Taxonomy of Image Provoking Behavior:*

TAXONOMY OF IMAGE PROVOKING BEHAVIOR

1.00

CONCRETE-IMAGERY

1.10 Teacher provides concrete experiences to provoke visual imagery.

1.20 Teacher provides concrete experiences to provoke auditory imagery.

1.30 Teacher provides concrete experiences to provoke organic, kinesthetic, or tactual imagery.

1.40 Teacher provides concrete experiences to provoke olfactory imagery.

1.50 Teacher provides concrete experiences to provoke gustatory imagery.

2.00

REPRESENTATIONAL

2.10 Teacher provides representational experiences to provoke visual imagery.

2.20   Teacher provides representational experiences to provoke auditory imagery.

2.30   Teacher provides representational experiences to provoke organic, kinesthetic, or tactual imagery.

2.40   Teacher provides representational experiences to provoke olfactory imagery.

2.50   Teacher provides representational experiences to provoke gustatory imagery.

3.00

ABSTRACT-IMAGERY

3.10   Teacher provides abstract experiences to provoke visual imagery.

3.20   Teacher provides abstract experiences to provoke auditory imagery.

3.30   Teacher provides abstract experiences to provoke organic, kinesthetic, or tactual imagery.

3.40   Teacher provides abstract experiences to provoke olfactory imagery.

3.50   Teacher provides abstract experiences to provoke gustatory imagery.

The order of the modes of imagery follows the frequency with which the type is encountered in the literature, with visual imagery being most predominant and gustatory imagery being least encountered.

Organic, kinesthetic, and tactual imagery are difficult to separate as all are related somatic functions. For the purposes of this taxonomy then, they have been grouped together.

Formulation of a Teacher Observation Instrument

The foregoing taxonomy was transformed into an observational instrument utilizing a sign system. The non-imaging concrete and abstract levels were added to obtain a complete measure of the teachers' behavior on the concrete-abstract continuum. A reliability study (Solomon 1968) produced data suggesting high reliability and validity and supported the ability of the instrument to discriminate between teachers. An inter-observer reliability of .89 with a level of significance of .001 was accomplished with a minimum of training.

FIGURE 1 Taxonomy of Image Provocation Profile

TOT   PROVOKES NO IMAGERY

.0   Uses Concrete Without Imagery

TOT   **1.00** USES CONCRETE TO PROVOKE IMAGERY

1.10 Provokes Visual Image

1.20 Provokes Auditory Image

1.30 Provokes Org, Kin, or Tact Image

1.40 Provokes Olfactory Image

1.50 Provokes Gustatory Image

TOT   **2.00** USES REPRESENTATION TO PROVOKE IMAGERY

2.10 Provokes Visual Image

2.20 Provokes Auditory Image

2.30 Provokes Org, Kin, or Tact Image

2.40 Provokes Olfactory Image

2.50 Provokes Gustatory Image

TOT   **3.00** USES ABSTRACTION TO PROVOKE IMAGERY

3.10 Provokes Visual Image

3.20 Provokes Auditory Image

3.30 Provokes Org, Kin, or Tact Image

3.40 Provokes Olfactory Image

3.50 Provokes Gustatory Image

TOT   PROVOKES NO IMAGERY

.00   Uses Abstract Without Imagery

The completed observational instrument was termed the *Taxonomy of Image Provocation Profile* (TIP Profile) and is shown in Figure 1 on the preceding page.

Directions

The *Taxonomy of Image Provocation Profile* provides a means of observing and recording the image provoking behavior of the teacher in the classroom.

There are twelve (12) separate 2-minute observation periods in each 24 minute visit to the classroom. During each of the two minute observation periods a check mark is placed in an appropriate imagery level category as the behavior is exhibited. Only if no imagery is provoked during 2-minute period should the PROVOKES NO IMAGERY section be marked. At the end of the 12th marking period totals should be added for each classification and recorded in the first column, headed TOT.

Patterns of Teacher Behavior

The development of the TIP Profile focused on theoretical aspects and reliability. In a more recent study carried out at West Virginia University (Solomon and Wood 1970) 71 students selected from the 250 students who were involved in student teaching were simultaneously observed utilizing four observational instruments including the TIP Profile. A look at their TIP Profile scores is revealing. (Figure 2).

FIGURE 2

TIP LEVEL	MEAN	S.D.
Concrete without Imagery	.41	1.53
Concrete with Visual Imagery	1.49	2.56
Representation with Visual Imagery	2.01	2.72
Abstract with Visual Imagery	4.10	5.59
Abstract without Imagery	5.97	5.46

As can be seen from the standard deviations, a broad spectrum of teacher behavior was observed within each level. Several other points can be noted. First, the frequency of observed behaviors indicates that teachers on the average exhibited more behavior on the abstract level than on any other level. Since the scoring of "abstract" on the instrument excludes behavior on imagery levels and tends to correspond to what is generally termed "lecture," lecture-type behavior excludes the forms of language that tend to be vivid. The next most frequent teacher behavior was abstract, lecture or expository type of teaching that does include image provocation, followed next in frequency by representational behavior. These teachers exhibited teaching in the concrete imagery level even less frequently and the concrete level almost not at all. The concrete levels being largely manipulative, it was dismaying not to find behavior of this type exhibited on a wider scale by the elementary teachers represented in the sample.

It was also determined (Figure 3) that visual imagery was the predominant form utilized by these teachers.

FIGURE 3

TIP LEVEL	MEAN	S.D.
Visual Concrete	1.48	2.56
Non-Visual Concrete	.87	2.20
Visual Representation	2.01	2.72
Non-Visual Representation	.61	1.26
Visual Abstract	4.10	5.59
Non-Visual Abstract	2.37	4.03

That the shift toward significantly less abstract behavior in the lower grades would reflect more appropriate behavior is assumed. A comparison of the 22 elementary teachers to the 49 secondary teachers in the sample showed just a slight decrease in level of abstraction with the corresponding slight increase in representation and concrete behavior.

A factor analysis suggested relationships between measures on all instruments. With regard to factors involving these imagery-related cognitive developmental levels measured by the TIP Profile it was found that (Figure 4) teachers displaying image-provoking behavior tended to use higher levels of cognition across any one of these developmental levels. Thus teacher application, translation (comprehension), and analysis as well as student application were found to accompany the imagery-related TIP measures. Conversely, the predominantly utilized abstract-without-imagery teacher behavior had a high negative loading with the previously mentioned factors suggesting that the higher levels of thinking do not accompany highly abstract teacher behavior.

FIGURE 4

VARIABLE NUMBER	IMAGERY	LOADING
52	Total Imagery	.97
46	Visual Concrete	.81
49	Non-Visual Representation	.80
48	Visual Representation	.77
50	Visual Abstract	.77
51	Non-Visual Abstract	.68
47	Non-Visual Concrete	.62
31	Student Cognition 4. Application	.51
21	Teacher Cognition 2. Translation	.36
23	Teacher Cognition 4. Application	.36
41	TPOR Experimentalism 6. Differentiation	.35
24	Teacher Cognition 5. Analysis	.34
45	Abstract Without Imagery	−.81

High levels of teacher cognition (analysis, synthesis, evaluation) are closely related to definite levels of cognition as measured by the Taxonomy of Image Provocation. It is interesting to note, however, that the highest levels of teacher cognition (synthesis and evaluation) are positively related to concrete classroom experiences, whether with or without imagery, and negatively related to abstract classroom experiences whether with or without imagery. It is the proximity to concreteness on this concrete-abstract continuum which appears to be congruent with high level teacher cognition. Evidence to support this conclusion may be found on Factor 7 and Factor 10. (Figures 5 and 6).

FIGURE 5

VARIABLE NUMBER	CONCRETE COGNITION vs ABSTRACT	LOADING
26	Teacher Cognition 7. Evaluation	−.65
47	Non-Visual Concrete With Imagery	−.45
36	Experimentalism 1. Nature of Situation	−.31
51	Non-Visual Abstract With Imagery	.35

FIGURE 6

VARIABLE NUMBER	CONCRETE *vs* ABSTRACT WITHOUT IMAGERY	LOADING
44	Concrete Without Imagery	.66
25	Teacher Cognition 6. Synthesis	.44
45	Abstract Without Imagery	−.32

Conclusion

This paper has focused on a means of determining teacher behavior as measured by an instrument based on a theoretically formulated concrete to abstract continuum. Used in conjunction with other measures of teacher behavior, patterns of teacher behavior and accompanying student response begin to emerge.

During the past year, the TIP Profile was utilized in the teacher training program at West Virginia University. In addition to developing the skills necessary to use the instrument in observations of simulated teaching, the pre-service teachers were able to demonstrate teaching behaviors at the various TIP levels so as to achieve any profile requested. The fact that they were able to modify their scores at will is evidence of an increased versatility in dealing with the presentation of subject matter at any given cognitive level.

References

David Ausubel, *The Psychology of Meaningful Verbal Learning.* New York: Grune and Stratton, 1963.

Benjamin Bloom (Ed.). *Taxonomy of Educational Objectives: Cognitive Domain,* New York: David McKay Company, Inc., 1956.

Daniel Brower. "The Experimental Study of Imagery: The Relative Predominance of Various Imagery Modalities." *The Journal of General Psychology.* 1947, 37, 199-200.

Jerome Bruner. "On Cognitive Growth," *Studies in Cognitive Growth: A Collaboration at the Center for Cognitive Growth Studies.* By Jerome Bruner, et al. New York: John Wiley and Sons, 1966.

Francis Galton. *Inquiries Into Human Faculty and Its Development.* New York: The MacMillan Co., 1883.

Gerard Solomon. The Classification and Measurement of Image Provoking Cognitive Behaviors of Science Teachers. *Unpublished Doctoral Dissertation,* University of Florida, 1968.

Gerald Solomon and Samuel Wood. Classroom Behavior Accompanying TIP Profile measures. Unpublished manuscript, mimeographed, available from authors, West Virginia University, 1970.

S. Wood, G. Solomon, and G. Deshpande. "Collecting and Analyzing Data Yielded by the Multidimensional Technique for Observing Classroom Behavior." Paper read at A.E.R.A., 1970.

5 *The Psychological Climate*

Overview

Teachers have long looked at teaching from the vantage point of psychology. To study teaching, they have used such concepts as anxiety, hostility, interpersonal relationship, and withdrawal. They have conducted investigations of the teacher's personality traits, especially those of the "effective" teacher. As part of their certification program, they have studied the principles of educational psychology as these relate to teaching. In short, the psychological perspective for the study of teaching is very familiar and widely accepted.

The reason is fairly obvious. The achievement of any goal is facilitated by a favorable emotional atmosphere, and the goal of gaining knowledge and skills is no exception. Furthermore, as shown by other articles in this book, learning of this type is only one goal of teaching. It is not surprising, then, that Rogers, Macdonald and Zaret, and Freud all point to the necessity for a good emotional tone in teaching and to the need for a favorable interpersonal relationship between the teacher and the student.

Educators generally agree that learning will most likely occur in a nonthreatening climate. (Climate is the tone of the interaction among people.) Stavsky, as cited by Tyler in her selection, even states that teaching is "basically an interpersonal relationship," which, with its proper techniques and devices, helps reduce or control anxiety and so promotes learning. Bills cites research which shows that when the teacher creates a favorable interpersonal relationship, that is, when the teacher is process-like, to use Bills's[1] term, the students feel more positive toward other students in the class. Also, this process-like behavior is seen by students as helpful to them in their fuller development. Furthermore, the process-like teacher shares decision-making with his students.

Because of these insights, the analysis of teaching from the psychological vantage point is fundamental. This analysis takes two forms in this Section: (1) the categorizing of classroom verbal behavior; and (2) the expository analyzing of teaching based on experience and previous research. Within each there is an article from two different psychological orientations, Freudian, or Second Force, and Humanistic, or Third Force. (For material on Behavioristic, or First Force, psychology the reader should see selections by Bloom and Gagné in Section 4.)

The articles by Freud and Tyler set forth the dominant ideas of Freudian psychology. (Anna Freud is the daughter of the founder of psychoanalytic psychology, Sigmund Freud.) Freud presents key ideas of Freudian psychology without much of the technical psychoanalytic language. Tyler, who bases her empirical system for categorizing verbal behavior on the work of Menninger, explicitly presents the concepts of psychoanalysis. Between the two the reader will readily get the key Freudian ideas of transference, resistance, discoverance, intervention, countertransference, ego, superego, and identification.

The articles by Rogers, Macdonald and Zaret, and Tuckman set forth key ideas of humanistic psychology. Rogers bases his article on his extensive experience and writings as a practicing psychotherapist, teacher of psychotherapists, and researcher. He, more than any other contemporary psychotherapist, has encouraged teachers to apply therapeutic concepts and principles to teaching. Rogers first sets forth the goals and conditions of learning in psychotherapy as he conceives it. Then he discusses the implications of these points for teaching. (He uses the word *education* here as a synonym for classroom teaching.) The reader will quickly notice that several of Rogers' ideas run counter to current teaching practices found in our schools, for example, testing and lecturing.

Macdonald and Zaret develop a system for categorizing the verbal behavior of the teacher and students based on the ideas of key Third Force psychologists, specifically citing Rogers, Rokeach, and Allport among others. These researchers use a process continuum going from opening behavior to closing behavior. Tuckman bases his research instrument on the work of Kelly and uses such terms as *warm, cold, fair,* and *unfair* to help specify the personal constructs people develop. From

[1]Robert E. Bills, "Insights for Teaching from Personality Theory: Intelligence and Teaching," in *The Nature of Teaching*, edited by Louise M. Berman (Milwaukee: University of Wisconsin-Milwaukee, 1963), pp. 49–64.

these four Third Force authors we get, then, some of the key concepts of humanistic psychology, such as unconditional positive regard, empathy, openness, warmth, congruence, acceptance, realness, dynamism, creativity, and self-actualization.

It is interesting to examine the three instruments developed by Tyler, Macdonald and Zaret, and Tuckman. The unit of behavior by Tyler, called an episode, is quite similar to the unit used by Bellack in Section 3. Both Tyler and Bellack categorize when the speaker changes. Tyler also categorizes when the speaker's meaning changes, and this is similar to the change in pedagogical function recognized by Bellack as an indication of a new pedagogical move. Tyler, moreover, utilizes as an indicator of intervention Bloom's taxonomy, which the reader can examine more fully in Webb's selection (Section 3).

Macdonald and Zaret incorporate categories from Gallagher and Aschner in the section on Cognitive Processes. In their report of results Macdonald and Zaret point out that the teacher gets the responses he solicits. This, they note, is corroborated by Gallagher and Aschner. They also comment about a teacher being locked in an open position. That is, some teachers may exhibit only one type of behavior pattern, and though it may be the open, or positive, position, it may not be always desirable. In the light of Flanders' (Section 2) firm statement that students who achieved the most learning were in classes exposed to flexible patterns of teacher influence, it is necessary to give added thought to this point.

Tuckman's instrument, as he explicitly notes, is not a category system for recording all teacher verbal and/or nonverbal behavior. Rather, it is an impression measure; that is, the observer gives his impression of the teacher after observing approximately forty-five minutes. Yet, Tuckman reports high reliability among observers, consistency over items, verifiable and reproducible data, discriminable differences between teachers and between teacher feedback conditions, and evidence of usability and practicality.

How adequate is the psychological framework for analyzing teaching? Since psychotherapy is most often a voluntary relation between one therapist and one client the question is whether the concepts and principles of psychotherapy (whether Freud's or Rogers') can be applied usefully to classroom teaching. If not directly applied, can they still be used to guide our analysis? It is meaningful to talk about teaching in such terms as Rogers' "significant learning"? If so, is it possible for classroom teachers to bring about "significant learning"? Is it meaningful to talk about teaching in such terms as anxiety, resistance, interpersonal relationship, transference, and hostility? In what ways does the employment of these concepts give us insight into teaching? Obviously, the authors in this section are convinced that such concepts are relevant to the study of teaching, as Macdonald and Zaret explicitly state at the end of their article. Many readers may wish to carry the discussion further.

Many questions for further research arise. For example, what is the relationship between a teacher's climate as measured by a psychoanalytic or humanistic instrument and the cognitive processes manifested in the verbal behavior in his teaching? To what extent does a teacher's own preference of psychological orientations influence the climate of his teaching? Is a particular psychological orientation more fruitful in studying teaching at the nursery school level? Elementary school level? High school level? College level?

20 Significant Learning: in Therapy and in Education

Carl R. Rogers

Presented here is a thesis, a point of view, regarding the implications which psychotherapy has for education It is a stand which I take tentatively, and with some hesitation. I have many unanswered questions about this thesis. But it has, I think, some clarity in it, and hence it may provide a starting point from which clear differences can emerge.

Significant Learning in Psychotherapy

Let me begin by saying that my long experience as a therapist convinces me that significant learning is facilitated in psychotherapy, and occurs in that relationship. By significant learning I mean learning which is more than an accumulation of facts. It is learning which makes a difference— in the individual's behavior, in the course of action he chooses in the future, in his attitudes and in his personality. It is a pervasive learning

Reprinted with permission of the Association for Supervision and Curriculum development and Carl R. Rogers from *Educational Leadership*, 16:232–242, January, 1959. Copyright © 1959 by the Association for Supervision and Curriculum Development.

which is not just an accretion of knowledge, but which interpenetrates with every portion of his existence.

Now it is not only my subjective feeling that such learning takes place. This feeling is substantiated by research. In client-centered therapy, the orientation with which I am most familiar, and in which the most research has been done, we know that exposure to such therapy produces learnings, or changes, of these sorts:

> The person comes to see himself differently.
>
> He accepts himself and his feelings more fully.
>
> He becomes more self-confident and self-directing.
>
> He becomes more the person he would like to be.
>
> He becomes more flexible, less rigid, in his conceptions.
>
> He adopts more realistic goals for himself.
>
> He behaves in a more mature fashion.
>
> He changes his maladjustive behaviors, even such a long-established one as chronic alcoholism.
>
> He becomes more acceptant of others.
>
> He becomes more open to the evidence, both to what is going on outside of himself, and to what is going on inside of himself.
>
> He changes in his basic personality characteristics, in constructive ways.[1]

I think perhaps this is sufficient to indicate that there are learnings which are significant, which do make a difference.

Significant Learning in Education

I believe I am accurate in saying that educators too are interested in learnings which make a difference. Simple knowledge of facts has its value. To know who won the battle of Poltava, or when the umpteenth opus of Mozart was first performed, may win $64,000 or some other sum for the possessor of this information, but I believe educators in general are a little embarrassed by the assumption that the acquisition of such knowledge constitutes education. Speaking of this reminds me of a forceful statement made by a professor of agronomy in my freshman year in college. Whatever knowledge I gained in his course has departed completely, but I remember how, with World War I as his background, he was comparing factual knowledge with ammunition. He wound up his little discourse with the exhortation, "Don't be a damned ammunition wagon; be a rifle!" I believe most educators would share this sentiment that knowledge exists primarily for use.

[1]For evidence supporting these statements see references (6) and (8).

To the extent then that educators are interested in learnings which are functional, which make a difference, which pervade the person and his actions, then they might well look to the field of psychotherapy for leads or ideas. Some adaptation for education of the learning process which takes place in psychotherapy seems like a promising possibility.

The Conditions of Learning in Psychotherapy

Let us then see what is involved, essentially, in making possible the learning which occurs in therapy. I would like to spell out, as clearly as I can, the conditions which seem to be present when this phenomenon occurs.

Facing a Problem

The client is, first of all, up against a situation which he perceives as a serious and meaningul problem. It may be that he finds himself behaving in ways which he cannot control, or he is overwhelmed by confusions and conflicts, or his marriage is going on the rocks, or he finds himself unhappy in his work. He is, in short, faced with a problem with which he has tried to cope, and found himself unsuccessful. He is therefore eager to learn, even though at the same time he is frightened that what he discovers in himself may be disturbing. Thus one of the conditions nearly always present is an uncertain and ambivalent desire to learn or to change, growing out of a perceived difficulty in meeting life.

What are the conditions which this individual meets when he comes to a therapist? I have recently formulated a theoretical picture of the necessary and sufficient conditions which the therapist provides, if constructive change or significant learning is to occur (7). This theory is currently being tested in several of its aspects by empirical research, but it must still be regarded as theory based upon clinical experience rather than proven fact. Let me describe briefly the conditions which it seems essential that the therapist should provide.

Congruence

If therapy is to occur, it seems necessary that the therapist be, in the relationship, a unified, or integrated, or congruent person. What I mean is that within the relationship he is exactly what he *is*—not a façade or a role, or a pretense. I have used the term congruence to refer to this accurate matching of experience with awareness. It is when the therapist is fully and accurately aware of what he is experiencing at this moment in the relationship, that he is fully congruent. Unless this congruence is present to a considerable degree it is unlikely that significant learning can occur.

Though this concept of congruence is actually a complex one, I believe all of us recognize it in an intuitive and common-sense way in individuals with whom we deal. With one individual we recognize that he not only means exactly what he says, but that his deepest feelings also match what he is expressing. Thus whether he is angry or affectionate or ashamed or enthusiastic, we sense that he is the same at all levels—in what he is experiencing at an organismic level, in his awareness at the conscious level, and in his words and communications. We furthermore recognize that he is acceptant of his immediate feelings. We say of such a person that we know "exactly where he stands." We tend to feel comfortable and secure in such a relationship. With another person we recognize that what he is saying is almost certainly a front or a façade. We wonder what he *really* feels, what he is really experiencing, behind this façade. We may also wonder if *he* knows what he really feels, recognizing that he may be quite unaware of the feelings he is actually experiencing. With such a person we tend to be cautious and wary. It is not the kind of relationship in which defenses can be dropped or in which significant learning and change can occur.

Thus this second condition for therapy is that the therapist is characterized by a considerable degree of congruence in the relationship. He is freely, deeply, and acceptantly himself, with his actual experience of his feelings and reactions matched by an accurate awareness of these feelings and reactions as they occur and as they change.

Unconditional Positive Regard

A third condition is that the therapist experiences a warm caring for the client—a caring which is not possessive, which demands no personal gratification. It is an atmosphere which simply demonstrates "I care"; not "I care for you *if* you behave thus and so." Standal (10) has termed this attitude "unconditional positive regard," since it has no conditions of worth attached to it. I have often used the term acceptance to describe this aspect of the therapeutic climate. It involves as much feeling of acceptance for the client's expression of negative, "bad," painful, fearful, and abnormal feelings, as for his expression of "good," positive, mature, confident and social feelings. It involves an acceptance of and a caring for the client as a *separate* person, with permission for him to have his own feelings and experiences, and to find his own meanings in them. To the degree that the therapist can provide this safety-creating climate of unconditional positive regard, significant learning is likely to take place.

An Empathic Understanding

The fourth condition for therapy is that the therapist is experiencing an accurate, empathic understanding of the client's world as seen from the inside. To sense the client's private world as if it were your own, but without ever losing the "as if" quality—this is empathy, and this seems essential to therapy. To sense the client's anger, fear, or confusion as if it were your own, yet without your own anger, fear, or confusion getting bound up in it, is the condition we are endeavoring to describe. When the client's world is this clear to the therapist, and he moves about in it freely, then he can both communicate his understanding of what is clearly known to the client and can also voice meanings in the client's experience of which the client is scarcely aware. That such penetrating empathy is important for therapy is indicated by Fiedler's research in which items such as the following placed high in the description of relationships created by experienced therapists:

> The therapist is well able to understand the patient's feelings.
> The therapist is never in any doubt about what the patient means.
> The therapist's remarks fit in just right with the patient's mood and content.
> The therapist's tone of voice conveys the complete ability to share the patient's feelings. (2a)

Fifth Condition

A fifth condition for significant learning in therapy is that the client should experience or perceive something of the therapist's congruence, acceptance, and empathy. It is not enough that these conditions exist in the therapist. They must, to some degree, have been successfully communicated to the client.

The Process of Learning in Therapy

It has been our experience that when these five conditions exist, a process of change inevitably occurs. The client's rigid perceptions of himself and of others loosen and become open to reality. The rigid ways in which he has construed the meaning of his experience are looked at, and he finds himself questioning many of the "facts" of his life, discovering that they are only "facts" because he has regarded them so. He discovers feelings of which he has been unaware, and experiences them, often vividly, in the therapeutic relationship. Thus he learns to be more open to all of his experience—the evidence within himself as well as the evidence without. He learns to *be* more of his experience—to be the feelings of which he has been frightened as well as the feelings he has regarded as more acceptable. He becomes a more fluid, changing, learning person.

The Mainspring of Change

In this process it is not necessary for the therapist to "motivate" the client or to supply the energy which brings about the change. Nor, in some sense, is the motivation supplied by the client, at least in any conscious way. Let us say rather that the motivation for learning and change springs from the self-actualizing tendency of life itself, the tendency for the organism to flow into all the differentiated channels of potential development, insofar as these are experienced as enhancing.

I could go on at very considerable length on this, but it is not my purpose to focus on the process of therapy and the learnings which take place, nor on the motivation for these learnings, but rather on the conditions which make them possible. So I will simply conclude the description of therapy by saying that it is a type of significant learning which takes place when five conditions are met:

When the client perceives himself as faced by a serious and meaningful problem;

When the therapist is a congruent person in the relationship, able to *be* the person he *is;*

When the therapist feels an unconditional positive regard for the client;

When the therapist experiences an accurate empathic understanding of the client's private world, and communicates this;

When the client to some degree experiences the therapist's congruence, acceptance, and empathy.

Implications for Education

What do these conditions mean if applied to education? Undoubtedly the reader will be able to give a better answer than I out of his own experience, but I will at least suggest some of the implications.

Contact with Problems

In the first place it means that significant learning occurs more readily in relation to situations perceived as problems. I believe I have observed evidence to support this. In my own varying attempts to conduct courses and groups in ways consistent with my therapeutic experience, I have found such an approach more effective, I believe, in workshops than in regular courses, in extension courses than in campus courses. Individuals who come to workshops or extension courses are those who are in contact with problems which they recognize as problems. The student in the regular university course, and particularly in the required course, is apt to view the course as an experience in which he expects to remain passive or resentful or both, an experience which he certainly does not often see as relevant to his own problems.

Yet it has also been my experience that when a regular university class does perceive the course as an experience they can use to resolve problems which *are* of concern to them, the sense of release, and the thrust of forward movement is astonishing. And this is true of courses as diverse as Mathematics and Personality.

I believe the current situation in Russian education also supplies evidence on this point. When a whole nation perceives itself as being faced with the urgent problem of being behind—in agriculture, in industrial production, in scientific development, in weapons development—then an astonishing amount of significant learning takes place, of which the Sputniks are but one observable example.

So the first implication for education might well be that we permit the student, at any level, to be in real contact with the relevant problems of his existence, so that he perceives problems and issues which he wishes to resolve. I am quite aware that this implication, like the others I shall mention, runs sharply contrary to the current trends in our culture, but I shall comment on that later.

I believe it would be quite clear from my description of therapy that an overall implication for education would be that the task of the teacher is to create a facilitating classroom climate in which significant learning can take place. This general implication can be broken down into several sub-sections.

The Teacher's Real-ness

Learning will be facilitated, it would seem, if the teacher is congruent. This involves the teacher's being the person that he is, and being openly aware of the attitudes he holds. It means that he feels acceptant toward his own real feelings. Thus he becomes a real person in the relationship with his students. He can be enthusiastic about subjects he likes, and bored by topics he does not like. He can be angry, but he can also be sensitive or sympathetic. Because he accepts his feeling as *his* feelings, he has no need to impose them on his students, or to insist that they feel the same way. He is a *person*, not a faceless embodiment of a curricular requirement, or a sterile pipe through which knowledge is passed from one generation to the next.

I can suggest only one bit of evidence which might support this view. As I think back over a number of teachers who have facilitated my own learning, it seems to me each one has this quality of being a real person. I wonder if your memory is the same. If so, perhaps it is less important that a teacher cover the allotted amount of the curriculum, or use the most approved audio-visual devices, than that he be congruent, real, in his relation to his students.

Acceptance and Understanding

Another implication for the teacher is that significant learning may take place if the teacher can accept the student as he is, and can understand the feelings he possesses. Taking the third and fourth conditions of therapy as specified above, the teacher who can warmly accept, who can provide an unconditional positive regard, and who can empathize with the feelings of fear, anticipation, and discouragement which are involved in meeting new material, will have done a great deal toward setting the conditions for learning. Clark Moustakas, in his book, *The Teacher and the Child* (5), has given many excellent examples of individual and group situations from kindergarten to high school, in which the teacher has worked toward just this type of goal. It will perhaps disturb some that when the teacher holds such attitudes, when he is willing to be acceptant of feelings, it is not only attitudes toward school work itself which are expressed, but feelings about parents, feelings of hatred for brother or sister, feelings of concern about self—the whole gamut of attitudes. Do such feelings have a right to exist openly in a school setting? It is my thesis that they do. They are related to the person's becoming, to his effective learning and effective functioning, and to deal understandingly and acceptantly with such feelings has a definite relationship to the learning of long division or the geography of Pakistan.

Provision of Resources

This brings me to another implication which therapy holds for education. In therapy the resources for learning one's self lie within. There is very little data which the therapist can supply which will be of help since the data to be dealt with exist within the person. In education this is not true. There are many resources of knowledge, of techniques, of theory, which constitute raw material for use. It seems to me that what I have said about therapy suggests that these materials, these resources, be made available to the students, not forced upon them. Here a wide range of ingenuity and sensitivity is an asset.

I do not need to list the usual resources which come to mind—books, maps, workbooks, materials, recordings, work-space, tools, and the like. Let me focus for a moment on the way the teacher uses himself and his knowledge and experience as a resource. If the teacher holds the point of view I have been expressing then he would probably want to make himself available to his class in at least the following ways:

He would want to let them know of special experience and knowledge he has in the field, and to let them know they could call on this knowledge. Yet he would not want them to feel that they must use him in this way.

He would want them to know that his own way of thinking about the field, and of organizing it, was available to them, even in lecture form, if they wished. Yet again he would want this to be perceived as an offer, which could as readily be refused as accepted.

He would want to make himself known as a resource-finder. Whatever might be seriously wanted by an individual or by the whole group to promote their learning, he would be very willing to consider the possibilities of obtaining such a resource.

He would want the quality of his relationship to the group to be such that his feelings could be freely available to them, without being imposed on them or becoming a restrictive influence on them. He thus could share the excitements and enthusiasms of his own learnings, without insisting that the students follow in his footsteps; the feelings of disinterest, satisfaction, bafflement, or pleasure which he feels toward individual or group activities, without this becoming either a carrot or a stick for the student. His hope would be that he could say, simply for himself, "I don't like that," and that the student with equal freedom could say, "But I do."

Thus whatever the resource he supplies—a book, space to work, a new tool, an opportunity for observation of an industrial process, a lecture based on his own study, a picture, graph or map, his own emotional reactions—he would feel that these were, and would hope they would be perceived as, offerings to be used if they were useful to the student. He would not feel them to be guides, or expectations, or commands, or impositions or requirements. He would offer himself, and all the other resources he could discover, for use.

The Basic Motive

It should be clear from this that his basic reliance would be upon the self-actualizing tendency in his students. The hypothesis upon which he would build is that students who are in real contact with life problems wish to learn, want to grow, seek to find out, hope to master, desire to create. He would see his function as that of developing such a personal relationship with his students, and such a climate in his classroom, that these natural tendencies could come to their fruition.

Some Omissions

These I see as some of the things which are implied by a therapeutic viewpoint for the educational process. To make them a bit sharper, let me point out some of the things which are not implied.

I have not included lectures, talks, or expositions of subject matter which are imposed on the students. All of these procedures might be a part of the experience if they were desired, explicitly or implicitly, by the student. Yet even here, a teacher whose work was following through a hypothesis based on therapy would be quick to sense a shift in that desire. He might have been requested to lecture to the group (and to give a *requested* lecture is *very* different from the usual classroom experience), but if he detected a growing disinterest and boredom, he would respond to that, trying to understand the feeling which had arisen in the group, since his response to their feelings and attitudes would take precedence over his interest in expounding material.

I have not included any program of evaluation of the student's learnings in terms of external criteria. I have not, in other words, included examinations. I believe that the testing of the student's achievements in order to see if he meets some criterion held by the teacher, is directly contrary to the implications of therapy for significant learning. In therapy, the examinations are set by *life*. The client meets them, sometimes passing, sometimes failing. He finds that he can use the resources of the therapeutic relationship and his experience in it to organize himself so that he can meet life's tests more satisfyingly next time. I see this as the paradigm for education also. Let me try to spell out a fantasy of what it would mean.

In such an education, the requirements for many life situations would be a part of the resources the teacher provides. The student would have available the knowledge that he cannot enter engineering school without so much math; that he cannot get a job in X corporation unless he has a college diploma; that he cannot become a psychologist without doing an independent doctoral research; that he cannot be a doctor without knowledge of chemistry; that he cannot even drive a car without passing an examination on rules of the road. These are requirements set, not by the teacher, but by life. The teacher is there to provide the resources which the student can use to learn so as to be able to meet these tests. There would be other in-school evaluations of similar sort. The student might well be faced with the fact that he cannot join the Math Club until he makes a certain score on a standardized mathematics test; that he cannot develop his camera film until he has shown an adequate knowledge of chemistry and lab techniques; that he cannot join the special literature section until he has shown evidence of both wide reading and creative writing. The natural place of evaluation in life is as a ticket of entrance, not as a club over the recalcitrant. Our experience in therapy would suggest that it should be the same way in the school. It would leave the student as a self-respecting, self-motivated person, free to choose whether he wished to put forth the effort to gain these tickets of entrance. I would thus refrain from forcing him into conformity, from sacrificing his creativity, and from causing him to live his life in terms of the standards of others.

I am quite aware that the two elements of which I have just been speaking—the lectures and expositions imposed by the teacher on the group, and the evaluation of the individual by the teacher, constitute the two major ingredients of current education. So when I say that experience in psychotherapy would suggest that they both be omitted, it should be quite clear that the implications of psychotherapy for education are startling indeed.

Probable Outcomes

If we are to consider such drastic changes as I have outlined, what would be the results which would justify them? There have been some research investigations of the outcomes of a student-centered type of teaching (1, 2, 3), though these studies are far from adequate. For one thing, the situations studied vary greatly in the extent to which they meet the conditions I have described. Most of them have extended only over a period of a few months, though one recent study with lower class children extended over a full year (3). Some involve the use of adequate controls, some do not.

I think we may say that these studies indicate that in classroom situations which at least attempt to approximate the climate I have described, the findings are as follows: Factual and curricular learning is roughly equal to the learning in conventional classes. Some studies report slightly more, some slightly less. The student-centered group shows gains significantly greater than the conventional class in personal adjustment, in self-initiated extra-curricular learning, in creativity, in self-responsibility.

I have come to realize, as I have considered these studies, and puzzled over the design of better studies which should be more informative and conclusive, that findings from such research will never answer our questions. For all such findings must be evaluated in terms of the goals we have for education. If we value primarily the learning of knowledge, then we may discard the conditions I have described as useless, since there is no evidence that they lead to a greater rate or amount of factual knowledge. We may then favor such measures as the one which I understand is advocated by a number of members of Congress—the setting up of a training school for scientists, modelled upon the military academies. But if we value creativity, if we deplore the fact that all of our germinal ideas in atomic physics, in psychology, and in other sciences have been borrowed from Europe, then we may wish to give a trial to ways of facilitating learning which give more promise of freeing the mind. If we value independence, if we are disturbed by the growing conformity of knowledge, of values, of attitudes, which our present system induces, then we may wish to set up conditions of learning which make for uniqueness, for self-direction, and for self-initiated learning.

Some Concluding Issues

I have tried to sketch the kind of education which would be implied by what we have learned in the field of psychotherapy. I have endeavored to suggest very briefly what it would mean if the central focus of the teacher's effort were to develop a relationship, an atmosphere, which was conducive to self-motivated, self-actualizing, significant learning. But this is a direction which leads sharply away from current educational practices and educational trends. Let me mention a few of the very diverse issues and questions which need to be faced if we are to think constructively about such an approach.

In the first place, how do we conceive the goals of education? The approach I have outlined has, I believe, advantages for achieving certain goals, but not for achieving others. We need to be clear as to the way we see the purposes of education.

What are the actual outcomes of the kind of education I have described? We need a great deal more of rigorous, hard-headed research to know the actual results of this kind of education as compared with conventional education. Then we can choose on the basis of the facts.

Even if we were to try such an approach to the facilitation of learning, there are many difficult issues. Could we possibly permit students to come in contact with real issues? Our whole culture—through custom, through the law, through the efforts of labor unions and management, through the attitudes of parents and teachers—is deeply committed to keeping young people away from any touch with real problems. They are not to work, they should not carry responsibility, they have no business in civic or political problems, they have no place in international concerns, they simply should be guarded from any direct contact with the real problems of individual and group living. They are not expected to help about the home, to earn a living, to contribute to science, to deal with moral issues. This is a deep seated trend which has lasted for more than a generation. Could it possibly be reversed?

Another issue is whether we could permit knowledge to be organized in and by the individual, or whether it is to be organized *for* the individual. Here teachers and educators line up with parents and national leaders to insist that the pupil must be guided. He must be inducted into knowledge we have organized for him. He cannot be trusted to organize knowledge in functional terms for himself. As Herbert Hoover says of high school students, "You simply cannot expect kids of those ages to determine the sort of education they need unless they have some guidance."[2] This seems so obvious to most people that even to question it is to seem somewhat unbalanced. Even a chancellor of a university questions whether freedom is really necessary in education, saying that perhaps we have overestimated its value. He says the Russians have advanced mightily in science without it, and implies that we should learn from them.

Still another issue is whether we would wish to oppose the strong current trend toward education as drill in factual knowledge. All must learn the same facts in the same way. Admiral Rickover states it as his belief that "in some fashion we must devise a way to introduce uniform standards into American education. . . . For the first time, parents would have a real yardstick to measure their schools. If the local school continued to teach such pleasant subjects as 'life adjustment' . . . instead of

[2]*Time,* December 2, 1957.

French and physics, its diploma would be, for all the world to see, inferior."[3] This is a statement of a very prevalent view. Even such a friend of forward-looking views in education as Max Lerner says at one point, "All that a school can ever hope to do is to equip the student with tools which he can later use to become an educated man" (4, p. 741). It is quite clear that he despairs of significant learning taking place in our school system, and feels that it must take place outside. All the school can do is to pound in the tools.

One of the most painless ways of inculcating such factual tool knowledge is the "teaching machine" being devised by B. F. Skinner and his associates (9). This group is demonstrating that the teacher is an outmoded and ineffective instrument for teaching arithmetic, trigonometry, French, literacy appreciation, geography, or other factual subjects. There is simply no doubt in my mind that these teaching machines, providing immediate rewards for "right" answers, will be further developed, and will come into wide use. Here is a new contribution from the field of the behavioral sciences with which we must come to terms. Does it take the place of the approach I have described, or is it supplemental to it? Here is one of the problems we must consider as we face toward the future.

I hope that by posing these issues, I have made it clear that the double-barrelled question of what constitutes significant learning, and how it is to be achieved, poses deep and serious problems for all of us. It is not a time when timid answers will suffice. I have tried to give a definition of significant learning as it appears in psychotherapy, and a description of the conditions which facilitate such learning. I have tried to indicate some implications of these conditions for education. I have, in other words, proposed one answer to these questions. Perhaps we can use what I have said, against the twin backdrops of current public opinion and current knowledge in the behavioral sciences, as a start for discovering some fresh answers of our own.

References

1. Volney Faw. "A Psychotherapeutic Method of Teaching Psychology." *American Psychologist* 4:104-09, 1949.

2. Volney Faw. "Evaluation of Student-Centered Teaching." Unpublished manuscript, 1954.

2a. F. E. Fiedler. "A Comparison of Therapeutic Relationships in Psychoanalytic, Non-directive and Adlerian Therapy." *Journal of Consulting Psychology* 14:436-45, 1950.

3. John H. Jackson. "The Relationship Between Psychological Climate and the Quality of Learning Outcomes among Lower-status Pupils." Unpublished Ph.D. thesis, University of Chicago, 1957.

[3] *Ibid.*

4. Max Lerner. *America as a Civilization.* New York: Simon & Schuster, 1957.

5. Clark Moustakas. *The Teacher and the Child.* New York: McGraw-Hill Book Company, 1956.

6. C. R. Rogers. *Client-centered Therapy.* New York: Houghton Mifflin Company, 1951.

7. C. R. Rogers. "The Necessary and Sufficient Conditions of Therapeutic Personality Change." *Journal of Consulting Psychology* 21:95-103, 1957.

8. C. R. Rogers, and R. Dymond, editors. *Psychotherapy and Personality Change.* Chicago: University of Chicago Press, 1954.

9. B. F. Skinner. "The Science of Learning and the Art of Teaching." *Harvard Educational Review* 24:86-97, 1954.

10. Stanley Standal. "The Need for Positive Regard: A Contribution to Client-centered Theory." Unpublished Ph.D. thesis, University of Chicago, 1954.

21 A Study of Openness in Classroom Interactions

James P. Macdonald and Esther Zaret

Background of the Study

What is essential to understanding the nature of teaching? How should teaching be conceptualized? These questions and others like them lead to a basic concern of many educational researchers and theorists. Behind these questions lies the desire to understand the nature of teaching in order that we may improve the selection, education, and performance of teachers; ultimately, improving the quality of learning in our schools. . . .

What is needed is a dynamic conceptualization which deals with human behavior in terms of a general dimension; a general dimension that can move freely among the levels of the teacher as a behaving person, the interactive context, and the children as behavers. Only when a concept of this order is available will it be possible to move freely in the analysis of teaching.

Reprinted with permission from *A Study of Openness in Classroom Interactions*. This investigation was supported (in part) by PHS research grant—MH 07563-01 from the National Institute of Mental Health, Public Health Service. (Numbering has been retained as it appeared in the original article.)

In recent years the behavioral sciences have discovered exciting new ways of looking at human behavior which have direct implications for our concern. One such approach found, for example, among the writings of Rogers (3), Schachtel (4), Rokeach (5), etc. gives promise for providing a conceptualization of the power, usefulness, and generality needed. Essentially, this is the idea of arranging behavior on a process continuum of openness as contrasted with compensatory and/or defensive behavior. Within this framework teacher and pupils as behaving persons, and the interactions between each, may be conceptualized. . . .

The open-closed analytical framework to be applied to classroom interaction in the present study has been developed from a general theoretical background based on the works of Allport (18), Kubie (19), Rogers (3), Rokeach (5), and Schachtel (4). . . .

Rationale of the Study

The proposed process continuum framework differentiates opening and closing teacher behavior in verbal interaction with learners.

At one end of the continuum, the open teacher, in process, exhibits maximal awareness and acceptance of the learner's frame of reference and his readiness to respond. Teacher interchanges with the learner will be differentiated and transaction-oriented, relating to the realities of the immediate interaction context, resulting in expanded opportunities for variations in learner behavior.

At the opposite end of the continuum, teacher behavior characterized by rigidity and judgmental authority is "closing" in two crucial aspects of teacher-learner interchanges: first, it limits the teacher's perceptual awareness of the learner's frame of reference and his readiness to respond; and, second, it restricts opportunities for variations in learner behavior.

It is hypothesized that the more "open" teacher, functioning at the optimal level of perceptual awareness of the learner, is more likely to make an effective spontaneous decision in direct response to the learner —a decision which will expand opportunities for variations in the learner's productive behavior. And further, an examination of these decisive teacher responses will reveal characteristic patterns of behavior which may be differentiated on a process continuum of opening to closing/defensive behavior. . . .

This study has focused on the interactive verbal behavior of teachers and learners in a specific instructional context—a social studies discussion and/or planning session. . . .

Figure 2 shows a diagrammatic sketch of an analytical framework which was derived from the theoretical perspective presented above, and further developed during the study. Essentially, this schema contrasts opening behavior with closing behavior on one process continuum in the classroom.

The descriptive behavioral terms in the diagram include representative responses found in interaction studies which appear to be most logically related to the framework of the process continuum. Similar descriptive terms were projected as guides for observation and analysis; in the course of the study modifications and additions were made resulting in the descriptive list found in Figure 2. . . .

Assumptions and Definitions of Concepts

The overall rationale and the definitions of concepts are based on several *assumptions about teaching behavior:*

FIGURE 2 Revised Analytical Framework

CLASSIFICATION OF VERBAL BEHAVIOR IN THE CLASSROOM

OPENING

	Teacher	Learner	
Transaction *Oriented* *Decisions*	Stimulating Supporting Clarifying Facilitating Elaborating Evaluating °Monitoring °Chairing Accepting	Discovering Exploring Experimenting Elaborating Qualifying Evaluating Synthesizing Explicating Deriving implications Divergent association Counter-responding	*Productive* *Behavior*
Role-expectancy *Oriented* *Decisions*	Directing Judging (Verdicts) Reproving Rejecting Ignoring Probing or priming °Monitoring °Chairing Factual dialogue (telling) Affirming	Guessing Confirming Acquiescing Following Parroting Counter responding (directing, judging, reproving rejecting, defending) Reproducing facts Reasoning based on given or remembered data	*Reproductive* *Behavior*

CLOSING

°Monitoring—calling on a student to respond; recognizing a volunteer response.
°Chairing—keeping a discussion going; no teacher talk.

The interaction flows primarily from teacher decisions, since almost all classroom behavior is either initiated by the teacher or is learner initiated behavior which is then accepted or rejected by the teacher. A relationship has been postulated between the teacher's mediating responses and possibilities for variations in the learner's ensuing responses. Thus, transaction-oriented teacher decisions would permit productive learner behavior; role-expectancy oriented decisions would promote reproductive learner behavior.

A. The teacher is the major agent of influence in the classroom.
B. Every teacher develops expectations regarding learner behavior; these expectations may be general or specific; these expectations may be explicitly or implicitly defined by the teacher.
C. The teacher continually makes decisions, either explicitly or implicitly expressed, which are compatible with his expectations for learner behavior, and which have a decisive effect on the course of action and interaction in the classroom.
D. Any area of teacher decision-making may be examined for fuller understanding, within a consistent and comprehensive framework of analysis.

The significant concepts to be defined are *critical incidents* and *critical shifts* in teaching behavior; *transaction oriented decisions* versus *role expectancy oriented decisions* in the teacher's mediating behavior; *productive* versus *reproductive* responses in learner behavior.

1. *Critical Incidents and Critical Shifts*

In describing "The Critical Incident Technique in the Study of Individuals" (21) John C. Flanagan has set forth a general definition of "critical incident":

> By an incident is meant any observable type of human activity which is sufficiently complete in itself to permit inferences and predictions to be made about the person performing this act. To be critical, an incident must be performed in a situation where the purpose or intent of the act seems fairly clear to the observer and its consequences are sufficiently definite so that there is little doubt concerning its effects.

In classroom verbal interaction the *critical incident* may be conceptualized as one or a series of related critical shifts which represent a readjustment in teacher strategy to facilitate learning. Harootunian (22) has recently called attention to the frequency of such critical shifts in teacher behavior and has emphasized the potential strategizing inherent in such teacher shifts. . . .

2. Analytical Schema for Classifying Verbal Behavior in the Classroom

2.1 *Transaction-oriented* versus *Role-oriented* teacher decisions. The study focused on a conceptualized "question-answer-response" flow of verbal action. In this sequence (QAR) the teacher's mediating response to the learner's answer was assumed to be the decisive factor in evoking or limiting productive learner behavior. In responding to the learner the teacher reflects his decision to continue the flow of action, or to shift and reorient classroom action to facilitate learning in accordance with his expectation for learner behavior.

In classifying teacher responses to the learner an attempt was made to differentiate between transaction-oriented and role expectancy-oriented teacher decisions. The conceptualized distinction is summarized as follows:

Transaction-oriented decisions were conceived as:
   (1) reflecting flexible teacher expectations.
   (2) accepting and expanding the learner's meanings (as revealed in his responses to teacher questions and statements).
   (3) promoting divergent, evaluative, and choice-making learner behavior.

Role expectancy-oriented decisions were conceived as:
   (1) reflecting rigid teacher expectations.
   (2) rejecting or proscribing the learner's meanings (as revealed in his responses to teacher questions and statements).
   (3) promoting convergent, non-evaluative learner behavior.

2.2 *Productive* versus *Reproductive* learner behavior.
The continuum of the range of variations in learner behavior includes four categories of the Aschner-Gallagher System (23), an adaptation of the Guilford structure of intellect model, for classifying productive thinking processes in the context of classroom verbal interactions.

In the present study *Productive* learner behavior includes the Aschner-Gallagher categories of evaluative and divergent responses; *Reproductive* learner behavior includes cognitive memory and convergent responses.

Research Plan

The specific aim of this study was an examination of classroom interactions from the viewpoint of the proposed process continuum of openness as contrasted with defensive and/or compensatory behavior in order to see if the behavior observed can be reliably identified, categorized, and analyzed in these terms.

The long term goal is to utilize the tested framework to generate hypotheses for large scale intensive studies involving increased effectiveness in teaching. . . .

Nine teachers, and their classrooms of students, from the Campus Elementary School of the University of Wisconsin-Milwaukee comprised the sample for the study.

Each classroom was visited during a planning and/or discussion period in the Social Studies program. The duration of this visit was from twenty to fifty minutes in each case. Tape recordings were made of these periods.

The tape recordings were transcribed and analysis of the data was made in terms of the analytical framework developed (Figure 2). The researchers' analysis was checked for reliability by submitting selected material to instructed judges for separate analyses. . . .

Analysis and Results of the Study

Reliability of the categorization process was checked by comparing trained and independent observers' responses to the categorization task in the areas of 1) critical shifts; and, 2) classroom verbal behaviors. . . . Having obtained acceptable reliability in classification, the transcripts were analyzed to see what kinds of patterns of interaction were in evidence.

Each teacher-pupil response sequence within each critical shift was analyzed and classified in terms of its closing or opening quality. The results of this analysis provided suggestive data concerning the following questions:

(1)—When teacher solicitation behavior is closed in nature will student response be closed? (and the reverse)

(2)—Can classroom interaction of individual teachers be characterized as essentially open or closed?

1. Analysis of the Teachers As a Group

Each teacher's shifts and the ensuing verbal behaviors of teachers and pupils within shifts were analyzed to see whether closed behavior on the part of the teacher (or open behavior) resulted in closed (or open) behavior on the part of students. A total of 147 shifts were identified in the nine transcripts. Analysis of paired or congruent (open-open or closed-closed) instances of verbal behavior revealed 127 cases of congruent behavior on the part of both teacher and pupil and 20 cases where there was a lack of congruence. Thus, congruence was found in 86% of the cases. Application of the sign test to the ratio of 127-20 shows that the ratio could occur by chance alone once every thousand times. (.001 level of significance).

2. Analysis of Individual Teacher's Patterns

A two by two table was constructed for each teacher after examination of their transcripts. Critical shifts were noted and the pairing of teacher-pupil behavior was made. Four categories for any pairing within a critical shift were possible. Figure 3 shows the possible categories.

FIGURE 3 Possible Pairing of Teacher-Pupil Verbal Behaviors

TEACHER

		Role	Transaction
LEARNER	Reproductive (role)		
	Productive (transaction)		

Thus, any set of paired responses within a critical incident could be categorized in one of four ways as shown in Figure 2.

    1—teacher role—learner reproductive
    2—teacher role—learner productive
    3—teacher transaction—learner reproductive
    4—teacher transaction—learner productive

The "pure" or expected cases, representing the 86% noted above which fall in the teacher role-learner reproductive and teacher transaction-learner productive categories, are pointed out by the diagonal line arrow in Figure 3. . . .

3. Conclusions drawn from the analysis of Individual Teachers' Classroom Classifications. Three general conclusions should be noted:

1. Significant (.05 level or beyond) congruence of pairs was found in 8 of the 9 individual teacher classrooms.

2. Teacher behavior was by and large, characterized to a significant degree (.05 level or beyond) by either transaction or role oriented behavior. Three teachers were significantly role oriented; four teachers were significantly transaction oriented; and, two teachers were mixed (i.e. not significantly oriented).

3. Learner behavior was, by and large, characterized to a significant degree (.05 level or beyond) by either reproductive or productive behavior. In five cases productive behavior was significantly (.05 level) present; in three cases reproductive behavior was characteristic, and in one case mixed behavior was characteristic.

Discussion

The results of this exploratory study must be held tentatively until further validation is forthcoming. Nevertheless, the percentage of agreement among those classifying behaviors would indicate that the classification system of the process continuum (opening–closing) is a promising tool for interaction research in classrooms.

This model of analysis was originally pursued, as mentioned earlier, with the hope that a global quality of classroom interaction could be identified to utilize across levels of teacher personality, social interaction, and other areas of teacher planning and operating in the classroom. The first step, an analysis at the social interaction level here, appears promising.

There is little doubt that behavioral phenomena are complex and the researchers do not wish to suggest otherwise. On the other hand, there would seem to be very little opportunity for effective utilization of verbal concepts by teachers in monitoring their behavior; or, for that matter, by researchers to make coherent sense out of complicated or partial analytic schemes unless classroom phenomena can be symbolized in relatively global and related terms.

The opening-closing process continuum does have theoretical corrolaries in personality and interaction dimensions, across grade levels, subject areas, and kinds of teacher decisions. As such, it would appear useful in light of the results of this study to pursue this conceptualization further.

Results of the patterns found among the nine teachers have little generality because of the nature of the sample. There is, however, some reason to suggest that these findings are indicative of promising hypotheses. Aschner and Gallagher (23), Guzak (24), and others have also found that teachers elicit the kinds of responses they ask for (in terms of level of thinking). The high percentage of congruent pairs noted in this study is in agreement with these findings in the sense that like begets like. Thus, open teacher (transaction oriented) behavior did appear to elicit open student (productive) behavior, and the reverse.

Though hardly startling as a finding this does at least underline the crucial significance of the teacher's role. The specific nature of the open learner behaviors which were (apparently) readily elicited by teachers is encouraging, inasmuch as they reflect a body of items classifiable loosely as inquiry or creative behaviors. The crucial significance of the development of learner inquiry and creative abilities has been fully expressed in much recent educational literature.

A further hopeful sign may be found in the variance among teachers in the study. Much recent research in classrooms has revealed the similarity in teacher patterns of behavior. Hughes (7), for example, reported the predominance of structuring activities, and the findings of Bellack (25), Flanders (6), and Perkins (10) illustrate a single teacher talk-content focus orientation. At least the present study suggests that teachers are capable of radically different behavior (transaction oriented versus role and needs oriented); and that this behavior can be said to characterize their interactions with learners. Whether some teachers are characteristically "open" in public school settings, however, remains to be seen.

The existence of mixed interactions in two cases raises a further point of interest. Flanders (26) hypothesizes that flexible teacher behavior (in his direct and indirect matrix) may be the most productive. It is worth reflecting upon whether teachers may, in terms of the proposed framework, be exhibiting behavior classifiable as "locked in an open position" as well as essentially opening or closing behavior.

A number of research possibilities appear to be opened by the study. Studies of comparative results with other frameworks, for example, seem to be in order. Further, studies utilizing this framework in relation to criterion variables in classrooms are feasible and desirable. One advantage this framework may have here, as suggested earlier, is that the model would seem to be predisposed to relate to non-achievement variables, such as self-direction, as well as to achievement criteria.

This study, then, is seen by the researchers as an initial exploratory attempt with highly tentative results, although the classificatory model appears to be feasible and useful. It would be less than truthful, however, if we failed to communicate the encouragement found in these results, and our positive convictions about the potential meaning and implications of the model.

References

1. Richard Turner, and Nicholas Fattu. "Skill in Teaching, A Reappraisal of Concepts and Strategies in Teacher Effectiveness Research," Bulletin of the School of Education, Indiana University, Vol. 36, No. 3, Bloomington, Indiana. ington, Indiana.

2. Arvil S. Barr, et al. "Wisconsin Studies of the Measurement and Prediction of Teaching Effectiveness—A Summary of Investigations," Dembar Publications, Inc., Madison, Wisconsin, 1961.

3. Carl Rogers. On Becoming a Person, Houghton Mifflin Company, Boston, 1961.

4. Ernest G. Schachtel. *Metamorphosis*, Basic Books, Inc., New York, 1959.

5. Milton Rokeach. *The Open and Closed Mind*, Basic Books, Inc., New York, 1960.

6. Ned Flanders. *Teacher Influences on Pupil Attitudes and Achievement: Studies in Interaction Analysis*, Cooperative Research Project. No. 397, Minneapolis, Minnesota, University of Minnesota, 1960.

7. Marie Hughes, and Associates. *A Research Report*, University of Utah, 1959.

8. B. Othanel Smith, and others. *A Study of the Logic of Teaching: A Report on the First Phase of a Five-Year Research Project*, Urbana, Bureau of Educational Research, University of Illinois, 1960.

9. Wright and Proctor. *Systematic Observation of Verbal Interaction as a Method of Comparing Mathematics Lessons.* Cooperative Research Project #816, U.S. Office of Education, Department of Health, Education and Welfare, St. Louis, Washington University, 1961.

10. Hugh Perkins. "A Procedure for Assessing the Classroom Behavior of Students and Teachers," *American Educational Research Journal.* Vol. I., No. 4 and Vol. II, No. 1, November, 1964 and January, 1965; pp. 249-260, and pp. 1-12.

11. Donald Medley. "Experiences with the Oscar Technique," *Journal of Teaching Education*, Vol. XIV, No. 3, September, 1963, pp. 267-273.

12. Anderson and Brewer. *Studies of Teachers' Classroom Personalities II: Effects of Teacher's Dominative and Integrative Contacts on Children's Classroom Behavior.* Applied Psychology Monographs, 1946, No. 8.

13. Heil, Powell and Feifer. Characteristics of Teacher Behavior Related to the Achievement of Children in Several Elementary Grades. Cooperative Research Project #7285, U.S. Office of Education, Department of Health, Education and Welfare, New York, Brooklyn College, 1960.

14. Mort Waimon. *Feedback in Classrooms: A Study of the Corrective Responses Made by Teachers as They Interact in the Teaching-Learning Process.* Paper presented at the American Educational Research Association Annual Meeting, February 1961, Atlantic City, New Jersey.

15. John Withall. "The Development of a Technique for the Measurement of Social-Emotional Climate in Classrooms." *Journal of Experimental Education*, 1949, 17:347-361.

15a. Newell, Lewis and Withall. "Use of a Communication Model to Study Classroom Interactions." Paper presented at American Educational Research Association, Annual Meeting, February 1961, Chicago, Illinois.

16. Robert Bills. "Being and Becoming." Paper presented at the Annual Meeting of the Association for Supervision and Curriculum Development, Las Vegas, Nevada, March 1, 1962.

17. H. H. Anderson. "Creativity and Education," Association for Higher Education College and University Bulletin, Volume 13, No. 14, Special Issue, National Committee on General Education, May, 1961.

18. Gordon Allport. *Pattern and Growth in Personality*, Holt, Rinehart, and Winston, New York, 1961.

19. Lawrence Kubie. "Research on Protecting Preconscious Functions in Education." Paper presented at Research Institute, Association for Supervision and Curriculum Development, Washington, D. C., 1961.

20. Carl R. Rogers. "A Process Conception of Psychotherapy." Paper presented at the Annual Conference of the American Psychological Association. New York, September 1957. (Mimeographed).

21. John C. Flanagan. "The Critical Incident Technique in the Study of Individuals." *Modern Educational Problems*, pp. 61-70, Seventeenth Educational Conference, New York City, October 1952 (Washington, D.C. American Council on Education).

22. Berj Harootunian. "The Teacher as Problem Solver: Extra-Class Decision-Making." Paper presented for *Symposium Curriculum and Instruction: A Dialogue on the Reconstruction of Theory.* 50th Annual Meeting, American Educational Research Association, February, 1966.

23. Mary Jane Aschner, and James Gallagher, et al. "A System for Classifying Thought Processes in the Context of Classroom Verbal Interaction." Champaign, Illinois: Institute for Research on Exceptional Children, 1965.

24. J. Frank Guzak. "A Study of Teacher Solicitation and Student Response Interaction About Reading Content in Selected Second, Fourth, and Sixth Grades." Doctoral Dissertation, University of Wisconsin, June, 1966.

25. Bellack, Arno, and Joel R. Davitz, et al. *The Language of the Classroom.* New York: Institute of Psychological Research, Teachers College, Columbia University, 1963. (Mimeographed).

26. Ned Flanders. "Teacher Influence in the Classroom." *Theory and Research In Teaching,* Arno Bellack (ed.) Teachers College, Columbia University Press, 1963, pp. 37-52.

Appendix

Following is a sample classroom transcript and analysis of the flow of verbal interchange for one teacher.

The classroom transcript shows the numbers (e.g. 1) of each unit and the critical shifts (marked /).

The analysis sheet shows how the flow was analyzed and classified. A plus (+) indicated a transaction orientation of a unit; A minus (−) indicates role orientation; and zero (0) refers to monitoring or chairing teacher behavior (classified as neutral).

Teacher #3 was classified as predominantly transaction oriented.

Record 3

1 TEACHER: Our plans for living things—the way we might be sharing
2 our information—could we do that now. You are just going to tell us
  your plans—you are not going to tell us anything of how—you are
3 just going to tell us how you plan to do it. You may even change
  your plans if you find you can't do everything the way you want it.
  / Now let's have some people tell us how you plan to share your
  information
4 about your animal or your living things— / Doug.
5 STUDENT: Well, I'm going to give some movies about the —the

6   likenesses and differences between a salamander and myself. And I'm setting for a movie already—I have done the likenesses and differences—not too many yet and I have seen how many legs on a salamander that we have now and if it is one that goes in water or lives on land or in water.

7   TEACHER: You are studying our salamander—our own salamander and how—

8   STUDENT: And how it gets its babies.

9   TEACHER: / You mentioned something about your photography—

10   STUDENT: Yes, and I will take the pictures with my camera of it to see how it acts when it is eating—I will try to get a picture of that—

11   of it eating, and, should I ask about an earthworm?

12   TEACHER: It's up to you.

13   STUDENT: / Could anyone bring an earthworm for the salamander.

TEACHER No. 3   Analysis of Verbal Interchanges

Verbal Unit #	Speaker	FLOW OF VERBAL ACTION Ongoing ⟵⟶ Shifting		Critical Incident	Classification of Verbal Behaviors	
1	T	Opening Statement		Opening	Intro-focusing	—
2	T	Opening Statement			Directing	—
3	T	Opening Statement			Elab-facilitating	+
4	T		T–State	1	Direct-monitoring	0
5	S	Answer			Reporting progress	+
6	S	Answer			Synthesizing	+
7	T	T–R–Q			Accepting	+
8	S	Counter R			Elaborating	+
9	T		T–R–Q	2	Support	+
10	S	Answer			Elaborating	+
11	S		⎧ S–Q ⎫		Permission for exploring	+
12	T		⎨ T–Answer ⎬		Support-facilitating	+
13	S		⎪ S–Q ⎪	3	Counter-facilitating	+
14	T		⎩ T–Monitoring ⎭	4	Monitoring	0

22 Teaching: the Application of Psychological Constructs

Bruce W. Tuckman

The Model

George Kelly (1955) in his *Psychology of Personal Constructs* postulates that ". . . a person's processes are psychologically channelized by the ways in which he anticipates events, . . . that a person anticipates events by construing their replications, . . . that each person characteristically evolves, for his convenience in anticipating events, a construction system embracing ordinal relationships between constructs, . . . that a person's construction system is composed of a finite number of dichotomous constructs." Put more simply, Kelly is saying that the central feature of human functioning is building a picture of reality, an ever-shifting one with recurrent patterns, that enables a person to deal with the future. By developing a set of personal constructs based on past experiences, we become capable of processing information contained in new experiences and, in turn, formulating a reaction to these experiences.

By focusing on the model a person constructs for representing or construing reality, Kelly gave impetus to a focus in social psychology on information processing. His suggestion that information processing might vary on a continuum of concrete to abstract gave rise to the development of a more delineated personality model by three of his former students, Harvey, Hunt, and Schroder (1961). They contended that people potentially pass through four stages of information processing, or conceptual systems, and more characteristically became arrested in one of the four. They called these systems absolute dependency, negative independency, conditional dependency, and interdependence, each system representing a more advanced state of conceptual complexity or abstractness than the one preceding.

In absolute dependence, conflict is resolved by appeal to authority, norms, and structure, while in negative independence forcing or pushing against authority is manifested as a conflict resolution mechanism. Conditional dependency is characterized by a connectedness and mutuality to the social system, while interdependency reveals a focus on problem-solving and the integration among alternatives. It is important to note that Harvey, Hunt, and Schroder viewed personal construct systems as vehicles by which persons deal with issues of control, interpersonal relations, and ambiguity.

The work of Kelly coupled with the work of Harvey, Hunt, and Schroder provides raw material for dealing with and theorizing about educational issues since teachers are principally confronted by problems of control, interpersonal relations, and ambiguity in classroom management (Tuckman, 1967).[1] Of particular interest here is the description and analysis of teaching behavior and teacher style. Murphy and Brown (1970) have shown a relationship between the personality construct system of a teacher and his teaching style using the Harvey, Hunt, and Schroder framework. More abstract teachers were found to be more reflective (that is, adaptive to change) and to reinforce search rather than attainment.

The result of the application of Kelly's psychology of personal constructs to education is a personal construct model of teaching which reflects itself both in a series of five propositions (based on Kelly's postulates) and a measurement technique which is appropriate for determining teacher behavior relative to the model.[2]

The first proposition to be offered is that *the teacher relates to the environment around him by means of a set or system of personal constructs which he uses as a vehicle for processing incoming information.*

---

[1]The author is himself a former student of Schroder's.

[2]It is noteworthy that the proposed model is as descriptive of the behavior of the measurer or theorist as it is of the behavior of the teacher, since it reflects his system of personal constructs, as inevitably any theory reflects the orientation of its builder.

The second proposition states that *these personal constructs act as a mediator between information which the teacher receives and subsequent behaviors that he emits.* If these propositions are valid, then the key to understanding teacher behavior and its relation to situational demands is to determine the nature of the personal constructs used by the teacher. By personal constructs we mean the kind of dichotomized considerations as creative-routinized, warm-cold, fair-unfair, etc., that are implied by Kelly's work.

We may take our arguments one step further and propose a third proposition that *the general kinds of personal constructs used by the teacher to construe his environment* (of which incidentally he is a part, perhaps the most critical part) *will also be the ones used by an observer to construe the behavior of a teacher in a classroom.* This is an important proposition because it enables an outsider to operate within the same construct system as an insider in judging the behavior of the latter. This is a necessary link if we are to presume to describe teaching from the vantage point of the observer with any hope of providing an honest reflection of the teaching process.

Our fourth proposition states that *personal constructs are organized into more stable and meaningful systems or clusters of constructs.* Our fifth proposition states that *the relative predominance of construct systems will reflect the characteristics of the situation, the disposition of the teacher, and the previous history of the teacher.* Rather than dealing with large numbers of individual constructs, we shall look for sets or systems of constructs that tend to relate or go together. Tendencies that teachers show on these construct systems can be expected to be different in different teaching situations such as in a large lecture hall before a hundred students as compared with twelve students in a seminar room. Other factors will also affect teacher behavior.

The preceding model of the teacher as information processer, following closely in the footsteps of Kelly, provides the basis for the development of a measuring instrument. If we view as the essence of teaching those constructs and construct systems that teachers use for converting classroom inputs into teaching behaviors, then our measurement procedure will consist of a set of relevant and reasonably general constructs.

The Measure

The measure is called the Tuckman Teacher Feedback Form (TTFF), so named because it was originally designed for purposes of giving teachers feedback; it appears in Figure 1 (Tuckman, 1971). As can be seen, it is a series of twenty-eight paired adjectives, each adjective having been paired with its approximate opposite, as opposed to its absolute opposite or negation. For example, "creative" is paired with "routinized" rather than with "noncreative". Each adjective pair represents a personal construct that can be used to construe the behavior of a teacher. The instrument may be used by any classroom observer—supervisor, trained observer, peer, or student, to describe the behavior of a teacher over approximately a forty-five-minute span of time. Rather than simply making notes, the instrument provides the observer with a more systematic means of recording his impressions of the teacher in the observation period.

Person Observed _____   Observer _____

Date_____

TUCKMAN TEACHER FEEDBACK FORM (Short Form)

1.	ORIGINAL	—: —: —: —: —: —: —:	CONVENTIONAL
2.	PATIENT	—: —: —: —: —: —: —:	IMPATIENT
3.	COLD	—: —: —: —: —: —: —:	WARM
4.	HOSTILE	—: —: —: —: —: —: —:	AMIABLE
5.	CREATIVE	—: —: —: —: —: —: —:	ROUTINIZED
6.	INHIBITED	—: —: —: —: —: —: —:	UNINHIBITED
7.	ICONOCLASTIC	—: —: —: —: —: —: —:	RITUALISTIC
8.	GENTLE	—: —: —: —: —: —: —:	HARSH
9.	UNFAIR	—: —: —: —: —: —: —:	FAIR
10.	CAPRICIOUS	—: —: —: —: —: —: —:	PURPOSEFUL
11.	CAUTIOUS	—: —: —: —: —: —: —:	EXPERIMENTING
12.	DISORGANIZED	—: —: —: —: —: —: —:	ORGANIZED
13.	UNFRIENDLY	—: —: —: —: —: —: —:	SOCIABLE
14.	RESOURCEFUL	—: —: —: —: —: —: —:	UNCERTAIN
15.	RESERVED	—: —: —: —: —: —: —:	OUTSPOKEN
16.	IMAGINATIVE	—: —: —: —: —: —: —:	EXACTING
17.	ERRATIC	—: —: —: —: —: —: —:	SYSTEMATIC
18.	AGGRESSIVE	—: —: —: —: —: —: —:	PASSIVE
19.	ACCEPTING (people)	—: —: —: —: —: —: —:	CRITICAL
20.	QUIET	—: —: —: —: —: —: —:	BUBBLY
21.	OUTGOING	—: —: —: —: —: —: —:	WITHDRAWN
22.	IN CONTROL	—: —: —: —: —: —: —:	ON THE RUN
23.	FLIGHTY	—: —: —: —: —: —: —:	CONSCIENTIOUS
24.	DOMINANT	—: —: —: —: —: —: —:	SUBMISSIVE
25.	OBSERVANT	—: —: —: —: —: —: —:	PREOCCUPIED
26.	INTROVERTED	—: —: —: —: —: —: —:	EXTRAVERTED
27.	ASSERTIVE	—: —: —: —: —: —: —:	SOFT-SPOKEN
28.	TIMID	—: —: —: —: —: —: —:	ADVENTUROUS

FIGURE 1. The Tuckman Teacher Feedback Form (TTFF)

Reprinted by permission of the author. Copyright © 1971.

The twenty-eight scales are from among a larger list of sixty-five paired adjectives that were originally tested to form the instrument. The original sixty-five were collected to cover the widest range of teaching behavior with an eye toward blanketing the four system types developed by Harvey, Hunt, and Schroder and described earlier. In other words, an attempt was made to cover the teacher as a structurer, the teacher as an individual force, the teacher as a sociable person, and the teacher as a problem-solver, four ways that teachers can deal with problems of control, interpersonal relations, and ambiguity. Choices of adjective pairs were broadly fitted to this formulation while attempting not to overlook other aspects of teaching such as mood (for example, cheerful—sad). The resulting list of sixty-five pairs was considered to be sufficiently broad for a first try with the instrument.

The procedure for scoring the TTFF is shown in Figure 2. Scores are obtained on each of four scales (described below). Scoring formulas involve pluses and minuses because adjective pairs appear with their "positive" pole on both left and right ends of scales to minimize response-set bias; constants are added to each formula to set minimum scores at one and thus avoid negative scores. On each factor, forty-three is the highest score obtainable.

Person Observed _____   **Observer** _____

Date_____

TUCKMAN TEACHER FEEDBACK FORM—FEEDBACK SUMMARY SHEET

A. *Item Scoring* Procedure

1. Place an "X" on one of the seven dashes between each pair of adjectives so as to describe your impression of the teacher.
2. Under the last set of dashes on the sheet of 28 items write the numbers 7-6-5-4-3-2-1. This will give a number value to each of the seven spaces between the 28 pairs of adjectives.
3. Determine the number value for the first pair, Original-Conventional. Write it into the formula given below on the appropriate line under Item 1.
   For example, if you place an "x" on the first dash next to "Original" in Item 1, then write the number 7 on the dash under Item 1 in the summary formula below.
4. Do the same for each of the 28 items. Plug each value into the formula.

5. Compute the score for each of the 4 dimensions in the Summary Formula.

B. *Summary Formula and Score for the Four Dimensions*

I. Creativity

Item (1 + 5 + 7 + 16) − (6 + 11 + 28) + 18
      (_ + _ + _ + _) − (_ + _ + _) + 18 = ____

II. Dynamism (dominance and energy)

Item (18 + 21 + 24 + 27) − (15 + 20 + 26) + 18
      (_ + _ + _ + _) − (_ + _ + _) + 18 = ____

III. Organized Demeanor (organization and control)

Item (14 + 22 + 25) − (10 + 12 + 17 + 23) + 26
      (_ + _ + _) − (_ + _ + _ + _) + 26 = ____

IV. Warmth and Acceptance

Item (2 + 8 + 19) − (3 + 4 + 9 + 13) + 26
      (_ + _ + _) − (_ + _ + _ + _) + 26 = ____

FIGURE 2. The Feedback Summary and Scoring Sheet for the Tuckman Teacher Feedback Form.

It must be pointed out that the TTFF item format was not only consistent with Kelly's approach to construing reality but was also equivalent to what Osgood, Suci, and Tannenbaum (1957) called the *semantic differential,* a technique designed to measure the meanings implicit in the judgment of social reality. The work of Osgood et al. revealed that general adjective pairs, when used to judge objects of attitudes, yielded the following three clusters or factors: evaluation (for example, good–bad), potency (for example, strong–weak), and activity (for example, active–passive). However, Osgood et al. pointed out that somewhat different factor structures result when the adjective pairs used are more specific and relevant to the object being judged, as would be true in the case of the Tuckman Teacher Feedback Form.

The set of sixty-five adjective pairs of the TTFF was given to eighty-four graduate students in education, and each was asked to use it to judge one of his/her graduate instructors. The resulting ratings were submitted to factor analysis, the results of which appear in Figure 3.

FACTOR 1 CREATIVITY		FACTOR 2 DYNAMISM	
Creative–Routinized	(.84)	Outgoing–Withdrawn	(.82)
Imaginative–Exacting	(.83)	Outspoken–Reserved	(.81)
Experimenting–Cautious	(.81)	Bubbly–Quiet	(.78)
Original–Conventional	(.77)	Extraverted–Introverted	(.78)
Iconoclastic–Ritualistic	(.72)	Aggressive–Passive	(.76)
Uninhibited–Inhibited	(.66)	Assertive–Soft-Spoken	(.73)
Adventurous–Timid	(.66)	Dominant–Submissive	(.71)

FACTOR 3 ORGANIZED DEMEANOR		FACTOR 4 WARMTH AND ACCEPTANCE	
Systematic–Erratic	(.83)	Warm–Cold	(.79)
Organized–Disorganized	(.76)	Sociable–Unfriendly	(.77)
Purposeful–Capricious	(.74)	Amiable–Hostile	(.76)
Conscientious–Flighty	(.71)	Patient–Impatient	(.74)
In Control–On The Run	(.62)	Fair–Unfair	(.72)
Observant–Preoccupied	(.58)	Gentle–Harsh	(.69)
Resourceful–Uncertain	(.55)	Accepting (people)–Critical	(.67)

FIGURE 3. Results of the Factor Analysis of the TTFF. (Numbers in parentheses represent factor loadings; N = 84 teacher observers.)

Figure 3 reveals the four principal factors that emerged from the analysis and were subsequently named: *creativity, dynamism, organized demeanor,* and *warmth and acceptance.* The seven adjective pairs having the highest factor loadings on each factor were taken from the original sixty-five to form the TTFF (short form) shown in Figure 1. Each factor can be considered to represent a cluster of constructs which both the teacher and the observer of teaching use to construe teaching behavior (that is, the result of the way the teacher processes information).

The *creative* teacher is seen as being not only creative but imaginative, experimenting, original, iconoclastic, uninhibited, and adventurous as well. This factor bears some relation to Harvey, Hunt, and Schroder's (1961) stage of interdependence which Tuckman (1967) has characterized as being a combination of abstractness in information processing and independence in terms of one's restrictedness only by the environment rather than by people in it. This type of teacher controls by his manipulation of the learning environment.

The *dynamic* teacher is seen as outgoing, outspoken, bubbly, extroverted, aggressive, assertive, and dominant. He is a personally forceful and commanding teacher and in some ways not unlike Harvey, Hunt, and Schroder's negative independent type. In essence, he uses "force" as a means to control student behavior and achieve goals.

The *organized* teacher is not only organized but systematic, purposeful, conscientious, in control, observant, and resourceful. This type of teacher controls in a more managerial capacity and bears some resemblance to Harvey, Hunt, and Schroder's absolute dependent type whose unilateral approach to training serves to reduce ambiguity and risk.

Finally, the *warm and accepting* teacher is in addition sociable, amiable, patient, fair, and gentle and thus achieves "control" by relating to his students, not unlike Harvey, Hunt, and Schroder's conditional dependency or mutuality type.

It is important to emphasize two points. First, consistent with Osgood, Suci, and Tannenbaum's (1957) work on the semantic differential, each of the twenty-eight scales on the TTFF cannot be considered an independent dimension, but those dimensions that fall on the same factor can be considered to *mean* the same (or similar) thing to the persons making the judgment. In terms of Kelly's formulation, it would be argued that in an area such as teaching, neither the teacher nor the observer can use as many as twenty-eight dimensions independently to construe the environment, and that consequently clusters or systems of constructs are employed. The second point is that all teachers exhibit some degree of each factor, assumedly as a function of their personality, training, and the situation in which they are teaching. We are ultimately then talking about differences in *degree* in construing teacher behavior along the four proposed dimensions.

Properties of the Measure

Let us examine existing evidence bearing on both the reliability and the validity of the TTFF. In the instance of *reliability,* it is of value to consider both the internal reliability of the instrument and its inter-rater reliability. As regards internal reliability, the factor analysis demonstrates a high degree of inter-item agreement within each factor as evidenced by factor loadings ranging from .55 to .84 (see Figure 3). Inter-rater reliabilities are reported by Tuckman, Cochran, and Travers (1973) for a pair of trained observers over fifteen observations as averaging .55 across the four dimensions. Most recently, corrected reliabilities ranging from .65 to .90 have been obtained over a sample of thirty-one open classroom teachers observed by a pair of observers (unpublished report). Walencik (1973) had high school students serve as the observers of student teachers (using an altered scoring procedure for the TTFF) and reported corrected correlations averaging .91 between arbitrarily designated class halves of sixteen-member classes across the dimensions of the TTFF.

On the matter of *validity,* the relationship between the TTFF and Student Opinion Questionnaire (SOQ; Bryan, 1963) has been examined as a test of concurrent validity. Walencik (1973) reports high correlations between TTFF scales and those SOQ scales that seem by wording that they should be measuring corresponding things. Moreover, the two instruments show moderate but significant correlations overall. To establish the construct validity of the TTFF, the research studies described below have been completed.

Research Applications

Tuckman, Cochran, and Travers (1973) used the TTFF to compare teachers trained in the use of open classroom philosophy and techniques to others not so trained. They found the open classroom teachers to be significantly more warm and accepting and to show a tendency to be more creative than the "traditional" teachers with no differences on the other two dimensions. Moreover, in comparing the scores of teachers on the four dimensions of the TTFF to measures of classroom management and process and to measures of subsequent student outcomes, the correlations shown in Figure 4 were obtained. These findings are consistent with one's expectations assuming the validity of the TTFF and hence provide some evidence of its construct validity.

The TTFF was designed primarily to be used for the modification of teacher behavior (Tuckman, 1971) and grew out of the work on teacher feedback done by Tuckman and Oliver (1968), Tuckman, McCall, and Hyman (1969), and Gage, Runkel, and Chatterjee (1960). Following the assumption that the instrument measured the behavior of the teacher on the four general construct systems described above, and hence held meaning for teachers in terms of how they processed information in their teaching environment and consequently reacted to situations of control, interpersonal relations, and ambiguity, it was reasoned that feedback in these areas would result in altered teaching behavior.

Spencer (1973) used the TTFF as part of a microteaching procedure with teachers about to begin their teaching careers. Prospective teachers were asked to rate their *ideal teacher* on the TTFF at the start and end of the training session. Some teachers were rated by their fellow trainees on the TTFF following microteaching, while others were not. Following feedback, a second lesson was taught and the TTFF used to judge performance in all instances. Follow-ups were done some months later by supervisors on selected teachers. Spencer found that teachers who received feedback on the TTFF changed their ideal (presumably a measure of their *teaching philosophy*) significantly more than teachers who did not receive TTFF feedback but who received "conventional" feedback (termed "unstructured" by Spencer), particularly on the dimension of warmth and acceptance. In other words, exposure to the

TTFF	Flexible Use of Space	Simultaneous Activity	Simultaneous Groupings	Teacher Structuring**	Teacher Soliciting**	Teacher Responding**	Teacher Reacting**	Student Structuring**	Student Soliciting**	Student Responding**	Student Reacting**	Attitudes Toward Self	Attitudes Toward School	Achievement***
			CLASSROOM PROCESS									OUTCOMES		
Creativity	.67*	.47*	.41*	.14	-.05	-.09	-.12	.40*	.06	-.17	.24	.32	.50*	.03
Dynamism	-.29	-.07	-.26	.41*	-.03	-.30	.44*	.08	-.45*	.12	-.31	.30	.14	.26
Organized Demeanor	-.06	-.21	-.60*	.16	.23	-.51*	.13	-.06	-.52*	.42*	-.23	.04	.01	.12
Warmth & Acceptance	.72*	.26	.14	-.07	.24	-.28	-.03	.12	-.14	.02	.22	.40*	.57*	-.16

*p = .01
**Bellack Coding Category (See Chapter 12 of this book. R.T.H., editor)
***California Achievement Test

FIGURE 4. Rank Order Correlations Between TTFF Scores and Measures of Classroom Process and Outcomes (N = 30)

TTFF increased a teacher's use of warmth and acceptance in construing his ideal teacher indicating an increasing sensitivity to this system.

Moreover, TTFF feedback caused teaching behavior to significantly improve (that is, change in the direction of the ideal)—more so than conventional feedback on warmth and acceptance and dynamism. Since the majority of Spencer's teachers were skilled craftsmen recruited directly out of industry and were about to enter teaching with no experience or training save Spencer's week-long workshop, the increasing emphasis placed upon warmth and acceptance constructs by the TTFF was considered an important accomplishment. It must be noted that the differences identified by Spencer were not reported three months later. Undoubtedly the use of another set of raters and smaller samples of teachers contributed to the absence of these differences.

Walencik (1973) worked with student teachers at a state college and had their high school students rate their behavior using the TTFF and a modified scoring procedure. Some of Walencik's student teachers received feedback on the TTFF while others received conventional supervision. Over all construct systems, student teachers who received TTFF feedback changed more than students not receiving such feedback, indicating the effectiveness of the TTFF as an element in the change process. Walencik also found change to be a function of the difference between actual behavior and ideal behavior, termed dissonance, which the TTFF apparently transformed from a change potential to an actual change.

While the above studies are not definitive, together they do indicate potentially effective uses for the TTFF. An additional study, presently planned, will employ a peer feedback approach with the TTFF at the two-year college level and will compare various techniques with which the feedback will be given. It will also provide another opportunity to examine the factor structure of the TTFF.

Conclusions

Remmers (1963) suggests that the following five factors be considered in evaluating a judgment-recording instrument for observations of teaching behavior: objectivity, reliability, sensitivity, relevance, and utility. Although considerably more work needs to be done with the TTFF to establish its psychometric credentials, it has to date yielded (1) verifiable and reproducible data (objectivity), (2) consistency over items and over judges (reliability), (3) discriminable differences between teachers and between teacher feedback conditions (sensitivity), (4) relatedness to the Kelly-derived construct systems and applicability to the real educational problem of changing teacher behavior (relevance), and (5) evidence of its efficiency and practicality in administration and use (utility).

The TTFF approach has been used with student judges, peer judges, and trained observers and has worked satisfactorily in each instance. It has been used as an element in a program aimed at changing teaching behavior and as a vehicle for judging the behavior of teachers trained in open classroom techniques. Open classroom teachers were found to score differently than conventional ones, the former being warmer and more creative. TTFF scores were also shown to be related to other classroom measures. Feedback from the TTFF was shown to be effective in causing new and prospective teachers to change both their behavior and their teaching philosophy within reasonably short periods of time.

As an instrument based on the psychology of personal constructs, the TTFF offers both the practitioner and the researcher a way to characterize teaching behavior without the training and time demands imposed by a coding system while yielding usable data on four major aspects of teaching behavior. It is not intended as a device for measuring all aspects of teaching behavior (for example, lesson-planning and testing are not explicitly dealt with) but does quickly and efficiently show how a teacher is seen as processing information within a social reality. Further studies, applications, and psychometric analyses will suggest considerations for additional uses of the TTFF. Users are encouraged to extend it in new but appropriate directions.

References

R. C. Bryan. *Reactions to teachers by students, parents, and administrators.* U.S. Office of Education, Cooperative Research Project No. 668. Kalamazoo, Michigan: Western Michigan University, 1963.

N. L. Gage, P. J. Runkel, and B. B. Chatterjee. *Equilibrium theory and behavior change: An experiment in feedback from pupils to teachers.* Report No. 6 in *Studies in the generality and behavioral correlates of social perception.* Urbana, Ill.: Bureau of Educational Research, College of Education, University of Illinois, 1960.

O. J. Harvey, D. E. Hunt, and H. M. Schroder. *Conceptual systems and personality organization.* New York: Wiley, 1961.

G. A. Kelly. *The psychology of personal constructs.* New York: Norton, 1955.

P. D. Murphy, and M. M. Brown. Conceptual systems and teaching styles. *American Educational Research Journal,* 1970, 1, 529-540.

C. E. Osgood, G. J. Suci, and P. H. Tannenbaum. *The measurement of meaning.* Urbana, Ill.: University of Illinois Press, 1957.

H. H. Remmers. Rating methods in research on teaching. In N. L. Gage, ed., *Handbook of research on teaching.* Chicago: Rand McNally, 1963.

M. Spencer. A study to evaluate the impact of structured and unstructured feedback to teachers. Unpublished doctoral dissertation, Rutgers University, 1973.

B. W. Tuckman. The application of the personality structure model in educationally-relevant research. Paper presented at meetings of Eastern Psychological Association, Boston, 1967.

B. W. Tuckman. Changing the behavior of teachers through feedback. Invitational paper presented at meetings of National Association of Elementary School Principals, Cleveland, 1971.

B. W. Tuckman, and W. F. Oliver. Effectiveness of feedback to teachers as a function of source. *Journal of Educational Psychology*, 1968, 59, 297-301.

B. W. Tuckman, K. McCall, and R. T. Hyman. The modification of teacher behavior: Effects of dissonance and coded feedback. *American Educational Research Journal*, 1969, 6, 607-619.

B. W. Tuckman, D. Cochran, and E. Travers. Evaluating the open classroom. Paper presented at meetings of American Educational Research Association, New Orleans, 1973.

V. J. Walencik. An experimental study to determine the effectiveness of feedback as a means of changing student teachers' humanistic behavior. Unpublished doctoral dissertation, Rutgers University, 1973.

23 The Role of the Teacher

Anna Freud

It is not a good practice for teachers to be confined to one age group because this encourages them to disregard the fact that any given age is merely a transitional stage within the whole process of childhood. It is important for the school teacher to have knowledge of children of all ages. The good teacher and child psychologist see every phase of childhood in terms of what has gone before and what will come afterwards. Teachers of children of every age should keep this outlook and not confine their interest to their own age group. It is a disadvantage for teachers of elementary school children that they do not see the earlier stages of infancy which have led up to the picture of the child as it is seen in the classroom.

Reprinted with permission from Freud, A., "The Role of the Teacher," *Harvard Educational Review*, 22, Fall, 1952, 229–234. Copyright © 1952 by President and Fellows of Harvard College.

The following paper is based on an informal lecture which Dr. Freud delivered to a group of students who are preparing for elementary and nursery school teaching at the Harvard Graduate School of Education. It is derived from notes taken by several students during the discussion and is presented as a reconstruction of her talk. The article has, however, been edited by Dr. Freud.

Dr. Freud began her discussion by telling the group that she had been a teacher earlier in her career, and used her observations from this experience as the starting point for her discussion. After spending five years teaching in elementary school, she began her more intensive psychoanalytical work with children of all ages.

What an enormous difference there is in the evaluation of the child's personality by the school teacher and by the parents. For example, when I used to work with one- and two-year-olds in a day nursery, I saw the children act within their community as full and independent personalities. These children asserted their wishes and influenced the conduct of the nursery school. For example, I would walk in and ask the nursery worker why the children had not yet gone out on the terrace. The teacher would say that Johnny was involved in work and had said they should wait, or Billy had said the weather wasn't fine enough. One day no one was eating lunch. It was because Jimmy had said the food wasn't good today, and the other children had followed his lead. Then one would meet these same "important" children on the street with their parents,—they would be pushed in prams, and appear in relation to the adults as small, insignificant infants.

This illustration led to a discussion of the three great dangers which threaten the school teacher. First, working too closely with children fosters a loss of perspective between the child's world and the adult world. The teacher who works with young children only sees them out of proportion. She gets caught up in the children's lives, loses her adult values, and begins to live in a children's world where everything comes down to the child's size.

Second, the teacher may come to look at childhood stages as valued within themselves, and not as a preparation for the future. One way to avoid this danger is for the worker with young children to develop an interest in later phases of development.

The third danger for the teacher is to attach herself to the individual child so much as to think of him as her own. Every teacher of young children is in a difficult emotional situation. It is only natural for her to develop strong positive feelings for the children on whom she spends so much of her care; she can hardly avoid valuing, and overvaluing them, in the manner of a mother. At the same time she has to accept the necessity that her children leave her after comparatively short periods and she has to avoid rivalry with the mothers of her children. Teachers who are too possessive in their attitude to the children will accomplish neither; they will suffer from the repeated separations and harden their personalities in defence against this experience; and they will get involved in battles with the mothers who are the legitimate owners of the child. There is one way for the teacher who wishes to escape this danger. Her interest in the individual child has to develop further until it becomes a more general and less personal interest in the whole process of childhood with all its implications.

At this point, a question was asked of Dr. Freud: *If we adopt this point of view, don't we become impersonal in our relations with the children?*

I don't think so. This way each child becomes a figure of real interest for the teacher. We ask how far he has gone in his development, how we can help him, which direction he is taking. It gives the possibility of looking at the child and wondering what is happening in him.

If the teacher sees in a child something that reminds her of her own childhood, she wants to help that child and save him from what she experienced. She will give him infinite patience and care. But what of the child who reminds her either of a brother with whom she fought constantly or of something in her own development which she cannot face? For every child who benefits because he means something in her life, another child suffers. This is the danger of the personal approach. It is too selective to want to work only with groups who need special help, such as deprived or retarded children. This is not a good basis for professional work because it means that in a subtle way the teacher identifies with the children she has chosen and is trying to help herself rather than the child. Since teaching is a profession, she ought to have an overall relationship with childhood. A teacher cannot be completely objective, but once she becomes interested in the processes of childhood, all children become interesting in a more objective way.

A question was raised: *Would you discuss the problem of the child who comes from a home in which he is emotionally deprived?*

To answer the question with a few historical facts: there was a time when teachers were interested only in the child's learning capacity; other sides of the child's life were added gradually. In Europe, about 1914 to 1918, teachers began to realize that the child's physical state had something to do with his learning capacity. Children were not getting sufficient food due to deprivations caused by the war, and it was noticed that the hungry child does not learn as well as the adequately fed. The first school meals were begun at this time. Then it was observed that the child without sufficient sleep could not learn well either. People realized that you can't deal with a child's intellect without taking care of his bodily needs first. The latter observation resulted in rest periods for younger children. The next step was the realization that affectional deprivation also influenced school behaviour. This came as a surprise because of the lack of knowledge concerning the connection between the emotions and learning. Equally, the influence of social conditions of the home upon the intellect became recognized. Thus teachers in time acquired knowledge concerning the child's bodily needs, his social environment, his emotional atmosphere, and his need for affection.

To satisfy a deprived child's need for affection the teacher may want to play the part of the mother. She had better know that in this case the child will cease to accept her in the teacher's role. The teacher's role is not that of a mother-substitute. If, as teachers, we play the part of a mother we get from the child the reactions which are appropriate for the mother-child relationship—the demand for exclusive attention and affection, the wish to get rid of all the other children in the classroom. This makes it more difficult to deal with the child. Although it fills a need of the child, it is not the teacher's role.

There is a difference in a child's attitudes toward his mother and toward his teacher. He wants to be loved by his mother, and doesn't want to be taught by her. His attitude toward his mother is a demanding one based on his instinctive wishes; his attitude toward his teacher is farther removed from drive-activity, it is one of willingness to give and take in. To illustrate: In the war-time nursery, the nurses who acted as mother-substitutes for the children separated from their families, could not function as teachers. Only when taken to another building and put with other nursery workers did the children behave as if in school.

It is inevitable that in the classroom the children will act out the attitudes which they transfer from home. But, normally, when the teacher stays within her role, the home situation does not develop fully in school. It is the privilege of the teacher to introduce the child to a new experience, to life within a social community, not merely to duplicate his experiences within the family.

Another question was raised: *Should the teacher try to help the problem child?*

It may depend on the child's age. Helping the child with personal problems by understanding them is within the teacher's role. But if this presupposes as close a relationship between the child and the teacher as between a child and a therapist, then it transgresses the limits within which the teacher can work. She can help the child by varying her demands on him and her behaviour toward him. But it should be remembered that the teacher is neither a mother, nor a therapist.

Another question was asked: *Should the teacher show affection to the children?*

The teacher with an objective attitude can respond warmly enough to satisfy the child without getting herself involved. In that way emotional involvement cannot develop to a dangerous extent.

On the whole, bodily contact should be left to the mother. This is true for children of all ages. The normal child will not make these demands for bodily contact in the classroom since they are satisfied at home. The child who doesn't have these contacts needs a mother-substitute, a function which—as said before—the teacher should not perform. The communication between teacher and child should take a form different from that of physical contact.

The question was asked: *What will be the teacher's interest in the child if her emotional approach has to be under such strict control?*

The teacher who has a firm grounding in psychoanalytic child psychology will look at the individual child in terms of his personality structure, i.e., not as a unified being but as a being consisting of several parts who, during his development, has to struggle to create an inner equilibrium, a state of harmony within himself. There are three agencies within the personality: (i) the drives, which clamour for satisfaction; (ii) the ego, which regulates drive satisfaction and establishes connections with the environment; (iii) the super-ego, derived from his identifications, which embodies the individual's demands on himself, his ideals, his morality. The teacher has to recognize in the child the working of these three agencies as well as their interactions.

So far as the detailed observation of children is concerned, the elementary school teacher is in a difficult position. By the time the child has reached school-age, much of the activity of his drives is under control, unconscious, and not visible on the surface; he would not be fit for school if his ego were not built up and functioning. The elementary school teacher therefore lacks the advantages of the nursery school teacher who sees the child during his early conflicts and struggles. Therefore it is of great advantage for the teachers of school children to observe infants in day-nurseries and even babies in their cribs. On the one hand they will realize how early the personality traits of the school child reveal themselves in the infant; on the other hand they will be impressed by the enormous changes which every individual undergoes in the first five years of his life, i.e., the long and strenuous way from the newborn with his primitive animal-like attitudes to the almost civilized human being as which the child presents himself at the beginning of his school career. Such observations will enable the teacher to understand the interactions between innate and environmental forces in the individual child.

A deeper understanding of personality structure will help teachers to avoid a common mistake: namely to approach children of varying ages in the same manner. At nursery age the teacher deals more or less directly with the child's instinctive wishes; she offers opportunities for satisfying wishes or restricts and deflects drive-activity by means of play-material. At school age the teacher only draws indirectly on drive-energy (as for instance in the sublimations); on the whole she deals with the ego and its intellectual interests. In moral matters the child with a fully developed superego has to be approached quite differently from one where this step in development has not taken place yet. Instead of receiving permission or being thwarted in his wish-fulfilments by the teacher he should be given scope to solve moral conflicts within himself, i.e., he should be approached indirectly through his ideals and values.

The question was asked in connection with Dr. Freud's discussion of drive development: *How far are the child's drives still visible in the elementary school period?*

The degree to which drives are still visible at school age varies from child to child, and according to his upbringing. After six years, the most common surface remants of past instinctive wishes are greediness, mouth play such as thumb-sticking, interest in lavatory matters, day-dreaming, masturbation, aggressiveness, and showing-off. Some children fail to outgrow the need for immediate drive satisfaction; they do not settle down to school occupations, but are always searching for immediate gratifications. They cannot wait or work for their pleasures. In this, they still have the attitudes of infants.

If the teacher observes behaviour remnants of early development, their occurrence can give clues to the inner life of the child as well as to his present stage of drive-development. Thumb-sucking, rocking, and dirty language do not indicate abnormality, but a stage of development over which the child has not yet achieved control. The teacher cannot do much to correct such behaviour unless she knows more about the relevant facts.

Curiosity is one of the early drives which can be used to the full by the elementary school teacher. The child's intellectual activity is a function of his mental apparatus activated by energy from the drives. The child's early curiosity concerning sex matters can be displaced most profitably to the school subjects, if these are selected carefully to come close enough to the child's original interests. But the progressive school has to accomplish more than provide the child with welcome outlets for his drive energy. Such "sublimation" of sexual curiosity will only be of real benefit if simultaneously the child is guided towards exchanging play for work, i.e., if he becomes able to pursue occupations which do not yield immediate and unrestricted fulfilment of his primitive wishes but lead to pleasurable experiences by more difficult circuitous routes.

24 The Utilization of Psychoanalytic Concepts for Assessing Classroom Transaction

Louise L. Tyler

Psychology and psychologists have long been sources of ideas about teaching. Recently, psychotherapists have been making a contribution to the topic. Carl Rogers succinctly presents the relationship as follows:

> Let me begin by saying that my long experience as a therapist convinces me that significant learning is facilitated in psychotherapy, and occurs in that relationship. It is learning which makes a difference—in the individual's behavior, in the course of action he chooses in the future, in his attitudes and in his personality. It is a pervasive learning which is not just an accretion of knowledge, but which interpenetrates with every portion of his existence.
>
> Now it is not only my subjective feeling that such learning takes place. This feeling is substantiated by research. . . . To the extent then that educators are interested in learnings which are functional, which make a difference, which pervade the person and his actions, then they might well look to the field of psychotherapy for leads or ideas. Some adaption for education of the learning process which takes place in psychotherapy, seems like a promising possibility.[1]

Reprinted with permission from *The Journal of Educational Research,* 60:260–266, February, 1967.

Stavsky, a clinical psychologist, takes a point of view which develops somewhat as follows: psychotherapy and education embody an interpersonal relationship between an adult and a child. Both teaching and psychotherapy reduce or control anxiety with the therapist working mainly through unconscious dynamisms of anxiety while the teacher works along an ego-building level. Stavsky states:

> From a psychotherapeutic point of view, teaching is basically an interpersonal relationship, which, with its proper techniques and devices, helps reduce or control anxiety and so promotes learning.[2]

As a result of material of this sort a search of the literature was made on psychotherapy (particularly along the psychoanalytic line) to obtain ideas as to the nature of the teaching-learning process. Fortunately, Karl Menninger in *Theory of Psychoanalytic Technique*[3] has elaborated in considerable detail upon the theory basic to psychoanalytic technique. In fact, this is the only work, that the author is aware of, which outlines a psychotherapeutic process in any detail.

Psychoanalytic Technique

According to Menninger, psychoanalytic therapy is considered a transactional process engaged in for the purpose of changing behavior. This idea, of course, is similar to statements made about education and is a further justification for going to psychoanalytic therapy for leads for investigating the teaching-learning process.

Menninger outlines four concepts: regression, transference and countertransference, resistance and interpretation, which are basic to understanding psychoanalytic technique. The concepts of transference and countertransference, resistance and interpretation seemed easily appropriate to the teaching-learning process.

Transference

Menninger holds that transference is "the unrealistic roles or identities unconsciously ascribed to a therapist by a patient in the regression of the psychoanalytic treatment and the patient's reaction to this presentation derived from earlier experience."[4] The patient may have warm and friendly feelings toward the therapist as well as cold and hostile feelings. These feelings are primarily a result of the patient's personality and are not due to the therapist's behavior. Reactions from the client stem from experiences with significant individuals—parents, siblings and others— during his early formative years. The question can be asked, does transference occur in teaching? Most teachers have been aware that students are responding "peculiarly" to them; students are behaving in "unnatural," "uncalled for" ways, that is, ways which are not appropriate to the situation. Some of the commonly encountered transference reactions are: (1) that the teacher is withholding and wishes to expose the student's ignorance; (2) that the teacher is reserved, cold, hostile; (3) that the teacher fails to give sufficient guidance and direction, and (4) that the teacher (in a team teaching situation) is "in love" with the other teacher.

Countertransference

With regard to countertransference, Menninger indicates that the psychoanalyst also has an unconscious attitude and that his reactions to the patients may contain strong irrational components. Manifestations of countertransference are: persistent drowsiness; a compulsive tendency to hammer away at certain points; dreaming about the patient; repeatedly experiencing erotic or affectionate feelings toward a patient. Is there evidence of countertransference in a classroom? Of course, for example, drowsiness, irritation at particular students, tendency to hammer away at a point.

Resistance

This is the concept which explains the trend of forces within the patient which opposes the ameliorative changes. Resistance may also be thought of as reluctance to change. Even though the patient is cooperative and eager to improve, he unintentionally but purposefully obstructs the treatment. Clinically, it is manifested by such behaviors as concealing facts and ideas, by an increased forgetting, by absences, and by prolonged silences.

In teaching, might there be any evidences of resistance? Certainly there are apparent analogies between teaching and psychotherapy. The student wants to learn, but learning ways of thinking which conflict with presently held ways is painful, so the student resists. Disturbance of previous skills and habits creates anxiety. In a classroom this is also manifested by such behaviors as absences, withdrawal from class, tardiness, and silence in class.

Interpretation

Menninger states that interpretation or intervention, as he chooses to call it, is the analyst's contribution to the therapeutic process. The analyst points to connections and implications of meanings which tend to elude the patient. He reminds the patient of forgotten statements or confronts him with discrepancies or self-contradictions. The purpose of interpretation is to have the patient see himself. Timing of interpretations is very important, and they should be "on time," and gently and kindly done.

TABLE 1. Indicators for Categories

	1. INTERVENTION (Interpretation)	2. COUNTER- TRANSFERENCE
INTELLECTUAL Knowledge Comprehension Application Analysis Synthesis Evaluation	Kind of questions and comments instructor makes according to Bloom Taxonomy. Subject matter: objectives, learning opportunities, etc.	*Positive*—Uncritical acceptance of ideas from certain students. *Negative*—Inability to understand ideas. Hammering away at a point.
INSTRUCTIONAL PROCESS	Comments by Instructor relative to: 1. Mechanics of classroom —noise, arrangement, windows, etc. 2. Announcements of meetings, examinations, due dates, etc. Discussion of biblio. outline, etc. 3. Statements evaluating place of. 4. Asking student to clarify inadequate verbal presentation. 5. Comments on purposes. 6. Ending a contribution.	a. *Positive;* Changing requirements because of sympathetic identification with student's difficulties. Changing procedure—giving answers because students request them or because of students having difficulties. b. *Negative;* Changing course requirements on basis of pique—assigning or giving exams, additional projects because of annoyance.
TEACHER	Statements or questions with regard to regression, discoverance, resistance to elements of the learning process.	

3. DISCOVERANCE (Disclosance)	4. RESISTANCE	5. TRANSFERENCE
Verbal recognition that one is not dealing with question. Tentative attempt to deal with question at appropriate level with degree of freedom from teacher. Asking of questions. Answering of questions at appropriate level. Presenting information.	Failure to answer at behavioral level desired. Talking about something else. Mild questioning. Tentative assertion of a different point of view. Strong, clear disagreement. Angry disagreement. Refuse to discuss. Inability to understand an idea after presented time and again. A "humorous" retort by a student in reference to a question.	Positive or negative reactions (Laughter) about ideas. Jumbled—inadequate presentation of ideas. Failure to understand ideas. Hammering away at a point.
1. Student asks for additional references on a topic. 2. Students ask about assignments, examinations, etc. 3. Students clarifying own ideas. 4. Students reply to quest of classroom procedure, etc.	Comments by students which indicate rejection or acceptance of procedure or materials used in class. Why don't you give us the answers? Anger, or pleasure about class procedure, examinations, etc. Fear of speech. Refusal to read materials. Taking role of teacher.	Acceptance or volunteering for assignments. Requesting change in assignments. Failure to understand assignments. Speaking or presenting ideas to fill the void. Giving polite responses that are irrelevant.
Statements which indicate instructor is an *instructor*, *not* an omnipotent being.	Statements about teacher that are complimentary or uncomplimentary. Silence. Laughter — "Please help me get started—. I try but I don't understand." Laughter.	Laughter. Comments about or to teacher that are not appropriate. Comments about or to teacher's likes or dislikes. Comments about or to teacher at a personal level.

T A B L E 1.   Indicators for Categories (Continued)

	1. INTERVENTION (Interpretation)	2. COUNTER- TRANSFERENCE
INDIVIDUAL STUDENTS	Statements or questions with regard to regression, discoverance, resistance to elements of the learning process.	a. *Positive;* Excessively trying to help student express ideas [Indicators: humorous (erotic) tone of voice for certain students]. a. *Positive;* Slower speech, laughter in voice, warm tone, inflection. b. *Negative;* Impatience, arguing with student [Indicators: humorous (aggressive), tone of voice.] b. *Negative;* Fast speech, irritated tone, inflection, rasping voice, humorous comment, laughter—aggresive—in tone.
GROUP	Statements or questions with regard to regression, discoverance, resistance to elements of the learning process.	a. *Positive;* Excessively friendly. b. *Negative;* Arguing with group.
SELF	Statements or questions with regard to regression, discoverance, resistance to elements of the learning process.	

Does teaching involve interpretation? Teaching, certainly, from one point of view, requires that teachers confront students with contradictions, discrepancies, and illogical statements for the purpose of having the student understand the kind of thinking he is doing. Timing or the "teaching moment" is also extremely important, and as in analysis interpretation should be gently and kindly done.

These ideas seemed promising enough for the author to formulate a pilot project utilizing mainly these concepts.

Procedure

The 12 class meetings of a graduate course in curriculum (19 students) were recorded on tapes. The microphone, of a foreign make, was obtained

3. DISCOVERANCE (Disclosance)	4. RESISTANCE	5. TRANSFERENCE
Questions about what a student is doing.		
Statements indicating insight into group behavior.	Arguing with instructor, fast speech—aggression.	Negative or positive reactions toward group's development of ideas.
Statements indicating insight into own understanding or behavior — (you'll accuse me of running along.)		

from a film producer in Hollywood. The tapes consequently are excellent, and probably only one or two percent of the verbal interaction has been unable to be transcribed.

Development of Indicators

After the course was completed the tapes were listened to for the purpose of developing some system of categorizing the verbal content. As the tapes were listened to, it became clear that the four concepts of transference, countertransference, resistance and interpretation were not sufficient to account for all the verbal interaction. Students were making comments which did not fit these categories. On returning to Menninger it was noted that he talked about the development of insight—this, for the author, was formulated into a dimension labeled Discoverance. The categories for this pilot study then became five: Intervention; Countertransference; Discoverance; Resistance and Transference. In Table 1 are listed some of the indicators for the five categories.

The above description seems to give the impression that it was a fairly routine and simple task to develop indicators for the categories. This is far from being accurate.

Indicators were formulated as a result of (1) close reading of Menninger's volume and attempting to translate his comments into types of verbal statements that students would make; (2) introspection by the author as to what her verbal statements meant; and (3) listening to tapes and translating verbal statements into types of indicators.

Classification of Data

Just as it was exceedingly difficult to formulate indicators so was it difficult to classify the verbal interaction. The method utilized was to listen to the tapes while following a transcribed record of the meetings. It was discovered that it was impossible to classify the verbal interaction by referring only to the transcribed tapes. The meanings that sentences have depend upon intonation, speed, quality of voice, emotion, and the like. In other words, the meaning any verbal interaction has is far from simply what the words mean, intellectually. It was necessary, in most cases, to hear how the words and sentences sounded. An example might be the word, "yes". Yes can be said in an encouraging accepting manner or in a defensive manner. In one case it might be an indicator of intervention while in another case an indicator of countertransference. Only by listening to the tape and reading the transcription at the same time was it possible to classify the interaction.

The most difficult problem at this stage of the research had to do with the decision as to what constituted a unit of talk. Most studies based upon analysis of verbal interaction use a time unit or a sentence unit. Ned Flanders who developed his well-known system for analyzing classroom interaction uses a three-second interval for classifying into ten categories verbal interaction. Robert Bales whose well-known system is widely utilized by social scientists uses the sentence as a unit. Both of these systems were considered but were rejected. The unit of talk that was developed was called an episode. In some cases an episode was one word ("Yes"); in some cases one sentence ("What were we to be doing tonight?"); in some cases an extended presentation ("I would like to eliminate the phrase school district because curriculum is made up of all the learning opportunities a student is exposed to whether structured or unstructured or prepared or unprepared. I think there is a formal curriculum but the informal curriculum has an influence on curriculum that needs to be conscious and planned for.").

What was desired in this study was to obtain a record of the nature of all the interaction between students and teacher, therefore an episode began with every speaker. This might mean that an episode could be one word—e.g. "Yeah." On the other hand an episode might run as long as several sentences or be an extensive presentation. In this case the discourse constituted an episode when its meaning was of one type, that is, it was classified as transference, resistance, and the like. However, a long presentation by one speaker might consist of three episodes because the meaning would shade from discoverance into transference back to discoverance.

The material from five class meetings was classified by two raters: the author and a research educationist. The meetings which were classified were the first and last and three spaced one month apart during the semester. The data as classified appear in Table 2.

Following are some illustrations of how the verbal interaction was classified according to the categories developed:

Speaker	Verbal Interaction	Classification
INSTRUCTOR	Mr. Johnson, what were we to be doing tonight?	Intervention—Instructional Process
	Laughter from group.	Transference—Teacher
STUDENT A	I've asked about five people so I think I have consensus.	Intervention—Teacher
INSTRUCTOR	I see.	Intervention—Instructional Process
STUDENT A	We were to be doing tonight?	Transference—Teacher
INSTRUCTOR	Yes.	Intervention—Instructional Process
INSTRUCTOR	You mean you're not clear.	Intervention—Individual Student
STUDENT A	Ah yes!	Discoverance—Self
INSTRUCTOR	You're not clear.	Intervention—Individual Student
STUDENT A	That is correct.	Discoverance—Self

TABLE 2. Percentage of Responses According to Psychoanalytic
Categories

	Teacher Responses				Student Responses					
	Intervention		Counter-transference		Discoverance		Resistance		Transference	
	No.	%	No.	%	No.	%	No.	%	No.	%
Date: Sept. 16, 1963 Topic: Overview of Course	91	55	20	12	29	18	8	5	17	10
Date: Sept. 30, 1963 Topic: Curriculum Definition	273	33	66	8	351	42	47	6	90	11
Date: Oct. 28, 1963 Topic: Subject Matter	218	35	65	10	234	37	49	8	59	9
Date: Dec. 2, 1963 Topic: Psychology .	243	38	10	2	242	38	35	6	102	16
Date: Jan. 6, 1964 Topic: Evaluation .	93	38	30	12	87	36	2	1	30	12
Totals	918	37	191	08	943	38	141	05	298	12

Validity and Reliability

It is customary in most research to first report reliability estimates; however, this study is going to be an exception. Validity will be discussed
first because aspects of validity have been emphasized.

Validity of the categories was established in several ways. First,
since the definitions of each category describe the kinds of things students and teachers do in the classroom, the instruments have face
validity. Second, the categorization made by the raters accounted for all
the interaction which occurred. This fact satisfied the criterion of in-
clusiveness of categories and provides evidence of validity.

Reliability of the raters was determined by a percentage of agreement. Approximately 20 percent of the verbal interaction on the five
meetings was scored independently by the two raters and the percentage
agreement ranged from 84 percent to 92 percent. Table 3 reports the data
on reliability.

Discussion

The attempt has been made to develop a system of categories for classifying the verbal interaction of a classroom according to psychoanalytic

TABLE 3.   Percentage of Agreement on Classification of Verbal
Interaction

	Percent of Agreement
Date: Sept. 16, 1963 Topic: Overview of Course	85
Date: Sept. 30, 1963 Topic: Curriculum Definition	84
Date: October 28, 1963 Topic: Subject Matter	87
Date: Dec. 2, 1963 Topic: Psychology	87
Date: Jan. 6, 1964 Topic: Evaluation	92

theory. This has been satisfactorily done. It has also been shown that raters can satisfactorily agree on the classification of the verbal interaction.

Of the total verbal interaction of the five tapes 45 percent is teacher talk and 55 percent is student talk. It can be noted from Table 2 that of the teacher talk 37 percent is intervention and eight percent is countertransference. Of the student talk 38 percent is discoverance, five percent is resistance and 12 percent is transference.

It can also be noted from Table 2 that teacher responses for individual meetings ranged from 40 percent to 67 percent of the total verbal interaction. Correspondingly student responses ranged from 33 percent to 60 percent of total verbal interaction.) It would be useful to compare the teacher's activity in this study with teachers from other studies on interaction done by Perkins and Flanders. These studies, however, used a time unit of teacher talk while this study did not; therefore, such a comparison is not possible.

In four out of five classes the student talk was greater than teacher talk. The first class was the exception and was probably a result of the fact that the instructor discussed the bibliography and the requirements for the class in considerable detail. Even with this limited talk by the teacher in most of the meetings, countertransference ranged from as low as two percent to as high as 12 percent.

The lowest amount of student talk occurred during the first meeting. In the other meetings student talk varied from 40 percent to 60 percent. There is occasionally discussion about the amount of resistance that is present in a class. Resistance appears to be rather limited—ranging from one percent to eight percent. What is of interest is the amount of transference which ranged from nine percent to 16 percent.

Now that it has been shown that a classroom can be analyzed according to concepts from psychotherapy, the next step will be to analyze many classrooms at the elementary and secondary level so that normative standards can be obtained relative to the amounts of transference, countertransference, et cetera, which occur. Also from psychoanalytic theory about the therapeutic process, a number of testable hypotheses about classrooms can be formulated. Some illustrations are the following: Classroom instruction is effective when there is a minimum of countertransference; the pattern of resistance will be low at the beginning of instruction, will rise, and then will drop; resistance will be high as long as the ideas that are introduced are incongruent with beliefs currently held by students.

A most fascinating idea to explore would be the pattern of activity in the classroom to note whether it has any similarity to the pattern of activity in therapy.

Conclusions

Out of this study the researcher primarily has come away with the thought that classroom interaction may be considered a complexly related intellectual and emotional activity.

There are the highly emotionally tinged reactions of resistance, of transference and of countertransference which make up approximately 25 percent of the total interaction. Classroom interaction is not neutral verbal interaction. If adequate insight is going to be obtained into the nature of classroom interaction, some further attempts must be made in the direction of exploring the hypotheses drawn from psychoanalytic theory.

FOOTNOTES

[1]Carl R. Rogers. "Significant Learning: In Therapy and in Education," *Educational Leadership* (January 1959), pp. 232–33.

[2]William H. Stavsky. "Using the Insights of Psychotherapy in Teaching," *The Elementary School Journal* (October 1957), p. 32.

[3]Karl C. Menninger. *Theory of Psychoanalytic Technique* (New York: Basic Books, Inc. 1958).

[4]*Op. cit.* p. 81.

6 *Games*

Overview

It would be difficult to deny, as we enter the last fourth of the twentieth century, that games are a significant aspect of American life. Sports capture the attention and devotion of a noteworthy segment of our population. This is best shown by the recent fantastic growth of professional football and basketball, as well as by greatly increased amateur participation in such sports as skiing, surfing, boating, bowling, and golf. Indeed, in some newspapers the sports section is as large as the news section or larger. Many men read the sports section of the newspaper first.

Furthermore, the language of games has become part of our daily vocabulary and thinking. Consider such statements as: "It's your turn to carry the ball." "He couldn't even get to first base." "That's a political football." "He struck out that time." "He's just a pawn in their plan." "He threw in the towel." A television detective series was entitled "Checkmate." Several plays dealing with games have appeared recently on Broadway, "That Championship Season" and "The Changing Room." There are many more such words, terms, and phrases, and we probably are not even aware of their origin in games.

It is no wonder, then, that educators have recently used this vantage point of games and sports and play to analyze teaching.[1] Since everyone knows about games, it is very easy to understand the analogies used, and

[1]Psychologists, too, have recently employed this perspective. See the works of Eric Berne and Thomas Szasz.

educators have not had to be concerned about using an unfamiliar
analogue. They have concentrated, instead, on identifying the similarities between teaching and games.

It is important here to keep in mind that the selections in this book
deal with the games vantage point for analyzing and understanding
teaching. This is quite different from the current popularity of simulation games as a method of teaching. We can use the games vantage point
for analyzing teaching whether or not the teacher is utilizing a simulation
game with the students. One is an observing, analyzing perspective; the
other is a teaching method.

In the selections that follow, Macdonald and Hyman present two
separate but overlapping sets of characteristics of games and play. They
then apply these characteristics to teaching. These articles employ such
concepts as rules, players, playing field, goals, and roles and use these
concepts to study teaching. Although similar, the articles differ insofar
as they abstract and outline different sets of characteristics. And these
complement rather than oppose one another.

The articles also differ in their specific approaches. Macdonald
identifies six *games in teaching* and then analyzes the factors he has
previously borrowed from Leary within each game. He later shows the
implications for educators of these concepts and games. Smith, Bellack
and his associates, and Hyman consider *teaching as a game*. Smith talks
about the player, coach, and referee. Hyman expands the analogy by
first classifying participants in the game into three categories and then
considering scorekeeper, spectators, rules committee, and waterboy as
well as player, coach, and referee.

Bellack and his associates present the rules of the classroom game
as derived from the empirical study presented in the section devoted
to the cognitive vantage point. The investigators conceptualized their
data in terms of the rules of the game since their initial framework is
derived from Wittgenstein's notion of a language game. This is itself a
metaphor. Though these rules stem from work with high school
classes studying a unit in economics, evidence from other studies seems
to show that they apply to a wide range of classes. The reader will notice
this in the selections by Flanders (Section 2), Hughes (Section 2),
Gallagher and Aschner (Section 3), and Maccia (Section 3), for example.
In regard to rules, the reader should note that Hyman speaks about two
types of rules, process and administrative. This distinction is made in
order to focus on the critical aspects of teaching.

An interesting feature of these articles is the justifications they
present for using the perspective of games. Macdonald draws on Western
analytic philosophy and Eastern mystic philosophy to arrive at a playful
way of talking about teaching that is quite serious in intent. For him, it

is a way of combining the best of two schools of philosophy, each of which has significance for teaching. As noted earlier, Bellack, too, draws upon analytic philosophy by way of Wittgenstein, the father of this school of thought. For Smith, the justification is simply the easy fit of the analogy.

The chief pedagogical implication of this vantage point is that teachers and pupils play various games and roles. Therefore, as Macdonald notes, we may describe and evaluate teaching in terms of the games and roles being played. To say that a teacher is sometimes effective and sometimes not is inadequate. It is more meaningful to say that he is an effective teacher in the information-giving game but not effective in the inquiry game. This procedure, of course, requires standards for effectiveness in each game. The need is to establish them for as yet they do not exist. This approach also gives us a way of selecting and grouping teachers, for example, into teaching teams. We may wish to put a teacher who excels at the dialogue game or coaching role on a team with another teacher whose forte is the information-giving game or player role. The assumption is that, once we are aware of the various games and roles, teachers and pupils will be able to choose and play as they want. That is, people can determine their behavior and are responsible for it. It is here that we see one connection between the games vantage point and the psychological one proposed by Rogers and others.

There are other connections, too, as the reader will quickly see. For example, the referee resembles the teacher who evaluates the pupil, as depicted by Flanders (Section 2) and Bellack. Yet there is a difference in that a failure on the part of a pupil as player does not reflect upon the referee, whereas a failure does reflect in some way on the teacher, as conceived in other frameworks. The waterboy in this perspective resembles the facilitating function of Hughes (Section 2). The reader should also note similarities between the concept of play and the concepts in Section 7 on Aesthetics, especially in the articles by Hallman and Eisner.

The previous paragraph hints at the issue of whether the games analogy is an adequate one for teaching. Though these four selections take the position that concepts from games can be successfully applied to teaching, there remains some doubt. The significant relationship of "when somebody wins, somebody must lose," which is basic to games, seems to be absent in teaching. Where is the win/lose idea in teaching? Also, by using the concept of games, how do we account for homework? In short, the reader should consider carefully the degree to which the games analogue is adequate for teaching.

If we assume the adequacy of this framework, the question still remains to be answered by future empirical work whether we can reliably identify different games and roles in teaching. What exactly do teachers do and say as they play the role of coach? What happens in the interaction between teacher and pupils when we emphasize or neglect the mastery game or referee role? How does teaching in the spirit of play affect the social climate or psychological climate of the classroom? The potential number of research projects growing out of this perspective is great but appears to be virtually untapped. The questions asked here are only a hint, as should be obvious to any player or spectator.

25 Gamesmanship in the Classroom

James B. Macdonald

A Playful Way of Talking About Teaching

How shall we talk about teaching? If its intent is the development of rationality, then how do we talk about how teachers develop student powers of rational thought?

Here it seems we have at least two sources of contemporary insight for helping us develop a playful language. These two are the analytic philosophers and the modern psychological mystics, especially those persons presently involved in the examination of and experimentation with consciousness-enlarging drugs such as LSD.

The common thread in these diverse enterprises is the concept of the game. In the one case, from Ludwig Wittgenstein comes the idea of language games. In the other instance, after the eastern mystics, come the modern western psychological philosophers, such as Timothy Leary, Alan Watts, and Aldous Huxley, who expand this concept to the reality game.

Without attempting to be accurate or to be faithful to either development, the central concept of teaching as a potential series of communication games would appear to have unusual free-floating and playful possi-bilities. Further, it is without doubt a valid way of talking, although there is no way of knowing at present how useful it can be.

Arno Bellack, in a study of teaching, talked about it as a language game. Now what I'm going to do today is talk about teaching as *games*.

However, what here carries the concept of the game to a much more general level is best described by Timothy Leary as follows:

> The use of the word "game" in this sweeping context is likely to be mis-understood. The listener may think I refer to "play" as opposed to stern, real-life serious activities of man. But as you shall see, I consider the latter as "game."
>
> All behavior involves learned games. But only that rare Westerner we call "mystic" or who has had a visionary experience of some sort sees clearly the game structure of behavior. Most of the rest of us spend our time strug-gling with roles and rules and goals and concepts of games which are implicit and confusedly not seen as games, trying to apply the roles and rules and rituals of one game to other games.
>
> A game is a learned cultural sequence characterized by six factors:
>
> 1. Roles: The game assigns roles to the human beings involved.
> 2. Rules: A game sets up a set of rules which hold only during the game sequence.
> 3. Goals: Every game has a goal or purpose. The goals of baseball are to score more runs than the opponents. The goals of the game of psychol-ogy are more complex and unimplicit but they exist.
> 4. Rituals: Each game has its conventional behavior pattern not related to the goals or rules but yet quite necessary to comfort and continu-ance.
> 5. Language: Each game has its jargon unrelated to the rules and goals and yet necessary to learn and use.
> 6. Values: Each game has its standard of excellence or goodness.

Teaching, then, can be considered a special kind of communication game or games, structured by our culture and learned by us. Each game has structure in the sense of Leary's six characteristics: roles, rules, goals, rituals, language and values.

This brings us to premise number three.[1] *Teaching is a set of com-munication games*. This paves the way for looking at common occurrences in classrooms from this perspective.

What follows, then, is the discussion of a number of teaching strate-gies as communication games, analyzed in terms of the six characteristics just discussed and their intent. The names of the "games" are drawn from experience and general knowledge of teaching and as such are purely suggestive of possibilities and labels.

[1]The first two premises in a section not included here are: There is no one reality in teaching; teaching is best characterized by its intent—the development of rationality. R.T.H., editor.

Games Teachers Play

The Information-Giving Game

The most common communication game in our high schools may be called information-giving. This game is exactly what it suggests. The teacher has information which he forms and manages to send to the student receiver. The receivers are expected to take in this information without distorting it and signal the teacher that they have the information. The media by which messages may be sent are variable, but the intent of the process is relatively constant.

The roles assigned are clear. The teacher possesses the information, or knowledge of avenues of access to this information. His role is to present to, or put students in contact with, the ideas or facts in the most effective manner. The student role is also clear. He is to receive the information and be able to show the teacher that he has possession of it.

1. *The game should be played seriously*—all participants are expected to accept the worth and significance of the game and to cooperate and perform in a serious work-like atmosphere.
2. *The teacher directs the game*—students are expected to take their cues for responding from the teacher. The teacher of course is responsible for initiating and soliciting responses.
3. *Attention and cooperation are expected*—students are expected to be attentive and to cooperate with the teacher to achieve the goals of the game.

The goals of the game are also fairly obvious. Students are expected to be able to reproduce the information presented in whatever form the teacher calls for. Their reproductions are graded and become part of the competitive interpersonal data of our society. The goals of the game vary. Some are, for example, to please the teachers, beat fellow students, win access to social mobility, or simply to know something.

Rituals are also involved. Students are expected (usually) to raise their hands before responding. Teachers are expected to have the last word and "cap" any set of responses. People take turns and talk one at a time; and all follow the special procedures for handing in assignments, taking tests, coming and going, and relating to each other.

The language of the game is essentially framed in a question-answer, lecture, and discussion format. Outside the classroom the teacher talks about individual "IQ's," meeting the "needs" of students, "gifted," "culturally deprived," and a host of other things. Inside the classroom the special language relates to cueing the smooth wording of the process. "Who would like to tell us about Charlemagne?" might be interpreted to mean "All right, let's get started; who is first?" Each teacher has her use of "good," "o.k.," and other phrases that are a distinctive use of language in the communication process.

The values of the game are found in achievement. Excellence means knowing the subject, and excellent teaching means getting the information across. Most often the standard is a comparative one, sometimes an absolute one, and infrequently an individual one.

Mastery

A subvariety of information-giving is the mastery game. In general it follows the same kinds of prescriptions as information-giving. However, the special context of drill and practice provides variation for this game.

The goals, for example, might be thought of as "over-learning" or habitualizing rather than "just" knowing. Many skills fall in this area and the basic intent is to take them into cognition and make them so automatic that cognitive awareness of them is no longer necessary for behavior.

The Problem-Solving Game

The next most common appearance in high school is the problem-solving game. The teacher role is to present, get students in contact with, or evolve a problem with them. The teacher often knows *the* or *an* answer to this problem, but if not he has knowledge of how to solve it or faith that it can be solved. Oftentimes problem-solving takes place in a project or "activity" format.

The student role is more active than in information-giving. He is now expected to take some initiative, to think about what he is doing as well as what he is learning. The goal of the game is to come up with some satisfactory resolution of the problem, and standards of excellence are applied in terms of the teacher's judgment of the exhaustion of relevant sources of data in relation to the level of maturity of the students.

Rules of the game are built around the expectation that students will define or see a problem and set out systematically and thoughtfully to solve it. Contrary to information-giving, it is now taboo to expect the teachers to provide answers. Language usage now shifts to terms such as "resource materials," "critical thinking," and analysis of the process of reflective thinking with such concepts as inference, data, and evidence becoming part of the setting.

The Discovery or Inquiry Game

The discovery or inquiry game is a variant of problem-solving. The major difference rests in the goals of the game. Each begins with discrepancies to be resolved, but in inquiry the goal is shifted from the solution to the *process* of solving a problem.

The teacher role is to set the circumstances for discrepant awareness on the part of students. Students are expected to search, manipulate, experiment, and seek actively.

The rituals in this case may often become the modes of inquiry and be in essence the goals. Thus, when appropriate, a student must use the ritual of scientific method, or of formal logic, or of aesthetic criticism, or of moral and ethical evaluation.

The value of the game is in the playing, intelligently and with spirit. The outcomes of the game are seen primarily in terms of the process utilized, and excellence becomes awareness of the process of inquiry.

The Dialogue Game

Upon occasion the communication game can actually move to the level of dialogue. In a true dialogue game the roles of all present are the same —the attempt to move the discussion to the revelation of insights not present in *any* participant at the beginning of the interaction.

The rules of the game are:

1. One participates as a total person, not as a role player.
2. One is expected to be open, to reveal himself, and to receive from and listen to others.
3. One must be disciplined. One is expected to participate and one is expected to participate in the context of the contribution of others.
4. One must respond to others and therefore be responsible in relation to them.

No contributions are rejected, criticized, or judged per se. Participants, however, are expected to discipline themselves by the monitoring of behavior which reflects personal needs to talk, show off, play one-upmanship, defend themselves, or pull rank. The goal is to explore beyond the present member-awareness for insights and implications about the material which produces an aesthetic response or an insight (Aha!).

Further, the goal is to relate the forms of content or subject matters to the vitality which originally produced them; to bring the meanings that come out of a student's living into conjunction with the meanings inherent in the subject matter. Excellence is assured by the feeling of time well spent and the satisfaction of new awarenesses.

Ritual and language will be loosened and, although the spatial arrangements of facilities for dialogue may reflect circular rather than linear patterns, time may be used more flexibly; and the use of judgmental terms will be negated.

The Clarification Game

Attempts to relate students to meanings and values are often found in clarification procedures. The teacher, in other words, attempts to elicit personal responses, reactions, and meanings to life and subject matter. The teacher's role is to focus the student inward and the student's role is to express attitude feelings, aspirations, values, and impressions and to reflect upon them.

The rules of the game are very open. The teacher must never judge any student response; he must never ask questions for which he has a predetermined answer but only questions for which an individual student could possibly have the answer. Students, on the other hand, must freely express their real feelings, concerns and meanings.

The goal of clarification is the development of values and commitments in the form of personal meanings attached to content. Standards of excellence are difficult to express, but if the process is satisfying the worth is assumed.

The language involves such phrases as "tell me more about that" or "now I see what you're saying," or "you mean to say . . . ?" All language involves "I feel," "I think," and other first-person reference. Again, ritual is caught in the use of time and space of a personal and flexible nature.

Potential Implications of the Communication Idea

Six teacher strategies were described as communication games. The question may shift to, "What relevance or insights for teaching can we glean from this description?"

I should like to reflect briefly upon four kinds: those for students, those for teachers, those for principals, and those for researchers.

The Student

Students rarely have any insight into the nature of the teaching role. They accept what the teacher does as natural, although they seldom know why he does things. Further, they realize that teachers expect certain things from them, but they are not really in control of their own responses in a rational way. Thus, when asked why they violate expectations, many can truly answer, "I don't know."

A major aid to improving the classroom situation could be found by developing the student's awareness of the communication games teachers play. Reflect for a moment upon what it might mean to students to understand what is happening to them, as well as what is expected of them as outcomes. The awareness of varying roles, rules, shifting goals, standards of value and appropriate ritual could incalculably improve the student's ability to participate and utilize the communication context. The simple fact of knowing which game is being played at what time would be a real revolution in insight.

Beyond this, the concept of games could well be a tremendous liberalizing and perspective-giving insight for students. As students come to realize that all cultural activities are games and that the "real" world out there and in the lunchroom is as much a game as the teaching-learning process they might better come to know themselves and to be able to choose rationally those social games in which they wish to invest their time and effort. (And in the process be able to play more expertly.)

The Teachers

If teachers came to understand the communication-game concept they might well realize the paucity of their use of potential learning contexts. One might be able to break down the dichotomous wall that exists in their minds today between teaching as information giving and "all that other impractical stuff." In its stead one could create a set of cognitive guiding-concepts known in terms of roles, rules, goals, rituals, language, and values—which could provide for teachers vehicles for self-insight and discovery, and which could be used as heuristic devices for developing a broader range of competencies.

At present, teachers do not possess a variety of models of styles or strategies to help them think rationally about teaching. Until we are able to provide models for them we cannot expect much change.

The Principals

Communication games provide tremendous possibilities for effective evaluation and improvement of teaching. The simple fact of rephrasing the question "How effective is a teacher?" to "How effectively is the teacher playing the communication game he has chosen?" "What is the teacher's repertoire of games?" and "Are chosen games appropriate to proposed outcomes?" could be a major step forward.

The value element would still be present in terms of valued games to play, but within that limitation the communication-game idea would appear to provide usable criteria for assessing teachers for the purpose of improvement.

Some of the criteria could be:

1. Does the teacher know what game is being played?
2. Do the students?
3. Is the game consistent? (i.e., within the rules, etc.)
4. Are the roles clearly delineated?
5. Are the rules clear?
6. Are the goals clear?
7. Is the language appropriate?
8. Are the rituals appropriate?
9. Are the standards known and clear?

The Researchers

In passing, a few comments for researchers seem relevant. One of the major problems with research in classrooms has been the failure to account for purposes of instruction within the research. To know that teachers are direct or indirect, for example, has little meaning outside the special communication context of the interaction (of which, hopefully, the development of rationality is the central intent).

Separating communication games by their various characteristics could provide clarity of conceptualization that is much needed and, in the process, could supply a list of variables that may be more productive. Just the simple matter of focusing some research on the variety of standards appropriate to different games would be a major improvement over the single-standard approach (achievement) now in vogue.

One final word of caution is in order. The position presented here is playful in mood though serious in intent. It is an attempt to build out of the particulars of teaching a framework which will, by its abstraction and generality, help bring new awareness of the particular, though perhaps not in specific terms of the abstraction itself. It would be well to heed T. S. Eliot's admonition:

> ... every attempt is a wholly new
> start, and a different kind of failure.

26 The Name of the Game is Teaching

Ronald T. Hyman

In all societies and cultures, everyone knows about games and their participants. Little girls and boys play London bridge, hide-and-seek, and Simple Simon. Older girls play hopscotch and jacks. Older boys play football, basketball, and other organized sports. Adults not only play games of their childhood but also learn new games, commercial games such as Scrabble and games in the public domain such as bridge and golf. Games are familiar to everyone—including teachers.

All games have certain common features:

1. Games have a goal or objective, e.g., to score the most runs in baseball, to score the most points in gin rummy, or to checkmate the king in chess.

2. Games are ordered by rules, and the goal is attained by playing according to the rules. If the rules are not obeyed, the game degenerates into chaos.

3. Games involve people who may be classified into three types: (a) Players—such as the fullback who actually scores the touchdowns in football; (b) Non-players—with a stake in the outcome of the game, such as coaches and managers, and (c) Non-players—without a stake in the outcome of the game, such as referees and scorekeepers.

Reprinted with permission from *Media and Methods*, 4:10–12, April, 1968.

4. Games involve a common playing area (a card table or a baseball diamond) and equipment with which to play the game.

These universally identifiable aspects of games can aid us in viewing teachers and pupils in action.

First, what is the goal of teaching? Learning! Teachers perform so that pupils can learn information, concepts, and skills. This is the primary but not exclusive goal of teaching. The primary goal is not good mental health or fun, though they do have a part in teaching.

Ideally, the teaching game is not competitive. The teacher and pupils are not opponents but have a common goal. In this way, the game of teaching differs from basketball and tennis in that what is gained (learned) by the pupil is not lost by the teacher. When the pupil improves, the teacher does not lose. On the contrary, only when the pupil improves, does the teacher win.

Second, the game called teaching operates on the basis of rules. Such rules as "The pupil may speak only when called upon," and "The pupils call the teacher *Mister* Jones while the teacher calls the pupils *John* and *Jane*," are in effect in virtually all classrooms. These rules may be labeled "administrative" rules. "Process" rules—those that govern the nature of the interaction between teacher and pupils—are the real focus of teaching. Process rules dictate, for example, that the teacher sets the topic to be discussed and decides on class activities such as lectures, films, and tests, that the pupil mainly responds to the teacher's questions, and that the teacher evaluates the pupil in his presence while the pupil evaluates the teacher with his classmates after the lesson is over. Unlike many of the administrative rules, these process rules are not written rules. Yet the process rules are strongly adhered to and, in effect, define the teaching game. They are as much in force as the written rules of tennis.

Third, who are the people involved in the teaching game? With few exceptions teaching involves two types of people, teacher and pupil. Usually there is one teacher and many pupils in any one teaching game. The teacher and pupils perform the roles of the three types of game participants noted before: players, non-players with a stake in the game, and non-players without a stake in the game. The game of football can be used to illustrate how the teacher and pupils take on these different roles.

The pupils are the halfbacks, fullbacks, and ends who score touchdowns, for it is they who are scoring (that is, learning) in the game. However, learning by the pupil does not preclude learning by the teacher, for teachers also learn during the game. The teacher may be likened to the quarterback whose primary function is to lead the other players in scoring points but who may, on occasion, score himself. Some pupil players run interference and block for the others, thus aiding them in their learning. They do so either at the request of the quarterback or at their own discretion. Hence, both teacher and pupil are players in the teaching game, the pupils mainly scoring the touchdowns.

The teacher is also the coach in the teaching game. He is the strategist who directs the play of his charges. As coach, the teacher determines when, how, and what the players will do. He plans schedules and instructs the pupils in the method of play which leads to learning. He teaches them how to listen, recite, gather information from reference books, take notes, prepare reports, and read the text. The teacher, like a coach who reviews the films of the previous week's game, goes over material previously learned and shows how the knowledge and skills gained may be applied in other situations. Perhaps most important of all the teacher as coach encourages his players while the game is in progress. As the pupils play, the teacher gives words of praise and urges them to continue learning. If the coach chastises his players, he does so only to bring about better performance.

The role of team manager (who ministers to the needs of all the players) also exists in the teaching game. The teacher and pupils share this role. They both erase the chalkboard, empty the pencil sharpener, distribute corrected homework assignments, and collect texts.

The role of referee is performed by the teacher in virtually all teaching games. The teacher as referee cites infractions of the rules and metes out appropriate penalties to the individual rule-breaker, or to the entire team. The teacher often says, "Remain after class a few minutes for doing that." It is rare that the pupil serves as referee although in some teaching games one or two pupils are in charge of noting minor infractions such as chewing gum or talking out of turn.

The role of scorekeeper also exists in the teaching game. The teacher usually performs this role. Only on occasion and only in certain teaching games do the pupils keep score. In such games the pupils suggest their score (grade, mark) to the official scorekeeper, the teacher.

From this analogy with football we see that the teacher and the pupils shift their roles during the teaching game, whereas in football different roles are performed by specifically designated people. The teacher and the pupils move from role to role. The teacher monopolizes a particular role or shares it with the pupils and vice-versa. Being alert to this shift in roles is crucial to understanding the teaching game. Unless one appreciates that the teacher performs many different roles during the game, he cannot comprehend the many acts performed. The game model demonstrates clearly and forcefully the multiplicity of roles performed by the teacher. Without the idea of teaching as a game before us, we would tend to forget this critical aspect of teaching, and this oversight leads many teachers to err in their judgment about what is going on in the classroom. That is, they fail to understand the nature of their roles.

It is also necessary to look at the role of rule-maker in games. The rule-maker may be an official committee, the creator of the game, some combination of these two, or even the players themselves. In the teaching game, some rules are made by people who are not participants in the game itself (such as the principal); however, most rules are established by the teacher and the pupils themselves. The degree of pupil participation in serving as rule-maker depends on the individual game situation. Generally, the teacher alone serves as rule-maker. It is he who makes explicit administrative rules (no gum chewing) and sets the stage for establishing the process rules (teacher talks three times as much as the pupils). Thus, it is interesting to note that the teacher not only makes the rules but, in addition, identifies infractions of the rules and metes out punishment as he performs the role of referee. It is interesting because in Western society the law-maker is generally not the judge. This unique aspect of the teaching game is often overlooked and often accounts for some of the statements about unfair behavior which pupils level at teachers. But this is the game as we know it.

Fourth, what are the playing field and equipment of the teaching game? Most games occur in a school classroom with desks and chairs. Today, teachers and pupils employ such equipment as films, film strips, recordings, slides, and broadcast media just as they do textbooks, paper, pencil, and chalkboard. The teaching game by its very nature necessitates equipment. What is more, the condition of the classroom and the equipment influence the game. A stuffy, undersized classroom with immovable desks and obsolete texts affects the teaching game just as a muddy field and a wet ball affect a football game.

Finally, we need to raise two questions regarding other aspects of the teaching game. First, players participate voluntarily in most games, and this largely accounts for the vitality and fun of the game. Does compulsory attendance in school affect the vitality of the teaching game?

Second, in most games players practice all week but score points only during the game. In the teaching game, students display their learning (that is, score points) not only during the actual game but during practice (homework) as well. Is the analogy therefore invalid?

To answer the first question, compulsory attendance does in some way detract from the spirit and fun of teaching in school. Teaching cannot always be exciting, but games are not always exciting either. To the second question, however, my answer is no. Though teaching and games are not identical, they are still similar enough to make the analogy helpful in understanding teaching in a special way.

If we as teachers wish to make teaching analogous to a game, then the key for doing it is our approach. The teacher establishes the tone of the situation. The environment he shapes not only affects how and what will be learned, but it contributes to the student's overall view of what teaching is all about and in what manner he will participate in it.

By keeping this model of teaching in mind the classroom teacher can create a more spirited and enthusiastic atmosphere. Perhaps the first and most important thing the teacher can do is to structure the situation so that he himself learns along with the pupils. The teacher can set up his game strategy so that the class inquires into areas which are open and which encourage *all* the players to score and win. For example, American history offers such areas as The Prevention of World War III and The Future of the Industrial City. Intellectual inquiry, rather than a re-hash of six or seven short homework study questions, can make the teaching game appealing.

In order to do this the teacher will need to sharpen up his coaching ability. The teacher as coach may need to teach his pupils new skills, e.g., to inquire intellectually into unsolved issues. This necessitates the continued observing and reviewing of the pupils' work. When the teacher criticizes a pupil's poor performance, he must do so according to intellectual standards and with a tone that will lead to subsequent improvement. This includes pointing out errors in logic, citing new references, and raising new questions. In this way, he need not feel guilty when he criticizes the student, and the pupil will learn how to play the game better. By concentrating on the roles of inquiring quarterback and coach, the teacher can profitably play down his role as scorekeeper.

One other procedure will help. The teacher can arrange for the pupils to play a variety of roles more often. As in baseball and football, the teacher as coach can call upon his better players to help him improve the play of others. Talented and expert players can give helpful hints and instruction to those who are in a slump. The pupils can serve as referees by judging debates and anonymously commenting on anonymous papers. Certainly players learn how to play any game, including the teaching game, from their teammates. This procedure will provide variety for the pupils and free the teacher from sole responsibility for specific roles. He will become more sensitive to the other roles he performs, especially the combination of rule maker and referee. By expanding the roles of the pupil, the teacher can infuse enthusiasm into the teaching game.

27 The Game of Thinking

B. Othanel Smith

When does one know the rules of a game, say, the game of checkers?
Suppose he says, "No, you can't make that move" when someone moves
a man backward, and he says this on any occasion when that move is
made. Should we say that he knows one of rules of the game, even
though he cannot give a sophisticated statement of it? I think we should
claim that he does know the rule. So it is with the rules of logic. To know
that affirming the consequent is invalid is to recognize such affirmation
when it occurs and to recognize thereby that the truth or falsity of the
conclusion is still up in the air. The particular verbal form in which the
rule is put is of no consequence in playing the game or in refereeing it.

The analogy between the game of checkers and thinking breaks
down at least in one significant respect. A player in checkers is always
called for infraction of the rules; learning to play the game entails learning
the rules. But with thinking it is different. A player in this game, except
among professionals, can take all sorts of liberties without anyone calling
him for infraction of the rules and without the player himself even knowing that he is breaking them. In some cases, however, he will pick up
certain logical rules in an *ad hoc* sense. Suppose a beginning high school

"The Game of Thinking" by B. Othanel Smith is reprinted with permission from
"Logic, Thinking, and Teaching," *Educational Theory*, 4:225–233, October, 1957.

student is given the following argument: If it rains, the streets are wet. The streets are wet. Therefore it rained. He will tell you quickly that the conclusion does not necessarily follow because the streets may be wet for some other reason. Perhaps the street sprinkler has come along. But when the content is unfamiliar and the argument complex, the student will seldom recognize the fallacy. He may fail to recognize the fallacy as such, if his reasoning is still at the level of concrete relations. Hence he could not go beyond cases of particular content. Nor could he recognize the fallacy in any general sense. Hence if the material relations in an argument go beyond his concrete knowledge, the student who has only an *ad hoc* command of the rules cannot detect logical mistakes. . . .

To continue a little longer in the metaphor, in the game of thinking the teacher is player, coach, and often referee. As a player, he engages students in thinking by asking questions and responding to their answers, by receiving questions and giving answers, and by many other devices and activities. In each of these there is a sort of give and take between teacher and students. But, having little knowledge of logic and being preoccupied with getting the student to understand facts and ideas, the teacher usually overlooks the logic of both his subject and of the class discussion. For instance, a history teacher discusses with his students the imperialism of a nation. He goes into the question of the extent and cause of the imperialism. But the concept of imperialism is not itself explicated, so that the students have varied notions of what is being talked about. The whole discussion is based on a vague and ambiguous term and thus thinking and learning are short-changed.

Now the teacher moves from the role of player to that of coach when he turns to the task of helping students work out a definition of imperialism. To handle this task, the teacher needs criteria by which to decide the adequacy of the definition worked out by himself and the students. As the teacher and students together analyze the concept of imperialism and give it the form of a definition, the teacher will help students from time to time to see what it means to define a term and to understand the kinds of rules by which the adequacy of a definition may be decided. He will show them, as appropriate occasions arise, that a definition lays down criteria for the use of a word, and that the definition we decide to give a word, or the usage we select, is related to the purpose we have in mind. He will show them that sometimes we define words by assigning whatever is named by the word to a class and then distinguishing it from other members of the class. On other occasions the teacher will show how to define words by pointing to instances, and in still other cases by reference to the operations we perform.

To reflect upon the work of the teacher is to see that there are many occasions when he could readily teach procedures of analysis and logical appraisal.

28 The Classroom Game

Arno A. Bellack, Joel R. Davitz, in collaboration with
Herbert M. Kliebard and Ronald T. Hyman

One way of conceptualizing these results[1] is in terms of the language game of teaching and learning. Despite the fact that the rules of this game are not explicitly stated for any of the players, our sample of teachers and pupils obviously followed a set of implicit rules with few deviations. These rules refine the teaching game. Although classes differ somewhat in details, for the purposes of an initial description of the classroom game, the results strongly support the assumption that common elements underlie much of the teaching game in that pupils and teachers follow a consistent pattern of language rules. It is as if the grammar of English had never been explicitly written, yet everyone generally spoke in essentially the same grammatical forms. It may be useful, therefore, to summarize these rules explicitly, *not as a prescriptive guide to future teacher behavior,* but rather, as a descriptive model of what actually occurs in classrooms like those in the present study.

Reprinted with permission from *The Language of the Classroom: Meanings Communicated in High School Teaching.* Arno A. Bellack and Joel R. Davitz in collaboration with Herbert M. Kliebard and Ronald T. Hyman. U.S. Department of Health, Education, and Welfare, Office of Education, Cooperative Research Project No. 1497. New York, Institute of Psychological Research, Teachers College, Columbia University, 1963.

[1]Results of the research reported in Section 3 on p. 177. R.T.H., editor.

The classroom game involves one person called a teacher and one or more persons called pupils. The object of the game is to carry on a linguistic discourse about subject matter, and the final payoff of the game is measured in terms of the amount of learning displayed by the pupils after a given period of play. In playing the game, each player must follow a specific set of rules. If one plays the role of teacher in this game, he will follow one set of rules; if one plays the role of pupil, he will follow a somewhat different, though complementary, set of rules. One is permitted some deviations from these rules and the subsequent pattern will characterize one's individual style of play. These deviations, however, are infrequent and are relatively minor in comparison to the general system of expectations. In fact, the first rule, which might be called "the rule of rules," is that if one is to play the game at all, he will consistently follow the rules specified for his role. Otherwise, the game cannot be played.

Within the general set of rules defining the game, there are individual differences among teachers and classes in style of play. In one classroom, the teacher may specialize in one kind of move or sequence of moves, while in another class the teacher may specialize in a slightly different pattern of discourse. Notwithstanding these variations in style and differences in specialization of moves, the game is always played by a consistent set of general rules. These are rarely made explicit during the course of play; more often, they are defined implicitly by the sequence of moves that actually occurs. Regardless of whether they are explicit or implicit, both teachers and pupils are responsible for playing by the rules of the game.

These rules will be presented in the following order: (1) rules for the role of teacher; (2) rules for the role of pupil; and finally, (3) general rules for all players.

Rules for the Teacher

If one plays the role of teacher in this game, he will obey the following rules:

1. The teacher will be the most active single person playing the game. This means that he will make the most moves; he will speak most frequently and his speeches will usually be the longest. He is permitted some flexibility in the exact amount by which his activity exceeds the total activity of all other players, but in general, the ratio of his speech to the speech of all other players will be 3 to 1 in terms of amount spoken, and 3 to 2 in terms of the number of moves made. Moreover, these ratios will remain constant over several class sessions, unless he directs another player to assume his role temporarily.

2. The teacher is responsible for structuring the form and content of the game. He will specify the subject matter of the game, and the rules for the game. Within any particular setting, as in various baseball parks, there will be specific ground rules. The teacher is responsible for setting these ground rules and for making them explicit to the other players. In addition to setting up the initial structure of the game, the teacher is responsible for launching new topics of discussion and for determining any changes that might occur in the form of play as the game proceeds.

3. The most frequent move of the teacher is called "soliciting." This is a directive move designed to elicit a specific response from the players called "pupils." Frequently, this move will be formulated in terms of a question, but may also be phrased in terms of a direct order, such as directing another player to speak, to open his book, or carry out any other action relevant to this game. If one plays the role of teacher, he is required to obey "the rule of proper questions"; that is, he must ask valid questions, stated in a logical form and concerned with substantive material so that some pupils in the game may be expected to answer. His intent must not be to trick the other players or pose impossible problems, but, rather, to formulate solicitations which will elicit from pupils legitimate responses that will move the game along.

4. After making a soliciting move, the teacher will normally expect a person playing the role of "pupil" to respond. It is then the teacher's responsibility to react to this response. Sometimes, he may react non-verbally, by nodding his head or perhaps by showing approval implicitly by moving to a new solicitation. In most instances, however, he is expected to react in an explicit fashion. Many of these reactions will be evaluative; that is, the teacher is expected either to approve or disapprove of the response made by the pupil player. In the majority of instances, his reaction will be at least somewhat positive. Frequently, he tells a pupil explicitly that he has made a "correct" or "good" response; in any case, he is expected at least to "admit" the pupil's statement, often by a short phrase such as "all right." When the teacher is forced, by the obviously incorrect nature of the pupil's response, to make a negative evaluation, usually he will not make this evaluation completely negative; that is, by reacting with such remarks as "No," or "You're wrong." Rather, he will offer some sort of qualifying evaluation, such as "Yes, but . . . ," or he will point out that the pupil's preceding response was not entirely correct or to the point.

5. In addition to reacting to immediately preceding statements, the teacher is also responsible for occasional summaries of larger parts of the discourse. This may simply be a repetition of several preceding responses or some form of integration of the earlier discourse. In this

respect, he is free to choose either the more repetitive or the more integrative style. When speaking the role of the teacher, one also has freedom to introduce, in summarizing reactive moves, additional logical and substantive meanings. Thus one may summarize by mere repetition, by more active integration, or by either repetition or integration plus additional meanings.

6. Although either the teacher or the pupil may express substantive and substantive-logical meanings, it is, primarily, the teacher who is responsible for expressing meanings relevant to instructional processes. A large proportion of these "instructional moves" will be reactions which are metacommunicative: reactive statements about another player's preceding statements. This sort of metacommunication is almost entirely within the teacher's domain of play; unless requested to do so, pupils will rarely make this kind of statement. Because metacommunicative statements are made rather infrequently in linguistic games outside the classroom, the teacher must take particular care in making them. For example, if one speaks the role of the teacher in the classroom, he will undoubtedly be required to play other games outside of the classroom with principals, supervisors, superintendents, etc. When playing this outside game, in contrast to his classroom role, it is likely that the teacher will not normally make reactive metacomments to the principal: telling him that he is wrong, his statement is false, or his response is off the point. But in playing the classroom game, this is one of his primary responsibilities, aimed at shaping the responses made by other players so as to bring them more into line with his expectations.

Other kinds of instructional statements made by the teacher will concern classroom procedures to be followed in playing the game and assignments to be prepared by students. From an instructional-logical point of view, these will consist largely of stating facts or making straightforward directive statements telling the pupils what to do. Rarely will the teacher ever express an opinion about instructional meanings or justify any opinions he might state about them.

Rules for the Pupil

If one speaks the role of the pupil, his responsibilities in playing the game are much more restricted than those of the person playing the role of teacher. The pupil must remember that his eventual performance on some measure of learning determines the final payoff of the game both for him and for the teacher; therefore, it is assumed that he will learn. Regardless of whether one learns, if he speaks the role of the pupil, he will obey the following rules:

1. The pupil's primary task in the game is to respond to the teacher's solicitations. This usually involves answering specific questions posed by the teacher, but may also involve following direct orders given by the teacher, such as "Open your book," or "Get up and shut the window." Whenever the teacher makes a soliciting move, the pupil will, if at all possible, attempt some form of response. The response may be right or wrong in terms of the teacher's expectations; it may be relevant or irrelevant to the ongoing game. In any case, the pupil is required to attempt some response to the teacher's solicitation. In extreme cases, the pupil may reply to a solicitation by saying, "I don't know" but this should be used rarely, if at all. The best policy for the pupil to follow in playing the game is "make a response whenever called upon."

2. The pupil does not structure the game; that is, he does not tell the teacher and other pupils what the game is to be about or how to play it. This is the task of the teacher. Occasionally, the pupil is called upon to give a report or to participate in a debate. This is a form of structuring, but pupils make such moves *only* when directed to do so by the teacher. Having fulfilled his assigned structuring obligation, the pupil will not structure again unless the teacher specifically directs him to do so.

3. In general, the pupil will keep his solicitations to a minimum. If he must solicit, he will restrict his questions to instructional matters. If absolutely necessary in order to continue playing the game, he may ask the teacher to clarify an assignment or explain some instructional procedure involved in the game. On the other hand, he does not solicit in regard to substantive matters, and certainly never makes a directive statement to the teacher such as "Speak" or "Get up and close the window." If the pupil makes such a solicitation, it is likely that he will be excluded from the field of play.

4. Even more important than the *don't* solicit rule is the *don't* react evaluatively rule. Under no condition is the pupil permitted to react evaluatively to a statement made by the teacher; that is, the pupil does not tell the teacher he is right or wrong, that he is doing well or doing badly. If the pupil has impulses in this direction, he must inhibit them, for they have no place in the classroom game. This applies both to positive and to negative evaluations of the teacher. Occasionally, the pupil may be asked to react evaluatively to another pupil's response. If asked to do so by the teacher, he may make this move; it should be brief and probably should not be too strong either in a positive or in a negative direction. Although not exactly achieving the status of a rule, the pupil should keep whatever evaluations he is asked to make as bland as possible.

5. A corollary of the "don't react evaluatively" rule is the general principle, "within the classroom, teachers speak The Truth." This principle holds by virtue of the teacher's role in the game and the rules

guiding pupils' play. Except under extraordinary circumstances, pupils overtly accept the teacher's statements as the spoken truth.

On the other hand, pupils may or may not speak "The Truth." If one speaks the role of pupil, he must remember that merely uttering a statement does not guarantee that it will be accepted as true. In fact, an important part of the teacher's responsibility is to challenge, though mildly, pupils' statements which he believes to be invalid. In certain classes, pupils may even be challenged occasionally by other pupils.

6. In some classes, pupils are expected to make reactions that carry no explicit evaluative meaning. This will depend upon the ground rules established by the teacher. The only guide one can follow is the expectation of the teacher: does he or does he not expect the pupil to react to other pupils' statements?

7. Finally, a pupil player should remember that his primary task is to respond to the teacher's solicitations and to perform well on the final payoff test. If he fulfills both of these obligations and does not usurp the role of the teacher, then he will most likely play the game successfully.

Some General Rules for All Players

In addition to the rules related to a specific role, there are some general rules that apply to all players. Regardless of the particular role one plays, he will obey the following rules:

1. The major part of the game will be played with the substantive meanings specified by the teacher's structuring of the game. From time to time, however, either player is permitted to wander from this central focus, sometimes to topics relevant to the substantive core of the game and occasionally to a topic which is thoroughly irrelevant to the principal subject matter. The teacher will usually initiate these off-target discussions, sometimes as a means of introducing or clarifying a substantive point. Occasionally a pupil player is permitted to introduce an irrelevancy, but this must not be done often in a single class session. The exact frequency depends upon the reactions of the person playing the role of teacher. In general, however, the discussion will take place within the substantive framework of the teacher's structuring.

2. From a substantive-logical or instructional-logical point of view, if the game is played within the substantive area of economics, or in any related subject area, the discourse will consist largely of empirical meanings. This means that for the most part, the moves will be statements either of fact or explanations; approximately 50 to 60 per cent of the speech will involve empirical meaning. Analytic meaning involving either definitions of terms or interpretations will be expressed much less fre-

quently. The frequency of evaluative statements will also be relatively low in comparison to empirical statements. Thus, expressions of personal opinion about economic policies or attempts to justify opinions will appear relatively infrequently. Players will, however, be free to report opinions of others, such as public figures, or to report the arguments used by others to justify their opinions. This does not mean that players are completely prohibited from expressing their own opinions and justifications, but that the general policy under which the game is played encourages the use of statements with empirical meaning.

3. As indicated in the preamble to this set of rules, one is permitted some deviations from the specified set of rules. In almost all instances, the range of these deviations depends upon the ground rules set by the teacher, which may be either explicit or implicit. In any event, one is responsible for learning and obeying these ground rules; for example, a teacher may vary his style of play so that he spends most of the game structuring, while the pupil's main task is simply to attend to the structuring and to respond whenever called upon to do so. A teacher may, on the other hand, choose to play the game principally as a question and answer exercise; if he so chooses, he is also responsible for reacting to pupil answers. The teacher may even choose a style of play characterized by a proportion of reactions larger than that usually seen in this game. If a pupil is indeed playing the game with such a teacher, his responsibility to react may be almost as compelling as his responsibility to respond. Thus, within the general rules of the game, the style of play may be modified in one way or another. Once the ground rules for a particular game have been set, however, it is wise neither for the teacher nor for the player to assume the other player's role. If one plays the role of teacher, part of his responsibility will be to set the ground rules and to see that these rules are obeyed in playing the game. In this sense, the teacher is expected to serve not only as coach and one of the players, but also as referee of the game. On the other hand, if one plays the role of pupil, he must learn the ground rules of the game even if the rules are not explicitly stated by the teacher.

4. In gauging wins and losses, players must remember that this is not a game in which one player, such as the teacher, wins while another player, such as one of the pupils, loses. Rather, there are relative degrees of winning and losing, and the teacher's winnings are a function of the pupils' performances. This is a peculiar, but important, characteristic of this game. While the teacher undeniably has the greater power and freedom in the course of play, he is ultimately dependent on his pupils for the degree of success he achieves in playing the game.

This feature of the game is a consequence of the criterion of success. The eventual aim of the game, the ostensible reason for the play, is the pupil's learning of substantive and substantive-logical meanings. Learning is usually measured by test performance; therefore, the teacher's success depends upon the pupil's test performance. If a pupil fails the test, implying that he has not learned, then the teacher, by implication, has not taught successfully. Thus, insofar as that pupil is concerned, the teacher has lost the game. A single teacher, of course, typically plays the game with many students, so that his wins and losses are scored over the total group of pupils, much as the team point system is used to score track meets. In calculating the results, several test failures may be offset by a number of brilliant test scores, although the precise formula depends upon the educational setting in which the game occurs. For some schools, success requires at least minimal performance by all pupils; in such schools, the teacher's overall score is considerably reduced for even one or two test failures, with proportionately less credit for high test scores. For other schools, a few exceedingly high scores overbalance a substantial number of low test results. In this latter setting, a few special pupil prizes, awarded by outside sources such as "Regents Scholarships" and "Merit Scholarships," may very well counterbalance many failures.

The general formula for computing a teacher's final score cannot be written because the weights assigned to various kinds of test scores depend upon other games played by other people. These outside players are called principals, superintendents, and school board members, and it would be wise for a person, when he begins to play the teaching role in a given setting, to determine the formula for success used by these outside players.

It is of historical interest to note that the general definition of success has changed over the years. Earlier forms of the teaching game were like other competitive games in which one person wins and another loses; the teacher was pitted against the pupil much like a baseball pitcher is pitted against the batter. But just as whist gradually evolved into bridge, the competitive type of the teaching game has changed to a more mutually dependent form of play.

In summary, it should be remembered that these are the rules of the game *as it is played, not necessarily as it should be played.* At this point, the concern is only with a description of the classroom game, and this description is summarized in the rules of the game. Depending upon one's opinion about what should occur in a classroom, the rules specified may or may not serve as prescriptions of teacher and pupil behavior. Regardless of any set of prescriptive guides that one might view as desirable, the rules thus far specified are based on a detailed analysis of what actually happened in the classrooms sampled.

7 *Aesthetics*

Overview

Of the vantage points considered in this book, the one of aesthetics is the most neglected. This neglect is evidenced by the paucity of material discussing teaching with the aid of such concepts as beauty, harmony, balance, rhythm, tempo, and form. Also, very few empirical studies have been conducted to describe what it is that constitutes artistry in teaching, or the art of teaching, or teaching as an art. Furthermore, programs for preparing teachers seldom devote attention to this perspective. The notion that teaching can fruitfully be viewed from an aesthetic vantage point comes as a pleasant surprise to many people already familar with other perspectives.

The reasons for this neglect are not at all clear. There have been articles and books dealing with the role of art and music in the schools, and of the role in the schools of aesthetics in general. There have also been articles and books claiming that teaching is an art, meaning by that phrase that there are currently no "scientific" laws one can apply in his search for what and how to teach. But in spite of this literature there has been precious little analysis of the act of teaching from the aesthetic point of view.

Precisely because of this lack, the three selections in this section are of particular interest. The authors here turn to aesthetics because our reliance on empirical findings simply has not paid off in results about ability of scientific studies to improve teaching and therefore call for

355

effective teaching. Seaberg and Zinsmaster explicitly mention the in-ability of scientific studies to improve teaching and therefore call for greater emphasis on intuition, the artist's sixth sense. Eisner makes this same point when he cites the inability of empirical investigations to identify the components of effective teaching. His search for an explanation leads him to the artistic concept of qualitative intelligence as an important component in teaching.

Seaberg and Zinsmaster forthrightly begin with the statement that teaching and directing have elements in common. Hence, they proceed to interview directors of choreography, plays, choral works, and orchestral works in an effort to identify key aspects of artistic behavior to be applied to teaching. Eisner justifies the aesthetic point of view by noting its contribution to learning. To the extent that teaching lacks the qualitative aspect, learning is impeded or hindered.

It is interesting to compare Eisner's unusual choice of nightclub comedian with Seaberg and Zinsmaster's choice of directors. In spite of the obvious differences in their work, the concepts of timing, pacing, atmosphere, and simultaneous harmony flow from the comedian and the directors and apply to the teacher. Likewise, the concepts of "on-the-spot shifts," "playing it by ear," intuition, and sensitivity to the ongoing situation further explicate the parallels between teaching and aesthetic activity. Also, the reader should note how Eisner draws upon such philosophers as Dewey and Aristotle, while Hallman mainly draws on Third Force (humanistic, existential) psychologists, such as May, Rogers, and Maslow.

Another reason why teaching is so seldom analyzed from the aesthetic point of view is that definitions of art differ widely. Philosophers have long differed on this topic, and one impact of the controversy may have been to discourage educators from entering the discussion. The few educators who have entered the discussion have not always agreed among themselves on what art is and what constitutes teaching as an art. Thus, the reader needs to scrutinize the overt and covert definitions used by the authors here.

Hallman's synthesizing article serves to focus our attention on the general topic of creativity. His four principles of creative teaching serve as a bridge between this section and the one on classroom psychological climate. He cites and draws upon Rogers, who is included in this book in Section 5, Schachtel, and others for his principles of creative teaching. These same researchers also serve as a foundation for other articles, especially the one by Macdonald and Zaret (Section 5). Hallman raises a significant point by connecting the self-actualizing person with an aesthetic need, an aesthetic drive. The interplay between aesthetics, creativity, and psychology is pertinent for the analysis of teaching. What role does the aesthetic drive, if there is one, play in teaching? How can we identify its manifestations during teaching?

Hallman further relates creativity to the cognitive processes vantage point (Maccia) by emphasizing the role of hypothetical thinking; to classroom social climate (Flanders) by discussing the role of freedom in creativity; and to communications (Packer and Packer) when dealing with the role of uncertainty. No doubt the reader will find other connections between this multifaceted article and others in this book.

But in at least two ways Hallman differs from, rather than complements, other authors. His use of the word *manipulation* is not at all the same as Gerbner's in the section on Communications. Nor is his definition of authoritarian behavior the same as Flanders' in the section on Social Climate. The reader is alerted to these differences as he himself interrelates the various perspectives and selections.

The implications for further research are many, as stated by Hallman. If this aesthetic perspective is to be fruitful, then much work lies ahead for educators. Is it possible to develop sensitive observational instruments based on such concepts as qualitative intelligence, timing, pacing, harmony, intuition, artistic vision, and aesthetic order.

If so, would data from high schools, elementary schools, colleges, and nursery schools differ? Would we get significantly different results in economics, art, music, biology, mathematics, and English classes? What is it that artistic teachers do and say that makes them artistic? What relation, if any, is there between achievement and the aesthetic atmosphere of the classroom as set by the teacher? How do we prepare teachers to teach artistically? These are but a few of the myriad of questions that need answering in this area, which more than any other lacks research.

29 Qualitative Intelligence and the Act of Teaching

Elliot W. Eisner

In this paper I would like to discuss a special variety of intelligence that is exercised in most teaching acts and to indicate how this type of intelligence contributes to the successful execution of those acts.

The need to develop fresh conceptions with which to analyze teaching becomes apparent to anyone who reviews the research on teacher effectiveness. While new developments in instructional practice are not scarce —note the advent of team teaching, programmed instruction, closed circuit and airborne television—research findings provide little evidence that the new teaching practices are leading to more efficient learning. Somehow research studies designed to assess the differential effects of various types of instructional procedures usually terminate as members of the not-so-exclusive club of "no significant differences."

New developments in theory are also plentiful. B. F. Skinner has operationalized his conceptions of learning through the teaching machine; Jerome Bruner has formulated a set of technologies through which

"Qualitative Intelligence and the Act of Teaching," by Elliot W. Eisner, is reprinted from *The Elementary School Journal*, 63: 299–307, March, 1963, by permission of The University of Chicago Press. Copyright © 1963 by The University of Chicago Press.

thinking occurs; and J. P. Guilford has developed a theoretical structure of the intellect which identifies some of the components that constitute human thought.

Although the theoretical positions of Skinner and Bruner differ in many ways, they both share the view that the process through which something is taught significantly affects the efficiency and the usefulness of the learning. In Skinner's view, efficiency is achieved if the learner can proceed through a program that consists of very small units of information so constructed that the student moves through them with minimum error. The student obtains immediate feedback to each response he makes and since ideally his responses to these programmed units are correct, he obtains positive reinforcement.

Bruner's approach to the problem of teaching and learning is quite different from Skinner's. Bruner has developed a conception of three technologies through which children and adults learn. These technologies are called the enactive, the ikonic, and the symbolic. Each provides the individual with a means of storing and retrieving data.

In a lecture on "The Nature of Intellectual Growth" given at the University of Chicago in November, 1962, Bruner said, "By enactive representation I mean a mode of representing past events through appropriate motor response. . . . Ikonic representation summarizes events by precepts and images, by the spatial, temporal, and qualitative structures of the perceptual field and their transformed images." The symbolic, which is employed when the individual acquires discursive language, is held to be the most economic and most flexible storage and retrieval system. It enables the individual to cope successfully with problems that might not be handled so well by the enactive and ikonic technologies.

Bruner believes that if teachers can identify the generic coding systems or structures that constitute the disciplines and if they can identify the dimensions of the conceptual unit that children can handle successfully, it will be possible to teach almost anything to almost anyone.

Although Skinner and Bruner differ with respect to the most efficient process through which learning takes place, they both hold that with the appropriate method, children would be capable of learning much that we now consider beyond their capacities.

J. P. Guilford has taken still another tack in his research, one that could lead to conclusions almost polar to those of Skinner and Bruner. Guilford has used factor analytic methods to formulate a structure of the intellect.

The building blocks of the structure are relatively specific abilities that fall into several major dimensions, among them the conceptual, the figural, and the structural. In each dimension, divergent or convergent thought processes may be used. By using the battery of tests that Guilford has constructed to measure these conceptualized unitary abilities, it is possible to obtain a psychometric profile of the trait abilities of different individuals. From such a profile one could conclude that the problem in formulating an educational program for a student is primarily a task of determining the kind of trait abilities he possesses and then designing an educational program appropriate for those abilities.

From such a conception one could also conclude that the likelihood of being able to teach almost anything to almost anyone is small and that it would be much more realistic to differentiate the educational diet for students having different patterns of trait abilities. Differences in education would not be merely a matter of using different methods, but one of differentiating the content of instruction.

Yet even with these new developments in educational practice and research, the problem of identifying the components of effective teaching still persists. This problem is so great and so central to education that competent observers like Guba and Getzels, reporting in the *Journal of Educational Psychology* (October, 1955) have concluded, "Despite a large number of investigations, relatively little more is known than was known [about teacher effectiveness] in 1900."

Perhaps recognition of ignorance is a form of knowledge, but with the vast sums spent on research (Herbert S. Conrad, director of Research and Statistical Service, U.S. Office of Education, reports that the U.S. Office of Education alone spends in excess of ten million dollars annually in support of educational research) and literally hundreds of research studies published each year, one may wonder why knowledge in this area is so scant. Why is it that after eighty years of psychological study in education the number of hard facts that can be passed on to teachers regarding the way teaching may be most effectively pursued is exceedingly small?

Plenty of hypotheses are available. One may claim that educational inquiry is much more complex than other types of inquiry and hence it will take more time to develop more effective methods of teaching. One may claim that the level of research competence of those working in educational research is too low. One might also postulate that educational research is dependent on research in other disciplines and cannot proceed any faster than research in those fields. Finally one may claim that educational research has far too long been concerned with descriptive studies and too little effort has been spent understanding how educational change may be most effectively engendered.

I am sure you can add more explanations to the list. Explanations are plentiful, and there is probably some truth in all of them. But perhaps educational research has found it difficult to produce significant findings on the conditions that make for effective teaching because it has neglected at least one very important component inherent in every teaching act—the teacher's use and control of the qualitative, an activity made possible through the use of what may be called *qualitative intelligence.*

I would like to develop this notion by looking at some of the assumptions that are employed in the education of prospective teachers. One of these assumptions is related to a kind of Platonism which holds that the most useful tool for good teaching is good theory. We implement this assumption by asking the teacher in training to take courses in educational psychology, in philosophy of education, in curriculum, and in methods of teaching various subject matters.

Student teaching is generally held off until the latter part of the student's program. This practice reflects the belief that if the student is to understand what he is to observe in the classroom, he needs some theoretical and conceptual tools. High-level comprehension of theory in learning, child development, and curriculum is supposed to provide the student, when he has completed student teaching, with the most useful tools for teaching. Indeed, these courses are considered so important that in most states an individual cannot be certified to teach unless he has taken and passed a specified number of them. Yet if one asks teachers how useful the theories provided in these courses are in teaching, one should not be surprised to find a lack of enthusiasm.

Now it may be that teachers underestimate the practical value of theory. But perhaps they do not. Perhaps much of what is most useful in teaching does not rest on theoretical considerations at all. Perhaps one reason why we have found it so difficult to identify the conditions that make for effective teaching is that we have neglected to consider the qualitative aspects of teaching and the qualitative intelligence of teachers.

Now it may be that teachers underestimate the practical value of theory. But perhaps they do not. Perhaps much of what is most useful in teaching does not rest on theoretical considerations at all. Perhaps one reason why we have found it so difficult to identify the conditions that make for effective teaching is that we have neglected to consider the qualitative aspects of teaching and the qualitative intelligence of teachers.

What is qualitative intelligence and what contribution does it make to the successful execution of the teaching act? Qualitative intelligence can be considered, in part, as the ability to formulate qualitative ends and to employ qualitative means in the efficient acquisition of those ends. In the relationship between such means and ends, qualitative thought is employed. After this rather abstract statement, I would like to describe some situations where qualitative intelligence is exercised.

Perhaps the most obvious examples are found in the activities of the musician and the visual artist, those most concerned with the qualitative. One of the primary tasks of the visual artist is the conception, control, and organization of qualities. A quality may be conceived of as the experience of anything sensible, provided that symbolic meaning of the sensible is disregarded. Such sensibles may be a product of the imagination as, for example, the experience you have when I suggest that you envision a brilliant arrangement of yellow and orange. Your experience in visualizing these colors is essentially qualitative.

Qualitative experience is also produced by the perception of physically real sensibles. Such sensibles may be experienced as either dominantly qualitative or symbolic. For example, the color red may be experienced qualitatively when it is experienced exclusively as color; symbolically, when it is conceived of as standing for *stop*.

Qualitative experience, therefore, is the sense of life one undergoes when conceiving or perceiving sensibles devoid of symbolic meaning. Qualitative intelligence is displayed in the degree to which qualitative ends are conceived and efficiently attained. The visual artist often conceives of a qualitative end, a particular mood or rhythm he wants to create, and controls qualities (color, line, shape, form, composition) so that this end is achieved. Qualitative concerns are expressed and qualitative intelligence is exercised in all walks of life by practically everyone.

You may be wondering what this has to do with teaching and with research that attempts to understand the conditions that contribute to effectiveness in teaching. The relationship between qualitative intelligence and teaching may become clearer if we examine one other domain in which qualitative intelligence is exercised, namely, acting.

Specifically, let us look at the night-club comedian, particularly the one who is able to change the form and content of his act as it unfolds. I have chosen a night-club comedian as an example because there are certain important parallels between his actions and those of a teacher and because the good ones display a very high degree of qualitative intelligence.

Here we see an individual whose task is to achieve a certain qualitative response in his audience. He conceives of qualitative ends—certain kinds of qualities we call laughter, joy, happiness—and engages in activities designed to elicit qualities that constitute those ends. In these activities he must pay attention not only to the symbolic meaning of his language but also to the rhythm, tempo, pace, and timing of his speech and actions.

He must listen with a qualitative ear to the qualities the audience generates, for a line late but a second is dead. He is able to perceive the qualitative flow of events and is able to control his actions—pace, tempo, timing, emphasis—accordingly, always relating his actions to the data (in this case, qualities) provided by the audience and the ends he wants to achieve. He literally knows how to play it by ear, to carry on a qualitative dialectic between the audience and himself.

There are several parallels between such actions and the actions of teaching. For one, the teacher, like the actor, is concerned with the control and guidance of a group of people. Whatever a teacher may wish to achieve in the classroom, the necessity of organizing and guiding human interests and actions is always present.

Further, teachers, like actors, attempt to communicate to groups of people in an audience-like situation, and while the ends of comedy and instruction differ markedly, both the actor and the teacher employ qualities to enhance communication; both must come through to the people with whom they work.

In addition, both the actor and the teacher must be able to control their actions in such a way as to capture the attention and interest of those to whom their message is directed. Knowing something and wanting to communicate it are hardly sufficient for achieving communication. The qualitative tone of a discussion or lecture is, as everyone knows, extremely important in determining not only the content of the message but the way it is considered after it is received.

Finally, much that the teacher tries to attain in the classroom is dominantly qualitative rather than dominantly symbolic or theoretical. This is especially true in subjects like poetry, history, art, music, and literature. In these subjects especially, the desired end of teaching is not limited to giving students a mere knowledge of a poem, a period, a painting, a symphony, or a plot, but also includes helping the students experience the qualities built into the work.

For example, a student whose experience of a symphony is limited to knowledge about its formal structure would miss experiencing whatever aesthetic quality it possessed. In history, a student who could not experience the qualitative *Zeitgeist* of the great events, people, and periods of the past, would have a limited historical experience indeed. Some subjects seem to be more concerned with symbolic or theoretical ends than others. While many might consider mathematics to be one such subject, it is well to remember that many of the greatest mathematicians considered the study of mathematics an aesthetic activity and looked upon the discovery or creation of new mathematical relations as comparable in aesthetic quality to any experience that can be derived from the arts. This suggests that purely conceptual or symbolic inquiries can have qualitative character. This aspect of qualitative experience, however, will not be discussed here.

What I am suggesting is that the acts of teaching and acting have important and significant parallels and that teaching, while concerned with some ends that are not relevant to acting, is concerned with many other ends that are. Intelligent control of qualitative elements necessary in acting is also necessary in teaching insofar as teaching is partly a task of acting and achieving communication between teacher and individual and group. The qualitative controls that teachers employ can enhance teaching and can be instrumental to theoretical ends embodied in certain subjects and can also be used to achieve qualitative ends incorporated in other subjects. Teachers who are able to control qualities intelligently are probably better able to produce the kind of classroom atmosphere that will facilitate the type of learning that they value.

Visits to a few classrooms will provide ample evidence of the fact that diverse qualities pervade different classrooms. In some classrooms the atmosphere possesses qualities that may be described as energetic, active, and enthusiastic; others might be described as languid, placid, and quiet; still others as monotonous, anxious, and rigid. Such atmospheres are a function of the classroom's qualitative components. Such components are the individual qualities generated by the students as they respond to and act upon the symbolic meanings and qualitative characteristics produced by others. Collectively, they produce what we commonly call *classroom atmosphere.*

I am not suggesting that classrooms can or ought to be kept at one qualitative level at all times. I am suggesting that the teacher, to the extent that he has qualitative control, can be effective in creating the type of classroom environment that is appropriate for different types of learning.

Primary-grade teachers are perhaps most likely to exercise such concerns and controls. These concerns and controls tend to diminish as one moves upward through the grades, so that by the time the student reaches college, the amount of variability in teaching strategies and in qualitative techniques is quite small compared with those in the primary grades.

Qualitative intelligence also makes possible the perception of the qualitative. I should point out that it is my view that intelligence is exercised in increasing degrees as man discriminates between more and more complex and subtle qualities. Discrimination between black and white, for example, is a simple task. Perception of discrimination of the subtle qualities in a Gauguin or in the counterpoint of Stravinsky is quite another matter. Sensitivity or appreciation of such qualities is a product of qualitative intelligence. Thus, I follow Dewey's lead that appreciation is a creative or intelligent act. The control of qualities can be achieved only when the actor is able to perceive the qualities that emerge from his ongoing activities. To be able to play it by ear means that one's decision-making is going to be made on the spot and that one will use, as those decisions, the qualitative and theoretical responses of the class or the audience.

We have long considered the preplanning of curriculum and the construction of lesson plans essential activities for effective construction. Yet relatively little attention has been paid to the type of immediate decision-making that all teachers engage in in the act of teaching.

We have also considered theoretical thought the most important and perhaps the only useful tool for making teaching decisions. I believe most of us who would teach would admit, if pressed, that the majority of our teaching decisions in the classroom are not made on the basis of theoretical considerations at all. Part of this is probably due to the limitations of theory in the behavioral sciences at the immediate decision-making level in the classroom. Human interactions are too rich to be adequately described by behavioral-science theory at its present state of development. As theory grows and as it becomes more complete, we may reach a point at which it may be more useful, but the likelihood of ever obtaining a network of theory adequate for directing all or most human action in the classroom seems to me to be small.

Aristotle was quite aware of the limitations of theory in practical realms. In his *Metaphysics* he distinguishes between three types of knowledge: the theoretical, which has as its end knowledge "of what is of necessity"; the practical-practical, knowledge whose end is action; and the practical-productive, knowledge whose end is making. Aristotle held that by their very nature the actions of men could not be understood with the certainty that was possible in the three theoretical sciences: theology, mathematics, and physics. And in the *Nicomachean Ethics* he says:

Our discussion will be adequate if it has as much clearness as the subject matter admits of, for precision is not to be sought for in all discussions any more than in all the products of the crafts . . . for it is the mark of an educated man to look for precision in each class of things just so far as the nature of the subject admits; it is evidently equally foolish to accept probable reasoning from a mathematician and to demand from a rhetorician scientific proof.

Here Aristotle tells us that the practical sciences cannot be known as well as the theoretical and also that the way in which they come to be known differs. Practical knowledge is acquired through experience in action; theoretical knowledge, through study. If we translate this view into expectations for theory and practice in preparing teachers, certain implications follow.

First, Aristotle's distinctions among the sciences suggest that theoretical knowledge is unlikely to be sufficient for guiding the teaching act, since by its nature teaching is a practical rather than a theoretical science. The great number of unique transactions occurring among individuals in the classroom is likely to make theoretical knowledge useful in only a suggestive way. Its application always needs to be tempered with art.

Second Aristotle's distinction between the practical and the theoretical implies that some things can be learned only through practical experience. The value that teachers generally place on practice teaching may be evidence of the fact that what they learn as classroom teachers, even in the role of the student teacher, could not be and was not learned in the university seminar. Some things, it seems, one may learn only through action.

Third, Aristotle's distinction between the practical and the theoretical suggests that if theoretical knowledge is to be of any use it needs to be learned in conjunction with or after practical experience in the classroom. Theoretical concepts are likely to have little meaning if the teacher in training is unable to link them to the practical matters of teaching. Current practices in teacher education proceed in just the opposite fashion: first the student learns theory, and only afterward does he try his hand at teaching.

Fourth, it suggests that if useful theory for teaching is developed, it will have to take into account what is appropriate for the particular teacher as well as for the class, since knowing depends as much on the nature of the knower as it does on that to be known. There is an idiosyncratic dimension to teaching that is unlikely to be defined by any single principle.

There are, I believe, certain relationships between Aristotle's conceptions of knowing and the type of knowing that Dewey discusses in *Art as Experience*. Each of these conceptions speaks to the question I raised in the earlier part of this paper, namely, why has research found it so difficult to identify the conditions that make for effective teaching. Dewey suggests in *Art as Experience* that the kind of knowledge and intelligence employed in the production of art is different in character from the kind of knowledge and intelligence employed in scientific inquiries. The artist, for Dewey, "knows" the rightness of a particular color or shape on canvas by its "feel"; the comedian knows he is pacing his dialogue correctly by the laughter of the audience; the teacher knows he is getting through to students by the qualities displayed in their behavior, qualities that often speak much louder than words. Dewey was aware of this way of knowing, and teachers with experience are aware of it as well. Perhaps if researchers were able to measure the extent to which individuals are aware of and able to control qualities and if institutions engaged in teacher-training could develop ways of fostering such intelligence, some of the conditions that contribute to effective teaching could be better understood and better developed.

It has been suggested that the type of intelligence that I am describing cannot be developed: we cannot teach students to be sensitive and, to use a term often used, intuitive to the qualitative happenings in a class.

It is often held that either you have this talent or you do not; either you are sensitive and responsive to such qualities or you are not. It seems to me that this point of view is based on a highly questionable conception of talent.

Such a view conceives of talent as a dichotomously distributed ability, a matter of all or nothing. But even sex, the geneticists tell us, is not a matter of all-or-nothing. One has merely to look at the kinds of qualitative intelligence that art, music, and acting schools develop to become convinced that almost anyone can increase his ability to cope intelligently with qualities. Not everyone can become a Rouault or a Barrymore, but almost everyone can become better able to conceive of and control qualities.

If intelligent control of the qualitative components of teaching is important in teaching, and I believe it is, then it might be well to try to help students who are preparing to teach to acquire such control and to consider it when we attempt to understand effective teaching. Perhaps recognition of this dimension of teaching is inherent when we say, as we have so often said, that teaching is both a science and an art. We imply that the scientific aspect of teaching relates to practice based on theoretical principles, the artistic, on those aspects of teaching governed by qualitative considerations. Perhaps it would not be too bizarre to propose that a good teacher of acting be on the staff of schools of education.

In developing the notion of the role of qualitative intelligence in teaching, I have risked overstating my case. I do not for a moment disregard the importance of subject-matter competence, personality disposition, or knowledge of useful theory in the behavioral sciences.

There is no single variable that is likely to define the effective teacher. There are probably many types of effectiveness in teaching, and perhaps the question that should ultimately be raised is "What teacher of what subject matter is effective with what students?" It seems likely that there is a high degree of specificity to effective teaching. Yet even with such specificity, one of the major components of teaching is acting, whether the teaching takes place in a lecture, in a large discussion group, or in a small seminar. The qualitative dimension of acting is always present and always important. To the extent that this aspect of teaching is disregarded or carried out unintelligently, to that extent is learning impeded. If greater understanding of the components of effective teaching is to be acquired and if skill in teaching is to be furthered, it would seem wise for teachers and researchers to take into account the qualitative components inherent in the teaching act.

30 Principles of Creative Teaching

Ralph J. Hallman

I. The Problem

It has been established that creative potentials exist commonly in all normal children [1] and also that there are theoretical grounds for believing that creativity can be taught.[2] But the teaching methods which can best elicit creative responses from pupils have not yet been clearly identified. This delay probably stems from the ambiguities which characterize both creative and teaching processes.

For example, the creative act cannot be deliberately planned. Creative teaching cannot be prescribed nor written into lesson plans. Consisting as it does of immediate encounters with specific problems and persons, it remains individualized. It can neither be fully explained nor accurately communicated in formal concepts. Rather, the teacher must himself invent creative techniques in the course of his day-by-day activities, and these techniques will appear as having been unforeseeable. Being un-

"Principles of Creative Teaching" by Ralph J. Hallman is reprinted with permission from *Educational Theory*, 15:306–316, October, 1965.

[1]Ralph J. Hallman, "The Commonness of Creativity," *Educational Theory*, XIII, 2 (April, 1963), 132–136.
[2]Ralph J. Hallman, "Can Creativity Be Taught?" *Educational Theory*, XIV, 1 (Jan., 1964), 15–23.

predictable, they confer freedom, for they encourage the teacher to react spontaneously to his concrete situation, to the cues which come directly from students, from the subject matter, and from the uniqueness of the problem at hand. They consist in the connecting of meanings which unforeseeably arise.

This paper makes the claim that certain principles can be identified which will assist the teacher in discovering these creative procedures.

II. The Principle of Suggestion

The principle of suggestion identifies the teaching *methods* which can most effectively promote creative tendencies in pupils. It defends indirect rather than direct methods of instruction as being appropriate to creativity.

This principle derives from three central features of the creative process; it is autonomous, spontaneous, and metaphoric. Its autonomy places the creative act outside the control of the deliberative faculties. Its spontaneity means that creativeness cannot be forced. It cannot be taught authoritatively. It can only be encouraged. Teaching becomes the art of suggesting, the art of supplying cues, indicating possibilities, associating apparent irrelevancies. It is itself a creative act. This is the third meaning: suggestion is metaphoric in nature. It stimulates associative tendencies, sets into motion connotative operations, and encourages combinatorial activity.

This process therefore calls for teaching techniques which are suggestive, flexible, experimental, imaginative, and manipulative. It is thwarted by methods which are authoritative and geared to the communication of predetermined truths. Suggestion emphasizes the importance of the unsaid, the seemingly unrelated, the apparently irrelevant. It produces quantities of ideas, concepts, imagery. It permits these to remain in a state of flux. It creates gaps in evidence, registers them, extends them, transplants them. It encourages the students' own metaphoric activity to fill in the gaps.

This principle can be clarified by reference to the methodology of John Dewey, who describes the process of learning as the clarification of uncertainties in our experience. Uncertainty brings out intelligence, and the intellect in turn functions to dispel uncertainty. It does so by identifying means and by charting directions toward which the given data point. These pointings are suggestions. For Dewey, they are tentative plans of action, or hypotheses. But they appear first as suggestions, for they reach beyond the immediately given. The process of entertaining suggestions is thinking, and thinking proceeds as a search for connections among consequences and antecedents. Consequently, every thought is creative. Every thinking act is an "incursion into the novel."

Creative teaching methods are also experimental. Again, Dewey's argument that the scientific method is the only means for bringing intelligence to bear upon human difficulties supports this position. Thinking, he says, begins in experience, and it ought to end in experience. It is the means for increasing efficiency in our living, and hence can never be separated from decision-making and from action. Experimentation deals with concrete troublesome situations; suggestions become instruments for clearing up the trouble.

Flexibility is the third characteristic of creative teaching. This quality belongs to the personal aspects of methodology. Individuals vary with respect to natural endowments, interests, and social histories. Managing these idiosyncratic factors such that they contribute to the creative process demands a maximum of flexibility. This means that classroom techniques will include not only the relatively stable procedures connected with all inquiry but also the improvisations necessary for handling unique events. Creative teaching methods will be directed by intelligence, but they will be continuously modified by the imaginative insights growing out of ongoing states of affairs.

Imaginativeness is the fourth characteristic of the suggestive method. As the only device for avoiding mechanical responses, an alert imagination becomes the heart of the creative act and the key to creative teaching. The very manner in which the imagination functions causes it to be creative. Though directed toward concrete, on-going experiences, it also reaches far back into experiences of the individual, and even of the race, and brings forward materials which combine with the immediately present data in exciting new ways. It adds meaning to experience.

Finally, the principle of suggestion calls for teaching methods which encourage the skillful manipulation of objective materials as well as of ideas. This emphasis on manipulative skill implies that creating is never complete unless some aspect of the environment has been changed. In the creative process, and in creative teaching and learning, acting and thinking are inseparably linked. The act of handling materials facilitates a sensing of the meaning of what is occurring in a given educational encounter.

The research literature which supports a methodology of suggestion comes invariably from those educators who are deeply concerned with problems of creativity. For example, Harold Rugg's last book, *Imagination*,[3] explores the connections between suggestion and hypnosis, between suggestion and the techniques of the Zen masters and the principles of Yoga and of Taoism. These studies convince Mr. Rugg that the techniques of suggestions as employed by mystics, poets, and intuitive philosophers in the West will eventually influence educational practices in the direction of creativity.[4]

[3]Harold Rugg, *Imagination* (New York: Harper & Row, 1963), Chapters 8–12.
[4]*Ibid.*, p. 210.

III. The Principle of Encounter

The principle of encounter identifies the kind of *curriculum* which facilitates creative teaching and creative learning.

Specifically, it asserts that the experimental situation, here defined as encounter, constitutes the basic unit in the educational process. It further describes this unit as a complex but integral whole involving the teacher, the pupil, and a particular subject matter. As used in this paper, the concept carries the meanings assigned to it by such therapists and educators as May,[5] Barron,[6] Schachtel,[7] and Dewey.[8] It is existential, problematic, purposive, open, unitary.

To define the curriculum as existential means that the one real datum which makes up the educative process is the existing pupils and the existing teacher who confront each other in a concrete, problematic situation. This confrontation has immediate import for their separate existences for the very reason that it is mediated by a real life problem. Each person in the encounter learns to participate in the inner experiences of the other because of the common circumstance which binds them together. These inner experiences are dynamic; they are movements—toward increased understandings, toward greater self-realization, toward creative development. Such encounters comprise the content of education. Out of them will come whatever learnings are available, whatever changes can be effected in both teacher and pupils, whatever expansion of consciousness may occur.

Barron refers to this existential quality of encounter as a "vitalizing transaction," which may be "as frail as love or blessedness." It is a live and growing thing, a personal relationship; and it becomes the purpose of psychotherapy, as well as of education, to nourish this relationship in constructive, self-initiating directions, to expand the range of choices among the participants and hence to provide for experiences of increased freedom.

To define encounter in terms of the problematic means that the engagement occurs in the first place because of the individual's basic need to establish productive relations with other people, and because he discovers in his experiences unsettled factors which inhibit these relationships. The encounter begins as indeterminate probings, as exploratory and experimental thrusts, as tensional and disturbing but wholly curious surveys and scannings.

[5]Rollo May (ed.), *Existential Psychology* (New York: Random House, 1961), p. 75. See also Rollo May, "The Nature of Creativity," *Creativity and Its Cultivation*, ed. H. H. Anderson (New York: Harper and Brothers, 1959), p. 58.

[6]Frank Barron, *Creativity and Psychological Health* (Princeton, N.J.: D. Van Nostrand Co., 1963), Chapter 7.

[7]Ernest G. Schachtel, *Metamorphosis* (New York: Basis Books, 1959), p. 240.

[8]John Dewey, *Democracy and Education*, Chapter 11.

Again, Dewey's view of the curriculum throws light upon this idea. He explains that the thoughtful modes of behavior are generated by the confrontation of unaccustomed elements, that these elements make the encounter a personal one. They bring to experience the qualities of immediacy and commitment. Active participation in the encounter dissolves away uncertainty, connects up meanings, overcomes cultural discontinuities, and consequently contributes to the achievement of inner freedom. Personal involvement brings the individual's own past to bear upon the problem at hand, and it evokes the cummulative culture of mankind. The past in all of its dimensions has its say, presents its constancies, and stands ready to be transformed into new expressions.

The function of the curriculum therefore is to strengthen the learner's relation to his world, which means to aid in the achievement of freedom, of responsiveness, and of responsibility—these ends are achieved as the student experiences purposiveness among elements of the encounter. Thus, the curriculum has not completed its work until its informational components have entered into the free play of imagination, until the learner has discovered within this information the connections which will carry his experiences forward, until he has imposed something of his own vision upon it. In short, the purpose of the curriculum is to stimulate the free play of imagination, to activate the student into creative ventures, and to provide for the added freedom which this kind of activity generates. Of the various characteristics of encounter, openness is probably the most important. It facilitates creativeness, permits freedom, and softens rigidity.

According to Rogers, openness means that the individual is able to perceive his world directly rather than through predetermined categories; it means that he is aware of the existential moment as it actually is. Openness is that condition within the individual which is most closely associated with creative potentiality; it is the opposite of psychological defensiveness and of rigidity; it is the permeability of boundaries among beliefs.

Discovered in therapy, openness becomes for Rogers a powerful educational weapon. It encourages individuals to become adaptive, to make responsible choices, to become more aware, self-expressive, and free to change.[9] It maintains the freshness of experience. In short, it makes the encounter creative. In Schachtel's words, it provides for an enlargement of personal experience.[10] According to Fromm, openness characterizes teaching at its best, as teaching is conducted, for example, by the Zen masters.[11] The only thing that the Zen master can teach, the only cur-

[9]Carl R. Rogers, "Learning to Be Free," *Conflict and Creativity*, p. 277.
[10]Ernest G. Schachtel, *Metamorphosis*, p. 240.
[11]Erich Fromm, "Psychoanalysis and Zen Buddhism," *Zen Buddhism and Psychoanalysis* (New York: Harper & Brothers, 1960), p. 116.

riculum he can follow, the only content which he can convey to the pupil is the pupil's own immediate existence.

The fifth characteristic of encounter refers to its integrated nature. It is a unitary act of perceiving, feeling, reflecting, willing. The whole person is involved. No boundary lines arise between the pupil and the subject matter, between the pupil and his tools, nor between the pupil and the teacher. More particularly there are no boundary lines between the categorized subject matters. Subject matter loses its logical orientation under manipulative, playful attitudes.

This aspect of encounter has far-reaching implications for the traditional curriculum. It suggests, for example, that when defined in terms of the hard core subjects the curriculum will not easily promote creativity. Since creativeness is the same wherever it occurs—the same in the arts, sciences, business affairs, and daily living—a curriculum which promotes creativity will find its organizing principle within the creative experience itself rather than in a systematized hierarchy of discrete subjects. For this reason it also rejects as incompatible the concept of general education, the theory that a well-rounded person can be developed by exposing him to a certain spread of courses, and the notion that enrichment counterbalances overspecialization.

Personality formation does not result from an exposure to a specified list of subjects. Growth toward selfhood is not necessarily nourished by general education courses, nor need it be thwarted by specialization. Variation in subject matter neither prevents nor cures overspecialization, alienation, or uncreativeness. The liberal arts may not serve as an antidote to the increasing particularization of knowledge; for the arts, no less than specialized courses, may produce only technically qualified individuals. The problem is not whether we should teach specialized courses, or general courses, or a scattering of subjects. The problem is to teach whatever we have at hand in a creative manner. When we teach creatively, any subject matter, however specialized or however general, will promote integration of the self.

Thus, traditional methods and curriculums tend to make technicians out of students. If the subject matter is literature, then pupils become literary technicians; if it is electronics, then they become electronic technicians. To be sure, technical knowledge and technicians are necessary in scientific, industrialized societies. This is not the argument. We must also have some assurance that literary and electronic technicians shall have also learned to function creatively and to appreciate creative products.

IV. The Principle of Therapy

The principle of therapy serves as the criterion for selecting educational *aims*. Applying this principle isolates creativity as a major goal, and it suggests the corollary aims of freedom, self-initiative, and responsibility. The achievement of these aims constitutes therapy just as it defines the educative process.

These concepts—creativity, freedom, initiative, responsibilty—are logically related. The creative imagination functions as an instrument for achieving freedom. It provides the individual with a wide range of adaptive responses and consequently extends the area of choice. But freedom implies the capacity to initiate one's own inquiries and to make one's own discoveries. And freedom, together with self-directing capacities, imposes the requirement that an individual accept an increasingly larger share of responsibility for choices and actions. Thus, when therapy or education is successful, the individual approaches the world creatively. He initiates his own encounters, and he takes responsibility for what he does.

This view has wide support among psychologists. Perhaps Carl Rogers has been most insistent in urging that education regard itself as therapy and that it pursue therapeutic goals. He argues that the aim of education is to assist students to take self-initiated action, to be responsible for such action, to become self-directive, to adapt flexibly to new situations, to cooperate effectively with others.[12]

The most important implication which psychotherapy has for the classroom teacher is its non-authoritarian attitude. Both Fromm and Rogers emphasize this requirement. Fromm again refers to the Zen masters, who seek no power of any kind over their pupils; who reject all authority except perhaps for their own particular specialties.[13] Rogers argues that the exercise of authority over pupils destroys creativeness and self-initiative. He explains that the teacher should never set lesson plans, lecture, evaluate, criticize, assign grades, or give examinations. He must only arrange opportunities for students to learn to become responsibly free.[14]

Few teachers are willing to reduce their authority so drastically, and Rogers agrees that the initial stages of this kind of education produce considerable chaos. But it is the only education which can help an individual to learn to be free. But what exactly does the teacher do to help pupils discover within themselves the grounds for directing their own affairs? Four things, Roger believes.

First, he can demonstrate his non-authoritarianism by placing complete trust in the pupil to choose his own way in learning and to discover his own information. It is because we distrust the student that we lecture him, assign tasks which *we* have selected, transmit to him *our* information, insist upon his following *our* directions. Second, the teacher can stand as a real person without sham or deceit. He serves as a model, provides resources, suggests. He shares the inner experiences of the learner, and in this encounter he begins to clarify his own feelings and to expand

[12]Carl R. Rogers, *Client-Centered Therapy* (Boston: Houghton Mifflin, 1951), p. 388.
[13]Erich Fromm, *Zen Buddhism and Psychoanalysis*, p. 124.
[14]Carl R. Rogers, *Conflict and Creativity*, p. 282.

his own consciousness. He begins to understand the student just as the student begins to understand him. He effects changes in the student by expanding his own awareness.

Third, he can become effectively non-authoritarian by learning to prize the student. Accepting the individual as inherently worthy permits him to enter into experiences of pupils in ways which can release creative tendencies. Encouraging the pupil to affirm the worth of his own existence also encourages him to accept others without defensiveness. Valuing self and valuing others characterize creative individuals.

Fourth, the teacher displays non-authoritarianism by his ability to understand the student's reactions from the inside, to be empathetically aware of the way the process of learning appears to the student.[15] Recognizing that this capacity is largely limited to trained therapists, Rogers nevertheless believes that it is also a condition of creative teaching. It is an act of encounter, an act of being fully engaged, fully open and responsible.

Non-authoritarianism thus becomes a major application of therapeutic principles to education. This attitude develops as the teacher builds into his own behavioral responses the traits of trust, honesty, acceptance, and empathy.

A second application of psychotherapy involves the counterpart to this attitude, namely, the achievement of self-direction on the part of the student. The principle of self-activity is of course time-honored in the history of educational philosophy. As used in this essay, it is not intended to express any new or unusual meanings. But it does require a new setting and a new emphasis. The new setting is its function in therapy; the new emphasis is its role in creativity.

Referring again to Zen, Fromm notes the importance of the Buddhist doctrine that no person can save another, that each man must save himself. Education likewise must remain a process of self-education; no one can teach another directly. The Zen master joins such other notables as Socrates in the emphasis on teaching as midwifery. The teacher can only provide his presence, his responsiveness, and the condition of openness. The kind of growth which involves personality formation occurs only as a result of what the pupil does to himself and for himself.

The therapists who have recently identified themselves as existentialists[16] agree in making the achievement of self-direction the most important new dimension in their system of therapy.

[15]Carl R. Rogers, *Conflict and Creativity*, p. 281.

[16]The following therapists contributed to the book, *Existential Psychology*: Rollo May, Gordon Allport, Herman Feifel, Abraham Maslow, and Carl Rogers. The existentialist movement now has its own publication, the *Review of Existential Psychology and Psychiatry*, which is edited by Adrian van Kaam. It lists twenty-one members on the editorial board, twelve of whom are doctors of medicine, indicating a strong emphasis on therapy.

Rollo May, a leading spokesman for this group, observes that there are in therapy, and in teaching, certain built-in tendencies which take away the student's decision making opportunities.[17] These pose a continual threat to his own growth. Every direct act which the teacher performs promotes the tendency on the part of the pupil to rely upon those activities, rather than his own, for his growth or for his failures. Yet it becomes precisely the aim of therapy, and of teaching, to support him in making decisions and in initiating behavior.

The existential therapists associate man's neurotic condition with his failure to learn to make decisions and to act upon them, and they therefore equate these learnings with therapy. May, for example, argues that the core of modern man's neurosis is "the undermining of his experience of himself as responsible, the sapping of his willing and deciding."[18] Therapy consists in encouraging man to accept responsibility; it consists in learning to be free.

Learning to become self-active and self-responsible becomes a central task in education. These learnings confer upon man his essential humanness. Says May, "Decision and responsibility are the distinctive forms of consciousness in the human being who is moving toward self-realization, integration, maturity."[19] Tillich also argues that these outcomes do not merely refer to what might be more or less preferable in human life; rather, they are the conditions of man's very existence. Says Tillich, "The power of deciding makes men human."[20]

Learning to become self-active and self-responsible are creative learnings. In the sense that the creative person is the self-actualizing person, the individual creates himself as he organizes his energies into patterns of living which are responsive to other persons. And the organization of his energies itself is an act of decision. Decision and action become essential to the creative life.

V. The Principle of Deferment

The principle of deferment describes the part which *evaluation* plays in the creative and educative processes.

Since this essay concerns itself primarily with the teaching side of education, the concept of deferment has been chosen to indicate the teacher's role in assigning value. It applies particularly to the judgments which

[17]Rollo May, *Existential Psychology*, p. 43.
[18]Rollo May, "Will, Decision, and Responsibility: Summary Remarks," *Review of Existential Psychology and Psychiatry*, Vol. 1, No. 3 (November, 1961), 250.
[19]*Ibid.*, p. 256.
[20]Paul Tillich, "Existentialism and Psychotherapy," *Review of Existential Psychology and Psychiatry*, Vol. I, No. 1.

are continually made in the daily operation of the classroom—making assignments, summarizing material, structuring class discussions, choosing goals, assigning grades. Deferment of the teacher's final judgments in these activities has one major purpose: it encourages self-initiative and promotes self-evaluation. The concepts which link up the attitude of deferment on the part of the teacher with self-evaluative tendencies on the part of the student form the meaning of this principle.

These concepts can be briefly summarized: the deferment of final solutions and choices stimulates the exploratory tendencies of students; such probings move beyond what is given to what is possible; the testing and choosing of possibilities characterize the creative process; the criteria for making these choices are personal and aesthetic; therefore, self-evaluation becomes the only basis for making choices which will carry forward the creative process. And finally, the capacity for self-evaluation calls for an independence of spirit and a feeling of self-worth.

The first of these ideas refers to the teacher's capacity to delay closure, to postpone the final settlement of a question which is under discussion, to entertain tentative conclusions. This does not mean that the student is left without direction or that his education deals with loose ends of information. But it does mean that the teacher refrains from imposing his own formal systems upon classroom activities in order to bring them to some predetermined end. The creative teacher avoids finalities. He continually shifts the limits of openness and closure as his emphasis moves from subject matter to pupil and back to his own concerns; balance between deferment and closure remains a precariously shifting one, as is the teacher's own involvement.

Hypothesizing is a second concept which enters into the meaning of deferment. Defined as the capacity to go beyond what is given, it serves as the logical connection between deferment and creativity. Deferment facilitates hypothesizing; hypotheses in turn reach beyond the data at hand; and going beyond the immediately given characterizes creative activity. To hypothesize means that the pupil freely engages in speculating, guessing, associating—in dealing with what is not yet present. And the environment which can best initiate and sustain this speculative venture is the condition of deferment.

The search for possibilities requires the acceptance of self as the source of judgment in making choices. Thus, self-evaluation becomes the third ingredient in the principle under discussion. At least three factors converge to make self-evaluation a necessary ingredient in creative education. First, creativity flourishes under conditions of conflict, ambiguity, and even chaos. Second, the creative individual functions as a self-assertive, independent person. Third, the grounds for judging original productions are personal, aesthetic ones.

Ample evidence has accumulated to support the view that creativity flourishes under conditions of conflict, that creative individuals prefer qualities of complexity, imbalance, and ambiguity and show an aversion to the settled, the symmetrical, and the ordered.[21] Tension forms part of the motivational drive of the creative person. Disorder arouses inventive tendencies and presents challenges to create new orders and more aesthetically satisfying structures. Hence, it is preferred by the gifted person.

This preference explains the creative person's predisposition to reject the conventional and to break up the orderly. For example, Barron finds that creativeness always involves an act of rejection preceding an act of construction;[22] and Golovin argues that every creative act both transcends prior experience and contains a revolt against it.[23] The very fact that creating entails abandonment of the status quo isolates the creative person and induces feelings of anxieties.

Thus, creative living and teaching inescapably incur certain risks, and this is why principles of creative teaching must emphasize the qualities of self-worth, self-reliance and self-responsibility.

The element of risk involved in creative acts, including creative teaching, has several dimensions. For example, the mere fact that creativity seeks out possibilities and rejects actualities poses a threat to the established order. Creativity is essentially revisionistic; in searching for novelty it rejects conformity. Risk arises in connection with any innovation. It consists in the fact that the individual must judge changes as occurring in the direction of improvement and of social cohesiveness. It consists in creating objects which may have no significance for culture and therefore which may disrupt communication among people. It consists in the possibility that his inner sense of values may err in the direction of eccentricity, that his choice of goals is spurious, that his impulse to be unique will remain an end in itself rather than a condition for further fulfillment, that his nonconformity is only a neurotic symptom rather than a source of courage. The risk consists in the possibility that symbolic freedom and rebellion will extend into overt aggression. Perhaps the real risk is that a sense of social sympathy will not grow to match his courageous strivings for self-hood.

But if creativity involves risk, it also holds out the possibility for deeply rewarding social relationships. Maslow discusses these possibili-

[21]Frank Barron, "The Disposition Toward Originality," *Scientific Creativity*, eds., C. W. Taylor and Frank Barron (New York: John Wiley, 1963), p. 146. See also Frank Barron, "Creative Vision and Expression in Writing and Painting," *The Creative Person*, The Institute of Personality Assessment and Research, University of California (Berkeley: Mimeographed, 1961), pp. II–1–19.

[22]Frank Barron, *The Creative Person*, p. II–10.

[23]N. E. Golovin, "The Creative Person in Science," *Scientific Creativity*, p. 16.

ties.[24] There is, he argues, a necessary connection between self-fulfillment and social sympathy. The individual who expresses in his living those values which he himself has created must of necessity express them in the form of social feelings. Thus, the two poles of individuality and conformity are complementary, not opposed. The more fully one actualizes himself, the more socially responsible he becomes.

An independence of judgment can easily run into self-assertiveness, into anti-social feelings of rebelliousness or exhibitionism; but these nevertheless belong in the creative environment, and it behooves the creative teacher to accommodate them in his classroom. These are not desirable forms of behavior, and they make teaching difficult. They add to the burden, as well as to the challenge, of creative teaching. How does the teacher channel such attitudes into productive activity?

For one thing, he can exploit an inherent dynamic of the creative drive itself, namely, its aesthetic component.[25] The creative individual accepts chaotic materials without threat because his own confidence assures him that he can impose an orderliness upon them which will be both aesthetic and accurate. He is strongly motivated by this need for aesthetic elegance. Physicists often argue that a theory is right because it is elegant. Maslow finds that this aesthetic need is invariably present in the behavior of self-actualizing people. Because these individuals make use of their unconscious urges without fearing them and accept their impulses without defending against them, they can release their creative energies into formal patterns of enjoyment.

Thus, the aesthetic drive which motivates the creative pupil places a powerful weapon into the hands of the teacher. As an internal force in the pupil, it is the counterpart of the creative teacher's own efforts. The teacher becomes a partner to the pupil. His deferring attitude joins the aesthetic tendency in the pupil to produce an autonomous functioning of the pupil's personality. It merges with the student's predispositions for self-discipline in the creative conduct of his life.

VI. Conclusion

The problem of how to educate for creativity remains among the most important of the unsettled questions in contemporary culture. It is an urgent question and merits the attention of our best minds. At stake is the possibility of a richer life for mankind generally, and at the same time the hope of discovering a therapeutic process which will cure souls.

[24]A. H. Maslow, *Toward a Psychology of Being*, Chapter 6.
[25]The nature and importance of the aesthetic drive in creativity is discussed in my article, "Aesthetic Motivation in the Creative Arts," which was published in the Summer 1965 issue of the *Journal of Aesthetics and Art Criticism*.

31 What Can Teachers Learn from Directors in the Performing Arts?

Dorothy I. Seaberg and Wanna M. Zinsmaster

Can teachers learn something about teaching from directors in the performing arts—dancing, music, acting? Certainly the classroom teacher and the director in the performing arts have much in common. Both work with individuals. Both work with prepared materials. Both work to help find life in the materials.

Since teaching and directing have elements in common, the actions unique to directing may be keys to artistic performance in teaching. No tools have been devised to study teaching as art. Therefore, the writers decided to interview directors to discover relationships between teaching and directing. We hoped that the behavior of directors would yield clues that would help us identify and study artistic aspects of teaching.

The writers designed fifteen questions to get at directors' personal outlook, intuitive behavior, and skills. Some questions asked the directors why they chose a particular art, what preparation they had for directing, and what they valued most in their preparation. Other questions focused on the relationship between intuitive actions and technical knowledge or skill, on interpersonal relationships between directors and performers,

Reprinted with permission from *The Elementary School Journal*, 72:167–175, January, 1972. Copyright © 1972 by the University of Chicago.

and on the use of materials. The responses of fourteen directors—four choreographers, five play and stage directors, and five choral and orchestral conductors—in the metropolitan New York area were taped and studied.

All the directors believed that the artistic response to problems in their work resulted more from intuition than from technique. In fact, many of the artists were unable to identify principles that guided their actions. Nearly all said that inspiration, enthusiasm, ability to communicate, good human relations, knowledge of structure, authenticity of their subject matter, and ability to identify with their materials were essential to their success as directors. Summaries and abstracts from the interviews that verify these generalizations are presented in this article (1).

Interviewer: What preparation did you have for your work?

All the conductors said that they had studied music in colleges and universities as well as privately with other conductors. The choreographers had studied dance and after dancing for a period of time began to choreograph. The directors began with study and experience in acting and moved into directing, sometimes without any formal training in directing. Seven of the interviewees who had formal training in schools had also studied or worked with outstanding individuals in their fields.

The artists valued the example set by virtuosos who were also master teachers. "Two professors really helped and inspired me to become a better musician," a musical director said. "I think you learn from great masters who teach."

A theater director credited a good liberal arts background: "My major in philosophy was most valuable because it gave me a survey of social psychology and all the various interrelated studies that are really the heart and soul of drama."

Interviewer: When you pick up the score or printed material, how do you know that it's worth producing?

All but two of the interviewees said that one could tell by looking at the material whether it had merit. "You read something, and you know that it will be successful. I don't know how you know," a play director remarked.

Another said, "Hopefully, you build up over the years a kind of inner radar that gives you a feeling something has occurred in the work that stimulates you. So much of it is intuitive."

Artists determine the worth of a piece for production mainly through intuition linked with experience—their emotional and analytical reactions. They visualize or hear a work as it would be if performed and determine whether it has contemporary appeal.

Interviewer: Do you envision an entire production in advance of working with the players just through reading the printed material, or does the picture emerge as you work with the players, musicians, or dancers?

Half of the interviewees said they envisioned a production before they worked with the players but they also allowed the performance to emerge as they worked. One play director responded:

"Some of it emerges as we're working with the players in rehearsal, but I try to envision some kind of thing . . . to a certain extent, not completely. Some things only start to show themselves as you work."

Two conductors said they had everything worked out before they went into the pit. The others said that there was no absolute rule, since many factors are involved.

Interviewer: How do you know when to add to or cut from printed materials?

Directors make changes as a result of their observation, study, and intuition. Shortcomings of performers, lack of clarity or continuity of the script, and audience response are the usual reasons for change.

"If the player is incapable of making a scene succeed," a play director said, "it's sometimes the better part of valor to cut the script."

A fencing choreographer said, "If suddenly I see that one part is lagging or not quite fitting the rest, we change it."

Interviewer: What kind of clues do you get from the first rehearsal?

Responses showed that, in the first rehearsal, the directing artists get clues about the performers' capabilities, backgrounds, understandings, and relationships to one another. The directing artists see which groups need to become true working units and which passages will benefit from further work or detailed rehearsal. The directors also discover ultimately how accurate they were in prerehearsal planning and where changes in the overall plan must be made.

A choreographer said, "You see what the people can do. Some people will take direction, and some are better if you don't direct them—if you let them play around. Some actors love to improvise and some don't and so you have to really feel your way and that's mainly what you learn."

Interviewer: How do you work with performers so that the production is the result of their creative response and not the imposition of your own ideas? How much of the finished product is imposed by you?

A conductor put it this way: "It depends upon the performer's ego, experience, and fame. I don't expect to have a carbon copy of the original. People are different, and so they want to interpret differently, but we do try to get them to do an honest role. . . . And then I do impose myself on tempos. . . . We cannot allow absolute freedom because anarchy steps in."

"The director has the function of stimulator, controller, coordinator, explainer, decision-maker, and demander of necessary results," another artist said.

In general, the directors believed that there is always some imposition by the leader. One cannot avoid imposition, since the material "goes through" the director to the performer. Nevertheless, performers do have some freedom for creative response.

Interviewer: Through what kind of working relationship with the performers do you get the best results?

The interviewees had various ways of approaching this problem:

"Of course they have to respect you for what you represent," one director said.

Two others responded:

"Part of working a group of people so that you get the best results out of them is being an amateur psychologist. You have to deal with different people differently. There are ways of asking for things, or even demanding things, so that the players respect you for it. You have to play it by ear with each person. Some people you get by cajoling, some by boosting their ego, some by just saying, 'Come on, you're a professional. Just let's work.' It's not a fast rule, and you have to have twelve different methods for working with twelve different people and hoping that each one will work right for you."

"It is my enthusiasm over the project and work atmosphere and a goal that is challenging for all of them. If I can generate the enthusiasm, they'll deliver to me 500 per cent more than I asked for. The director to me is the guy to set the tone and create the atmosphere."

Some of the interviewees said that humor alleviates tension. One choreographer said that she believed the "best results are obtained by being very available to the dancers. . . . It all depends on the person you're dealing with. But I think always it's like teaching: The less frightening you are, the more available, the more open you are, the better your results."

Interviewer: How do you go about creating the atmosphere for the kind of action (or in the case of music, the kind of mood) you desire?

Eleven of the artists indicated that they helped the performer feel what they, the directors, feel about the music or the characters to be portrayed:

"When it comes to the actual performance where you can't even explain in words, there is something that you can do with your hands, with your face, with your eyes, with your body, with whatever it is that kind of gets either tremendous intensity or complete serenity or some other kind of color."

Responses indicated that directors created atmosphere chiefly by being catalysts or by helping performers visualize action or mood. Directors get results through words and gestures that stimulate the imagination. Performers capture a feeling for atmosphere or mood by empathizing with the director. It behooves the director, therefore, to experience the work of art so intimately that his feelings exude from him. A spirit of camaraderie helps.

Interviewer: How do you know how to use each person's potential to the best advantage?

Many agreed that this question really could not be answered. Six responded that the director must use his intuition and do a lot of "playing by ear."

A choral director said, "You work at the medium level. The brightest ones, the best singers, are held back by the slowest ones. You don't go at the pace of the slowest ones or else you lose the brightest ones, but you take every advantage you can of the ability of your good ones to lead."

According to a play director, "It depends on whether you yourself fundamentally respect the actor. I don't mean that you think he's the greatest actor in the world, but respect him as a person who's going to give something, and you're going to work along with him."

Others said that, in the performing arts, an artist is hired for what he has achieved, his demonstrated potential. However, directors also discover potential intuitively through observing the performer in action. Casting is based on the director's discoveries about what a performer can do. In working out a production, the most effective ways for helping the artist do his best seem to be to foster good human relations and to respect the performer's uniqueness.

Interviewer: How important are timing and pacing to the entire performance?

Everyone: Terribly!!!

Interviewer: How do you tell when pacing is right? How do you plan for it?

No stock answer to this question was apparent. Some artists are guided by instinct or intuition; some work indirectly, stressing what is happening in the scene and building the pacing into the text. Some make up the pacing as they go along; others work out the pacing in advance of rehearsal.

The artists emphasized the need to develop a sense of timing and pacing. The most difficult task the artist has is to build the pacing into the production without calling attention to the fact that it is being done.

Interviewer: How do you know when to re-do a scene or rehearse a section of a musical score again?

This group of artists had several ways of deciding when to re-do a scene or a section of a musical number. The chief ways were intuition, artistic sensitivity, or technical know-how.

A conductor said, "You have to answer the question, will fixing and replaying help it? Or will leaving it alone help it? Or will doing it with everybody help it? Or should you wait and just do it with one or two instruments? I can't answer you generally how you know when or where, but there is a reason for doing it each time."

One respondee said, "There is such a thing, too, as overworking a section of script or musical score to the point of frustration and diminishing returns."

Interviewer: How do you know when a performance is ready for an audience?

Six directors said facetiously, "The opening date determines that."

Another said, "The more experienced you are, the better guess you can make, but you don't always make the right one."

Interviewer: Are there any specific principles you rely on to guide your work?

Few were able to give a definite answer. Three replied that there are no definite principles. Others indicated that they worked from technique rather than principles. However, a play director said:

"I think that directors are moving closer towards choreography, because they've found that to make the theatre exciting enough for an audience, now, the quality and texture of the event that you see must be heightened in a way that is not often done by some of the more realistic drama. We have to find those basic human actions that are central to our existence and make them exciting and vivid."

A theatrical director said, "You must proceed from the meaning that the musical composition or play is trying to convey."

Judging from the replies, perhaps principles of operation are too closely bound up with technique to make them readily discernible to most artists. Or perhaps the principles are too close to the directors, too deeply ingrained to be apparent.

Interviewer: What relationships do you see between teaching and your art?

The most striking likenesses mentioned were the need for inspiration and enthusiasm, the need for communication and good human relations, and the need to know the materials in teaching and the other arts.

An orchestra conductor said, "Well, it's entirely a teaching process. I would say the two are inseparable, but I wouldn't say 'instructing'; I would say 'showing'—communicating a final result to someone who may only see a part of it at the beginning."

A play director said, "Ideally, directing is different from teaching because in teaching your obligation is to the student indirectly. In directing your obligation is to the finished work of art and that determines choices that you make in directing a play."

Another play director said, "I found out very quickly that if you try to teach when you're directing, you're going to be in trouble. I see myself as a catalytic agent guiding and pushing a show towards a complete dramatic picture that is in the back of my mind, but I can't teach the actors anything. I have to encourage them to do themselves."

Implications for Teaching

Certain relationships between the arts of conducting, directing, choreography, and teaching were apparent in this study. The interviews revealed that underlying types of actions, judgments, and necessary decisions are mutual concerns of these artists. As in counterpoint in music, directors and teachers must keep many facets of their craft in simultaneous harmony. All face common problems in selecting, rehearsing, and staging a show.

Teachers as well as directors must envision and judge the effectiveness of the materials in advance of their use. Both make judgments that affect the productivity of the participants in the creative process of performing or thinking. These judgments largely determine the quality of interpersonal relationships and working atmosphere. The artist decides on the amount of repetitive practice needed and determines when the production is ready or when the learner is ready for next steps.

Materials and plans often need modification. They can be effective only if they are changed. The teacher, like the director, must develop the ability to look at materials and see them "come to life." The teacher must also consider the significance of material in relationship to pupils, where they live, and the time in which they live. If the teacher does not "feel good" about the materials, it is likely that they will not succeed.

The ways materials are put together, timed, and paced are crucial. Interest is maintained by timing and pacing, but the most difficult task for artist or teacher is to build the pacing into the production without calling attention to the fact that it is being done.

The teacher, like the director, envisions and develops an overall plan of action but finds that as he works with the participants he must make changes. The teacher observes the pupils as they become involved with the materials and picks up clues for change. Thus the artist teacher knows the materials and envisions them, but lets part of his plan emerge as he works with the participants.

The teacher, during the first use of materials, gains information for developing his plan. He discovers pupils' capabilities for handling the material. He may also discover that the participants are not a working unit ready to undertake a specific task. Then he ceases to work on the material itself and seeks to develop a working group.

Like the artist, the teacher makes some imposition on the pupils. The very choice of material involves imposition. Actually, teaching, like the performing arts, involves some imposition and some creative response from the pupils. But the goals of education may not be attained if the teacher imposes too much without helping the pupil find his way or his answers.

There are tests to help the teacher determine the readiness of a group or an individual for an activity, but the teacher does not really know whether the pupils are ready until his audience responds. Is it possible that the teacher, like the artist, must develop a sense of the rhythm and the flow of ongoing classroom activities to help him become more sensitive to readiness? The artists often spoke of intuition, feeling, and sixth sense. Do teachers need training in one of the performing arts to develop these qualities?

The teacher, like the director, must learn to relate to people in ways that fit him. The more ways the teacher is able to respond, the more likely it is that he can react to each pupil as an individual. Like the director, the teacher gains respect through his knowledge, his technical know-how, and the way he works with the participants.

Much as the director sets the atmosphere for the performance, the teacher sets the classroom tone through leadership and example. The responses of the artists suggest that the teacher's gestures, facial expression, intonation, and manner of speech may be as important as what he says. An atmosphere of excitement can pervade the learning process when the teacher is imaginative and identifies enthusiastically with the content he teaches.

The directors stressed intuition as a guide to action, but they also said that techniques were totally at their command. Were the directors saying that they are free to follow intuitive hunches because their skills function automatically? One wonders whether teachers who have a large repertoire of techniques and lesson designs at instant command are more able to follow intuitive hunches and make on-the-spot shifts in their teaching.

The study gave support to the idea of using "the self" or "the person" as an instrument in teaching (2). Teachers should be encouraged to be experimental in teaching and to follow hunches and educated guesses. They should be encouraged to develop their individuality and to be open to their own experience in teaching.

Although the study was exploratory and not definitive, it suggests that here is an important lead worth following. For example, master teachers could be interviewed or their actions could be studied to verify the implications pointed out in this study. Perhaps new clues for artistic teaching would be found.

Scientific studies have not carried us very far in the improvement of teaching. Perhaps it is time in teacher education to stress intuition, the artist's sixth sense. The aesthetics of teaching have barely been studied and may prove fruitful in further investigation.

References

1. Wanna M. Zinsmaster and Dorothy I. Seaberg. *Contributions from the Field of Directing in the Performing Arts to the Field of Teaching.* Monograph. New York: Tri-University Project in Elementary Education, New York University, 1968.

2. Arthur W. Combs. *The Professional Education of Teachers.* Boston: Allyn and Bacon, 1965.

8 *Nonverbal Communication*

Overview

The interest in nonverbal communication in teaching has blossomed. No doubt this interest has resulted from the general attention to nonverbal communication by anthropologists and sociologists. Perhaps the three best-known scholars are Birdwhistell, Hall, and Goffman, who, through their research and writings in nonverbal communication, have influenced educators.[1] Birdwhistell uses the term *kinesics* and has developed a complex system for recording nonverbal behavior. Another term is *body language,* which is the title of a recent best-selling book by Fast,[2] a popularizer of this subject.

But there is more to nonverbal communication than the physical gestures that the term *body language* generally connotes. Teachers communicate nonverbally not only with their hands and facial expressions but also by the very space they use when they teach and the time chosen to travel to that space.

The three selections here are significant in that each presents an observation system for empirically studying nonverbal behavior. As Flanders notes in Section 2, it is more difficult to get agreement on the meaning ascribed to nonverbal behavior than it is to reach agreement on

[1]R. Birdwhistell, *Kinesics and Context* (Philadelphia: University of Pennsylvania Press, 1970); E. Hall, *The Silent Language* (Garden City, N.Y.: Doubleday, 1959); E. Hall, *The Hidden Dimension* (New York: Fawcett World Library, 1966); E. Goffman, *The Presentation of Self in Everyday Living* (New York: Doubleday, 1957).

[2]J. Fast, *Body Language* (New York: M. Evans Co., 1970).

the meaning ascribed to verbal behavior. Yet, Galloway, Grant and Hennings, and Koch have successfully created instruments for categorizing nonverbal behavior.

Galloway's instrument overlaps with certain ideas in the section on Social Climate. Galloway states in his field study that he built the subcategories for encouraging and inhibiting communication upon the work of Flanders and Hughes (Section 2), to name but two sources. A careful comparison of this instrument with the articles by Flanders and Hughes will reveal the points in common. Indeed, the third part of the Galloway selection presents a system for matching Galloway's continuum with Flanders' interaction analysis.

Grant and Hennings' selection focuses on three types of instructional motions—conducting, acting, and wielding. Grant developed the category system for nonverbal activity in her doctoral dissertation under the supervision of Arno Bellack. Hence, it is no coincidence that Grant and Hennings relate their teacher motions to Bellack's (Section 3) pedagogical moves in an attempt to combine the nonverbal and verbal dimensions to teaching.

Koch does not relate his work to any particular person, though it appears that he is influenced more by anthropologists than by other educators. Koch's list of thirty-five nonverbal observables ranges from breathing and hand movements to room appearance and territoriality. Other than classifying a nonverbal behavior as positive or negative, Koch ascribes no particular meaning to his specific nonverbal behaviors. Koch, in contrast to both Grant and Galloway, whose original works involve elementary teachers, studies junior and senior high school teachers.

The comparisons of these articles with each other and with other selections in this book are fruitful. For example, Galloway and Koch refer to the use of space and territoriality, a dimension of classroom teaching often neglected by observers. The reader would do well to compare these authors with each other and then with Adams and Biddle (Section 2), who refer to location as one dimension of their study, citing Hall's work on space. Similarly, the reader should compare the concept of conducting offered by Grant and Hennings and their data on conducting with the concept of controlling offered by Hughes (Section 2). The reader also might well ask where Grant and Hennings' conducting lies on Galloway's continuum of encouraging to inhibiting.

Since the nonverbal vantage point has now blossomed, it is not surprising that the authors of these three selections are quite strong in their call for teacher training in the observation and deliberate improvement of nonverbal communication.

The research questions arising from this vantage point abound. For example, will teachers trained in nonverbal communication be more congruent than those not so trained when verbal and nonverbal behaviors are compared? To what extent can teachers change their nonverbal behavior? Can teachers be trained to reduce the distance they maintain from students and the lack of interest they show for students? (See Koch's data on distance and interest.) Can teachers be trained to increase the amount of acting motions relative to controlling motions? Does the amount and type of nonverbal behavior correlate with a teacher's age, teaching speciality, and sex? Do the three systems by Galloway, Grant, and Koch apply to all levels of teachers, elementary to college?

32 Nonverbal Communication in Teaching

Charles M. Galloway

1. Nonverbal Communication*

Many teachers rely upon words and verbalisms to convey meaning during instruction. They believe that teaching is telling. They readily accept the notion that to be instructive is to be verbal, or, that to be verbal is to be instructive. They view words as the very miracles of learning. "How many times will I have to *explain* this?" "Haven't I *explained* that a hundred times already?" "Were you listening when I *told* you that?" "Alright, everybody pay attention—I am only going to *say* this one more time." Although these statements by teachers do not characterize teaching, they do portray a reliance on the power of words.

Teachers constantly check on the fidelity of student verbal remarks by reading their nonverbal cues, but they miss the fact that by interpreting and inferring from these nonverbal expressions, pupils obtain the full impact of teacher motivations and feelings. It is much more "fun" to think that enlightenment is one way—that teachers are free to observe and read the behaviors of students with an open license. But the real point is that

*Reprinted with permission from *Theory Into Practice*, 7:172–175, December, 1968.

teachers convey information to students through nonverbal behavior, and this is what it is they overlook.

Words and verbalisms may be the preferred symbols of coming to know, but they do not represent the only means of knowing. Nonverbal cues and clues represent elegant signs for conveying and receiving information, for actions do speak as loud as words—perhaps, louder.

To recognize that how we say something is as important as what we say is difficult to grasp because little conscious thought is given to the process of providing information through nonverbal action. We are usually *unaware of our own awareness.*

Immediately understanding another and having the other understand us is commonly referred to as empathy. In fact, most of us believe that the most personal and valid kinds of information can be discovered this way. Yet, we rarely attribute our understanding to the influence of nonverbal communication. It is by reacting to the nonverbal cues of others —to their facial expressions, movements, postures, mannerisms, vocal tones, gestures, energy changes, etc.—that we pick up information which we use in deciding what to do next and in determing what our role needs to be. All of this expressive activity seems so natural and spontaneous to us that we overlook the fact that we influence and are influenced by others through nonverbal action.

Nonverbal cues may also be calculatingly managed to achieve a desired effect, to effect an impression, or to convey an attitude. The females of our culture have long since learned the significance of exchanging mutual glances with males. This is perhaps the most efficient and quickest way for two parties to convey immediate attraction for each other. You do not engage in a warm mutual glance with another if you are disinterested. Females understand the consequences of mutual glances so well that they are capable of looking around, through, and by a male to avoid his gaze and to avoid attention. They do this without drawing attention to themselves. It seems natural. Yet, the motive for action may be intentionally conceived and the expression deliberately managed.

We engineer expressions to convince others how we wish to be viewed. Such is the case when we take a driver's test to obtain a license, go to church, or listen to an instructor in a classroom. We may begin by deliberately engineering our performance to convince an observer of the realness of our participation, but there is a very good chance that we too begin to believe that our performance is authentic.

Whether nonverbal cues are spontaneously expressed or deliberately managed, either condition influences perceptions. While it is often difficult to detect the difference between the two kinds of cue-giving, nonverbal information facilitates efforts to understand others and to be understood. Whether a person deliberately chooses to react to nonverbal cues or whether he unconsciously does so, the crucial conclusion is that expressive cues influence perceptions. Both teachers and students take the expressive state of the other as symptomatic of inner feelings and attitudes. These cues are not taken at face value, but inferences are made from them to determine what to believe. Sometimes students will respond to a precise expression and know that a teacher is angry and hostile or sad and depressed. Teachers often read the facial expressions of a student to discover whether he is elated or unhappy.

In a psychological sense, teacher-pupil contacts are distinguished by spontaneity and immediate response. Therefore, nonverbal reactions are especially prominent for the formation of attitudes since they stem from unwitting responses. Not only are teachers quite likely to be unaware of their own behavior, but they can unwittingly reveal feelings to students that are not in their own best interests. Teachers must be on the alert to discover these possibilities after they occur, for the probability of preventing their occurrence is quite difficult. To increase an awareness of the psychological consequences of what is ordinarily out-of-awareness is a step in the right direction. Attitudinal displays and emotional reactions are not peculiar to classrooms, but the need to be open to the meaning of their appearance is greater than imagined.

In any classroom the exchange of messages that are nonverbal in character often plays a more significant role in student learning than the formal teaching which takes place. Throughout a teaching day, there are many occurrences which have an impact on the course and direction of classroom activity and which shape the contextual meaning derived from a situation. These are nonverbal phenomena that involve the use of the body, use of space, and even use of time. Not only do they minimize verbal messages, but they become the real focus of attention—the idea that lingers long after the event has passed. Why this should be so is most difficult to determine, but the character and influence of these events speak for themselves.

Use of Space

Classrooms are usually divided into territories where a teacher and students occupy space. Some arrangements are traditional, with the teacher's desk at the front of the room and students seated in rows. Other arrangements of desks and furniture are more imaginative. A change in a spatial arrangement influences the potential meaning of a learning context.

Teacher Travel

Where and when a teacher chooses to travel in a classroom signifies meaning. Some teachers move around their desks as if they were isles of security. They rarely venture into the territories of student residence unless they wish to check or monitor seatwork. To move forward or away from students signifies relationships.

Use of Time

How teachers use their time indicates the value and importance they place on something. Spending little time on a topic or passing by it can indicate no interest or knowledge about the topic. Teachers do not ordinarily recognize the meanings of their use of time, but students can frequently relate what a teacher's preferences are and what the teacher dislikes.

Control Maneuvers

Teachers engage in various nonverbal tactics to control the behavior of students. These silent expressions serve as singular events to remind students of teacher expectations. For example, a teacher often indicates inability to hear due to a classroom noise, places finger to lips, stands with hands on hips and stares in silence, scans room to see who is not working, records in grade book while student reports, or raises brow or uses eyes to gain attention.

The acts of a teacher suggest a reflection of the teacher's self. By interpreting and inferring from nonverbal cues, pupils attempt to obtain a fuller understanding of the teacher. Since pupils assume that these cues are more consonant with the actual feelings and thoughts of a teacher, pupils who detect contradictions between verbal and nonverbal behavior will accept the nonverbal as more valid. Therefore, what a teacher says makes little difference if it is incongruent with what he does. When there is an incongruency between the verbal and nonverbal, students are troubled by the dilemma, and they see through to the teacher's real self.

Communication theorists vary considerably in their views of human interaction, and models of the process can be needlessly abstract. Explanations range from the Shannon-Weaver model, which describes electronic communication, to the Ruesch-Bateson description which includes anything to which persons can assign meaning. However, the four major ingredients that researchers agree are common to human communication are: (1) sender, (2) message, (3) channel, and (4) receiver.

A sender of communication has ideas, interests, information, needs, and sentiments which he attempts to encode in the form of messages. Given a sender who sends messages, a channel is necessary. The channel is the carrier of messages, the medium, or the vehicular means for transmitting messages. The communication channels are the verbal and the nonverbal skills possessed by the sender and the sensory skills possessed by the receiver. Once the message is decoded by the receiver, it has reached a destination which can be considered the response, interpretation, or meaning the receiver assigns to the message. If the receiver answers, the communication cycle begins anew.

The teacher's nonverbal behavior constitutes a model that represents six dimensions of nonverbal activity on a continuum ranging from encouraging to restricting communication, as follows:

TEACHER COMMUNICATION
Encouraging–Restricting
Congruity–Incongruity
Responsive–Unresponsive
Positive–Negative Affectivity
Attentive–Inattentive
Facilitating–Unreceptive
Supportive–Disapproving

Congruity–Incongruity

This dimension refers to the congruity or incongruity that exists between the voice, gesture, and actions of the teacher and the verbal content communicated by the teacher. Congruity occurs when the teacher's verbal message is supported and reinforced by nonverbal behaviors to the extent that there is consonance between verbal intent and nonverbal referents. A mixed message or incongruity exists when there is a discrepancy or contradiction between the verbal message and nonverbal information.

Responsive–Unresponsive

A responsive act relates to modifications in the teacher's behavior as a result of feedback. Verbal feedback occurs when the teacher hears himself talking, but nonverbal feedback is based on the reactions and responses of pupils to the teacher. A responsive act occurs when the teacher alters the pace or direction of a lesson as a result of a detection of misunderstanding or feelings by pupils. Operating on the basis of pupil behavior the teacher uses feedback data to "feedforward" with changed information. Unresponsive acts are an ignoring of or an insensitivity to the behavioral responses of pupils.

Positive–Negative Affectivity

Positive nonverbal expressions convey warm feelings, high regard, cheerful enthusiasm, displays of liking, and acceptance. Negative nonverbal expressions convey aloofness, coldness, low regard, indifference, or display of rejection.

Attentive–Inattentive

Nonverbal expressions may imply a willingness to listen with patience and interest to pupil talk. By paying attention, the teacher exhibits an interest in pupils. By being inattentive or disinterested, the teacher inhibits the flow of communication from pupils, and neither sustains nor encourages sharing information or expressing ideas.

Facilitating—Unreceptive

The teacher is facilitating when acting to perform a function which helps a pupil, usually in response to a detection of pupil needs, urgencies, or problems. This may be in response to a pupil request or a nurturant act. An unreceptive act openly ignores a pupil when a response would ordinarily be expected, may ignore a question or request, or may be a tangential response.

Supportive—Disapproving

Expressions supportive of pupil behavior or pupil interactions manifest approval, indicate being strongly pleased, exhibit encouragement, or connote enjoyment or praise. Disapproving expressions convey dissatisfaction, discouragement, disparagement, or punishment. The expression may be one of frowning, scowling, or threatening glances.

Viewing a teacher's nonverval communication as an encouraging to restricting continuum has the advantage of being related to the communication process and of being indicative of subsequent interpersonal relationships between a teacher and pupils. The model is also useful in regarding the potential influence and consequence of a teacher's nonverbal behavior with pupils. This conceptualization reflects a process point of view: an action system of nonverbal behaviors that exists in dynamic relationship to the continuing influence of the teacher and pupil in interaction.

A requirement of communication in the classroom is that the symbols a teacher chooses from his repertoire must satisfy his own peculiar requirements and meaning and must evoke a similar meaning in the pupil. Communication is successful when the teacher and pupil agree on the interpretation that should be put on the message. Perfect communication is rarely achieved, however, because words are at best mediating symbols between the expressed intent of an inner state of being and the achieved effect they elicit.

Because we can hear ourselves when we talk, adjustments can be made in the intent of our verbal speech. If something uttered verbally does not sound appropriate, it can be restated—we can correct our messages to others. Oral communication permits this marvelous facility for receiving instantaneous feedback of what has been said. Teachers have in fact often suggested that they were not precisely sure of what they thought until they heard themselves speak. Our words become data not only for others but for ourselves, and we can capitalize on our utterances as sort of a feedback-loop to determine if our words meet our test of intent and meaning.

Feedback data from our expression of nonverbal cues are not, however, so easily available; the process is different. We cannot see ourselves when we behave. If we lived in a "world of mirrors" perhaps nonverbal cues could be as easily manipulated as verbal behavior, but this is not the case. We have to rely on the reactions and responses of others in order to comprehend our nonverbal effect in a situation. In the classroom, attending to the responses of students is the major source of information. Teachers differ markedly in their ability to be sensitive to the behavior of youngsters toward them and to use it as feedback data.

The prospect of training teachers to become more knowledgeable of nonverbal cues is in the process of greater development. For the present, it must be stressed that a greater openness to the occurrence of nonverbal events and expressions, plus a greater awareness of student behavior, is the major key. The feedback-loop for the nonverbal is necessarily contingent in great part on the reflective mirror of student reaction and response.

References

Basil Bernstein. "Social Structure, Language, and Learning," *Educational Research*, June 1961, 3, 163-76.

Herbert Blumer. "Social Attitudes and Nonsymbolic Interaction," *Journal of Educational Sociology*, May 1936, 9, 515-23.

Charles Darwin. *The Expression of Emotions in Man and Animals*. New York: Philosophical Library, 1955.

Helen H. Davidson and Gerhard Lang. "Children's Perceptions of Teachers' Feelings Toward Them Related to Self-Perception, School Achievement, and Behavior," *Journal of Experimental Education*, December 1960, 29, 107-18.

Joel R. Davitz, et al. *The Communication of Emotional Meaning*. New York: McGraw-Hill, 1964.

David Efron. *Gesture and Environment*. New York: King's Crown Press, 1941.

Charles M. Galloway. "An Exploratory Study of Observational Procedures for Determining Teacher Nonverbal Communication," doctoral dissertation, University of Florida, 1962.

Charles M. Galloway. "Teacher Nonverbal Communication," *Educational Leadership*, October 1966, 24, 55-63.

Erving Goffman. *The Presentation of Self in Everyday Life*. New York: Doubleday and Co., 1959.

Edward T. Hall. *The Silent Language*. New York: Doubleday and Co., 1959.

Andrew W. Halpin. "Muted Language," *School Review*, Spring 1960, 63, 85-104.

Watson Labarre. "The Cultural Basis of Emotions and Gestures," *Journal of Personality*, September 1947, *16*, 49-68.

Jurgen Ruesch. "Nonverbal Language and Therapy," *Psychiatry*, November 1955, *18*, 323-30.

Jurgen Ruesch and Gregory Bateson. *Communication: The Social Matrix of Psychiatry*. New York: W. W. Norton and Co., 1961.

Jurgen Ruesch and Weldon Kees. *Nonverbal Communication*. Berkeley: University of California Press, 1956.

Claude Shannon and Warren Weaver. *The Mathematical Theory of Communication*. Urbana, Illinois: University of Illinois Press, 1949.

E. Paul Torrance. "Teacher Attitude and Pupil Perception," *Journal of Teacher Education*, March 1960, *11*, 97-119.

2. Categories for Observing Teacher Nonverbal Communication°

The investigator constructed seven observation categories for observing a teacher's nonverbal communication with pupils in instructional settings. The pupose of arriving at the categories was to enable observers to make inferences at the time a nonverbal behavior was enacted by a teacher. When a communicative act occurred, which was related to the category system, observers recorded a number representative of the category. . . . In short, seven categories of a teacher's communicative behavior were recognized which were assumed to be heavily influenced by nonverbal expressions. Three of the categories were considered as encouraging communications, and three were considered as inhibiting. The neutral category of pro forma was considered as neither encouraging nor inhibiting. . . .

Encouraging Communication

1. *Enthusiastic Support.* A nonverbal expression implying enthusiastic support of a pupil's behavior, pupil interaction, or both. An expression that manifests enthusiastic approval, unusual warmth, or emotional support; being strongly pleased. An expression that exhibits strong encouragement to pupil. Examples of nonverbal determinants are as follows:

   1. *Facial expression.* Any expression that implies support or approval of some behavior or interaction occurring in the classroom. Any facial expression that connotes enjoyment, pleasure, or satisfaction with the pupil, or the topic.
   2. *Action.* Any movement or action that portrays enthusiastic approval and active acceptance in an approving way, e.g., a pat on the back,

°Reprinted with permission from Charles M. Galloway. "An Exploratory Study of Observational Procedures for Determining Teacher Nonverbal Communication." University of Florida, Gainesville, 1962. (Unpublished doctoral dissertation.) pp. 65, 67-68, 146-149.

or a warm greeting of praise. An act that endorses approval of the pupil, and gives strong encouragement.
3. *Vocal language.* Any voice quality indicating pleasure or warm acceptance. The use of the voice through intonation or inflection suggest approval and support.

2. *Helping.* A responsive act that relates to modifications in the teacher's behavior which suggest a detection of expressed feelings, needs, urgencies, problems, etc., in the pupil. A communicative act that performs a function which helps a pupil or answers a need. An act that meets a pupil's request; a nurturant act. This act is the spontaneous reaction that the teacher manifests in the form of an actual response. It may be either intellectually supporting, or problem-centered. Examples of nonverbal determinants:

1. *Facial expression.* An expression that implies, "I understand," or "I know what you mean," which is followed up by some kind of appropriate action. An expression that is consistent and sensitive to the pupil's need. A facial expression that registers an acceptance and an understanding of a pupil's problem.
2. *Action.* A movement or action that is intended to help or perform a function for the pupil. The action of the teacher is consistent with the need expressed by the pupil. Any action that suggests understanding and assistance.
3. *Vocal language.* A vocal utterance that is acceptant and understanding. The voice may be tender, compassionate, or supportive; or it may be a laugh or vocalization that breaks the tension.

3. *Receptivity.* A nonverbal expression that implies a willingness to listen with patience and interest to pupil talk. By paying attention to the pupil, the teacher exhibits an interest in the pupil, and implicitly manifests approval, satisfaction, or encouragement. Such a nonverbal expression implies to the pupil that "lines of communication are open."
1. *Facial expression.* Maintains eye contact with pupil in a systematic fashion, exhibiting interest in pupil, pupil's talk, or both. Facial expression indicates patience and attention. Other expressions suggest a readiness to listen, or an attempt at trying to understand.
2. *Action.* The teacher's demeanor suggests attentiveness by the way the total body is presented and movements used. An expressional pose or stance that suggests alertness, readiness, or willingness to have pupils talk. Teacher may be paying attention to pupil talk, even though eye contact is not established. A moving gesture that indicates the pupil is on the "right track." A gesture that openly or subtly encourages the pupil to continue.

3. *Vocal language.* A vocal utterance or vocalization that augments pupil talk, or that encourages the pupil to continue. An utterance indicating "yes-yes" (um-hm), "go on," "okay," "all right," or "I'm listening." Although in a sense, the utterance can be characterized as an interruption, it in no way interferes with the communication process; indeed, such a vocalization supplements, and encourages the pupil to continue.

4. *Pro forma.* A communicative act that is a matter of form, or for the sake of form. Thus, the nature of the act, whether it is a facial expression, action, or vocal language, conveys little or no encouraging or inhibiting communicative significance in the contextual situation; a routine act. When the pupil is involved in a consummatory act, or when it is appropriate or unnecessary for the teacher to listen or to respond, pro forma applies.

Inhibiting Communication

5. *Inattentive.* A nonverbal expression that implies an unwillingness or inability to engage attentively in the communicative process, thus indicating disinterest or impatience with pupil talk. By being inattentive or disinterested the teacher inhibits the flow of communication from pupils.
   1. *Facial expression.* Avoids eye contact to the point of not maintaining attention; exhibits apparent disinterest, or impatience with pupil by showing an unwillingness to listen.
   2. *Action.* An expressional pose or movement that indicates disinterest, boredom, or inattention. A demeanor suggesting slouchy or unalert posture. Body posture indicates "don't care attitude," or an ignoring of pupil talk. Postural stance indicates internal tension, preoccupation with something else, or apparently engrossed in own thought. Either a moving or completed hand gesture that suggests the teacher is blocking pupil talk, or terminating the discussion.
   3. *Vocal language.* A vocal utterance that indicates impatience, or "I want you to stop talking."

6. *Unresponsive.* A communicative act that openly ignores a pupil's need, or that is insensitive to pupil's feeling; a tangential response. Display of egocentric behavior or a domination of communication situation by interrupting or interfering in an active fashion with the ongoing process of communicating between pupils, or from pupil to teacher. An annoying, or abusive act; or a failure to respond when a response would ordinarily be expected by ignoring a question or request.
   1. *Facial expression.* An expression that is troubled, unsure, or unenthused about the topic in question. An expression that threatens

or cajoles pupils; a condescending expression, as unsympathetic expression; or an impatient expression. An obvious expression of denial of feeling of pupil, or noncompliance with a request.

2. *Action.* Any action that is unresponsive to or withdrawing from a request or expressed need on the part of the pupil. An action that manifests disaffection or unacceptance of feeling. A gesture that suggests tension or nervousness.

3. *Vocal language.* A vocalization that interferes with or interrupts ongoing process of communication between pupils, or from pupil to teacher. Such a vocalization, when it is an obvious interruption, appears unresponsive to the flow of communication and to the pupils.

7. *Disapproval.* An expression implying strong disapproval of a pupil's behavior or pupil interaction. An expression that indicates strong negative overtones, disparagement, or strong dissatisfaction.

1. *Facial expression.* The expression may be one of frowning, scowling, threatening glances. Derisive, sarcastic, or disdainful expression may occur. An expression that conveys displeasure, laughing at another, or that is scolding. An expression that "sneers at" or condemns.

2. *Action.* Any action that indicates physical attack or aggressiveness, e.g., a blow, slap, or pinch. Any act that censures or reprimands a pupil. A pointed finger that pokes fun, belittles, or threatens pupils.

3. *Vocal language.* Any vocal tone that is hostile, cross, irritated, or antagonistic to pupil. The vocalization is one of disappointment, depreciation, or discouragement. An utterance suggesting unacceptance.

3. Summary Combining Nonverbal with Verbal Categories*

This Summary represents a system to match Galloway's continuum with Flanders' (Section 2) system of interaction analysis. Each of Flanders' ten categories has a nonverbal extension with the exception of the first, which does not need one. The observer categorizes every three seconds, as with Flanders alone, and writes down the number of the appropriate verbal category. By marking a slash (encouraging) or dash (restricting) to the right of recorded tallies, an observer can record both the verbal and nonverbal dimensions. A circled number is used to enclose the tally when teacher behavior is solely nonverbal. In this way it is possible to categorize verbal (via Flanders) and nonverbal (via Galloway) behavior simultaneously.

*Reprinted with permission from *Theory Into Practice*, 7:177, December, 1968.

SUMMARY of Categories for Interaction Analysis Using Nonverbal Categories

	VERBAL (Flanders)	NONVERBAL (Galloway)	
		ENCOURAGING	RESTRICTING
TEACHER TALK — Indirect Influence	1. ACCEPTS FEELING	1. –	11. –
	2. PRAISES OR ENCOURAGES	2. CONGRUENT: nonverbal cues reinforce and further clarify the credibility of a verbal message.	12. INCONGRUENT: contradiction occurs between verbal and nonverbal cues.
	3. ACCEPTS OR USES IDEAS OF STUDENT	3. IMPLEMENT: implementation occurs when the teacher actually uses student's idea either by discussing it, reflecting on it, or turning it to the class for consideration.	13. PERFUNCTORY: perfunctory use occurs when the teacher merely recognizes or acknowledges student's idea by automatically repeating or restating it.
	4. ASKS QUESTIONS	4. PERSONAL: face-to-face confrontation.	14. IMPERSONAL: avoidance of verbal interchange in which mutual glances are exchanged.
TEACHER TALK — Direct Influence	5. LECTURES	5. RESPONSIVE: change in teacher's pace or direction of talk in response to student behavior, i.e., bored, disinterested, or inattentive.	15. UNRESPONSIVE: inability or unwillingness to alter the pace or direction of lecture disregarding pupil cues.
	6. GIVES DIRECTIONS	6. INVOLVE: students are involved in a clarification or maintenance of learning tasks.	16. DISMISS: teacher dismisses or controls student behavior.
	7. CRITICISMS OR JUSTIFIED AUTHORITY	7. FIRM: criticisms which evaluate a situation cleanly and crisply and clarify expectations for the situation.	17. HARSH: criticisms which are hostile, severe, and often denote aggressive or defensive behavior.
STUDENT TALK	8. STUDENT TALK-RESPONSE 9. STUDENT TALK-INITIATION	8. & 9. RECEPTIVE: involves attitude of listening and interest, facial involvement, and eye contact.	18. & 19. INATTENTIVE: involves a lack of attending eye contact and teacher travel or movement.
	10. SILENCE OR CONFUSION	10. COMFORT: silences characterized by times of reflection, thought, or work.	20. DISTRESS: instances of embarrassment or tension-filled moments, usually reflecting disorganization and disorientation.

33 Motions and the Teacher

Barbara M. Grant and Dorothy Grant Hennings

Turn off the audio in a classroom, and observe a teacher in action. The teacher pulls down a map . . . points to a location on the map . . . adjusts his glasses . . . points to a child to respond . . . shakes his head . . . scratches his chin in a way typically his own . . . moves to the chalkboard . . . picks up a piece of chalk . . . again scratches his chin in that typical way . . . points with the chalk to a second child . . . nods . . . writes the word "China" on the board . . . moves away from the board . . . turns back to the board to dot the "i" . . . drops the chalk . . . slips his hand into his pocket . . . takes his hand out of his pocket to straighten his jacket . . . puts his hand back into his pocket . . . walks toward a child in the front row . . . picks up the child's paper . . . adjusts his own glasses . . . looks at the paper . . . holds the paper so that the child can see it . . . points to a word on the paper . . . shakes his head. . . .

Turn down the volume in a second classroom. There a teacher perches in a relaxed way on the edge of a desk. He looks down at a book in his hand . . . looks up . . . nods to a student . . . then nods to a second student . . . moves his right hand from a position on his hip to the corner of the book . . . turns the page . . . scratches his ear . . . puts his hand back on his hip . . . nods to a third child. . . .

Reprinted by permission of the publisher from Barbara M. Grant and Dorothy Grant Hennings, *The Teacher Moves* (New York: Teachers College Press, Copyright 1971 by Teachers College, Columbia University), pp. 8–24.

Even the most casual, untrained observer can note differences in the kinds of motions these teachers employ, in the purposes for which they use physical motion, and in the meanings they are trying to communicate nonverbally. The trained researcher, using a classification system, is at the opposite end of a continuum; he can analyze such differences with a high degree of reliability. The classroom teacher who has understanding of how motions can be used in the classroom can go beyond even the trained observer; he can learn to produce sequences of motions that add to rather than detract from his verbal teaching.

Instructional and Personal Motions

What are the kinds of motions a teacher uses? Research evidence indicates that teacher motion can be reliably classed as instructional or personal. When categorizing was done by student teachers trained in the use of the two categories, reliability coefficients of .94 to .99 were obtained. These high coefficients seem to suggest that use of the two categories—instructional and personal—is one positive way to look at non-verbal teaching.

Instructional Motions

What is an instructional motion? When the teacher in the example above pulls down the map, picks up the chalk to write on the board, or turns the page of a book, he is readying his materials for teaching. When he points to the map or writes the word "China" on the board, he is focusing the attention of his students. When he points or nods to a child, he may be asking, "Jack, what is the answer?" Each of these motions is instructional because it facilitates teaching. Each is part of a sequence through which the teacher is guiding students in their learning.

Instructional motions are as integral a part of the teaching act as are verbal components. They communicate meanings that are essential in teaching. Motions may "say": "Look here!" "Very good, Susan." "*This* is the important part." "Be quiet!" "Let's get ready." "Let's hurry." "You're next." "*This* is what I mean." "This is what it looks like."

Although instructional motions are integral parts of teaching sequences, these motions are not necessarily performed consciously by the teacher. The teacher may have learned "pointing" to such an extent that this motion has become a natural component of his repertoire of motions; he uses his body without being totally aware of what he is doing.

Of course, many instructional motions are performed consciously by the teacher. The teacher who walks over to the light switch and flicks the lights to get attention is using a device that is part of the stock-in-trade of a teacher. Likewise, the primary school teacher, who reaches for a piece of chalk and breaks it in two before writing, is acting on a principle; she does not want the chalk to squeak.

Personal Motions

How do these motions differ from those that can be called personal? The teacher scratches his ear, puts his hand into his pocket and then takes it out, tugs on his newly sprouting goatee, straightens his jacket, adjusts his glasses. His female equivalent, meanwhile, is playing with her pendant necklace, twisting her engagement ring, adjusting her skirt as she sits down on a low chair, tucking her hair back behind her ear. All of these motions are personal or self-adjusting because they are aspects of the teacher's humanness; they are not employed directly to aid in the learning process.

At times, the teacher uses personal, self-adjusting motions to achieve a more balanced state; he uses them to release tension and to achieve a more relaxed or comfortable bodily position. For instance, he may cross his legs, uncross his legs, lean back in his chair, straighten his body, drop his hand down to his side, clasp his hands, place his elbow on the desk, prop himself against the desk, sit down on a chair. He may put his hands into his pockets, rest his face on his hand, tap his finger on the desk, fan himself with a piece of paper.

Similarly, the teacher may use personal motions in adjusting articles on his body for social or practical purposes. The female teacher who adjusts her short skirt is employing bodily motion for this purpose as is the teacher who adjusts his glasses before looking at a student's paper. Teachers have been recorded on video-tape in the process of adjusting an earring that has fallen off and a slip strap that has fallen down; they have been recorded pulling down a sweater that has ridden up and placing a bobby pin back in the hair.

To some extent, motions may also be symptoms of inner conditions— a cold, a headache, a preoccupation with something else, a momentary itch; to some extent they may be indicative of a transition or change in mood. The teacher rubs the back of his neck, scratches his cheek, takes out a handkerchief, blows his nose, rubs his eye.

Bodily actions known as mannerisms fall into the personal category. We can all remember a teacher who showed marked or excessive adherence to a particular way of using his body—the one who was always twisting his arm behind his neck to scratch, the one who continually was winding his watch, the one who seemed never to stop pacing back and forth, the one who repeatedly pushed back her bangs.

The percentage of personal motions used in a classroom is amazingly high when one considers that such bodily action does not necessarily contribute positively to the instructional process. Of all the motions used by our case study* teachers, 22.1 per cent were personal, and 77.9 per cent were instructional. The verbal equivalents of such personal motions are not that frequent. Teachers do remark: "I am tired." "Opps, I'm going to sneeze." "Excuse me." "Oh dear, I dropped my earring." Yet classroom observation of teachers uncovered only several instances of such verbal, personal actions.

Looking At Instructional Motions

Through studying teacher behavior recorded on video tape, we have identified three categories of instructional motions—conducting, acting, and wielding. Student teachers using these categories have been able to analyze teacher motions with a high degree of reliability; reliability coefficients ranged from .97 to .94. (See Appendix, Table A-1.) This section describes each of the categories.

1.0 Conducting

A teacher physically conducts a class by involving one, some, or all of his students in the lesson. In conducting he uses motions that enable him to control student participation and obtain attending behavior.

1.1 CONTROLLING PARTICIPATION. Physical motions *control participation* by focusing attention on materials, objects, persons, or even symbolic representations. These motions also indicate who the participants should be, when they should participate, and for how long; in a sense they halt or exclude interaction, elicit a physical response, rate a response, or answer the verbal or non-verbal inquiries of students. In addition, the motions regulate the flow, speed, and intensity of the verbal interaction. Examples, taken from actual classroom performances, are:

> moving the head to survey the group
> pointing to a child to begin
> turning to focus on a child
> pointing the microphone from a tape recorder at a child to indicate
>   begin
> using index finger to connect one child's remarks to another child's
> leaning forward toward a child
> cocking head in a questioning way
> cupping hand behind ear
> shrugging shoulders

*The study involved five experienced teachers, men and women, representing grades one through five. In each class there were approximately thirty pupils of various backgrounds. R.T.H., editor.

raising hand to communicate "Would you raise your hand when you want to speak?"

1.2 OBTAINING ATTENDING BEHAVIOR. *Obtaining attending behavior* is another aspect of the conducting act. Motions that obtain attending behavior usually occur prior to the launching of a lesson or during a transitional period within the lesson. They tend to vary from teacher to teacher; but in essence, they are all used for the same purpose—to acquire a spreading stillness or period of tranquility when every eye is focused on the teacher. Such motions are also used to gain the attention of a child who is misbehaving or a group of children who are not conforming to the established behavior pattern. Some examples are:

> clapping hands to gain the attention of the group
> tapping bell
> playing a note on the piano
> placing finger to lips
> holding up hand toward child to indicate: stop misbehaving
> clicking the light switch
> touching child on shoulder
> walking toward front of the room and standing still
> holding up hand to class group: quiet down
> pushing down start button for recording purposes: please be quiet
> because we are recording

That conducting motions can occur in repetitive patterns is evident. A cycle may get under way with the tapping of a bell to obtain attending behavior. The tap may be followed by surveying, pointing, nodding motions. Such a sequence can be repeated over and over again during a lesson.

2.0 Acting

A teacher uses bodily motion to amplify and clarify meanings he is trying to communicate. These motions emphasize or illustrate; in combination they also enable a teacher to make meanings more clear by the complete acting out of words, concepts, or objects, as in role playing and pantomime.

2.1 EMPHASIZING. To *emphasize* a word or group of words a teacher may move his hand as he says the important words. He may swing his head to give emphasis to a word as when he says "No!" to a child. Sometimes he may move his entire torso, as when he moves his body to emphasize the rhythmic flow of language. And sometimes he may gesture with a microphone, chalk, or pointer to emphasize one aspect of the lesson. Some examples are:

    moving finger up and down as he speaks
    giving head a sharp jerk
    moving hand as he says word

2.2 ILLUSTRATING.   To *illustrate* a teacher may use his hands to describe nonverbally some word, concept, or object under consideration. For instance, a teacher may move his hand in a circular pattern to describe what is meant by a spiral; he may point to indicate a direction in which the class should walk. Examples of illustrating are:

    showing the movement of the wind
    showing the size or shape of an object
    indicating what time it is
    counting the numbers on his fingers
    illustrating concepts such as "to go away from" and "to go up"
    referring to someone who has previously spoken

2.3 ROLE PLAYING OR PANTOMIMING.   In a third type of acting, *role playing or pantomiming,* the teacher actually pretends to be an object, an animal, or a character. In this respect his entire body gets into the act. Examples of possible role playing motions are:

    taking on the role of an announcer
    imitating a tiger
    pretending to be a wilting daisy or a flat tire
    hopping like the bunny in the story
    playing dead

Although acting motions aid in the communication of meanings in the classroom, they also serve as interest-provoking devices; and because they do engender interest, they may enable a teacher to maintain student attention after attention has been gained through conducting motions. As a result of this dual function, acting motions serve a valuable purpose in the classroom.

3.0 Wielding

The teacher interacts with objects, materials, or parts of the room by using wielding motions.

3.1 DIRECT WIELDING.   A teacher may wield directly by touching, handling, or maneuvering "things" in the class. He *wields directly* when he is:

    picking up book, pen, pencil, pointer, etc.
    flipping pages in book

placing cover on the back of felt pen
adjusting shades in the classroom
placing globe on floor
holding down rewind button on tape recorder
placing book in lap
using eraser to erase board
writing words for his own use on paper while sitting at desk
writing sentences on board to be used later in the lesson as an
    exercise or assignment

3.2 INDIRECT WIELDING.   A teacher may *wield indirectly* by surveying, scanning, looking at, or reading things in the classroom environment; in this instance, the teacher does not come into direct bodily
contact with the materials, but rather makes motions as he brings his
eyes to a point where they can focus on some written or concrete
material. A teacher wields indirectly when he is:

surveying or scanning books on shelf
standing in front of bookshelf looking for a particular book
looking down at book to read sentence
dropping head toward book to check answer
leaning over books on shelf to select book
glancing at clock to check time
looking down at watch to check time

3.3 INSTRUMENTAL WIELDING.   The teacher also wields when he
makes motions that enable him to interact with the physical environment
of the classroom. These motions involve movement toward objects, materials, or part of the room. Because these motions are instrumental to
the actual maneuvering of objects or materials, they can be called
instrumental wieldings; a teacher wields instrumentally when he is:

walking back to desk
walking over to bookshelf
turning to write an assignment on easel or board for use later on in
    the lesson
walking over to tape recorder to turn off the machine

All wielding motions are not necessarily carried through to a logical,
intended end. For instance, a teacher may begin to walk toward the
tape recorder in a motion that would be classified as "instrumental to
wielding" but never get to complete the action and turn on the recorder.
Some other classroom event or a simple change of mind may interfere

with the completion of the task. All wieldings, therefore, are not productive in terms of carrying the teaching step by step to an end point; some wieldings might even be considered abortive.

Just because a teacher's body comes into contact with an object does not mean that his motion involves a wielding act. A teacher often comes into physical contact with objects in the environment when he is conducting, especially when he is controlling participation. When he touches the chalkboard just beneath a word written there, he may be focusing attention on that particular word; and thus it is a conducting act he is performing rather than a wielding act.

The Meaning of Motions

Throughout this discussion, it probably has become obvious to the reader that the motions of a teacher take on meaning only within the context in which they occur. For instance, a pointing of the finger does not always mean the same thing. Depending on the context, a pointing motion may mean:

> Let's go this way.
> Be quiet, Tracy.
> You recite, Wendy.
> This is the item we will take next.
> Look here.

Likewise, with a nod. A nod may mean:

> Good response.
> This is the end of the lesson.
> Interesting!
> What is the answer, Frank?
> Yes, you may leave the room.

What in one instance may be a motion used to control participation in another case may be a motion that obtains attending behavior, in another a motion that emphasizes, and in still another a motion that wields. One must look at the actual instructional setting to determine the meaning communicated.

Facial Expressions

So far little has been said about the teacher's facial expressions, and yet the facial muscles of most teachers are in a continual state of motion. Teachers smile, frown, grimace, wrinkle their foreheads, pull up their noses, squint, bite their tongues, make a "long face," grin, smirk, beam, and even wiggle their ears.

Instructional Motions

Classroom observations of teaching behavior as well as study of video tapes of classroom action indicate that teachers use movement of facial muscles in much the same way as they use other bodily motions. Many of a teacher's facial expressions are related to the instructional process and can be categorized as conductings, actings, and wieldings.

In using facial conductings to control participation, the teacher:

> smiles at a child, meaning "You answer."
> grins at a child, meaning "We're on the right track."
> smiles at the entire class, meaning "Let's begin."
> beams from ear to ear, meaning "Excellent."
> wrinkles his forehead, meaning "Let's think about that again."

In using facial conductings to obtain attending behavior, the teacher:

> frowns at a child, meaning "Stop fooling around."
> raises his eyebrows, meaning "Pay attention."
> squints at a child, meaning "What are you up to back there?"

In using facial actings to emphasize, the teacher:

> opens his eyes wide on an important statement, indicating "This is significant."
>
> opens his mouth wider as he says an important word.

In using facial actings to illustrate, the teacher:

> puts on a downcast expression while reading a story to show "This is how the child felt."
>
> puffs up mouth and blows out to illustrate "This is the wind."

In using facial actings to pantomime or role play, the teacher:

> puckers up his mouth and "pulls down" his eyes to show "This is what the evil troll looked like."
> puffs out his cheek to make himself look like a chipmunk.

In using facial expressions to wield, the teacher:

squints to read a title on the shelf.
twitches his eye as he reads.

Personal Motions

Facial motions not only are instructionally oriented but also are personal, self-adjusting. The most significant of these motions are those that fall into the category of mannerisms—motions that are repeated incessantly and often are distracting to a listener: the licking or biting of the lips, the clenching of the teeth accompanied by a tightening of cheek muscles.

Not all self-adjusting motions of the face are mannerisms. Just as in the case of other motions, facial expressions can be a reaction to inner conditions or means of adjusting articles on one's body. The teacher who sniffs his nose may be suffering from a cold; the one who wiggles his nose may have a passing itch. Then again that wiggle of the nose may be a way of pushing up one's eye glasses which have slipped down.

Analyzing Facial Expressions

To study facial expressions even with video-taping procedures is an almost impossible task. First, it is often difficult at a distance to determine whether a teacher's expression is a grimace or a frown, a smile or a beam. Then too facial expressions are more a continual state of being—happy, sad, in-between, or even a mask of inner feeling. For these reasons, we have not analyzed facial expressions using statistical techniques and we did not include them in any mathematical interpretation of teaching. Rather we looked at these motions separately in a rather subjective way.

This is not to suggest that facial expressions are an insignificant part of teaching. Just the opposite is true. The expression on a teacher's face may reassure a child, set the climate for the day, or even irritate another child. A child can "read" a teacher's expression, "Miss Jackson is in a bad mood today" and translate that into his own behavior, "I'd better watch out." Or conversely, "Miss Jackson is in a good mood—she won't send me to the office today!"

Motion in the Classroom

What is the teacher doing when he teaches? At the physical level, he is performing as a conductor, using gestures and motions that often bear a striking resemblance to the gestures and motions of a musical conductor. The teacher is also performing as an actor, building interest and clarifying meanings with his body. In addition, he is performing as a technician, wielding aspects of the environment. Finally, the teacher is performing as a human being, bringing with him into the classroom personal motions that do not have an instructional purpose. Each of the categories of physical motion is, thus, based on a nonverbal teaching role.

Although the teacher performs nonverbally as conductor, actor, technician, and person, he does not play each role in equal proportions. It has already been noted that of all the motions used by a sample of teachers, 77.9 per cent were instructional, 22.1 per cent were personal. In the same pilot study on which this book is based, it was also discovered that in the sample group of case study teachers certain instructional motions tend to predominate. The relative proportion of motion types is shown below in Table 1.

Analysis of these data reveals that this restricted population of case study teachers used more "conducting" motions than "acting" or "wielding" motions. These teachers as a group used very few "acting" motions. Within the conducting category the teachers primarily employed motions that controlled student participation in the learning situation; relatively few motions (less than six per cent) were used to obtain attending behavior. Of course, the teachers in this population were highly experienced. The new teacher might find himself using a greater number of such motions.

A Simple Design for Looking at Teacher Activity

Let us now look at a typical classroom episode and analyze the kinds of motions the teacher is using. In so doing we shall consider each of the physical motions in terms of the categories already developed.

T A B L E 1.   How the Teacher Moves

1.0 Conducting			62.5%
	1.1 Controlling Participation	57.04%	
	1.2 Obtaining Attending Behavior	5.47%	
2.0 Acting			8.8%
	2.1 Emphasizing	4.25%	
	2.2 Illustrating	4.45%	
	2.3 Role Playing or Pantomiming	.05%	
3.0 Wielding			28.7%
	3.1 Direct Wielding	11.63%	
	3.2 Indirect Wielding	7.87%	
	3.3 Instrumental Wielding	9.24%	

The Framework

INSTRUCTIONAL MOTIONS.   This category comprises motions that deal with teaching purposes and processes.

    1.0 Conducting: Motions that enable the teacher to control the participation and obtain attending behavior of students. These motions serve to involve the students either verbally or nonverbally.

        1.1 Controlling participation

        1.2 Obtaining attending behavior

    2.0 Acting: Motions that enable the teacher to clarify and amplify meanings by holding the attention of students.

        2.1 Emphasizing (word or group of words)

        2.2 Illustrating (words or concepts)

        2.3 Role playing or pantomiming (objects, animals, characters)

    3.0 Wielding: Motions through which the teacher interacts with aspects of the physical environment—objects, materials, or parts of the room.

        3.1 Direct wielding (touching, handling, maneuvering)

        3.2 Indirect wielding (scanning, looking at, reading: motions made in)

        3.3 Instrumental Wielding (movement toward)

PERSONAL MOTIONS.   This category comprises motions that deal with human purposes and processes.

The teacher says	The children say	The teacher moves
		Walks to the board
		Picks up the chalk
		Tries to write with the chalk but finds it doesn't work
		Looks down at it
		Tries to write with the chalk
		Drops it into the tray
		Picks up another
		Writes on board "The *quaq* _____ is a *floop* _____ ."
Can someone give me real words to put in this sentence?		Turns to the class
		Brushes hand against nose
		Pushes up glasses
		Surveys class
Leslie?		Points to child
	Leslie says: "The dog is a collie."	
Yes.		Nods
		Turns to the board
		Writes dog under *quaq*
		Writes collie under *floop*
		Turns back to the class

The teacher says	*The children say*	*The teacher moves*
Another?		Walks toward Fred, who is not paying attention
		Waves hand at him
		Surveys class
		Points to another child whose hand is raised
	Jack says: "The car is a Ford."	
That's right Jack, "The car is a Ford."		Uses hand as he talks to stress car and Ford
		Walks back to the board
		Writes car under dog
		Writes Ford under collie
		Walks to desk
		Picks up open book
		Scans the page to find another sentence
Let's look at this sentence next.		Returns to the board
		Writes on the board: "The *drikle* gave us some *lacks.*"
Read this sentence and substitute real words for *drikle* and *lacks.*		Turns to the class
		Pumps hand on *drikle* and *lacks*
		Surveys group
		Nods at Tracey
	"The butcher gave us some meat."	
		Turns to the board
		Writes "butcher" under "drikle"
		Writes "meat" under "lacks"
		Surveys class
Frank?	"The cow gave us some milk."	
		Writes "cow" under "butcher"
		Writes "milk" under "meat"
		Drops the chalk
		Turns to the class
		Pulls down his sweater
Let's look at all the words which you have given me: dog, collie, car, Ford, butcher, meat, cow, milk		Folds arms
		Unfolds arms
		Moves finger up and down as he says each word in the sequence
		Moves finger against nose
What are all these words?		Points toward Alex
		Walks toward Fred
		Shakes head at Fred

The Episode

There is a fifth grade lesson in which the teacher is developing the concept of what a noun is. His physical motions are indicated on the right.

His verbal motions are given at the left. The children's comments are noted in the center column to make the meanings of the action clearer to the reader.

During this episode the teacher makes more than forty physical motions. Yet, it is obvious to anyone who has concentrated on study of teacher motions that the number of physical motions is not abnormally high. Teachers in practice tend to be active—perhaps because teaching involves the use of audio-visual, concrete materials: chalkboards, projectors, pens, pencils, paper, books, etc.: perhaps because teaching involves keeping students' attention focused on the subject; perhaps because teaching involves housekeeping tasks: answering telephones, arranging window blinds, opening and closing windows.

What kinds of motions does this teacher make? First, the teacher makes a number of motions that are clearly personal, self-adjusting acts. When the teacher brushes his hand against his nose, he is reacting to some internal bodily condition. When he pushes up his glasses and pulls down his sweater, he is simply adjusting a part of his clothing for practical reasons. When he folds and unfolds his arms, he is taking on a new bodily stance as a means of relaxing.

The other motions he makes are related to the instructional process. As the teacher walks to the board at the beginning of the sequence, the children are expected to follow along with his motions; the motions focus the children's attention. These motions are part of the conducting act, specifically controlling participation. The same can be said of most of the initial motions, other than the interaction with the chalk:

> walks to the board
> tries to write
> tries to write again
> writes on the board "The *quaq* is a *floop*."

The following motions can also be considered in that category:

> points to Leslie
> nods
> turns to board
> writes
> turns back to class
> points to another child.

In the next sequence within the episode the teacher uses conducting motions to obtain attending behavior:

> walks toward Fred, who is not paying attention
> waves hand at him.

These motions communicate to Fred: "I know that you are not paying attention. Stop that!"

On several occasions the teacher uses hand motions that can be considered acting-emphasizing:

> uses hand as he talks to stress car and Ford
> pumps hand on "drikle" and "lack"
> moves finger up and down as he says each word.

These motions add meaning to the utterances they accompany; they clarify what is being said.

The next sequence of motions is again an attempt to control participation by conducting:

> walks back to the board
> writes car under dog, Ford under collie.

These are conducting motions that focus attention because students are supposed to follow these motions.

On the other hand, when the teacher walks to the desk to check the book to determine what the next example will be, the students are not expected to follow his motions. The motions, therefore, are not conducting activities. Rather he is wielding:

> walks to desk (instrumental wielding)
> picks up book (direct wielding)
> scans the page for another word (indirect wielding).

The motion of walking to the desk is instrumental to wielding, for it gets the teacher in a position to wield. The picking up of the book is a direct wielding, for it involves the actual maneuvering of an object. The scanning of the page is an indirect wielding; it involves motions made as the eyes are used to read.

If we return to the introductory sequence of motions, we note some additional "direct wieldings":

> picks up chalk
> drops chalk
> picks up another piece of chalk.

There is also an indirect wielding:

> looks at chalk.

These again are wieldings, for the students are not expected to focus on the chalk. When he tries to use the chalk to write, however, that is a different situation; he expects the students to focus on his activity and, therefore, is controlling participation.

Most of the remaining motions are conductings to control participation:

> returns to board
> writes on board "The drikle gave us some lacks."
> turns to class
> nods at Tracey
> turns to board
> writes "butcher"
> writes "cow"
> turns to class
> points to Alex.

Each of these motions focuses attention on the subject of the lesson or identifies participants.

The final motions involving Fred are disciplinary and are to obtain attending behavior:

> walks toward Fred
> shakes head at Fred.

Analysis of Episode

Within this episode the use of the body in the instructional process is rather typical of teacher performance in a discussion situation. The teacher is primarily using conducting motions basically to control participation and to a much lesser extent to obtain attending behavior. Acting motions are rather infrequent as is generally true; the only use is to emphasize, which in most classroom situations is more common than the use of pantomiming motions.

Since this teacher was working within a chalkboard-book lesson format, wieldings employed were rather limited to interaction with the chalk and the book. Wieldings, of course, would be more frequent and varied in situations in which the teacher uses paper, scissors, tape-recorders, maps, projectors, crayon, paint pots, scientific equipment.

One warning must be interjected at this point. It would be unfortunate to characterize in a general way this teacher's performance based on this very limited teaching sample of less than two minutes. Teachers do vary in their physical activity from one episode to another. That this is true can be understood by considering just how a cold can affect the personal motions of a teacher. The brushing of the nose might be a cold-associated motion that would not reappear in future episodes. Similarly if the teacher were using an overhead projector rather than the chalkboard, a different sequence of motions would result. If we sample episodes from a number of lessons, however, and find the same approximate numbers and kinds of bodily motion often appearing, we can begin to characterize the teacher's general patterns of motion.

When we looked at the classroom activity of a group of teachers whose behavior was analyzed in detail, we found that a single short episode taken from each of five lessons produced a rather consistent picture of the teacher's performance. Teachers do tend to have their own typical repertoire of motions upon which they draw again and again.

34 Nonverbal Observables

Robert Koch

> *Fie, fie upon her!*
> *There's language in her eyes,*
> *her cheek, her lip.*
> *Nay, her foot speaks; her wanton*
> *spirits look out at every*
> *joint and motive of her body.*
>
> Shakespeare: *Troilus and Cressida*

This paper is part of a systems analysis begun during the fall semester of 1970, and conducted by the School Psychology Department of George Peabody College.

A junior and a senior high school in Davidson County, Tennessee were selected for the analysis; they will be referred to as Junior and Senior Schools.

There were two major reasons for undertaking a systems analysis of Junior and Senior Schools. The first was to gather information on patterns of interaction among members of the schools' social system to study

Reprinted with permission from *Theory Into Practice*, 10:288–294, October, 1971.

how these patterns related to the achievement of the schools' goals, and to make the data available to the faculties to aid in their own assessments of their schools. The second reason was for purposes of training students in the School Psychology Training Program at George Peabody College.

My part in this analysis was observing the extent and nature of the nonverbal communication that occurred in randomly selected classrooms.

Teacher and student interviews and informal conversations were conducted to supplement the one hour classroom visitations. Also some isolated incidents were observed by chance and noted for their nonverbal content.

What is Nonverbal Language?

Any message sent or received, independent of the written or spoken word, is an instance of nonverbal language. It can even be distributed among and around the very words themselves, as loudness or silences.

C. W. Morris's (1946) definition will not be used here. He says that language consists of signals which both the receiver and sender are aware of. This seems to be a definition of communication. In using spoken language, the sender usually knows what he has said, but the receiver may not, as in the case of a language unknown to him, or an unusual accent, or a sprinkling of scientific terms or polysyllabic words. In these last examples, communication to the degree intended did not take place, but language was used. Neither the sender nor the receiver needs to understand the message, or even be aware of it, in order for it to be called language.

Nonverbal messages abound, and we "read" a lot of them without being aware of doing so. Consider the umpire's "You're out" signal; a stethoscope extending out of a white coat pocket; the hippie's hair and beads; the soldier's posture; the occupational stigmata of the restaurant cook's pallor and numerous thin-line horizontal burns on his lower forearms. These are nonverbal signals that tell us something. How can a boy accurately pick out, in a new school, the boys he can "lick" and the ones he can't, almost at first glance?

A List of Nonverbal Observables

This paper deals with the quantity and type of nonverbal cues that were observed in various randomly selected classrooms in a junior and a senior high school. Other than classifying a nonverbal signal as positive or negative, no meanings will be assigned to the items below. However, the reader will automatically assign judgments; otherwise, the nonverbal data are meaningless. To say that a wind blew through the window of the classroom is only physics if the children's reactions aren't noted. Were they pleased with its cooling effect or were they chilled by it?

The nonverbal behaviors observed included the following:

1. Gestures
2. Hand movements
3. Foot movements
4. Voice variations
5. Silences
6. Facial expressions
7. Eye-Language
8. Head movements
9. Nose movements
10. Lip movements
11. Postures
12. Gaits
13. Body shape and tonus
14. Skin: pallor, flushing, sweating
15. Ties
16. Territoriality shown
17. Proximity used
18. Handwriting
19. Art, drawing, doodling
20. Laughter
21. Breathing
22. Tactility
23. Prearranged signals
24. Clothes, hair, jewelry
25. Occupational stigmata
26. Use of time
27. Lack of essentials
28. Lack of expected reaction
29. Status moves or acknowledgment
30. Room appearance and arrangement
31. Modality for presenting lesson: visual, auditory, kinesthetic
32. Rituals and stereotyped behavior
33. Scratching, self-stroking
34. Toying with objects
35. Hesitations

To list all the ramifications of the above would require a paragraph for some, a page for others, and a chapter for still others. British anthropologist Brannigan (1969) has listed 135 gestures and Birdwhistell (1970) claims 20,000 facial expressions are somatically possible.

The Need for Knowledge of Nonverbal

Shertzer (1968) says, "Understanding by the counselor of the client, then, is the ability to infer meaning and significance from the student's verbal and nonverbal behavior, and at the same time the client is giving a verbal message, the counselor is sending, nonverbally, interest, boredom, etc."

According to Dr. Ruth Strang (1965), "Acceptance of the student may be indicated by the interviewer's bodily position, facial expression, gestures."

Milton Hahn and Malcolm MacLean (1955) say, "Our biggest criticism of counselors and teachers is that they either talk too much or too little, ignoring the highly significant elements of nonverbal (both their own and the student's) cues which are as basic to communication as words."

Steiner (1965) says vast domains of meaning are the province of nonverbal language: "Verbal language can deal only with surfaces . . . reality begins where verbal language leaves off."

Results of a study by Davidson and Lang (1960) imply that teachers communicate different feelings toward children: "Teachers vary in their inclination and/or their capacity to communicate favorable feelings. It seems urgent that teachers be helped to recognize the significance of the feelings which they express toward children, consciously or unconsciously."

Halpin (1960) states that training programs for school teachers "ignore the entire range of nonverbal communication, the muted language in which human beings speak to one another more eloquently than with words."

Ernest Beier tells a story about an elderly teacher, Miss R., that makes our point well. A nonverbal observer had been called into the case to find out why her discipline was deteriorating.

He reported that when Miss R. entered her room, she looked confused. This emotional climate was created by an uncertain gait, a bewildered facial expression, and she watched the floor as though she might stumble. She ignored the noisy class and they her. They went on talking.

She sat at her desk, fumbled with books, laid them aside, reached for them again, found passages, and marked these with hastily torn slips of paper.

Suddenly she looked up as though aware for the first time that others were about, picked out a single student, glared, and threatened to send him to the principal. The class was silent just a moment, then ignored her and resumed making noise. The one student heeded her admonition. Evidently they had learned that she would carry out her threats, but only to the one addressed.

She began her lesson. She knew her subject, but sounded bored. Nonverbal cues were clearly communicated to the class by her facial expression, her monotone, and her stance. Her class responded appropriately with yawns.

She paid good attention to any single student working at the board, but ignored the group as if they weren't there.

She did not smile, stand near or touch anyone, or meet gazes with eye contact.

The children, as though testing the limits, grew noisier, walked about, punched each other, ignored the lesson. She, perhaps rightly, made no attempt to reach them by raising her voice, and they couldn't have heard the lesson above the bedlam.

The consultant later told her that she communicated interest in one student at a time. This communicated the impression that she was afraid to deal with the group. Then he went over her other nonverbal errors and showed her how to correct them.

Plan of Observation

A cluster incident refers to a happening. Let's say a boy comes in late to class and presents an admission slip from the office, then takes his seat. From a constellation of verbal and nonverbal signals, the observer detects a main theme: for example, the boy is nervous and anxious and the teacher is disturbed. This is described in sentences under the heading "Cluster Incident" because a cluster of nonverbal events contributed to the main theme. Then a single cue can be assigned meaning. A frown alone, out of context, might mean concentration, but in the incident above, probably means annoyance.

Under *Cluster Incident* are words such as *Gestures* and *Posture*, each followed by a short blank. After the cluster incident is described in sentences, the teacher's nonverbal behavior that accompanied it is charted with numerals in the short blanks. The numerals are taken from a second sheet listing possible variables, e.g. *Gestures* has 15 numbered choices.

For example, a 2 next to *Facial* on the form represents a frown. Besides *Gestures* the observer may put 4, 8. These denote inner-directed and forceful. *Posture* may get a 3 (rigid) and *Eyes* might be left blank because the observer wasn't close enough or in a position to see changes in luster or size of pupils.

The beginning nonverbal observer may become confused, because so much happens nonverbally! One can shut off his verbal output, but not his nonverbal. Example: A silence can have dramatic meaning: turning away and ignoring people is nonverbal chatter. Imagine entering a classroom where every person is talking at once. One would concentrate on the voices he wanted to hear, filtering the input. Nonverbal may be handled the same way.

Becoming alerted to the concept of nonverbal can do much for the beginner. At Peabody, as the year progressed, we were aware that students had become convinced that nonverbal language existed and was important.

Though many signals are idiosyncratic, the beginning observer understands many things as soon as he begins to look for them. See how that superintendent ends an interview by starting to shuffle papers; that principal by scooting his chair back and tensing his body trunk as he grips the chair arms in both hands; and that supervisor by glancing at her watch. These actions could be unconscious or deliberate. Soon the neophyte sees examples of nonverbal everywhere: That boy who eats lunch alone at a back table and blocks the rest of the seat by sitting at the entrance end. The woman who didn't fix up a bit for the pastor's visit.

Observation Results—Raw Data

Only behaviors of twelve teachers while teaching classes are shown below. Isolated events happening elsewhere are reported later.

A trait or a nonverbal signal had to be a regularly occurring event to be reported. Examples: "Smiles . . . 6," or "Touched students . . . 1," means six teachers smiled a good deal of the time and one teacher touched students often. Isolated events, e.g., one smile or one touch during an hour's teaching would not be included.

Eye-contact		Voice (Continued)	
Met students' gazes	11	Repetition of words	0
Avoided eye contact	1	Too soft to hear well	0
		Sniffs	0
Walking and Gait		Shrillness	0
Vagrant, peripatetic, restless		Tremulous	0
moving about	2	Words spaced out	0
		Too high pitch	0
Voice		Nasal	0
Shows anger	0	Scratchy	0
Choking	0	Dialect (Southern)	2
Uses filler-talk	0	Good clear voice	10
Grunts	0	Mispronunciations	
Interrupts students	1	Oil = oll	
Too loud	0	Senator = sinater	
Overtalkative	0	tar = tor	2

Facial
Bites lip	0
Blinks	0
Frowns	0
Furtive glances	1
Glares	0
Excessive mouth movements	1
Raises eyebrows	0
Stares	0
Tears flow easily	0
Grins	1
Smiles	6
Quickly flashed smile	2
Thin-lipped painful smile	1
Too serious, never smiles	2

Student Behavior
Black students clustered in peripheral groups	4
Black students seem free of tension	12
Students seek attention by talking out	1

Teacher Dress
Appropriate	10
Ostentatious	1
Over-dressed	1
Neat	12
Dirty	0
Colors match	12

Proximity
Stood close to students	4
Approached middle distance	0
Stayed as far as possible	8
Leaned over students' work	2

Territoriality Shown 0

Gestures
Many	4
Few	7

Gestures (Continued)
None	1
Gives directions with	2
Agitated, rapid, useless hand flutters	1

Molar Impression
Aloof, bored, disinterest	1
All business, we've got a lesson to cover	12
Angry attitude	0
Anxious	0
Calm	12
Shows empathy or sympathy	3
Forceful personality	6
Frustrated air	0
Positive learning situation: students eager, interested	3
Negative learning situation: students turned off	1
Neutral learning situation: if you want to learn, ok; if not, it's your business	8
Teacher lectures, little student discussion	9
Negative use of time	0
Noisy room, teacher ignoring	3

Hands
Clasped	0
In pockets	1
Fists	0
Juxtapositional	1
Preening	4
Restless	4
Stroking face	3
Touching face	5
Tapping, drumming	0
Toying with objects	2
Tremor	0
Scratching body	2
Immobile hands	1
Touch jewelry	2

Teacher Sitting		Use of Nonverbal (Cont.)	
Sits while teaching	3	Sarcastic verbally	1
Immobile	1	Sarcastic nonverbally	3
Relaxed	2	Gave verbal reinforcement	4
Rigid, tense	1	Gave nonverbal reinforcement	4
Use of Nonverbal		Gave little reinforcement	7
Used a lot	3		
Used moderate amounts	2	**Quasi-Courtship Used**	**0**
Used little or none	7		
Gave directions verbally	12		
Gave directions nonverbally	3	**Quasi-Courtship Disclaimers**	**0**

Raw-Data Conclusions

There was a scattering of negative nonverbal traits and mannerisms idiosyncratically distributed. One teacher seemed bored with it all, and this attitude was reflected by the students. One teacher avoided eye contact with the students, though not with the observer. Two had hard-to-understand voices. Then there was a scattering of nervous mannerisms that were distracting—useless, agitated hand gestures, mouth movements, repeated touching of hair or face, and scratching.

More widespread was the long distance from pupils maintained by some teachers, nonverbal putting down of students, and neutral learning situations.

In general there is much more positive than negative nonverbal in the two schools that were observed, but it is regretted that only 25% of the classes were really enthusiastic and only a similar percentage of teachers communicated interest in students.

Positive signals used by the majority of the teachers were eye contacts, task-oriented, in-command miens, adequate voices, appropriate dress, and frequent smiles. Relaxed students were a vivid nonverbal sign that much is good in Junior and Senior Schools.

An Observed Cluster Incident

We have been told that, in case of nonagreement between a sender's verbal and nonverbal communication, the nonverbal will be believed (Galloway, 1970). T. Kaul (1971) has verified this in experiments at The Ohio State University.

It was exciting, then, for this observer to see such an episode unexpectedly unfold. A thirty-year-old white female teacher was telling her class of eleventh graders about the horrendous conditions of the early slaughterhouses in Chicago—the cruelty to the animals—the unsanitary conditions. Vividly experiencing the impact of her own words, her nonverbal showed extreme distaste of these happenings, though her voice, strangely enough, was rather emotionless and routine. Her eyes distended showing much white; her breathing quickened. This was the only time during the class period when she left her desk and approached the students, coming quite close. Forceful, chopping gestures were made with her left forearm, her elbow fixed, her fingers in rigid curvature as though gripping a baseball.

Note-taking forgotten, the class absorbed the emotional nonverbal message. They sat up straighter, eyes glued to the teacher's face. The boys' faces assumed grim, compressed-lipped expressions while the girls winced at gory parts, their shoulders moving slightly forward and upward in contiguity with a squinting of eyes and a tightening of lips.

One girl was not involved emotionally and sat slumped in her seat, feet spread, knees straight with a heel against the floor in each aisle. Her eyes flicked about the room while a pencil gripped between the extended index and middle fingers made rapid arcs at right angles to the fingers. One almost expected a yawn.

At certain places in the lecture, events were described which were not especially exciting by themselves (bristles were removed, the meat cooled, etc.), but the teacher's negative nonverbal continued, perhaps from inertia. At these points there was incongruity—verbal did not agree with nonverbal—yet the class believed the nonverbal, paid scant attention to the words' content, and continued their wincing and grimacing.

An Observed Nonverbal Incident

A black administrator, in charge of discipline, was wont to stand on the cafeteria steps at lunchtime, eyes casting about for miscreants. Head and trunk immobile, right hand on hip, elbow thrust into view, feet in a wide stance, he drew many a furtive glance from the passing and eating students. Baleful and threatening, he reminded the observer of a prison guard. Suddenly a motion caught the observer's eyes—the sphinx had moved! He had stepped one step forward, and now with both hands on hips, stared at a black girl. What crime she had committed is not known. She seemed to sense the concentrated gaze and glanced at him, then away, then back again. With a slow deliberate movement, his right hand moved off the hip, up the trunk to eye-level, then outward, ending stiff-armed, index finger extended and aimed at the girl. Motionless perhaps four seconds, the hand suddenly snapped palm up and toward the man in a "come here" gesture, then slowly found the hip again.

Realizing that she was the object summoned, she awkwardly rose and slowly approached him. As she approached, the man's gaze was fixed beyond her at the back of the room, and halfway, the girl faltered and stopped as though there was a possibility that she hadn't been summoned after all. Instantly the stare found her and she resumed her approach. The gaze again sought the back of the room.

The girl mounted two steps, paused, then continued hesitatingly to the top. He let her stand a few seconds, then, without once looking at her, slowly withdrew a small notebook from his pocket, flipped to an empty page, and holding it in position for writing, reached for a pencil with the other hand. The pencil point positioned itself for writing and only then did his eyes move—they dropped to the notebook.

The girl seemed to understand the routine and began speaking—probably giving identifying information.

After he finished writing, the routine was reversed and when the gaze again was afar and the hands back on the hips, the girl realized that she was dismissed and scurried off throwing one quick glance over her shoulder at him.

The observer was not able to watch the rest of the students' reactions to this little drama, but quick glances revealed that most students simply ignored it.

A Portion of a Taped Interview

Teacher: Give me a short definition of nonverbal, then we can go from there.

Interviewer: Have you ever known something about someone that wasn't said to you? No one told you?

Teacher: Yeah, for instance, that J_____ dame hates me.

Interviewer: If she didn't say so, how do you know? Perhaps she is very fond if you.

Teacher: (laughing) That would be the day! No, I can just tell—like she won't speak if she can get out of it—pretends to be engrossed in papers in her hands or something like that. And her eyes . . . well, they're sort of frosty, if you know what I mean.

Interviewer: That's nonverbal. You picked up signals and read them. You simply compared the signals to past experiences.

Teacher: Then I've been using nonverbal all my life. But how can you nonverbal guys say emphatically and without reservation that from, say facial expression and posture, you felt that the man was physically tired? How do you know that he is not sick or mentally depressed?

Interviewer: Well, actually we don't. Notice you said, "felt he was tired." We qualify conclusions. Sometimes we are guilty of your charge, but it's assumed—I mean, if I say he's tired—that the listener will understand that at best it is conjecture, an educated guess. I just had a thought (voice enthusiastic); you realized a minute ago that a fellow could be sick, or tired, or disturbed, and that the nonverbal cues might all look alike. So you know more about nonverbal than you realized!

Teacher: Now, I've read some stuff—like if a girl crosses her legs a certain way . . . perhaps like the Freudians, you are reading too much into too little.

Interviewer: That's huckster-writing. No nonverbal observer would use a single cue, no more than you would a single word. In many cases, the verbal actually sends the message and the nonverbal is used to attach affect or to see if the speaker really meant the words. A fellow named Albert Mehrabian says only 7% of a message is verbal.

Teacher: 7%? He's gotta be wrong. I think words are the best way . . . Let me think . . . Suppose the nonverbal person went by the crossed legs and I went by the word, "Bed?" that she said to me. I bet I'd be more sure than he would.

Interviewer: With just crossed legs to go by, I dare say you would! But let's isolate the pure word. You're sitting back-to-back with a woman and she says, "bed." You've got nothing but a word. But when *you* said "Bed?" before, you put a lot of nonverbal into it. You put a vocal inflection at the end, turning it into a question, and you tossed your head sideways toward a certain bedroom, and you tried to put a sexy expression on your face, but it didn't come off. (laughter)

Teacher: I'll have to practice. (laughter)

Interviewer: Anyhow, any number of people, I think Eric Berne is one, claim that the sexier a woman acts and looks, the more chance that she's a teaser . . . so in the "will she or won't she" cases, knowing what nonverbal is valid is the thing. But let's take your *bed* example a little further to show you that we don't use one clue. Actually you would have been reading a lot of nonverbal that led up to that one word. Maybe you had felt her heart beating while you danced and she gave your hand a couple of quick squeezes or breathed harder. Then her eyes—they really talk.

Teacher: Like a girl I was dancing with once during the war. She actually reached and grabbed me. That was one nonverbal message I read loud and clear! (laughter)

Proposed Followup

It seems valid to assume that most faculties could benefit from being trained to use more nonverbal signals of a positive nature.

Verbally telling a student, "I like you; I accept you; I expect you to learn," will not suffice if the accompanying nonverbal is saying, "But you and I both know I don't and you won't."

Rosenthal's (1968) findings that teachers' expectations *are* realized, that teachers can "will" a child to learn, must have a nonverbal basis. No other answer explains the phenomenon (Christiansen, 1970).

Teacher Training

Nonverbal training of teachers should first be cleared with the school administration, starting with the principal. The next step involves contacting the Faculty Advisory Committee, and securing their blessing. They would be asked to "spread the word" so that the next step would not meet the usual resistance to a new idea.

At a general teachers' meeting the plan would be explained in general terms and volunteers enlisted.

There can be little success without the use of volunteers, but here may lie some difficulties. Volunteering teachers may be a different sort from abstainers who will comprise the controls. Might not the volunteering teachers need improvement less? Also, volunteers are apt to be younger than nonvolunteers.

The volunteers would then each be observed while teaching to establish baselines for future reference. Voices would be taped.

This would be followed by a meeting where the nonverbal concept would be discussed and a hand-out describing positive and negative nonverbal signals would be given for home reading.

After the first meeting and the home reading, they would have enough information to start using proximity, tactility, face work, eye contact, and so on.

Soon would follow another meeting where specifics would be dealt with. Volunteers would relate experiences in attempting the new medium. Some role-playing, sensitivity encounters and previously practiced skits would be used. The actors in some cases would be comprised of the teachers present, and in others by the Student Drama Club. After viewing, the audience would react. Like videotape (which might be used), a skit can be rerun to impress its point or to clear up an obscure part. Skits and role-playing help to increase teachers' abilities to "read" the nonverbal of their students. The writer presented such skits under Dr. Ernest Siegel at the University of New Mexico and they were very successful.

One lady, playing the part of a high school student who resents her mother's quasi-courtship flirting, remarked after the skit, "Golly, even though it was all make-believe, I could feel the tension build in the audience. It was like real and I really felt like that girl felt by going through her emotions."

Proposed Study

A dissertation proposal is being prepared at this time based on the above Teachers' Training Program.

Randomly selected classes of the teachers who received nonverbal training will be matched with control groups on as many variables as is practical.

Paper and pencil instruments will be used to measure the attitudes of students toward themselves, their teachers, certain school subjects, and learning. These will be administered to both experimental and control groups.

Teachers' attitudes will be plumbed with a similar device, and like the students' will be administered pre- and post-intervention.

A behavior rating scale, pre and post, will measure positive and negative behavior of students in the experimental and control groups (Haring and Phillips, 1962).

Achievement tests are regularly given, both spring and fall, in the school system that will house the study. Achievement scores gains for the school year will be compared among groups. Certain randomly selected students' individual gains will be compared, subject by subject, with achievement score gains in other years.

References

E. G. Beier. *The Silent Language of Psychotherapy*. Chicago: Aldine Publishers, 1966, pp. 180-93.

E. Berne. *Games People Play*. New York: Grove Press, 1968.

R. L. Birdwhistell. *Kinesics and Context*. Philadelphia: University of Pennsylvania Press, 1970.

R. Brannigan. "Man's Silent Signals: Nonverbal Vocabulary of Gestures and Expressions." *Time* (13 July 1969): 86.

J. E. Christiansen, President Emeritus, North West Community College, Powell, Wyoming, 1970 (in conference).

H. H. Davidson and G. Lang. "Children's Perceptions of Teachers' Feelings Toward Them Related to Self-perception, School Achievement, and Behavior." *Journal of Experimental Education* 24 (December 1960): 107-18.

C. M. Galloway. The Ohio State University, Columbus, Ohio, 1970 (in correspondence).

A. W. Halpin. Muted Language. *School Review* (Spring 1960): 85-104.

N. Harring and E. Phillips. "Proposed Rating Schedule for Classes of Exceptional Children. In *Educating Emotionally Disturbed Children*. New York: McGraw-Hill Company, 1962, pp. 303-11.

T. Kaul. School of Psychology, The Ohio State University, Columbus, Ohio, 1971 (in colloquium).

A. Mehrabian and M. Wiener. "Non-immediacy between Communication and Object of Communication in a Verbal Message." *Journal of Consulting Psychology* 30 (1966): 5.

D. Morris. *The Naked Ape.* New York: Delta, 1969.

R. Rosenthal and L. Jacobsen. *Pygmalion in the Classroom.* New York: Holt, Rinehart and Winston, 1968.

E. Siegel. Home-study, New York City Public Schools, 1970 (in conference).

R. Strang, Professor Emeritus, Columbia University, 1964 (in correspondence).

9 *Strategies*

Overview

This section is different from the others. In the preceding eight sections it is fairly easy to abstract concepts shared by the authors. In the section on aesthetics, for example, such concepts as beauty, form, balance, and conflict unify the various articles; and in the section on communications, the concepts of input, output, channel, message, and feedback are held in common by the authors. But in this section it would be difficult to find a unifying set of terms for the selections. This section serves as a culmination of the others, for a strategy is a deliberate pattern of actions aimed at achieving a specific goal. A strategy comes after we determine the goal and understand fully the nature of the activities to be performed. Thus, we need a strategy, or strategies, to achieve certain cognitive behavior or to bring about a particular climate in the classroom. In these two senses, at least, this section stands apart from the others.

Moreover, the articles in this section do not concentrate on describing or analyzing the nature of strategy but rather present primarily strategies for teaching. Socrates presents a strategy to show that there is no such thing as teaching but only recollection; Oliver and Shaver present two teaching styles, or strategies, for presenting public issues, and in an updating of their article Shaver and Larkins present a third style; Taba and Elzey present an analysis of teacher-pupil interaction aimed at getting pupils to perform on various levels of three cognitive tasks; Suchman presents a strategy for teaching the pupil an inquiry strategy in science;

and Broudy offers three prescriptive styles for improving teaching. Resnick focuses on describing teacher behavior in the informal British infant school where the strategy employed is popularly known as "open education."

The concept of strategy is used in situations where attainment of one's goal is blocked by someone or something. To overcome the conflict posed by the opposition, whatever it is, a strategist maps out his plan of attack according to the strengths of his forces and his opponent. He carefully interrelates the order and timing of his actions. He even plans for possible retreating and regrouping actions. He takes into account his opponent's possible behavior. His strategy, in short, is a plan for the most efficient and quickest victory in light of his opponent's position and the prevailing general conditions.

It is no wonder, then, that strategy is first and foremost a concept used by the military. In war we have the prime example of someone deliberately and forcefully countering the actions performed against him. Strategy is also employed in such games as chess, tennis, and basketball, in which one person or team matches ability with another person or team with the intention of overcoming competition. Strategy is used in other situations, too, where there is conflict, as in political contests, world diplomacy, labor-management relations, and race relations.

As always, we must ask whether the concept of strategy and its accompanying concepts of attack, retreat, force, enemy or opponent, and timing can be meaningfully applied to teaching. Are there sufficient similarities with war and chess, for example, to warrant the use of the concept of strategy in teaching? Many would strongly argue that there are, that strategy applies closely to teaching. It applies because there are specified goals to be attained in the classroom and because a variety of means can be used to attain them. Furthermore, teachers and pupils often see each other as opponents, not only for leadership control of classroom activities, but also in a battle of wits related to the topic at hand.

Some would argue that strategy applies to teaching just as it applies to any situation where goals are to be attained. That is, strategy in teaching is a plan for achieving the goal of learning, but that goal in no way implies a victory for the teacher and a defeat for the pupil. The teacher and pupil are to be viewed as cooperating in a plan that benefits both of them but primarily the pupil. In the sense that a teaching strategy is a plan to attain certain goals and to guard against undesirable results, the concept of strategy is meaningful for teaching.

Obviously, the authors in this section feel that strategy does apply to teaching, whether they say so explicitly or by implication. According to Taba and Elzey, "the chief task of teaching . . . is to determine the order of learning tasks and to pace each step appropriately. This is a crucial point in the formulation of teaching strategies, and one against which current teaching methods commit the greatest errors." Perhaps the most famous teaching strategy is the one named after Socrates. The famous selection from the Meno illustrating the Socratic style is a demonstration to Meno of how to conduct inquiry. Socrates employs his particular strategy, while at the same time commenting about it, so that Meno will understand it. Also, he talks about geometry, as opposed to such concepts as virtue and piety. A careful reading and analysis of this selection from Plato will reveal the elements of Socrates' strategy. The reader is asked to consider which points are crucial to this style of teaching.[1] (I use the term *teaching* in spite of Socrates' objection.) For example, is it possible to employ the Socratic strategy if we do not accept the fact that man acquires his knowledge not in this life but at some other time? Is it possible to use this strategy with areas of mathematics other than geometry? Can we use it with history? With economics? With literature? With biology? With physics? With art? With music? If this strategy cannot be used with a particular subject, then we must consider in what ways this subject differs from geometry.

A further clue about the Socratic strategy appears in the article by Oliver and Shaver. In their research on teaching social studies within a framework of public issues, these researchers set forth several dimensions for describing the act of teaching. Then, within these dimensions, they describe two styles, one of which is the Socratic analytic strategy. It will be helpful to the reader to use their specification of the Socratic style as a means of examining the selection from Plato.

Broudy presents three strategies of teaching and discusses the characteristics of each. He then goes on to show the effect of the wonder machines of modern electronic technology on these three strategies, especially on didactics. The addendum, which comes from his book on the public schools, clearly and specifically indicates how these three strategies apply to the elementary and secondary levels of teaching. Obviously, Broudy's points on didactics, heuristics, and philetics pertain to all levels of teaching, but there is a matter of differing proportions of each depending on level.

Taba speaks of strategies for teaching thought processes. By analyzing classroom discourse along three dimensions—designation, function, and levels of thought—Taba and her associates are able to describe the flow of classroom talk and the effect of various strategies on the thought processes performed verbally. This is similar to Oliver and Shaver's attempt to study the effect of the recitation and Socratic styles on learning outcomes and teaching behavior.

---

[1]For an analysis of Socratic teaching and suggestions for implementing this strategy see Ronald T. Hyman, *Ways of Teaching* (Philadelphia: J. B. Lippincott Company, 1974).

Suchman differs from the others in that his strategy is, in essence, to teach a strategy. Suchman is interested in having the pupils inquire productively, and therefore his approach is to teach the pupils a strategy. Part of the teacher's strategy is to present a concrete problem and then to require the pupils to solve that problem by asking only questions that can be answered yes or no. Though Suchman concentrates on the three stages for pupil inquiry, the reader will easily be able to extract the components and justification of the teacher's strategy.

Three studies in this section deal with the analysis of teacher-pupil verbal behavior. Taba and Elzey, Oliver, Shaver, and Larkins, and Resnick analyze classroom discourse. The reader may wish to compare their three sets of categories. Furthermore, since these are all involved in content analysis, it would be worthwhile to compare them to the studies in the section on Cognitive Processes.

A word about the units of behavior used in these three investigations is appropriate. Taba and Elzey, and Oliver and Shaver use the unit of thought, though they define it in different ways. Resnick categorizes "each utterance" (statement or question) by the teacher.

It is important to note that none of the three units of behavior is a time unit. The reason appears to be the belief that strategies will not be found in any given sample of time. Also, a short time period will quite likely fragment an existing strategy.

It is appropriate to comment on the Shaver and Larkins updating of the original study by Oliver and Shaver. Shaver and Larkins conducted their study in a rural-suburban high school on the outskirts of Ogden, Utah, rather than in the original New England junior high school setting. Moreover, the Utah researchers added a third style of teaching, seminar teaching, to the original Socratic and recitation styles. In seminar teaching "the students are presented with a case, as with the recitation and Socratic discussions, told that their task is to discuss the case, trying to identify the issue it poses and coming to a decision about the issue, applying the concepts that had been studied in the regular class meetings. The teacher's role, the students are told, is to answer questions that they might have (to serve as an information-idea source) and occasionally to help structure the discussion by suggesting relevant concepts."[1]

Resnick's is one of the few studies that reports data on the observation of teachers in an open education environment. One other study is referred to by Tuckman (Section 5) as he reports data from a study on open education in New Jersey modeled on the British informal teaching strategy. Resnick is struck by the high percentage of questions asked by

[1]James P. Shaver and A. Guy Larkins, *The Analysis of Public Issues: Concepts, Materials, Research*, Final Report to the U.S. Office of Education, Project #6-2288 (Logan, Utah: Utah State University, Bureau of Educational Research, 1969), p. 213.

the informal teacher, a finding which parallels the research in public school classrooms. The high percentage of questions is particularly significant in light of Resnick's intention to establish categories "intended to reflect the activities observed" in the British informal infant classrooms. She is probably the first one to publish this somewhat unexpected characteristic of open education.

As already pointed out, this section relates to all of the other eight sections. Most directly it relates to the cognitive processes vantage point, as the titles of the articles alone suggest, and to the classroom phychological climate. The concept of strategy is readily found in Section 6, Games, in the Smith and Macdonald articles. Finally, the reader may wish to compare Resnick's emphasis on questioning with many other selections which also highlight questions, especially Taba in this section, Bellack (Section 3), and Gallagher and Aschner (Section 3).

Further research on the topic of teaching strategies is clearly needed. We need to be able to describe the elements of the strategies many teachers do in fact use and to measure the effect of these strategies upon students and teachers. The six problems for research suggested by Oliver and Shaver are sufficient to suggest the direction of future thought and work. If strategies are as important to teaching as Taba and Elzey claim, the task facing educators will be challenging and enormous.

35 The Meno

Plato

Soc: . . . In that confiding, I will gladly inquire with you into the nature
of virtue.

    Meno: Yes, Socrates; but what do you mean by saying that we do not
learn, and that what we call learning is only a process of recollection?
Can you teach me how this is?

    Soc: I told you, Meno, just now that you were a rogue, and now you
ask whether I can teach you, when I am saying that there is no teaching,
but only recollection; and thus you imagine that you will expose me in a
contradiction.

    Meno: Indeed, Socrates, I protest that I had no such intention. I only
asked the question from habit; but if you can prove to me that what you
say is true, I wish that you would.

    Soc: It will be no easy matter, but I am willing to do my best for you.
Suppose that you call one of your numerous attendants, whichever you
like, that I may demonstrate on him.

    The Dialogues of Plato: The Meno, translated by Benjamin Jowett, is reprinted by
permission of The Clarendon Press: Oxford, 4th Edition (Vol. I) 1953. (Diagrams do
not appear in the original Greek text. I have modified the diagram which appears in
this 1953 edition, added others, and inserted markings in the dialogue to aid the reader.
R.T.H., editor.)

Meno: Certainly. Come hither, boy.

Soc: He is Greek, and speaks Greek, does he not?

Meno: Yes, indeed; he was born in the house.

Soc: Attend now, and observe whether he learns of me or only remembers.

Meno: I will.

Soc: Tell me, boy, do you know that a figure like this is a square?

Boy: I do.

Soc: And you know that a square figure has these four lines equal?

Boy: Certainly.

Soc: And these lines which I have drawn through the middle of the square are also equal?

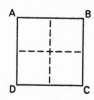

Boy: Yes.

Soc: A square may be of any size?

Boy: Certainly.

Soc: And if one side of the figure be two feet long (AB) and the other side two feet (AD), how much will the whole be? Let me explain: if in one direction the space was two feet long, and in the other direction one foot, the whole space would be two feet taken once?

Boy: Yes.

Soc: But since this side is also two feet, there are twice two feet?

Boy: There are.

Soc: Then the square is twice two feet?

Boy: Yes.

Soc: And how many are twice two feet? Count and tell me.

Boy: Four, Socrates.

Soc: And might there not be another figure twice as large as this, but of the same kind, and having like this all the lines equal?

Boy: Yes.

Soc: And how many feet will that be?

Boy: Eight feet.

Soc: And now try and tell me the length of the line which forms the side of that double square: this is two feet—what will that be?

Boy: Clearly, Socrates, it will be double.

Soc: Do you observe, Meno, that I am not teaching the boy anything, but only asking him questions; and now he fancies that he knows how long a line is necessary in order to produce a figure of eight square feet; does he not?

Meno: Yes.

Soc: And does he really know?

Meno: Certainly not.

Soc: He fancies that because the square is double, the line is double?

Meno: True.

Soc: Now see him being brought step by step to recollect in regular order. (*To the boy.*) Tell me, boy, do you assert that a double space comes from a double line? Remember that I am not speaking of an oblong, but of a figure equal every way, and twice the size of this—that is to say of eight feet; and I want to know whether you still say that a double square comes from a double line?

Boy: Yes.

Soc: But does not this line become doubled if we add another such line here? (add BE to AB; BE = AB)

Boy: Certainly.

Soc: And four such lines, you say, will make a space containing eight feet?

Boy: Yes.

Soc: Let us describe such a figure: Would you not say that this is the figure of eight feet?

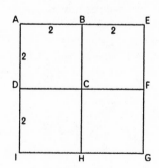

Boy: Yes.

Soc: And are there not these four divisions in the figure, each of which is equal to the figure of four feet?

Boy: True.

Soc: And is not that four times four?

Boy: Certainly.

Soc: And four times is not double?

Boy: No, indeed.

Soc: But how much?

Boy: Four times as much.

Soc: Therefore the double line, boy, has given a space, not twice, but four times as much.

Boy: True.

Soc: Four times four are sixteen—are they not?

Boy: Yes.

Soc: What line would give you a space of eight feet—for that gives a fourfold space, of sixteen feet, does it not? (AE yields a square of 16 feet)

Boy: Yes.

Soc: And the space of four feet is made from this half line? (AB yields a square of 4 feet)

Boy: Yes.

Soc: Good; and is not a space of eight feet twice the size of this (ABCD), and half the size of the other (AEGI)?

Boy: Certainly.

Soc: Such a space, then, will be made out of a line greater than this one (AB), and less than that one (AE)?

Boy: Yes; I think so.

Soc: Very good; I like to hear you say what you think. And now tell me, is not this a line of two feet (AB) and that (AE) of four?

Boy: Yes.

Soc: Then the line which forms the side of the eight foot space ought to be more than this line of two feet (AB) and less than the other of four feet (AE)?

Boy: It ought.

Soc: Try and see if you can tell me how much it will be.

Boy: Three feet.

Soc: Then if we add a half to this line of two, that will be the line of three. Here are two (AB) and there is one (BJ); and on the other side, here are two also (AD) and there is one (DL) and that makes the figure of which you speak?

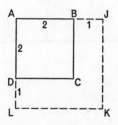

Boy: Yes.

Soc: But if there are three feet this way (AJ) and three feet that way (AL), the whole space will be three times three feet?

Boy: That is evident.

Soc: And how much are three times three feet?

Boy: Nine.

Soc: And what was to be the number of feet in the doubled square?

Boy: Eight.

Soc: Then the eight foot space is not made out of a line of three feet?

Boy: No.

Soc: But from what line?—tell me exactly; and if you would rather not reckon, try and show me the line.

Boy: Indeed, Socrates, I do not know.

Soc: Do you see, Meno, what advances he has made in his power of recollection? He did not know at first, and he does not know now, what is the side of a figure of eight: but then he thought that he knew, and answered confidently as if he knew, and felt no difficulty; now he feels a difficulty, and neither knows nor fancies that he knows.

Meno: True.

Soc: Is he not better off in knowing his ignorance?

Meno: I think that he is.

Soc: If we have made him doubt, and given him the 'torpedo's shock', have we done him any harm?

Meno: I think not.

Soc: We have certainly, as would seem, assisted him in some degree to the discovery of the truth; and now he will wish to remedy his ignorance, but then he would have been ready to tell all the world again and again that the double space should have a double side.

Meno: True.

Soc: But do you suppose that he would ever have started to inquire into or to learn what he fancied that he knew, though he was really ignorant of it, until he had fallen into perplexity under the idea that he did not know, and had desired to know?

Meno: I think not, Socrates.

Soc: Then he was the better for the torpedo's touch?

Meno: I think so.

Soc: Mark now the further development. I shall only ask him, and not teach him, and he shall share the inquiry with me: and do you watch and see if you find me telling or explaining anything to him, instead of eliciting his opinion. Tell me, boy, is not this a square of four feet which I have drawn?

Boy: Yes.

Soc: And now I add another square equal to the former one?

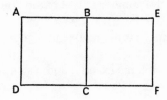

Boy: Yes.

Soc: And a third, which is equal to either of them?

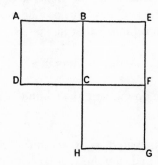

Boy: Yes.

Soc: Suppose that we fill up the vacant corner?

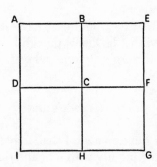

Boy: Very good.

Soc: Here, then, there are four equal spaces?

Boy: Yes.

Soc: And how many times larger is this space (AEGI) than this other (ABCD)?

Boy: Four times.

Soc: But we wanted one only twice as large, as you will remember.

Boy: True.

Soc: Now, does not this line, reaching from corner to corner, bisect each of these spaces (DB, BF, FH, HD)?

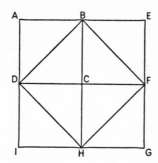

Boy: Yes.

Soc: And are there not here four equal lines which contain this space? (DB = BF = FH = HD; they contain space DBFH).

Boy: There are.

Soc: Look and see how much this space is.

Boy: I do not understand.

Soc: Has not each interior [line] cut off half of the four spaces?

Boy: Yes.

Soc: And how many such spaces are there in this section (DBFH)?

Boy: Four.

Soc: And how many in this (ABCD)?

Boy: Two.

Soc: And four is how many times two?

Boy: Twice (that is, DBFH is twice as big as ABCD).

Soc: So that this space (DBFH) is of how many feet?

Boy: Of eight feet.

Soc: And from what line do you get this figure?

Boy: From this (DB).

Soc: That is, from the line which extends from corner to corner of the figure of four feet?

Boy: Yes.

Soc: And that is the line which the learned call the diagonal. And if this is the proper name, then you, Meno's slave, are prepared to affirm that the double space is the square of the diagonal?

Boy: Certainly, Socrates.

Soc: What do you say of him, Meno? Were not all these answers given out of his own head?

Meno: Yes, they were all his own.

Soc: And yet, as we were just now saying, he did not know?

Meno: True.

Soc: But still he had in him those notions of his—had he not?

Meno: Yes.

Soc: Then he who does not know may still have true notions of that which he does not know?

Meno: Apparently.

Soc: And at present these notions have just been stirred up in him, as in a dream; but if he were frequently asked the same questions, in different forms, he would know as accurately as anyone at last?

Meno: I dare say.

Soc: Without anyone teaching him he will recover his knowledge for himself, if he is merely asked questions?

Meno: Yes.

Soc: And this spontaneous recovery of knowledge in him is recollection?

Meno: True.

Soc: And this knowledge which he now has must he not either have acquired at some time, or else possessed always?

Meno: Yes.

Soc: But if he always possessed this knowledge he would always have known; or if he has acquired the knowledge he could not have acquired it in this life, unless he has been taught geometry. And he may be made to do the same with all geometry and every other branch of knowledge; has anyone ever taught him all this? You must know about him, if, as you say, he was born and bred in your house.

Meno: And I am certain that no one ever did teach him.

Soc: And yet he has these notions?

Meno: The fact, Socrates, is undeniable.

Soc: But if he did not acquire them in this life, then he must have had and learned them at some other time?

Meno: Clearly he must.

Soc: Which must have been the time when he was not a man?

Meno: Yes.

Soc: And if there are always to be true notions in him, both while he is and while he is not a man, which only need to be awakened into knowledge by putting questions to him, his soul must remain always possessed of this knowledge; for he must always either be or not be a man.

Meno: Obviously.

Soc: And if the truth of all things always exists in the soul, then the soul is immortal. Wherefore be of good cheer, and try to discover by recollection what you do not now know, or rather what you do not remember.

Meno: I feel, somehow, that I like what you are saying.

Soc: And I too like what I am saying. Some things I have said of which I am not altogether confident. But that we shall be better and braver and less helpless if we think that we ought to inquire than we should have been if we thought that there was no knowing and no duty to seek to know what we do not know;—that is a belief for which I am ready to fight, in word and deed, to the utmost of my power.

Meno: There again, Socrates, your words seem to me excellent.

Soc: Then, as we are agreed that a man should inquire about that which he does not know, shall you and I make an effort to inquire together into the nature of virtue? . . .

36 Teacher Style and the Analysis of the Student-Teacher Dialogue

Donald W. Oliver and James P. Shaver

A Broader View of Discussion Style

Although we can dissect the dialogue into any number of appropriate dimensions, and identify teaching behavior along these dimensions, we recognize, at least intuitively, that there may well be certain *general* styles of teaching which are commonly observed. In dealing with the problem of describing these general styles, an important question arises: Which of the various dimensions set forth should be considered central, and which should be considered secondary in the definition of such styles? In determining the effect of a general style of teaching on learning outcomes, for example, is it more important that teachers be alike in the posture used, in the intellectual operations performed, in the amount and direction of affectivity shown, or in all three areas? Experimentally, there are at least two strategies one might use in answering this question. One might obtain a large sample of teachers, give them the same materials to teach, ask

Reprinted with permission from Chapter 12 of *The Analysis of Public Controversy: A Study in Citizenship Education.* U.S. Department of Health, Education, and Welfare, Office of Education, Cooperative Research Project No. 8145. Cambridge, Harvard Graduate School of Education, Harvard University, 1962.

them to direct the class's attention toward the analysis and clarification of controversial political issues, observe the range and profiles of behavior that follow and relate these to learning outcomes. Or, one might define two or more particular styles of teaching along those dimensions of behavior that one felt were critical, train teachers to play the styles, observe to what extent the dimensions of teaching not included in the definition were also affected by the different styles, and again determine the relationship of behavioral dimensions to student learning. In the long run, we are saying that our ability to identify and differentiate teaching styles is justified by the kinds of predictions we can make about learning outcomes. No matter how different two teaching styles may appear to an observer, with or without the tools of systematic observation, they are "significantly different" from an educational standpoint only if they lead to different learning outcomes.

In our own work we have chosen the latter course: To define styles according to certain conceptual dimensions, train teachers to play these styles, and observe what differences occur, if any, in behavior as well as differences in the learning outcomes of students. We might illustrate this approach by describing two style models we have investigated experimentally. We have called these styles "recitation" and "Socratic" teaching.*

RECITATION TEACHING. Probably the basic characteristic of recitation teaching is the teacher's attitude toward and control of knowledge. He provides through reading assignments—usually a text—and through his role in class discussions the correct information which the students are to know. The teacher expects the student to respond when called upon to fill in the sequence of information which the teacher wishes to develop in class. This involves mainly relating personal experiences or repeating or paraphrasing what the teacher or a text has said, although it may require the use of some independent thought, such as reorganizing previously read material or applying it to a new situation. In essence, then, evidence of learning is contingent upon the extent to which the student can respond to questions regarding information given him by the teacher, either in class or through texts and other media.

SOCRATIC TEACHING. Socratic teaching, as we have conceived it, is clearly adversarial. When the center of discussion is a controversial political topic—as in our work—Socratic teaching requires that the student do more than describe the controversy in the terms in which the teacher, or assigned materials, have presented it. Rather, the Socratic teacher requires the student to take a position on the issue, state that position, and defend it. Here the emphasis is not only on knowledge provided by the

---

*See the addendum for a third style, seminar, added in a later research project. R.T.H., editor.

teacher, as background for the discussion, but on the process by which the student arrives finally at a decision about the topic under consideration, on the careful consideration of alternative decisions, and on the utilization of analytic concepts and strategies, regardless of the position which is finally reached.

Describing General Styles Dimensionally

While these brief descriptions of the two styles suggest that we "know" what are, in fact, the differences between Socratic and recitation teaching, when one begins to perform as a teacher, the general descriptions very quickly prove themselves inadequate. It is this fact that has led us to the more microscopic dimensional analysis. We found we needed a more precise and reliable way of describing the teaching performance than casual recall based on anecdotal records. It should be clear, however, that the microscopic analysis does not replace the general style description. Theoretically, it will simply provide us with a more precise way of defining "natural" teaching styles.

To illustrate how these two levels of description are related, below we have defined some of the similarities and differences between Socratic and recitation teaching according to the dimensional analysis given previously [in this report and outlined here].

STATEMENT POSTURE.   Recitation teaching is characterized by a high frequency of "stating" and "question asking," with less emphasis on "questioning" or "expressions of self-doubt." With its adversarial nature, Socratic teaching shows a much higher frequency in "questioning" responses.

DISCUSSION POSTURE.   Recitation teaching tends to be descriptive; it is assumed that the truth of the situation is available and that one has only to present and clarify information or an analytic structure by which information can be organized. The attempt to push the student toward a personal decision in which values are at stake is inappropriate for this style. The Socratic style is clearly dialectical. It assumes that the problem can be clarified only in an adversarial context in which various points of view can be presented and defended.

Both recitation and Socratic teaching may emphasize either substantive or analytic responses. The recitation teacher, however, will be concerned with the substance of the issue only insofar as he is interested in clarifying it and presenting the correct position. In the process of clarifying, he may well be analytic, asking that his students explain, "What are the possible ways one might look at this problem?" The concepts which the students apply to this analysis will be those given them by the teacher as correct. The recitation teacher will often avoid giving an answer to the substantive issue, feeling that here knowledge is not certain so he should only attempt to present his students with the knowledge and concepts which they should use in resolving the problem *outside* of the school. In using the Socratic style, on the other hand, the teacher focuses directly on the substantive issue and possible answers to it. From time to time, however, the Socratic teacher may depart from the dialectical posture and treat the problem analytically in order to facilitate conceptualization of the problem. The structure used for such an analysis by the Socratic teacher may have been taught in a descriptive manner, or if the teacher maintains a "pure" style throughout, will likely have evolved from a dialectical discussion of the proper framework for viewing controversial political issues.

STATEMENT TYPES. Recitation teaching involves mainly factual claims. The teacher tends to deal with descriptions of reality, rather than with the truth or goodness of these descriptions. The recitation teacher in maintaining the sequence of his lesson—to the extent that it is successfully programmed—tends to proceed by gradual, well-related steps, using a great many summarizing, repeating, and focusing statements. The Socratic teacher, on the other hand, in dealing with political controversy, tends to ask for value judgments and to challenge them. Factual claims will deal mainly with the background to the issue and as support for value statements. There is also a sequential factor involved in Socratic teaching. It is likely to involve an emphasis on factual statements and questions as the discussion gets under way with the emphasis on value issues coming later. Recitation teaching, as far as we have been able to ascertain, does not reflect any sequential pattern.

INTELLECTUAL OPERATIONS. Except for the fact that the Socratic teacher is engaged in an adversarial role, there is no reason to expect that Socratic teaching will evidence any different patterns of critical thought than will recitation teaching. The recitation teacher may question relevance, ask for or give evidence, or ask his students to qualify statements. However, our experience is that the Socratic teacher does use more of these operations dealing with political controversy. It is also likely that because the teacher and students are engaging in controversy rather than talking about it, the intellectual episodes are more complex than in recitation teaching.

THE PROCEDURAL DIMENSION. Procedurally, we have considered the teacher as the channelizer of a dialogue between him and the students, regardless of which of the two styles he is using. This, perhaps, points up our cognitive bias. It seems to us, however, that it is more fruitful to investigate procedural style differences within a limited context of general classroom procedures. If, for example, the teacher ordinarily withdraws to the back of the room to let students run the discussion, this is less a matter of style than general pedagogical methodology. The concept of style for us assumes a common curriculum, common objectives, and a common procedural context. Variations that occur with this much held constant, then, we would denote "style." The number of times a teacher is required to act procedurally to control deviance, for example, would be a matter of style.

THE AFFECTIVE DIMENSION.   Theoretically, one may not link high or low affectivity with any particular style. In practice, the Socratic discussion tends to be highly charged with negative affect because of the open controversy on the cognitive level, which spills over into the affective domain.

Utility of a Dimensional Analysis of Teacher or Discussion Style

We are suggesting here, as indicated by our previous discussion, that a dimensional analysis of teacher style might be useful in a number of ways. First, it allows us to define general teacher style more precisely. Instead of beginning with polar constructs such as student-centered—teacher-centered or democratic-autocratic, for example, and developing categories to differentiate the poles, we define a number of dimensions of teaching, and then proceed to identify the characteristics of a teacher whom one would judge to be "student-centered," "democratic," "truth-seeking," or "Socratic." Thus, we are not trapped with a conceptualization of teacher behavior that works with only limited types of teaching.

Second, it allows us to describe variations in teaching styles which may or may not significantly affect learning outcomes. Instead of setting up styles in terms of single dichotomies and defining these operationally with "good" and "bad" categories, we can attempt to identify commonly observed styles of teaching, and determine which elements in the style, when varied, will or will not affect learning outcomes. Thus we can develop an empirical approach to the evaluation of teacher style. In the Socratic style, for example, we can ask whether the affective overflow which occurs when the student feels a personal threat to his ideas is a necessary part of the style, or is a low affect Socratic just as effective? In other words, is it the logical performance of the teacher which makes the learning more or less effective (if it is), or is it the logical performance plus the affective charge injected into the discourse?

From a research point of view this methodological approach allows us to investigate a number of interesting problems:

1. Is it possible for individual teachers to manipulate their behavior and play more than one style, or must we identify teachers who have natural styles we wish to investigate and compare?

2. If it is possible for teachers to manipulate their style, and play more than one style, what are the variations that occur within a single style, and are there overlapping areas in which one style cannot be differentiated from another?

3. Assuming that students were subjected to two quite different teaching styles on a systematic basis over a sustained period of time, under what conditions would this difference result in any different learning outcomes?

4. What is the relative importance of the intellectual or other personal characteristics of students, the style of teaching, and the personality of the individual teacher in effecting learning outcomes?

5. Is it possible to develop an observational instrument to describe not only the general style factors of the teacher, but also sufficiently complex intellectual processes that occur in the classroom, so that it can be used to assess learning outcomes?

6. How difficult is it to train teachers to operate consistently from a particular teaching style, and are there personality factors which make certain teachers incapable of learning some styles of teaching?

In our own work we have focused mainly on the first five questions, and have simply sidestepped the last question by selecting teachers for our research who were sufficiently flexible to teach in a variety of ways. It should be noted, however, that most of the people who have taught for our experimental program could handle Socratic teaching with ease, and had more difficulty avoiding challenging the student's value position and initiating an adversarial dialogue. The problem of teacher training, therefore, would seem to be not only whether or not the teacher is sufficiently quickwitted and flexible to perform in a dialectical context (the major problem of beginning teachers), but also whether or not he can tolerate giving doses of "truth" when they are called for. And the problem here may stem from basic temperamental differences among people, something professional educational programs can probably do little about. (Analogously, there may be temperamental as well as intellectual characteristics which cause some physicians to specialize in surgery and others to specialize in internal medicine.)

The Two Styles Investigated

In the course of our work we have focused mainly on the analysis, conceptual differentiation, and quantification of two complex teacher styles.

We have called them the Recitation-Analytic Style (RA) and the Socratic-Analytic Style (SA).* Since we have already described the distinctions between recitation and Socratic teaching, the following brief operational definitions of the two styles should be adequate.

Recitation-Analysis

Recitation-Analysis (RA) as we define it involves the following steps:

1. A controversial case is read aloud.
2. The students are first asked to describe what took place in the case in their own words. This step is called *descriptive recitation.*
3. Students are then asked to tell why the situation in the case might be considered either good or bad. Students are not to give a personal evaluative reaction. They are to begin the analysis of the case by using the thought process concepts. This involves:
   (a) Describing the conflict in the case according to general social and political values;
   (b) Telling what important factual assumptions relate to the conflict;
   (c) Telling what analogies one might give to put the values in this particular case in perspective;
   (d) Telling what consequences one might anticipate if any of the possible decisions suggested in the case were made;
   (e) Telling whether any words in the cases might create special definitional problems;
   (f) Telling how one goes about dealing with these definitional problems;
   (g) If there are questionable factual assumptions in the case, telling what evidence the students might gather to support a particular claim, and what evidence already in the case supports any particular claim; and,
   (h) Telling whether there are any rhetorical devices, such as the use of loaded words, which might influence one's judgment.
4. Students then summarize what particular alternative decisions are available in this particular case, and what important considerations one might take into account in arriving at an intelligent qualified decision.

In the initial stages of RA teaching much of the analysis and application is simply explained to the students by the teacher. As the treatment proceeds, however, the students carry out more of the analysis without

*See the addendum for seminar style. R.T.H., editor.

the teacher's help, and they are simply told whether or not the analytic concepts are correctly applied.

Socratic-Analysis

Socratic-Analysis (SA) involves the following steps.

1. A controversial case is read aloud to the students. (Same as RA).
2. The teacher first asks students to recite events in the case to assure himself that the major points are understood.
3. The students are then asked what their personal feelings are about the situation described.
4. After several students have given an evaluative reaction, and a description of their position justifying the reaction, the teacher begins a period of intensive questioning, concentrating on one student at a time.
   (a) If a student simply says, "This situation is bad," the teacher then asks him to explain what is so bad about it. The student then usually repeats his position.
   (b) The teacher appears enlightened and then verbalizes for the student, if he has not done so for himself, a general social value which supports his position, or the violation of which disturbs him. The teacher then attempts to persuade the whole class to agree with the student's position. Usually most students will agree, since controversial cases tend to be loaded in one direction.
   (c) The teacher then presents a second situation (telling it as an informal story) which illustrates the same values in conflict as those described in the case, except that the value loadings are reversed. For example, if a Negro sit-in case is presented which stresses equal opportunity as good and ignores the value of property rights, an analogy might be used to present the confiscation of American property in Cuba by Castro, which would make the importance of property rights more salient.
5. Usually students are unable to resolve the inconsistency between their feelings about the case and the analogy. They know that both involve the same value conflict, but they are sympathetic to equality in one and property in another. When the students have reached some degree of agitation, the teacher suspends the intensive questioning and asks the student to deal with the contradiction analytically. He shows the student how to qualify his position, how to question the factual assumptions the teacher commonly

makes, and how to deal with the definitional licenses the teacher takes. This step is much the same as step three in RA teaching.

SA teaching is an attempt to teach the student to think on two levels simultaneously while he is discussing a case. The student must deal with the problem of persuading the teacher that he is taking a reasonable position with respect to the problem presented in the case. This is the argumentative level. At the same time, he must see that this can be done more effecivtly by using the political values and critical thinking concepts taught earlier. This is the analytic level. Initially, even after the students are taught the analytic concepts, few see their relevance to the controversial discussion. They tend to argue "blindly" in the sense that they have no conscious framework by which to analyze the nature of the problem. The teacher can argue more forcefully, because he can anticipate how to maneuver the student into unavoidable inconsistencies. We attempted to teach this two level consciousness by bringing the argument to a halt after a period of frustration, and asking the student to apply the concepts to this particular argument. If the student is unable to do this, the teacher "explains" the argument in terms of the analytic concepts. ("I am attacking your value by the use of this analogy. You can counter this analogy with one of your own, qualify your position and make the analogy less relevant, or you can find some important difference between the situation in the analogy and the situation in the case, which also makes the analogy less relevant.")

After some analysis the argument may or may not resume. This depends on the timing and the enthusiasm of the class. While initially, the class is a patchwork of two phases: Socratic questioning→ analysis and application of concepts→ Socratic questioning, the teacher works in the direction of less and less analysis as the students become more proficient in using the concepts to guide their arguments. The tone of the class theoretically should move from a strictly adversarial one to one of a mutual search between teacher and students for an intelligent position in the case.

In comparing the *Socratic* element of SA teaching with RA teaching, there are two striking differences. First, Socratic teaching demands relatively long interchanges between student and teacher. The student cannot be led into an evaluative or definitional inconsistency in one or two statements. The teacher must first establish what the student's position is, suggest exceptions through analogies or counter cases or through contradictory evidence, and counter the student's defense. RA teaching, on the other hand, deals with the problem presented in the case only from an abstract position, never from the point of view of the student's personal commitment. The teacher would ask, for example, "What are some of the ways we might deal with the problem presented in this case?" Several different students can then summarize alternative positions in a sentence or two. The teacher might then ask, "What is the relative importance of the two conflicting values in this case when we consider this particular position. . . . ?" Although one position may be given sustained analysis in RA teaching, no person is asked to defend the position, and thus, no person becomes involved in a protracted dialogue with the teacher.

Second, as we have already noted, the level of affect in Socratic teaching tends to be high. In RA teaching the student is asked only to apply a set of analytic concepts to a particular case. The student has no commitment to the analytic content other than its existence as something that the teacher has taught him. Nor is he asked to state a commitment to a position in the case. Misapplication of a concept requires an immediate corrective response from the teacher. In a Socratic discussion, however, the teacher has no immediate responsibility for the inconsistencies or "holes" in the student's position in the argument. The student has autonomy to accept any position he chooses as long as he can withstand the teacher's probing. The student becomes excited and often agitated because he sees that two values, which he himself holds and is committed to in the argument contradict one another. It is this dissonance in his own position which usually provokes his affective responses, rather than his particular commitment to one position or another, or the disagreement between himself and teacher, although the impact of the latter cannot be discounted. . . .

Research in Teaching Style

Our first systematic experiment in teaching style was set up to test some initial ideas about distinctions in the teaching styles which we planned on using as a basis for more extensive experimental teaching. In this experiment we asked two major questions:

1. Is it possible for individual teachers to manipulate their behavior and play either a Socratic or recitation role when called upon to do so, or must we identify teachers who have natural Socratic and recitation styles
2. If it is possible for teachers to manipulate their general style of teaching, what variations occur within a single style, and are there overlapping areas in which one style cannot be differentiated from another?

The instrument developed primarily to differentiate recitation from Socratic teaching was used in an attempt to answer these questions. A brief description[28] of it is called for before discussing the experimental results.

TEACHING STYLE CONTENT-ANALYSIS: FORM A. The central problem in developing an observational system for the quantified description of teacher behavior such as that in which we are interested, is to develop a set of categories which will have meaning in terms of the specific teaching styles to which it is to be applied. The instrument, i.e., Form A, which we are discussing here actually is composed of two sets of categories. Categories 1 through 6 (as shown in Table 12.1) are affective categories; categories 7 through 12 are cognitive categories; and categories 13 and 14 are procedural. In scoring, then, the observer must infer the cognitive significance of verbal behaviors, as well as their affective implications. Each scorable act is categorized in a cognitive category *and* in an affective category—including the categories which indicate that either a cognitive or affective message was not discernible. For scoring purposes, the cognitive and procedural categories are grouped together so that no double scoring takes place between them (or it would be a triple scoring scheme)....

The primary function of the cognitive categories is to answer questions about differences between the cognitive messages expressed in discussions led by teachers using the two teacher styles. Central to the description of the two styles is the extent to which teachers using each deal with *descriptions* of the controversial case at either the specific or analytic levels as opposed to dealing with the evaluation of events presented in the cases. Categories 8 and 9 are set up specifically to identify differences of this kind. Category 7 (suggests inconsistency) is meant to identify the attempt by the teacher to arouse personal value conflicts on the part of the student by suggesting that he is making contradictory decisions in similar situations (the case and an analogy). Category 12 (analogy) thus has obvious significance. Categories 10 and 11 were employed to make the cognitive subsystem exhaustive.

The procedural categories provide a meaningful exhaustive category system which allows us to gather data about possible procedural problems incidental to the styles. They may also be useful at some later point when and if we compare teaching styles which differ mainly in the procedural area. It should also be pointed out that although we may *think* the behavior of teachers who are role playing recitation-analytic and Socratic-analytic teaching differ significantly, we will not know this until the assumption has been tested by some such scheme as we are here describing.

[28]For a more extensive and detailed treatment of the thought immediately behind this instrument and of the instrument itself, the reader is referred to James P. Shaver, "A Study of Teaching Style." Doctoral Thesis, Harvard Graduate School of Education, 1961. (Footnote numbering is retained as it appeared in the original article.)

T A B L E 12.1 Brief Definitions of the Categories in a Preliminary
Observational System for the Description of Teacher Style

Affective or Socio-emotional Categories

1. SOLIDARITY—Status raising language or tone of voice; strong approval or acceptance of another person. Often indicated by enthusiastic acceptance of another's ideas.
2. LOW POSITIVE AFFECT—Signs of mild approval or acceptance of another person, or of his ideas.
3. TENSION RELEASE—Action interpreted as tension reducing or attempting tension reduction, e.g., laughing or telling a joke.
4. TENSION—Behavior indicative of a state of tension, such as stuttering or becoming tongue-tied.
5. LOW NEGATIVE AFFECT—Statements or acts indicating mild disapproval or rejection of another person, e.g., disbelief of, skepticism about, a statement by the other person.
6. ANTAGONISM—Deflating, derogatory, or highly negative statements or actions.
   NEUTRAL—Acts or statements with no affective message discriminable by the observer.

Cognitive Categories

7. SUGGESTS INCONSISTENCY—An attempt to lead another person to see inconsistencies in his values, claims, or definitions.
8. DESCRIPTIVE—Statements which describe events, i.e., make claims about what reality is like, was like, or will be like.
9. EVALUATIVE—Statements which evaluate events, i.e., statements of like or dislike, right or wrong, good or bad.
10. REPEATS, SUMMARIES, FOCUSES—Statements that restate what has happened during the discussion, or bring attention to what is happening or going to happen.
11. CLARIFICATION—Statements that attempt to clarify the content of the discussion, i.e., clear up the meanings of statements or specific words.
12. ANALOGY—Statements wetting up for consideration a situation similar to the one under discussion. The situation set up may be hypothetical or one which it is claimed existed, exists, or will exist.
    NON-COGNITIVE—Acts with no cognitive—including procedural—message discriminable by the observer.

Procedural Categories

13. DIRECTS TASK-ORIENTED BEHAVIOR—Statements directed at controlling behavior which is in line with the task of the group, or at delineating what that behavior will be.
14. CONTROLS DEVIANT BEHAVIOR—Statements directed at controlling behavior which detracts from the accomplishment of the group task.

It should also be mentioned that unitization, i.e., the breaking of behavior into bits to be categorized, was based on the "single item of thought." In general, the unit to be categorized was the simple sentence, with complex sentences usually scored as individual units, but with compound sentences broken into their component parts.

Reliability Attained

Bale's adaptation of Chi-Square was used to estimate reliability for the study presented below. . . . All of the Chi-Square values are well below the maximum allowable to meet the criteria we adopted—a probability of .50.

DISCUSSIONS FOR EXPERIMENT ONE.   Using, then, the observational instrument which has been described, an experiment was carried out to determine whether the same teachers could use two styles as different as the Recitation-Analytic and the Socratic-Analytic.

First the basic concepts to be used in the analysis of societal issues were presented to the seventh grade students. Then a series of 14 cases was used to begin the teaching of the process by which the analytic concepts were to be applied to concrete problems. Each case was to serve as the basis for a one-period discussion and was not embedded within a total unit framework—except that each case had in common a problem in civil rights as its focus. It was during this period that the Project teachers first attempted a sustained treatment according to the two different teaching styles.

The ten class periods were spent in the discussion of cases based upon U. S. Supreme Court cases presenting instances in which decisions had to be made in regard to the application of basic principles of American government—freedom of speech, religious freedom, due process, etc. Each case presented a specific situation involving a conflict between at least two principles. The cases were very brief, two to four double-spaced pages, and were designed as a simple vehicle by which the student could be introduced to the application of the concepts and operations of critical thought to situations of societal conflict.

The teachers were instructed to use at least the first twenty to twenty-five minutes of each class period leading a discussion using the style assigned to that particular group. These first twenty to twenty-five minutes were tape recorded for later scoring with the Form A instrument. In line with the objectives of the Project, this initial discussion was to lead into an analysis of the cases in an attempt to get the students to apply critical thinking skills to the problem under discussion. The teachers were thoroughly familiar with the teaching objectives and the conceptual framework, and all had practiced both teaching roles. In addition, some time had been spent in discussions among the teachers trying to anticipate particular stylistic problems which might arise. In this particular experiment, we were interested only in measuring the initial Socratic phase of the Socratic-Analytic style as compared with Recitation-Analytic.

STYLE CONFIRMATION.   In scoring the tape recordings, we were first interested in determining whether or not there were over-all differences in behavior—that is, differences that held up when all categories were compared at once—when the teachers were using the two styles. For each of the four experimental teachers, we sampled six discussions in which the teacher was trying to use each of the two styles. This was a total of twelve discussions for each teacher. (Because of varying rates of interaction, and some variation in length of scoring time, the frequencies of interests in each category were converted to proportions so as to provide a common base for comparison.)

The basic question at this point, then, is: How are style differences as interpreted and played by the teachers reflected in the over-all quantitative description of the teachers' behavior obtained with the observational instrument? Did the teachers in fact succeed in playing the two different styles (at the abstract level of our categories)? . . . The ratio testing the interaction between style and category is significant beyond the .001 level.

Therefore, with the conclusion that the teachers were able to effect great over-all differences in style, a second question becomes pertinent: Which of the individual categories contribute to these global differences? The following generally stated hypotheses, in conjunction with Table 12.5, suggest the categories in which we would expect to find stylistic differences particularly reflected.

1. In the area of affect we would anticipate that while recitation teaching is going to require more low positive affect in carrying out its general program of reinforcement of correct responses, there is no reason to expect more highly loaded positive affect, or solidarity. Moreover, the highly argumentative Socratic situation should reflect a greater amount of both low negative affect and antagonism than the recitation. And we expected the teachers to use more tension release—telling of jokes and laughing—with the Socratic style in order to keep tension under control. The affect-laden Socratic situation also would lead to a prediction of fewer affectively neutral acts.

2. Because of the differing focuses of discussion with the two styles, the teachers should make more descriptive statements with the recitation style, and ask for more evaluations with the Socratic style. It is presumed that Socratic teaching will emphasize consideration of inconsistencies in the student's position, and therefore the teachers will suggest more evaluative inconsistencies with this style while avoiding a statement of their own positions. While the argumentative situation might have indicated such a result, we did not anticipate that Socratic teaching would necessitate any greater amount of disagreement with descriptive statements made by students.

3. Two categories seem rather directly related to the different nature of lesson organization for the two teaching styles. While Socratic teaching involves an intensive and lengthy intercourse with individual students centered around the values expressed by the student, recitation teaching requires planning organized around the teacher's conception of the adequate treatment of the problem. It is necessary, as recitation moves from one student to another and as each responds to the teacher's queries, that this organizational structure be maintained. We therefore would expect that the recitation teaching would result in a greater proportion of acts in the repeats, summarizes, and focuses category. This same factor might well have a similar effect in the clarification category.

4. It is obvious from our stylistic models that Socratic teaching should result in many more analogies than would be the case with recitation teaching.

5. A high frequency behavior categorized in the category of direct task-oriented behavior is calling on students. Because of the difference in duration of periods of student-teacher interaction, we can expect a greater proportion of categorizations in this category when the recitation style is to be in use.

T A B L E 12.5   Predicted Differences in Categorizations of Behavior for Teachers Attempting to Use the Two Styles

Category*	Style for Which Greater Proportion Predicted	Fate of Hypothesis
Solidarity	No Difference	Rejected
Low Positive	Recitation	Accepted
Tension Release	Socratic	Rejected
Low Negative	Socratic	Accepted†
Antagonism	Socratic	Accepted
Neutral	Recitation	Accepted
Evaluative, Gives	No Difference	Rejected
Evaluative, Asks For	Socratic	Accepted
Suggests Inconsistency, Evaluative	Socratic	Accepted
Descriptive	Recitation	Accepted
Disagreement with Description	No Difference	Rejected
Repeat, Summarize, Focus	Recitation	Accepted
Clarification	Recitation	Rejected
Analogy	Socratic	Accepted
Directs Task-Oriented Behavior	Recitation	Accepted

*Categories are not included in which there were insufficient frequencies for analysis or which were not considered central to the styles.

†This was not accepted in the later research by Shaver and Larkins, p. 221. (See Overview to this section for reference.) R.T.H., editor.

A brief comment is in order on those which were rejected. While the teachers did use more behavior categorized as solidarity when using the recitation style, this seems to be a reflection of the reinforcing function. But this result raises the question of the appropriateness of timing of that solidarity and tension release evidenced during Socratic teaching. The greater proportion of evaluative statements during Socratic teaching probably reflects two factors: the difficulty of talking about value issues without expressing one's own commitments; and, the expression of one's own values in order to draw out value statements on the part of students. It should be noted that the difference is between about one percent on the one hand and two and one-half on the other. That the teachers disagreed with more descriptive student statements while using the Socratic style is probably a function of the argumentative nature of Socratic discussions, as well as a reflection of the success of recitational programming—i.e., setting up a series of questions based on assigned material and sequenced so that student errors in response are avoided. The lack of difference in clarification simply indicates that the discussion needs to be clarified at certain points with either style.

Results of the Comparison Between Recitation and Socratic Groups

The most obvious fact about the [test] results of the differential treatment experiment is that groups taught by the two treatments turn out to behave in an astonishingly similar way on all measures of learning outcomes administered. This result is consistent with general findings in "methods" research. Few experiments, however, have operated under such carefully controlled curricula, or have actually demonstrated marked differences in teaching style quantitatively, as we have. Regarding the general finding we might make the following comments.

1. .The instruction was probably generally very effective across styles. All teachers were selected not only because of their ability to play to style roles well, but also because of their general excellence as teachers. The materials were especially prepared to teach a particular analytic framework. The teachers were involved in the development of the materials, the preparation of lessons based on the materials, as well as the actual teaching. With this combination of resources, it is reasonable to assume that a powerful instructional situation resulted, regardless of the particular style employed by the teacher.

2. All measures except SIAT* No. 4 (the Socratic Discussion Test) assessed the student's use of analytic concepts either implicity in the substance of an argument or explicitly in a non-stress situation. It is therefore surprising, actually, that the recitation groups did not perform consistently better on all measures other than SIAT No. 4. Since the analytic framework was learned as well by the Socratic groups, one might assume a tremendous redundancy of treatment, so that despite much less explicit discussion of the framework in the Socratic groups, they grasped certain basic elements of the system as well as did the recitation groups. It is very difficult to explain, however, why the Socratic groups did not do better on SIAT No. 4. Two of the most plausible explanations might be explored. First, there may be something deficient in the

*SIAT is an acronym for Social Issues Analysis Test. R.T.H., editor.

test. The most obvious deficiency, we think, is in the amount of behavior sampled (actually only 15 minutes). While this gives us a great deal of behavior when compared with pencil-and-paper tests (some 225 acts), it constitutes a very brief discussion. It also makes the assumption that there is homogeneity across topics which may be used as the basis of such a discussion. This assumption requires further exploration. Second, there may be something deficient in the instructional situation: the students may have been too young to gain substantial benefit from use of the analytic concepts in a persuasive situation; or the treatment may have been too brief to have made a significant impact. It is our impression that both of these situations may, to some extent, be true. We would say that *most* of the students had difficuly translating the analytical framework into a usable tool when engaged in a dialectical discussion. Whether this difficulty is related to intellectual maturity, or whether it is a general phenomenon is difficult to say.*

It is very possible that there is an interaction between individual personality characteristics and the student's ability to benefit from one style or the other. In other words, some students may learn from one style and be inhibited by the other style, and *vice versa*.

Addendum: Seminar Style*

In seminar discussions, the teacher plays much less of a leadership role than in either recitation or Socratic discussions. The burden of discussion and analysis rests with the students; the teacher as seminar leader provides focusing statements and questions, and serves as a resource person. His questions are largely open-ended, guiding the discussion as necessary, but putting the burden of analysis on the students. Because of this role it

---

*In later research, Shaver and Larkins (see Overview to this section) write, "The results of the tests for style effects can be summarized very easily: There was no significant difference among the teaching styles on any of the dependent variables. It will be remembered that the dependent variables included a standardized test of critical thinking (the Wagmis Test), two Harvard Project paper-and-pencil tests of critical thinking (SIAT No. 1 and No. 2), a measure of interest in social issues (the Headlines Test), two U.S.U. Project paper-and-pencil tests of knowledge (the Negro Unit Test and the Final Exam), the Total Valued Acts (TVA) in student discussions as scored with ACOS (Analytic Content Observation System), and student evaluations of the course. In short, style had no systematic effect discernible with the project's measures, design, and analysis." (p. 245).

*Reprinted with permission of the publisher and authors from *Instructor's Manual for the Analysis of Public Issues Program* by J. P. Shaver and A. G. Larkins, Boston: Houghton Mifflin Company, 1973. pp. 89–90. This is based on the authors' research project cited in the Overview to this section.

is difficult to provide a lesson plan. A seminar discussion involves the following steps:

1. The teacher tells the students that they will be expected to carry much of the weight of the discussion, although he will on occasion ask questions and serve as a resource person.
2. The teacher tells the students that they should attempt to decide on a policy to handle the issue in question. In doing so, they should:
   a. decide what issue or issues the case poses;
   b. clarify any language problems that arise during the discussion or interfere with arriving at a decision;
   c. raise and try to answer any factual questions that are important to arriving at a decision;
   d. identify and weigh the values that need to be considered in arriving at a decision.
3. A controversial case is read aloud by one of the students.
4. The teacher should then initiate the discussion by saying something like, "I suggest that you start by identifying and agreeing upon the issue or issues posed by the case."
5. At this point, the teacher's role becomes that of gently prodding the students to be certain that the issue is defined, and that the necessary definitional, factual, and value questions are raised. The teacher should ask such questions as:
   a. "Are you certain that you have defined the issue explicitly enough?"
   b. "Do you all agree with Johnny's statement of the issue?"
   c. "Have you clarified all the important words in the case?"
   d. "Are there other important factual questions that need to be answered before deciding on a policy?"
   e. "Are you satisfied with the evidence for that factual claim?"
   f. "If you took the opposite stand on this issue, what values would you use to support your position?"
6. Usually, seminar discussions will end with the teacher asking the group to summarize the discussion, including stating the issue, possible solutions to it, and important considerations in arriving at a policy. Many times, a good follow up assignment (sometimes an alternative to a summary at the end of the discussion) will be to have each student write a brief position statement on the issue.

Recitation, Socratic, and Seminar Methods Compared

The three discussion styles can be contrasted in terms of the degree of teacher-student initiative, the amount of pre-planned discussion structure, and the emotional tone. In terms of teacher-student initiative, the teacher is clearly the focal point in recitation and Socratic discussions. In seminar discussions, the teacher asks questions, but they are posed for the students to deal with in their discussion with one another. Because of student expectation, the teacher may have to make his change in role explicit for seminar discussions. It may be necessary to make statements such as: "I would rather that the group dealt with that question": "Why don't you pose that question to the group?"; "Please don't look to me for answers"; "Those are the kinds of questions I would like you to deal with as a group." The teacher may even have to remove himself physically from the group (by standing or sitting outside the discussion circle, by moving to a different part of the room, or even by leaving the room) for a while so that the students will become accustomed to not turning to him for answers or for indications that their responses are correct.

In terms of lack of pre-planned structure, Socratic and seminar discussions are fairly similar. That is, in both, the teacher's questions depend in large part on the course of the discussion as it is set by the students' responses. This is even more true of seminar discussions than of Socratic ones. In Socratic discussions, the teacher is at the focal point as leader; in seminar discussions, the teacher plays a subsidiary role as he or she helps the group to grapple with the issue. Although the questions asked in seminar and recitation discussions may look similar, the difference is in their interrelation. In recitation discussions, the teacher has a sequence of questions planned to cover the case; in seminar discussions, the questions asked and the order in which they are asked depend on how the students proceed. Also, in recitation discussions, the students give their answers to the teacher; in seminar discussions, the teacher throws the questions out to the group and the students answer one another.

We have already noted the almost inevitable emotional impact of Socratic discussions because of the emphasis on conflicting beliefs and the adversarial nature of the teacher's role. On the other hand, what emotion there is in recitation discussions comes from much "softer" indications of incorrect responses and from the reinforcing of correct responses. Seminar discussions usually fall between the other two in emotional loading. They may become more heated as students study the analytic concepts and learn to ask probing questions about one another's positions. Because of the teacher's central role in recitation and Socratic discussions, he or she is in good position to control the emotional level of the discussion. In seminar discussions, the teacher will, on occasion, need to intervene for that reason—again, however, putting the burden of discussion and analysis back on the students with questions such as, "Have you stopped to think why the discussion is becoming so heated?", or "Can you suggest ways in which the use of language might help to lessen the emotion in this discussion?"

37 Inquiry Training in the Elementary School

J. Richard Suchman

Skills of scientific inquiry are being taught to elementry school children at the University of Illinois through the use of motion pictures and verbal "experimentation." For the past three years, a research project known as the Illinois Studies in Inquiry Training[1] has been experimenting with the teaching of strategies and tactics of scientific inquiry to children who learn to apply them in question-and-answer investigations. Short films of physics demonstrations pose problems of cause and effect. The children learn to attack these problems with questions by which they gather data and perform imaginary experiments. The teacher provides the answers to the questions.

A portion of a typical session would go something like this: (The children have been shown a film of the "Ball and Ring" demonstration.)[2]

Reprinted with permission from *The Science Teacher*, 27:42–47, November, 1960.
[1]This project is supported by a grant from the U.S. Office of Education, Department of Health, Education, and Welfare and by The Research Board of the University of Illinois.

[2]A brass ball just fits through a brass ring. The ball is then heated and placed on the opening of the ring which is held in a horizontal position. It does not slip through at once but is held in place by the ring. After some time has passed the ball drops through.

PUPIL: Were the ball and ring at room temperature to begin with?

TEACHER: Yes.

PUPIL: And the ball would go through the ring at first?

TEACHER: Yes.

PUPIL: After the ball was held over the fire it did *not* go through the ring, right?

TEACHER: Yes.

PUPIL: If the ring had been heated instead of the ball, would the results have been the same?

TEACHER: No.

PUPIL: If both had been heated would the ball have gone through then?

TEACHER: That all depends.

PUPIL: If they had both been heated to the same temperature would the ball have gone through?

TEACHER: Yes.

PUPIL: Would the ball be the same size after it was heated as it was before?

TEACHER: No.

PUPIL: Could the same experiment have been done if the ball and ring were made out of some other metal?

TEACHER: Yes.

Such questioning continues for about thirty minutes as the children gather data, identify variables and determine their relevancy to the problem, and formulate hypotheses of cause and effect which they test experimentally. No data are given that the children do not obtain through observation or from the teacher's "yes" or "no" answers to their highly structured questions.

To these children and others who are inquiring into the causes of physical phenomena, science is the discovery of new relationships. Children sometimes discover by accident; and sometimes "discovery" is carefully contrived by a skillful teacher. Whichever way it occurs, children are typically thrilled by the sudden new insights, and the learning that results has deep roots. But if we are going to teach the child how to discover meaningful patterns independently and consistently in a highly complex environment, we must teach him how to probe aggressively, systematically, and objectively, and how to reason productively with the obtained data. In other words, we must teach him the skills of inquiry.

Objectives

Inquiry training is designed to supplement the ordinary science classroom activities. It gives the child a plan of operation that will help him to discover causal factors of physical change through his own initiative and control, and not to depend on the explanations and interpretations of teachers or other knowledgeable adults. He learns to formulate hypotheses, to test them through a verbal form of controlled experimentation, and to interpret the results. In a nutshell, the program is aimed at making pupils more *independent, systematic, empirical, and inductive* in their approach to problems of science.

The Strategy of Inquiry

The children are given a general three-stage plan to guide them in their investigations and help them develop a logical, systematic approach. Each stage has its own goal and a set of tactics helpful in attaining it.

Stage I. Episode Analysis

Goal: The identification, verification, and measurement of the parameters of the problem.

In order to perform the operations of this stage, the child must learn to use a set of categories to describe and analyze each episode. Taken together, these categories form a logical system in which each element has an established relationship to the others. The episode-analysis categories are as follows:

1. *Objects:* Objects are the easiest elements for the children to recognize. Familiar objects that are clearly visible pose no problems. The chief difficulty is identifying *all* the objects, whether or not they are visible, familiar, or seemingly unimportant. Included in this category are *systems,* two or more objects combined to form a functional unit. As such they have certain properties that the objects do not possess separately. Water is an object; a beaker is an object. A beaker of water may be regarded as a system.

2. *Properties:* Properties relate to both objects and systems. A property of an object is its predisposition to behave a certain way under a given set of conditions. Properties may be identified through experimentation. By placing an object under varying conditions and observing the resulting changes, a person can determine as many of its properties as he may desire. The identification of objects by their properties is generally more useful than identification by name.

3. *Conditions:* Conditions pertain to the state of objects or systems. While the identity of an object remains constant, its conditions may change. Conditions are identified by observation or measurement.

4. *Events:* Events are defined as changes in the conditions of objects or systems. If an object moves, evaporates, expands, or merely gets hotter, an event has taken place. Events are the consequences of

changing the conditions of objects or systems. The type or amount of change that is necessary to produce a given event is a function of the properties of the objects and systems involved.

Using a question-asking strategy to obtain the kinds of information defined by this system of descriptive categories, the child can collect and organize data which provide grist for the mill of inductive investigations.

Episode analysis involves a number of tactical operations. Careful observation must be supplemented by instrumentation and measurement. Many parameters or condition changes are not directly observable, yet may be critical factors in the causation of an event. If the child confines his attention to those variables which are striking or obvious, he is bound to overlook many highly significant dimensions. A thorough and orderly assessment of the objects, conditions, and events of an episode increases the probability of gathering all of the significant data.

One problem is that people tend to perceive new events and situations as total patterns (Gestalts) unless they have a specific set to analyze and a system of categories on which to base an analysis. Total perceptions may be superficial and misleading, causing children to make false analogies to similar total patterns. It is typical, for example, for children to conclude that a bimetallic strip is melting when it is held in a horizontal position over a flame so that it bends downward. The total pattern of this episode is identical to others in which a heated object melts. Yet a careful analysis would reveal the fact that the melting point of the metals is never even approached when the bending occurs.

Stage II. Determination of Relevance

Goal: The identification of the conditions that are necessary and sufficient to produce the events of the episode.

Not all the parameters identified in Stage I are critical. Often many can be changed without altering the events of the episode. The process of determining criticalness is accomplished through experimentation. Various conditions and objects are changed, one at a time, through a series of controlled verbal experiments. The effects of these changes on the events of the episode are noted. Obviously, only when critical conditions are changed, will events change. Thus, experimentally, the child can determine the relevant variables. This is strictly an empirical solution to the problem of causation. It brings the child halfway to the ultimate goal of understanding the causation of events. More complete comprehension includes the recognition of the events as necessary consequences of universal principles that make a certain set of conditions necessary and sufficient. Stage III is devoted to the search for these principles.

Stage III. Education of Relations

Goal: The formulation and testing of theoretical constructs or rules that express the relationships among the variables of the observed physical event.

During this phase, experimentation is still the principal tool of inquiry, but each experiment is designed as a critical test of some hypothetical construct. Obviously, the scope of operations must extend well beyond the domain of the original event. This stage demands a higher degree of conceptual sophistication, flexibility, and imagination than the others. The problem of designing an unequivocal test for an hypothesis can be as taxing as formulating the hypothesis itself. The child sees his objective as the discovery of rules that express the relationship between variables. He learns that the value of any rule he constructs is a function of (1) its validity within a specified realm of applicability and (2) the scope of this realm.

The Method of Inquiry Training

During the past three years the inquiry-training program has evolved into a somewhat structured pedagogical procedure. At the fifth-grade level, ten seems to be the optimum group size. With classes of thirty or more, the remaining children serve as nonparticipating observers who have an important evaluative role. Rotation permits all children to participate in turn. The training sessions are about one hour long and thus far have been held at weekly intervals, although we now believe that more frequent intervals and shorter sessions would be desirable.

Practice, corrective feedback, and exposition are incorporated into each training session. While they are generally applied in a regular sequence, a degree of flexibility in their use is maintained. A typical training session is organized in the following way.

Presenting the Problem

A silent motion picture of a physics demonstration provides the problem episode. Typical of the demonstrations used is the "Collapsing Varnish Can."[3] As any teacher of science knows, children who do not have well-developed, operative concepts of atmospheric pressure and condensation are exceedingly perplexed by this demonstration. In producing the current series of stimulus films—40 demonstrations in all—we tried to capitalize on this perplexity to provide an intrinsic motivation for inquiry. Our

---

[3]The condensation of water vapor inside a corked varnish can reduces the inside pressure and permits the can to be crushed by the atmospheric pressure.

technique is predicated on the belief that the drive to "find out why" can surpass in sustained motivational power almost any other classroom incentive.

In addition to their motivational function, the films pose cause-and-effect problems in very specific terms. They make available some parameters and suggest areas where important additional parameters might be sampled. In short, the films provide a portion of empirical experience which the child must then relate to his conceptual systems. To the extent that these systems are not sufficiently developed to accommodate the experience, he must expand and strengthen them through inquiry until he is capable of explaining the episode.

The Practice Session

Immediately upon seeing the film, the children begin the inquiry process. All probes are verbal, originate from the children, and must be so phrased as to be answerable by "yes" or "no." Keeping the inquiry at the verbal level permits the teacher and the rest of the group to keep track of most of the information the children are obtaining. The questions must originate from the children because the selection and design of questions are as much a part of inquiry as the interpretation one makes of the answers. The questions must be answerable by "yes" or "no" because in this way only can the child be discouraged from transferring control of the process to the teacher. "Yes" or "no" questions are hypotheses. The teacher in answering merely establishes the tenability of the hypothesis. If the children were permitted to ask, "Why did the can collapse?" the responsibility for selecting the kind of information to be supplied next would be on the shoulders of the teacher. The children would thus be relinquishing their roles as inquirers by returning to the traditional dependent role of obedient listeners and memorizers. This would inhibit the occurrence of inquiry behavior.

The children have two types of questions available to them as information-gathering tools. In identifying parameters in Stage I they may simply ask questions of verification. Since the film provides stimuli that are one step removed from firsthand experience, the children have recourse to verification questions to confirm or test their hunches as to the identity of objects and their conditions at any given time during the episode. They may also need to check the specifics of the observed events, *e.g.*, what happened when. As indicated previously, adequate verification and identification of parameters is an essential first step.

The second type of probe is the experimental question. The child states a set of conditions and postulates a resulting event. The question is answered by the teacher in terms of whether the postulated event will or will not be the result. If the conditions of the experiment are not complete or clear enough to permit the teacher to give an unequivocal answer, he may say, "That all depends" or "Tell me more." Either of these answers tells the child that his experiment has not been sufficiently controlled. Presumably every experimental question is a test or part of a test of an unstated hypothesis. If the child suspects that the cork in the varnish can was a necessary condition for the collapse of the can, he might ask, "If the cork had not been placed in the mouth of the can before the can was cooled, would the same result have occurred?" The teacher's answer of "no" supports the hypothesis that the corking of the can is a necessary condition and tends also to lend support to an hypothesis that the can must be kept airtight while it is being cooled. *But the child must make these inferences himself from the empirical data he obtains.* He cannot test his hypothesis *directly*, even if such questions are phrased as "yes"- "no" questions. If the child had asked, "Does the cork have anything to do with the collapsing of the can?" the teacher does not answer the question. Such a query tends to tap the *teacher's* understanding of the relationships involved. The child is asking the teacher to make certain inferences *for him* and in so doing is relinquishing some of his own responsibility in the inquiry process. Such questions are frequently asked by children, even after they have been trained for several months. The standard response by the teacher is, "What could you do to find that out for yourself?" This retort, without the slightest note of admonition, puts the responsibility right back where it belongs.

The Critique

Generally the inquiry session is terminated by either the achievement of the objectives, the inability of the children to proceed without further conceptual development, or the expiration of time. The latter is usually the case. Following the inquiry session is the "critique," a period in which the strategy and tactics of the group are reviewed and evaluated by the teacher, the nonparticipating members of the class, and the members of the participating group itself. It has been our practice to tape record each inquiry session and utilize the tapes as a point of departure. But we now feel that this is not entirely necessary, particularly if the critique immediately follows the inquiry session. Immediate "feedback" has long been recognized by psychologists as an important condition for effective reinforcement. Some comments and suggestions by the teacher are best made during the course of the inquiry session itself. If this practice is followed to excess, however, the children may be distracted too often from the physics problem at hand. This may impair their efficiency in this work.

The principal function of the critique is to correct weaknesses in the inquiry of the children and to build up a repertoire of tactics that will increase their accuracy and productivity. At times, the critique becomes something like a lecture-discussion in which the teacher may be trying to help the group conceptualize the general design of inquiry strategy. Sometimes special recordings of model inquiry sessions are played. These provide clear examples of the strategies and tactics that the teacher wants the children to utilize.

The critique is indispensable; when it is eliminated morale slips and inquiry becomes progressively worse.

Conclusion

Preliminary analysis of the results of three pilot studies suggests the following conclusions about inquiry training.

The inquiry skills of fifth-grade children can be improved over a fifteen-week period as a result of the methods described herein. Most of the children who receive training become more productive in their design and use of verification and experimentation. They develop a fairly consistent strategy which they can transfer to new problem situations. They make fewer untested assumptions; they formulate and test more hypotheses; and they perform more controlled vs. uncontrolled experiments in the course of their inquiry.

The children have little apparent desire to improve their inquiry skills per se. The chief motivating force is the desire to comprehend the causation of the observed episodes. An explanation by the teacher might satisfy this desire, but in the absence of such explanations the children accept inquiry as a means to their goal. Whenever inquiry is not directly related to the satisfaction of their need to "find out why," they show little interest in the strategies and tactics being discussed. Thus methods for constant improvement are desirable.

Our final conclusion for the present is that inquiry skills cannot be successfully taught to this age group as an isolated content area. The major focus in elementary science education should remain the *content* rather than the *methods* of science. Inquiry training and abundant opportunities to attain new concepts *through* inquiry, however, seem to produce increments in the understanding of content as well as an important new grasp of the scientific method and proficiency in its use.

38 Teaching Strategies and Thought Processes

Hilda Taba and Freeman F. Elzey

The development of critical thinking has figured as an important objective
of education for a long time. Yet, the implementation of this objective in
curriculum construction and teaching has been sporadic and ineffective
for a variety of reasons.

First, thinking has been treated as a global process. Consequently, the
problem of defining thinking is still before us, as is the need to identify
its specific elements, especially in terms which are helpful to planning
effective teaching strategies. In a jungle of definitions, thinking has meant
anything that goes on in the head, from daydreaming to creating a concept of relativity. Neither has knowledge of the development of thinking
been too adequate. While Piaget has spent his lifetime in studying the
development of thinking and has produced a quantity of reports, until
recently, his work received scant attention in the United States.

Implementation of thinking as an educational objective has also been
handicapped by several questionable assumptions. One rather widely
accepted assumption is that reflective thinking cannot take place until a
sufficient body of factual information is accumulated. Teaching which

Reprinted with permission from *Teachers College Record*, 65:524–534, March,
1964.

follows this assumption stresses factual coverage and burdens the memory with unorganized and, therefore, rather perishable information.

An opposite, but equally unproductive, assumption is that thought is an automatic by-product of studying certain subjects and of assimilating the end-products of disciplined thought. Some subjects are assumed to have this power independently of how they are taught or learned. Inherently, memorizing mathematical formulae or the steps in mathematical processes is assumed to be better training than memorizing cake recipes, even though both may be learned in the same manner and call for the same mental process—rote memory.

The combination of these factors has prevented the focusing of attention on the development of teaching strategies designed to stimulate productive and creative thought. The curriculum is seldom organized to focus on active discovery and the use of abstract ideas. Classroom learning experiences are not usually designed to provide a cumulative sequence in the maturation of thought which is at once psychologically sound and logically valid.

All this has contributed to considerable underachievement in the mastery of autonomous and disciplined thought processes. Hence, a rather frequent criticism of current teaching-learning procedures is that they tend to cultivate passive mastery instead of an active discovery of ideas— a tendency to follow "recipes" in solving problems instead of analyzing them and searching for generalizations with which to organize the needed facts and to plan an attack on them (1, 3).

Cognition Revisited

Recently, there has been a renewed interest in the study of cognitive processes in general and thinking in particular. For example, Bartlett (1) and Rokeach (15) have been concerned with open and closed thought. Getzels and Jackson's study (8) of creativity and Gallagher's study (7) of productive thinking employed the classification of divergent and convergent styles of thought. Sigel (16) has been interested in the relationship of styles of organizing and labelling to personality dynamics.

The difficulty with such studies is that the findings about general cognitive styles fail to shed light on the processes by which these styles are acquired. Consequently, the data cannot be translated into guidelines for more effective teaching.

The study of thinking in elementary school children, on which this paper is based, set out to examine the processes of thought in the classroom in terms which are capable of shedding a light on the learning and teaching of certain cognitive skills in the school setting. The fundamental assumption was that thought consists of specific, describable processes which are subject to training, not in some category of powers which are inherent in the individual. Therefore, the study sought to create categories for analyzing thought which described learnable, and therefore also teachable, processes of thought. Specific processes in three cognitive tasks were identified: (1) concept formation, (2) the making of inferences and the induction of generalizations from interpretations of specific data, and (3) the application of generalizations to explain new phenomena and to predict the consequences of certain events and conditions. Critical thinking *per se* was excluded because the curriculum offered meager opportunities for its development.

The study was also conducted under conditions which presumably offered optimal conditions for the training of thought processes. First, the 20 elementary classrooms involved followed a social studies curriculum which centered on a series of basic ideas and was organized for an inductive discovery and development of these ideas. In addition, the curriculum outline also included a planned sequence of learning experiences designed to enhance the development of generalizations and their application to solving problems (4).

Finally, the design for the study provided for special training of the teachers in the analysis of thought processes and in devising effective teaching strategies for their development. In other words, the study proposed to explore thinking under conditions which included the twin impact of the curriculum and of specified methods.

The Theoretical Framework

The study, as well as the curriculum which provided the context for it, and the training of teachers were based on several concepts regarding the nature of thought and its development. First among these was the idea that the maturation of thought follows an evolutionary sequence in which the simpler mental operations form a basis for the creation of the increasingly more complex and abstract mental structures. For example, the learning experiences in the curriculum outlines were arranged so that each preceding step developed skills and cognitive operations which constituted a prerequisite for the next more complex or more abstract mental operations. The cycle of these operations usually began with the analysis of a concrete instance of the general idea on which the unit was centered and ended with the formulation of the idea and its application to new problems and situations (4, 18).

The exploration of the logical structure of the three cognitive tasks with which the study was concerned revealed another, more specific series of hierarchically ordered sequences of thought processes.

1. For example, the sequence in concept formation begins with enumeration of concrete items, such as listing the differences one would expect to encounter when traveling in Latin America. The next step is that of grouping these items on some conscious basis, such as deciding the basis on which to group together "climate," "weather," and "altitude." The process ends with the labeling of classifications, such as deciding to subsume a group of items under "standards of living." These steps constitute a necessary sequence in the sense that each preceding step is a prerequisite for mastering the next one. Underlying the steps are still other cognitive processes, such as differentiation of certain properties of phenomena or events with some degree of precision and an ability to abstract common elements and to determine the basis on which to group and label them.

2. In a similar manner, the logic of interpreting information and making inferences involves the assimilation of specific points of information, followed by relating several points to each other and making inferences or generalizations which go beyond that which is explicitly given.

3. The process involved in applying known facts and principles is a bit more complex, involving as it does divergent lines of prediction as well as the hierarchies of leaps in each according to the distance, ranging from the most immediate consequences to the most remote—such as predicting that water will bring grass, in comparison to predicting that the presence of water will cause nomads to cease to be nomads and turn to building cities.

The logic of the sequential steps in this process is not entirely clear. This unclarity is reflected in the rating scheme used. Obviously, the individual must draw upon his memory for the relevant information to form any predictions at all. But he must also relate this information to the requirements of the situation and to construct the parameters of conditions necessary for the predicted consequences to occur. This process entails both the construction of chains of consequences, such as water → growing crops → settling down → building cities, and the perception of the logical relationships between the conditions and consequences.

The chief point about the sequences in the development of thinking is that a deficiency in mastering the first step, such as the analysis of concrete instances, leads to incapacity to function on the level of the final step, such as the formulation of generalizations. The chief task of teaching, then, is to determine the order of learning tasks and to pace each step appropriately. This is a crucial point in the formulation of teaching strategies, and one against which current teaching methods commit the greatest errors.

Cognitive Commerce

The concept that the cognitive operations are an active transaction between the individual and his environment or the material was another idea which influenced the design both of the curriculum and the study. Children inevitably build mental schemes with which to organize the information they encounter. The quality of the learinng experiences determines the degree of productivity of these schemes. All learning experiences teach what Harlow (*10*) calls "sets to learn." Depending on the teaching strategies employed, children may learn to look for the structure of the problems set by the learning tasks or for arbitrary procedures. They may acquire a disposition to search for relationships and patterns among ideas and facts, or to look for single "right answers."

When the teaching strategies pay little attention to creating models for thinking, children tend to acquire faulty or unproductive conceptual schemes with which to organize information or to solve problems. For example, procedures such as asking students to name important cities in the Balkans, without revealing the criterion of importance or without developing such a criterion with the class, leave students no alternative but to guess what the teacher wants or to recollect what the book said about the matter. Repeated experiences of this sort cause students to adopt irrational, unproductive, and arbitrary models of thinking and a dependence on memory rather than on judgment or inference.

Burton (*2*) cites an extreme example of an irrational or mechanical model or schema. He describes an elementary school child who made good grades in arithmetic because she "came up" with the right answers. When asked how she decided when to use which process, she explained her method as follows: "I know what to do by looking at the examples. If there are only two numbers I subtract. If there are lots of numbers, I add. If there are just two numbers and one is smaller than the other, then it is a hard problem. I divide to see if it comes out even, but if it doesn't, I multiply." Evidently this child had built a scheme to fit the manner of presentation of problems in the arithmetic book. By applying the scheme, she was also learning an unproductive model of thinking or a "set" which excluded understanding the structure of the problems.

The idea of thought as an active organization of mental processes underscores the importance of addressing teaching strategies to the development of autonomy and productivity. Effective teaching is seen as consisting primarily of what we get out of the children instead of what we put into them (*16*). In other words, helping students to develop a basis for and a method by which to judge the importance of cities may be of greater value than their simply knowing which cities are important.

Of special relevance is the idea that thought matures through a progressive and active organization and reorganization of conceptual structures. The individual fits the information he receives at any moment into the conceptual scheme he already possesses. When the requirements of the situation do not fit his current scheme, however, the individual is forced to alter it or to extend it to accommodate new information. Piaget (14) calls this fitting process "assimilation" and the process of alteration "accommodation."

This process suggests a teaching strategy which includes a rotation of learning tasks, calling for the assimilation of new information into the existing conceptual scheme with information that requires an extension and reorganization of the scheme (12). Prolonged assimilation of facts without a corresponding reshaping of the conceptual schemes with which to organize them is bound to retard the maturation of thought. On the other hand, a premature leap into a more complex or a higher level of thought is likely to immobilize mental activity and cause reversion to rote learning or, at any rate, to a lower level of thought. Students need a sufficient amount of assimilation to have the "stuff" to think with. But they need equally a challenge to stretch their modes of thinking and their conceptual schemes. An appropriate transition from one to the other demands a proper match between the current level and that which is required. Determining the proper match is perhaps one of the most difficult tasks in teaching and constitutes, in effect, a new concept of readiness and pacing. This task is complicated by the fact that the mastery of abstract communications, such as language and number, often masks the actual level of thinking. Verbalization may deceive the teacher and lead him to assume that thinking is more advanced than it is and, hence, to pushing the child's verbal habits of learning beyond his level of thinking (13).

Reasonable Hopes

It seems reasonable to assume that, given an adequate analysis of the learning processes involved in certain important cognitive tasks, and teaching strategies which effectively implemented the principles of sequence, of active mental organization, and of adequate rotation of assimilation and accommodation, it should be possible for all students to achieve higher levels of cognitive operation than seems possible under current teaching. Furthermore, it is not beyond possibility that by far the most important individual differences may be found in the amount of concrete thinking an individual needs before formal thought can emerge. This difference may distinguish the slow but capable learner from one who is incapable of abstract thought. It is not beyond possibility, therefore, that many slow learners can achieve a high level of abstract thought, provided that they have the opportunity to examine a greater number of concrete instances than the teaching process typically allows. The employment of teaching strategies which are scientifically designed for the development of cognitive skills may make it possible to develop cognitive processes at a much higher level and in a greater number of students.

This rationale set certain requirements for the methodology of studying the development of thought processes in the classroom. It required, first, securing records of classroom transactions. Second, it required a multi-dimensional analysis of these transactions in terms of what the teacher does, of what the responses of the students are, and of the product of the interaction.

Four discussions were taped in each of the 20 classrooms. Because the curriculum outline projected learning activities, it was possible to place each taping at a point in a sequence at which a specified cognitive task of concern to the study occurred. The first taping was made during the very first class session in which enumeration, grouping, and classification was the chief task. The next two tapings recorded discussions involving interpreting data and formulating inferences from them: one an interpretation of a film, and another at a point at which students reported information from preceding research, compared and contrasted their data, and attempted to express their findings in generalizations. These tapings were taken at the midyear. The final taping, at the end of the year, was of discussions involving application of previously learned knowledge to predicting consequences from described hypothetical conditions.

Units and Scores

One problem in analyzing classroom transactions for the purpose of describing thought processes is to decide on units of analysis which are at once capable of being scored accurately and which express sensible units of thought. In this study, the time sampling was discarded in favor of a "thought unit." "Thought unit" was defined as a remark or series of remarks expressing a more or less complete idea, serving a specified function, and classifiable according to a level of thought. It is, therefore, possible for one word or an entire paragraph to be designated as a "thought unit." For example, the word "cement," when it occurs in the process of enumerating materials for building houses, is considered a thought unit. So is a paragraph, such as "The people in the other country do not have electric saws and things that the men in this country use to build houses. The children help chop the wood and can do a lot of things to help build the houses. But the children over here cannot do very many things because of the danger."

In order to describe simultaneously the teaching acts and the levels of thinking of students, the verbal transactions were "scored" by three different "ratings." The first is that of *designation*. It describes the source of the thought unit—whether it emanated from the teacher or from the student and whether the person is giving or seeking information. The code symbols for designation are *child gives* (CG), *child seeks* (CS), *teacher gives* (TG), and *teacher seeks* (TS).

The rating of *function* describes how a thought unit functions in the context of discussion. When applied to remarks or questions by teachers, these ratings may be used to describe teaching strategies which affect the subsequent thought of children.

Two large groups of function ratings may be distinguished: (1) questions or statements made by the teacher or the students which are psychological or managerial in their function and unrelated to the logic of the content. Statements of this type include those that express agreement (A), approval (AP), disagreement (D), disapproval (Dp), management (M), and reiteration (R). (2) The second group includes teacher or student statements which function to give direction to discussions, but which at the same time can be rated according to the logic of content. Such ratings include focusing (F), refocusing (F2), change of focus (FC), deviating from focus (Fd), controlling thought (C), extending thought on the same level (X), and lifting called to a higher level (L).

The third rating, called *levels of thought*, describes both the student's and the teacher's verbal behavior by specifying the logical quality and the level of thought expressed. A separate rating scheme was developed for each of the three cognitive tasks. For each of these tasks, categories were established which represent the hierarchical levels of thought, according to their level of abstraction and complexity. These categories refer to the specific thought processes which need to be mastered in a sequential order, because performing on the preceding level is a prerequisite to being able to perform on the next. Thus, the rating scheme represents the developmental sequence for each cognitive task. In addition, within each category, distinctions were made between the irrelevant, the disconnected, and the related information or content.

The rating scheme used for designating the levels of thought for each of the cognitive tasks is as follows:

COGNITIVE TASK: Grouping and labeling[1] (giving or seeking)

    10 specific or general information outside of focus
    11 specific or general information within focus

[1]Categories in the 20 series were originally reserved for "general information" but were later combined with the 10 series.

12 specific or general information with qualifications
30 grouping information without basis
31 grouping information with implicit basis
32 grouping information with explicit basis
40 categorizing information without basis
41 categorizing information with implicit relationships between items
42 categorizing information with explicit relationships between items

COGNITIVE TASK: interpreting information and making inferences:
(giving or seeking)

10 specific or general information outside of focus
11 specific or general information within focus
12 specific or general information with qualifications and relationships
50 specific reason or explanation that does not relate to the information
51 specific reason or explanation that relates or organizes the information
52 specific reason or explanation that states how it relates or organizes the information
60 irrelevant or incorrect inference which is derived from information
61 relevant inference which is derived from information
62 relevant inference which is derived from information and expresses a cause and effect relationship, explanation, consequence, or contrast
70 relationship between information which implies an irrelevant or incorrect principle or generalization
71 relationship between information which implies a principle or generalization
72 principle or generalization which is derived from information

COGNITIVE TASK: predicting consequences (giving or seeking)

90 correcting the cause or condition
Establishing parameter information
100 relevant information
101 relevant information for establishing the total parameter (if-then) or for a particular hypothesis or prediction
102 relevant information for the total parameter or any particular prediction with appropriate explanation
Establishing parameters of conditions
110 irrelevant or untenable condition for the total parameter or for the particular prediction or hypothesis
111 relevant condition without connecting it with relevant information
112 relevant condition and information and establishing logical connection between them
Prediction: Level one, immediate consequences
Level two, remote consequences
120-220 incorrect or out of focus prediction
121-221 prediction with no elaboration
122-222 prediction accompanied by explanation, qualification, differentiation, comparison, or contrast
123-223 prediction accompanied by a stated or implied principle

In determining the level at which to rate a particular thought unit, it was necessary to consider the context in which the thought unit occurs. For example, the statement, "a hammer, because you can drive large nails with it," may be rated as "specific information with qualifying statement" if it is offered in response to the task of naming tools used in building a house; it merely gives additional information about the hammer and does not constitute a reason for naming "hammer." If the focus is on identification of tools most useful to primitive people, however, the same response would be rated as "relevant inference derived from information," because the phrase is an explicit reason for naming "hammer."

Function and Level

In describing the effect of teaching strategy on thought levels, four groups of function rating are especially important: focusing (F), extending the thought on the same level (X), lifting thought to a higher level (L), and controlling thought (C). Focusing establishes both the topic and the particular angle for its treatment. It sets the cognitive task. For example, the statement by the teacher, "If the desert had all the water it needed, what would happen?" establishes the central focus for discussion and calls for prediction of consequences.

The coding system also specifies the shifts in subject matter (change of focus), the degree to which the teacher finds it necessary to bring the discussion back to the original topic (refocus), and the number of times that the discussion wanders from the subject (deviation from focus).

A statement of the teacher or a child is coded as extension of thought (X) when it gives or seeks additional information or provides elaboration and clarification on an already established level. The following example illustrates a series of extensions on the level of providing specific information:

(1)	C	Malobi took the money home with her.	CC 11
(2)	T	What did Malobi do with the money?	TS 11
(3)	C	She saved it.	CG 11X
(4)	C	She put it underground.	CG 11X
(5)	C	She put sticks and tin over it.	CG 11X
(6)	C	Before she did that, she put it in a little pot.	CG 11X

A thought unit is functioning to lift the level of thought whenever the teacher or child seeks or gives information that shifts thought to a higher level than had previously been established. In the following example, the teacher attempts to lift the level of thought from giving information to explanation:

(1)	C	They carried things in baskets on their heads.	CG	11
(2)	T	Explain why.	TS	61L
(3)	C	I suppose they can carry more things that way.	CG	61L

A question may function to extend the thought in one context and to lift it in another, as illustrated in the following example:

(1)	C	They were working fast on the house.	CG	11
(2)	T	Why?	TS	51L
(3)	C	They wanted to get the house done before the rain came.	CG	51L
(4)	T	Why?	TS	51X
(5)	C	Because unless it is finished, the rain will destroy it.	CG	52X

The inquiry on line two is rated as teacher seeking to lift the level of thought from the established level of giving specific information to the level of inference. The child's response provides the reason on the level sought by the teacher. The same inquiry on line four and the child's response on line five function to extend the thought because the level at which the question is asked has already been established.

Controlling of thought occurs when the teacher performs a cognitive task that students should be induced to do. This is the case when the teacher gives a category for classification, an inference in interpretation, or a prediction in the task of applying principles.

Strategic Patterns

As elements of teaching strategy, the frequencies of these functions may represent either effective or ineffective teaching strategies. For example, frequent shifts in focus may be needed at some points in the discussion to introduce sufficient information to form a basis for comparison and generalization. Other tasks may require that the discussion remain on one focus long enough to provide full treatment of the subject before proceeding to another, higher level of thought process. Frequent refocusing may indicate a faulty handling of the sequence in thought processes, which results in the necessity for constantly having to bring the children back to the focus. This multiple coding scheme makes it possible to depict the flow of the classroom discussion by charting the sequences of transactions between the teacher and the children, the changes in the level of thought during the discussion, and the effect of these strategies upon the level and the direction of thought. The flow of thought can be reconstructed even though the specific content of the discussion is not given.[2] For example, an empirical sequence of thought may, when trans-

[2]Charts based on empirical observation will be published later as a part of the report to the US Office of Education of a study of "Thinking in Elementary School Children" (Project No. 1574).

lated from the code, be read as *child gives specific information, teacher seeks an extension of that information, child provides the requested extension, teacher seeks to lift the level of thought from the "information" level to the "reason" level, child provides a reason as requested by the teacher, and teacher gives approval to the child.* In a similar manner, any sequence of ratings can be reconstructed from the observationally developed flow charts.*

When the flow charts identify individual children, then one can describe the characteristic modes and levels of thought of particular pupils, such as a tendency to operate only on the level of concrete information or on the level of inference and generalization, the tendency to remain focused or to stray from the focus, to give relevant or irrelevant information, etc. It also permits the accounting of the frequencies of the various thought patterns which prevail in the classroom group and the discrepancies between what the teacher seeks and how the children respond.

Data of this sort depict the various strategies which teachers may employ and their consequences. For example, when the teacher attempts to raise the level of thought very early in the discussion, this typically results in the children's returning to a lower level and in their inability to sustain discussion at the higher levels of thought. On the other hand, a strategy representing an effective pacing of shifting the thought onto higher levels seems to follow a characteristic course. The level of seeking information is sustained for a considerable time during the first portion of the discussion. Grouping is requested only after a large amount of information has been accumulated. The result is that in a fairly brief period, children transcend from grouping to labeling and then to providing reasons for labeling and to inferences.

Other strategic patterns that have been empirically identified include the teacher's repeated attempts to steer discussion to the inferential level without permitting the development of a body of needed information; in such a case, the children repeatedly return to the information level. Or when there is constant change of focus, the children's thought alternates between several levels, is not sustained at the higher level, and gradually stabilizes on the most primitive one.

Some Implications

This multidimensional analysis of classroom transactions has several advantages. First, by combining the description of the teacher's acts in terms of their explicit functions with the assessment of the logical quality of

*See the addendum to this article for two such charts selected from the full report. R.T.H., editor.

student responses, it is possible to evaluate the impact of the teacher's behavior in terms of its productivity. This addition of the dimension of the logical quality of the content of thought carries the analysis of classroom transactions a step beyond what has been available to date. Most current studies of classroom transactions concentrate more or less exclusively on the analysis of the psychological functions of teaching acts (5, 11). This emphasis has evoked the criticism that teaching is explained and controlled exclusively in terms of psychological principles and that the logic of teaching and of its product in learning is overlooked (17).

A further advantage lies in the fact that, in addition to describing the impact of teaching exclusively in terms of the frequencies of specific acts, this scheme permits studying the cumulative impact of certain patterns or combinations of acts, including their pacing. It is at this point that a transfer is made from the study of teaching acts to the study of teaching strategies. Flanders (6) has taken a step in this direction by describing the points of shift in the nature of teaching acts.

Finally, the scheme permits the examination of the effect of teaching strategies in terms of a measurable change in a specified outcome—levels of thinking in this case—and thus frees the study of teaching from the necessity of inferring the effect from the assumed consequences of the frequencies of certain types of teacher behavior.

A preliminary analysis of the typescripts of classroom discussion reveals an enormous influence of teacher behavior on the thinking of students. This impact is exercised in a variety of ways: by the nature of the questions asked, what the teacher gives to the students or seeks from them, the timing of these acts in the total sequence, which ideas are picked up for elaboration and which are passed over, points at which approval and disapproval are given, etc. For example, the focus which the teacher sets determines which points students can explore and establishes the models for thought they can practice. Of great importance is the sequence of mental operations called for and the appropriateness of this sequence to developing productive thought models.

It seems clear, further, that the level of thinking attained is influenced not only by the nature of the single act by a teacher just preceding a given response. The level of thought attained seems to be determined by the whole pattern of transactions: the particular combination of focusing, extending, and lifting; the timing of these acts; the length of time spent on a particular focus, such as exploring specific descriptive information before examining causes or attempting explanation; the distance between the mental operations of the students at the moment from the level required by the teacher, and the points at which the teacher seeks information from students and gives it. These combinations, not merely the frequencies alone, constitute a teaching strategy.

Only a casual identification of these strategies is available at the moment of writing this article. The variations in the patterns are too numerous to permit analysis by ordinary means. The staff, in cooperation with experts in computer programming, has developed a high-speed computer program designed to aid in accounting for these patterns. Such a computer program should permit the identification of the elements and the cumulative patterns of strategies associated with high and low performance.[3]

The findings so far suggest that if the acquisition of skills in autonomous thinking is to be a realistic objective, a much more thorough study of and experimentation with the appropriate teaching strategies and their impact on the development of thinking is called for. As Flanders (6) suggests, any step in the direction of specifying productive teaching strategies should lead to a more adequate understanding of the connection between teachers' behavior and student response. A scientific mapping of such strategies should also add considerably to the developing theory of instruction, and especially to our understanding of the conditions which maximize the development of higher mental processes on the part of all students, not only the intellectual elite.

References

1. F. E. Bartlett. *Thinking: an experimental and social study.* New York: Basic Books, 1958.

2. W. N. Burton. *The guidance of learning activities.* New York: Appleton-Century, 1952.

3. G. T. Buswell and B. Y. Hersch, *Patterns of solving problems.* Berkeley, California: Univer. California Press, 1956.

4. *Contra Costa County Social Studies Units, Grades 1-6.* Pleasant Hill, California: Contra Costa County Schools, 1959.

5. N. A. Flanders. *Teacher influence, pupil attitudes, and achievement.* Pre-publication manuscript of a proposed research monograph for the U. S. Office of Education, Cooperative Research Branch, Washington, D.C., 1960.

6. N. A. Flanders. Some relationships between teacher influence, pupil attitudes, and achievement. Ditto *MS* of a chapter submitted to the AASA, the NTBA, and the NEA Classroom Teachers Division. No date.

7. J. J. Gallagher, Mary Jane Aschner, Joyce M. Perry, and S. S. Afaar. A system for classifying thought processes in the content of classroom verbal interaction. Ditto MS. Urbana, Ill.: Institute for Research on Exceptional Children, Univer. Illinois, 1961.

8. J. W. Getzels and P. Jackson. *Creativity and intelligence.* New York: Wiley, 1962.

9. J. P. Guilford. Basic conceptual problems in the psychology of thinking. *Annals NY Acad. Sci.,* 1961, *91,* 9-19.

[3]Such a computer program has been devised by P. J. Stone and M. S. Smith as a general sequence analyzer, planned to identify recurrent patterns in a list of events.

10. H. F. Harlow. The formation of learning sets. *Psychol. Rev.*, 1949, *56*, 51-60.

11. Marie Hughes, *et al. Development of the means for the assessment of the quality of teaching in elementary school.* (Mimeo.) Salt Lake City: Univer. Utah, 1959.

12. J. McV. Hunt. *Experience and intelligence.* New York: Ronald Press, 1961.

13. E. A. Peel. *The pupil's thinking.* London: Oldbourne, 1960.

14. J. Piaget. *The psychology of intelligence.* London: Routledge, Kegan Paul, 1947.

15. M. Rokeach. *The open and closed mind.* New York: Basic Books, 1960.

16. I. Sigel. Cognitive style and personality dynamics. Interim report, Merrill-Palmer Institute, 1961.

17. B. O. Smith. Concept of teaching. *Teach. Coll. Rec.*, 1960, *61*, 229-241.

18. Hilda Taba. *Curriculum development: theory and practice.* New York: Harcourt, Brace & World, 1962.

Addendum: The Patterns of Classroom Interaction*

Figure 1 presents the first 40 thought units in a third grade tapescript. In this flow chart, the thought units are represented by equal intervals on the horizontal axis and their level on the vertical axis. Thus, the systematic progression of the thought units and the relative levels of thought can be presented diagrammatically. The thought units of the teacher are indicated by "T" along the horizontal axis. The horizontal arrows, such as appear for thought units 7 and 13, represent the teacher's request for an extension of the thought expressed just prior to these units. The vertical arrows shown for thought units 9, 15, 28, and 36 depict the teacher's attempts to lift the thought to a higher level. Thought unit 10 (L), indicates that the child complied with the teacher's request for a lift in level and produced a thought unit at the 41 level. The other letters represent other function codings such as reiteration, approval, agreement, etc.

By examining the chart, the flow of thought can be reconstructed even though the specific content of the discussion is not given. For example, the sequence of thought presented in thought units 12 through 17 may be read as: child gives specific information (unit 12); teacher seeks an extension of that information (unit 13); child provides the requested extension (unit 14); teacher seeks to lift the level of thought from the "information" level to the "reason" level (unit 15); child provides a reason as requested by the teacher (unit 16); teacher gives approval to the child (unit 17).

*Reprinted with permission from *Thinking in Elementary School Children* by Hilda Taba, Samuel Levine, and Freeman F. Elzey. U.S. Department of Health, Education, and Welfare, Office of Education, Cooperative Research Project No. 1574. San Francisco, San Francisco State College, 1964.

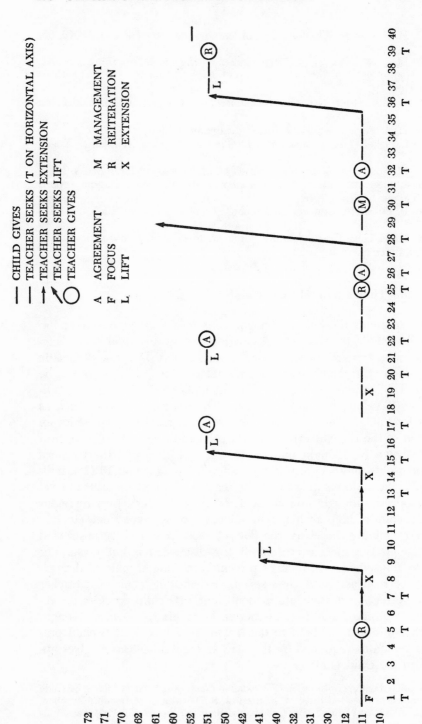

FIGURE 1 Flowchart of Classroom Interaction

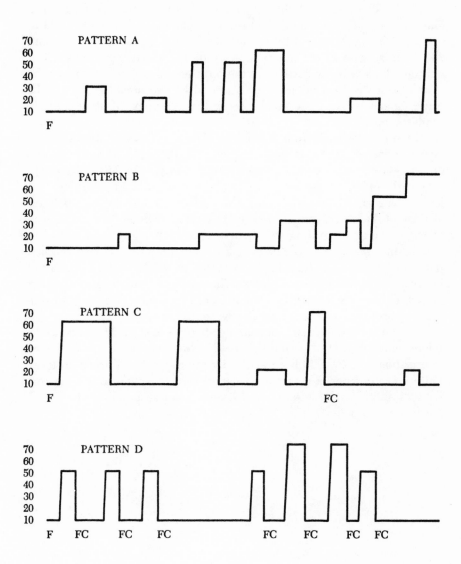

FIGURE 2 Class Discussion Patterns

Other patterns can be depicted by this method. For instance, the child gave an unsolicited lift at unit 21 which was approved by the teacher at unit 22. The discussion then dropped back to the information level at unit 23 where it stayed until the teacher attempted to lift the thought at unit 28. This was unsuccessful as indicated by the child's response at unit 29 which is again at the information level. The teacher sought a lift at unit 36 which was successful and the level of thought seems to now be sustained at the "reason" level as indicated by the units 37 through 42. Any sequence of codings can be reconstructed from the flow chart in similar manner.

Figure 2 presents four simplified class discussion patterns which depict various strategies teachers may employ. Pattern A illustrates a type of discussion in which the teacher attempts to raise the level of thought very early in the discussion. This results in the children returning to a lower level, and their inability to sustain discussion at the higher levels of thought. Pattern B depicts a type of discussion which demonstrates an effective pacing of shifting the thought onto higher levels. The level of seeking information is sustained for a considerable time during the first portion of discussion. Grouping is requested only after a large amount of information has been accumulated. The result is that, in a fairly brief period, children make the transitions from grouping to labeling, to providing reasons for labeling, and, finally, to inferences.

In pattern C the teacher repeatedly attempts to steer discussion to the inference level without permitting the development of a body of needed information and the children repeatedly return to the information level. Pattern D illustrates a constant change of the focus, with the result that thought alternates between several levels, is not sustaintd at the higher level, and gradually stabilizes on the most primitive one.

39 Didactics, Heuristics, and Philetics

H. S. Broudy

I

The multitudes of prescriptions for the improvement of teaching, especially in college, fall roughly into three categories:

1. Put order in your materials, in your presentations, and your testing. Connect new material with what has already been studied; reward frequently and promptly. Don't befuddle the students with zigs and zags. Don't surprise them. Let them know what you expect; be fair, don't spring quizzes, don't test on material that has not been discussed in class or definitely assigned. Let us call these and similar exhortations advice on how to improve one's *didactics*, that is, the imparting and reinforcing of skill and knowledge. All learnings that can be made explicit and the criteria for which are explicit can be included under didactics. Most of the instruction at any level of school falls into the domain of didactics, and possibly as much as 80 percent of all undergraduate collegiate instruction is didactical.

Reprinted with permission from *Educational Theory*, 22:251–261, Summer, 1972.
This article was commissioned for presentation to a symposium on instruction held by the North Central Region Colleges of Agriculture held at Allerton House, University of Illinois, June 27–29, 1971.

The major trouble with didactics is that what they impart is only indirectly and incidentally related to the life interests of the learners at the time of teaching. Hence didactics depend on extrinsic motivation. One might think that after twelve years of pupillage, the college student would be thoroughly conditioned to studying well whether he was interested in the assignment or not. For many college students this apparently is not the case. They are still amateurs in studentship, that is, they do well when they feel like it, unlike the pro who does well whether he feels like it or not. For such students good teaching means, "Make it relevant" and this, in turn, means, "connect it with my sex life, money, popularity, or political commitments." We take it for granted that little children have to be motivated in this way; we try to connect didactics with play activities in which they have an intrinsic interest. The college student insisting on being interested before he will consent to study is asking for the prolongation of his pedagogical infancy into the domain of adolescent problems. Unfortunately, when knowledge is organized for didactics, it is packaged in a logical and not necessarily a psychological order. The logically simple elements of a discipline are used to build up a complex system of ideas. But what is logically simple, e.g., the nucleus of an atom (relatively to the whole atom) may not be psychologically simple at all. It may be highly abstract and extraordinarily remote from the direct perceptual experience of the learner. One has to take on faith the notion that an ice cream cone is a mass of restless atoms. Hence all logically organized subject matters run the risk of irrelevance to a given learner's existential predicaments, i.e., his life concerns.

2. The second type of prescription exhorts the instructor so to manage instruction that the student thinks for himself. This thinking for himself can mean that he discovers the solution to a problem, or that he achieves an insight into a situation, or that he arrives at an induction in some field of particulars, or that he does something creative. I shall call the method of teaching that is designed to promote discoveries by the pupil heuristics. The classic examples of heuristical teaching are supplied by Socrates. One is the demonstration in the *Meno* in which Socrates elicits from the slave boy the proof of the Pythagorean theorem, even though the slave boy had never studied geometry. Although this demonstration is often cited as an example *par excellence* of Socratic teaching, it is less characteristic of Socrates than the dialogues in which the teacher and his student seek for a definition of courage, piety, temperance, etc. In these dialogues the student is led to discover how little he understands the moral principles to which he is committed and how dull are the logical tools he employs in thinking about them.

In our own time the problem-solving method of teaching as articulated by John Dewey is an example of heuristic teaching. Combinations of Socratic questioning and Deweyan problem-solving are to be found in the more recently publicized learning by discovery theories.

Heuristic teaching solves the problem of relevance by beginning with the learner's predicaments. The difficulties with heuristic teaching are (a) one can't hope to cover a field of knowledge systematically or exhaustively as one can by didactics; (b) one can't plan instruction in any great detail and (c) it is difficult to test for heuristical results, e.g., critical thinking, creativity, etc., so that the tests for heuristical teaching tend to become tests of didactics.

Before going on to the third type of teaching, which I shall call philetics, it may be appropriate to comment on some of the relationships between didactics and heuristics. If the students have already mastered a given body of facts and principles, e.g., as in chemistry or economics or history, these can be used in heuristic teaching to solve problems, carry on discussions, gain insights, etc. For example, the principles of chemistry and economics might be used profitably in the discussion of famines in underdeveloped countries. (This is quite different from learning the principles of chemistry and economics by studying famines in underdeveloped countries.) If principles and facts have not been studied systematically, then the heuristic approach is restricted to the facts and generalizations that the students have discovered for themselves or to common knowledge. While discussion restricted to these intellectual resources is not without value and can indeed be exciting to the participants, it is not accompanied by that advance in sophistication that we expect from formal schooling.

Very often the choice between didactic and heuristic teaching depends on the scholastic accomplishments of the student. Well-grounded high school graduates may be ready for the heuristic approach in such fields as the basic sciences, literature, and history, whereas poorly prepared high school graduates may not be. Since high schools do not, as a rule, give formal instruction in economics, psychology, sociology, and anthropology, heuristic approaches that presuppose systematic work in these areas cannot be substituted for didactical instruction in these areas.

The distinction between didactics and heuristics is not synonymous with that between beginning and advanced courses. Some advanced courses are used for the formal exposition of the more complex phases of a subject. Some use laboratory work as the heuristic phase of a course that is didactical in its lectures and discussions. On the other side, a beginning course in law or agriculture, especially for the nonprofessional, might well be heuristic, i.e., deal with problems that disclose the general nature of inquiry and practice in these fields.

3. The third type of improvement in teaching I shall call philetics derived from the Greek *philos* (loving). This prescription urges that the

secret of successful teaching is love—the love of the teacher by the learner and presumably vice versa. The lady who in 1971 was named teacher of the year when interviewed on television said that the secret of her success was just plain love. If one loves pupils, she intimated, everything else will straighten itself out. On questioning she did betray a pedagogical sophistication that seemed to go beyond philetics, but she seemed reluctant to take anything away from love.

Just what sort of love is recommended in philetics is not easy to define. At various times the teacher is urged to be a pal, a big brother, a father figure. One historian of education (Marrou) has argued that the deep attachment of Greek youth to their mentors had a homosexual character, and one gets whiffs of this in the remarks of Alcibiades to Socrates. Plato, of course, would have wanted such liaisons to remain Platonic, but it would be surprising if some of them did not go beyond that.

At any rate, concern for the pupil's development both intellectually and as a person is the criterion in philetics. Given this philetic relationship, it is held that motivation and mastery will take care of themselves. This is explained by the hypothesis that the love relation removes the psychological blocks to learning—insecurity, fear of failure, fear of rejection, alienation from peers and parents, and a thousand other emotional ills to which adolescents are heir.

There are some difficulties of course with philetics as a style of teaching. One is that there is no intrinsic relationship between learning X and being in love with the teacher of X. Hence motivation is even more extrinsic than in didactics, which comes out when the teacher-friend gives out poor grades to student-friend. This is likely to ruin a beautiful friendship. For another matter, the psychic needs of students vary even more than their intellectual ones, and to treat any more than a handful of them as persons in any serious sense of that word is probably beyond the capacity of most instructors.

The love of students is manifested in many ways. Generally it expresses itself in a teacher's willingness to spend considerable time outside of class in talking with them about their problems, educational and personal. There is an old saw to the effect that teaching keeps one young because one is renewed by the youth of the students. Perhaps one has to remain young to maintain a genuine fondness for the young, a sense of duty alone will take the teacher only so far, as a rule, not far enough.

In recent years the complaint has become endemic that students do not have access to faculty for the kind of personal relationships they want. A multitude of schemes for counseling and advising have not satisfied the complainants, and perhaps because formal procedures cannot take the place of a genuine desire to be with students and to become involved in their problems. I suppose that American undergraduates yearn for something comparable to the tutor available to the Oxbridge undergraduate—an intellectual mentor who not only knows the academic ropes but who to some extent also becomes identified with the tutee's academic career.

Formal interviews with professional counselors, interviews with the professor during his stated office hours, and even informal beer sessions at the faculty member's home or in one of the academic pubs—these do not add up to the tutor's continuing concern for the tutee. For the tutor knows what the tutee is reading and writing. There is discussion about books and authors and whatever else may stir their interest. Nobody knows as much about a student as does his tutor. A few American schools provide some version of this tutorial relation, but it is a rare phenomenon. Whether the rarity is caused solely by its expensiveness I do not know, but there is no doubt that it is a very expensive form of instruction.

A teacher whom students rate highly is likely to be one who is around the office a lot and whom they do not need an appointment to see. But this means spending one's time on something other than writing an article or doing research in the laboratory or jetting all over the country for conventions and consultations. The latter activities contribute to the faculty member's guild visibility, something that impresses the dean much more than it does the undergraduate student. Accordingly, when students complain that faculty are inaccessible it will not do to retort that one has office hours or that one occasionally invites students to his home. For what they have in mind is a personal concern in their academic and personal welfare.

At the American university something like the tutorial relationship is available to the good doctoral student from his advisor. The latter often regards the student as an embryonic junior colleague in his field of study. The advisor takes the student's personal and domestic problems very seriously and identifies with his career. The undergraduate, especially if he has no field of specialization, cannot generate this sort of interest in a faculty member, but something like it, I believe, is what he craves.

Many of the so-called cluster colleges and residential colleges try to recruit staff who feel about undergraduates as university professors feel about their promising doctoral students. The more expensive independent secondary schools were able to find such faculty, and no doubt there are still some small liberal arts colleges with a sizable complement of Messrs. Chips. In the modern large university, faculty attracted to the young tend to fall into three groups: first, the younger faculty members who are political activists and who find allies among students; second, men who are not drawn to research or scholarly work as such; and third, men who would like to get away from conventionalized teaching—especially didactics.

By and large, the first two sorts listed above do not have a bright future in the high-grade university, for they are not going to rise very high in the guild status system. The third is more promising—if we can relieve the professoriate as a whole of the burden of didactics. The move toward cluster and residential colleges on the university campus is an acknowledgment of a genuine need of adolescent students who not only want to further their education, but who also want to solve the problem of completing their adolescence. But the cluster college is at best an oasis for a relatively small portion of the student body, and one must still conclude that the better the university academically, the less likely is it to be a good place for living through the storms and stresses of adolescence.

Whether the large university can provide its undergraduates, or some of them, with the proper philetics, i.e., collegiate staff interested as much in students as in research, consultation, and other high status guild activities, remains to be seen. I doubt it. Perhaps a more viable solution is to begin induction into the guild earlier, i.e., during the freshman and sophomore years—but this would mean the virtual elimination of general or liberal undergraduate education. Nevertheless, there is some reason to believe—although there is no time to discuss it here—that we shall be moving in that direction, at least in the university. Professional and pre-professional curricula (such as engineering and agriculture) have no special problems in this regard; and the pattern they have established may well become the dominant one.

II

We have now distinguished three types of teaching strategy or teaching style. They differ in the kinds of results they can achieve, and although they are related, they are relatively independent of each other; being good or bad in one tells us much less than we'd like to know about being good or bad in the other two. This is so because, for one thing, teachers do not deliberately develop all three. Indeed, they may become habituated into one of them and not pay much attention to the others. This is especially so with university teachers.

Nevertheless, it is probably the case that a student or teacher will prefer one of these three types of instruction or instructional style and be more at home in it than in the other two. Perhaps the catalogue descriptions of course offerings should indicate the instructor's teaching style so that the student may be appropriately attracted or forewarned. Likewise, somewhere on the student IBM card, his or her style of learning might also be recorded, so that the computer can bring about more happy instructional matings. Instructors who use one style have to make provisions for the type of outcome stressed by the other two. Good didacticians have to find ways of activating the learner so that he does something more than regurgitate inputs; good heuristicians have to find ways of covering the required range of material, and the master of philetics must be able to coax his charges into studying something other than their own personality problems.

As we view the developments in communication media, the question arises as to whether or not the traditional dominance of didactics in formal schooling can survive. That it is the dominant mode of instruction is a fact, as is proved by the frantic efforts of educational reformers to get away from it. It had its origin in the scarcity of study materials. This put a premium on compendia of information that could be read out loud slowly enough for the student to make his own book. The invention of printing relieved this stricture no little, but it gave the teacher a new opportunity, viz., to do something other than read out loud from his book. He could spend his time testing whether the pupils had read the book (reciting) or he could supplement the book either by adding to it or interpreting it. To do either, he had to have knowledge other than that in the text. Now if he really had something important to add to the text, it would seem natural that he would write a book of his own—a commentary, a gloss, or a new text. Teachers with lesser talents could then spend their time hearing pupils recite from the new textbook. Inasmuch as what was to be learned was explicit and since it was to be used as learned, that is, replicated, didactics was the most feasible method of teaching. Heuristics were unnecessary, for there was little for the student to discover for himself or to figure out for himself, and philetics was unnecessary also because nobody was under the illusion that happiness was the normal state for anybody, and least of all for schoolboys.

The new communication and recording media have affected didactics in two important ways:

1. They have made available to the student a variety of informational resources. He is no longer wholly dependent on textbooks or on formal courses. I take it this needs no elaboration here.
2. They have put into question whether for didactics one needs the teacher at all.

The second development deserves some discussion. Anything that any teacher can utter can be put down in print or on tape or on videotape. Once captured and made replicable, the need to utter it is gone. Hence the most brilliant heuristic lesson, if put on tape, becomes a product that can be used didactically. At this point I cannot refrain from remarking that the Xerox machine and its cousins have made a profound change in didactics. In previous days, reading, especially outside reading, meant careful digesting of the material into a small number of notes (mnemonic devices). In reviewing one's notes for the exam, the original material had to be reinstated. Both of these processes—organizing material for reinstatement and the effort to reinstate—had real educational value for the student. For this reason skipping classes all semester and relying on friends' lecture notes was risky. But with the Xerox machine these activities are defeated. No digesting is necessary. Neither, presumably, is class attendance, because everything the instructor could utter in the classroom he could make available to the student ahead of time in one form or another. Hence the logical form upon which all didactics converge is programmed instruction, or, where the hardware is available, computer-aided instruction.

Of course, the hardware is not yet available in sufficiently inexpensive form to permit didactics to follow its logic into practice. Neither is the software for that matter. But I believe it is only a matter of time before it will do so. When one considers that computer-aided instruction not only presents learning tasks in carefully paced sequences, adapts the pace to the individual's ability to perform, evaluates the performance and attends without fuss and resentment to all the dreary chores of didactics, then all intelligent teachers should look forward to it as to the Promised Land.

I realize that many college teachers do not. This is attributed to their fear of being displaced and/or to the restriction of their teaching ability to didactics. I believe we shall go forward faster in the improvement of teaching if we do not confuse these alleged causes. Consider the fear of being displaced. I have found some evidence for the charge, but when I inquired more deeply, I found it to be rooted in the belief that didactics had to be supplemented by judicious heuristics and philetics, and this they rightly believe the machine cannot do. Teachers do not fully realize, however, how much of their energy is spent in dull drill, testing for retention, remedial work; how much these chores turn them not only into machines but into machine-like policemen who keep unwilling noses to unwanted grindstones.

The solution is to give over the mechanics of didactics to machines, not because didactics are unimportant, but because they are adaptable to machine operations, whereas heuristics and philetics are not.

This brings up a somewhat different but no less important reason for supporting the transfer of the mechanics of didactics to machines. Only to the machine-like aspects of instruction can quantity production methods and economies be applied. Large classes (a somewhat crude form of mass production) are defensible in didactics. So are televised lectures and demonstrations, provided it is not expected that the heuristics and philetics are to be done en masse as well.

The import of using quantity production methods cannot be overestimated, if one is to take seriously the promise of post-secondary schooling for all who want a crack at it. The mixing of didactics, heuristics, and philetics into one package makes this impossible. Either it applies mass-production methods to heuristics and philetics, or it wastes expensive staff time on the mechanics of didactics.

The high art of teaching is displayed in heuristics when a student is helped to discern what he has not seen, understood, or appreciated before. For this develops the intellectual powers of the student. This helping can take many forms, as has already been indicated. It depends largely on the teacher being able to imagine where the block to the student's understanding lies. It also depends on one's ingenuity to imagine what device would *remove* the block. Further, one needs to be concerned enough about the student to want to bring the transformation about. If an academic is not really good at heuristics and doesn't care enough about individual students to worry about their insight or lack of it, then teaching is *not* for him; scholarship perhaps, but not teaching.

Heuristics and the accompanying philetics are encounters between two or only a few individuals at a time. They require dialogue, conversation, which are costly in terms of time and staff. These resources will not be available if didactics continue to be the paradigm of teaching. Relieved of the didactic burden, the professor who also professes teaching might take on a number of tutees in his field. Or he might undertake small seminars with undergraduates. There are numerous variations of this idea which I do not propose to enumerate at this time. The important point is that all devices for tutorial work are extraordinarily costly in terms of staff time. As matters now stand, every effort to find that time raises the spectre of increasing staff. The alternative is to ask faculty members to do some of this tutorial work as an overload.

Although one can always find a number of dedicated enthusiasts who will volunteer for such an overload (their philetic sense is usually over-developed), the results, while welcome, are not universally desirable. Either the volunteers are too busy to do their "thing" for more than a semester or so, or a haven is created for philetics who are disinclined to work at systematic scholarship either in teaching or in research. Unless one is ready to create a free university within the regular university, the philetic volunteers can easily undermine systematic instruction and therewith the rationale for higher education.

For these reasons, it seems to me that any institution or any department that seriously contemplates putting a large proportion of its resources into heuristics would be well advised to deal with the problem of didactics *first*. If didactics can be done inexpensively—and preferably with the help of mass production techniques—then it makes sense to exhort the faculty to give more heed to teaching, especially the teaching of undergraduates.

Most efforts to reform undergraduate teaching in the university founder because the precautions about didactics have not been taken. It is thought that a mere determination by the faculty member to "love students" and to neglect his research are sufficient.

For reasons already indicated, I believe this faith to be misguided.

III

Granted that the problem of didactics can be solved—as I think in principle it can be—will professors become good teachers automatically? Or will one have to select those who have a special talent for it? Or will it be necessary for the guild to include as a prerequisite for admission some training in heuristics and philetics?

There is a sense in which heuristics in teaching goes with talent for discovery in other directions. It calls for an intuitive sense for the importance of problems and an equally intuitive sense for the example that simplifies complexity and concretizes abstractions. Whether this can be acquired I do not know. If any aspect of intelligence is native, this probably is. To the extent that this is the case, good heuristic teachers will have to be selected from those academics who already have some talent for it.

But this selection is not the same as the plea for senior faculty members to teach introductory survey courses. This is asking them to do didactics, and I think we can understand now why this approach to the improvement of teaching is futile. If, however, the senior faculty member has a taste for heuristics, the plea could be quite fruitful.

The situation is not altogether different with the younger staff members. They inherit as the newest comers to the guild the least interesting form of teaching, viz., didactics. If they accept it with good grace, they nevertheless look forward to relief from it. Yet there may be among the younger faculty those with a bent for heuristic teaching and sufficient philetic potential to get satisfaction from doing it.

Identifying these talents and utilizing them for teaching would therefore be the sensible thing for the Dean to do—provided, of course, that the necessary didactics could be done in another way. If not, the Dean will continue what is by now standard practice, or, may we say, standard malpractice. That is to say, the Dean calls on his junior staff to give the didactics—the large introductory survey courses, the required courses, . . . the ones which get the lowest ratings by students.

This brings me to the relation of didactics, heuristics, and philetics to the evaluation of instruction. This topic has agitated campuses everywhere for reasons that are at times puzzling.

Prima facie, the argument that the student, the consumer, is the best judge of the product (teaching) has a great deal of plausibility. Yet among many faculty members there is a reluctance—at times amounting to fierce resistance—to accept this argument. Unless one assumes what is very unlikely, viz., that this reluctance is a result of irrational fear, then the anomaly deserves our attention.

First off, does the consumer have criteria for judging the product—the teaching performance? There is one criterion on which his judgment is beyond challenge, viz., his *satisfaction*. The student is the final judge of what he likes. But what does he *like?* Does he *like* a didactic, heuristic, or philetic teacher? Surveys of student opinion rarely tell us. A good heuristic teacher to a student who is looking for straightforward didactics is sure to be rated poorly. So may a good didactician by somebody who says that he lacks "warmth." I shall not belabor the point. I would insist, however, that students' evaluations say less about an instructor's teaching than on the relation of that teaching to their own style of learning.

Student satisfaction is a valid criterion for evaluating teaching, but is it the only valid one? There are, it seems to me, at least two others equally so. One is peer judgment of procedural adequacy. The other is quality of learning results. I shall not do much with the latter because of the difficulties of measuring how much or how well something is learned, although grades are supposed to be such a measure. Yet although course grades and achievement tests do pretty well in measuring the results of didactics, they are not very illuminating with respect to the results of heuristics and philetics.

The results of such teaching may not be evident at the end of the course or until many years later or never. The most important event in my own scholastic career was the choice by a seventh-grade teacher for my essay to be read out loud before the class. At that moment she created in my mind a delusion about my literary ability which has affected my entire career. Intellectually she made a mistake, but philetically she was a very effective teacher, whether she meant to be or not.

Clearly, to evaluate such complex results in terms clear cut enough to satisfy the skeptics prone to tough talk about accountability is out of the question. Hence, of the three measures of teaching, one is incurably subjective and another hopelessly indeterminate. And oddly enough, the more subtle the teaching is heuristically and philetically, the more difficult it is to get reliable measures in terms of either consumer satisfaction or learning results.

For these reasons procedural adequacy should be one of the criteria in the evaluation of teaching. By peer judgment of procedural adequacy I mean the sort of testimony that makes it logically possible for the surgeon to say, "The operation was successful but the patient died," or for the lawyer to claim that he had argued the defendant's case well, but that the court found him guilty.

These locutions make sense only if it is possible to validate the procedure independently from the result. Indeed no suit for malpractice—always instigated because of unsatisfactory results—could be defended if this kind of validation were *not* possible. Teaching, if it is to be defended against analogous charges, must also have access to this type of defense.

However, whence comes this validation? Not from the client who is or is not pleased with the result. It must come from one's peers by virtue of their expertise, which, in turn, has been legitimated by membership in the guild. Within each intellectual discipline and within each well-developed profession canons of inquiry and expertise are acknowledged by the accredited members.

Some such judgment on teaching by one's peers should certify as to procedural adequacy. This should not be excessively difficult, especially so far as didactics are concerned. Examination of syllabi, reading lists, examinations will enable one's peers to make a judgment as to adequacy. Visits to the classroom would be necessary to judge rapport, clarity of presentation, quality of language, discussion, and the like.

Judgment by peers is *minimally* necessary for the defense of the teacher against charges of malteaching and nonteaching, but it is both necessary and minimal. Necessary because without it the teacher is at the mercy of subjective student judgments. Minimal because procedural adequacy is never sufficient justification. Surgeons who lose too many patients cannot continue to justify themselves by procedural correctness. Procedural correctness, like consumer satisfaction and good results, are each grounds for believing that the teacher is doing *something right*, but none by itself is a guarantee that he is doing everything right.

However, in peer judgment, as in other modes of evaluation of teaching, the distinction among didactics, heuristics, and philetics is necessary, for each has some characteristics which it does not share with the others. To judge them by criteria not appropriate to them exacerbates the confusion and only muddies the argument about the improvements of teaching.

My purpose in this paper has been to distinguish three types of teaching not for the sake of making distinctions, but rather to show that failure to observe them may account for some of our difficulties in improving college teaching. (I believe the argument would hold equally well at other levels of teaching.) The key to any substantive reform in teaching lies in the possibility of displacing didactics as the dominant paradigm of instruction in formal schooling. I say "displace" rather than "dispose of" because what didactics accomplish is essential and cannot be accomplished by heuristics or philetics or even a combination of them. Displacing didactics, I submit, means giving them over to some form or forms of programmed instruction, preferably those which can utilize mass production techniques, and independent study on and off campus.

Such a displacement, I have argued, will help meet the current cries of students for relevance, the ambivalent attitude of faculty toward teaching undergraduates, and help straighten out some of the anomalies involved in the evaluation of teaching. These clarifications cannot come about so long as didactics, heuristics, and philetics, variables with a high degree of independence, are lumped together in the complex ordinarily referred to as "teaching."

Application to Elementary and Secondary Schools*

Insofar as relevance is relevant to schooling, it has to do with the strategy and tactics of instruction: the tasks chosen for the pupil to work at and the way these tasks engage the pupil and teacher. Bringing the abstraction level of the task into congruence with the abstraction potential of the pupil is the key to the strategy of instruction. The difference in abstraction potential of pupils in the elementary, secondary, and collegiate schools seem to require different mixes of what I have called didactics, heuristics, and philetics.

In the elementary school the strategy of instruction could be:

1. Didactics for certain skills in language, writing, and computation.

2. Heuristics, or the method of learning by discovery, for a varied assortment of items in history, mathematics, geography, and science.

3. Philetics to provide a psychologically healthy relationship between teacher and pupil, between pupil and pupil, as well as to promote conditions favorable to school attendance and learning.

This perspective represents a fairly broad consensus among educational theorists, if the extremists are left off, namely, the traditionalists, who regard all but didactics as a betrayal of the school, on one end, and the acute philetics, who regard nothing but love of children as relevant to instruction, on the other.

Given this strategy of instruction for the elementary years, that of the secondary school, grades seven through twelve, might be as follows:

1. Didactics for the key concepts of the basic disciplines: in mathematics, science, and the humanities.

2. Heuristics for discovering the ingredients of the dominant social problems of the culture, including the skills of collective deliberation about these problems.

3. Philetics for coping with the difficulties of adolescent adjustment to problems of schooling and personal development.

This general design makes didactics the central mode of instruction in the secondary school, and it does so on the supposition that at this level all adolescents will master—to their individual optimum capacity—the basic, key concepts of the intellectual and humanistic disciplines that supply the categorical maps that we call the human heritage.

*From *The Real World of the Public Schools* © 1972 by Harry S. Broudy. Reprinted by permission of Harcourt Brace Jovanovich, Inc., pp. 184–185, 188–189.

This design has as its justification the fact that for a fairly large minority of the population high school will be the terminal of formal schooling, and, if the categorical system we call the cultural heritage is to be taught to all of our citizens, it had better be done in the secondary school. On the other hand, the emphasis on the discipline-centered curriculum in the secondary school presupposes that a highly differentiated system of vocational training will be available to all graduates of high school . . . .

Given these factors and the rationale that I have tried to sketch in, one might argue that some such general scheme as the following would provide the kind of relevance that legitimately could be demanded of formal schooling.

1. Kindergarten and preschool: heuristics (learning by discovery) for everything and everyone; philetics (love) for everyone in all situations.

2. Elementary grades one through six: didactics for certain symbolic skills; heuristics for such knowledge as seems necessary to supplement that acquired informally through the media and the milieu; philetics for motivation.

3. Secondary school grades seven through twelve: didactics for the key concepts of the basic intellectual disciplines and the humanities for the collective deliberation on social problems that require interdisciplinary or multidisciplinary thinking; philetics for emotional adjustment of adolescents to their peers, to society, and to themselves.

4. Higher education A (general education): heuristics to synthesize previous departmentalized study; philetics for rapport between faculty and student, and between student and student.

Higher education B (professional and preprofessional) didactics for specific knowledge and skill; heuristics and practical experience for everything else; philetics for acute maladjustment.

Should this scheme become the normal one, much of the just criticism of the educational system as a whole could be obviated. Rote learning and recall constitute most of the drudgery of schoolwork, but a legitimate reduction—never a complete elimination—is now possible and justifiable. Didactics could be concentrated in the secondary school but only for the *key* concepts and relations. Elsewhere necessary didactics could be relegated to computer-aided instruction or some variant of programmed instruction. The importance of this shift from didactics to heuristics cannot be overestimated, because the educational system has been erected on the supposition that if the school did not stock the minds of the young with retrievable skills and knowledge, nothing else would. This assumption is no longer needed—at least not in the simple form in which we have held it. And yet the degree to which we continue to operate on that assumption is revealed if one examines the routine of a typical college student.

40 Teacher Behavior in the Informal Classroom

Lauren B. Resnick

This paper represents an attempt to describe systematically the behaviour of the teacher in an informal, or "open" classroom. It derives from a concern with the ways in which the teacher in such a setting performs the critical functions of maintaining purposeful activity on the part of the children, directing them to tasks and activities she deems appropriate, and engaging in direct instruction of various kinds. The data to be reported were collected in an infant school in a working-class district in Southeast London. The school was an extremely "informal" one; even in the basic skill areas of mathematics and reading there were no regularly assigned lessons or scheduled activities. As a result, the total burden of instruction had to be carried by the informal and unprogrammed encounters between teacher and child (and, of course, between children, and between child and "material"). Thus, it provided an excellent setting in which to study the characteristics of teacher behaviour in an individualized educational system in which formal statement of objectives, evaluation and "programmed" materials of most kinds were not used.

Reprinted with permission from *Journal of Curriculum Studies*, 4:99–109, November, 1972.

Method of Observation

Since no systematic observation instruments for informal classrooms were available at the time this study was conducted, it was necessary to develop one specifically for this study. The categories for coding teacher behaviour were developed after about two weeks of daily visits to the classrooms in the school and extended talks with the head teacher and some classroom teachers.* The categories were intended to reflect the activities observed in these particular classrooms rather than to test any particular theoretical position concerning appropriate or inappropriate

TABLE 1 Categories for Observation of Teacher Behaviour in an Open Classroom

Q_m	A question from the teacher directed to one or more children. Subscripts indicate content: m = "management" (What kind of paper do you want? When do you want to finish? Where is the tape?)
Q_p	p = "personal" (Did you go with your brother? Did your mother like it? Whose room is being painted?)
Q_s	s = "substantive" (How many over here will balance these? Which word says "little"? What letter is missing?)
Wh	Teacher asks child *What* he is going to do.
D_m	A direction to the child to do something or work on a particular task. Subscripts have same meaning as for Q-code.
D_p	
D_s	
I_m	Teacher gives information to child. Subscripts have same meaning as for Q-code.
I_p	
I_s	
Pr	Teacher praises child or child's work.
N	Negative statement to child (That isn't good. Stop that.)
W	Teacher writes or spells a word for child (when child is writing); or teacher reads a word for child when child is reading.
H	Teacher helps child (implies physical aid, as in crafts, art, moving furniture, finding things, etc.).
Wr	Teacher writes from child's dictation.
Rd	Teacher reads a story to child.
P+	Teacher gives permission to child.
NP	Teacher does not grant permission when child asks.
Del	Teacher asks child to wait.
R	Unclassifiable response.
A	Teacher speaks to another adult.

*A full description of the observational procedure, including reliability estimates, is available in the following report, available from the Learning Research and Development Center, University of Pittsburgh, Pittsburgh, Pennsylvania 15213, U.S.A.: L. B. Resnick, *Teacher Behavior in an Informal British Infant School*, Learning Research and Development Center, University of Pittsburgh, 1971.

teacher behaviour. The coding scheme was discussed with each teacher who was observed, and several modifications were made on the basis of the teachers' suggestions. The categories used in the final set of observations are listed and briefly defined in Table I.

Systematic use of these categories made it possible to encode each remark (question or statement) by a teacher and divide this stream of remarks into "brief interactions" (four or fewer remarks to a particular child or group) and "extended interactions" (five or more remarks to a child or group). It was possible to determine the average number of each kind of interaction that occurred in a given time period. Further, it was possible to note when a new interaction "interrupted" one already going on (i.e., cases when the teacher temporarily attended to a new child and then returned to continue the original conversation), and whether each interaction was initiated by a child or by the teacher.

Observations were conducted in four different classrooms. Two teachers were observed for one period (approximately two hours) each; two were observed for two such periods. By combining and comparing the data in various ways it is possible not only to describe the characteristic behaviour pattern of the teachers observed, but also to estimate the function of each specific type of interaction in the total classroom process. In this way, quantitative data on teacher behaviour in the classroom can be used to suggest some of the critical characteristics of informal styles of teaching.

General Patterns of Interaction

In each of the classrooms observed the same general pattern of teacher behaviour was evident. This pattern consisted of extended substantive conversations with one or a small group of children interspersed with very brief interactions, frequently initiated by children. Children requesting momentary help, information, permission to engage in some activity, or simply recognition of their work, approached the teacher, who repeatedly interrupted her more extended conversations to deal with these momentary needs. Typically, the teacher then returned to the interrupted conversation. Between extended conversations the teacher herself might initiate brief interactions, sometimes substantive and sometimes concerned mainly with focusing the child's attention on a particular task.

The data on frequency and initiation of teacher-child contacts* offer some suggestions as to how it is possible to maintain an adequate degree of organization and teacher guidance in a setting in which children have

*Detailed data for these and other variables discussed in this article are available in the report cited above. All specific comparisons mentioned in this article have been found to be characterized by statistically significant differences, according to tests described in the longer report.

so many choices and work on such varied activities. There were, on the average, about two interactions per minute, including both extended and brief exchanges. Each teacher engaged in many more brief than extended interactions, and there was a tendency towards a high degree of child initiation for brief interactions, while teachers generally initiated the bulk of the extended interactions. As a result, in part, of permitting child-initiated interruptions of more extended conversations, children's demands for attention were met fairly quickly. Using the data on number of interactions per minute one can estimate that if each interaction involved a single child (many of the extended ones actually involved small groups), and if a new child was contacted with each new interaction, then about six different children would experience direct teacher contact in each three-minute interval. At this rate of contact, the teacher could speak at least briefly with every child in a class of forty once every twenty minutes, *if she distributed her attention fairly evenly among the children present.*

No systematic observations were made in the present study of the extent to which attention was evenly distributed. The observer's impression, however, reinforced by comments of the teachers observed, is that in any given period certain children received the bulk of attention while others were largely ignored. If this impression of uneven distribution were to be substantiated, it would pose the following important sets of questions: (*a*) Do the same children receive the bulk of the attention from day to day and week to week? If so, (*b*) Which children receive the most attention? That is, is the teacher's response dependent heavily on which children approach her, or does she successfully seek to interact with children who are less aggressive or less "teacher-oriented"? Does the teacher attend significantly more to children she "likes" or believes to be more intelligent? Finally, (*c*) What are the effects of attention, or lack of it, on children? Although there are many other educational influences in the classroom—particularly in an informal and individualized classroom —it seems likely that the quantity and quality of teacher attention is a powerful variable in accounting for a child's responses to school and to learning tasks. Thus the questions just raised are crucial to an understanding of the effects of informal instructional methods on children of different characteristics.

Character and Function of Extended Interactions

Between ten and nineteen per cent of the teacher's interactions with children are extended conversations, and between forty-one and fifty-five per cent of her total remarks form part of one of these extended conversations. Thus, in terms of teacher time in the classroom, extended interactions are a dominant feature. Indeed, these conversations seem to provide the major opportunity for direct instruction by the teacher in the informal classroom. As such, it is important to understand their character and to attempt to assess their function within the total process of the classroom.

Table 2 (first column of data) shows the coding categories into which the remarks forming part of extended interactions fell. The percentages given are averages for all four teachers observed. The most

T A B L E 2 Mean Per Cent of Remarks in Each Category for Extended and Brief Interactions

	Extended Interactions	Brief Interactions
Q_s	50.4	16.9
Q_p	4.3	1.2
Q_m	1.8	4.0
Wh	2.3	2.4
I_s	7.1	4.8
I_p	—	.3
I_m	.1	1.7
D_s	10.4	7.1
D_p	—	—
D_m	2.6	12.1
P	.8	8.7
NP	.1	2.1
Del	—	1.1
W	1.9	3.0
H	3.9	4.0
Wr	.8	1.6
Rd	.4	.3
Pr	3.1	5.9
N	—	2.5
R	6.8	14.5

striking feature of these data is the high percentage of questions directed by the teacher to the child. Between forty-five and sixty-nine per cent of the total number of remarks are questions of one type or another. Of these questions, the vast majority are substantive in nature (Q_s). That is, they are questions related to the content of the task the child is working on. A much smaller percentage are personal in nature (Q_p) concerned with the child's feelings or with something he or his family has done or is planning to do (a holiday trip, for example). These personal questions occur largely in connection with writing and art work and reflect the teachers' attempts to use these activities as a means of encouraging self-expression in the children as well as for skill development. Finally, there is a group of questions concerned with the "management" of instruction (Q_m). These concern where or with whom the child would like to work, what materials he plans to use, and the like. They are closely related to questions coded in the Wh category, which ask a child what he is going to work on, and which are a major means for some teachers of getting children to focus on an activity and of controlling "drifting" behaviour.

The precise nature of substantive questions varies, of course, with the kind of work the child is doing. In order to characterize the teachers' questioning strategies, several separate observational periods, when no quantitative data were taken, were devoted to recording *verbatim* the teachers' questions, together with the type of work being done by the child to whom each question was addressed. Table 3 lists a small sample of the questions recorded in this way and the following discussion of types of questions refers to the material listed there.

Writing

This was a dominant activity in each of the classrooms observed. The child was encouraged first to draw a picture, or series of pictures, to illustrate any of them which he found interesting. When completed, the child brought his picture to the teacher, and the teacher, usually after engaging the child in conversation concerning the picture, wrote the "story" dictated by the child. The child was then sometimes asked to read what had been written, or to copy the words immediately below the teacher's writing.

TABLE 3 Sample Teacher Questions

WRITING
  Story questions
  1. Who usually wears a crown?
  2. Do they wear it all the time?
  3. Have you got a dog? What do you call him?
  4. A car goes in there, does it?
  5. Then how are you going to make the tire mended again?
  6. That's a giant doing all these footsteps, then?
  7. What's happening here?

  Writing and Spelling questions
  8. Which word is longer? What does it begin with?
  9. You tell me which word is "gold".
  10. What shall I write?
  11. How do you always spell "ing"?

ART (drawing and painting)
  12. Who is this?
  13. Who is bigger, mummy or daddy?

T A B L E 3 (continued)

14. Is she smiling?
15. Is he a big man or a little man?
16. How many houses have you got here?

READING
17. Where have they gone to?
18. What is the boy's name?
19. What do you think she says?

MATHEMATICS
Counting materials
20. How many nails?
21. Do you know how many rows altogether?
22. And how many rows has each row got?

Measuring and weighing materials
23. So he took how many minutes then? (Children are using a stop-watch)
24. Is that the right length?
25. Suppose you have a stone. Would you need more Plasticine or the same? Try it.

Other materials
26. How many pages will that make if we fold it? (writing)
27. Is it as long as that piece of material? (sewing)
28. Which is longer, this brick or this brick? (bricks)
29. Which one do you think has more water in it? (cooking)
30. Which does feel heavier? (water-play)
31. Who knocked down more? (skittles game)

CRAFTS AND COOKING
Cooking
32. What did you put in to make it that colour?
33. What have you got to do with tins to stop cakes from sticking?
34. Why do you make them greasy?
35. What do you need to bring?

Craft
36. What have you put in there to stuff it? (sewing)
37. What will happen if I don't tie tightly enough? (tie-dyeing)
38. What can you do (if wood is too heavy for you to carry?)

SCIENCE
39. What is it he's eating?
40. Has he got teeth?
41. Where is he (a bird) going to live?

MANAGEMENT
42. Who would like to work with Keith on the paints?
43. Have you finished playing with the bricks?
44. Are they really mixed up (the paints), Alan?
45. Do you want to finish it now or later?
46. Who's going to go first?
47. Can you find two bits of paper like that or will one be enough?
48. What did you want it for?
49. What are you going to do this time?

More advanced children did as much as possible of the original writing themselves, asking for spellings as required, and using a personal "word-book", or small dictionary consisting of words he himself had requested in the past.

Substantive questions in the writing area were of two major types: (a) those concerned with encouraging the child to tell the story—that is, with "drawing out" both language behaviour and, where possible, the personal meaning of the experience being represented (questions 1–7); and (b) those concerned with problems of writing and spelling (questions 8–11). Occasionally, the conversation surrounding a story prompted extensive discussion of some aspect of the child's personal life (e.g., question 3). Occasionally, too, there was an attempt to use the story as the basis for engaging the child in some general reasoning or information exchange (e.g., question 5).

Art (painting and drawing)

Questions based on children's art work largely share the character of the "story" questions in the writing area. Children's art productions were viewed as an occasion for stimulating general language development and for exploring the child's own interests, as indicated by the content of his art work. Sometimes, as in the case of writing, art activities were used as an occasion to prompt general reasoning or information exchange (e.g., questions 13, 15, 16).

Reading

Reading "lessons" generally consisted of the child reading a book, chosen for his level of reading skill, aloud to the teacher. The teacher helped in the mechanics of reading and asked questions concerning the story. With children not yet able to read on their own, the teacher typically read the story to the child, stopping after each page to question him about the story and pictures. Questions 17–19 are examples of the types of questions used during these reading sessions.

Mathematics

In the school in which these observations were taken, there was very little use of formal mathematics materials. There was a "maths" area in each classroom, with objects to count, measuring instruments, and the like. However, this was typically not a prominent area in the room, and was not richly supplied.* Nevertheless, there was considerable attention paid by the teachers to the development of mathematical concepts, using such formal material as was available and attracted the child's attention, and

---

*This relative lack of materials such as Cuisenaire, Unifix or Dienes in this school reflected a deliberate decision, expressed on several occasions by the head teacher, to try to relate mathematics learning to general and practical experience rather than to set it off as a special subject of study.

also making use of all of the craft and other activity resources of the classroom. Table 5 lists both the types of activities used in developing mathematical concepts and some of the questions used (questions 20–31).

Craft and cooking activities

In addition to their function in developing mathematical concepts, these activities were used to stimulate planning activities and to elicit descriptions of work after completion. Questions 32–38 are examples of the use of craft and cooking activities for this purpose.

Science

The science area in each room typically consisted of some live animals and plants, and some physical science materials such as magnets, prisms, and colour paddles. The animals usually attracted the most attention, as indicated by the questions listed (questions 39–41). On the whole, science materials were not heavily used by the teachers observed as a medium of basic instruction.

Playhouse/dress-up area (Wendy House)

Although rather prominent in terms of physical space devoted to it, this area seemed to evoke few substantive exchanges between children and teacher in any of the classrooms observed. There were children in and around the Wendy House most of the time, but the teachers apparently had not developed strategies for integrating the activities in these areas. into the mainstream of instruction. This being the case, the Wendy House functioned largely as a play area for the children.

Management questions

The last set of questions in Table 3 (questions 42–49) are the "management" questions, coded Q_m and Wh in the observations. These questions are included in order to convey a sense of the way in which the teacher, while requiring the child to engage in some focused activity, nevertheless frequently found ways of providing the child with choices concerning exactly what would be worked on and how the activities would be carried out. Although direct instructions to children to carry out certain tasks were more frequent than questions of this type, the presence of these management questions nevertheless contributed to a sense that the child was expected to make decisions concerning the learning process for himself.

Character and Function of Brief Interactions

Brief interactions comprised eighty to ninety per cent of the total number of interactions in the classrooms observed. The second column of data in Table 2 shows the coding categories into which the remarks forming part of brief interactions fell. Comparison with the distributions for extended interaction indicates that brief interactions are characterized by relatively fewer questions and more "management" directives (D_m category). There are also many more remarks concerned with giving or withholding permission (P, NP, and Del categories), and somewhat more praise and negative statements (Pr and N). The differences in types of remark reflect the relatively greater "management" as opposed to "instructional" load borne by the brief interactions. The relatively greater number of uncodable teacher responses (R) in the brief interactions further reflects this character, since remarks coded R were frequently those which had no real "content", but which served to let the child know that the teacher was attending to him.

As has been indicated, a large percentage of brief interactions is child-initiated. Table 4 indicates the distribution into coding categories of remarks forming part of brief interactions, broken down according to who initiated the interaction. Comparison of these two distributions shows that child-initiated interactions contain fewer questions, a great deal

TABLE 4 Mean Per Cent of Remarks in Each Category for Teacher-Initiated and Child-Initiated Brief Interactions

	Teacher-Initiated	Child-Initiated
Q_s	23.3	13.6
Q_p	1.4	1.2
Q_m	5.7	3.1
Wh	4.7	1.2
I_s	5.7	4.3
I_p	.4	.2
I_m	1.4	1.9
D_s	7.6	6.8
D_p	.4	—
D_m	19.5	8.2
P	.9	12.6
NP	.4	3.1
Del	.9	1.2
W	.4	4.3
H	5.2	3.4
Wr	1.4	1.7
Rd	.4	.2
Pr	2.8	7.5
N	3.8	1.9
R	8.5	17.5

more giving of permission, and somewhat more praise and negative statements. These comparisons suggest that much of the "management" load is borne by child-initiated interactions. Further, a relatively large proportion of the child-initiated interactions can be shown to be "interruptions" of the teacher's conversation with another child, and this finding suggests that interruptions play a particularly heavy management function in these classrooms. As has been suggested earlier, it seems likely that a teacher who did not respond to children's requests for attention, even when she sometimes had to interrupt another activity to do so, would not maintain an adequate degree of contact with the children in an informal classroom.

Discussion

The data reported here have permitted a descriptive characterization of certain features of informal teaching and have provided the basis for clarifying how some key instructional and management functions are met in the open classroom. It remains now to consider the social and intellectual consequences of the teaching styles described, and their implications for the kind of learning that is likely to take place in informal settings.

As has been noted, the most striking feature of the data is the predominance of questions from the teacher to the child. The likely effects of teaching through questions are several. Perhaps most important, the teacher, as she questions, "models" an attitude of inquiry and investigation towards all events in the environment. Very probably, many children begin to imitate this questioning; certainly such an outcome is among the goals frequently espoused by proponents of informal teaching. At the very least, it is a hypothesis worth serious investigation, such investigation undoubtedly requiring observation of children's behaviour in the classroom, and perhaps outside, over extended periods of time.

A second effect of questioning, most evident in the "story" questions surrounding writing and art work, is probably to communicate to the child a sense of interest in his communicative efforts. The effects of such an expression of interest ought to be seen not only in a greater tendency on the part of the child to engage in communicative acts, but also in generally higher self-evaluations. Again, these are effects frequently claimed for informal teaching, but there is little "hard" evidence for them; they deserve serious attempts at evaluation.

Finally, the use of questions as a means of fulfilling the management functions of the classroom contributes to a sense that children must make choices—and commitments—concerning both the content and the manner of their work. Although there were generally fewer questions of this type than there were direct task setting statements (D categories), the presence of even a small percentage of management-oriented questions probably reflects the informal educator's concern for helping children to take responsibility for their own learning activities—thus becoming "autonomous" rather than externally directed learners. Here again, research assessing the long-term effects of engaging children in active choice behaviour is needed, together with investigation of a still wider range of techniques for encouraging and promoting self-directed learning.

As this discussion has suggested, the informal teaching behaviours described here have features which seem especially well suited to developing attitudes of inquiry, strong self-evaluation, and self-direction in children. To what extent do these same teaching styles contribute to the acquisition of basic skills and concepts, such as reading and mathematics? Since there are no formal means of assuring that the child works on tasks suited to his current level of development in any particular area, the child's acquisition of basic skills in an informal environment depends on a combination of two factors: (a) the extent to which the child is able to extract from a complex and "distracting" environment those tasks that optimally "stretch" his current repertoire of skills and concepts—i.e., the extent to which he can "programme" his own learning; and (b) the extent to which the teacher, on the basis of informal observation and evaluation and her own knowledge of the structure of the subject-matter, can guide the child to appropriate tasks. In addition, the informal method of teaching depends upon a subtle blending of "self-motivated" learning on the part of the child, the setting of expectation for performance by the teacher, and both peer and teacher reinforcement of intellectual effort.

The data presented here do not permit any direct assessment of how successfully these factors interact in the classrooms studied. Nor, for that matter, is there a great deal of detailed research from other sources, particularly on children's ability to programme their own learning in various kinds of environments, a capacity that is very likely related to aspects of self-motivation, as has been implied in the writings of Montessori, Piaget, Hunt, and others. Nevertheless, it seems important to raise these questions in the present context, since they suggest the kinds of research that will be needed if we are to develop and extend ways of simultaneously maximizing skill development and the attitudes of involvement and responsibility in learning described above.

INDEX

(Page numbers in italics refer to main discussions.)

A

Actors, teachers as, 364
Aesthetics and creativity, 380, 381-89
Affect, student, *66-75*, 87, 103
Analogies for teaching, 4-5, 8 (*see also* Teacher roles)
Anderson, H. H., 112
Art as Experience (Dewey), 367
Aschner-Gallagher System, the, 287
Atkinson, R. C., 239
Ausubel, David P., 257
Authoritarian behavior in teaching, 91, 112
Authority in teaching, 74, 89, 90, 115, 121, 135, 137, 375

B

Bales Interaction Process Analysis, the, 48
Barron, Frank, 372
"Basic concepts" in teaching, 5
Behavior modification, teaching as, 105 ff.
Bellack, Aron, 332
Bettleheim, Bruno, 3
Binary digits, 40
"Bits" of information, 40-42, 43
Bloom, Benjamin S., 208, 209
Body language, 391
Boredom, student, 277
Bower, G. H., 242
"Brainwashing," 6-7

C

Case-study method, the, 48-55
Categories, application of, 52-55, 56;
and the Bales Interaction Process Analysis, 48; of classroom interaction, 223-27, 285-87; of cognitive behavior, 184-91, 192-97, 490-91; in communication, 47 ff.; of nonverbal behavior, 402-6, 417-19, 427; of student behavior, 316-26; of teacher behavior, 516; of teacher feedback, 78-81; of teacher influence, 119-22; of verbal behavior, *253-64* (*see also* Observation instruments) CCOS (*see* The Classroom Creativity Observation Schedule)
Cherry, Colin, 46
Choreographers, teachers as, 381-89 passim
Circular reinforcement, 43
Clarification game, the, 335-36
Clarke, M. C., 242
Classroom Creativity Observation Schedule, the, 221-29
"Classroom encounter," 58
"Classroom game," the, 130
Classroom interaction: affect in, *66-75*, 87, 103, 459, 465, 468; analysis of, 118-26, 127-34, 151-60, 181-92, 224-26, 315-26; assumptions in, 66; authority in, 74, 89, 90, 115, 121, 135, 375; categories of, 223-27, 285-87; as a clarification game, 335-36; as "classroom encounter," 58; as "classroom game," 130; as "classroom meeting," 103, 104; climate of, 89-93, *111-26*; coding of, 60-61, 67-73, 106-7,

527

37-38; heuristics, *501-14*; and
hypothetical thinking, 203-5; and
indirect teaching, 115, 117, 119-20,
121, 124, 125, 128, 130, 370 ff.; as
information processing, 236, 239; and
information theory, 35-36; imagery in,
253-64; memory in, 237, 242-43, 244;
models of, 236-43; motivation in,
273-74, 277; and philetics, *501-14*;
prerequisites for, 241-42; and problem
solving, 235; and programmed
instruction, 105-7; and productive
behavior, 285, 287, 289; and
psychotherapy, *269-81*; and qualitative
intelligence, 259-68 passim;
reinforcement in, 247, 249, 251; and
repetition, 237-39; retrieval in, 240,
244; reviews in, 244; "significant,"
269-81 passim; and Skinnerism, 247-51;
and social conflicts, 95; and
socialization, 98, 154, 299; and student
affect, 87; and teacher authority, 74,
89, 90, 115, 121, 135, 137, 375; and
teacher expectations, 285-87, 289-90;
and teacher personality, 296-306; and
uncertainty, 40-42, 43
Leary, Timothy, 331, 332
Lecturing, 156
Lesson plans, 253
Lifting thought, 492-93, 495
Lippitt, R., 112

M

Mann-Whitney *U* Test, the, 189
May, Rollo, 377
Memory, 237, 242-43
Menninger, Karl, 316, 317
Meno, The (Plato), 445-53
Messages: believability of, 32; clarity of,
32; context of, 25, 26, 33; criteria for,
31; and mass media, 33-34; perception
of, 24; selection of, 25; terms of, 29;
truth of, 31; validity of, 31
Minnesota Attitude Inventory, the, 126
Models: of communication processes, 18,
22, 24-29, 160; game, 339-43, 345, 347;
Guilford, of the Structure of Intellect,
287; of learning, 236-43; mathematical,
4; PIT, 61-63; problems of, 4; of
reality, 295-96; scale, 4; the teacher
as, 4, *98-110*, 375; of the teacher,
296-306; of teaching processes, 4, 222;
theoretical, 4; of thinking, 487
Models and Metaphors (Black), 4
Mother-substitutes, 311
Motivation, 120, 224-25, 273-74, 277
Motor skills, 20
Moustakas, Clark, 276

N

M. S. A. I. (*see* the Minnesota Student
Attitude Inventory)
Negative dependency, 296
"Noise," 20
Nonverbal communication: categories of,
402-5, 417-19, 427, 430-32; cluster
incidents in, 429, 432-33; continuum of,
399-400; as control, 398-99, 410-11;
definition of, 426; for emphasis,
411-12; encouragement of, 402-4;
feedback from, 400; inhibition of, 404-
5; instructional, 408-9, 410-14, 415-16;
models of, 18; and the observation
instrument, 10; personal, 409-10; the
teacher's, 407-23 passim;
self-awareness of, 396; and teacher
training, 436-37; time in, 398

O

Observation instrument, the: arbitrary
time units in, 11; the Bales Interaction
Process Analysis, 48; categories in, 10,
11, 12-13; and chi-squares, 466;
Classification of Verbal Behavior in the
Classroom, 285-91, 293-94; for
classroom creativity, 221-29; for
classroom interaction, 57; classroom
protocol analysis, 170-71; the
Flanders' Interaction Analysis, 63;
the Guilford Classification system,
184-92; Interaction Analysis Summary,
406; the Mann-Whitney *U* Test, 189;
the Minnesota Student Attitude
Inventory, 126; and nonverbal
behavior, 10, 429-35; for the "open"
classroom, 516-17; point of view in, 18;
psychoanalytic, 315-26; purpose of,
12; rating scales in, 10, 11;
recitation-analysis, 461-62, 468-71;
reliability, 12, 214, 226-27, 261, 302,
305, 324, 466-68; the Social Issues
Analysis Test, 470; Socratic-analysis,
462-64, 468-71; the Spaulding
Interaction System, 66-75; for student
perception of teacher feedback, 78-88;
the Taxonomy of Cognitive Behavior,
208-216; the Taxonomy of Image
Provoking Behavior Profile, 253-64;
for teacher style, 465-66, 469;
theoretical bases for, 209-11, 221,
254-56; "thought units" in, 12; the
Tuckman Teacher Feedback Form,
297-306; types of, 10-12; validity of,
214, 226-27, 261, 302-3, 305, 324;
vantage point of, 10, 12

socialization, 98, 154, 167; Socratic, 100, 445-53, 456-57, 458, 462-64, 468-71, 472-73; student-centered, 48-53, 54-55, 103, 157, 222; and subject matter (*see* Subject matter); and systems management, 107-9; task-oriented, 222; and teacher assumptions, 26, 28, 29, 30, 33; and teaching machines, 281; and the therapy principle, 374-77; thought levels in, 490-93, 494, 495, 500; and transaction, *151-60*, 284-87, 289-90; and transference, 316-17, 319, 321-25; value levels in, 332-37
Teaching, observation of (*see* Observation instrument, the)
Teaching, processes of: affect in, 495, 496; ambiguity in, 303; analogies for, 4-5, 8; as art, 24, 31, 109, *381-89;* assumptions in, 26, 30, 31, 33; authoritarian, 91, 112; authority in, 74, 89, 90, 115, 121, 135, 137, 375; as behavior modification, 105 ff.; believability in, 32; and the case-study method, 48-53, 54-55; circular reinforcement in, 43; and the classroom climate, 224-25; classroom encounters in, 58; and the "classroom meeting," 103, 104; coding in, 60-61, 67-73; and cognitive behavior (*see* Cognitive behavior); and communication (*see* Communication); conditioned responses in, 236-38; connectionist, 236 ff.; context of, 25, 26, 28, 30, 31, 33; control in, 37-39, 130, 138, 139-43, 249, 301, 303, 410-11, 492-93; and counseling, 102-4; and counter-transference, 317, 318, 320-25; criticism in, 109, 131-32; and curriculum (*see* Curriculum); and cybernetics, *35-46;* and the deference principle, 377-80; dialogue in, *455-73;* and diagnosis, 104-7, 109; and didactics, *501-14;* and discipline, 139; and discoverance, 321, 322, 325; and discovery methods, 101, 321, 322, 325; dominative patterns in, 90; emphasis in, 363, 411-12; and the encounter principle, 372-74; encouragement in, 131, 133, 137; and entropy, 44-45; experiment in, 109, 371; extending thought in, 492-93; feedback in (*see* Feedback); films in, 475; flexibility in, 115-16, 126, 371; flow charts of, 67, 72, 185, 493-94; focusing thought in, 492-93, 495; function levels in, 490-93; as a game, 335-36, 339-43, 345, 347-

54; goals in (*see* Teaching, goals of); and "guided discovery," 101; and heuristic, *501-14,* "humanistic," 106; as humanization, 22-24, 30-32; and hypothetical thinking, 203-5; and I/D ratios, 128, 130; and i/d ratios, 128, 130; imagery in, *253-64;* imaginativeness in, 371, 373; indirect, 115, 117, 119-20, 121, 124, 125, 128, 130, 370 ff.; inference levels in, 500; influence in, 114, 115, 117, 119-20, 124, 125, 286; as information dissemination, 40 ff., 154 ff., 236, 239, 295; and information theory, 35-46; intuition in, 66; inquiry methods in, 101; and inquiry training, 475-82; institutional events in, 58-59, 60; institutional level in, 23, 32-34; integrative patterns in, 90; as interpersonal relationships, 265; intuition in, 381-89 passim; as "language game," 167, 177-78; leadership in, 89; and learning (*see* Learning); lecturing in, 156; and lesson plans, 253; lifting thought in, 492-93, 495; and manipulation, 29; and mass media, 33-38; and mass-production, 32; "mechanistic," 106; mood in, 299; motivation in, 120, 224-25, 273-74, 277; nonverbal communication in (*see* Nonverbal communication); observation of (*see* Observation instruments); open, 37-38, 108, 141, 143, 283-91, 293-94, 515-26; the organization function in, 24, 31, 154; pacing in, 363; personal events in, 59-60; and philetics, *501-14;* point of view in, 26, 28, 30, 33; policing in, 109; power in, 89; problem-setting in, 100-2; and programmed instruction, 104-7; psychological constructs in, 295-306; and psychotherapy, 274-81, 372; public criteria in, 139, 141, 143; and qualitative intelligence, 358-68; and reality therapy, 103; and recitation, 141, 145, 456, 458, 461-62, 468-71, 472-73; reinforcement in, 247, 249, 251; and repetition, 237; resistance in, 317, 319, 321-25; resource provision in, 276-77; respect in, 144; rituals in, 332, 333-37; roles in (*see* Teacher roles); rules of, 167, 177 ff., 332, 333-37, 339-43, 345-46, 347-48, 350-54; the "science function" in, 24, 31; self-analysis in, 29, 32, 66, 73, 396; and self-government, 33-34; seminar, 471-73; and sensitivity training,